Interior Construction & Detailing

for Designers and Architects

David Kent Ballast, AIA

Professional Publications, Inc.
Belmont, CA

Disclaimer

This book is intended to be used by knowledgeable professionals as a general reference source and as a guide for developing their own details within the context of their specific designs. Where appropriate, the reader should seek additional professional advice or consult original sources for more detailed information.

The information presented in this book has been compiled from many sources including industry standards, building codes, manufacturer's literature, and technical reference works, as well as the author's own experience. Every effort has been made to present reasonably accurate information; however, it is difficult to ensure that all the information given is entirely accurate and the possibility of error cannot be entirely eliminated. The publisher and the author do not warrant the techniques and methods presented in this book. This book and the materials contained herein have not been examined for safety engineering, consumer or workplace safety, or similar or dissimilar laws or regulations. The author and publisher assume no liability or responsibility for any injury and/or damage to persons or property that is incurred as a consequence, directly or indirectly, of the use and application of any of the contents of this book.

Trademark List

Contraflam®	VEGLA–Vereinigte Glaswerke GmbH
Teflon®	E.I. DuPont De Numours and Company
Romex®	GK Technologies, Incorporated
Permalam®	American Laminators Association
Masterformat®	Construction Specification Institute, Inc. and Construction Specifications Canada

Acquisitions Editors: Elizabeth Fisher and Wendy Nelson
Production Editor: Lisa Rominger
Copy Editor: Patricia C. Walter
Book Designer: Jennifer Pasqual Thuillier
Typesetter: Jennifer Pasqual Thuillier
Illustrator: David Ballast
Proofreaders: Mia Laurence, Jessica R. Whitney-Holden, Cris Triebsch
Cover Designer & Cover Photo: David Bergeron

INTERIOR CONSTRUCTION & DETAILING FOR DESIGNERS AND ARCHITECTS

Printed in the United States of America

ISBN: 0-912045-67-1

Professional Publications, Inc.
1250 Fifth Avenue, Belmont, CA 94002
(650) 593-9119
www.ppi2pass.com

Current printing of this edition: 7

Library of Congress Cataloging-in-Publication Data

Ballast, David Kent.
    Interior construction & detailing for designers and architects /
David Kent Ballast.
      p.   cm.
    Includes bibliographical references and index.
    ISBN 0-912045-67-1
    1. Building--Details. 2. Building. 3. Interior architecture.
I. Title. II. Title: Interior construction and detailing for
designers and architects.
TH2025.B35 1994
721--dc20
                              93-48254
                                CIP

TABLE OF CONTENTS

LIST OF FIGURES

LIST OF TABLES

ACKNOWLEDGMENTS

I thank the many people who helped me with the development and publication of this book. Credit goes to Michele Guest, Registered Interior Designer, and Hubert I. McDaniel, ASID, IBD, IDEC, for their reviews of the initial proposal and early chapters. Thanks also goes to Robert D. Troy, architect and Registered Interior Designer, for his thorough technical review and his many helpful suggestions that have made the material clearer.

The great people at Professional Publications did a fine job, as always, of getting everything on paper and between the covers. Special thanks to acquisitions editor Wendy Nelson for following the project through from conception to completion and to Lisa Rominger and her production staff for taking care of the thousands of necessary details.

And for this newest printing, I would also like to thank Jessica R. Whitney-Holden, Production Manager and also the proofreader on this project; Kate Hayes, copy editor; and Cathy Schrott, typesetter.

The Construction Specifications Institute, Inc. (CSI) and Construction Specifications Canada (CSC) also graciously allowed me to use both the Masterformat® system for numbering many of the sections and the Masterformat® index.

INTRODUCTION

Good interior construction design and detailing require a broad range of knowledge about materials, finishes, construction assemblies, mechanical and electrical systems, building codes, and planning standards. This book is a comprehensive reference text on these topics for interior designers and architects involved in commercial and residential construction.

Interior architecture is a specialty in itself; however, until now no book has covered the broad spectrum of knowledge required for competent interior design and detailing. Many books on interior design lack data about construction, mechanical and electrical systems, code requirements, and other subjects that were once thought to be the exclusive province of the architect. Architectural books stop short of covering all of the specialty materials and methods necessary for sophisticated interior detailing. This book brings together information from the two fields.

The merger of what has typically been thought of as strictly architectural or interior design knowledge reflects the changes now taking place in the professional design fields. Three of the most prominent changes are given here.

First, the required knowledge base of interior designers is continually expanding. This is reflected in the increasingly complex work interior designers are undertaking, the knowledge needed to take the National Council for Interior Design Qualification (NCIDQ) examination, the rigorous standards set by the Foundation for Interior Design Education Research (FIDER) for accreditation of interior design schools, and expanding title and practice legislation for interior designers across the United States and Canada.

Second, many architectural and interior design firms are merging as a result of economic conditions along with the need to practice more efficiently and to offer a broad range of services. Whatever the reasons, architects and interior designers need to better understand each other's specialized knowledge to work together.

Finally, more architectural firms are only doing interior design work as a way either to survive difficult economic times or to increase business and profits. Architects, previously untrained in the specialized area of interior design, need additional information to practice competently.

Even though what has historically been thought of as separate—that is as either interior design or architecture work—is merging, regulatory constraints have been slow to keep up. Most building departments still require the stamp of a licensed architect for many types of interior construction work shown in this book. Because a specific type of work is included in this book does not mean that it is the province of the interior designer or that a licensed architect is not required to assist with design and drawing preparation. However, the interior designer should know what is required both when working with an architect and for accurate preliminary design purposes, so that a design project gets started in the right direction.

The subject matter in this book is generally organized in the same way interiors are constructed. The early chapters describe construction components that give form to all interior spaces in all types of interior construction. These include the elements of partitions, ceilings, doors, hardware, glazing, and woodwork. Chapters in the middle of the book cover finish materials applied to the structure of the building. Finally, supplemental topics are discussed, such as acoustics, security systems, mechanical and electrical coordination, barrier-free design, and building codes.

Throughout the book, more detailed, supplemental information is given in separate sidebars. This allows the main text to be read without interruption by reference information, which not all readers want to review on the first reading. Although the scope of the book includes much more than just product and construction information, five-digit Masterformat® numbers have been included in headings when appropriate. These are the standard numbers developed by the Construction Specifications Institute, Inc. (CSI) as part of their Masterformat® system, which is a system of numbers and titles for organizing construction information. A separate Masterformat® index is included at the back of the book.

Because the United States has been slow to convert to the metric system, the measurements in the book are based on the standard English units of measure. The corresponding metric, or SI (Système International d'Unités), units are included in parentheses immediately after the English units. This will assist designers in becoming familiar with the SI system while considering readers who are already using it. In addition, because the Department of Commerce will require all federal designs for renovation and new construction completed after January 1994 to be done only in metric units, many designers and architects will be required to use the system. In the text, the SI numbers are followed by the units, such as mm for millimeters or kg for kilograms. However, to avoid clutter, only the SI numbers are given on the illustrations (in parentheses immediately after the English units); units such as millimeters are not included. Following standard conventions, all distance measurements in the illustrations are in millimeters, unless specifically indicated as meters. For example, a dimension on a drawing may be shown as 4 1/2" (114), which means that it is 4½ inches in English units and 114 millimeters in SI units. A distance of 30' (9.1 m) means that the distance in English units is 30 feet and the distance in SI units is 9.1 meters.

1

PARTITIONS

Partitions define space, support doors and interior glazing, interface with ceilings, anchor woodwork, contain electrical and plumbing systems, and provide the base for a majority of decorative finishes. The commonly used partition types include gypsum wallboard, lath and plaster, masonry, and glass block.

GYPSUM WALLBOARD PARTITIONS [09250]

Gypsum wallboard is the most common and most versatile of all partition types. It consists of a gypsum core sandwiched between heavy paper or other materials. Wallboard is factory-formed into standard-size sheets ready for dry application to a variety of framing methods. Because of its many advantages, it is the most common material used for constructing partitions and ceilings in both residential and commercial construction. New products include wallboard manufactured with gypsum and fiber from recycled newspaper.

Gypsum wallboard is used on studs for partitions, over furring to cover other rough walls or columns, and on structural or suspended framing for ceilings. In some situations it can be directly applied to concrete block and other substrates with mastic.

Wallboard components

Although the term "gypsum wallboard" (or "gyp board" for short) is often used to describe a construction component, such as "a gyp board ceiling," the component is actually an assembly of several individual pieces. A typical gypsum wallboard system consists of framing to which the gypsum wallboard is attached. The corners and exposed edges of the frame are covered with trim, then the joints are finished with reinforcing tape and joint compound. This results in a smooth surface that is ready for final finishing with paint, wall covering, or other decorative finish.

Gypsum wallboard

Gypsum wallboard is manufactured in panels 4 and 4½ ft (1200 and 1372 mm) wide and 8, 10, 12, and 14 ft long (2400, 3000, 3600, and 4200 mm). Special 1-in. (25 mm) thick core board used for shaft enclosures is manufactured in 2 ft widths. The length depends on the requirements of the job, but contractors generally use the longest practical length to minimize the number of joints.

Standard gypsum wallboard is available in thicknesses of ¼, ⅜, ½, and ⅝ in. (6.4, 9.5, 12.7, and 15.9 mm). A relatively new product that is ¾ in. (19 mm) thick is also available, which carries a 2-hour fire rating. This allows a 2-hour-rated partition to be constructed with a single layer without resorting to a standard two-ply application.

The thickness used depends on the particular application, frame spacing, and building code requirements. For most commercial and high-quality residential work, ⅝-in. (16 mm) thick wallboard is used. A thickness of ½ in. (12.7 mm) is commonly used in residential projects and for some commercial applications, such as furred walls. Table 1.1 gives general guidelines for determining wallboard thickness based on frame spacing.

Other applications require different wallboard thicknesses. For example, a ⅜ in. (9.5 mm) thickness is used in some double-layer applications or when wallboard is applied over other finished walls in remodeling work. A thickness of ¼ in. (6.4 mm) is used for forming curved surfaces and for providing new finishes over old wall and ceiling surfaces. Double-layer applications are used when additional fire resistance is required or for extra acoustical benefits.

Gypsum wallboard is available in a variety of types and edge treatments. The most common wallboard has tapered edges on the face side along the long dimension of the panel and square edges at the ends. The tapered edges allow for application of reinforcing tape and joint compound without causing bulges at the joints. Square edge panels are used where appearance is not a factor, for base layers of two-layer applications, and veneer plaster work.

In addition to the standard paper-faced gypsum wallboard, several other types are available. The types commonly used for interior construction are discussed.

Fire-rated gypsum wallboard

Fire-rated gypsum wallboard, commonly designated as Type X, must be used where fire-rated partitions or coverings are required. It has a specially formulated core containing mineral additives that improve the wallboard's fire resistance.

Water-resistant wallboard

Water-resistant wallboard is used as a backing for adhesive-applied ceramic tile and similar finishes in moist areas, such as showers or where the wallboard may be exposed to moisture during construction. However,

Table 1.1 Wallboard thickness based on frame spacing	Application	Frame spacing, in. (mm)	
		16[1] (406)	24[1] (610)
	Partitions	½[2] (12.7)	⅝ (15.9)
	Ceilings	½[2] (12.7)	⅝ (15.9)
	Furring	½ (12.7)	½ (12.7)
	Mastic applied	⅜[3] (9.5)	⅜[3] (9.5)

[1] On center.
[2] Required fire rating may dictate the use of ⅝-in. (15.9 mm) Type X wallboard in some cases.
[3] No frame.

Detailing curved partitions with gypsum wallboard

Gypsum wallboard partitions may be constructed with single curved surfaces by bending thin wallboard and attaching it to closely spaced studs. The amount of curvature (minimum radius) depends on wallboard thickness and whether the wallboard is applied dry or wet. When applied dry, it is usually installed horizontally and is gently bent while being attached to the studs. When applied wet, the wallboard face is moistened and then attached to studs. After drying, the panels regain their original hardness. Generally, ¼-in. (6.4 mm) or ⅜-in. (9.5 mm) panels are used in multiple layers. Table 1.2 gives the minimum radii possible when using wallboard for curved surfaces, both wet and dry. These dimensions are approximate. Exact numbers may vary depending on individual manufacturer's recommendations.

Table 1.2 Minimum bending radii for gypsum wallboard

		Minimum radius, ft (mm)	
Application	Panel thickness, in. (mm)	Long dimension perpendicular to framing, ft (mm)	Long dimension parallel to framing, ft (mm)
Dry bending	¼ (6.4)	5 (1500)	15 (4600)
	⅜ (9.5)	7.5 (2290)	25 (7600)
	½ (12.7)	20 (6100)	—
	½ [2¼ in. layers]	5 (3050)	—
Wet bending [1]	¼ (6.4)	2 (600)	—
	⅜ (9.5)	3 (900)	—
	½ (12.7)	4 (1200)	—
	½ [2¼ in. layers]	2 (600)	—

[1] Dimensions are for gypsum wallboard applied to a 4-in. (100 mm) partition.

Source: United States Gypsum Company.

Composition of Type X gypsum wallboard

In general, gypsum wallboard is an excellent fire barrier because of its basic composition, hydrous calcium sulfate. Gypsum is about 50 percent water by volume and when subjected to heat the water of crystallization is turned into steam. Because this process takes time and requires a great deal of heat, the gypsum remains incombustible and insulates the nonexposed side against heat transfer. However, because the gypsum shrinks as the crystallized water is driven off during a fire, pure gypsum board develops cracks and allows fire and heat to pass through. Type X gypsum board is manufactured with vermiculite, glass fiber, and other additives that offset shrinkage and increase durability.

for heavy-duty commercial showers and applications that are continuously wet, it is better to use ceramic tile on a Portland cement plaster setting bed or a glass mesh mortar unit as described in Chapter 10. Today, for most residential and commercial construction, other types of cementitious panel products are used in place of gypsum wallboard in showers. Water-resistant wallboard is also available as a fire-rated product.

Foil-backed wallboard

Foil-backed wallboard provides a vapor barrier to prevent the transmission of water vapor into exterior wall and ceiling spaces. It is installed with the foil-backed side facing the framing members. It is not commonly used for interior construction, but may be required when remodeling exterior walls or ceilings.

Figure 1.1
Metal stud
wall framing

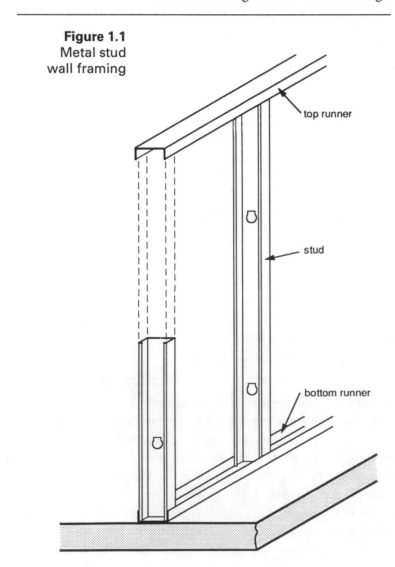

Pre-finished gypsum wallboard

Pre-finished gypsum wallboard is available with various types of vinyl wallcovering already applied. However, instead of being installed like regular wallboard, it is used with demountable partition systems. It slips into bottom and top runners, and various types of concealed clips connect the edges to each other. Once installed, a thin vertical joint exists where one panel is butted up against the next. For very large projects, the wallboard can be manufactured with a custom wall covering of the type, pattern, and color specified by the designer.

Framing

Gypsum wallboard framing for vertical construction, such as walls or furring, can be either wood or metal. (For ceiling framing, see Chapter 2.) Wood is used in residential construction and occasionally in smaller commercial projects. Metal studs are commonly used in commercial construction because they are noncombustible, lightweight, and easy to work with. Metal framing may be used in residential construction; however, residential contractors prefer wood stud walls because they can double as load-bearing walls.

Wood framing

Wood framing for gypsum wallboard partitions consists of two by four (2 × 4-in.) wood studs (actual size 1½ in. × 3½ in. or 38.1 × 88.9 mm) spaced 16 in. (406 mm) or 24 in. (610 mm) on center, although 16-in. spacing is more common, especially for residential construction. These spacings are used because they are even subdivisions of the 4 ft width and 8, 10, and 12 ft lengths of gypsum wallboard. For ceilings, the wallboard is generally attached directly to wood joists or ceiling rafters, which are also spaced 16 in. on center.

Metal framing

Metal framing is light gage, galvanized steel formed in a variety of sizes and shapes. Although metal stud partitions are usually nonload-bearing they can be load-bearing if heavy gage, structural steel studs are used.

Load-bearing walls require calculations and sizing by a structural engineer, but the gypsum wallboard is applied directly to the studs as with any other partition.

Metal studs are available in several gages (thicknesses). The most common thicknesses are 25-gage (0.0188 in. or 0.48 mm), 22-gage (0.0284 in. or 0.72 mm), and 20-gage (0.0344 in. or 0.87 mm). The 25-gage thickness is used most often for studs and other metal framing. Heavier gages are used for very tall partitions, when the partitions must support unusual loads, and for framing door openings. For load-bearing partitions, exterior walls, and other heavy loading conditions, 12-, 14-, 16-, or 18-gage structural steel studs can be used.

Metal studs are manufactured in a C shape with small flanges, as shown in Figure 1.1. Openings are prepunched along the length to allow for the passage of electrical conduit and other wiring. Metal studs are available in depths of 1⅝, 2½, 3⅝, 4, and 6 in. (41.3, 63.5, 92.1, 101.6, and 152.4 mm). These depths are the sizes labeled on construction drawings. The exact width of a stud is not critical and varies slightly depending on the manufacturer. It is usually about 1¼ in. (32 mm).

Metal studs are placed vertically and, like wood studs, are spaced either 16 in. or 24 in. (406 or 610 mm) on center. However, 24-in. spacing is commonly used for most nonload-bearing commercial construction because it is more economical and minimizes construction time. Metal studs must be framed into runners both at the floor and ceiling, as shown in Figure 1.1. The runners are C-shaped metal fabrications, without flanges or prepunched holes, and are the same width as the studs. The runners are attached to the floor and upper support first and then the studs are slipped into the runners and attached with self-tapping screws or a crimping device. Other stud shapes are also available for special uses, such as stairway shaft framing.

The depth of a steel stud is generally determined by the height of the partition. The most common metal stud size (depth) used in commercial construction is 2½ in. (63.5 mm), although 3⅝-in. (92.1 mm) studs are also frequently used. A 2½-in. stud is generally adequate for normal ceiling heights (8 to 10 ft) and also allows clearance for electrical boxes, wiring, and small plumbing pipes. Table 1.3 gives an abbreviated listing of maximum partition heights based on stud depth. Although one stud size may be sufficient for structural purposes, larger sizes may be required to accommodate plumbing pipes and recessed items, such as medicine cabinets or pocket doors.

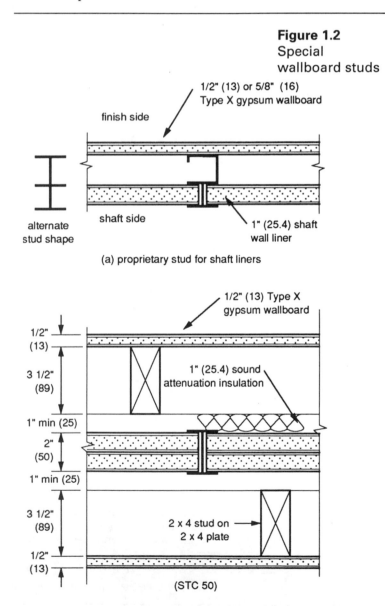

Figure 1.2
Special wallboard studs

(a) proprietary stud for shaft liners

(b) H stud for area separation partitions

Special framing

Specially shaped metal studs are used for specialized partitions. For example, various configurations of proprietary studs are used for shaft wall liners in fire stairs, elevators, and dumbwaiters. See Figure 1.2(a). These allow the wallboard to be applied from one side only and provide a 2-hour-rated separation, as required by building codes. H-shaped studs are used for area separation walls to provide a fire break between adjacent apartments or condominiums, or anywhere such a partition is required. They can be used with other metal stud construction or with wood frame construction, as shown in Figure 1.2(b).

Wood and metal furring

Furring consists of smaller framing members, either wood or metal, that only provide a base for attachment of gypsum wallboard to one side of some other construction, which is not appropriate for direct attachment of the wallboard. First, the furring is attached to the substrate behind it, such as a concrete or masonry wall, and then the wallboard is screwed to the furring. The furring can also be free-standing when the application is to use wallboard to cover up

Table 1.3 Maximum partition heights based on stud depth			Structural criteria			
		L/120 at 5 lb/ft[1] Spacing, ft-in. (mm)		L/240 at 5 lb/ft[1] Spacing, ft-in. (mm)		
Stud depth, in. (mm)	Gypsum board layers	16 in [2] (406)	24 in.[2][3] (610)	16 in.[2] (406)	24 in.[2] (610)
1⅝ in. (41.3)	One	11 ft (3353)	**10 ft** **(3048)**	8 ft 9 in. (2667)	7 ft 11 in. (2413)
	Two		**12 ft 4 in.** **(3759)**		9 ft 9 in. (2972)
2½ in. (63.5)	One	14 ft 8 in. (4470)	**13 ft 5 in.** **(4089)**	11 ft 8 in. (3556)	10 ft 8 in. (3251)
	Two		**15 ft 10 in.** **(4826)**		12 ft 7 in. (3835)
3⅝ in. (92.1)	One	19 ft 5 in. (5918)	**17 ft 3 in.** **(5258)**	15 ft 5 in. (4699)	13 ft 8 in. (4166)
	Two		**19 ft 5 in.** **(5918)**		15 ft 5 in. (4699)
4 in. (101.6)	One	20 ft 8 in. (6299)	**18 ft 5 in.** **(5613)**	16 ft 5 in. (5004)	14 ft 7 in. (4445)
	Two		**20 ft 8 in.** **(6299)**		16 ft 5 in. (5004)

[1] L/120 refers to the maximum allowable deflection based on the length L of the stud. Partition heights are the heights from the bottom runner to the top runner, not the finished ceiling height.
[2] On center.
[3] Figures shown in bold type are the most common.

Source: ASTM C 754; Copyright ASTM. Reprinted with permission.

some other construction. For example, a finished, square column can be built around a rough, unfinished, structural concrete column.

There are several types of furring, as shown in Figure 1.3. When wood furring is used, it measures a minimum of 1 × 2 in. (actual size ¾ × 1½ in.) (19.1 × 38.1 mm) if it is directly attached to another solid wall, such as concrete block. If the furring is applied perpendicular to the other studs, or if a greater depth is required, a 2 × 2-in. (51 ×51 mm) piece must be used.

There are three common types of metal furring. The most common is the metal furring channel, sometimes called a hat channel because of its cross-sectional shape. See Figure 1.3(b). The channel is attached to other construction, such as a concrete block wall or ceiling framing, providing a surface to which the gypsum wallboard can be screw-attached. Furring channels are usually spaced 16 in. or 24 in. (406 or 610 mm) on center. Resilient channels are similar to hat channels, but are manufactured with legs of unequal length so that only one edge touches the framing. See Figure 1.3(c). This avoids a rigid connection between the gypsum wallboard and the stud wall or ceiling structure

and reduces sound transmission through the wall or ceiling. To accommodate electrical conduit, switch boxes, and insulation, Z-furring channels provide more depth than standard metal furring channels. See Figures 1.3(d).

Standard trim [09270]

Because the edges of gypsum wallboard are ragged when cut, they must either be concealed or finished with prefabricated trim. The most common trim is made from galvanized steel in a few common configurations. Other types of proprietary trim are available in aluminum in a variety of shapes to accommodate many detailing conditions. Vinyl trim is also made to finish off common edge conditions. There are six common trim shapes used for gypsum wallboard.

Corner bead trim

Corner bead trim is L-shaped with legs of equal length, about 1 in. (25.4 mm) long. See Figure 1.4(a). It is used at all exposed exterior corners. Once applied, the metal is covered with joint compound, then sanded smooth ready for painting or other finishing.

Figure 1.3
Common types of furring

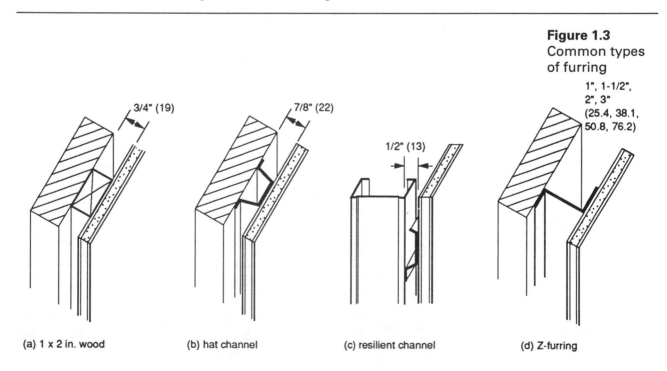

1", 1-1/2", 2", 3" (25.4, 38.1, 50.8, 76.2)

3/4" (19)   7/8" (22)   1/2" (13)

(a) 1 x 2 in. wood   (b) hat channel   (c) resilient channel   (d) Z-furring

LC bead trim

LC bead trim is used where the edge of the gypsum wallboard is exposed. See Figure 1.4(b). This trim requires finishing with joint compound; however, once finished, it gives a neat, clean edge that does not look like a metal edge. Because of its U shape, LC bead trim must be installed before the wallboard is installed, or at the same time. LC bead is its generic name, and contractors sometimes call it U-bead or J-bead. Also, manufacturers have different numerical designations for it.

L bead trim

L bead trim is similar to LC bead but does not have the back flange; therefore, it can be installed after the wallboard. See Figure 1.4(c). This is an advantage when remodeling and when trim is used to make final dimensional fits next to millwork, door frames, and other construction. Like LC bead, L bead must be finished with joint compound.

U bead trim

Like LC trim, U bead trim fits over the edge of the wallboard; however, it does not require finishing. See Figure 1.4(d). As a result, the metal is visible on the wallboard surface. This trim is used where appearance is not critical or where finishing costs must be minimized.

LK bead trim

LK bead trim is similar to LC trim; however, it has a small V edge that must be fitted into a slot in the construction (usually wood) to which the wallboard is attached. See Figure 1.4(e). Because of this installation method, LK bead trim is adjustable and can be used for wallboard measuring ⅜ in., ½ in., or ⅝ in. (9.5, 12.7, or 15.9 mm), or in situations where the wood trim is not exactly plumb. This trim must also be finished with joint compound.

Control joints

A control joint is used when movement in large expanses of gypsum wallboard is expected. See Figure 1.4(f). Generally, this is not a problem with interior construction for two reasons. First, there is very little expansion and contraction caused by temperature variations; second, most wallboard surface areas are limited by the size of rooms and spaces. Occasionally, on surfaces such as ceilings in very long corridors, large rooms, or where there is a building expansion joint, wallboard expansion joints are required. They are generally used at distances not to exceed 50 ft (15 m) when an unbroken surface exceeds that dimension, or when movement is expected.

Figure 1.4
Standard wallboard trim types

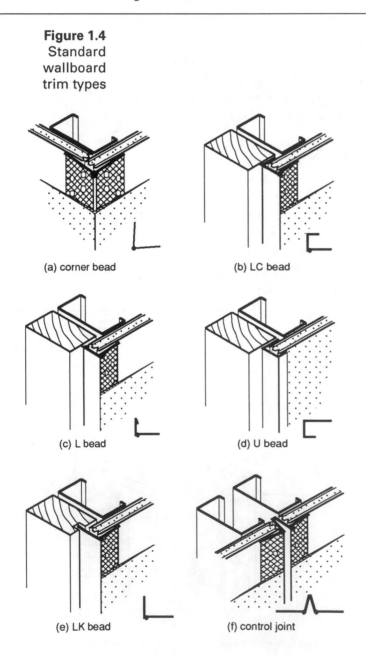

(a) corner bead

(b) LC bead

(c) L bead

(d) U bead

(e) LK bead

(f) control joint

Proprietary gypsum wallboard trim

For situations where the standard wallboard trim will not work, there are various types of proprietary trim available from several manufacturers. Proprietary trim is usually made from extruded aluminum and allows detailing of reveals, rounded edges, and other configurations that would otherwise not be feasible. Figure 1.5 gives four examples of proprietary wallboard trim.

Reinforcing tape, joint compound, and finishing

After gypsum wallboard is nailed or screwed to the framing, the holes and joints must be covered. For joints, joint compound is placed along the crack, and either paper or fiberglass reinforcing tape is embedded in the compound and troweled smooth. After it has dried, another layer of compound is applied, troweled smooth and feathered farther out onto the wallboard, allowed to dry, then sanded. This process is repeated. At this point, when the joint compound blends smoothly with the wallboard, the surface is ready for finishing. A similar three-coat process is used to cover nail or screw holes, except that no tape is used.

Once the wallboard is installed and readied for finishing, it can be primed and painted for a smooth finish. Textured coating, which is applied before painting, provides an alternative to a smooth finish and is often preferred by contractors because it hides minor surface imperfection. A variety of treatments is available, from a fine, sandy finish to a heavy, coarsely textured finish. One of the most common is the "orange peel" texture.

Fire and sound ratings

Two of the most important qualities of gypsum wallboard partitions are fire resistance and sound rating. Gypsum wallboard is a good material for both because gypsum is inherently fire resistant, as described previously, and is very dense, making it a good barrier for sound transmission. Because there are dozens of ways a partition can be built, knowing what type of fire resistance (if any) and acoustic qualities are needed help determine the exact partition construction.

Partition fire ratings are specified as 1-hour, 2-hour, 3-hour, and 4-hour. A 1-hour partition, for example, will theoretically prevent fire and smoke from passing through the partition for a period of at least one hour. The ratings are established by an

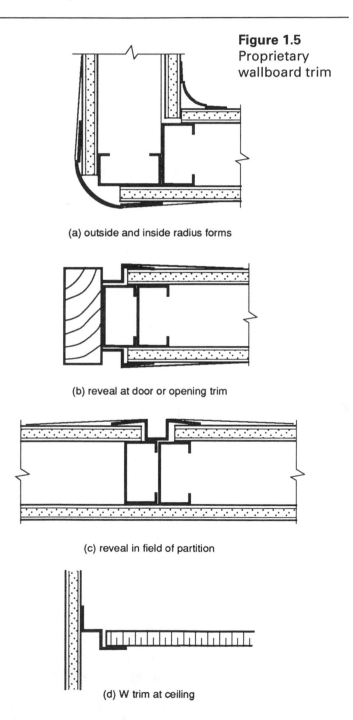

Figure 1.5
Proprietary wallboard trim

(a) outside and inside radius forms

(b) reveal at door or opening trim

(c) reveal in field of partition

(d) W trim at ceiling

independent testing laboratory. A partition is built and subjected to a standard test fire, and the results are measured. In addition to partitions, gypsum wallboard can also be used to protect columns, beams, and other building components.

For interior construction 1-hour-rated partitions, and occasionally 2-hour-rated partitions, are required. One-hour partitions are used for separating corridors from lease space, separating houses from their attached garages, and separating one type of occupancy from another. Two-hour partitions are used to enclose vertical shafts, such as stairways and elevators. Some architectural applications, such as some types of occupancy separations, require 3-hour or 4-hour protection.

Partitions are also given sound ratings based on laboratory testing. These ratings usually appear along with the fire ratings in various reference tables and publications. In most cases, the rating is the STC number, or sound transmission class. This is an average rating of the resistance to transmission over a wide range of frequencies. The higher the number, the better the partition is in reducing sound transmission. Some approximate STC ratings are given in Figure 1.21. Refer to Chapter 11 for more information on acoustics.

Typical partition construction

Figures 1.6–1.8 show three of the most common types of gypsum wallboard partitions. One is the standard wood frame partition used in residential construction. The other two are metal frame partitions commonly used in commercial construction.

Standard types of gypsum wallboard finish

The following levels of wallboard finish have been standardized in the gypsum wallboard industry and are described in *Recommended Specification of Levels of Gypsum Board Finish* published by the Gypsum Association. The levels provide a way to specify the exact requirement for any project. This is important because factors such as lighting conditions and paint type can affect the appearance of the surface if it is not finished properly. For example, strong sidelighting from a window perpendicular to a partition can accentuate minor flaws and dents in the wallboard.

Level 0: Requires no taping, finishing, or accessories.

Level 1: Joints and interior angles have tape embedded in joint compound with the surface free of excess joint compound. This level is used for plenums above ceilings and other areas not normally open to view.

Level 2: All joints and interior angles have tape embedded in joint compound and one separate coat of compound applied over all joints, angles, fastener heads and accessories. This level is used where water-resistant backing board is used as a substrate for tile and in other areas where appearance is not critical.

Level 3: Similar to Level 2, except that two coats of joint compound are used and the surface is free of tool marks and ridges. This level is used where the surface will receive heavy- or medium-textured finishes or where heavy-grade wall coverings are to be applied.

Level 4: Similar to Level 3, except that three coats of joint compound are used. This level is used where light textures or wall coverings will be applied or where economy is of concern. Gloss, semigloss, and enamel paints are not recommended over this level of finish.

Level 5: Similar to Level 4 except that a thin skim coat of joint compound is applied over the entire surface. This level is used where gloss, semigloss, enamel, or nontextured flat paints are specified or where severe lighting conditions exist.

Figure 1.6
Standard wood
frame partition

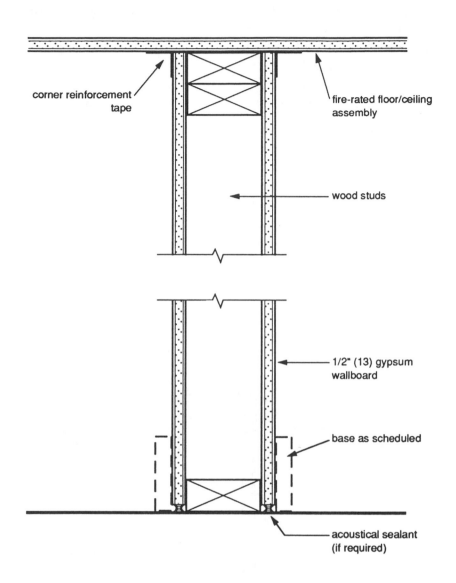

corner reinforcement
tape

fire-rated floor/ceiling
assembly

wood studs

1/2" (13) gypsum
wallboard

base as scheduled

acoustical sealant
(if required)

The Uniform Building Code (UBC) and other model codes specify the exact requirements for the application of both single-ply and two-ply gypsum wallboard, including framing member spacing, wallboard thickness, types and spacing of fasteners, and joint treatment. Some of these are specified in Tables 43-B and 43-C of the *Uniform Building Code* (and similar tables in other model codes). Detailed construction requirements can also be found in such publications as the Underwriters Laboratories' *Building Material Directory,* the Gypsum Associations' *Fire Resistance Design Manual,* and manufacturers' product literature, as well as other reference books.

In addition, the UBC requires water-resistant gypsum board to be used as a base for tile and wall panels, tub and shower enclosures, and water closet compartment walls. However, water-resistant gypsum wallboard cannot be used over vapor barriers, in areas of high humidity (such as saunas, steam rooms, or gang showers), or on ceilings.

**Building code
requirements
for gypsum
wallboard**

Figure 1.6 illustrates a residential wood frame partition. These partitions are constructed with two by four studs 16 in. (406 mm) on center, covered with one layer of gypsum wallboard on each side. Because of the way the board is installed, there is usually about a ¼-in. to ½-in. (6 to 12 mm) gap at the floor, which is concealed by the base.

Figure 1.7 shows a typical nonrated partition used in commercial construction to economically divide spaces when fire separation, sound control, and security are not critical considerations. The partition is built from the floor to the underside of the suspended ceiling, with the plenum space above the ceiling left open.

This standard partition is constructed by attaching the bottom runner to the floor with power-actuated fasteners (or other means) and attaching a corresponding top runner to the ceiling grid with screws or rivets (or other types of fasteners). The studs are slipped between the runners and attached to them with self-tapping metal screws. Application of the gypsum wallboard and finish base completes the construction.

In most cases, ⅝-in. (15.9 mm) wallboard is used because of the typical 24-in. (610 mm) spacing of studs, but ½-in. (12.7 mm) wallboard may be applied to studs spaced 16 in.

Figure 1.7
Standard
floor-to-ceiling
steel stud
partition

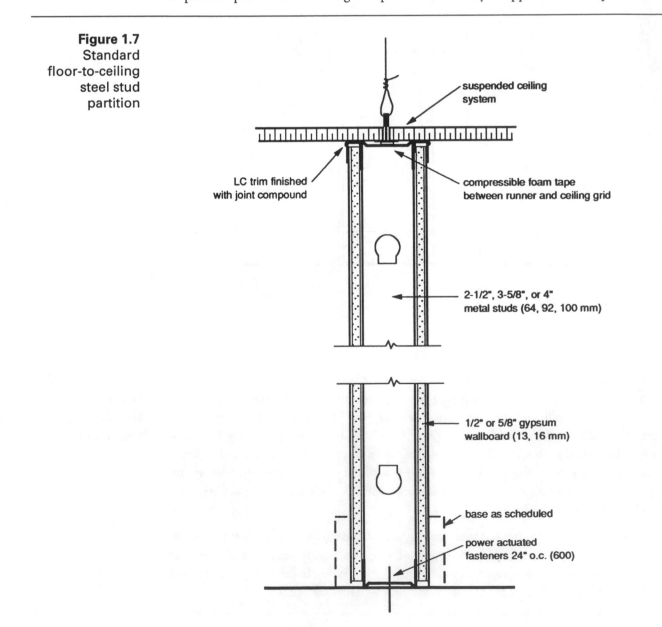

suspended ceiling system

LC trim finished with joint compound

compressible foam tape between runner and ceiling grid

2-1/2", 3-5/8", or 4" metal studs (64, 92, 100 mm)

1/2" or 5/8" gypsum wallboard (13, 16 mm)

base as scheduled

power actuated fasteners 24" o.c. (600)

(406 mm) on center. Wallboard ½ in. (12.7 mm) thick is sometimes applied to metal studs 24 in. (610 mm) on center to reduce costs.

Steel studs that measure 2½ in. (63.5 mm) are generally used for usual ceiling heights of 8 ft to 9 ft (2438 to 2743 mm), but 3⅝-in. (92.1 mm) studs can be used when additional cavity depth is needed for pipes or recessed items. The exposed edge of the wallboard near the ceiling should be finished with some type of trim.

Although wallboard may be applied with the length parallel to the studs (vertically) or with the length perpendicular to the studs (horizontally), most contractors prefer to apply it horizontally. For partitions, if the ceiling height is 8 ft 1 in. (2464 mm) or less, it is best to apply wallboard horizontally in the longest lengths practicable for the following reasons:

• It results in fewer joints, which means faster and less costly finishing.

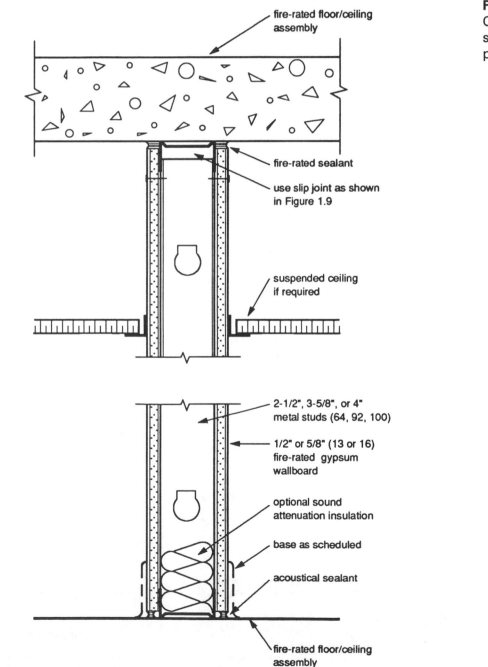

Figure 1.8
One-hour-rated slab-to-slab partition

fire-rated floor/ceiling assembly

fire-rated sealant

use slip joint as shown in Figure 1.9

suspended ceiling if required

2-1/2", 3-5/8", or 4" metal studs (64, 92, 100)

1/2" or 5/8" (13 or 16) fire-rated gypsum wallboard

optional sound attenuation insulation

base as scheduled

acoustical sealant

fire-rated floor/ceiling assembly

• It places the horizontal joint at a convenient height for finishing.

• It ties more studs together, making the installation stronger.

• It puts the strongest dimension of the wallboard across the studs.

Figure 1.8 shows a 1-hour fire-rated partition used in commercial construction. This partition type is commonly used to separate an exit corridor from adjacent spaces and when the building code requires a 1-hour separation. It is also used when acoustical control is needed between two spaces but not a fire separation. If the partition is used for sound control, acoustical insulation should be detailed within the stud space as well. Refer to the next section on special partition construction for examples of acoustical partitions. There are other construction assemblies that provide 2-hour, 3-hour, and 4-hour ratings; however, these are seldom encountered in most interior construction. One exception is 2-hour-rated partitions that are required around vertical enclosures, such as stairways.

Although there are many variations of 1-hour-rated partitions, all these partitions must be built with Type X gypsum wallboard and must extend to the structure above. All joints, edges, and penetrations

Partition cracking in high-rise buildings

All buildings move to one extent or another, thus causing cracking of materials that are rigidly attached to the structure. This problem is especially prevalent in high-rise buildings where structural movement, movement caused by floor deflection, and expansion and contraction are more pronounced than in residential and smaller commercial buildings.

Most wallboard cracking in high-rise buildings is caused by partitions that are rigidly attached to walls, columns, beams, or floor slabs without provisions for such movement. When a floor slab deflects it can put enough pressure on a slab-height partition to cause it to crack. This can be avoided by detailing a slip joint as shown in Figure 1.9. This joint seals the partition to the slab, while allowing some movement.

In addition, when high-rise buildings sway under wind load, they move from side to side. Figure 1.10 shows another type of slip joint that can be used between the edge of a partition and an exterior window mullion. Figure 1.11 shows a perimeter relief joint where a partition abuts a column or structural wall.

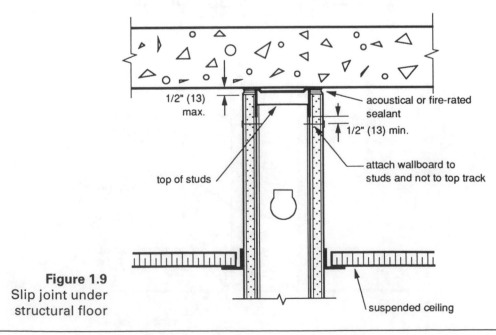

1/2" (13) max.

acoustical or fire-rated sealant

1/2" (13) min.

top of studs

attach wallboard to studs and not to top track

Figure 1.9
Slip joint under structural floor

suspended ceiling

must be sealed. If ducts pass through the wall, they must have a fire damper at the wall line. Electrical boxes may be placed in the wall but are limited to one box on one side of the wall in each space between studs.

This kind of partition should be provided with a slip joint at the structural floor or roof, as shown in Figure 1.9. The space between the structural slab and the top of the gypsum board must be sealed with fire-rated caulking compound. In addition, if the top of the partition abuts a fluted metal deck, the voids must be sealed with appropriate fire-rated material.

Two other common partition details include 2-hour-rated partitions and chase walls. Figure 1.12 illustrates a typical 2-hour-rated partition developed by using a double layer of Type X wallboard on each side of metal studs. It is also possible to use proprietary ¾-in. (19.1 mm) thick wallboard in a single layer.

Figure 1.13 shows a chase wall, which is a double row of studs braced together and spaced far enough apart to accommodate plumbing pipes. Chase walls can also be used to recess large elements, such as bookcases and cabinets. If sound control is

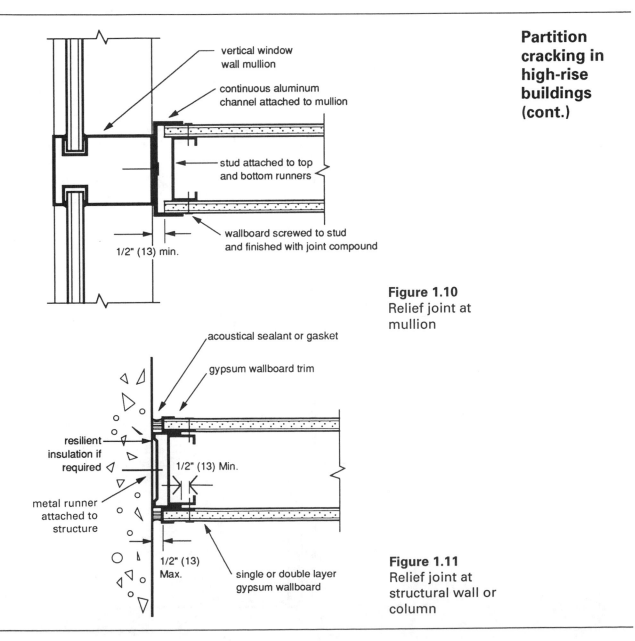

Partition cracking in high-rise buildings (cont.)

vertical window wall mullion

continuous aluminum channel attached to mullion

stud attached to top and bottom runners

wallboard screwed to stud and finished with joint compound

1/2" (13) min.

Figure 1.10
Relief joint at mullion

acoustical sealant or gasket

gypsum wallboard trim

resilient insulation if required

1/2" (13) Min.

metal runner attached to structure

1/2" (13) Max.

single or double layer gypsum wallboard

Figure 1.11
Relief joint at structural wall or column

required, extra layers of wallboard are applied or resilient furring channels are used.

For soffits above cabinets, lockers, and similar items gypsum wallboard can be framed down from the ceiling, as shown in Figure 1.14. In residential construction, two by twos or two by fours are used instead of the metal framing shown in the commercial detail of Figure 1.14.

Special partition construction

Detailing often requires special partition construction for acoustical separation, shaft lining around stairways and dumbwaiters in high-rise buildings, and column enclosures to maintain the required fire rating for structural elements.

There are many available acoustical partition designs depending on the degree of sound reduction desired. Some of the more common ways of detailing partitions are illustrated in Figures 1.15–1.20. For partitions with a single row of studs, additional sound attenuation for standard partitions is achieved by adding more layers of wallboard, by using resilient channels, by using

Figure 1.12
Two-hour-rated
partition

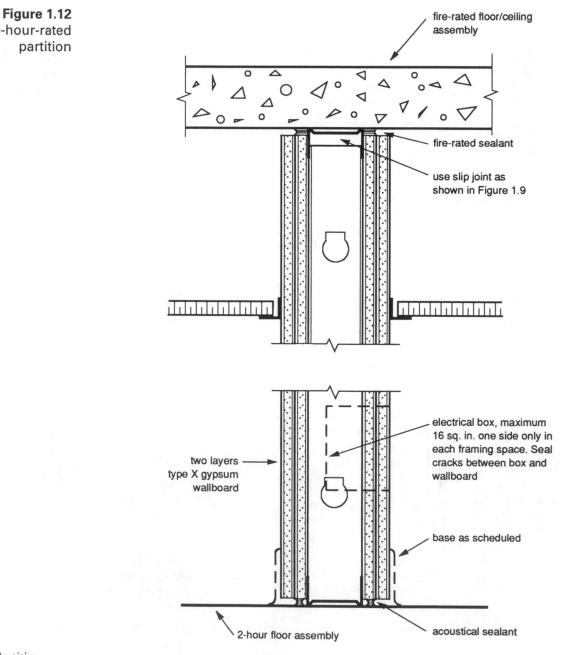

fire-rated floor/ceiling
assembly

fire-rated sealant

use slip joint as
shown in Figure 1.9

electrical box, maximum
16 sq. in. one side only in
each framing space. Seal
cracks between box and
wallboard

two layers
type X gypsum
wallboard

base as scheduled

2-hour floor assembly

acoustical sealant

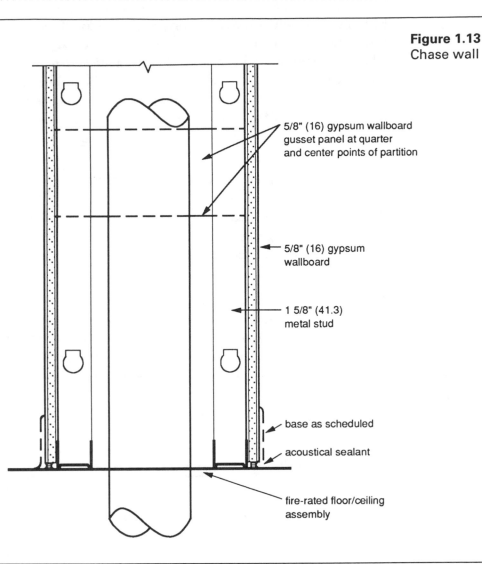

Figure 1.13
Chase wall

5/8" (16) gypsum wallboard
gusset panel at quarter
and center points of partition

5/8" (16) gypsum
wallboard

1 5/8" (41.3)
metal stud

base as scheduled

acoustical sealant

fire-rated floor/ceiling
assembly

The sound transmission class (STC) of a construction assembly is a quick way to evaluate the relative effectiveness of the assembly in reducing sound transmission. It uses a single number to represent the average sound loss. For more information on acoustics, refer to Chapter 11. Table 1.4 gives some STC ratings and a subjective description of their effect on speech. Higher ratings may be required to reduce the sound transmission of music, machinery, and other types of noise.

**STC ratings
and what
they mean**

Table 1.4
STC ratings and
what they mean

STC	Subjective effect
25	Normal speech can be clearly heard through the barrier.
30	Loud speech can be heard and understood fairly well.
35	Loud speech is not intelligible but can be heard.
42–45	Loud speech can only be heard faintly. Normal speech cannot be heard.
46–50	Loud speech is not audible. Loud sounds other than speech can only be heard faintly, if at all.

batt insulation within the stud cavity, or with some combination of all these methods. High attenuation partitions, such as those shown in Figures 1.17 and 1.18, usually require a double row of studs to physically separate one side of the partition from the other.

In all types of acoustic partitions, simply detailing the partition is not enough. Special attention must also be placed on observing the construction to verify compliance with the drawings, sealing all penetrations, and using the appropriate types of doors and frames.

Although 2-hour-rated shaft lining partitions are usually part of the architectural design of a building, interior construction sometimes requires an enclosed stairway.

This usually occurs when a new stairway is constructed in a high-rise building for a multifloor tenant. Two-hour-rated shafts are also required for vertical transportation systems, such as dumbwaiters. It is useful to know the size requirements for detailing such an opening so that plenty of space can be provided early in the design phase. One method of detailing a partition around a stairway that bypasses an intermediate floor is shown in Figure 1.19. The exact configuration may vary depending on the structural system used.

Fire protection of structural elements is another condition that is usually part of the architectural design of a building. However, new construction is often required during remodeling when old column covers are

Figure 1.14
Soffit detail

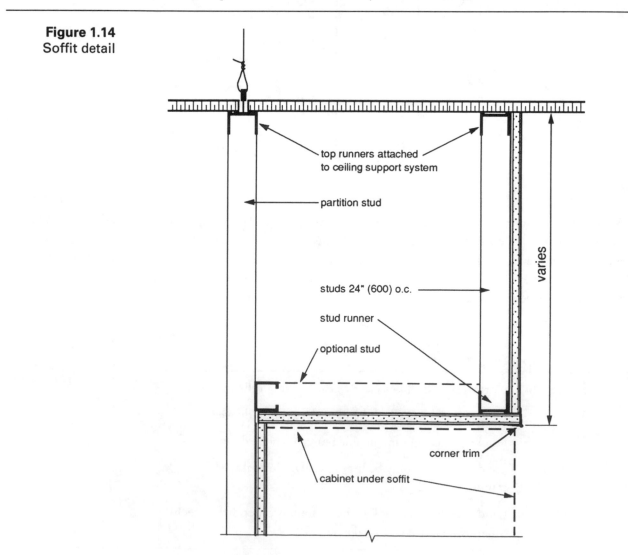

top runners attached to ceiling support system

partition stud

studs 24" (600) o.c.

stud runner

optional stud

corner trim

cabinet under soffit

varies

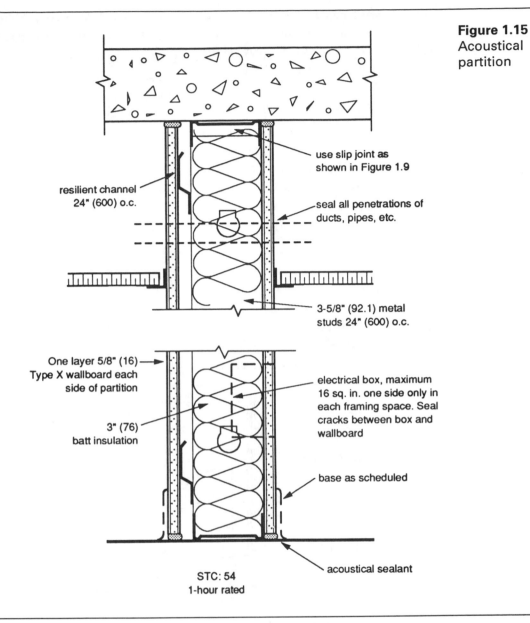

Figure 1.15
Acoustical
partition

use slip joint as
shown in Figure 1.9

resilient channel
24" (600) o.c.

seal all penetrations of
ducts, pipes, etc.

3-5/8" (92.1) metal
studs 24" (600) o.c.

One layer 5/8" (16)
Type X wallboard each
side of partition

electrical box, maximum
16 sq. in. one side only in
each framing space. Seal
cracks between box and
wallboard

3" (76)
batt insulation

base as scheduled

acoustical sealant

STC: 54
1-hour rated

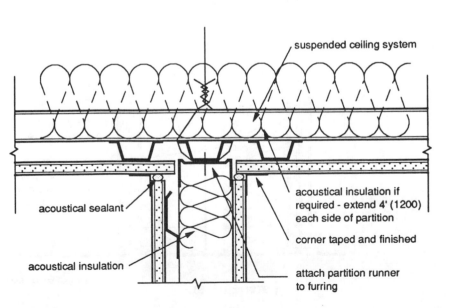

Figure 1.16
Acoustical
partition at
suspended
wallboard
ceiling

suspended ceiling system

acoustical sealant

acoustical insulation if
required - extend 4' (1200)
each side of partition

corner taped and finished

acoustical insulation

attach partition runner
to furring

stripped away. Figure 1.20 shows one method of enclosing a steel column that otherwise had not been protected with spray-on fireproofing. Refer to Chapter 17 for more information on how to determine hourly rating requirements for structural elements.

Although there are many variations of gypsum wallboard partitions, those discussed in this section are the most common for the majority of interior construction. The final decision usually takes into account cost, fire-rating requirements, acoustical separation needs, and ease of construction.

The partitions discussed in this section are sketched in Figure 1.21 along with a description of their construction, their fire ratings, and their acoustical STC ratings. Some additional partitions are also included that are variations of the ones discussed.

Coordination with other construction components

Developing partition details requires coordination with other construction elements and conditions. Some of the things to consider in addition to fire and sound ratings include the following: vertical deflection of floor structures, horizontal movement, support for heavy loads, total partition depth, and partition anchors.

Vertical deflection

In many cases, it is simply a matter of nailing, screwing, or using power-actuated fasteners to rigidly attach the bottom and top runners of a partition to the floor and ceiling. In other cases, movement of the structure must be provided for, as discussed in the previous section.

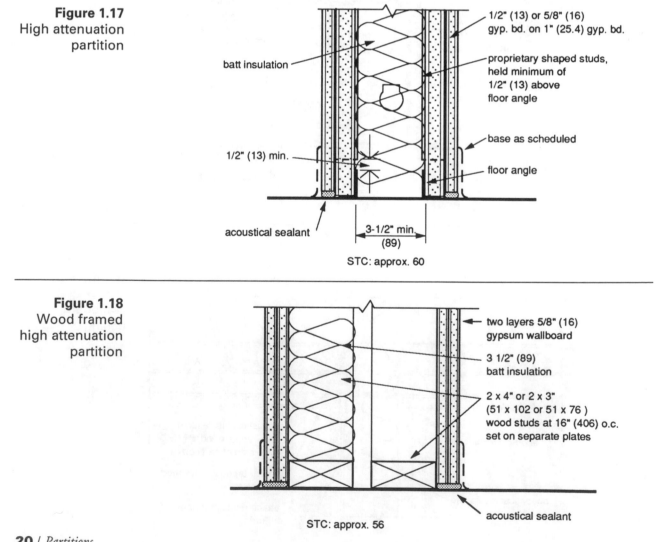

Figure 1.17
High attenuation partition

batt insulation

1/2" (13) or 5/8" (16) gyp. bd. on 1" (25.4) gyp. bd.

proprietary shaped studs, held minimum of 1/2" (13) above floor angle

base as scheduled

floor angle

1/2" (13) min.

acoustical sealant

3-1/2" min. (89)

STC: approx. 60

Figure 1.18
Wood framed high attenuation partition

two layers 5/8" (16) gypsum wallboard

3 1/2" (89) batt insulation

2 x 4" or 2 x 3" (51 x 102 or 51 x 76) wood studs at 16" (406) o.c. set on separate plates

acoustical sealant

STC: approx. 56

Horizontal movement

In tall buildings, wind loading on the exterior wall or windows causes a slight horizontal movement. If a partition is rigidly attached to a window mullion or flexible wall, the gypsum wallboard may crack. This was also discussed in the previous section.

Support for hanging heavy loads

Standard gypsum wallboard partitions constructed with metal studs will only support moderate loads. Although there are various types of screws and bolts that can be used to hang pictures and lightweight shelving, blocking must be shown on the drawings when heavy loads are involved. This blocking is either ¾-in. (19 mm) plywood or solid wood and is placed within the wall cavity, set between the studs, and attached to them. The wood blocking provides a solid substrate into which screws can be driven to support cabinets, paneling, and other wall-hung items.

Partition depth

If plumbing pipes, recessed equipment, or other large items must be built into the walls, a stud size must be specified that accommodates the largest item. For very deep built-in items, a chase wall must be detailed, as shown in Figure 1.13.

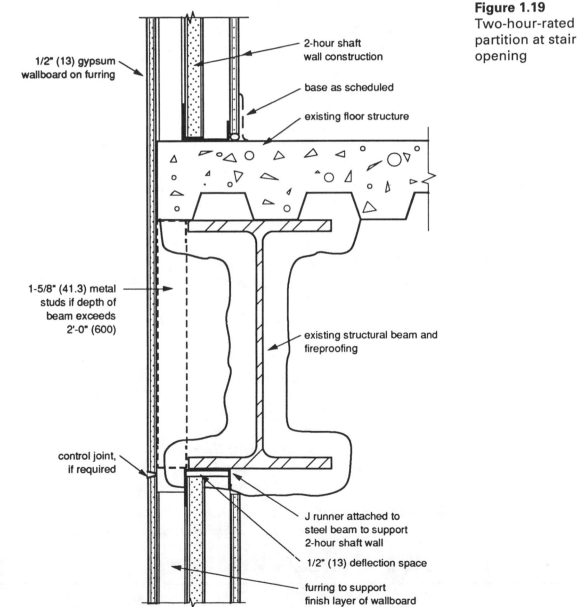

Figure 1.19
Two-hour-rated partition at stair opening

1/2" (13) gypsum wallboard on furring

2-hour shaft wall construction

base as scheduled

existing floor structure

1-5/8" (41.3) metal studs if depth of beam exceeds 2'-0" (600)

existing structural beam and fireproofing

control joint, if required

J runner attached to steel beam to support 2-hour shaft wall

1/2" (13) deflection space

furring to support finish layer of wallboard

Figure 1.20
Two-hour-rated
column cover

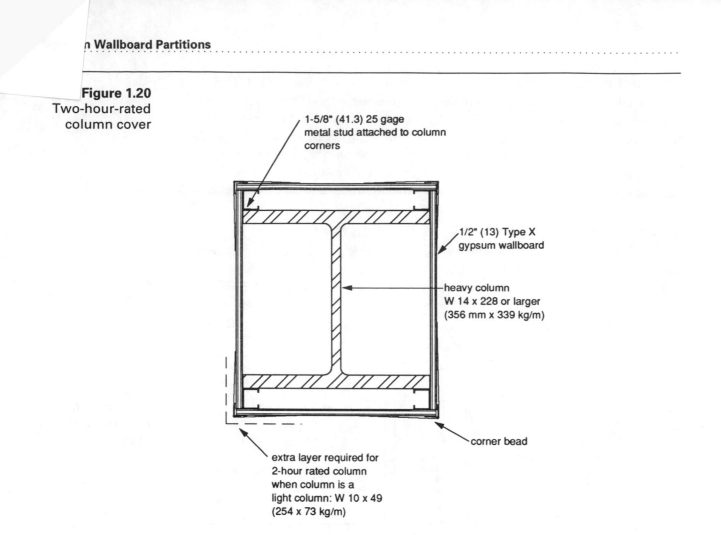

1-5/8" (41.3) 25 gage
metal stud attached to column
corners

1/2" (13) Type X
gypsum wallboard

heavy column
W 14 x 228 or larger
(356 mm x 339 kg/m)

corner bead

extra layer required for
2-hour rated column
when column is a
light column: W 10 x 49
(254 x 73 kg/m)

Applicable standards for gypsum wallboard partitions

American Society for Testing and Materials (ASTM):

ASTM A-653	*Specification for Sheet Steel, Zinc-coated (Galvanized) or Zinc-Iron Alloy-Coated by the Hot-dip Process*
ASTM C-36	*Specification for Gypsum Wallboard*
ASTM C-442	*Specification for Gypsum Backing Board*
ASTM C-475	*Specification for Joint Compound and Joint Tape for Finishing Gypsum Board*
ASTM C-514	*Specification for Nails for the Application of Gypsum Wallboard*
ASTM C-630	*Specification for Water-resistant Gypsum Backing Board*
ASTM C-645	*Specification for Nonload (Axial) Bearing Steel Studs, Runners (Track), and Rigid Furring Channels for Screw Application of Gypsum Board*
ASTM C-754	*Specification for Installation of Steel Framing Members to Receive Screw-attached Gypsum Wallboard, Backing Board, or Water-resistant Backing Board*
ASTM C-840	*Specification for Application and Finishing of Gypsum Board*
ASTM C-1002	*Specification for Steel Drill Screws for the Application of Gypsum Board or Metal Plaster Bases*

Gypsum Association (GA):

GA-216	*Recommended Specifications for the Application and Finishing of Gypsum Board*
GA-600	*Fire Resistance Design Manual*

Figure 1.21
Common
partition types

Partition	Description	Fire rating	STC	Figure reference
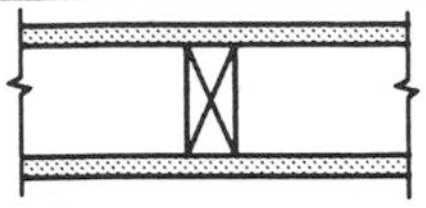	1/2" (12.7 mm) wallboard each side 2" x 4" (51 mm x 102 mm) wood studs 16" (406 mm) on center. One-hour rating with 5/8 (15.9 mm) Type X wallboard.	3/4-hr.	+30	1.6
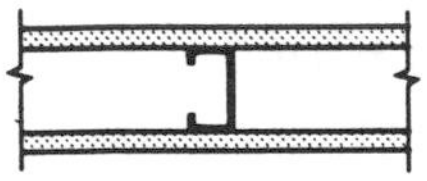	5/8" (16 mm) wallboard each side 2-1/2" (64 mm) metal studs 24" (610 mm) on center to underside of suspended ceiling.	None	±40	1.7
	5/8" (16 mm) type X wallboard each side 2-1/2" (64 mm) metal studs 24" (610 mm) on center built to underside of slab above with 1-1/2" (38 mm) sound attenuation insulation.	1-hr.	±47	1.8
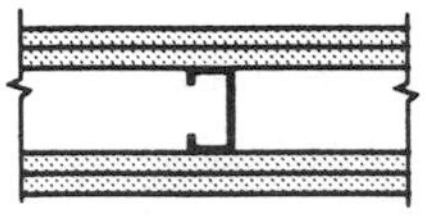	Two layers 5/8" (16 mm) type X wallboard each side 2-1/2" (64 mm) metal studs 24" (610 mm) on center built to underside of slab above. Adding 2" (51 mm) sound attenuation insulation blanket raises STC to about 56.	2-hr.	±48	1.12
	5/8" (16 mm) type X wallboard each side 3-5/8" (92 mm) metal studs 24" (610 mm) on center. Wallboard one side mounted on resilient channels 24" (610 mm) o.c. with 3" (76 mm) sound attenuation insulation in stud cavity.	1-hr.	±54	1.15
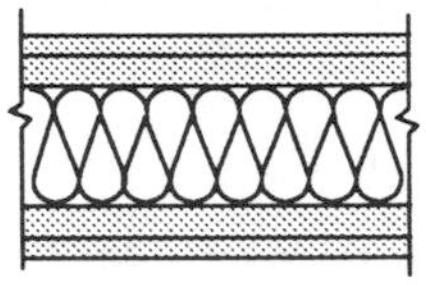	1/2" (13 mm) wallboard on 1" (25.4 mm) wallboard liner panels on proprietary studs. Liner panels spaced 3-1/2" (89 mm) apart with cavity filled with 3" (76 mm) sound attenuation insulation. Bead of acoustical sealant on vertical center line between panel edges.	3-hr.	±60	1.17
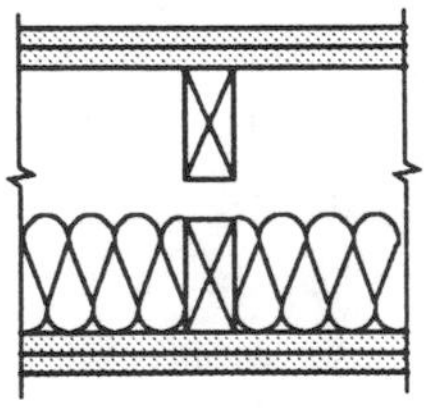	Two layers 5/8" (16 mm) type X wallboard on 2 x 4" studs 16" (406 mm) o.c. on separate plates. 3-1/2" (89 mm) sound attenuation insulation in cavity.	2-hr.	±56	1.18
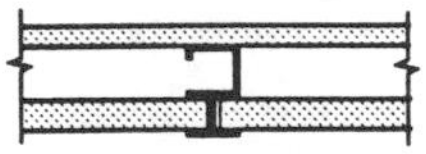	5/8" (16 mm) type X wallboard on proprietary studs 24" (610 mm) o.c. with 1" (25.4 mm) wallboard panel on shaft side.	1-hr.	±35	1.2(a)
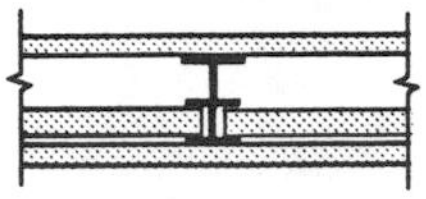	5/8" (16 mm) type X wallboard each side proprietary studs 24" (610 mm) o.c. with 1" (25.4 mm) wallboard liner panel set between studs.	2-hr.	±41	1.19
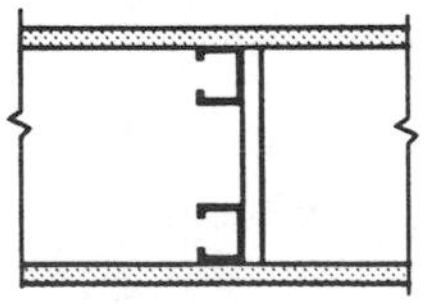	5/8" (16 mm) type X wallboard each side 1 5/8" (41.3 mm) studs 24" (610 mm) o.c. with 5/8" (16 mm) wallboard gusset panel attached at quarter points and center point. Adding 3-1/2" (89 mm) sound attenuation insulation raises STC to about 52.	1-hr.	N/A	1.13
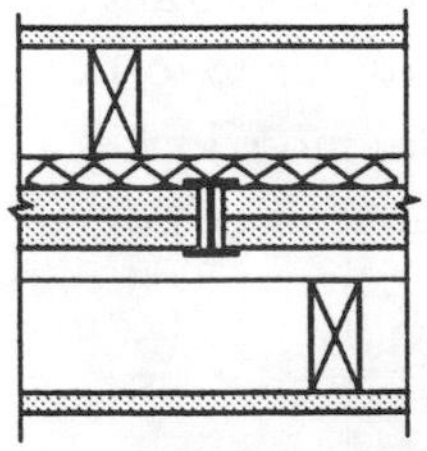	1/2" (13 mm) wallboard on 2 x 4" studs 16" (406 mm) o.c. with two layers 1" (25.4 mm) wallboard set between H-studs 24" (610 mm) o.c. 1" (25.4 mm) sound attenuation insulation on one side of double 1" panels.	2-hr.	±50	1.2(b)

Partition anchoring

In commercial construction, partitions are often only built to the underside of the suspended acoustical ceiling. The top runner is fastened to the ceiling grid, and this is all that holds the upper portion of the partition in place. When heavy doors or cabinets are placed on the wall, it is often necessary to provide additional braces extending from above the ceiling to the structural floor above. These braces are called *kickers* and are usually metal studs that can be screwed to the top partition runner through the ceiling.

LATH AND PLASTER PARTITIONS [09200]

Gypsum wallboard has supplanted plaster as the typical partition material because of its lower cost, easier and faster application, and the ready availability of material and workers able to install it. However, plaster has many advantages that gypsum wallboard cannot duplicate: it can be applied to form single or double curves, it can be molded into ornate decorative pieces for either new or remodeling work, and it can be finished with a wide variety of textures. Functionally, it is very abrasion resistant, and it is water resistant if Portland cement is used.

Plaster partition components

Plaster is a cementitious material that is applied to a surface in a plastic state and subsequently sets, or hardens, to a rigid state. The most common plasters used today for interior finishing are some combination of a cementitious binder, either gypsum or Portland cement, with lime, water, and aggregates of sand, vermiculite, or perlite.

The two cementitious binders used represent the two broad categories of plasters: gypsum and Portland cement. Gypsum plaster is used for most interior applications. Portland cement plaster is used in interiors where wetting, steam, or severe dampness is expected. When Portland cement plaster is used on the exterior of a building it is often called stucco.

Plaster

There are various formulations of plastering material to suit different conditions and to enhance the material's strength, abrasion resistance, and water resistance. Most partitions can be constructed with gypsum plaster troweled to a smooth finish. When water resistance is required, Portland cement plaster over metal lath is used because moisture can cause gypsum plaster to deteriorate. When extreme abrasion resistance is needed, keene's cement is used. This is a mixture of pure, completely dehydrated gypsum and lime putty.

For added texture, strength, sound reduction, and workability, various gradations of sand are added to the mixture. Aggregates of pumice, perlite, or vermiculite can also help reduce shrinkage, extend finish coverage, lower cost, and increase plasticity. Unique decorative effects can be achieved by adding unusual materials, such as straw or wax. Pigments can be added to the plaster mix to create integral color.

Special effects available with plaster include scagliola, sgraffito, marezzo, and fresco. Scagliola is plaster applied and painted to give the appearance of marble. Sgraffito is a plastering process that uses two or more layers of different-colored plasters. While the plasters are still soft, part of the top layer is scratched off to expose the layer or layers below. Marezzo is another type of imitation material formed with colored keene's cement and precast on a glass or marble bed. Fresco is the painting of freshly spread plaster before it sets.

The two basic types of plaster construction are standard lath and plaster and veneer plaster over gypsum board lath. The standard lath and plaster construction method is the traditional type, where several coats of plaster are applied over some type of open lath that is attached to studs or some other type of framing. It is even possible to form solid plaster partitions two or more inches thick; however, this technique is seldom used today. The veneer plaster method substitutes a special type of gypsum wallboard for the open lath. The wallboard is applied to wood or metal studs and a very thin coat of plaster from ⅟₁₆ in. to ⅛ in. (1.6 to 3 mm) thick is applied over the wallboard to form a uniform, homogenous surface.

Portland cement plaster can also be applied directly to concrete or masonry surfaces, but this is not a common use for interior applications. It is generally preferable to attach furring strips over the wall and apply a veneer plaster system onto the furring.

Metal lath [09250]

Expanded metal lath is used in standard lath and plaster construction. There are various types, but the three most common for interior use are shown in Figure 1.22. Diamond mesh lath as shown in Figure 1.22(a) is used over studs or other framing by attaching it with wire ties. This type of lath can be shaped into single curves or shaped and molded into complex, double curves. It is also available in a self-furring type for use in column fireproofing and replastering old surfaces.

Flat rib metal lath, shown in Figure 1.22(b), is more rigid than diamond mesh lath and is used for flat ceilings and in other applications where extra rigidity is needed. Rib metal lath, shown in Figure 1.22(c), is available with either ⅜-in. (10 mm) or ¾-in. (19 mm) ribs spaced about 4 in. (100 mm) apart. This is used for studless, solid partitions or where rigidity is needed over widely spaced framing.

Gypsum lath [09205]

Gypsum lath is used for veneer plaster installations. This is similar to gypsum wallboard, with the exception that the paper surface is specially formulated to provide a good plaster bond. The paper face is usually light blue and is sometime referred to as "blueboard." Fire-rated gypsum lath must be used for rated partitions.

Trim

For both types of plaster construction various trim types are used for outside corners, in framed openings, and where the plaster abuts another material. These trim pieces are very similar to those used for gypsum wallboard construction.

Typical plaster construction

In the standard lath and plaster construction method, plaster is applied in three coats over wire lath. See Figure 1.23. The first coat is

---

Building codes specify the requirements for plaster mixes for various applications, frame spacing, the types and application of gypsum and metal lath, and the exact method of applying the lath and plaster. Refer to the appropriate model code for specific requirements.

Building code provisions for plaster construction

Figure 1.22
Expanded metal lath

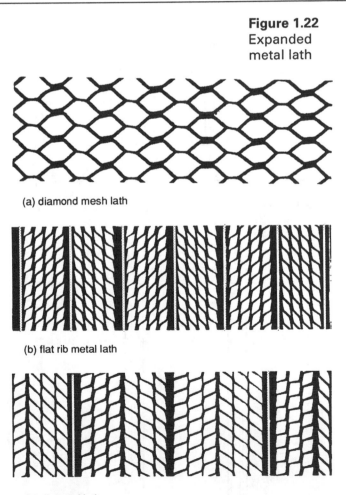

(a) diamond mesh lath

(b) flat rib metal lath

(c) rib metal lath

called the *scratch coat* and is about ½ in. (12 mm) thick. Before it sets, the scratch coat is roughened with deep ridges to provide a good base for mechanical bonding of the next coat. The second coat, or *brown coat*, is about ¼ in. (6 mm) thick and is used to bring the surface to a true level and near its final position. The *finish coat* of about ⅛ in. (3 mm) provides the final smoothing and surface texture. Sometimes only two coats are used, primarily in preparation for applying ceramic tile.

Figure 1.23
Traditional
three-coat
plaster partition

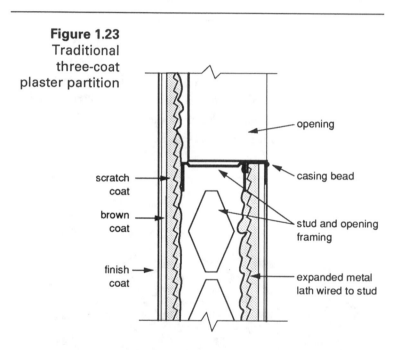

scratch coat

brown coat

finish coat

opening

casing bead

stud and opening framing

expanded metal lath wired to stud

Figure 1.24
Veneer
plaster partition

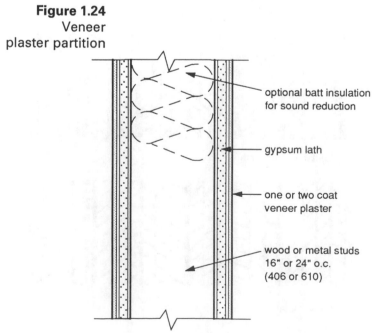

optional batt insulation for sound reduction

gypsum lath

one or two coat veneer plaster

wood or metal studs 16" or 24" o.c. (406 or 610)

Veneer plaster has many of the advantages of three-coat plaster, but only one of its disadvantages. It provides a very hard, durable surface that can be treated with a variety of textures and finishes and is faster and less expensive to construct. In addition, there is not as much moisture involved during interior construction. The only disadvantage is that gypsum lath is not appropriate as a base in wet areas such as showers and around tubs. Cement backing boards are used in residential construction or in other moderately wet construction areas. Standard lath and plaster systems are used for extremely wet, commercial applications. A typical veneer plaster partition is shown in Figure 1.24. The veneer may be applied in one or two coats.

Variations of the typical partition shown in Figure 1.24 include using two layers of fire-rated gypsum lath to achieve a 2-hour rating, adding batt insulation to improve the sound attenuation properties of the partition, and using resilient channels to further improve sound attenuation.

Stud spacing depends primarily on the type and weight of the lath and the weight of any surfacing material, such as ceramic tile. Metal studs measuring 2½ in. (63.5 mm) should be spaced 16 in. (406 mm) on center. See Table 1.5 for recommended stud spacing.

Glass-reinforced gypsum [09540]

The term glass-reinforced gypsum (GRG) refers to a broad class of products manufactured from high-strength, high-density gypsum reinforced with continuous filament glass fibers or chopped glass fibers. It is also known as fiberglass-reinforced gypsum (FRG) and glass-fiber-reinforced gypsum (GFRG).

GRG products are used for decorative elements, such as column covers, arches, coffered ceilings, ornate moldings, light troughs, and trim. They are premanufactured products made by pouring GRG into molds. After setting, the products are shipped to the job site for installation and final finishing. They can be finished with any kind of material that can be put on plaster or gypsum wallboard. An unlimited variety of shapes can be manufactured that would otherwise be too expensive or impossible to achieve with site-fabricated lath and plaster.

Design tips

Here are some design tips for glass-reinforced gypsum that will save time and reduce costs.

• Design GRG components so that only one side is exposed. Because of the way GRG

Lath type	Wood studs, in. (mm)	Metal studs, in. (mm)
Diamond mesh, 2.5 psy[1]	16 (406)	12 (305)
Diamond mesh, 3.4 psy	16 (406)	16 (406)
Flat rib lath, 2.75 psy	16 (406)	16 (406)
Flat rib lath, 3.4 psy	19 (483)	19 (483)
⅜-in. rib lath, 3.4 psy	24 (610)	24 (610)
⅜-in. gypsum lath	16 (406)	16 (406)
½-in. gypsum lath, 1-coat system	16 (406)	16[3] (406)
½-in. gypsum lath, 2-coat system	16/24[2] (406/610)	16/24[3] (406/610)
⅝-in. gypsum lath, 1-coat system	16/24[2] (406/610)	16/24[3] (406/610)
⅝-in. gypsum lath, 2-coat system	24[2] (610)	24[3] (610)

Table 1.5 Maximum spacing of studs for plaster partitions

[1] psy = weight of lath in pounds per square yard. Verify with specific manufacturer's recommendations.
[2] Spacing of 24 in. may require special joint treatment. Follow manufacturer's recommendations.
[3] Assemblies using metal studs and gypsum base require paper joint tape and setting-type joint compound.

Source: United States Gypsum Company.

Security partitions

For durable, thin, smooth finish partitions in jails, vaults, and other security areas, it is possible to construct a solid plaster partition that resists breakthrough and ballistic attack. A special, heavy-gage, perforated steel sheet is used in the center of the partition and high-strength plaster is applied to the steel sheet. A finish coat of 3000 psi or 20,684 kPa (psi-pounds per square inch; kPa-kilopascals) compressive strength plaster is then applied over the solid base coat. Although not appropriate in every instance, this type of partition is thin (from 3½ in. to 4½ in. (89 to 115 mm), lightweight, and easy to maintain and repair.

is molded, the back side is rough and shows the reinforcing and stiffing ribs.

• Minimize the number and detail of components on a job. The more unique molds that have to be made, the higher the cost.

• GRG shapes should only be used as decorative covers—not for bearing loads.

• Detail corners so that components can be removed easily from the molds. This means providing curves or draft angles and avoiding 90° angles or details that make it impossible to remove a casting from a mold.

• GRG components are attached to framing with screws, adhesive, or hanging. Follow the manufacturer's recommendations for specific details.

• Openings for mechanical and electrical penetrations can be made in the field.

• Transitions from curved GRG shapes to flat gypsum wallboard should be made so that the GRG curved component extends about 2 in. (50 mm) into the flat wallboard. This allows the joint to be floated together easily.

• Joint alignment tolerances should not exceed ⅛ in. (3 mm), and joint width should not exceed ⅜ in. (10 mm).

Coordination with other construction components

• Mounting strips or wood cleats for attachment of medium-to-heavy cabinets and other loads should be bolted to metal studs.

• Steel door frames used with plaster partitions should be at least 16-gage steel.

• Control joints or relief joints should be placed where a plaster partition abuts a structural element, where a partition run exceeds 30 ft (9.1 m), and where a building expansion or control joint occurs. Full height doors can be used as control joints.

• Metal studs for partitions faced with ceramic tile should be a minimum of 20-gage, 3⅝-in. (92.1 mm) deep, spaced 16 in. (406 mm) on center.

• The total thickness of the scratch and mortar coating as the base for ceramic tile should not exceed 1 in. (25.4 mm).

MASONRY PARTITIONS

Masonry is a term that includes brick, concrete block, glass block, structural clay tile, terra cotta, and gypsum block. Masonry is usually part of the architectural design of a

Applicable standards for plaster partitions	American Society for Testing and Materials (ASTM):
	ASTM C-28 *Specification for Gypsum Plasters*
	ASTM C-35 *Specification for Inorganic Aggregates for use in Gypsum Plaster*
	ASTM C-37 *Specification for Gypsum Lath*
	ASTM C-59 *Specification for Gypsum Casting and Molding Plaster*
	ASTM C-61 *Specification for Gypsum Keene's Cement*
	ASTM C-150 *Specification for Portland Cement*
	ASTM C-206 *Specification for Finishing Hydrated Lime*
	ASTM C-207 *Specification for Hydrated Lime for Masonry Purposes*
	ASTM C-587 *Specification for Gypsum Veneer Plaster*
	ASTM C-588 *Specification for Gypsum Base for Veneer Plasters*
	ASTM C-631 *Specification for Bonding Compounds for Interior Gypsum Plastering*
	ASTM C-841 *Specification for the Installation of Interior Lathing and Furring*
	ASTM C-842 *Specification for the Application of Interior Gypsum Plaster*
	ASTM C-843 *Specification for the Application of Gypsum Veneer Plaster*
	ASTM C-844 *Specification for the Application of Gypsum Base to Receive Gypsum Veneer Plaster*
	ASTM C-847 *Specification for Metal Lath*
	ASTM C-897 *Specification for Aggregate for Job-Mixed Portland Cement-based Plasters*

building. However, there are times when interior construction requires a masonry, nonload-bearing partition for special purposes or to match existing construction. Most often, masonry partitions are concrete block or glass block.

Concrete block [04220]

Concrete block is manufactured with cement, water, and various types of aggregate, including gravel, expanded shale or slate, expanded slag or pumice, or limestone cinders. It is hollow and its size is based on a nominal 4-in. (100 mm) module which includes an allowance for ⅜ in. mortar joints. One of the most common sizes is an 8 × 8 × 16-in. unit (203 × 203 × 406 mm), which is actually 7⅝ in. (193.7 mm) wide, 7⅝ in. high, and 15⅝ in. (396.9 mm) long. Common nominal thicknesses are 4, 6, 8, and 12 in. (102, 152, 203, and 305 mm). Various sizes and shapes are manufactured for particular uses.

Concrete block is laid up in a staggered bond with horizontal joint reinforcement placed every 16 in. (406 mm) on center vertically. As the partition is being laid, door and glass frames are set in place and anchored with special masonry anchors laid in the joints.

Structural clay tile [04210]

For interior partitions, glazed structural clay tile is typically used where a hard, durable, nonstaining, easily cleaned partition is required, such as in hospitals, institutions, and food processing plants. Glazed tile is available in 8 × 16-in. and 6 × 12-in. sizes (203 × 406 mm and 152 × 305 mm), in thicknesses of 2 in., 6 in., and 9 in. (51, 152, and 225 mm). It is available in several preformed trim shapes, such as bull-nose, wall and end caps, curved inside, and curved outside corners. It is also available in a variety of colors and finishes. Specified in the correct thickness for the height, glazed structural clay tile provides a finished partition in one construction operation.

Coordination with other construction components

- The load bearing capacity of existing floors for new masonry must be verified by a structural engineer.

- In existing construction, new steel reinforcing may need to be anchored to existing floors and walls to tie new masonry walls to the existing building. This must be designed by a structural engineer.

- Electrical and plumbing requirements may increase the difficulty and cost of using masonry for interior partitions.

- Increased sound attenuation properties can be achieved by filling the hollow cells of concrete block with sand or grout.

- Rough wood framing is required in a masonry opening to provide a solid base for wood doors and frames.

- Whenever possible, the heights and widths of openings in masonry should be based on the nominal module of the masonry, usually 4 in. (102 mm), so that excessive cutting of masonry is not required.

GLASS BLOCK PARTITIONS [04270]

Glass block is manufactured either as a hollow or solid unit with a clear, textured, or patterned face. It is a popular choice for interior use when a combination of light transmission, privacy, and security is required. Solid block can also be used for flooring if the flooring is supported correctly.

Generally, glass block does not provide rated fire resistance; however, some assemblies are now available that qualify as 30-minute and 45-minute fire-rated enclosures in 1-hour-rated walls. Underwriters Laboratories has given some manufacturer's blocks 60-minute or 90-minute ratings in openings up to 100 ft² (9.29 m²) if no dimension is greater than 10 ft (3050 mm). Exact requirements vary, and some controversy exists concerning fire-rated glass block used for interior walls and openings; therefore, check with local codes.

Glass block components

Glass block is manufactured in a nominal thickness of 4 in. (102 mm) and in face sizes of 6 × 6, 8 × 8, 12 × 12, and 4 × 8 in. (152 × 152, 203 × 203, 305 × 305, and 102 × 203 mm). The two standard thicknesses are 3⅛ in. and 3⅞ in. (79.4 and 98.4 mm). The thinner block is commonly used for interior partitions. Other sizes are available from foreign manufacturers. Glass block is available in clear, textured, or patterned faces, and special blocks made by most manufacturers can be used to form 90° angles and end caps.

Standard glass block assemblies

Glass block walls are laid in stack bond (with joints aligned rather than staggered) with mortar and horizontal and vertical reinforcement in the joints. Because of the glass expansion coefficient and the possibility of floor structure deflection and other building movement, it is good practice to provide expansion strips at the tops and sides of glass block partitions. Figure 1.25 shows typical detailing for the sill and head of an interior glass block wall, and Figure 1.26 shows jamb and vertical joint details. A steel stiffener similar to the section shown in Figure 1.26 is required when a block partition exceeds the maximum sizes allowed by the building code. An alternate type of stiffener is illustrated in Figure 1.27.

Because glass block cannot be load-bearing, individual interior panels are usually limited by code to about 250 ft². Each panel must be supported both horizontally and vertically by a suitable structure and by expansion joints provided at the structural support points.

Custom glass block assemblies

If the appearance of a frame overlapping the block is objectionable, the block can be set flush with the steel frame if special detailing is used. This is done by both horizontal and vertical reinforcement using panel anchors that are rigidly attached to the bottom and top framing members. See Figure 1.28. This detailing also eliminates the need for intermediate vertical stiffeners, if allowed by the local building code.

Curved glass block partitions

The minimum radius of a partition is determined by the block thickness. Assuming that a wedge-shaped head joint measures ⅛ in. (3 mm) on the inside and ⅝ in. (16 mm) on the outside, the minimum radii for curved partitions are shown in Table 1.6.

Figure 1.25
Glass block partition at sill and head

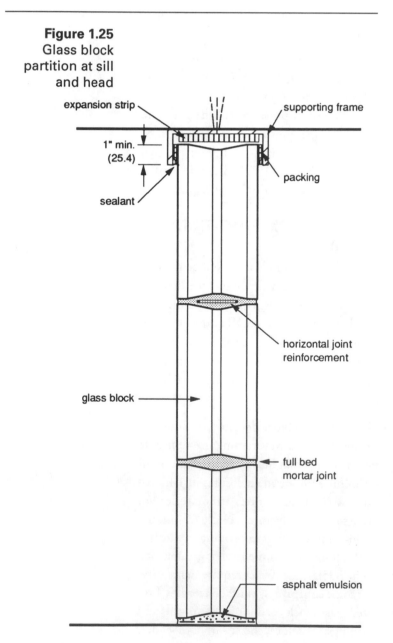

expansion strip

supporting frame

1" min. (25.4)

packing

sealant

horizontal joint reinforcement

glass block

full bed mortar joint

asphalt emulsion

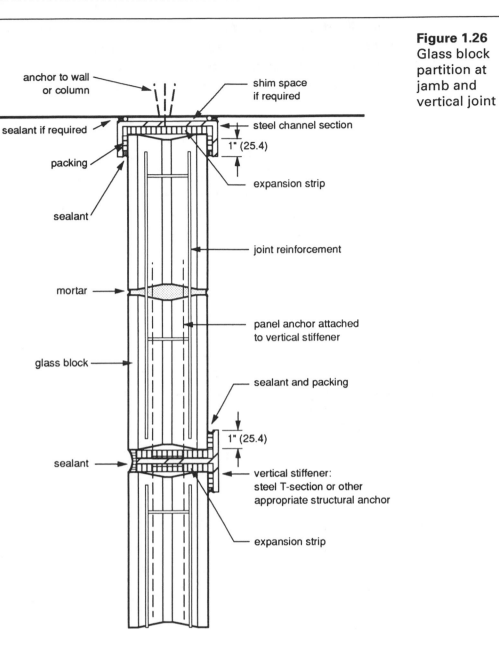

Figure 1.26
Glass block
partition at
jamb and
vertical joint

anchor to wall
or column

shim space
if required

sealant if required

steel channel section

1" (25.4)

packing

expansion strip

sealant

joint reinforcement

mortar

panel anchor attached
to vertical stiffener

glass block

sealant and packing

1" (25.4)

sealant

vertical stiffener:
steel T-section or other
appropriate structural anchor

expansion strip

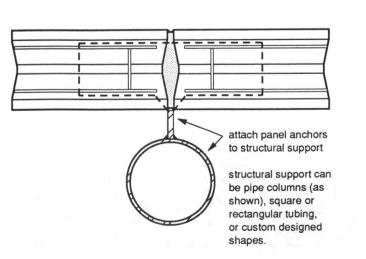

Figure 1.27
Intermediate
stiffener behind
glass block
partition

attach panel anchors
to structural support

structural support can
be pipe columns (as
shown), square or
rectangular tubing,
or custom designed
shapes.

Coordination with other construction components

• The width and height of the opening should be an even multiple of the size of the glass block used.

• The deflection of the floors, beams, or other structural members supporting the glass block must not exceed L/600. Verification by a structural engineer is necessary.

• Intermediate vertical stiffeners, as shown in Figure 1.26 or 1.27, are required at every change of direction in a multicurved wall and at every location where a curve joins a straight section.

DEMOUNTABLE PARTITIONS [10615]

Demountable partition components

Demountable partitions consist of a system of individual components that can be quickly assembled, disassembled, and reused with nearly-total salvageability. Demountable partitions differ from operable partitions, as described in Chapter 3, in that demountable partitions are intended to remain in place as standard partitions, while operable partitions act as special doors to open and close space frequently.

Demountable partitions allow space to be reconfigured quickly and easily as needs change. Because the components are prefinished and designed as a system, they can be rearranged and combined with new components, such as doors and glazing panels, without messy demolition and damage to adjacent construction. They can also make initial construction faster because flooring, ceilings, lighting, and mechanical work can be completed first and the partitions installed later. Although demountable partitions have higher initial costs than standard partition construction, life-cycle costs are lower because of the savings in material and labor costs in places where space plans are changed frequently.

Typical partition construction

The configuration and design of individual components varies with each manufacturer, but generally consist of four components: floor runners, ceiling runners, stud sections with clips to hold the panels, and prefinished gypsum wallboard panels. The panels are typically covered with vinyl wallcovering in a range of standard colors and patterns, although custom finishes are possible on large jobs. Panels are usually 24 in. or 30 in. (610 or 762 mm) wide to work with common building planning modules of 4 ft or

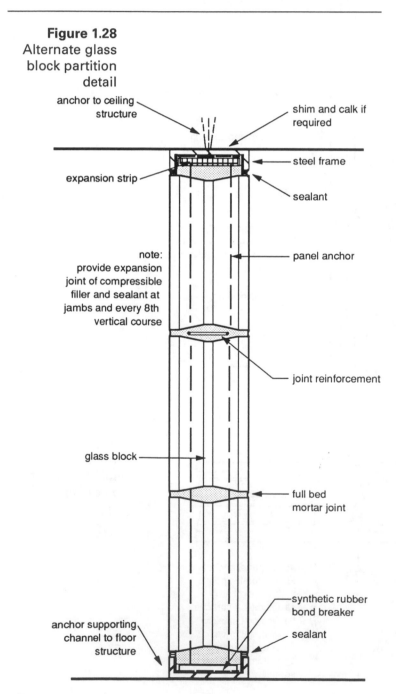

Figure 1.28
Alternate glass block partition detail

anchor to ceiling structure

shim and calk if required

expansion strip

steel frame

sealant

note: provide expansion joint of compressible filler and sealant at jambs and every 8th vertical course

panel anchor

joint reinforcement

glass block

full bed mortar joint

synthetic rubber bond breaker

anchor supporting channel to floor structure

sealant

5 ft (1220 mm or 1524 mm). When a partition is completed, there are small vertical joints between the panels and the top track is visible as it overlaps the panels at the ceiling. A manufacturer's standard base trim snaps on at the floor line.

In addition to the basic components, all manufacturer's systems have door frames, glazing, bank rails, openings, and similar common components. Some manufacturers also provide for hanging shelves and furniture components in slots between the panels.

The bottom track can rest directly on the structural floor or finished floor like a standard gypsum wallboard floor runner. As shown in Figure 1.29, tracks are also available with spikes extending below the runner, allowing the runner to be placed directly over carpeting without crushing it. When the partition is moved, the previous partition's location is less noticeable. The top track is attached directly to the suspended ceiling system, as with standard construction, except that the flange of the

track overlaps the panel and is visible in the final installation.

Partition systems can be either progressive or nonprogressive. In a progressive system the first panel must be placed before the second panel, which must be placed before the third panel, and so on. When the partition is taken down, the reverse order must be followed. In a nonprogressive system the panels are independent and can be removed

Block size, in. (mm)	Minimum radius inside, in. (mm)
4 (100 mm)	32 (813)
6 (150 mm)	48½ (1232)
8 (200 mm)	65 (1650)
12 (300 mm)	98½ (2500)

Table 1.6 Minimum radii for curved glass block partitions

Building code requirements for glass block

Building codes limit the maximum size and maximum unsupported length of unsupported glass block panels. These requirements are summarized in Table 1.7. When panels larger than these sizes are required, stiffeners similar to those shown in Figures 1.26 or 1.27 must be provided. The Uniform Building Code also requires that at least a 3-in. (76 mm) thick block be used, that reinforcement be of minimum No. 9 gage wire, and that mortar joints be from ¼ in. to ⅜ in. (6 mm to 10 mm) thick. Although the UBC does not specifically require interior glass block partitions to have expansion joints, it is good practice.

	Interior walls		
Building code	Area, ft² (m²)	Height, ft (mm)	Width, ft (mm)
Uniform Building Code (UBC)	250 (23.2)	25 (7620)	25 (7620)
Standard Building Code (SBC)	250 (23.2)	25 (7620)	25 (7620)
Basic Building Code (BBC)	–	–	–

Table 1.7 Maximum glass block panel sizes for interior partitions based on building code limitations[1]

[1] Panels between 144 and 250 ft² (13.4 and 23.3 m²) are permitted if they are braced by a special stiffener.

Figure 1.29
Demountable
partition

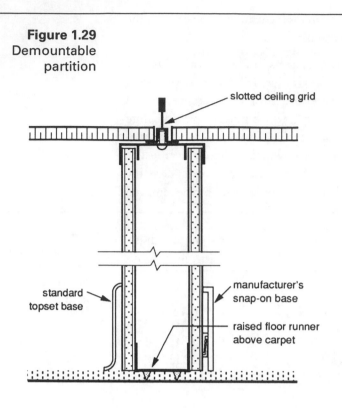

slotted ceiling grid

standard
topset base

manufacturer's
snap-on base

raised floor runner
above carpet

or replaced individually. Although progressive systems have a lower initial cost than nonprogressive panels, they are much less flexible.

Coordination with other construction components

Demountable partition systems are only cost-effective if they are coordinated with other building components and systems, including lighting, HVAC (heating, ventilating, and air conditioning), window mullions, and a suspended ceiling system. Space plans should be laid out on the building grid, which should also coincide with the ceiling grid. In this way, the relocation of lights, HVAC diffusers and grilles, and sprinkler heads is minimized when partitions change. Slotted suspended ceiling grids should be used, which allow the top track to be screwed into the grid without damaging its appearance when the track is moved.

2

CEILINGS

In addition to providing the finish surface for a space, ceilings form part of a system that accommodates lighting, partition attachments, supply- and return-air grilles and diffusers, speakers, and other construction components. Because ceilings are dominant design features and have many functional requirements, their detailing is critical.

Ceilings can be classified into three groups based on how they are attached to the structure. They can be suspended from the structure, attached directly to the structure, or the structure and the finish ceiling can be the same component. Figure 2.1 illustrates this ceiling classification system and the variations possible within each group. The most common construction method for residential ceilings is gypsum wallboard placed directly on the floor joists or ceiling joists with mechanical attachment using screws or nails. In most commercial construction, the ceiling is a wire suspended system supporting a finished surface of acoustical tile, gypsum wallboard, or other decorative material. This provides a flat ceiling surface for partition attachment, lights, and acoustical treatment and allows the space above the ceiling, called the *plenum*, to be used for mechanical systems, wiring, and other services.

SUSPENDED ACOUSTICAL CEILINGS [09510]

Suspended acoustical ceilings are the most common type for commercial construction. They consist of thin panels of wood fiber, mineral fiber, or glass fiber set in a support grid of metal framing that is suspended by wires from the structure. The tiles are perforated or fissured in various ways to absorb sound. Although acoustical ceilings absorb sound, they do not prevent sound transmission to any appreciable extent. The advantages of suspended acoustical ceilings include low cost, fast installation, sound control, flexibility, adaptability to lighting and mechanical services, and easy accessibility to the plenum.

Acoustical ceiling components

Acoustical ceiling tiles and the metal supporting grid are available in a variety of sizes and configurations. The most common type is the lay-in system in which panels are simply laid on top of an exposed T-shaped grid system. See Figure 2.2(a). A variation of this is the tegular system that uses panels with rabbeted edges, as shown in Figure 2.2(b).

Systems are also available in which the grid is completely concealed. Concealed systems

Figure 2.1
Ceiling
classification

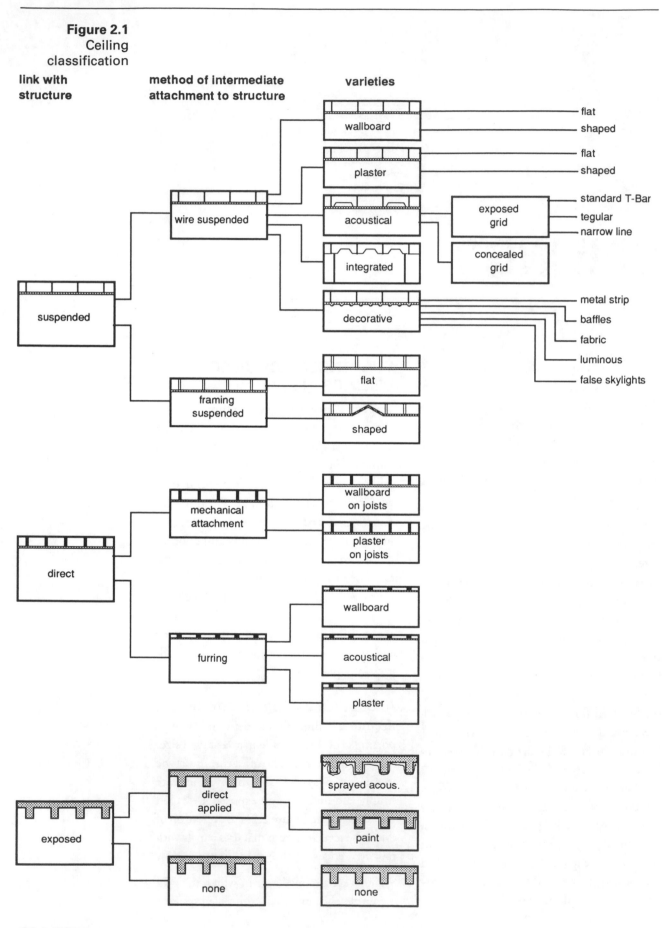

typically use 1 × 1-ft (300 × 300 mm) tiles with either square or beveled edges. Beveled-edged tiles are better than square-edged tiles because the slight bevel helps prevent edge chipping and conceals minor misalignments between tiles. See Figure 2.2(c). Whichever system is used, the tile at the perimeter walls is supported by a ceiling angle. This angle is also used to support light fixtures mounted next to the wall.

Manufacturers offer many types of grid shapes and sizes. Some of these are shown in Figure 2.3. Refer to manufacturer's catalogs for current information on the availability of acoustical tiles and support systems.

The most common tile and grid sizes for lay-in acoustical ceiling systems are 24 × 24 in. (600 × 600 mm) and 24 × 48 in. (600 × 1200 mm).

A 20 × 60-in. (500 × 1500 mm) size is also available for use in buildings with a 5-ft working module so that three panels fit within one 60-in. (1500 mm) grid. This allows office partitions to be laid out on the 5-ft module lines without interfering with HVAC (heating, ventilating, and air conditioning) registers and special 20 × 48-in. (508 × 1219 mm) light fixtures located in the center of a module. The system is most often employed when demountable partitions are used. Partitions can be moved easily without disturbing most of the lighting and HVAC system. See Figure 2.4.

Other types of suspended systems that provide acoustical properties are also available. These include metal strip ceilings, wood grids, and fabric-covered acoustical batts. All serve the same purpose: they provide a finished ceiling to absorb rather than reflect sound (like a gypsum wallboard ceiling does) to reduce noise levels within a space while providing easy plenum access.

Standard ceiling assemblies

Suspended acoustical ceilings are installed by attaching hanger wires to the structural

floor or roof and using these wires to support lengths of the grid system spaced 4 ft (1200 mm) on center. Cross tees are then snapped into prepunched holes in the main runners every two feet. If the grid size is 24 × 24 in. (610 × 610 mm), additional cross tees are placed in the center of the 24 × 48-in. (610 × 1219 mm) grid. A ceiling angle is placed around the perimeter of the room and around columns and other obstructions. See Figure 2.5. The tiles are placed within the grid and odd-sized tiles are cut to fit nonstandard

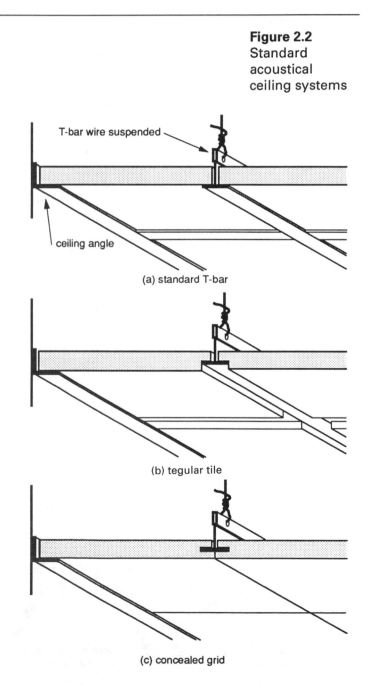

Figure 2.2
Standard acoustical ceiling systems

(a) standard T-bar

(b) tegular tile

(c) concealed grid

T-bar wire suspended

ceiling angle

openings. Tiles are easily cut to accommodate holes for lights, sprinklers, and other penetrations. Retention clips can be installed above the ceiling to prevent people from pushing the tiles out of the grid or for fire-rated ceiling assemblies when retention is required.

Concealed spline ceilings use a similar suspension system, with the exception that special cross members are required. These cross members fit within slots that have been cut into the edges of the tiles. Various systems are used to install the last pieces of tile and close up the ceiling. In addition, special components are required that allow tiles to be removed to gain access to the space above. Although exact details vary with each manufacturer, there are two types: downward accessible and upward accessible.

In the downward accessible system, an access clip mounted to the framing or a special tool is required to pull a unit of two tiles loose by pivoting them from one end. After the unit is removed, the adjacent tiles can be removed if necessary. In an upward accessible system, a unit of two tiles is pushed up from a pivot point at one end and removed. Additional tiles can then be removed by slipping out intermediate splines.

In either system, the percentage of the total ceiling area that is accessible can be specified based on the amount of access required. For example, if a 25 percent accessible ceiling is specified, then one-fourth of the tiles should consist of units of two tiles that can be easily removed. Upward accessible ceilings are preferable to downward accessible ceilings because the tool used to pull down the tiles usually causes the tile edges to chip. After a time the ceiling becomes unsightly. In an upward accessible system, the tiles rest in place on concealed Z-clips, and all that is required to remove them is a push up. In order to identify which tiles are accessible, some manufacturers place a small pin in the corner of the removable tile.

Suspended ceilings are installed level to a tolerance of ⅛ in. in 12 ft (3 mm in 3660 mm). Because ceilings are almost always more level than floors, critical dimensions are often measured from the ceiling down. In addition to flat ceilings, suspended acoustical systems can accommodate vertical rises and sloped sections with standard suspension system components.

In commercial construction, the space above a suspended ceiling is frequently used as a return-air plenum. Return-air grilles are set

Figure 2.3
Ceiling grid types

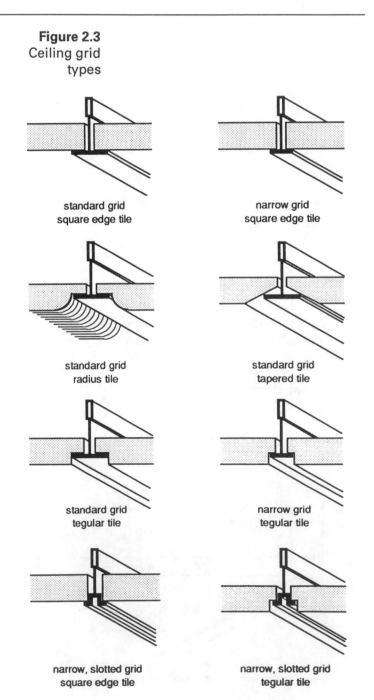

standard grid
square edge tile

narrow grid
square edge tile

standard grid
radius tile

standard grid
tapered tile

standard grid
tegular tile

narrow grid
tegular tile

narrow, slotted grid
square edge tile

narrow, slotted grid
tegular tile

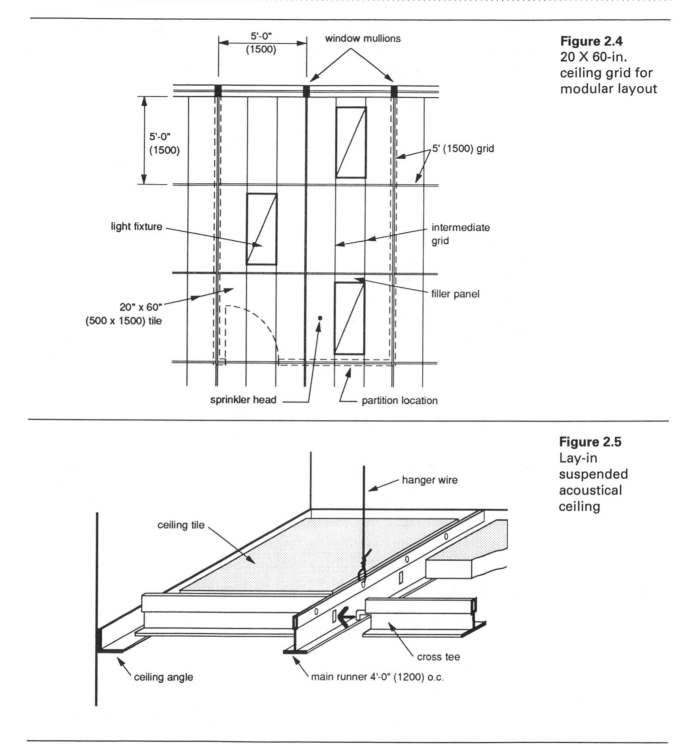

Figure 2.4
20 X 60-in. ceiling grid for modular layout

Figure 2.5
Lay-in suspended acoustical ceiling

Although adjacent tiles of concealed spline ceilings are installed nearly flush, tolerances between tiles can be critical if artificial or natural light grazes across the ceiling. Variations between tiles of as little as 0.005 in. (0.127 mm) can cause objectionable shadows that emphasize any joint unevenness. Ambient lighting or rooms with a lot of reflected light are preferable. If grazing light is going to be present, cardboard splines can be installed in all joints of a concealed spline ceiling. Although it adds to the initial cost and makes removal more difficult, the splines force the tiles into closer alignment. Bevel-edged tiles can also be used to conceal misalignment.

Maintaining the flush appearance of concealed spline ceilings

in the grid and return-air passes through the grilles, through the ceiling space, and back to a central return-air duct or shaft that connects to the HVAC system. If this is the case, building codes require that no combustible material be placed above the ceiling and that all plastic wiring be run in metal conduit. Some codes allow wiring used for telephone, computer, low-voltage lighting, and signal systems to be exposed if it is approved plenum-rated wiring.

Suspended ceilings may be rated or non-rated. If they are fire rated, it means that they are part of a complete floor/ceiling or roof/ceiling assembly that is rated. Ceiling systems in themselves cannot prevent the spread of fire from one floor to the next. Rated acoustical ceiling systems consist of rated mineral tiles and rated grid systems, which include hold-down clips to keep the panels in place and expansion slots to allow the grid to expand when subjected to heat.

Special ceiling assemblies

Because acoustical ceilings cannot stop sound from passing through them, plenum sound barriers are required above partitions that extend from the floor to the underside of the suspended ceiling when acoustical privacy is needed. There are several ways to achieve this without breaking the ceiling grid. The easiest and least expensive way is to lay fire-rated sound attenuation insulation on top of the ceiling tile for a distance of about 4 ft (1200 mm) on either side of the partition line, as shown in Figure 2.6. While this provides some sound control, noise can still pass through the ceiling of one space into the plenum, through the plenum over the insulation, and into the adjacent room.

If the ceiling grid cannot be broken, a better solution is to suspend a partition from the structural floor above down to the top of the ceiling grid and apply one layer of gypsum wallboard to it. The crack between the bottom runner and the top of the ceiling tile is filled with sound attenuation insulation. Alternately, sheet lead can be suspended from the structural floor above down to the ceiling. Both of these methods are awkward to build and add to the cost of the ceiling; however, they offer better sound attenuation than insulation laid on ceiling tile. Refer to Chapter 11 for more information on acoustical design and details of plenum barriers.

Building code requirements for suspended acoustical ceilings

The Uniform Building Code (UBC) and other model codes specify the finish and construction requirements for suspended ceilings. As with any finish material, the ceiling tile must meet the particular flame spread limitations for the occupancy group and space in the building where the ceiling is being used. Nearly all acoustical ceiling tiles have a Class A rating; therefore, this usually is not a problem.

The codes also require that all of the suspension system components be noncombustible, and the codes specify the minimum size of hanger wires based on the type of installation and the area of ceiling that is supported.

For ceilings that are part of a complete floor/ceiling assembly, certain construction details must be followed. For example, when a ceiling forms the protective membrane for a fire-resistive assembly, the UBC sets limits on the number and size of openings in the ceiling for items such as duct openings, lights, and electrical boxes. In addition, approved barriers must be placed over light fixtures. These consist of gypsum wallboard sheets laid over recessed fluorescent light troffers or semirigid mineral-wool board tied together into boxes that fit over the fixtures.

Seismic restraint may also be required, as discussed in the next section.

In some areas of the United States, special seismic restraint detailing is required for suspended ceilings. Because seismic restraint requirements are evolving, check with the local building code and building official to determine current rules. Codes may require ceiling suspension systems to be designed to withstand the force of earthquake loads, or they may refer to ASTM E-580, *Recommended Practice for Application of Ceiling Suspension Systems for Acoustical Tile and Lay-in Panels in Areas Requiring Seismic Restraint,* which is based on early recommendations of the Ceilings & Interior Systems Construction Association (CISCA). CISCA has recently updated its work and published recommendations for direct-hung ceiling suspension systems for all seismic zones in the United States. For zones 0, 1, and 2, these are found in *Recommendations for Direct-hung Acoustical Tile and Lay-in Panel Ceilings, Seismic zones 0–2.*

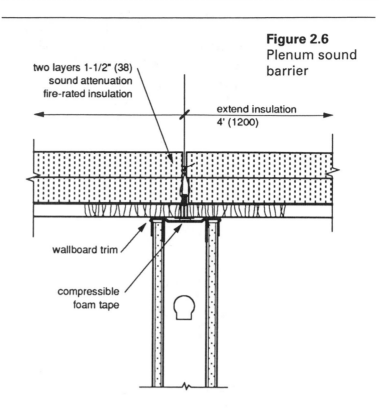

Figure 2.6
Plenum sound barrier

two layers 1-1/2" (38) sound attenuation fire-rated insulation

extend insulation 4' (1200)

wallboard trim

compressible foam tape

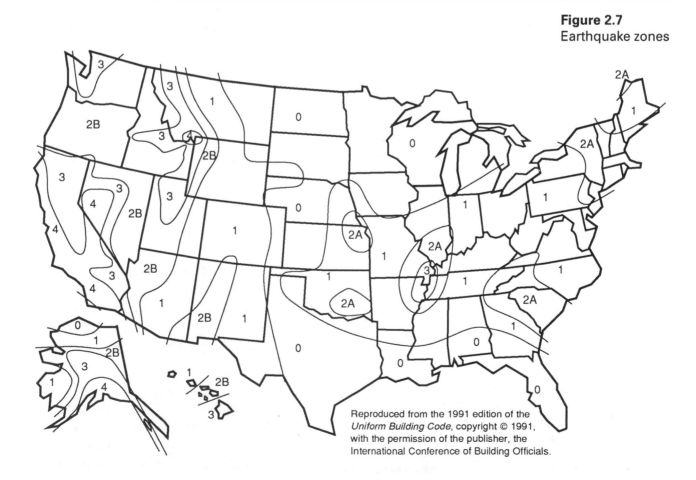

Figure 2.7
Earthquake zones

Reproduced from the 1991 edition of the *Uniform Building Code,* copyright © 1991, with the permission of the publisher, the International Conference of Building Officials.

The United States is divided into five zones representing the relative risk from potential earthquakes. Zone 0 includes areas with the least risk, while zone 4 includes the greatest risk areas, such as California. Figure 2.7 shows the approximate location of the seismic zones in the United States.

Figure 2.8
Partition bracing for zones 3 and 4

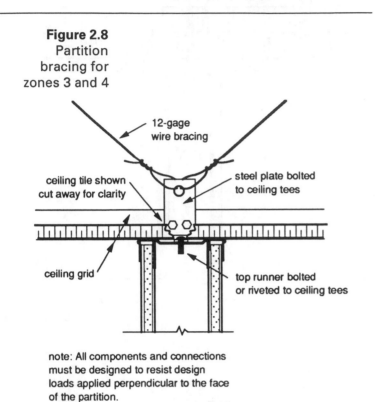

12-gage wire bracing

ceiling tile shown cut away for clarity

steel plate bolted to ceiling tees

ceiling grid

top runner bolted or riveted to ceiling tees

note: All components and connections must be designed to resist design loads applied perpendicular to the face of the partition.

Figure 2.9
Detail of runners at perimeter partition

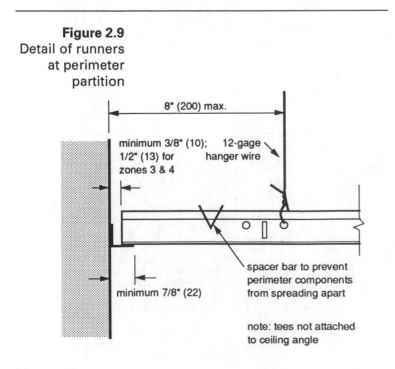

8" (200) max.

minimum 3/8" (10); 1/2" (13) for zones 3 & 4

12-gage hanger wire

minimum 7/8" (22)

spacer bar to prevent perimeter components from spreading apart

note: tees not attached to ceiling angle

For zones 0 and 1, CISCA recommends that individual light fixtures or other types of equipment that weigh 56 lb (25.4 kg) or less and that are typically supported by the ceiling grid have two No. 12 gage wire hangers attached at opposite corners. Although these wires must be slack, they would prevent the fixture from falling if the ceiling grid deformed or broke. Fixtures heavier than 56 lb should be supported independently of the structure. Additionally, CISCA recommends that the intersection of the main runner and cross runners have an average ultimate test strength of 60 lb (27.2 kg) or more in both tension and compression.

For buildings in zone 2, CISCA recommends the same specifications as for zones 0 and 1 along with four others. These are summarized below; however, exact requirements must be verified with the local building code.

• The actual average weight of the ceiling system, including lights and air terminals, should be 2.5 lb/ft² (12.2 kg/m²) or less. All other items should be supported independently.

• The ceiling system should not be used to provide lateral support for partitions. Instead, the partitions should be braced with detailing similar to that shown in Figure 2.8 so that the ceiling membrane can move laterally.

• Ceiling angles should provide at least a ⅞-in. (22 mm) ledge, and there must be at least a ⅜-in. (10 mm) clearance from the edge of the tile to the edge of the wall. This is shown in Figure 2.9.

• The perimeter main runners and cross runners must be prevented from spreading without relying on permanent attachment to the ceiling angle.

The requirements for buildings in zones 3 and 4 are much stricter and require more elaborate detailing. The suspension system must be of intermediate-duty or heavy-duty type and must have lateral force bracing 12 ft (3600 mm) on center in both directions, with the first point within 6 ft (1800 mm) from each wall. As illustrated in Figure 2.10, these points of lateral bracing must provide support in all four directions and must have rigid struts connected to the structure above to prevent uplift as well as to support gravity loads. Additional wire supports are also required for all runners at the perimeter of the room within 8 in. (200 mm) of the wall. Clearances from the end of the runners to the partition must be ½ in. (13 mm) instead of ⅜ in. (9.5 mm). Complete detailing recommendations can be found in the *Guidelines for Seismic Restraint Direct Hung Suspended Ceiling Assemblies, Seismic zones 3 & 4*, published by CISCA.

Coordination

Because ceilings serve so many purposes in today's construction in addition to acoustical control, there are many elements that must be coordinated with the selection and detailing of ceiling systems. These elements can include recessed lights, duct work, sprinkler piping, fire alarm speakers, smoke detectors, drapery pockets, and other recessed items.

Surface-mounted items

All the mechanical, electrical, and architectural items that must be mounted on the ceiling should be considered. They must be located consistent with the design plan, while satisfying the limitations of function and code requirements. These items may include lighting fixtures, HVAC air grilles and registers, speakers, smoke detectors, sprinkler heads, fire alarms, and signs.

Recessed lights

The space above suspended ceilings is packed with ducts, conduit, and piping. It must be verified that there is sufficient clearance for recessed lights, coffers, and other specified design features.

Plenum space

If the plenum is being used for return-air as part of the mechanical system, only noncombustible materials can be used in the plenum space. For example, the use of wood blocking, even if it is fire-retardant treated, is generally not permitted. Wiring must be in conduit or be the approved plenum-rated type. Exact requirement must be verified with the local building code.

Access

If there is a great deal of mechanical equipment, valves, electrical junction boxes, and other items requiring access, a ceiling system must be selected that is easy to open up and return into place without damage or soiling the visible system components.

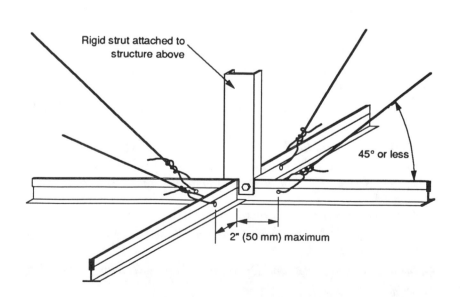

Figure 2.10
Ceiling grid bracing

Rigid strut attached to structure above

45° or less

2" (50 mm) maximum

Remodeling work

In remodeling work, painting existing acoustical tiles is sometimes seen as an economical way to refinish ceilings. However, painting destroys the acoustical value of the tiles. Instead, replacing or cleaning the tiles should be considered.

Heavy loads

When partitions extend only to the suspended ceiling, additional bracing may be required for heavy loads suspended on the partition, such as bookcases. Additional bracing will prevent wall shake from heavy doors being closed and can be used for earthquake bracing in zones 3 and 4. Bracing may consist of diagonal studs screwed through the ceiling into the top runner of the partition and secured to the structural floor above.

Demountable partitions

If a demountable partition system is used, a ceiling suspension system with a continuous slotted grid or other provisions for attachment should be selected. Doing so will prevent marring of the grid when the top runner of the partition is removed and reinstalled.

Drapery pockets

It must be verified that there is enough clearance to recess drapery track or horizontal blinds if required by the design.

GYPSUM WALLBOARD CEILINGS [09250]

Gypsum wallboard ceiling components

Gypsum wallboard for ceilings is either ½ in. (13 mm) or ⅝ in. (16 mm) thick, depending on the frame spacing. Wallboard ½ in. thick is generally used for framing 16 in. on center (406 mm); wallboard ⅝ in. thick is used for framing 24 in. (600 mm) on center. As with partitions, contractors prefer to use the longest lengths practicable to minimize the number of joints.

When wallboard is attached directly to structural framing, such as joists, the only other components to the assembly are fasteners, tape, and joint compound. Screws are almost always used for both ceiling and partition construction because they are faster and easier to install and do not pull out of the framing.

When wallboard is suspended, a framing grid of 1½-in. (38 mm) steel channels and furring channels are suspended from the structure above like an acoustical ceiling. These components are discussed in the next section.

Applicable standards for suspended acoustical ceiling systems

American Society for Testing and Materials (ASTM):

ASTM C-423   *Test Methods for Sound Absorption and Sound Absorption Coefficients by the Reverberation Room Method*

ASTM C-635   *Metal Suspension Systems for Acoustical Tile and Lay-in Panel Systems*

ASTM C-636   *Installation of Metal Ceiling Suspension Systems for Acoustical Tile and Lay-in Panels*

ASTM E-580   *Recommended Practice for Application of Ceiling Suspension Systems for Acoustical Tile and Lay-in Panels in Areas Requiring Seismic Restraint*

ASTM E-1264   *Standard Classification for Acoustical Ceiling Products*

Ceilings & Interior Systems Construction Association (CISCA):

     Recommendations for Direct-hung Acoustical Tile and Lay-in Panel Ceilings, Seismic zones 0–2

     Guidelines for Seismic Restraint Direct Hung Suspended Ceiling Assemblies, Seismic zones 3 & 4

Standard ceiling assemblies

Gypsum wallboard ceilings are either directly attached to structural framing or suspended like an acoustical ceiling. For residential construction, wallboard is screwed directly to the ceiling joists. Wiring and heating ducts are concealed between the joists. If a small additional space below the joists is required, furring is used. Larger spaces for ducts or dropped soffits are made by boxing in with wood framing and applying the wallboard over it.

Because commercial construction typically requires clear space above the ceiling for piping, electrical conduit, HVAC duct work, and sprinkler pipes, gypsum wallboard ceilings are applied to a suspended grid of framing members. Figure 2.11 shows the typical construction. Steel channels measuring 1½ in. (38 mm) are located 4 ft (1200 mm) on center and are suspended from the structural floor or roof above with wires spaced 4 ft on center. Metal furring channels (hat channels) are attached to the main runners either 16 in. or 24 in. on center, with the wallboard screwed to them. For most commercial construction 24-in. (600 mm) spacing is used with ⅝-in. (16 mm) wallboard.

Although gypsum wallboard ceilings in commercial construction provide a smooth, uninterrupted finished ceiling, they lack the easy accessibility of suspended acoustical ceilings. Because of this, where access to valves, junction boxes, fire dampers, or other equipment or services is required, access panels must be installed in the ceiling. These are prefabricated steel units with a hinged door that allow the wallboard to be framed into them. They are available in several standard sizes, but a 24-in. (600 mm) square door is usually sufficient. Unfortunately, if the design intent is to build a smooth ceiling, access panels interrupt the appearance and become unsightly after they are used a few times. Cracks develop in the joint compound around the frame, and the finish becomes soiled. If possible, wallboard ceilings should be limited to areas not requiring access panels, or the mechanical and electrical engineers should be requested to locate new equipment away from intended wallboard ceilings.

Custom ceiling assemblies

In addition to a flat ceiling, gypsum wallboard can be formed into nearly any configuration. Stepped, sloped, coffered, vaulted,

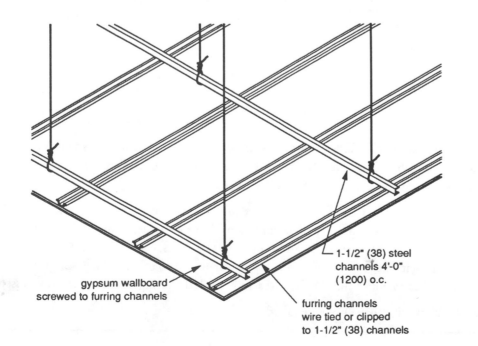

Figure 2.11
Suspended gypsum wallboard ceiling

gypsum wallboard screwed to furring channels

1-1/2" (38) steel channels 4'-0" (1200) o.c.

furring channels wire tied or clipped to 1-1/2" (38) channels and arched ceilings are all possible using various combinations of suspended framing and studs to form the basic shape. For curved shapes, the minimum radii for forming curved partitions given in Table 1.2 are applicable.

When acoustical control is required in residential construction, resilient channels are attached to the joists and sound attenuation insulation placed between the joists. One typical assembly is shown in Figure 2.12.

Coordination

• Fire-rated floor/ceiling assemblies require the use of Type X gypsum wallboard.

• Light troffers, air terminals, and other heavy equipment should be supported separately.

• In commercial construction, the location of valves, junction boxes, and other mechanical and electrical equipment must be coordinated to eliminate or minimize the need for access panels.

Figure 2.12
Gypsum
wallboard
ceiling on
wood framing

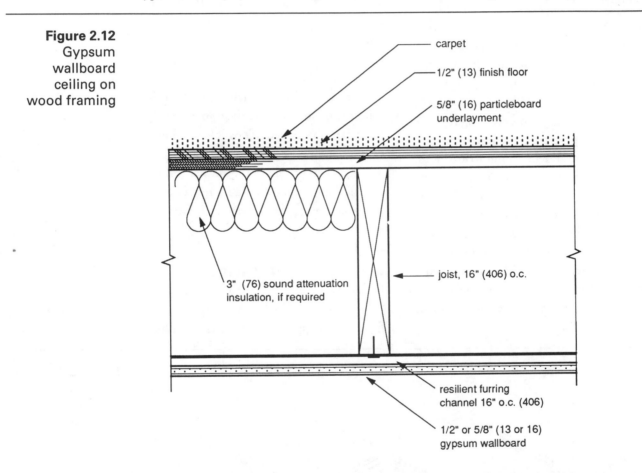

carpet

1/2" (13) finish floor

5/8" (16) particleboard underlayment

3" (76) sound attenuation insulation, if required

joist, 16" (406) o.c.

resilient furring channel 16" o.c. (406)

1/2" or 5/8" (13 or 16) gypsum wallboard

Building code requirements for gypsum wallboard ceilings

As with acoustical ceilings, model codes require that the entire suspension system be noncombustible. The codes also specify the minimum size of hanger wires based on the type of installation and the area of ceiling that is supported.

For ceilings that are part of a rated floor/ceiling assembly, certain construction details must be followed. For example, when a ceiling forms the protective membrane for a 2-hour-rated, fire-resistive assembly, the UBC limits openings for pipes, electrical outlet boxes, and ducts to an aggregate area of no more than 100 in.^{2} for every 100 ft^2 of ceiling area (0.0645 m^2 per 9.3 m^2). Access doors must be fire-rated and match the rating of the floor/ceiling assembly.

Seismic restraint may also be required.

- For sloped, vaulted, or arched ceilings, it must be verified that there is no interference from duct work, piping, or other obstructions.

PLASTER CEILINGS [09200]

Plaster ceiling components

Lath and plaster ceilings are constructed similarly to lath and plaster partitions. Like their partition counterparts, lath and plaster ceilings cost more than gypsum wallboard ceilings and are more difficult to construct. However, they can easily be curved in two directions to form complex shapes. Full, three-coat Portland-cement plaster ceilings are used most often when ceramic tile must be applied in a continuously wet environment, such as a public shower or a steam room. They are also used in remodeling work when ornate or complex moldings and decorative castings are required.

Standard ceiling assemblies

A typical commercial plaster ceiling assembly is shown in Figure 2.13. A framework is suspended from the structure like a gypsum wallboard ceiling. However, instead of using wallboard, expanded metal lath is wired to the framework and the plaster is applied, usually in a three-coat application process.

In a traditional plaster ceiling for residential construction, metal lath is attached to the ceiling joists and a two- or three-coat plaster application process is used. Refer to Chapter 1 for information on standard plaster construction.

When curved shapes are required, the suspended framing is shaped into the approximate configuration of the ceiling and wire lath bent to conform to the final profile. The application of the plaster completes the final shape. Large templates are sometimes used to make sure the entire length of a curved shape has a consistent profile. Like plaster partitions, a ceiling can be finished in a variety of textures.

As with partitions, veneer plaster construction can also be used. Gypsum lath is screwed to the framing and a thin veneer coat of plaster approximately ⅛ in. (3 mm) thick is applied.

Custom ceiling assemblies

For decorative work, complex moldings are formed by cutting a piece of sheet metal or wood to conform to the desired profile. A large amount of plaster is applied in place and the metal template is run along the length of the molding to shape it. When

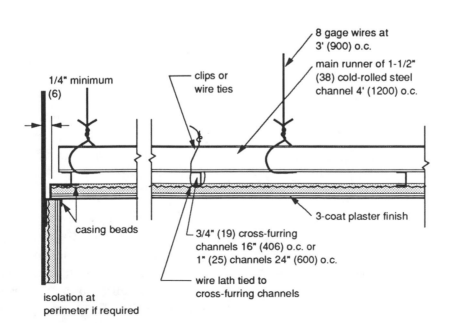

Figure 2.13
Typical plaster ceiling construction

8 gage wires at 3' (900) o.c.

main runner of 1-1/2" (38) cold-rolled steel channel 4' (1200) o.c.

clips or wire ties

1/4" minimum (6)

casing beads

isolation at perimeter if required

3-coat plaster finish

3/4" (19) cross-furring channels 16" (406) o.c. or 1" (25) channels 24" (600) o.c.

wire lath tied to cross-furring channels

moldings cannot be formed in place, they can be cast in molds and attached to the walls and ceilings.

Coordination

• In commercial construction, heavy loads, such as large light fixtures and mechanical equipment, should be suspended independently from the structure above.

• Perimeter isolation joints, as shown in Figure 2.13, should be used where the ceiling is adjacent to a structural element or dissimilar partition, where other vertical penetrations occur, and where building movement can be expected.

• Control joints should be detailed when a ceiling dimension exceeds 50 ft (15 m) in either direction when perimeter relief joints are used, or when it exceeds 30 ft (9 m) when perimeter relief joints are not used.

LINEAR METAL CEILINGS [09545]

Linear metal ceilings are suspended systems that use lengths of prefinished aluminum sections. These sections are clipped to carrier sections that are suspended with wires attached to the structure above. The exact configuration of linear metal ceilings varies with each manufacturer, but a typical section is shown in Figure 2.14. The visible pieces are available in a variety of sizes and shapes and in painted and anodized finishes. There is usually a gap between each piece to provide for both some sound absorption and return-air movement. If additional acoustical control is needed, acoustical batts can be laid on top of the ceiling. Each manufacturer provides accessories for trimming around walls, light fixtures, and other openings.

DECORATIVE SUSPENDED CEILINGS [09545]

Many other types of decorative suspended ceilings are available. They are all suspended with either wires or threaded rods anchored to the structure above. The visible, finished portion of the ceiling can be vertical metal baffles, wood strips, mirrored panels, open grids of aluminum or wood, or other proprietary systems. Refer to manufacturer's catalogs for availability and exact installation details.

INTEGRATED CEILINGS [13020]

Integrated ceilings are suspended ceiling systems specifically designed to accommodate acoustical ceiling tile, light fixtures, supply- and return-air grilles, fire sprinklers, and partition attachment in a consistent, unified way. There are many proprietary systems, each with its own characteristics; however, all are intended to be used in commercial applications where the partitions, lights, and other elements connected with the ceiling change frequently. Most of the systems are designed to work with standard building planning grids of 4 ft (1200 mm) or 5 ft (1500 mm).

All of the components are designed for maximum reusability and flexibility. Light fixtures usually have plug-in connectors, and HVAC system air terminals are connected with flexible ducts so all services can be relocated easily. The top track of demount-

Figure 2.14
Linear metal
ceiling

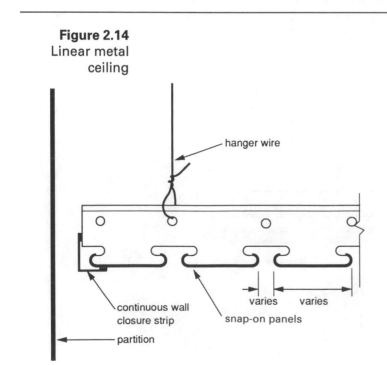

hanger wire

continuous wall
closure strip

snap-on panels

varies   varies

partition

able partitions screw or clip onto a specially designed grid. Refer to manufacturer's catalogs for availability and exact installation details.

Integrated ceilings are more expensive than standard acoustical ceilings but can be economical when frequent changes to space plans are made. However, before deciding on an integrated ceiling system, a life-cycle cost analysis should be made to determine if the cost savings of frequent changes offsets the higher initial cost.

ABUSE-RESISTANT CEILINGS [09515]

Abuse-resistant ceilings include a range of products that are designed to resist one or more of the following kinds of abuse:

- Environmental damage such as humidity, atmospheric corrosion, and surface moisture

- Contact from objects striking the ceiling such as balls, mop handles, and other thrown objects

- Frequent access to the plenum

- Deliberate abuse such as vandalism

- Deliberate attempts to gain unauthorized access to the ceiling space

Abuse-resistant ceilings are commonly detailed and specified for areas in schools, hospitals, industrial plants, and security or detention facilities. They include various types of acoustical suspended ceiling systems as well as plaster and built-up gypsum wallboard systems.

Suspended acoustical abuse-resistant ceiling systems use several types of tiles depending on the severity and type of abuse expected. For light abuse such as in commercial kitchens, the tiles are mineral-based or glass-fiber-based construction with plastic, fiberglass, fabric, aluminum, or other metal-membrane-faced overlays. For heavier use there are snap-in metal panels with perforated steel, stainless steel, or aluminum facings backed with acoustic material. For maximum security and durability, metal plank systems can be used. These consist of linear pans of heavy-gage steel securely attached to wall-mounted angles with tamper-resistant fasteners.

As with standard suspended-ceiling systems the grid is supported with wires, but where penetration to the plenum space must be restricted, compression members are typically installed at 48 in (1220 mm) on center to resist uplift of the grid. To resist incidental uplift, the panels are attached to the grid with clips. For more secure installations, special metal panels can be used that snap under a bulb tee of the grid, locking the tile in place and making removal impossible except with obvious damage.

Plaster systems use a hard finish coat over plaster base coats that are spread on heavy, expanded metal lath. Gypsum wallboard systems use multiple layers of wallboard separated by heavy-gage expanded metal lath. A veneer coat of dense plaster is applied to the exposed surface to increase surface durability. Although both plaster and wallboard systems provide the necessary degree of abuse resistance, they result in poor acoustical performance.

3

DOORS

oors are available in a variety of materials and operating methods to meet many functional and aesthetic needs. There are dozens of standard designs for interior use. Doors and frames can also be custom detailed to meet particular project requirements. This chapter discusses how to select and detail the best door assembly for any situation and then reviews the various types of doors available for interior use.

SELECTION AND DETAILING PROCEDURES

Door classifications

A door can be classified by the function it serves, its operation, and the material from which it is made. Each classification is useful in its own way to help select the best door type for a particular situation. Doors for interior use can serve one or more of the following functions:

- Control passage
- Provide visual privacy
- Provide sound privacy
- Provide security
- Provide fire and smoke resistance
- Provide light control
- Provide radiation shielding
- Serve a decorative function

Door operation refers to the way the door opens and closes. The common operation types and variations are shown in Figure 3.1. Each operating method has its own advantages and disadvantages, as summarized in Table 3.1.

Swinging doors

Swinging doors provide easy and convenient operation, are simple to install, can be fire rated, and can accommodate many people. The three common variations of swinging doors depend on how they are suspended. These include the typical hinged door, pivoted doors, either center-hung or offset, and balanced doors, which reduce the force required to open the door. Balanced doors are typically used as entrance doors where wind or air pressure makes it difficult to open the door.

The double-acting door is another type of swinging door. It uses special hinges or center-hung pivots that allow it to operate in either direction. Double-acting doors are good for situations requiring quick passage without having to use an opening device, such as a commercial kitchen. Because of the nature of their operation they cannot be used as exit doors and cannot be sealed against sound or light.

Table 3.1
Door types—
advantages and
disadvantages

Door operation type	Advantages	Disadvantages
Swinging		
Hinged	Ease of use and installation Inexpensive Can be fire rated Wide variety of hinge styles	Appearance of hinges sometimes undesirable
Offset pivoted	Ease of use Closer can be part of pivot Can be fire rated Can accommodate very heavy doors Minimal hardware appearance	More expensive than hinges Floor closers require solid flooring and adequate thickness to accommodate closer
Center-hung pivoted	Ease of use Closer can be part of pivot Allows door to swing both ways Support hardware is fully concealed Can be fire rated Can accommodate very heavy doors	More expensive than hinges Floor closers require solid flooring and adequate thickness to accommodate closer Height limitations required to avoid bowing
Balanced	Little effort required to operate	Expensive Clear width reduced when open
Double acting	Easy operation both ways	Cannot be used as exit door Dangerous unless glass light provided
Sliding		
Pocket	No operating space required	Awkward for frequent use Difficult to seal against light or sound Cannot be used as exit door
Bi-pass	No operating space required	Awkward for frequent use Difficult to seal Cannot be used as exit door
Surface	No operating space required	Appearance of hardware Cannot be used as exit door
Folding		
Bi-fold	Minimum operating space	Awkward to use Cannot be used as exit door
Accordion	Useful for subdividing space Inexpensive	Poor as a sound barrier Cannot be used as exit door Limited finishes and colors available
Special		
Operable partition	Good for very large openings Good sound barrier Wide choice of finishes	Expensive Cannot be used as exit door
Overhead coiling	Automatic closing of large openings for security or fire separation	Appearance when closed Requires large space for housing Cannot be used as exit door
Revolving	Accommodates large numbers Prevents air infiltration Types available for darkrooms	Only appropriate for entrance doors Requires large space Expensive Cannot be used as exit door

Sliding doors

Sliding doors are appropriate when space is tight. They have many disadvantages. They are not good for frequent use, they are awkward to open and close, and they are difficult to seal against sound and light. In addition, they are not acceptable for exit doors.

Folding doors

Folding doors are also good where space is limited. However, like sliding doors, they have disadvantages. They are not good for normal passage and are best used for closets and other minor spaces. Accordion folding doors can be used as space dividers but are limited in maximum size to about 20 ft (6 m) high by 40 ft (12 m) wide.

Special doors

Movable walls can be classified as special doors. They are used to divide very large spaces. They are composed of individual solid sections of material that fit tightly together when closed. When open, the sections come apart and slide into a storage area. Movable walls are suspended from ceiling tracks and usually include provisions for sealing the wall against sound transmission.

Other types of special doors can be used for interior construction, but they are not as common as other types. Overhead coiling doors, for example, are sometimes used for securing large openings during off-hours. They can also act as automatic-closing fire doors for large openings.

Figure 3.1
Door classification by operation

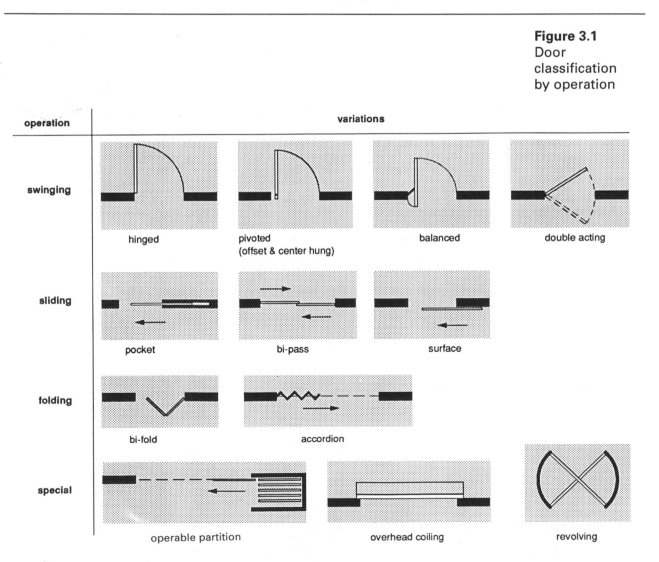

Revolving doors are commonly used for building entrances to prevent air infiltration and to accommodate many people. However, they are not acceptable as exit doors or accessible doors. Smaller revolving doors are available that provide seals against light for darkrooms.

Door types and materials

Doors are also classified by their type and the material from which they are made. Common door types include flush, panel, louvered, sash, glass, and Dutch. Common materials for doors include wood (and wood with plastic laminate facing), steel (also called *hollow metal*), aluminum, glass, and other metals, such as brass, bronze, and stainless steel. Combinations are also possible, such as ornamental sheet metal laminated to wood or steel doors. Not all door types are available or possible in all materials. The common type and material combinations are shown in Figure 3.3. Many variations are possible within most of the type/material combinations.

Components of opening assemblies

There are four major components of a door system: the door itself, the frame, the hardware, and the partition in which the frame and opening are placed. Each must be coordinated with the others and must be appropriate for the function of the door as well as the design intent. This concept is especially important when detailing and specifying fire-rated opening assemblies. As with door types and materials, there are many possible combinations and variations of these four components, but some are never used. For example, a steel door is never placed in a wood frame, but wood doors are commonly set in steel or aluminum frames.

Door handing

The standard method of referring to the way a door swings is called the *door hand* or the *handing* of the door. Handing is used by designers, specifiers, and hardware suppliers to communicate how a door swings and what kind of hardware must be supplied for a specific opening. Some hardware will only work on a door that swings a particular way because of the way the strike side of the door is beveled. Hardware that can work on any hand of door is called *reversible*, or *nonhanded*.

The door hand is determined by standing on the outside of the door, as shown in Figure 3.2. The exterior of a building is considered the outside, as is the hallway side of a room door, the lobby side of a door opening into a room, or the room side of a closet door. In situations where the distinction is not clear, such as between two offices, the outside is considered the side of the door where the hinge is **not** visible.

When standing on the outside looking at the door, if the door hinges on the left and swings away, it is a *left-hand door*. If it hinges on the right and swings away, it is a *right-hand door*. If the door swings toward you, it is considered a *left-hand reverse* or a *right-hand reverse*, depending on the hinge location. Sometimes a left-hand reverse door may be referred to as a right-hand door and a right-hand reverse door as a left-hand door, but it is better to use the correct terminology.

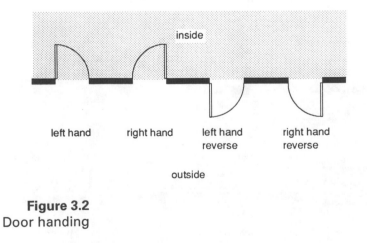

Figure 3.2
Door handing

The most common types of partitions for interior construction include gypsum wallboard on either wood or metal studs, plaster on either wood or metal studs, and masonry, either exposed or covered with gypsum wallboard or plaster. Specific detailing conditions for these partition types are shown in the following sections.

Design and detailing

Selecting, designing, and detailing a door assembly follows a logical sequence of steps. The order of decision may vary slightly from one project to the next, but all of the steps must be considered.

1. Determine the primary function or functions of the door and the method of operation. The spaces or rooms on either side of the door and specific programmatic requirements determine what function the door will serve. Operating types are determined by considering the following:

- Code requirements
- Frequency of use
- Opening size
- Ease of operation
- Security
- Sound privacy
- Light control
- Cost
- Availability

Table 3.2 shows the commonly used types and materials for the required functions and can be used as a guide in making preliminary selections.

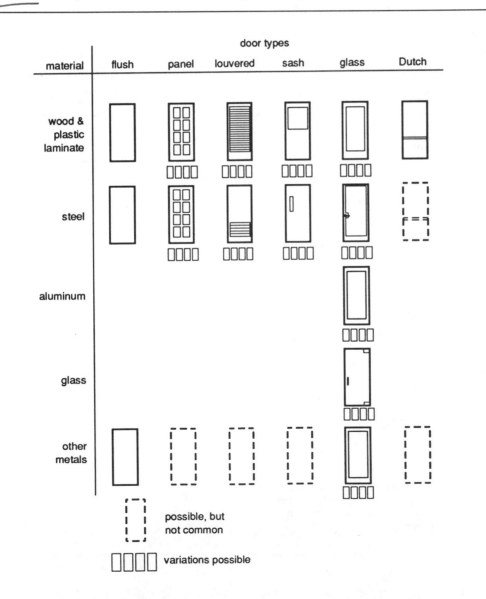

Figure 3.3
Door classification by types and materials

Often, the specific functional requirements determine what door and frame material to use when several types are possible. For example, a low level of security can be accomplished with a solid core wood door, while greater security requirements may require a heavy gage steel door.

2. Determine the desired appearance of the door and the opening. This is a design decision based on the program and the design concept of the entire project. Some questions to ask include: Should the opening be emphasized, standard, or concealed? Should the door finish match or contrast with the partition? Should the frame be emphasized or minimized? Should the hardware be emphasized, standard, or concealed? What finish should the hardware have? Does it meet accessibility requirements?

3. Determine the type and material of the door. This depends on both the functional requirements and the aesthetic goals of the project. For example, if a wood door is used, a paneled door may be more appropriate than a flush door for a traditional design.

4. Decide on the door size. Door width is primarily determined by functional requirements; door height is generally determined by cost and aesthetic considerations. A 36-in. (914 mm) door is the minimum allowed for an exit door. A 36-in. door also provides a 32-in. (813 mm) clear opening that is required for accessibility. Wider doors may be needed where large objects will be moved through; narrower doors may be acceptable for infrequently used doors, such as closets and residential bathrooms.

While 80-in. (2032 mm) and 84-in. (2134 mm) high doors are standard sizes, taller doors may be desirable. For instance, many designers prefer full-height doors, which are as high as the ceiling.

5. Decide on the frame type. Considerations for this decision include the desired appearance, fire-rating requirements, security

Door terms

Figure 3.4
Door opening
terms

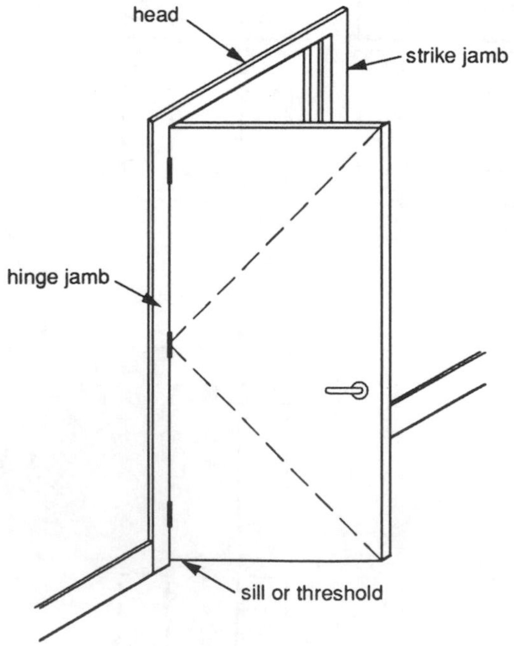

note: dashed lines used on construction drawings to indicate how door swings when drawn on a two-dimensional elevation.

The terms used to describe parts of a door opening are illustrated in Figure 3.4. To differentiate between the two jambs, the side where the hinge or pivot is installed is called the *hinge jamb,* or *hinge side,* and the jamb where the door closes is called the *strike jamb, strike side,* or *latch side* of the door.

needs, partition type, and anchorage for closers. In some cases, frames are not even required. Blind doors, for example, can be mounted on pivots, finished the same way as the partition, and set in openings without any trim, thereby minimizing their presence.

6. Determine hardware types for the desired appearance and functional requirements. How a door is hung and operated affects both its appearance and how the construction is detailed. In some cases, such as with fire-rated door assemblies, only certain types of hardware can be used; in other cases, there is a wide variety to choose from. Refer to Chapter 4 for more information on hardware.

7. Determine frame substrate conditions. All frames must be attached to the partition framing. The conditions on all four edges of

a door opening can affect how the frame is detailed. For example, heavy doors or doors that receive rough use may require extra studs or other bracing to prevent wall shake or cracked finishes.

Some of the more important detailing considerations for a door opening are summarized in Figure 3.5. Additional questions to consider when planning and detailing doors include the following:

• For doors in corners, is the hinge jamb far enough away from the wall and perpendicular to the door to allow the door to open at least a full 90°, with space for the door handle, door stop, and other hardware?

• For doors serving many people, do the doors open at least 110°?

• Are vision panels included in double-acting doors?

		Functions						
Operation		Control passage	Visual privacy	Audio privacy	Security	Control fire/smoke	Control light	Control radiation
Swinging	Hinged	W, S, A, B, T	W, S, A, B, T	W, S, B, T	W, S, B, T	W, S, B, T	W, S, B, T[1]	S[2]
	Pivoted	W, S, A, G, B, T	W, S, A, B, T	W, S, B, T	W, S, B, T	W, S, B, T[1]		
Sliding	Pocket	W	W				W	
	Bi-pass	W	W					
Folding	Bi-fold	W	W					
	Accordion	W, V	W, V					
	Movable wall	W, S, A	W, S, A	W, S	W, S		W, S	
Special	Overhead coiling	S	S		S	S[3]		
	Revolving	S, A, G, B			S, A, G, B			

Table 3.2
Door classifications by function, operation, and material

W = Wood
S = Steel
A = Aluminum
G = Glass
B = Bronze, brass, etc.
T = Stainless steel
V = Vinyl

[1] Limited fire ratings with wood.
[2] Special shielding required.
[3] Not for exiting.

• Is protection required on the door in the way of armor plates, kick plates, edge guards, and similar hardware?

• Will the door swing clear of carpeting, uneven floors, and other obstructions?

• If used, can gaskets and sound seals be readjusted after a period of use?

• If the frame and door are wood, is the wood species compatible with surrounding wood trim and other mill work and furniture on the job?

• Will concealed doors operate freely after the application of finish material?

• Does the door operate within the maximum force requirements for accessibility?

• Is there sufficient space on either side of the door to meet accessibility requirements?

• Do door tolerances need to be specified differently from industry standards?

• Are doors recessed so that they do not interfere with traffic on the opening side?

Fire-rated doors

When a building code requires that a partition be fire rated then all openings, such as doors, glazing, ducts, and louvers, in that partition must also be fire rated. A protected opening is considered an *opening assembly*, but in the case of doors it is usually referred to as simply a fire-rated door.

Fire door classifications and ratings

A *fire-rated door* is defined as a door assembly that has been tested by an independent laboratory to determine that it is capable of withstanding a measured temperature without failure for a specific length of time. The assembly consists of the door itself, the frame,

Figure 3.5
Door detailing
considerations

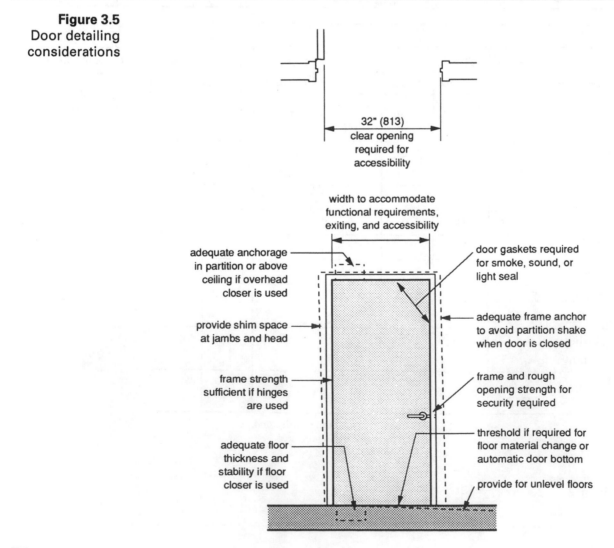

32" (813)
clear opening
required for
accessibility

width to accommodate
functional requirements,
exiting, and accessibility

adequate anchorage
in partition or above
ceiling if overhead
closer is used

provide shim space
at jambs and head

frame strength
sufficient if hinges
are used

adequate floor
thickness and
stability if floor
closer is used

door gaskets required
for smoke, sound, or
light seal

adequate frame anchor
to avoid partition shake
when door is closed

frame and rough
opening strength for
security required

threshold if required for
floor material change or
automatic door bottom

provide for unlevel floors

and the hardware used on the door and frame. The classification is stated in hours or minutes, and some doors are also given a corresponding letter designation. The required rating for a door depends on the rating of the wall or partition in which it is placed and the use of the wall or partition. Table 3.3 lists fire door classifications and highlights the three types most commonly used in interior design work.

Most commercial interior design only requires the use of a 20-minute-rated door in a 1-hour-rated corridor or where a smoke and draft assembly is required; or a ¾-hour-rated door in a 1-hour occupancy separation or in a 1-hour-rated exit stair enclosure. For multifloor projects, a 1½-hour-rated door must be used in a 2-hour-rated exit enclosure (stairway).

Some codes, such as the UBC, also require that a 20-minute door be a "tight fitting smoke and draft assembly." T that the listed gasketing must b both jambs and the head to pr from passing through when closed.

For fire-rated door assembli or hollow metal doors may types of wood doors can I 1½ hours, but wood frames can used in 20-minute assemblies. For ratings above 1½ hours on doors and 30 minutes or more for frames, hollow metal must be used. However, some jurisdictions allow aluminum door frames for 45-minute assemblies.

Because exact provisions vary among local building codes, the exact requirements must be verified with the code having jurisdiction. Refer to Chapter 17 for more information on code requirements for opening assemblies.

Fire door rating (hr)	Opening class	Use of wall	Rating of wall (hr)
3	A	Fire walls Fire separations	3 or 4
1	B	Vertical shafts Exit stairs Occupancy separations	1
½		Limited application	1 or less
1½ ¾	D E	Severe exterior exposure Exterior exposure	2 or more 1 or less

Table 3.3
Fire door classifications

Note: Classifications in the shaded areas are those most commonly used for interior design. Because exact provisions vary among building codes, the requirements must be verified with the code having jurisdiction.

Additional considerations for detailing fire-rated doors

• Nearly all requirements for fire-rated doors apply to other than one- and two-family dwellings. Most codes require the use of a solid core door to separate a house from an attached garage.

• Combustible floor coverings cannot extend through the door opening unless the flooring has, at minimum, a Class II rating.

• The type and amount of glass used in fire-rated doors is limited. Refer to Chapter 17 for exact requirements.

• Generally, modifications to a fire-rated door cannot be made on the job site. All cutting, fitting, and hardware preparation must be done in the factory.

• There is a maximum allowable dimension of ½ in. (12.7 mm) from the bottom of the door to the top of allowable floor coverings and a maximum of ⅜ in. (9.3 mm) to the top of a raised noncombustible sill.

• The maximum size of a single-leaf, fire-rated door is 48 in. (1219 mm) wide and 96 in. (2438 mm) high for doors with panic hardware. The maximum height is increased to 10 ft (3048 mm) when other types of hardware are used. Pairs of doors can be up to 8 ft wide.

• A minimum of 6 in. (152 mm) must be maintained between the edge of a door and any cutouts for glazing and louvers.

• If assemblies must conform to UBC 7-2 for positive pressure, fire testing intumescent material may need to be mortised into door edges or frames.

Labels and listing for fire ratings

When a door opening assembly is used, the door, frame, and closer are required to be labeled and the other hardware must be labeled or listed. A *label* is a permanent identifying mark attached to the door or frame by a testing organization that indicates the component is in compliance with the standard tests for fire doors and with the National Fire Protection Association's

Standard NFPA 80, which governs the installation of fire doors. A *listed* device is a product that has been shown to meet applicable standards for use in fire-rated assemblies (including NFPA 80) or that has been tested and found suitable for use in a specific application.

Tests for fire-rated doors

There are two primary industry standard tests used in connection with fire-rated doors. NFPA 80, *Standard for Fire Doors and Windows,* deals with the construction and installation of fire doors; NFPA 252, *Standard Methods for Fire Tests of Door Assemblies,* is the standard method for testing fire doors. UL 10B is another designation for essentially the same NFPA 252 test.

WOOD DOORS AND FRAMES [08200]

Wood doors are the most common type for both residential and commercial construction. They are available in a variety of styles, methods of operation, sizes, and finishes. As shown in Figure 3.3, there are six common types of wood doors: flush, panel, louvered, sash, glass, and Dutch.

Types of wood doors

Flush wood doors

Flush wood doors are made of thin, flat veneers laminated to various types of cores. They are either hollow core or solid core. Hollow core doors are made of one or three plies of veneer on each side of a cellular interior. The frame is made of solid wood, with larger blocks of solid wood where the latching hardware is located. Hollow core doors are used where only light use is expected and cost is a consideration. They cannot be fire rated.

Solid core doors are made with a variety of core types depending on the functional requirements of the door. Cores may be particleboard, staved lumber (solid blocks of wood), or mineral core for fire-rated doors.

There are four basic types of cores for flush wood doors: hollow core, particleboard core, staved core, and mineral core. Figure 3.6 illustrates these types and some of their variations as classified by the Architectural Woodwork Institute (AWI).

A standard hollow core door has either one or three plies of veneer on either side of a ladder, mesh, or cellular core. The door is framed with a 2¼-in. (57 mm) thick rail on the top and bottom and 1-in. (25 mm) thick stiles. A solid lock-block is provided on each side for application of hardware. Institutional hollow core doors are also available that have wider stiles and rails and an intermediate crossrail.

Particleboard core doors use mat-formed particleboard with a density of 28 to 32 lb/ft³ (448 kg/m³ to 513 kg/m³). These doors are faced with two or three plies of wood veneer, plastic laminate, or hardboard that is suitable for painting.

Staved core doors use solid blocks of wood with the end joints staggered in adjacent rows. Like particleboard core doors, the facing can be multiple plies of wood veneer, plastic laminate, or hardboard. Both particleboard core and staved core doors can be used where a 20-minute or ½-hour fire-rated door is required.

Mineral core doors are used when fire ratings of ¾, 1, and 1½ hours are required. The core is a mineral composition within a frame of treated, solid wood stiles and rails (see the section on panel doors) faced with wood veneer or plastic laminate constructed according to NFPA 80 and designed to meet the test requirements of UL 10B and NFPA 252.

Core types for wood doors

Figure 3.6
Wood door core types

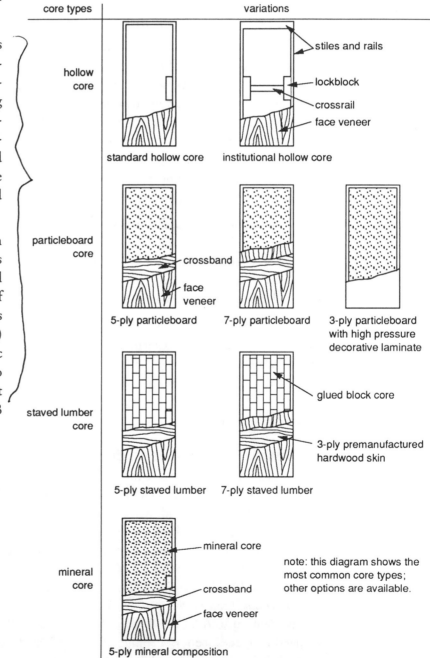

core types | variations

hollow core
standard hollow core   institutional hollow core
stiles and rails
lockblock
crossrail
face veneer

particleboard core
5-ply particleboard   7-ply particleboard   3-ply particleboard with high pressure decorative laminate
crossband
face veneer

staved lumber core
5-ply staved lumber   7-ply staved lumber
glued block core
3-ply premanufactured hardwood skin

mineral core
5-ply mineral composition
mineral core
crossband
face veneer

note: this diagram shows the most common core types; other options are available.

Solid core doors are used for their fire-resistive properties, as acoustical barriers, for security, and for their superior durability. Solid core doors are available with fire ratings of 20-, 30-, 45-, 60-, and 90-minutes.

The face veneers of wood doors are made from any available hardwood species using rotary-cut, plain-sliced, quarter-sliced, or rift-cut methods, just as wood paneling discussed in Chapter 6. Veneers of hardboard suitable for painting and plastic laminate are also available.

Special function wood flush doors

A sound retardant door is often thicker than 1¾ in. (44 mm) and has a core with a special damping compound. Sound retardant doors are usually furnished with special gasketing and automatic door bottoms to complete the installation. They are specified by including the required sound transmission class coefficient (see Chapter 11).

Lead-lined doors are manufactured with a continuous lead sheet in the center of the door or between the crossbanding and the core. The thickness of the lead may be specified to meet the functional requirements of the project.

Electrostatic shield doors are manufactured with wire mesh in the center or between the crossbanding and the core. The mesh is grounded with electrical leads through the hinges to the frame.

Standards for flush wood door

Two organizations develop the most commonly used standards for flush wood doors. One is the National Wood Window and Door Association (NWWDA), and the other is the Architectural Woodwork Institute (AWI). The NWWDA publishes I.S. 1-A, *Architectural Wood Flush Doors* and I.S. 1-R, *Residential Wood Flush Doors*. I.S. 1-A is nearly identical to AWI standards and includes three grades of doors: Premium, Custom, and Economy. The NWWDA are considered minimum standards for construction and can be used by themselves to specify wood doors for many interior applications. The AWI standards are classified into the same three groups, but generally exceed the NWWDA standards and have a different method of specifying doors. For most commercial interior design work it is best to use the AWI standards or NWWDA I.S. 1-A for specifying wood doors.

Panel doors

Panel doors are constructed of solid pieces of wood that frame various types of panels. Because the vertical wood frame pieces are called *stiles* and the horizontal framing members are called *rails,* paneled doors are also called stile and rail doors. Any number of panels can be constructed, and the door is described by the number of panels it has. For example, a door with six panels is called a six-panel door. There are also standard number designations developed by the National Wood Window and Door Association (NWWDA) for doors with typical panel configurations.

The panels can be framed into the stiles and rails in a number of ways. Figures 3.7(a) and 3.7(b) show two typical panel door constructions. A wide variety of panel doors are available as catalog items from many manufacturers, including doors with glass panels. Panel doors can also be custom designed and detailed.

Louvered doors

A louvered door has a solid wood stile and rail frame with wood slats set at an angle to allow air flow through the door. The slats can be set to prevent all vision or to allow some vision. They can also be adjustable. They are commonly used for closet doors and other areas where ventilation is required.

Sash doors

Sash doors are flush- or panel-type doors having one or more pieces of glass. Standard sash doors are available from a variety of manufacturers, and custom sash sizes and configurations can be designed. The glass lights are framed into the stiles and rails in much the same way as panel doors, with the exception of removable stops that allow the glass to be installed and replaced. When

most of the door consists of multiple sash lights it is called a French door.

Glass doors

Glass doors differ from sash doors in that most of the door is one piece of glass set in a solid wood frame. Sash doors and glass

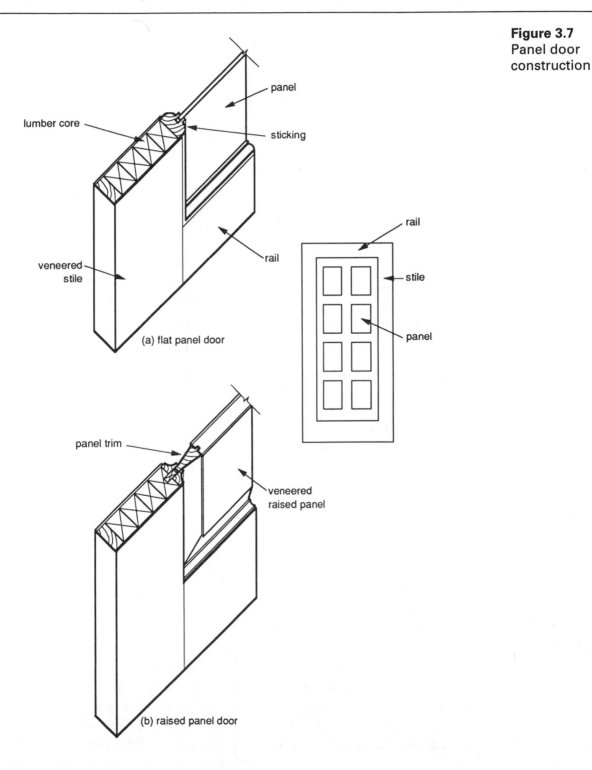

Figure 3.7
Panel door construction

doors allow vision and light to pass through, while controlling passage.

Dutch doors

Dutch doors are two-piece doors that allow the top half to be opened while the bottom half remains latched. The two halves can be latched so that the entire door operates as a standard door. The halves can be flush, paneled, or sash type. Dutch doors prevent, or at least discourage, passage when the lower half is latched, provide an unobstructed view, and allow objects to be passed through the opening.

Wood door specifications

Wood doors can be custom made to any size. However, standard widths are 1 ft 6 in., 2 ft, 2 ft 4 in., 2 ft 6 in., 2 ft 8 in., and 3 ft (457, 610, 711, 762, 813 mm). Standard heights are 6 ft 8 in. (2032 mm) and 7 ft (2133 mm). Higher doors, often used in commercial construction, are available. Hollow core doors are commonly 1⅜ in. (35 mm) thick and solid core doors 1¾ in. (44 mm) thick.

Frames for wood doors can be wood, steel (hollow metal, discussed in the next section), or aluminum. In custom details, wood doors can also be set on pivots in an opening without a frame as described later in this chapter.

The following are standard clearances between a door and its frame for wood doors. Clearance dimensions are subject to a tolerance of ± 1⁄32 in. (0.8 mm).

> At hinge jamb: ⅛ in. (3 mm)
> At lock jamb: ⅛ in. (3 mm)
> At head: minimum ⅛ in. (3 mm)
> At meeting edges of door pairs: ⅛ in. (3 mm)

UNDERCUTS

Undercut dimensions can be labeled on the drawings, but there is a maximum of ¾ in. (19 mm) from the bottom of the door to the top of a noncombustible floor and ⅜ in. (9.5 mm) maximum to the top of a noncombustible sill.

Standard assemblies

In addition to the door and the partition, standard wood door assemblies consist of three major parts: the head/jamb frame itself, casing trim to cover the space between the frame and the partition, and the stop. In addition, all wood frames require a shim space so that the frame can be set plumb and level within the rough opening of the partition. Wood doors are beveled at 3° or ⅛ in. in 2 in. (3.2 mm in 50.8 mm) on the strike side to prevent the edge of the door from scraping the jamb as the door opens. A common wood frame jamb is illustrated in Figures 3.8(a) and 3.8(b). Although the stop and casing trim are shown as simple shapes, any molding profile can be used. Pre-hung doors are available that include the door, frame, and hinges in one package.

The decision concerning the type of frame to use for a wood door depends on the appearance desired, the type of partition the opening is being installed in, fire rating requirements, the security needed, and the durability desired. For example, wood frames are generally only available for use in 20-minute fire door assemblies. Doors that require higher ratings must be set in steel frames. When appearance is important, labeled steel frames are available that are covered with a thin lamination of real wood veneer.

Figures 3.9(a)–3.9(f) illustrate several possible combinations of wood frame profiles set in various types of partitions.

Custom assemblies

By definition, custom wood door frame assemblies include a limitless variety of configurations. Some or all three of the major component parts of a standard assembly may be omitted, but certain functional requirements must be met. First, there must be some way to hang the door, either with hinges, pivots, or an overhead track. Some type of jamb frame is required if hinges are used. For frameless openings, the door must be supported with a pivot or track. Second, there must be some way to stop the door. If a standard continuous trim stop is not used, a metal angle or block must be provided either in the head section or the strike jamb. In some cases, stopping action can be provided by a door closer. Third, there must be some way to operate the door with a handle, knob, pull, or other hardware, as discussed in Chapter 4.

Optional components of a custom opening detail include a method to lock the door and a method to seal the openings between the door and frame. However, for many interior door assemblies these options are not required.

Figures 3.11–3.13 illustrate some commonly used custom door opening details.

Figure 3.8
Standard wood door frame

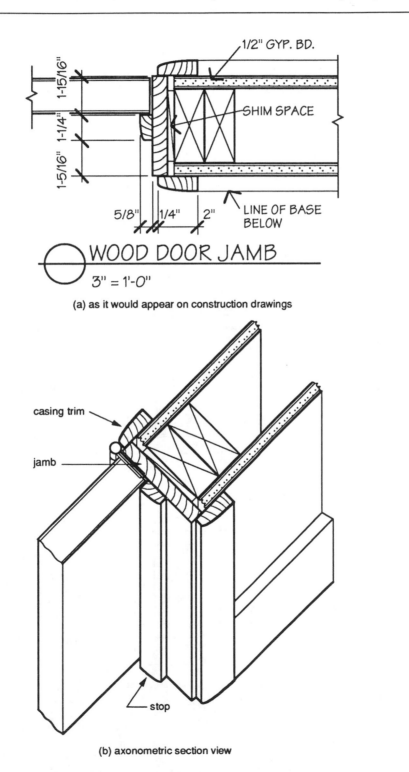

1/2" GYP. BD.

SHIM SPACE

1-15/16"
1-1/4"
1-5/16"

LINE OF BASE BELOW

5/8"   1/4"   2"

WOOD DOOR JAMB
3" = 1'-0"

(a) as it would appear on construction drawings

casing trim

jamb

stop

(b) axonometric section view

The drawings show jamb details, but the head details are similar. If a threshold is required it can be set flush with adjacent flooring materials or raised slightly above the finish floor. Thresholds of wood, stone, and metal are commonly used. Standard aluminum thresholds can also be used where cost is a consideration or where a special sound, weather, or light seal is required.

Coordination

Designing and detailing custom door assemblies, and even some standard door assemblies, requires coordination between the door components and other construction elements. The following list summarizes some of the things to consider.

- Wood blocking at jambs is generally required in metal stud partitions.
- Casing trim should be thick enough to provide a stopping point for the wall base.
- Hardware, louvers, and glass lights must be listed or labeled to be used in a labeled door.
- Smoke gaskets may be required for some fire-rated doors.

Figure 3.9
Common wood door frame variations

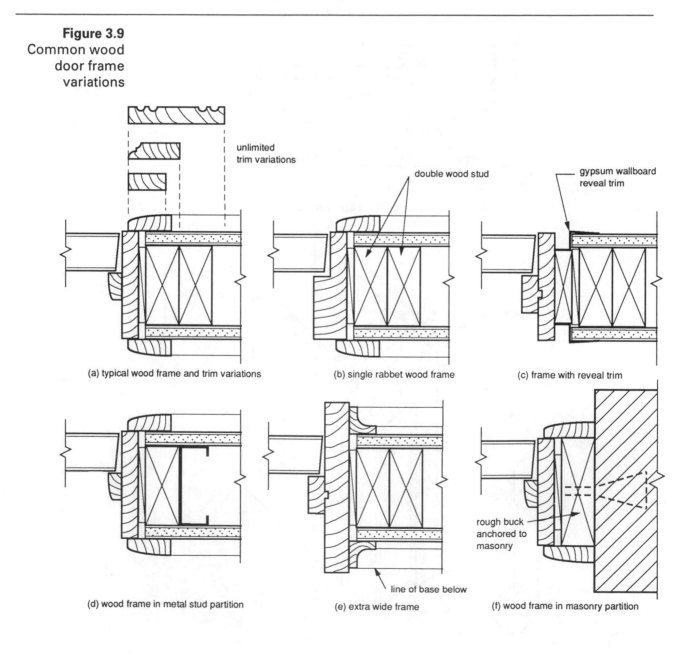

(a) typical wood frame and trim variations

(b) single rabbet wood frame

(c) frame with reveal trim

(d) wood frame in metal stud partition

(e) extra wide frame

(f) wood frame in masonry partition

Figures 3.10(a) and 3.10(b) show the industry standard dimensions for wood door frames, along with ways in which hinges are applied to doors and frames. These dimensions are useful when standard hinges and doors are used, but may be modified when detailing a door within a custom frame assembly. Maintaining standard dimensions simplifies detailing and minimizes the cost and difficulty of building the detail.

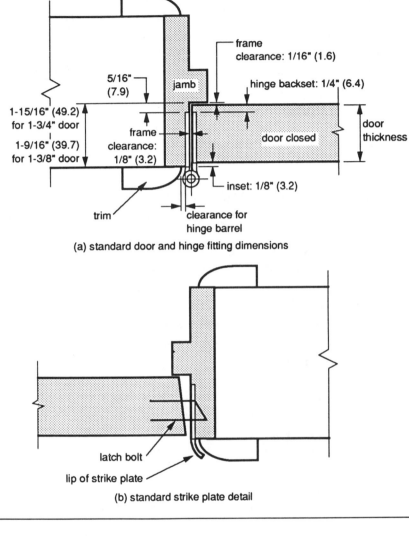

(a) standard door and hinge fitting dimensions

(b) standard strike plate detail

Figure 3.11
Wood frame without casing trim

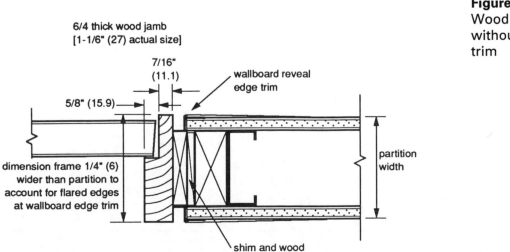

American National Standards Institute (ANSI):

ANSI/DHI A115.W2   *Preparation of 1¾ in Flush Wood Doors for Series 4000 Bored Locks and Latches*

ANSI/DHI A115.W3   *Preparation of 1⅜ in Flush Wood Doors for Series 4000 Bored Locks and Latches*

ANSI/DHI A115.W6   *Preparation of 1¾ in Flush Wood Doors for Double-Type Locks*

ANSI/DHI A115.W8   *Preparation of 1¾ in Flush Wood Doors for Bored Auxiliary Deadlocks and Deadlatches*

ANSI A117.1   *Specifications for Making Buildings and Facilities Accessible to and Usable by Physically Handicapped People*

Architectural Woodwork Institute (AWI):

Architectural Woodwork Quality Standards, Section 900, Door Frames; Section 1300, Architectural Flush Doors; Section 1400, Stile and Rail Doors; Section 1500, Factory Finishing

American Society for Testing and Materials (ASTM):

ASTM E-119   *Fire Tests of Building Construction and Materials*

Door and Hardware Institute (DHI):

DHI-WDHS-3   *Recommended Hardware Locations for Wood Flush Doors*

National Fire Protection Association (NFPA):

NFPA 80   *Standard for Fire Doors and Windows*

NFPA 252   *Standard Methods for Fire Tests of Door Assemblies* (same as UL 10B)

National Wood Window and Door Association (NWWDA):

I.S. 1-A   *Industry Standard for Architectural Wood Flush Doors*

I.S. 1-R   *Industry Standard for Residential Wood Flush Doors*

I.S. 6   *Industry Standard for Wood Stile and Rail Doors*

Underwriters Laboratories (UL):

UL 63   *Safety Standard for Fire Doors and Frames*

Std. 10B   *Fire Tests of Door Assemblies* (same as NFPA 252)

Uniform Building Code (UBC):

UBC 7-2   *Fire Tests of Door Assemblies*

• A steel or aluminum frame may be required for some fire-rated doors.

• Floors must be of adequate thickness and stability to support floor closers.

• Partitions or ceilings must be of adequate stability to support overhead closers.

• Hard-surfaced thresholds should be used when automatic door bottoms are installed.

STEEL DOORS AND FRAMES [08110]

Steel doors and frames, often referred to as *hollow metal*, are the most common type of metal door assemblies. Aluminum, stainless steel, and bronze (discussed in later sections), are also used. Steel doors are seldom used for residential construction but are frequently used in commercial construction because of their durability, security, and fire-resistive qualities. However, steel doors manufactured to resemble paneled doors and filled with polyurethane or polystyrene insulation are being used more often for residential entrance doors because of their added durability and insulative qualities.

Steel door construction

Steel doors are constructed with faces of cold-rolled sheet steel. The steel face is attached to cores of honeycomb kraft paper, steel ribs, mineral fiberboard, polyurethane, polystyrene, or other materials. The edges are made of steel channels, with hardware locations reinforced with heavy gage steel. Mineral wool or other materials are used to provide sound-deadening qualities, if required.

Steel door and frame gages

Twenty-gage steel is used for Standard Duty, Grade I doors, 18-gage steel for Heavy-duty, Grade II doors, and 18-gage, 16-gage, or 14-gage for Extra Heavy-duty, Grade III doors. Lighter or heavier gages are available from some manufacturers for special needs. Table 3.4 gives the recommended gages for various steel doors and frames.

Steel door grades

Steel doors are classified into three grades by the Steel Door Institute. Each grade is further subdivided into models indicating the type of construction. Table 3.5 lists the grades and models and their corresponding gages. Full flush design means that each door face is fabricated from a single sheet of steel with no visible seams on the surface of the faces. Seamless design is identical to full flush with the added provision that no visible seams are permitted along the vertical edges of the door.

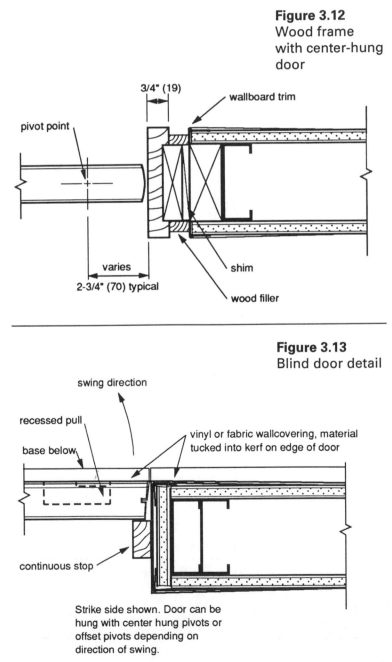

Figure 3.12
Wood frame with center-hung door

3/4" (19)
wallboard trim
pivot point
varies
2-3/4" (70) typical
shim
wood filler

Figure 3.13
Blind door detail

swing direction
recessed pull
base below
vinyl or fabric wallcovering, material tucked into kerf on edge of door
continuous stop

Strike side shown. Door can be hung with center hung pivots or offset pivots depending on direction of swing.

Building type	Frame gage[1]	Door face gage[1]
Apartments		
Main entrances	16, 14, or 12	16 or 14
Apartment entrances	18 or 16	20 or 18
Bedrooms	18 or 16	20
Bathrooms	18 or 16	20
Stairwells	16, 14, or 12	18, 16, or 14
Schools		
Entrances	16, 14, or 12	16 or 14
Classrooms	16	18
Toilets	16, 14, or 12	18, 16, or 14
Gymnasiums	16, 14, or 12	18, 16, or 14
Cafeterias	16, 14, or 12	18, 16, or 14
Stairwells	16, 14, or 12	18, 16, or 14
Hotels/motels		
Main entrances	18 or 16	20 or 18
Room entrances	18 or 16	20 or 18
Bathrooms	18 or 16	20
Closets	18 or 16	20
Stairwells	16, 14, or 12	18, 16, or 14
Storage and utility rooms	18 or 16	20 or 18
Hospitals		
Main entrances	16, 14, or 12	16 or 14
Patient rooms	16	18
Stairwells	16, 14, or 12	18, 16, or 14
Operation and exam rooms	16, 14, or 12	18, 16, or 14
Kitchens	16, 14, or 12	18, 16, or 14
Industrial		
Entrances	16, 14, or 12	16 or 14
Offices	18 or 16	20 or 18
Production	16, 14, or 12	16 or 14
Toilets	16, 14, or 12	18, 16, or 14
Tool and trucking	16, 14, or 12	16 or 14
Offices		
Entrances	16, 14, or 12	16 or 14
Individual offices	18 or 16	20
Closets	18 or 16	20
Toilets	16, 14, or 12	18, 16, or 14
Stairwells	16, 14, or 12	18, 16, or 14
Mechanical rooms	16, 14, or 12	18, 16, or 14

Table 3.4
Recommended gages for steel doors and frames

[1]These are manufacturer's standard gages. See Table 3.5.

Steel door frames

Steel door frames are used for either steel doors or wood doors and are made from sheet steel bent into the shape required for installation of the door. Frames are constructed of 18-, 16-, 14-, or 12-gage steel depending on the grade level of the door and the specific application. Table 3.6 gives the recommended frame thickness based on the door grade and model. Table 3.4 also gives the recommended frame gages for various applications. Different types of anchoring devices are used inside the frame to attach it to the partition. A floor anchor is also used at each jamb when the frame is installed before the partition.

Steel frames are manufactured as one piece, welded frames, knock-down (KD) where

Grade	Model	Description	MSG gage[1]	Minimum thickness, in. (mm)
I[2]	1	Full flush	20	0.031 (0.787)
	2	Seamless	20	0.031 (0.787)
II	1	Full flush	18	0.042 (1.067)
	2	Seamless	18	0.042 (1.067)
III	1	Full flush	16	0.053 (1.346)
	1A	Full flush	14	0.067 (1.702)
	2	Seamless	16	0.053 (1.346)
	2A	Seamless	14	0.067 (1.702)
	3	Stile and rail	18[3]	0.042 (1.067)

Table 3.5
Standard steel door grades and metal thicknesses

[1] MSG is manufacturer's standard gage.
[2] Grade I is available in 1⅜ in. (35 mm) thickness as well as 1¾ in. (44 mm) thickness. Grades II and III are only available in 1¾ in. thickness.
[3] Stile and rails of 16-gage.

Reprinted with permission from ANSI/SDI-100-91, copyright 1991 by the Steel Door Institute.

Door grade	Door model	Door gage	Frame gage
I	1 and 2	20	18 or 16
II	1 and 2	18	16
III	1, 2, and 3	16	16 or 14
III	1A and 2A	14	14 or 12

Table 3.6
Steel frame thickness based on door grade

Reprinted with permission from ANSI/SDI-100-91, copyright 1991 by the Steel Door Institute.

the two jamb sections and the head section are shipped to the job site as separate pieces, or as slip-on frames. One-piece frames must be set in place before the partition is constructed; knock-down and slip-on frames can be set after gypsum wallboard partitions are built. Slip-on frames are not available with welded corners and should be avoided if the appearance of a joint is objectionable.

Specifications

Steel doors and frames are available in the full range of fire ratings, from 20-minute to 3-hour ratings. Steel frames are used almost exclusively for openings that must be rated over 20 minutes, although qualifying aluminum frames may be rated up to 45 minutes.

Although metal doors can be custom made in almost any practical size, standard widths are from 2 ft (600 mm) to 4 ft (1200 mm) in multiples of 2 in. (50 mm). Standard opening sizes are listed in Table 3.7.

The following are standard clearances between a door and its frame for steel doors. Clearance dimensions are subject to a tolerance of ± 1/32 in. (0.8 mm).

At hinge jambs: 1/8 in. (3 mm), maximum

At head: 1/8 in. (3 mm), maximum

At meeting edges of door pairs: not more than 1/4 in. (6 mm) but 1/8 in. (3 mm) for fire-rated door openings

Undercut dimension: 3/4 in. (19 mm)

Between door face and door stop: 1/16 in. (1.6 mm)

Table 3.7
Standard opening sizes for steel doors

1¾ in. doors (44 mm)		1⅜ in. doors (35 mm)	
Width	Height	Width	Height
2 ft (610)	6 ft 8 in. (2032)	2 ft (610)	6 ft 8 in. (2032)
2 ft 4 in. (711)	7 ft (2134)	2 ft 4 in. (711)	7 ft (2134)
2 ft 6 in. (762)	7 ft 2 in. (2184)	2 ft 6 in. (762)	
2 ft 8 in. (813)	7 ft 10 in. (2388)	2 ft 8 in. (813)	
2 ft 10 in. (864)	8 ft (2438)	2 ft 10 in. (864)	
3 ft (914)	8 ft 10 in. (2692)	3 ft (914)	
3 ft 4 in. (1016)	10 ft (3048)		
3 ft 6 in. (1067)			
3 ft 8 in. (1118)			
3 ft 10 in. (1168)			
4 ft (1219)			

Standard assemblies

The three most common types of metal doors are flush, sash, and louvered. Flush doors have a single, smooth surface on both sides; sash doors contain one or more glass lights; and louvered doors have an opening with metal slats to provide ventilation. Many standard configurations of sash and louvered doors are available, as well as doors with both louvers and glass.

Steel frames are generally made from one piece of sheet steel bent into the required profile. Figures 3.14(a) and 3.14(b) show one of the most common frame profiles, along with some standard dimensions and the terminology used to describe the parts. Frames can also be custom fabricated into a variety of sizes and shapes within the limits of the machinery used to form them. Figures 3.15(a)–3.15(e) illustrate several possible combinations of steel door frames set in various types of partitions.

Custom assemblies

Most custom steel door assemblies are unique because of the size or shape of the frame. The frame profile shown in Figure 3.14 is the most common. Other profiles are possible; however, the minimum face dimension is usually 1 in. because of limitation on the brake presses used to form the frame. Unusual designs must be verified with a hollow metal door manufacturer to be sure that its fabrication is possible. Figures 3.16(a) and 3.16(b) show some examples of custom frames.

Coordination

Designing for hollow metal work requires some of the same coordination as for wood doors and frames. In addition, consider the following items in detailing:

• Knock-down or slip-on frames are easier to install than one-piece welded frames in gypsum wallboard partitions, but the joints are visible.

Figure 3.14
Standard steel
door frame

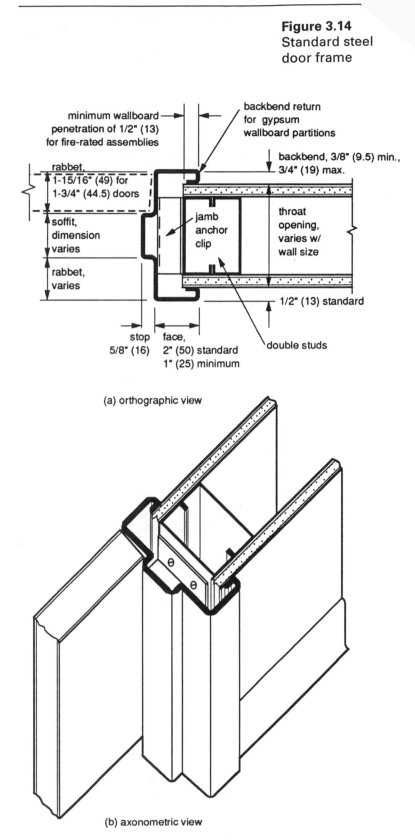

(a) orthographic view

(b) axonometric view

• Cutoff (or sanitary) stops that do not extend to the floor should be used where ease of cleaning around the frame is important.

• Mineral-core, flush wood doors may be used with steel frames for fire ratings up to 1½ hours.

• Rubber silencers must be provided in strike side of door frame.

• Full-height doors in partitions that extend only to a suspended ceiling may require extra bracing from the head frame to the structure above the ceiling.

ALUMINUM DOORS AND FRAMES [08120]

Aluminum is commonly used as stile and rail material for glass doors and as door frame material for both aluminum glass doors and wood doors. A few manufacturers also offer flush, sash, and louvered doors faced with aluminum. Aluminum door

Figure 3.15
Common steel door frame variations

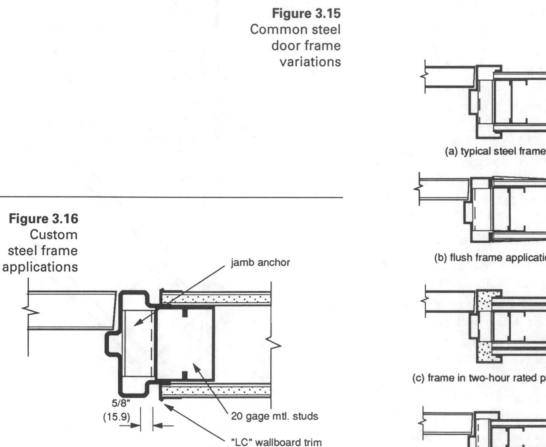

(a) typical steel frame

(b) flush frame application

(c) frame in two-hour rated partition

(d) single rabbeted frame in narrow partition

(e) frame in masonry wall

Figure 3.16
Custom steel frame applications

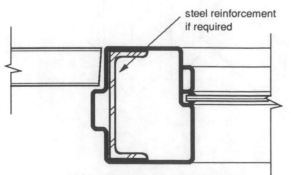

jamb anchor

5/8"
(15.9)

20 gage mtl. studs

"LC" wallboard trim

(a) frame shaped for flush application with reveal

steel reinforcement if required

(b) frame between door and sidelight

American National Standards Institute (ANSI):

ANSI/ISDSI 100	*Door Size Dimensional Standard and Assembly Tolerance for Insulated Steel Door Systems*
ANSI/ISDSI 102	*Insulated Steel Door Systems—Installation Standard*
ANSI/ISDSI 103	*Acoustical Performance Standard for Insulated Steel Door Systems*
ANSI/SDI 100	*Recommended Specifications for Standard Steel Doors and Frames*
ANSI/SDI A123.1	*Standard Nomenclature for Steel Doors and Steel Door Frames*
ANSI A224.1	*Standard Test Procedure and Acceptance Criteria for Prime Painted Steel Surfaces for Steel Doors and Frames*

American Society for Testing and Materials (ASTM):

ASTM E-119	*Fire Tests of Building Construction and Materials*

Door and Hardware Institute (DHI):

Recommended Locations for Builders' Hardware for Custom Steel Doors and Frames
Recommended Locations for Architectural Hardware for Standard Steel Doors and Frames

Hollow Metal Manufacturers Association (HMMA):

HMMA 860	*Guide Specifications for Hollow Metal Doors and Frames*
HMMA 861	*Guide Specifications for Commercial Hollow Metal Doors and Frames*
HMMA 862	*Guide Specifications for Commercial Security Hollow Metal Doors and Frames*
NMMA 863	*Guide Specifications for Detention Security Hollow Metal Doors and Frames*

National Fire Protection Association (NFPA):

NFPA 80	*Standard for Fire Doors and Windows*
NFPA 252	*Standard Methods for Fire Tests of Door Assemblies*

Steel Door Institute (SDI):

ANSI/SDI 100	*Recommended Specifications for Standard Steel Doors and Frames*
SDI-105	*Recommended Erection Instructions for Steel Frames*
SDI-106	*Recommended Standard Door Type Nomenclature*
SDI-107	*Hardware on Steel Doors (Reinforcement—Application)*
SDI-108	*Recommended Selection and Usage Guide for Standard Steel Doors and Frames*
SDI-109	*Hardware for Standard Steel Doors and Frames*
SDI-110	*Standard Steel Doors and Frames for Modular Masonry Construction*
SDI-111	*Recommended Standard Details for Steel Doors and Frames*
SDI-113	*Test Procedure and Acceptance Criteria for Apparent Thermal Performance for Steel Door and Frame Assemblies*
SDI-114	*Test Procedure and Acceptance Criteria for Acoustical Performance for Steel Door and Frame Assemblies*
SDI-116	*Standard Test Procedure and Acceptance Criteria for Rate of Air Flow Through Closed Steel Door and Frame Assemblies*
SDI-117	*Manufacturing Tolerances for Standard Steel Doors and Frames*
SDI-118	*Basic Fire Door Requirements*

Underwriters Laboratories (UL):

UL 63	*Safety Standard for Fire Doors and Frames*
Std. 10B	*Fire Tests of Door Assemblies*

Uniform Building Code (UBC):

UBC 7-2	*Fire Tests of Door Assemblies*

frames are most commonly used in interior construction to frame wood doors when a lightweight, easily assembled frame is required. Aluminum frames are also used in many demountable partition systems (see Chapter 1) or when a complex frame profile is required. Because aluminum frames are manufactured by extrusion, intricate shapes can be formed easily.

Components

Aluminum frames are constructed of one or more pieces of extruded aluminum. The exact configuration and size of a frame depends on the manufacturer's proprietary system, but most are a double-rabbeted shape with a continuous stop, similar to a steel door frame. One noticeable difference is that aluminum frames have sharp corners, as opposed to the slightly rounded corners of steel frames. This is because aluminum frames are extruded.

Standard assemblies

Figure 3.17 shows a typical aluminum frame with a separate, continuous anchor member that is attached to the gypsum wallboard partition. The finished jamb and the door stop are attached to the anchoring subassembly to complete the installation. Other types of aluminum frames have separate jamb pieces and casing trim, similar to wood frames. The door stops may have individual silencers or a continuous wool pile sealer.

Aluminum frames are available for 20-minute fire-rated opening assemblies. Smoke gaskets are also available where they are required by code.

Custom assemblies

Many proprietary shapes, sizes, and finishes of aluminum frames are available from several manufacturers. If quantities are sufficient, custom extrusion dies can be made to order so that project-specific frame profiles can be manufactured. Curves, angles, and ornate profiles are all possible with custom extrusions.

Coordination

• Most manufacturers offer a complete system of extrusion sizes and shapes for door frames as well as glass sidelight framing, bank railing, and partition track.

• Other metals in contact with the frame should be stainless steel or zinc. Contact with other dissimilar metals should be prevented with bituminous paint or nonmetallic gaskets to prevent galvanic action.

• Aluminum framing used with demountable partition systems may be used with prefinished panels of gypsum wallboard in place of standard wallboard construction.

GLASS DOORS [08450]

Glass doors refer to those constructed primarily of glass with fittings to hold the pivots and other hardware. Sometimes they are called *all-glass doors*. Their strength depends on the glass rather than the framing. Doors with large lights of glass framed with wood, steel, aluminum, or other metals are discussed in other sections.

Components

Glass doors are generally constructed of ½-in. (13 mm) or ¾-in. (19 mm) tempered glass with fittings and operating hardware as required by the installation. Common door sizes are 36 in. (914 mm) wide and

Figure 3.17
Typical
aluminum frame

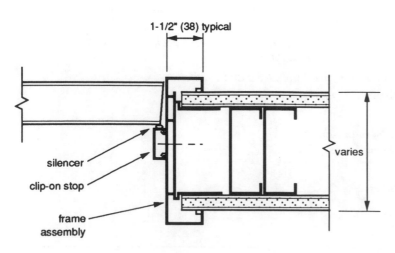

1-1/2" (38) typical

silencer

clip-on stop

frame
assembly

varies

7ft (2,134 mm) high, although many designers prefer to specify glass doors at the same height as the ceiling.

Some typical glass door configurations are shown in Figures 3.18(a)–3.18(d). The minimum configuration requires some type of door pull and a corner fitting at the top and bottom (sometimes called the *shoe*) to hold the pivots. In lieu of corner fittings, some manufacturers provide hinge fittings that clamp on the glass and support the door in much the same way as a standard hinged door. If a lock is required, the bottom fitting may be continuous across the door to allow for a dead bolt to be installed. Some designers prefer continuous fittings on both the top and bottom.

Because a full glass door is a potential hazard and extra strength is required, the glass must be tempered. Any holes, notches, or other modification to the glass must be made before it is tempered. As a result, the design and detailing of glass doors must be finalized when the construction drawings are issued. Before glass doors are manufactured, the designer receives shop drawings to confirm that the manufacturer will make the door according to the original design intent.

The glass may be clear, tinted, or patterned, depending on the design requirements. Special designs, lettering, and logos can be etched into the glass as well, if deep etching is done before the glass is tempered.

Standard assemblies

Glass doors can be used alone and set within a wall opening with or without a frame, or they can be installed between glass sidelights. If glass sidelights are used, the same type of fitting used on the door is generally used to support the sidelights. Although jamb frames of aluminum, wood, or ornamental metal can be used, they are not necessary and the glass sidelights can be butted directly to the partition or held away a fraction of an inch. Figures 3.19(a)–3.19(c) shows some standard glass door jamb assemblies and associated jamb details.

Figure 3.20 illustrates a typical vertical section through a full-height glass door.

Custom assemblies

In a sense, all glass doors and their associated framing are custom designs because each installation is manufactured to meet the specific project requirements of size, metal finish, door pull type, and so forth. However, the most common assemblies described in the preceding section may be considered standard because they are used so often and present no significant manufacturing or installation challenges.

Custom assemblies generally involve installations with unusually large doors or sidelights, bent glass, custom-designed fittings, unusual glass support or suspension systems, or special hardware. Some custom assemblies require the use of a specific manufacturer's proprietary system, while

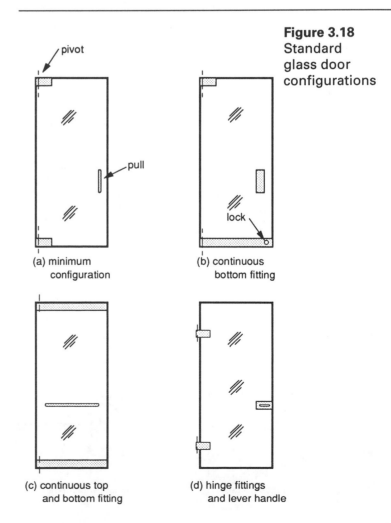

Figure 3.18 Standard glass door configurations

(a) minimum configuration

(b) continuous bottom fitting

(c) continuous top and bottom fitting

(d) hinge fittings and lever handle

others can be built using standard component parts installed by a glazing contractor.

Glass doors may be part of an all-glass entrance system that does not use visible framing members. Instead, special fittings clamp onto the surrounding glass and contain the top pivot for the door and latching hardware. See Figure 3.22. The glass panels surrounding the door are usually set in framing that is flush with the floor and ceiling so it is not visible. Refer to Chapter 5 for information on concealed glazing framing.

Coordination

Glass doors, their hardware, and any glass sidelights are usually supplied by one manufacturer and installed by the glazing contractor as a complete package. Therefore, most of the required coordination of design elements is verified during bidding and production of shop drawings. However, there are several items that the designer should consider during design and construction document production.

• Verify if glass doors are allowed by the local building code and what type of hardware is required.

• If the door extends to the underside of a suspended ceiling, adequate bracing for the top pivot must be provided. If the space above the ceiling is a return-air plenum, wood blocking is not allowed; all bracing must be noncombustible.

• If a floor closer is used, verify that the floor structure is thick enough and provides enough support for the depth of the closer housing.

• Thresholds are optional for glass doors; however, access to the cover plate over any floor closer mechanism must be maintained.

• Overhead closers may be located in the top rail fitting or in a transom bar if sufficient anchorage is provided. Verify availability with the manufacturer.

Figure 3.19
Standard glass door installations

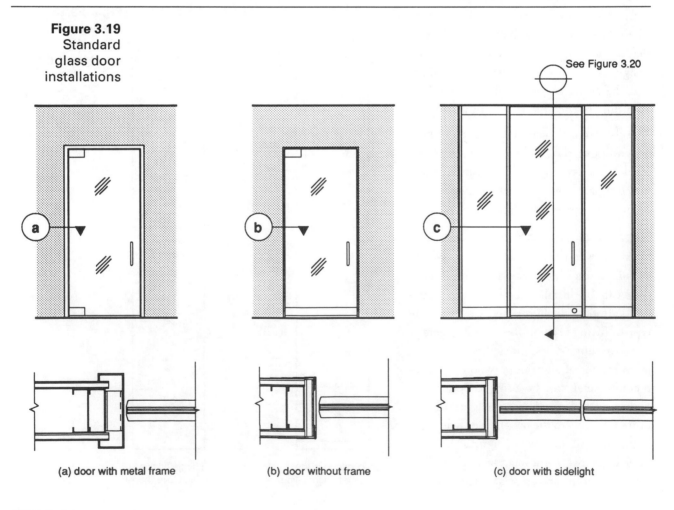

(a) door with metal frame   (b) door without frame   (c) door with sidelight

METAL DOORS [08100]

Metal doors include those constructed primarily of some metal other than steel or aluminum. This includes bronze, brass, and stainless steel or doors clad with sheets of decorative metal. In some cases, wood, aluminum, or steel doors are used for structural support and are simply clad with thin sheets of the finish metal. If door framing is required, it is clad with the same material.

Metal doors may be custom fabricated to the designer's plans or one of several manufacturer's proprietary decorative metal doors may be selected from a catalogue. If decorative metal is being added to a standard door, the hinges or pivots must be capable of supporting the extra weight, and the framing must allow for the increased thickness of the door. If hinges are used, wider hinges than normal may be required to accommodate the extra thickness.

Stainless steel doors

Stainless steel doors are the most common type of metal door after hollow metal and aluminum. The advantages of stainless steel doors include corrosion resistance (to humidity, coastal salt spray, and industrial environments), low maintenance, durability, cleanability, and appearance. For interior

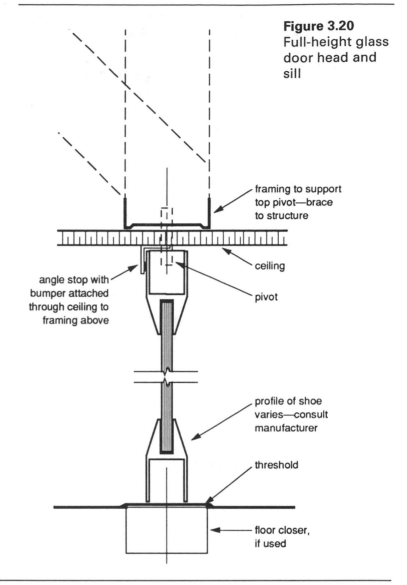

Figure 3.20
Full-height glass door head and sill

framing to support top pivot—brace to structure

ceiling

pivot

angle stop with bumper attached through ceiling to framing above

profile of shoe varies—consult manufacturer

threshold

floor closer, if used

Because all-glass doors cannot be fire rated, they cannot be used where a protected opening is required in a fire-rated partition. When they are allowed and serve as exit doors, the type of hardware used must conform to the requirements of the building code in force. Some codes and local amendments are more restrictive than others and may prohibit the use of a simple dead bolt in the bottom rail fitting. Instead, special panic-type hardware is available for glass doors that allows the door to be locked from the outside (and operated with card keys or keypads, if necessary) but still allows the door to be unlatched and opened from the inside in a single operation without any special knowledge or effort, if handicapped accessability is not a consideration. See Figure 3.21.

Building code requirements for all-glass doors

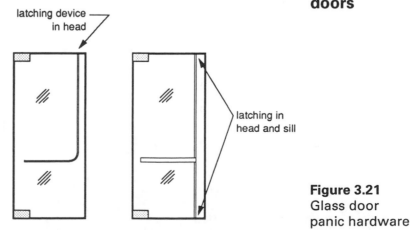

latching device in head

latching in head and sill

Figure 3.21
Glass door panic hardware

applications, stainless steel doors are commonly specified for food preparation areas, clean rooms, industrial plants, swimming pools, and public areas where intentional or accidental damage is expected. For example, a stainless steel door with a swirl or distressed finish hides scratches and is easy to maintain.

Stainless steel doors are constructed similarly to hollow metal doors, with face sheets bonded to honeycomb or vertical stiffener cores. Polystyrene insulating cores can also be used. The most common steel alloy used is 304, but for more corrosion resistance, alloy 316 should be specified. Whatever type of alloy and construction is used, all components of the door

Applicable standards for glass doors

Consumer Product Safety Commission (CPSC):
CPSC 16 CFR 1201 *Safety Standards for Architectural Glazing Materials*

American National Standards Institute (ANSI):
ANSI Z97.1 *Safety Glazing Material Used in Buildings, Safety Performance Specifications, and Methods of Test*

American Society for Testing and Materials (ASTM):
ASTM C-1048 *Specification for Heat Treated Flat Glass*

Figure 3.22
All-glass entrance system

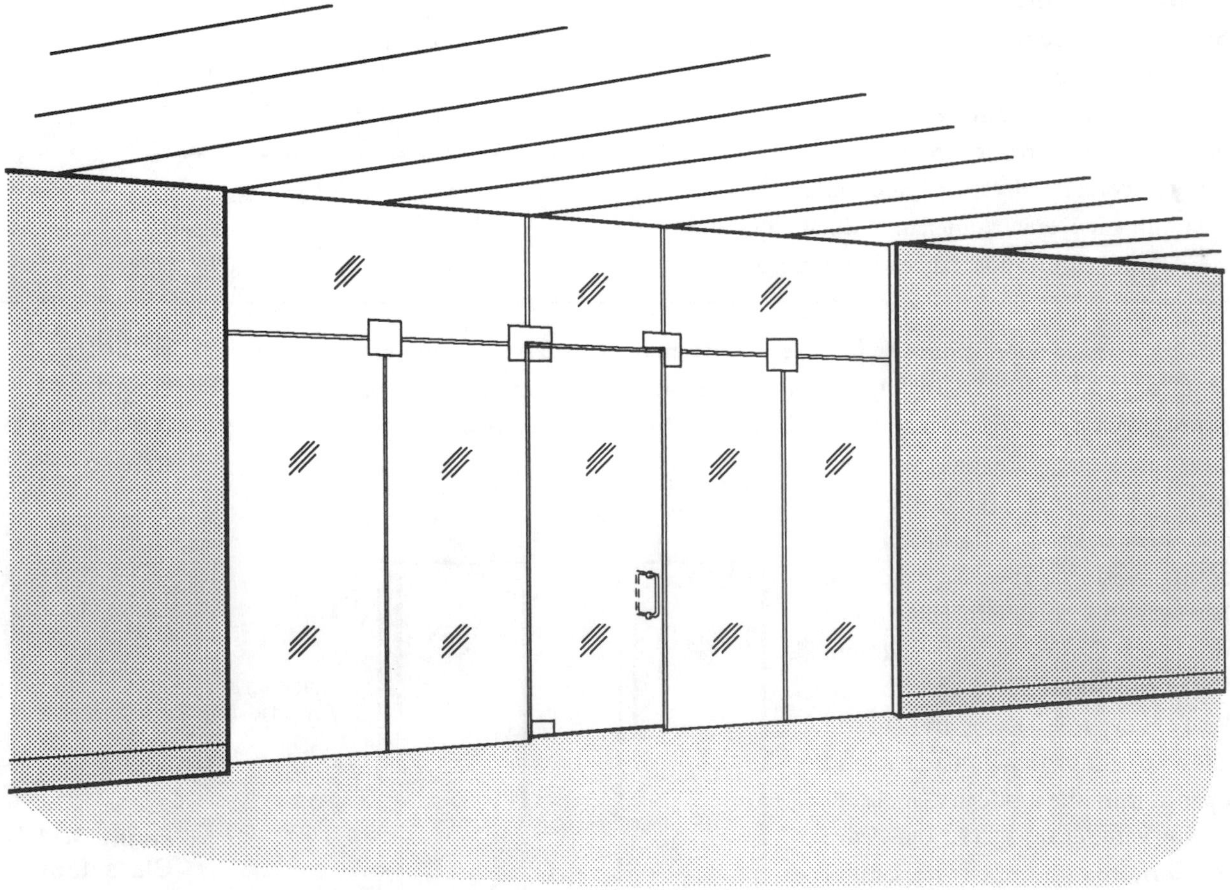

and hardware should be of stainless steel to avoid galvanic corrosion.

While any standard stainless steel finish can be specified for doors, a No. 4 finish is quite common. This consists of fine parallel lines giving a dull finish that hides minor scratches. Refer to Table 7.3 for a listing of common stainless steel finishes. However, many other finishes are possible. These include swirl, distressed, and abrasive blast finishes as well as selective etching and embossing. Coloring is also possible, but it is easily scratched so it should be limited to the recessed portions of embossed finishes.

SPECIAL DOORS
Folding and accordion doors [08350]

Two types of special doors commonly used to close large openings or divide rooms are folding doors and accordion doors. When they are used as room dividers, they are called *folding* or *accordion partitions*.

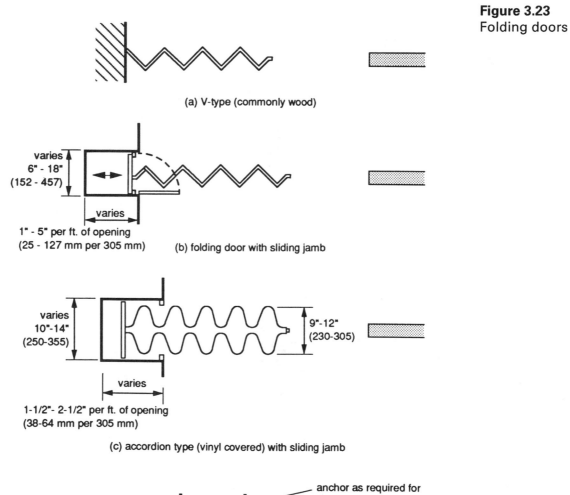

Figure 3.23
Folding doors

(a) V-type (commonly wood)

varies
6" - 18"
(152 - 457)

varies

1" - 5" per ft. of opening
(25 - 127 mm per 305 mm)

(b) folding door with sliding jamb

varies
10"-14"
(250-355)

9"-12"
(230-305)

varies

1-1/2"- 2-1/2" per ft. of opening
(38-64 mm per 305 mm)

(c) accordion type (vinyl covered) with sliding jamb

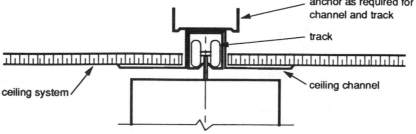

anchor as required for channel and track

track

ceiling system

ceiling channel

(d) typical ceiling detail

Folding doors are made of multiple units of relatively narrow vertical slats hinged together so that the door can be folded against the jamb. They are made from a wood core and are covered with wood veneer, vinyl, or plastic laminate. Accordion doors have a folding steel framework and are covered with a continuous sheet of vinyl. See Figures 3.23(a)–3.23(c).

Both folding and accordion doors are suspended from a track mounted on or concealed within the ceiling, as shown in Figure 3.23(d). They can be used singly or in pairs for very large openings. The leading edge of

the door has a continuous latching strip that mates with a closure strip mounted on the jamb. If the folding door is concealed within a pocket, it usually has a sliding jamb, as shown in Figure 3.23(c), that pulls out flush with the finished wall when the door is completely closed.

Folding and accordion doors are relatively inexpensive and are a good choice for dividing small openings. However, their maximum size is limited to about 40 ft (12 m) wide and 20 ft (6 m) high. Some manufacturers make accordion partitions that can close off a 60-ft (18 m) wide opening. They can be used in straight

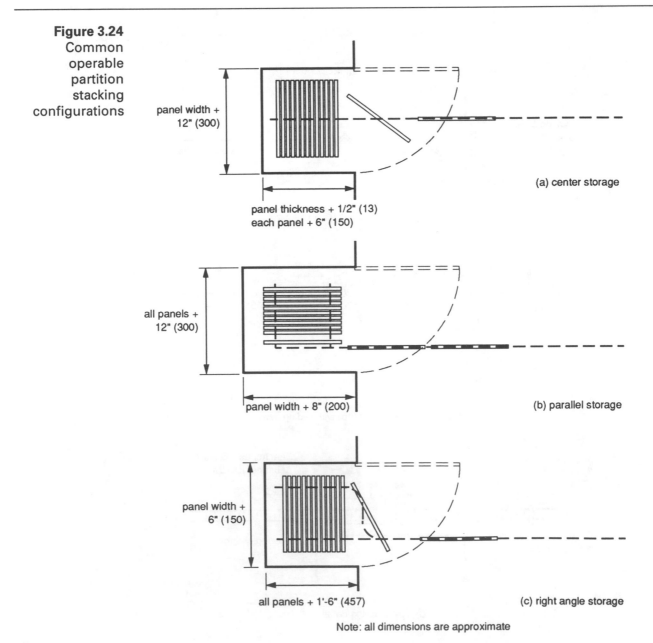

Figure 3.24
Common operable partition stacking configurations

panel width + 12" (300)

panel thickness + 1/2" (13)
each panel + 6" (150)

(a) center storage

all panels + 12" (300)

panel width + 8" (200)

(b) parallel storage

panel width + 6" (150)

all panels + 1'-6" (457)

(c) right angle storage

Note: all dimensions are approximate

runs or on a curved path. Electrically driven doors are available. The range of available colors and materials is also limited to what each manufacturer provides, unless the supplier offers custom color choices.

Although some types of these doors are manufactured to reduce sound transmission, their sound attenuation capabilities are limited to provide a sound transmission coefficient (STC) of about 40. Therefore, they should not be used where acoustical control is critical. (See Chapter 11 for a discussion of STC values.) In these situations operable partitions should be used instead.

Folding doors and accordion doors cannot be used as exit doors, and they are not typically fire rated as an opening assembly. One manufacturer, however, does make electrically driven, automatic-closing partitions that have been tested and approved for ⅓-, ¾-, 1-, and 1½-hour fire ratings. Most manufacturers do offer finishes with a Class I fire rating.

Operable partitions [10650]

When very large rooms must be subdivided and sound control is critical, such as in meeting rooms or hotel ballrooms, an operable partition should be used. These are systems of individual panels suspended by a track in the ceiling similar to folding doors. Unlike folding doors, however, operable partitions use fairly wide panels, typically from 3 to 5 ft (0.914 to 1.52 mm), that move independently (some systems use individual pairs of panels that are hinged).

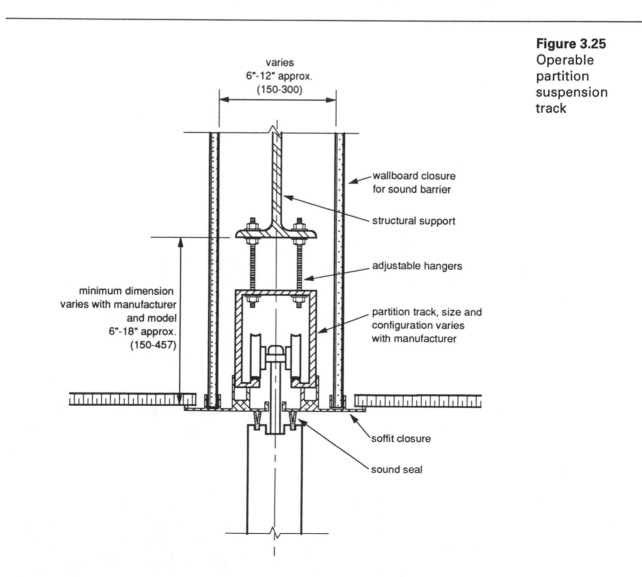

Figure 3.25
Operable partition suspension track

varies
6"-12" approx.
(150-300)

minimum dimension varies with manufacturer and model
6"-18" approx.
(150-457)

wallboard closure for sound barrier

structural support

adjustable hangers

partition track, size and configuration varies with manufacturer

soffit closure

sound seal

The panels can be manually operated or electrically driven. When fully closed, the edges of each panel are tightly sealed against the adjacent panels. Special sealing methods at the floor and top track provide a tight sound seal at these locations as well. Operable partitions can close off openings up to 48 ft (15 m) high with unlimited widths.

The panels are much thicker, typically from 3 to 6 in. (76 to 152 mm), and heavier than folding doors, and with STC ratings up to 58, they provide a more massive barrier to sound transmission. Generally, the panels can be finished to match the other walls in the room. When necessary, passage doors can be placed within one panel to allow access through the wall without opening the entire assembly.

Operable partitions are usually concealed within a separate pocket space. The exact method of stacking and track arrangement varies with each manufacturer and the requirements of the individual project. Figures 3.24(a)–3.24(c) show some common stacking configurations.

Because operable partitions are heavy, each manufacturer's track must be supported by structural steel above the ceiling. This must be designed by a structural engineer and coordinated with the partition manufacturer's track system. Figure 3.25 shows a "generic" detail of a suspension track. All details and dimensions must be verified for specific installations.

Overhead coiling doors [08330]

When large openings need to be closed for fire separation or security reasons and appearance is not a consideration, overhead coiling doors can be used. They are not intended for frequent passage, but to close off an opening for an extended period of time or to automatically close off an opening during a fire. For example, a private stairway opening may require an automatically closing fire-rated door to isolate one floor from another. Because an overhead coiling door is not intended for passage, it cannot be used in an exit corridor unless an approved exit door is located adjacent to it.

Overhead coiling doors require a large space above the ceiling for the housing and motor and steel tracks on each side of the opening. With careful detailing, however, only a narrow slot is required at the ceiling and the jamb tracks can be recessed within the walls. Figures 3.26(a) and 3.26(b) show a typical head and jamb detail for an overhead coiling door.

Overhead doors can be manually operated or motor driven. For interior design applications a motor driven door should be used with a fail-safe feature so it will close during a fire even if power is interrupted.

Figure 3.26
Overhead
coiling door
details

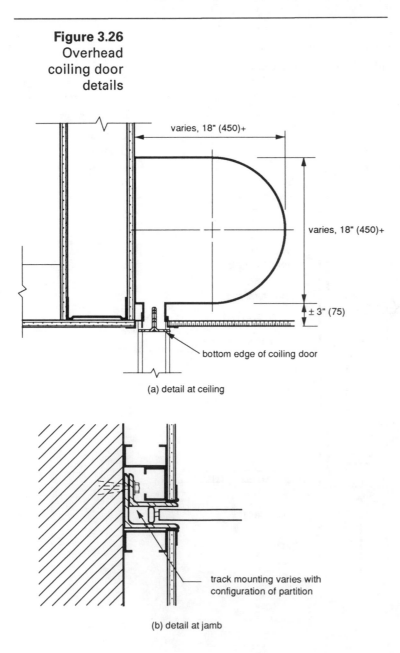

varies, 18" (450)+

varies, 18" (450)+

± 3" (75)

bottom edge of coiling door

(a) detail at ceiling

track mounting varies with configuration of partition

(b) detail at jamb

4

HARDWARE

There are two major categories of hardware: finish hardware and cabinet hardware. The former includes all hardware required to support and operate full-size doors, while the latter is used for smaller cabinet doors and other architectural woodwork. This chapter discusses finish hardware only.

Hardware is critical to door functioning, accessibility, and life-safety requirements, and is also a major design feature. Its style, detailing, and finish should complement other design features.

In most situations, the interior designer can be assisted with hardware selection and detailed specification writing by hardware suppliers or hardware consultants. However, every designer should know enough about hardware availability, function, and application to make intelligent preliminary decisions that are consistent with the functional and aesthetic needs of a project.

Selection of hardware involves the following criteria:

Opening constraints. These include the door type, the frame type, the size of the opening, and the frequency of use.

Code requirements. If the hardware is being used on a fire-rated door, the hardware must be listed or certified for use on such doors.

Accessibility. The hardware must be usable by the physically disabled, as prescribed by the local building code and the Americans with Disabilities Act. Refer to Chapter 18 for detailed information on accessibility requirements.

Security. The degree of security required affects not only the type of lock used but also the method of hanging the door and installing other components.

Appearance. The style and finish of hardware should be consistent with the design concept of the space in which the doors are used.

Special considerations. Requirements such as light proofing, radiation protection, acoustic control, concealed door design, or other unusual design criteria dictate special hardware.

DOOR MOUNTING
Hinges [08710]
The typical way to mount a door is to use hinges. The most common type of hinge consists of two leaves with one or more knuckles on each leaf. The knuckles are attached with

a pin that can be either removable (the standard) or nonremovable for security installations. The knuckles and pin form the barrel of the hinge, which is finished with a tip. Most hinges have three knuckles on one leaf and two on the other. There are four standard types of hinges: full-mortise, half-mortise, half-surface, and full-surface.

Standard hinges

The full-mortise hinge is also called a butt hinge (or butt, for short). It is the most common type and is designed so that both leaves are fully mortised into the frame and the edge of the door. See Figure 4.1(a). When the door is closed, only the barrel of the hinge is visible. Full-mortise hinges are

Figure 4.1
Common hinge types

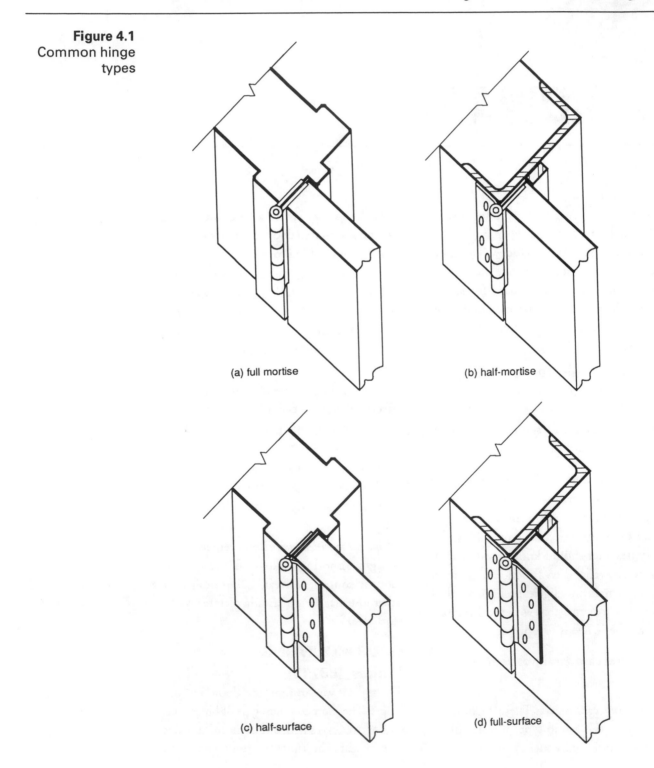

(a) full mortise

(b) half-mortise

(c) half-surface

(d) full-surface

used when both the door and the frame can be mortised.

Half-mortise hinges are designed so that one leaf is mortised into the edge of the door, while the other leaf is surface mounted to the frame. See Figure 4.1(b). These are used when the frame cannot be cut away, such as in a steel channel frame.

In half-surface hinges, one leaf is mortised into the frame. The other is surface applied to the door face and secured with through bolts. See Figure 4.1(c). These are used on extremely large doors and other types of composite doors that cannot be mortised.

Full-surface hinges are designed to be surface mounted to both the frame and the door when mortising is not possible, such as on a kalamein (metal-clad) door hung on a steel channel frame. See Figure 4.1(d). Full-surface hinges are seldom used for interior applications.

Special hinges

There are also special types of hinges. Raised barrel hinges are used when there is no room for the barrel to extend past the door trim. The barrel is offset from its normal position to allow one leaf to be mortised into the frame. This is shown in Figure 4.2. Swing clear hinges have a special shape that allows the door to swing 90° or 95° so that the full opening of the doorway is available, as shown in Figure 4.3. Without a swing clear hinge, standard butt hinges decrease the opening width by the thickness of the door when it is open 90°.

Other types of specialty hinges are also available, as illustrated in Figures 4.4(a)–4.4(d). Electric hinges allow low-voltage power to be run from the frame into the door to control electric locks, hold-open devices, or security alarms. Invisible hinges are completely concealed within the edge of the door and frame and are only partially visible when the door is open. Wide throw hinges are used where the barrel of the hinge and the door in the open position must clear

molding or other protrusions. Pivot reinforced hinges have an integral plate on one of the leaves perpendicular to the leaf that is screwed into the top or bottom of the door. They are used to support doors subject to a high frequency of use and abuse, such as in schools, institutions, and public buildings. Continuous hinges are also available that support the door along its entire length, distributing the weight along a much larger area and eliminating localized stress.

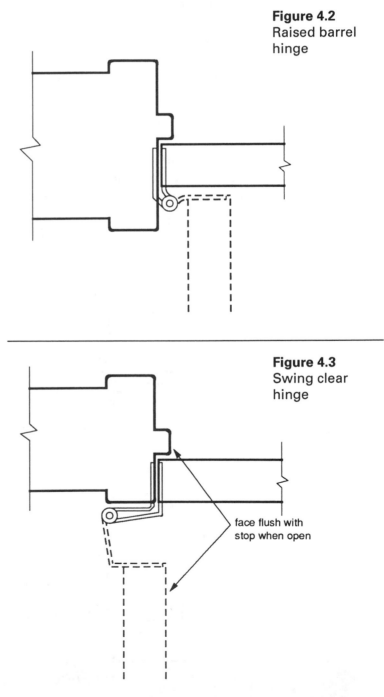

Figure 4.2
Raised barrel hinge

Figure 4.3
Swing clear hinge

face flush with stop when open

Selecting hinges

A standard procedure is used to determine the type, size, and number of hinges to be used on a door.

1. Determine the hinge type. This depends on the type of door and frame and includes the full-mortise, half-mortise, half-surface, full-surface, or other specialty hinges as required.

2. Determine the weight and bearing of the hinge. This depends on the door weight and frequency of use. Hinges are available with or without ball bearings in three types: standard weight, plain bearing; standard weight, ball bearing; and heavy weight, ball bearing. Table 4.1 gives some common applications and the recommended hinge type. Ball bearing hinges are required for fire-rated assemblies and on all doors with closers.

3. Determine the hinge size. Hinge sizes are described by two numbers, such as 4¼ × 4½ in. The first number represents the height of the hinge in inches, not including tips. The second number represents the width of

the hinge when it is open. Standard widths include 3½, 4, and 4½ in. (89, 102, and 114 mm). Standard heights include 3, 3½, 4, 4½, 5, 6, and 8 in. (76, 89, 102, 114, 127, 152, and 203 mm).

The required width for full-mortise hinges is determined by the width of the door and the clearance required around the jamb trim. One rule of thumb is that the width of the hinge equals twice the door thickness, plus trim projection, minus ½ in. (13 mm). If the fraction falls between standard sizes, use the next larger size.

The height of the hinge is determined by the door thickness and the door width, as indicated in Table 4.2.

4. Determine the number of hinges required. The number of hinges is determined by the height of the door. Numbers of hinges are commonly referred to by pairs; one pair meaning two hinges. Doors up to 60 in. high (1500 mm) require 2 hinges (1 pair), although some lightweight residential doors over 60 in. can be mounted with only

Figure 4.4
Specialty hinges

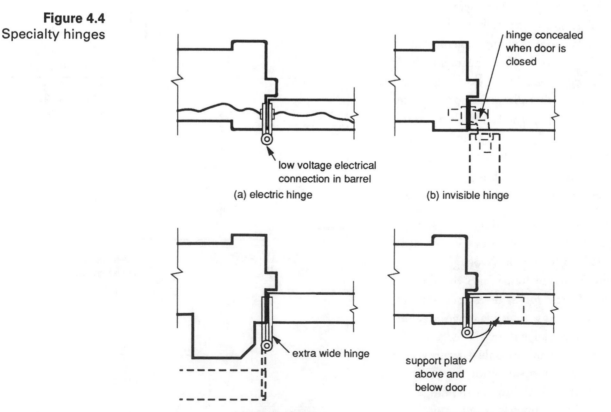

(a) electric hinge — low voltage electrical connection in barrel

(b) invisible hinge — hinge concealed when door is closed

(c) wide throw hinge — extra wide hinge

(d) pivot reinforced hinge — support plate above and below door

Application	Estimated frequency (daily)	Frequency classification	Hinge type
Large department store entrance	5000		
Large office building entrance	4000		
School entrance	1250		
School toilet door	1250	High	Heavy weight, ball bearing
Theater entrance	1000		
Store or bank entrance	500		
Office stairwell	500		
Office building door	400		
School corridor door	100		
Office building corridor	75	Medium	Standard weight, ball bearing
Store toilet door	60		
Residential entrance	40		
Residential door	25		
Residential corridor door	10	Low	Standard weight, plain bearing
Residential closet door	6		

Door thickness, in. (mm)	Door width, in. (mm)	Height of hinge, in. (mm)
¾ to 1⅛ (19 to 29)	to 24 (610)	2½ (64)
1⅜ (35)	to 32 (813)	3½ (89)
1⅜ (35)	over 32 to 37 (over 813 to 940)	4 (102)
1¾ (44)	to 36 (to 914)	4½ (114)
1¾ (44)	over 36 to 48 (over 914 to 1219)	5 (127)
1¾ (44)	over 48 (over 1219)	6 (152)
2, 2¼, 2½ (51, 57, 64)	to 42 (to 1067)	5 (heavy weight) (127)
2, 2¼, 2½ (51, 57, 64)	over 42 (over 1067)	6 (heavy weight) (152)

Table 4.2
Hinge sizing for height

two hinges. Doors from 60 in. to 90 in. (1500 to 2290 mm) require 3 hinges (1½ pair), and doors 90 in. to 120 in. (2290 to 3050 mm) require 4 hinges (2 pair).

5. Determine the type of base metal. The base metal comprises the structural part of the hinge and is the metal to which the finish is applied. The type of base metal required is determined by atmospheric conditions, fire-rating requirements, and the final appearance desired. The available base metals include steel, brass, bronze, and stainless steel. For interior applications, any of these base metals may be used. However,

fire-rated doors must have hinges with a base metal of steel or stainless steel. Not all finish coatings are available on every base metal. Refer to the section on materials and finishes near the end of this chapter for more information.

6. Determine the finish coating on the hinges. The available hardware finishes are listed at the end of this chapter.

7. Determine the tip design desired or required. Most manufacturers offer a variety of tip designs for the barrels of hinges. See Figures 4.5(a)–4.5(f). Typical types are the flat button, hospital, and oval head. Flat button tips are the most common and are furnished if not specified otherwise. Flush tips are concealed within the knuckle. Hospital tips have a sloped end to make cleaning easy and to prevent attachment of ropes or cords in psychiatric wards and jails. Other tips available from some manufacturers include ball tips, steeple tips, and flush tips. Other decorator tips are available for some hinge varieties. Consult individual manufacturer's catalogs for availability.

Pivots

Pivots provide an alternative way to hang doors, where the appearance of hinges is objectionable or where a frameless door design may make it impossible to use hinges. Pivots are used in pairs with the bottom pivot mounted in or on the floor and a corresponding unit mounted in the head frame. They may be center hung or offset. Tall and heavy doors require offset pivots with one or more intermediate pivots. For tall doors, intermediate pivots are required to keep the door from warping; for heavy doors, they are required for additional support. Center-hung pivots allow the door to swing in either direction and are completely concealed. Offset pivots allow the door to swing 180°, if required. Pivots can be used alone, as shown in Figure 4.6(a)–4.6(d) or they can be part of a closer assembly, as discussed in the section on Closing Devices.

Figure 4.5
Hinge tip designs

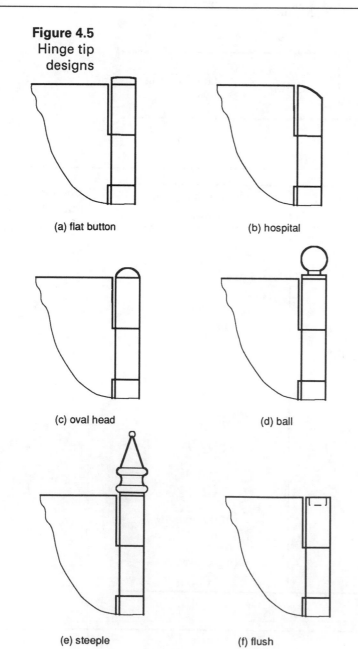

(a) flat button

(b) hospital

(c) oval head

(d) ball

(e) steeple

(f) flush

Because of the way center-hung pivots operate, they cannot be used with a door stop on the same side of the door on both jambs. This makes it difficult to seal the door against sound or light transmission on the hinge and strike sides, although a flexible strip of wool pile or synthetic stripping can be rabbeted into the edges of the door. The rotation point of a center-hung pivot is typically located 2¾ in. (70 mm) from the edge of the frame, but it can be located anywhere along the door. For example, a series of doors with the pivot located in the center of the door width can be used to make a "louvered" opening between two rooms. See Figure 4.7.

As shown in Figure 4.6, offset pivots can be used in standard framed openings with door stops, but the corner of the door opposite

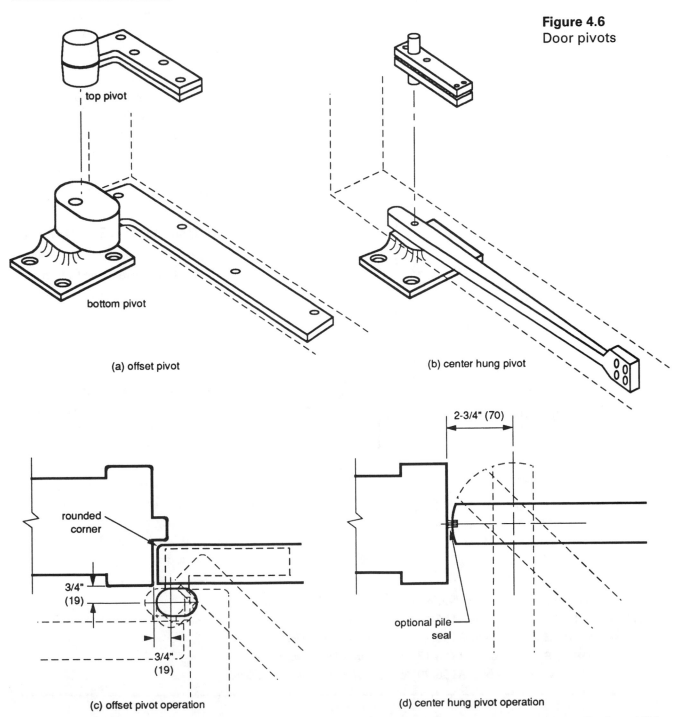

Figure 4.6
Door pivots

top pivot

bottom pivot

(a) offset pivot

(b) center hung pivot

rounded corner

3/4"
(19)

3/4"
(19)

(c) offset pivot operation

2-3/4" (70)

optional pile
seal

(d) center hung pivot operation

the pivot must be slightly rounded so this corner does not scrape against the stop as the door opens.

Concealed door detailing

Pivots are often used to detail concealed doors, those designed to appear to be part of the partition in which they are placed. Center-hung pivots, or closers, are especially useful because they are completely concealed by the top and bottom edges of the door and require no door frame. Figure 4.8 illustrates one method of detailing a door that is flush with the partition and that uses a minimum of visible hardware.

Other mounting hardware

Pocket doors and sliding doors are suspended with rollers from tracks in the head frame. Hardware is also available to allow doors to be supported by rollers that run on floor tracks. These are used for very heavy doors or where movement of the bottom edge of the door must be restricted.

Special proprietary pocket pivot and continuous hinges are available that can be used on fire-rated doors while concealing much of the hardware. These are used where appearance is important but where building codes require labeled hardware.

OPERATING DEVICES [08710]

Operating devices are used to open and close doors. These devices can range from simple push plates to power-assisted mechanisms. In some cases, such as with locksets, the method of securing the door is integrated with the method of operating the door.

Latchsets and Locksets

A latchset is a device that operates a door and holds it in the closed position by means of a retractable latch. A doorknob or lever handle can be used both to provide a gripping surface and to operate the latching device. In most cases, a lever handle is needed to meet accessibility requirements. A lockset does the same job, but also has a method for locking the door.

Figure 4.7
Center-hung pivots used in multiple door opening

Figure 4.8
Concealed door details

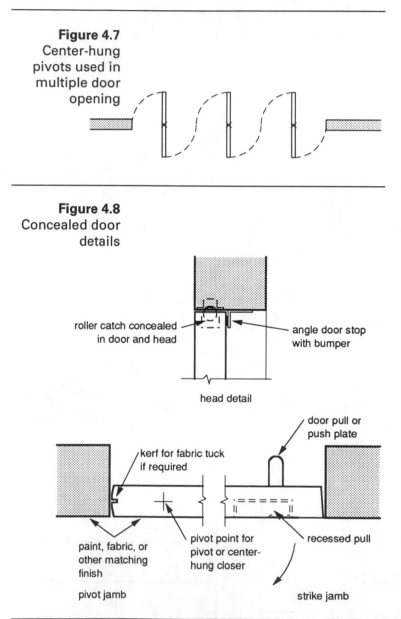

roller catch concealed in door and head

angle door stop with bumper

head detail

door pull or push plate

kerf for fabric tuck if required

paint, fabric, or other matching finish

pivot point for pivot or center-hung closer

recessed pull

pivot jamb

strike jamb

Applicable standards for hinges and pivots

American National Standards Institute (ANSI):

ANSI A156.1	*Butts and Hinges*
ANSI A156.7	*Template Hinge Dimensions*
ANSI A156.17	*Self Closing Hinges and Pivots*
ANSI A156.20	*Strap and Tee Hinges and Hasps*

There are four types of latches and locks: mortise, preassembled, bored, and interconnected. These are shown in Figures 4.9(a)–4.9(d). Another type, the integral, is no longer produced in the United States, but is still found in older buildings. Each of the four types is designated by a corresponding series number, as standardized by the American National Standards Institute (ANSI). Mortise locks are designated as Series 1000, preassembled locks as Series 2000, bored locks as Series 4000, and interconnected locks as Series 5000. Series 3000 was used for integral locks.

Mortise locks

A mortise lock or latch is installed in a rectangular area cut out of the door. It is generally more secure than a bored lock and offers a much wider variety of locking options. Mortise locks allow the use of a deadbolt and a latchbolt, both of which can be retracted in a single operation. A variety of knob and level handle designs can be used

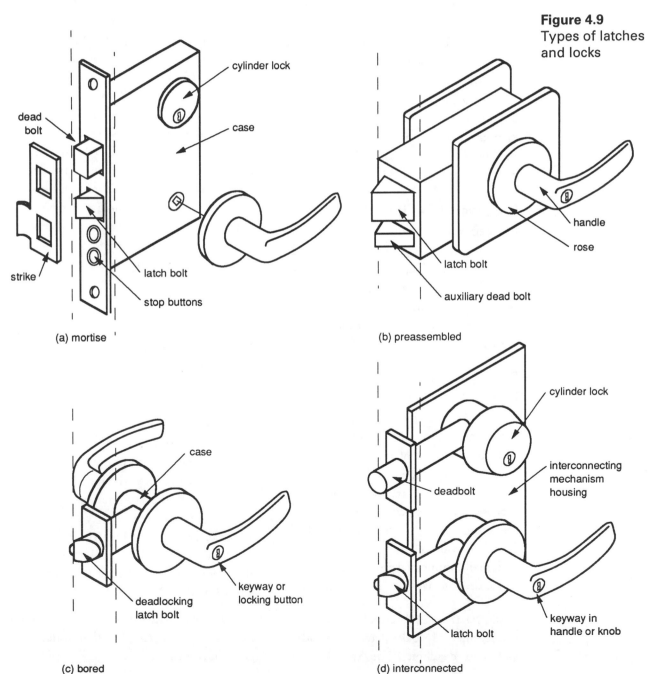

Figure 4.9
Types of latches and locks

(a) mortise

(b) preassembled

(c) bored

(d) interconnected

with the basic mechanism. Mortise locks are available in two classifications of grades, one for operation and one for security. There are three levels for each, Grade 1, Grade 2, and Grade 3. The grade level for each classification is expressed separately. Grade 1 is the highest level for operation.

Grade 1 offers the highest security, while Grade 3 offers the lowest level of security. Levels of security for entire door assemblies are also established by ASTM (American Society for Testing Materials) F-476. (See applicable standards for operating devices in this chapter). These are designated by two digit numbers. Grade 40 is the highest level of security and is used for commercial buildings. Grade 30 is used for medium-to-high security areas, such as small commercial buildings. Grade 20 is used for low-to-medium security, such as apartment houses and hotels. Grade 10 is for the lowest required level of security, single family residential.

Preassembled locks

Preassembled locks and latches are also called unit locks. They arrive from the factory as a complete unit. They are slid into a notch made in the edge of the door and require very little adjustment. Preassembled locks are seldom used today and are only available in Grade 1.

Bored locks

Bored locks and latches are also called cylindrical locks or latches. They are installed by boring holes through the face of the door and from the edge of the door to the other bored opening. Bored locks are relatively easy to install and are less expensive than mortise locks; however, they offer fewer operating functions than mortise locks. Bored locks are generally used in residential and small commercial projects. Like mortise locks, they are available in three grades.

Interconnected locks

Interconnected locks have a cylindrical lock and deadbolt. The two locks are interconnected so that only a single action of turning a knob or lever on the inside releases both bolts.

With all types of latches and locks, either a door knob or lever handle may be used to operate the latching device. In most cases, a lever handle is required to meet requirements for accessibility.

Standard function designations

When used in the context of hardware, the word *function* refers to the mechanical operation of a lock or latch, the method of locking and unlocking, and the position, rigidity, and operability of the various parts of the hardware. Function designations have been standardized by the American National Standards Institute (ANSI) as sponsored by the Builders Hardware Manufacturers Association (BHMA). These function designations can be used to specify the desired operation without using specific proprietary manufacturer's names or numbers. However, many manufacturers make special latchsets and locksets that do not have corresponding ANSI function numbers.

Each function is specified with a number, a description of its common application, and a detailed explanation of the function. The detailed explanation describes three elements: (1) the operation of the lock or latch from either side of the door in the unlocked mode, (2) the method of locking from the outside and inside, and (3) the method by which unlocking is accomplished from the outside and inside. Although the description indicates the common usage of the function, it does not restrict its use. For example, a store door lock can be used in applications other than retail stores. Overall, there are 54 different functions described by the ANSI standards.

Latchset and lockset functions are summarized in Appendix A-1. Full descriptions are given in Appendix A-2.

Exit devices

Exit devices, commonly called *panic hardware*, are used where required by building code for safe egress by many people. Push bars extending across the width of the door on the push side operate side latches or vertical rods that disengage latches at the top and bottom. The vertical rods can be surface mounted or concealed in the door. Exit devices are intended to operate the door by pushing on a horizontal bar or push pad without any special knowledge or complex actions in the event of panic. Electrified panic hardware can be used where access from the outside is controlled with keypads or card readers, but where completely failsafe, manually operated exiting is required from the inside.

Pulls and push plates

Push plates and pull bars are used to operate doors that do not require automatic latching. Push plates and pull bars are available in a variety of designs and are commonly used on doors to toilet rooms and commercial kitchens. For doors that swing only in one direction, a combination push plate and pull bar can be used.

Power-assisted openers

Power-assisted doors are activated by a push button, pressure pad on the floor, infrared beam, or other electronic means. They are most often used for interior construction where handicapped accessibility is required.

Several types of openers are available, including those mounted at the head of the door and those concealed in the floor. The head-mounted door openers are usually surface-applied to the head of the door frame and operate the door with an arm assembly similar to a standard door closer. These are commonly used in retrofit applications where installation is fairly easy.

In-floor power-assisted openers are completely concealed but generally have to be installed at the same time the door and frame are installed. They are available in either center-hung or offset-hung styles and can operate doors mounted on pivots or butt hinges. These openers require a large pit in a concrete floor for mounting. Required pit depth ranges from about 6 in. to 7 in. (152 mm to 175 mm). For other types of floor construction or where the required depth is not available, the power mechanism can be mounted from the ceiling of the floor below with a drive shaft extending through the floor to the door.

CLOSING DEVICES

Closers are devices that automatically return a door to its closed position after it is opened. They also control the distance a door can be opened, thereby protecting the door and the surrounding construction from damage.

Closers can be surface mounted on either side of the door or on the head frame. They

---

American National Standards Institute (ANSI):

ANSI A156.2	*Bored and Preassembled Locks and Latches*
ANSI A156.3	*Exit Devices*
ANSI A156.10	*Power Operated Pedestrian Doors*
ANSI A156.12	*Interconnected Locks and Latches*
ANSI A156.13	*Mortise Locks and Latches*
ANSI A156.19	*Power Assist and Low Energy Operated Doors*

American Society for Testing and Materials (ASTM):

ASTM F-476	*Test Methods for Security of Swinging Door Assemblies*

Underwriters Laboratories (UL):

Std. #305	*UL Standard for Safety Panic Hardware*

Applicable standards for operating devices

also can be concealed in the frame or in the door. In addition, closers can be integrated with pivots mounted in the floor or ceiling.

Surface-mounted closers [08710]

There are four basic types of surface-mounted door closers. They are categorized as to how they are mounted to the door and jamb and where the hardware is located, that is on the push or pull side of the door. Figure 4.10 illustrates regular arm, slide track, top jamb, and parallel arm door closers.

The regular arm application is used where a door swings into a room and the closer is mounted on the pull side of the door (the room side). When a door opens out and the closer should be mounted on the push side (inside the room), either a top jamb or parallel arm application can be used. A parallel arm application helps prevent vandalism because the arms are mostly concealed below the head frame. However, the

power efficiency of the parallel arm application is less than that of the regular arm application.

Closers are available in three grades, Grades 1 to 3. Grade 1 is the most durable and is used for doors that have a high frequency of use and abuse. Closers are also rated by "size," which refers to the size of the internal spring mechanism that determines the closing force. Sizes range from 2 to 6; the higher the number, the greater the closing force. Closers with greater closing force are required for wide doors or heavy doors. Two types of adjustable closers are available, the 50 percent adjustable and the fully adjustable. The 50 percent adjustable closers are furnished with springs between sizes 2 and 6, but the closing force can be increased 50 percent above the spring size. The fully adjustable closers are not sized, but can be adjusted through the complete range of sizes. Adjustable closers are available for barrier-free applications so that the maximum

Figure 4.10
Surface-mounted door closers

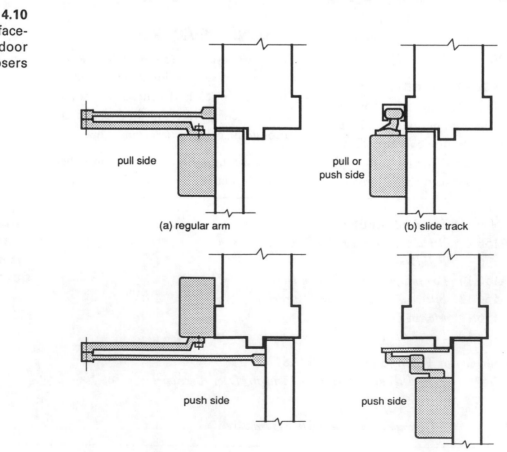

(a) regular arm

pull side

(b) slide track

pull or push side

(c) top jamb

push side

(d) parallel arm

push side

opening resistance can be set to 5 lb (2.2 N) for interior, non-fire-rated doors.

Closers are spray painted in aluminum, bronze or tan colors. The Builders Hardware Manufacturers Association (BHMA) finish designations include 689, aluminum paint; 690, dark bronze paint; 691, light bronze paint; and 692, tan paint. They may also be specified as 600, prime paint.

Concealed closers

As illustrated in Figure 4.11, door closers can be concealed in the head frame or the door itself. However, it is generally best to avoid closers concealed in the door because anchoring is not as strong as it is in the head frame. Doors measuring 1¾ in. (44 mm) must be used so that the entire mechanism can be concealed without the use of face plates. The head frame must be large enough to accommodate the closer selected.

A number of options are available for both surface-mounted and concealed closers. Hold-open closers have arms that can be set to hold the door in the open position until it is disengaged. However, these types cannot be used on fire-rated doors. Delayed-action closers momentarily hold the door open before starting the closing cycle to make it easier for people to pass through the opening.

Pivot closers

Pivot closers incorporate both a pivot and a door closer in one mechanism. The door operation works in the same way described earlier in the section on pivots. Pivot closers are available for either center-hung or offset-hung doors. Pivot closers can be mounted either in the floor or above the door for center-hung doors, while floor closers can only be used for offset-hung doors. Because a closer is subjected to a great deal of torque during operation, overhead closers should only be used on lightweight doors up to about 200 lb (91 kg). If a frameless door installation is used, the overhead closer must also be securely mounted in the door frame or above the ceiling. Floor mounting is the preferred installation method for pivot closers and must be used for heavy or very wide doors.

Floor closers are typically installed in concrete floors with a cement case, around which grout is poured to securely anchor the mechanism. They can be installed below wood floors as long as sufficient anchorage is provided. When installation is complete, only an access plate is visible. Thresholds can also be specified that cover the mechanism and extend across the width of the door. Low-profile closers are available for thin-slab concrete floors or for areas where clearance is limited.

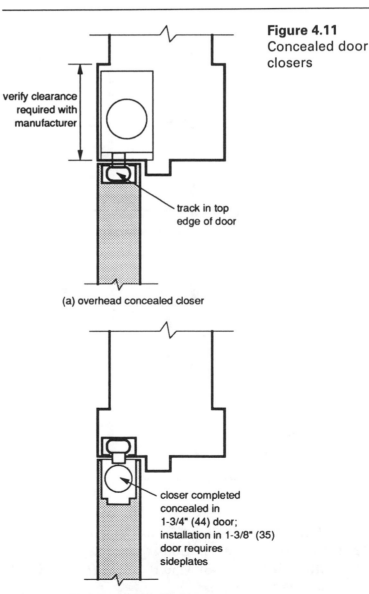

Figure 4.11
Concealed door closers

verify clearance required with manufacturer

track in top edge of door

(a) overhead concealed closer

closer completed concealed in 1-3/4" (44) door; installation in 1-3/8" (35) door requires sideplates

(b) closer concealed in door

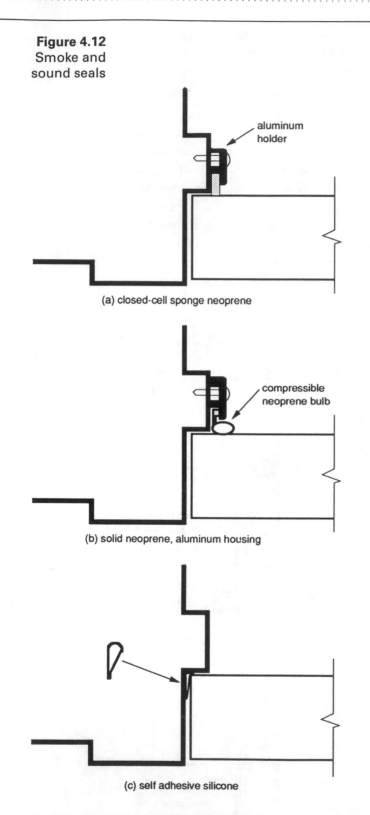

Figure 4.12
Smoke and
sound seals

(a) closed-cell sponge neoprene

aluminum
holder

(b) solid neoprene, aluminum housing

compressible
neoprene bulb

(c) self adhesive silicone

Floor closers are available in different models to support weights of up to 1250 lb (567 kg) for offset-hung doors and 1000 lb (454 kg) for center-hung doors. Hold-open and nonhold-open floor closers are available, with openings limited to 85°, 90°, 95°, or 105°. For high traffic areas, heavy-duty models are available.

Closers with integrated smoke detectors

Surface-mounted closers can be used to hold open a door under normal circumstances, but can also be used to automatically close a door when smoke is detected. These closers can be wired to sound an alarm upon activation and to close other doors without built-in smoke detectors. The limitations of use on these types of closers must be verified with local building and fire codes.

All types of closers must satisfy accessibility requirements. Closers must have their sweep periods adjusted so that, from an open position of 70°, the door will take at least 3 seconds to move to a point 3 in. (75 mm) from the latch, as measured to the leading edge of the door.

DOOR SEALS [08710]

Door seals are used along the edges of doors to provide tight seals against smoke, light, and sound. Different types of neoprene, felt, metal, polyurethane, and vinyl are available in many configurations, three of which are shown in Figures 4.12(a)–4.12(c). Refer to manufacturers' catalogs for specific sizes, materials, and available configurations.

Smoke seals

Fire-rated seals are required on fire doors to prevent both smoke from passing through and drafts. They are similar to light and

---

Applicable standards for closing devices

American National Standards Institute (ANSI):

ANSI A156.4   *Door Controls*

ANSI A156.15   *Closer Holder Release Devices*

sound seals, but have been tested by an approved laboratory and certified for use on fire doors. They are used on the head and jamb sections.

Light and sound seals

As with smoke seals, door seals for blocking the passage of light or sound are available in many configurations for jambs, head, and threshold. The compressible material used most often is neoprene. Double door seals can be used, when a high level of sound isolation is needed as illustrated in Figure 4.13. This type of construction is usually limited to sound studios, stages, and other occupancies where sound isolation is critical.

Automatic door bottoms

Figures 4.12 and 4.13 both show construction methods only at the jambs and head of a door. When the undercut between the bottom of a door and the floor or threshold needs to be sealed (as with all light and sound seals and some fire doors) an automatic door bottom must be used.

Automatic door bottoms are devices that are mortised or surface applied to the bottom of the door to provide a sound or light seal. When the door is open the seal is up; as the door is closed a plunger strikes the jamb and forces the seal down against the floor. See Figures 4.14(a)–4.14(c). If carpeting is being used in two rooms separated by a sound door, the opening should be detailed so that there is a solid, smooth surface below the door bottom. This provides for a tight seal against the floor. Alternately, a threshold can be used to provide for a double seal as shown in Figure 4.14(c); however, this is usually less desirable for most applications because it projects above the plane of the floor.

DOOR SECURITY [08710]

Several types of manual and electrically operated locking hardware are available. This section discusses manual locks; electrically operated locks are discussed later in this chapter.

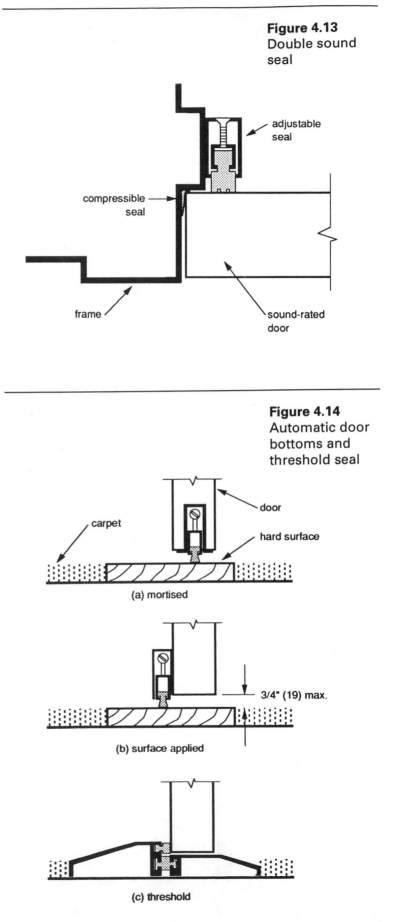

Figure 4.13
Double sound seal

Figure 4.14
Automatic door bottoms and threshold seal

(a) mortised

(b) surface applied

(c) threshold

Locksets

Locksets combine an operating device, either a knob or lever handle, with a mechanism for locking a door. The four major types of locksets are discussed in the section on operating devices. The most appropriate lockset type must be selected based on the degree of security required. Bored locksets are sufficient for residential and many types of commercial projects. Mortise locksets and interconnected locks provide greater security and a broader range of functions for many commercial applications.

Deadbolts

A deadbolt is a lock component with an end that extends from the lock front by action of the lock mechanism. When the door is

Figure 4.15
Flush bolts

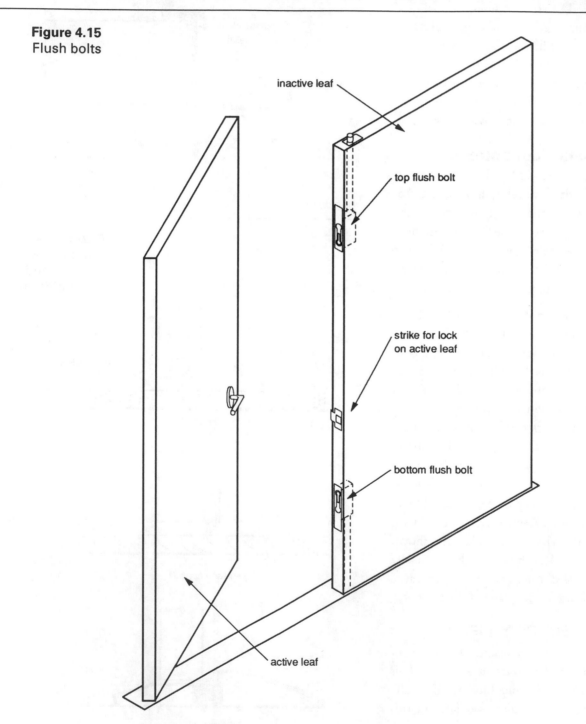

inactive leaf

top flush bolt

strike for lock
on active leaf

bottom flush bolt

active leaf

closed and locked, the bolt cannot be retracted with end pressure.

Deadbolts are used for added security but their use is limited to single family residences and guest rooms of hotels and motels by most building codes. Even when their use is allowed, most codes require that deadbolts be operable from the inside without a key or tool, which means they must have a thumb turn on the inside. If the extra security of a deadbolt is required, a mortise lock with a deadbolt or an interconnected lock can be used. Both are constructed so that all the latches and bolts are retracted with a single operation of the knob or lever handle. Refer to Table 4.3 for a summary of the standard deadbolt functions.

Flush bolts

Flush bolts are devices mortised into the edge of the door that allow a bolt to be extended into the head frame or the floor by manually flipping a lever. See Figure 4.15. Flush bolts are used on pairs of doors so that the inactive leaf can be locked, thereby providing a fixed strike against which the active leaf can lock. Flush bolts require both an awkward manual operation to unlatch and the active leaf to be open before unlatching can occur. Because of these requirements, flush bolts are prohibited on exit doors and on many other doors by most building codes. Their use is generally limited to openings where an occasional wide opening is needed for access but where only the active leaf is used on a daily basis. Automatic flush bolts, however, may be used on exit doors.

Keying

Keying refers to a system of matching keys to specific locks and door openings and determining which key will operate which lock. For example, everyone in an office must have his own key that operates both his personal office door and the front door. Furthermore, that key should not open other personal office doors or doors to rooms with restricted access. However, one person may need a key that can operate everyone's office door. In addition, building management must have a key that opens every door in the building.

Keying is based on different levels of access to locks as diagrammed in Figure 4.16. At the lowest level is the change key, which operates an individual lock. Change keys may be keyed alike or keyed differently. If

Figure 4.16
Keying

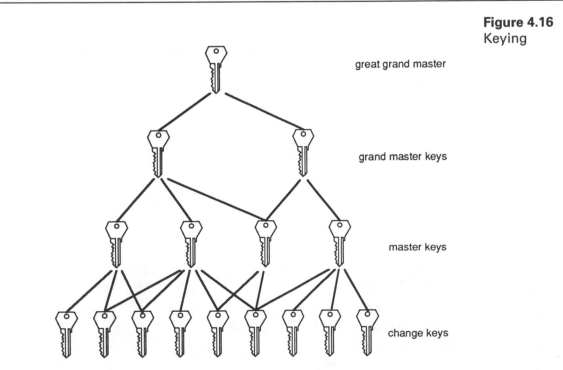

great grand master

grand master keys

master keys

change keys

keyed alike, one key operates two or more locks. If keyed differently, each lock has a different key. A master key operates any number of locks with different change keys. A grand master key operates all locks operated by two or more master keys. A great grand master key operates all the locks operated by the various master keys and the grand master keys.

For very large buildings or multiple building complexes, it is also possible to have a great great grand master key. During construction there may be a construction key that temporarily operates all locks until the permanent keying system is established. This prevents construction workers and others from having functioning keys after construction is completed.

MISCELLANEOUS HARDWARE [08710]

Coordinators

For pairs of doors to be fire rated, building codes require the gap between the two doors to be covered with an astragal. An astragal is a flat plate mounted along the edge of one door (designated the active leaf) that overlaps the second door (designated as the inactive leaf) when the doors are closed. If the active leaf closes before the inactive leaf, the astragal prevents the inactive leaf, from closing completely. A door coordinator prevents this from happening by momentarily holding the active leaf open slightly until the other door closes. The active leaf then closes, sealing the opening. Coordinators are mounted on the head frame and usually work in conjunction with automatic flush bolts, which latch the doors to the head frame and the floor.

Door stops and bumpers

Some method of keeping doors from damaging adjacent construction is required. Closers will do this to some extent, but floor stops or wall bumpers provide more consistent protection. These devices are small metal

Figure 4.17
Miscellaneous door hardware

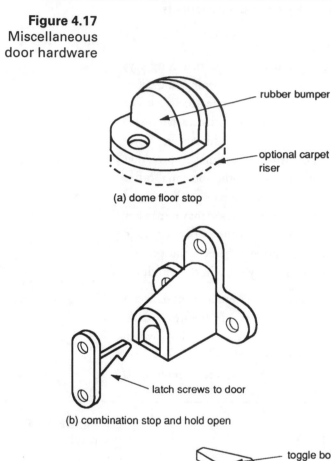

(a) dome floor stop

rubber bumper

optional carpet riser

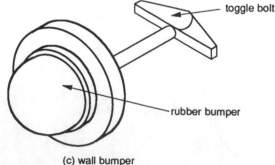

latch screws to door

(b) combination stop and hold open

toggle bolt

rubber bumper

(c) wall bumper

Applicable standards for door protection	American National Standards Institute (ANSI):
	ANSI A156.2 *Bored and Preassembled Locks and Latches*
	ANSI A156.3 *Exit Devices*
	ANSI A156.12 *Interconnected Locks and Latches*
	ANSI A156.13 *Mortise Locks and Latches*

fabrications with rubber bumpers attached. Several types of stops and bumpers are available from various manufacturers. Some of the more common ones are shown in Figures 4.17(a)–4.17(c). Metal door frames also use silencers, which are small pads of rubber mounted into small holes along the door stop to cushion the door when it is closed.

Thresholds

Thresholds are used where floor materials change at a door line, where a hard surface is required for an automatic door bottom, or where minor changes in floor level occur. There are dozens of different types of thresholds, but only those that conform to accessibility requirements should be used. Refer to Chapter 18 for barrier-free code requirements.

Astragals

Astragals are vertical members used between double doors to seal the opening, act as a door stop, or provide extra security when the doors are closed. An astragal may be attached to one door leaf or may be a separate unit against which both doors close. If the pair of doors is fire rated and an overlapping astragal is used, the doors must be provided with a door coordinator, as described above.

Protective coverings

Metal plates can be attached to wood doors to protect the surface from damage. Mop plates extend the full width of the door, minus 1 in., and are about 6 in. (150 mm) high. As the name implies, a mop plate protects the bottom of the door from damage during cleaning operations. Kick plates are similar but are placed slightly higher. Armor plates also extend the full width of the door, but are mounted higher to protect

against damage caused by people pushing the door open with trays and other objects held at waist level.

Door holders

Overhead holders are devices used to hold doors open until they are manually released. Usually they are straight bars or telescoping bars with a pivot that slides along a track that is recessed in the top edge of the door. The door is closed by pushing the door slightly beyond its open position to disengage the hold-open device. Door holders cannot be used on fire-rated doors where codes require automatic-closing doors.

ELECTRONIC HARDWARE [08740]

Electronic hardware includes devices that control or monitor door openings using electric or electromechanical means. Because electronic hardware and security systems can be complex, a qualified hardware or security consultant should be employed for specialty installations. Local building codes must also be consulted because some electronic hardware devices do not qualify as allowable exit devices. If an exit door is electronically locked and controlled from the outside, most codes require that exiting be possible from the inside by a purely mechanical action of the locking device. This action must not depend on any power supply or deactivation of the lock on the inside by the person exiting.

There are hundreds of products available, ranging from simple intrusion detection devices to biometric readers than can unlock doors by identifying a person's retina, voice, or fingerprint. This section briefly describes some of the commonly used devices.

American National Standards Institute (ANSI):
ANSI A156.6 *Architectural Door Trim*
ANSI A156.8 *Door Controls (Overhead Stops and Holders)*
ANSI A156.16 *Auxiliary Hardware*

Applicable standards for miscellaneous hardware

Electric locks

An electric lock maintains a mortise or bored lockset in the locked position until a signal is activated by some type of regulating device. Regulating devices can include wall switches, push buttons, card readers, key switches, computerized controls, automatic timing devices, security consoles, and other sophisticated control devices. Electric locks can also be specified so that they automatically open if there is a power failure. In either case, the inside knob or handle mechanically unlatches the door for exiting at any time.

A variation of the electric lock is the electric latch. This device is typically in a position to hold the latchbolt of the lock so that the door cannot be opened. On activation, the electric latch pivots slightly, allowing the door to be opened. From the inside, the mechanical operation of the knob or handle retracts the latch allowing exit regardless of the position of the electric latch. Electric latches have the advantage of not requiring any power to be run to the door; all wiring is done in the door jamb. Electric locks require the use of electric hinges or other power-transfer devices to make the low-voltage wiring connections from the door frame to the mechanism in the door.

Electric bolts

Electric bolts are devices separate from the operating hardware of a door. They can be mounted in the strike jamb or head of a door. In the typical locked position, a bolt extends from the unit into a strike in the door. A push button, card reader, or other regulating device activates a solenoid, which retracts the bolt. Fail-safe units are available that open when there is a power failure. Electric bolts are generally not allowed on exit doors because there is no sure way to mechanically open the door if the bolt does not retract.

Card readers

A card reader is one type of regulating device that reads a magnetic code on a small plastic card when the card is inserted into the reader. If the reader detects a valid code, the switch is activated and the door is unlocked. Card readers can also be used to send a signal to a central monitoring computer. The computer keeps track of whose card was used to open which door and when the entry was made. In addition, the computer can control the times of the day particular doors can be opened by particular cards. Card readers are usually mounted on the partition near the door they control. They also can be part of the lockset, such as the card readers typically used in hotels. Card readers can also be concealed behind the finish of the partition. To gain access the person must know where the card reader is concealed. The device is activated by pressing the card against the partition.

Keypad devices

An alternative to the card reader is the keypad in which a coded number must be entered to gain access. The keypad device can be a separate unit mounted near the door or can be part of the door knob or lever. For additional security, keypads can be used with card readers.

Magnetic hold-open devices

While exit doors must have closers, most codes allow them to be held in an open position if they can be closed automatically upon activation of a smoke detector or other approved fire signal. One method of doing this is to use a closer with an integrated smoke detector, as described previously. Another way is to use a magnetic hold-open device, which is an electromagnet mounted on a wall or the floor that makes contact with a metal plate attached to the door. Upon activation by a central alarm signal or a smoke detector, or upon a power failure, the electromagnet releases and the door closes.

Delayed-exit devices

Delayed-exit devices resemble standard exit devices (panic hardware) but are designed to

BHMA no.	Finish description	Base material	BHMA category	Nearest former US no. designation
605	Bright brass, clear-coated	Brass	A	US3
606	Satin brass, clear-coated	Brass	A	US4
609	Satin brass, blackened, relieved, clear-coated	Brass	C	US5
611	Bright bronze, clear-coated	Bronze	A	US9
612	Satin bronze, clear-coated	Bronze	A	US10
613	Satin bronze, dark-oxidized, oil-rubbed	Bronze	B	US10B
616	Satin bronze, blackened, relieved, clear-coated	Bronze	C	US11
617	Bright bronze, dark-oxidized, relieved, clear-coated	Bronze	C	US13
618	Bright nickel, clear-coated	Brass, bronze	A	US14
619	Satin nickel-plated, clear-coated	Brass, bronze	A	US15
620	Satin nickel, blackened, relieved, clear-coated	Brass, bronze	C	US15A
623	Light-oxidized, statuary bronze, clear-coated	Bronze	C	US20
624	Dark statuary bronze, clear-coated	Brass, bronze	C	US20A
625	Bright chromium-plated	Brass, bronze	A	US26
626	Satin chromium-plated	Brass, bronze	A	US26D
627	Satin aluminum, clear-coated	Aluminum	A	US27
628	Satin aluminum, clear-anodized	Aluminum	A	US28
629	Bright stainless steel	Stainless steel	A	US32
630	Satin stainless steel	Stainless steel	A	US32D
632	Bright brass-plated, clear-coated	Steel	E	US3
633	Satin brass-plated, clear-coated	Steel	E	US4
639	Satin bronze-plated, clear-coated	Steel	E	US10
640	Oxidized satin bronze-plated	Steel	B	US10B
645	Bright nickel-plated, clear-coated	Steel	E	US14
646	Satin nickel-plated, clear-coated	Steel	E	US15
648	Nickel-plated, blackened, relieved, clear-coated	Steel	C	US17A
649	Light-ozidized bright bronze-plated, clear-coated	Steel	C	US20
651	Bright chromium-plated	Steel	E	US26
652	Satin chromium-plated	Steel	E	US26D
656	Light-oxidized satin bronze	Steel	C	US13
666	Bright brass-plated, clear-coated	Aluminum	E	US3
668	Satin bronze plated, clear-coated	Aluminum	E	US10
694	Medium bronze painted	Any	A	—

Compiled from ANSI/BHMA A156.18-1987, copyright 1987, by Builders Hardware Manufacturers Association.

Table 4.3
Selected hardware finishes

stay locked for a fixed time (usually 15 to 30 seconds) after the bar is depressed. During that time an alarm sounds to allow response to an unauthorized door opening. Delayed-exit devices are used where both security and life safety are required. In an actual emergency, the delay is bypassed and the device unlocks upon activation from the building's fire alarm or other emergency system.

For more information on building security systems refer to Chapter 14.

MATERIALS AND FINISHES

Hardware is available in a wide variety of finishes, the choice of which depends primarily on the desired appearance and the required durability. Standards for describing and comparing finishes are detailed in the *American National Standard for Materials and Finishes* (ANSI/BHMA A156.18) published by the American National Standards Institute (ANSI) and sponsored by the Builders Hardware Manufacturers Associations

(BHMA). This standard provides a three-digit code to describe the finish and the base metal on which the finish is applied. These are summarized in Table 4.3, along with the older US (United States) designations that are sometimes found in the literature.

There are 10 base material categories listed for hardware in ANSI/BHMA 156.18: (1) cast, forged, or extruded brass or bronze, (2) wrought brass or bronze, (3) cast, forged, or extruded aluminum, (4) wrought aluminum, (5) stainless steel, (6) malleable iron, (7) cast iron, (8) wrought steel, (9) zinc alloy, and (10) optional material, as determined by the manufacturer. The four base metals used for most finish hardware include steel, stainless steel, bronze, and brass. In many instances, the base metal can be important in specifying the hardware. For example, fire-rated doors must have hinges made from steel or stainless steel, even though any plated finish can be applied over the base metal. In other instances, plated finishes on pulls, levers, and other frequently used items can wear off

Comparing hardware finishes	Because various finishes can be applied to different base materials and some finishes are considered unstable, the ANSI/BHMA 156.18 standard establishes five categories of finishes, A, B, C, D, and E, and describes a method for comparing finishes on different hardware items. The Builders Hardware Manufacturers Association has match-plate samples available for purchase with samples of categories A, B, and C finishes.

When comparing category A finishes, such as chrome, brass, and stainless steel, with a match-plate sample, the two finishes are considered comparative if they appear the same when viewed 2 ft apart (600 mm) and 3 ft away (900 mm) under the same lighting conditions and on the same relative plane. The finishes in category A offer the highest potential for consistency in appearance on different hardware items throughout a project.

Category B finishes are considered unstable, such as 613, oil-rubbed bronze. Finish inconsistencies can occur based on variations in alloys and base materials. Category B finishes are required to match only when compared to the same finish on the same alloy or base material.

Because category C finishes are hand applied, they are intended to be compatible with each other, rather than matching exactly. Category D finishes are for protective applications only and are not considered for appearance. Category E finishes are intended to be matched with comparable finishes from categories A, B, and C. Many finishes applied to steel, aluminum, and plastic are category E finishes.

with time; therefore, it is better to specify a finish with the same type of base metal even though the base metal may cost more. Some finishes, such an oil-rubbed bronze, wear and change color with time from the salt content in perspiration.

Some hardware finishes are more commonly used than others; therefore, manufacturers keep these items in stock. Other infrequently used finishes must be manufactured based on a specific order and the lead time in getting hardware can be substantial.

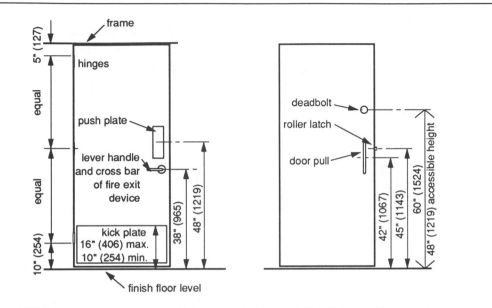

Figure 4.18
Standard hardware mounting heights

All model codes refer to standards developed by the National Fire Protection Association, which include NFPA 80, *Standards for Fire Doors and Windows*, NFPA 252, *Fire Tests of Door Assemblies*, and NFPA 105, *Recommended Practice for the Installation of Smoke-control Door Assemblies*.

Building code requirements for exit door hardware and accessibility

The Uniform Building Code requires exit doors to meet the following requirements. The other model codes have similar requirements.

• Exit doors must be operable from the inside without the use of a key or any special knowledge or effort.

• Panic hardware must be mounted at a height between 30 in. and 44 in. (760 mm and 1118 mm) above the floor. The unlatching force cannot exceed 15 lb (66.7 N).

• Panic hardware is required for Group A occupancies, Group E occupancies with occupant loads greater than 50 and from corridors, and for Group I occupancies that have occupant loads greater than 50. (See Chapter 17 for information on occupancies and occupant loads.)

• Exit doors must have closers or other approved self-closing or automatic-closing devices. Any device that holds open a door must release upon activation of a smoke detector or power failure.

• Hinges must be steel or stainless steel of the ball bearing type.

• Doors must be provided with an automatic latch that secures the door when it is closed.

• The floor level at a door cannot be less than ½ in. (13 mm) below a threshold if the door is part of an accessible route.

Finally, hardware for doors must meet the requirements of the Americans with Disabilities Act and applicable provisions of ANSI A117.1, *Specifications for Making Buildings and Facilities Accessible to and Usable by Physically Handicapped People*.

COORDINATION

Mounting heights

Although hardware can be mounted any-where on a door, there are standard heights for various hardware items. These are shown in Figure 4.18. Unless otherwise noted on the drawings or specifications, door and hardware suppliers and contractors locate the hardware as shown in the illustration. Maximum mounting height for any accessible hardware is 48 in. (1220 mm).

Hardware schedules

Before a project can be bid on or a construction price negotiated, the interior designer must prepare a hardware specification list, which gives a general listing of the items necessary for the operation of doors and the level of quality desired for a particular project. Later, based on this specification, the hardware supplier compiles a thorough hardware schedule that contains all the details necessary to order from the factory.

On the hardware specification list, the various hardware items needed for each type of door on the job are grouped into hardware sets and each set is given a sequential number. Each set includes a unique collection of hardware that may apply to one door or to several doors. The door schedule contains a separate column, which lists the hardware group that each door requires.

5

GLAZING

Over the past several years, there have been dozens of new technological developments in glass products. Along with traditional glazing materials, these have given designers a variety of new ways to solve functional problems and have opened up exciting decorative possibilities.

COMMON GLASS TYPES [08810]

In the building trades *glazing* is the installation of glass in framing. The word *glazing* also refers to glass used in the construction of a building. There are a number of common types of glass that are available for interior use, which are described in this section. Special glazing will be discussed in the next section.

Float glass

Float glass is the most common type of glass produced. It has replaced plate glass, which was in common use until about 15 to 20 years ago. Float glass is manufactured by pouring molten glass onto a bed of molten tin until the glass floats to a smooth surface. It is then slowly cooled, or *annealed*, and cut into the required lengths for further processing. Float glass is produced clear, but it can

be tinted blue, bronze, gray, or green. For interior use, it is employed in small openings or where safety glazing is not required.

Float glass is available in thicknesses of ⅛, 3/16, ¼, ⅜, ½, ⅝, and ¾ in. (3.0, 5.0, 6.0, 10.0, 12.0, 16.0, and 19.0 mm). Other thicknesses are available, but not frequently used for interior applications.

When higher strengths are required, heat-strengthened glass can be used. However, this type of float glass is generally used only for exterior windows.

Tempered glass

Tempered glass is produced by subjecting float glass to a special heat treatment. The glass is heated to about 1150°F, after which both surfaces are cooled rapidly. This produces compressive forces on the surfaces and tensile forces in the core. Under uniform loading, tempered glass is about four times stronger in tensile bending strength than float glass of the same thickness. Therefore, it resists impact much better than float glass. In addition to its extra strength for normal glazing, tempered glass is considered to be safety glass, so it can be used in hazardous locations (discussed later in this chapter). If it breaks, it breaks into very small, cubical pieces instead of into dangerous shards.

Tempered glass is available in thicknesses from ⅛ in. (3.0 mm) to ⅞ in. (22.0 mm). For interior use ¼ in. (6.0 mm) thickness is common. The maximum dimensions for tempered glass vary depending on thickness, ranging from 42 × 84 in. for ⅛-in. glass to 74 × 110 in. for ⅞-in. glass (1067 × 2134 mm for 3.0 mm glass to 1880 × 2794 mm for 22.0 mm glass).

One of the disadvantages of tempered glass is that it must be ordered to the exact size required for the final installation because once it is tempered it cannot be cut, drilled, or deeply etched. In addition, tempering may produce slight distortions in the field of the glass as well as near the tong marks for vertically tempered glass.

Tempered glass also bows or warps slightly during the heat treatment. The distortion can take the form of a slight S shape or, more commonly, a long arch. When two or more large pieces of tempered glass are butt-joined without a frame, the bows should be oriented the same way so there is not a gap perpendicular to the plane of the glass at the midpoint.

Bow tolerances for tempered glass

Glass can be tempered in a horizontal position or by suspending it vertically with tongs. If tongs are used, there will be marks near one edge of the glass that should be concealed with framing. For glass thicknesses up to ⅜ in. (9.5 mm), the centerline of the tong marks cannot be more than ½ in. (12.7 mm) from the edge of the glass. For glass thicknesses over ⅜ in., the center line of the

Table 5.1
Bow tolerances for tempered glass

Length of edge, in. (mm)	Nominal glass thickness			
	⅛ in. (3.0 mm)	¼ in. (6.0 mm)	⅜ in. (10.0 mm)	½ in. (12.0 mm)
18–36 (457–914)	3/16 (4.8)	⅛ (3.2)	3/32 (2.4)	1/16 (1.6)
36–48 (914–1219)	9/32 (7.1)	3/16 (4.8)	⅛ (3.2)	3/32 (2.4)
48–60 (1219–1524)	⅜ (9.5)	9/32 (7.1)	3/16 (4.8)	⅛ (3.2)
60–72 (1524–1829)	½ (12.7)	⅜ (9.5)	¼ (6.4)	3/16 (4.8)
72–84 (1829–2134)	⅝ (15.9)	½ (12.7)	5/16 (7.9)	¼ (6.4)
84–96 (2134–2438)	¾ (19.0)	⅝ (15.9)	⅜ (9.5)	9/32 (7.1)
96–108 (2438–2743)	⅞ (22.2)	¾ (19.0)	½ (12.7)	⅜ (9.5)
108–120 (2743–3048)	1 (25.4)	⅞ (22.2)	⅝ (15.9)	½ (12.7)

Source: ASTM C 1048
Copyright ASTM. Reprinted with permission.

tong marks cannot be more than ¾ in. (19 mm) from the edge of the glass. Regardless of which method is used some distortions occur, the most noticeable of which is bowing. Bow tolerances depend on the thickness of the glass and the length of its longest edge. Table 5.1 shows some selected values for thicknesses and sizes normally used in interior design work.

Laminated glass

Laminated glass consists of two or more layers of glass bonded together by an interlayer of polyvinylbutyral. The glass can be clear or tinted float glass, tempered glass, or heat-strengthened glass. When exceptional impact or ballistic resistance is required, heat-strengthened glass can enclose one or more layers of polycarbonate laminated with interlayers of polyvinylbutyral or polyurethane. Polycarbonates are thermoplastic resins that are dimensionally stable and have high impact strength.

Traditionally, laminated glass used for interior applications has been clear. However, recent developments have provided the interior designer with a wide range of decorative possibilities. These are discussed in the next section on special glazing.

When laminated glass is broken, the interlayer holds the pieces together even though the glass itself may be severely cracked. Laminated glass fabricated with tempered glass or polycarbonate is used where very strong glazing is required. Float glass or tempered glass can be used where acoustical control is needed. It can be bullet resistant and provides high security against breakage (intentional or accidental). Some combinations of glass and plastic thickness qualify as safety glazing and can be used in hazardous locations.

Laminated glass is available in thicknesses from ¹³⁄₆₄ in. to 3 in. (5.2 to 76 mm). Most typically, thicknesses used for interior design projects range from ⁹⁄₃₂ in. to ¾ in. (7.1 to 19.0 mm). These thicknesses consist of from two plies of ⅛-in. (3.0 mm) glass to two plies of ⅜-in. (10.0 mm) glass. Maximum sheet size is 84 × 160 in. (2134 × 4064 mm). The polyvinylbutyral interlayer thickness can be specified from 0.015 in. to 0.090 in. (0.381 to 2.286 mm) or more.

Laminated glass is excellent where high strength or acoustical control is required. It qualifies as safety glazing and can be cut in the field. However, its impact resistance is low unless tempered or heat-strengthened glass is used. Refer to Chapter 11 for more information on the use and detailing of laminated glass for acoustical control.

Wired glass

Wired glass has a mesh of wire embedded in the middle of the sheet. The two wire patterns generally available are hexagonal and square shapes. The surface can be either

Applicable standards for glazing

American National Standards Institute (ANSI):
ANSI Z97.1   *Safety Glazing Materials Used in Buildings—Safety Performance Specifications and Methods of Tests*

American Society for Testing and Materials (ASTM):
ASTM C-1036   *Specification for Flat Glass*
ASTM C-1048   *Specification for Heat-treated Flat Glass*

Consumer Product Safety Commission (CPSC):
16 CFR 1201   *Safety Standard for Architectural Glazing Material*

National Fire Protection Association (NFPA):
NFPA 80   *Standard for Fire Doors and Windows*

smooth or patterned. Wired glass is used primarily in fire-rated opening assemblies, where it is required by most building codes. To be used as fire-resistant glazing, it must meet the requirements of the National Fire Protection Association's NFPA 80, or be classified by Underwriters Laboratories as a fire-resistant glazing. Wired glass cannot be tempered and, therefore, does not qualify as safety glazing for hazardous locations.

Fire-rated wire glass openings are limited to a maximum size of 1296 in.² (0.836 m²) and a maximum dimension between framing of 54 in. (1372 mm).

Figured/patterned glass

This specialty glass is made by passing a sheet of molten glass through rollers on which the desired pattern is pressed, which may be on one or both sides. Vision through the panel is diffused, but not totally obscured; the degree of diffusion depends on the type and depth of the pattern. The exact type of pattern and the available sizes depend on the individual manufacturer.

Mirrored glass

Mirrored glass is produced by depositing a thin film of metal or metallic oxide on one surface of the glass. Because the reflective surface is fragile, a protective backing is applied. Mirrors can be made from standard float glass or from tempered glass, where safety glazing is required.

Mirrors should be installed using mechanical methods rather than simply applying the mirror to a backing with mastic. J-moldings, frames, or clips can be used. Mirrors can also be installed by drilling holes and using screws or special rosettes. A rubber sleeve should be placed around the fastener to prevent direct contact between the glass and fastener.

Transparent, or two-way, mirrors can be used to provide vision through the glass from one direction and a mirrored appearance from the other. These are used where undetected observation is required, such as in detention facilities, psychiatric centers, and gambling casinos. In order for transparent mirrors to work, the lighting level in the room to be observed must be at least five times greater (10 times is even more effective) than in the observation room. The mirror should be installed with the coated side to the observed (lighter) room.

Decorative glass

Decorative glass differs from the glass types mentioned above in that it is installed, and in most cases, manufactured by artists or craftspersons as a one-of-a-kind installation. The design possibilities of decorative glass are limitless and give the designer a large palette from which to work. There are dozens of different types of decorative glass. Some of the more common ones are described below.

Beveled glass

Beveling produces a decorative edge to a sheet of glass. The most common treatment is a simple, sloped, polished surface. However, more elaborate carvings are possible, such as multifaceted bevels, bull-nose shapes, or more complex curved profiles. The beveled portion can be smooth or etched. The angle and length of the bevel can also be specified.

Etched glass

Etched glass is created by using acid or sandblasting techniques to remove a portion of the glass surface. When the etching becomes very deep, it is often called carved glass. Glass can be etched uniformly (frosted) or in geometric patterns, with lettering, or with elaborate designs, as the skill of the artist allows. When properly illuminated and positioned in front of the correct color and shade of background, carved glass has a dramatic, luminescent quality.

Etching can be done on several types of glass, depending on the depth of the etch and the thickness of the glass. Light etching, such as frosting, can be done on float glass, tempered glass, laminated glass, and insulated glass as thin as ⅛ in. (3 mm). Slightly deeper etching must be done on glass at least ¼ in. (6 mm) thick. Medium etching or carving requires at least ⅜-in. (9 mm) glass, while some heavy carving may only be done on glass ½ in. (12 mm) or thicker. If tempered glass is required for deep etching, the etching or carving must be done before the glass is tempered. Light etching may be done after tempering.

Stained glass

As one of the most common forms of decorative glazing, stained glass can produce vivid, dynamic murals or area separation partitions. Used against an exterior window, stained glass can reveal a never-ending combination of colors and patterns. Although traditionally used in religious settings, stained glass has been applied to all types of residential and commercial design by artists working in a variety of areas.

Stained glass is produced by adding metal oxides to the glass during manufacturing. It is typically used in relatively small pieces to create a particular pattern or image. The individual glass pieces are set in H-shaped *cames* made from lead or zinc. The entire assembly is set in a heavier frame, which the interior designer needs to accommodate in the construction detailing. If stained glass is in a location where it might be damaged or is used in ceilings, an additional piece of clear tempered or laminated glass or plastic (if allowed by the local building codes) should be placed over it for protection.

Hand-blown glass

Hand-blown flat glass is made by blowing a large bubble or cylinder of glass with a traditional blow pipe and then cutting the cylinder and unrolling it flat. Because of the way it is made, hand-blown glass sheets are fairly small, but have unique irregularities that make them desirable for decorative glass designs.

Hand-blown glass may be clear or colored, and there are several effects that can be created. Flashed glass uses a double layer with one clear layer and a thin layer of colored glass. Crackle glass is made by dipping hot glass in water to produce a webbed pattern. Seedy glass is produced by blowing the glass before the silica and other material are completely refined. The effect is one of small particles on the glass that scatter light.

Cathedral glass

Cathedral glass is machine formed by rolling molten glass across rollers that impress patterns or textures on one side, while the other remains smooth. After cooling, the glass is textured and transparent.

Opalescent glass

Opalescent glass is machine formed by mixing one or more colors with the glass. The final product is translucent and has a marbleized appearance.

Painted glass

Painted glass is made by applying vitreous paints to clear glass and then firing the glass

---

Because of the reflective and transparent qualities of glass, special care needs to be taken when illuminating space or objects near glass. For most clear glass, light should be directed at objects and surfaces beyond the glass rather than at the glass itself. However, for etched glass, the frosted part of the glass needs to be illuminated for maximum effect.

There are two ways to do this. One way is to use directional lights from above on the etched side of the glass so that the light interacts with the rough surfaces, highlighting them and causing them to "glow." The other way is to use edge lighting with fluorescent lights. One or more edges of the glass are detailed in such a way that the light is centered on the thickness of the glass. Unfortunately, because the glass absorbs so much of the light coming from the edge, edge lighting is not effective past about 18 in. (457 mm) from the light source.

Lighting etched glass

a kiln until the applied material fuses to the glass. The same piece may be fired several times to create layers of color and texture. Because of the technique used, painted glass can have smaller and more intricate designs than stained glass.

Dichroic glass

Dichroic glass is manufactured by depositing a thin evaporative coating of any one of various metals to the glass while it is in a vacuum. The resulting glass shows colors that change depending on the viewing angle and the transmission or reflection of light.

Cast glass

Cast glass pieces are produced by pouring molten glass into a mold that is made by pressing a positive model into specially prepared sand. The resulting piece is usually fairly thick and can be used for exterior as well as interior applications.

Cast glass can be made in a variety of colors, but in general the pieces must be fairly small. Although cast glass is usually done on a custom basis, some manufacturers mass-produce cast glass for wall and floor tiles.

Kiln-formed glass

Kiln-formed glass is flat glass that is heated just enough to cause it to sag over a mold. The resulting piece has the sculptural relief and texture of the mold while the other side remains smooth. Typical thicknesses range from ¼ in. to ½ in. (6 mm to 12 mm). Pieces up to 4 ft (1200 mm) wide × 8 ft (2400 mm) long can be formed. Kiln-formed glass can be tempered, drilled, notched, and fitted into other building components, making it a functional as well as decorative construction element.

SPECIAL GLAZING [08810]

Glazing technology is one of the fastest growing areas of building product innovation. There are dozens of products under development or on the market that provide a variety of functional and decorative possibilities.

This section reviews special glazing that is useful for interior design applications.

Fire-rated glazing

There are five types of glazing that can be used in fire-rated partitions: wired glass, clear ceramic, gel-filled glass, tempered glass, and some types of glass block. Glass block is discussed in Chapter 1.

Wired glass has traditionally been the only type of glazing permitted in fire-rated assemblies, such as partitions, doors, and windows. Wired glass is ¼ in. (6 mm) thick and when installed in a steel frame carries a 45-minute fire rating in sizes up to 1296 in.^{2} or 9 ft^2 (0.84 m^2) with no dimension exceeding 54 in. (1372 mm). This makes it possible to use wire glass in 1-hour-rated corridor partitions, and 45-minute-rated doors. For one- and 1½-hour-rated doors, the maximum size is 100 in.^{2} (0.0645 m^2). Some building codes allow larger sizes of wired glass to be used as sidelights in corridor walls but, technically, wired glass over 9 ft^2 has not been tested and therefore has not been given a 45-minute rating.

Although the wire in wired glass helps to hold the glass together during a fire, it is about half as strong as annealed glass of the same thickness. It is not considered safety glazing as is tempered glass, but most building codes allow it to be used in hazardous locations only if it is required as a fire barrier. In these cases, the fire-safety requirement overrides the safety glazing requirement if the two are in conflict. However, if wired glass is only used within the strict limitation of 9 ft^2 this is also the size below which a glazed opening does not have to have safety glazing, even if it is in a hazardous location.

The second type of glazing is not a glass at all but a visually clear ceramic that has a higher impact resistance than wired glass and a low expansion coefficient. The ceramic "glass" produced from one manufacturer carriers 1-hour fire rating in sizes up to 1296 in.^{2} (0.84 m^2) and a 3-hour rating in sizes up to 100 in.^{2} (0.0645 m^2). It is only ³⁄₁₆ in. (4.8 mm) thick and is available in sizes up to 48 × 96 in. (1200 × 2400 mm). It is available with polished or patterned surfaces. Although some forms of ceramic glass do not meet safety glazing requirements, there are laminated assemblies that are rated up to 2 hours and are impact safety-rated, meeting the requirements of both ANSI Z97.1 and 16 CFR 1201. For the exact thicknesses required, maximum sizes, and safety requirements for various fire ratings, manufacturers' catalogues should be consulted.

One proprietary product (Contraflam®) is a glazing system that uses two or three layers of tempered glass with a clear polymer gel in between. When subjected to fire, the gel turns opaque, thus retarding the passage of heat. This protects the nonexposed pane of glass. This product is available with 30-minute, 60-minute, and 90-minute ratings, depending on the thickness and number of glass panes used. The maximum sizes allowed are shown in Table 5.2. Although this product can be used in larger sizes than ceramic glazing, qualifies as safety glazing, and has higher fire ratings, it must be set in frames in strict accordance with the manufacturer's requirements.

The fourth type of fire-rated glazing is tempered fire-protective glass. It is rated at a maximum of 30 minutes because it cannot pass the hose-stream test, but it does meet the impact safety standards of ANSI Z97.1 and 16 CFR 1201. It is ¼ in. (6 mm) thick with maximum areas of 2905 in.^{2} (1.87 m^2) for use in doors and 4626 in.^{2} (2.98 m^2) for use in areas other than doors. The maximum dimension of any one length is 35.75 in. (908 mm) for doors and 49.875 in. (1267 mm) for other areas.

Rating	Maximum size allowed mm (in.)	Overall thickness mm (in.)
30-minutes	1435 × 2000 (56½ × 78¾)	31 (1¼)
60-minutes	1200 × 1800 (48 × 72)	41 (1⅝)
90-minutes	1200 × 1600 (48 × 63)	72 (2¹³⁄₁₆)

Source: Manufacturers' literature.

Table 5.2
Maximum sizes and thicknesses for fire-rated, gel-filled glazing

Building code requirements for fire-rated, glazed opening assemblies

There are three critical functional requirements that fire barriers, such as partitions, doors, and glazing, must meet: (1) they must restrict the passage of flame; (2) they must limit the spread of smoke; and (3) they must retard the transmission of heat. One of the reasons that it is difficult for glazing assemblies to have very high fire ratings in large sizes is that, while they can restrict the passage of flame and limit smoke spread (assuming the glazing stays intact), most products do not provide insulation against heat transmission. During a fire, if a combustible object is near one side of a piece of glazing, it is possible for the transmitted heat alone to ignite the object. It is not necessary for a flame to penetrate an opening.

Most codes require that one-hour-rated corridor partitions have 45-minute-rated opening protection. This includes doors and glazing. Other types of one-hour-rated partitions require 60-minute-rated opening protection. These partitions include occupancy separations and one-hour-rated stairways. Refer to Chapter 17 for more information on code requirements.

Bent glass

Bent glass is flat glass that has been shaped while hot into cylindrical or other curved surfaces. Bent glass can be plain annealed glass up to 1 in. (25.4 mm) thick, or tempered, laminated, insulating, wire, or patterned glass. The maximum sizes available in different types depend on the capabilities of individual manufacturers, as do the minimum and maximum radii for bends. Maximum sizes are about 4 × 8 ft (1200 × 2400 mm). Generally, the minimum radius depends on the thickness. For ¼-in. (6 mm) glass, the minimum radius for a 90° bend is about 8 in. (200 mm); the maximum radius is about 60 in. (1500 mm).

Decorative laminated glass

Several manufacturers now offer laminated glass with an interlayer of opaque or translucent, colored film; wire mesh; rice paper; fabric; and other materials. One product uses a film with a tiny dot pattern printed black on one side and colored on the other. The effect is that when viewed from one side the glass looks transparent (but slightly tinted), and when viewed from the other side the glass looks opaque. This offers visual privacy. In order for the effect to work, the opaque side (which can be printed with colors and patterns) must be at least 30% brighter than the transparent side.

Electrochromic glass

This type of glass changes from translucent to transparent with the application of an electric current. It can be used in place of drapes or blinds in applications where privacy is sometimes required when clear glass is used. When the current is turned off the glass appears milky white. When a standard 120 volt current is applied, the glass turns transparent. The effect is made possible by using a thin liquid crystal film sandwiched between electrically conductive coatings and two lights of laminated glass. Application of an electric current aligns the crystals perpendicular to the plane of the glass, making it appear clear. Electrochromic glass is very expensive and currently requires a constant voltage to maintain transparency. It is possible that further research may produce results that will reduce cost and require current only when the glass is changing.

Other special glazing types

There are several other types of special glazing, but most of them are designed for exterior windows to reduce solar heat gain and loss, and otherwise modify the effects of climate on energy requirements. Photochromic glass, for example, changes its tint in response to light level changes. Thermochromic glass changes in response to temperature changes.

Other glass products provide electromagnetic shielding to prevent interference to sensitive computer or communications equipment from outside sources, such as radar waves. Traditionally, glass with a wire mesh was used to prevent interference, but one manufacturer now has a clear glass product that provides the same shielding.

The type of glass used for exterior windows can have a significant effect on interior materials. Clear float glass allows ultraviolet light to enter. Fabrics and other finishes fade as a result, including many types of window coverings. If clear glass is present, fade-resistant window coverings should be specified and detailed in such a way as to protect interior furnishings and finishes. An alternative is that the furnishings and finishes themselves should be fade resistant. If tinted, reflective, or other type of glass is present that minimizes ultraviolet transmission, fading of interior materials is less of a problem.

FRAMED GLAZING [08810]

The most common interior glazing installation consists of glass set in wood, steel, or aluminum frames. Because interior glass does not have to withstand wind loads or be weather sealed, the size of the framing members is not as critical as for windows, and it can be eliminated in some cases. This is frameless glazing and is discussed in the next section. If the glazed opening must be fire rated, most codes require that a steel frame be used and that fastening and other details meet particular criteria.

Wood framing

Figures 5.1 and 5.2 illustrate jamb details for two common interior glass framing methods. Figure 5.3 shows the corresponding sill and head detail for the jamb shown in Figure 5.2. As with wood doors (Chapter 3), the exact profile of the frame and trim can vary according to the functional and aesthetic needs of the installation.

Some detail requirements are common to all wood frames. Like door framing, a glass frame should have at least ¼ in. (6 mm) of shim space on all sides of the rough opening to allow the frame to be leveled and plumbed. The glass frame should also allow some way to conceal the space between the frame and the partition. At least one of the stops holding the glass in place must be removable to allow for original installation and subsequent glass replacement. If the glazing is installed in a metal stud partition, most mill

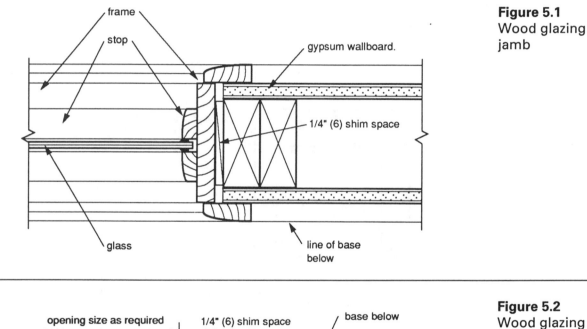

Figure 5.1
Wood glazing jamb

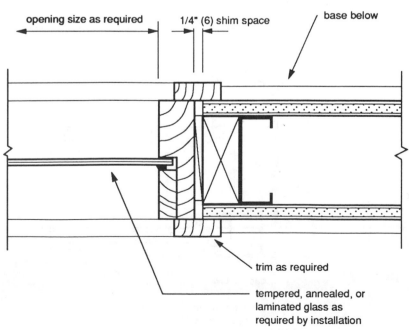

Figure 5.2
Wood glazing jamb with flush stop

Figure 5.3
Head and sill of
wood frame

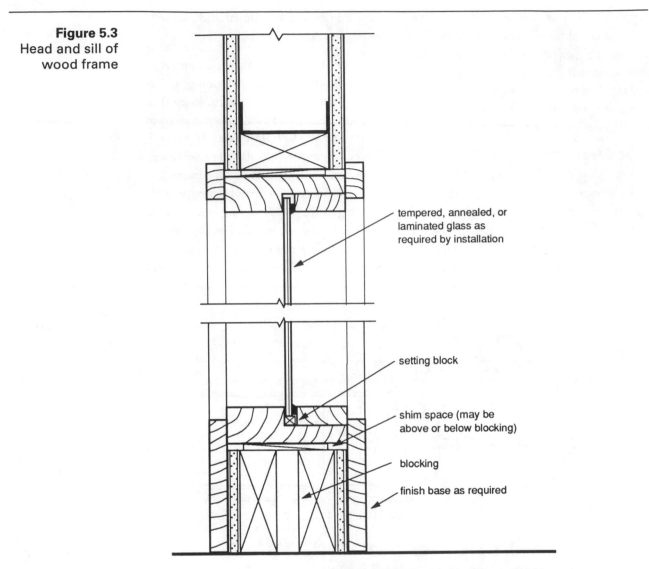

tempered, annealed, or
laminated glass as
required by installation

setting block

shim space (may be
above or below blocking)

blocking

finish base as required

Note: if the sill is raised much above the height
of the base, the space below the sill is framed
as a partition instead of with blocking.

Figure 5.4
Double-rabbet
steel frame

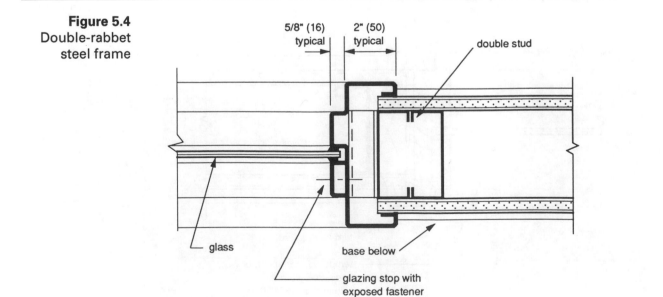

5/8" (16)
typical

2" (50)
typical

double stud

glass

base below

glazing stop with
exposed fastener

shops and carpenters prefer to have solid wood blocking into which they can attach the jamb frame.

In most cases, the glass should not come in contact with the frame. The glass should rest on setting blocks located at the quarter points of the sill (two setting blocks one-quarter of the way in from the edges of the glass). The space between the face of the glass and stops should be filled with one of several appropriate glazing compounds. For interior glazing, this is usually silicone sealant or a preformed glazing tape of neoprene or other elastomeric material. In some instances, small pieces of glass can be held in place directly against wood stops. However, this is generally not recommended because uneven or point pressures can cause the glass to crack.

Generally, ¼-in. thick (6 mm) glass should be used for most interior glazing. Small

For standard glazing methods, framing clearances are the dimensions from the face and edges of the glass to the frame. For interior glazing, these dimensions are not as critical as for windows because there is no wind load or thermal movement. However, some recommended minimum dimensions are shown in Table 5.3.

Framing clearances for interior glass

Table 5.3
Recommended face and edge clearances for interior glass

Thickness in. (mm)	Minimum clearance		
	Face	Edge	Bite
⅛ (3)	⅛ (3)	¼ (6)	⅜ (10)
³⁄₁₆ (5)	⅛ (3)	¼ (6)	⅜ (10)
¼ (6)	⅛ (3)	¼ (6)	⅜ (10)
⁵⁄₁₆ (8)	³⁄₁₆ (5)	⁵⁄₁₆ (8)	⁷⁄₁₆ (11)
⅜ (10)	³⁄₁₆ (5)	⁵⁄₁₆ (8)	⁷⁄₁₆ (11)
½ (13)	¼ (6)	⅜ (10)	⁷⁄₁₆ (11)

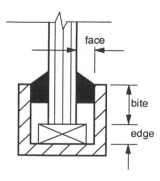

Note: Verify the dimensions with the manufacturer.

Reprinted with permission from *Glazing Manual,* copyright 1986, Flat Glass Marketing Association.

openings, such as pass-through windows or observation ports, can be glazed with double-strength ⅛-in. (3 mm) or ³⁄₁₆-in. (5 mm) glass. Thicker glass is used for very large openings or where the glass is adjacent to a glass door without a frame. Tempered or laminated glass must be used in hazardous locations. Refer to a later section of this chapter for detailed requirements for safety glazing.

Figure 5.5
Single-rabbet
steel frame

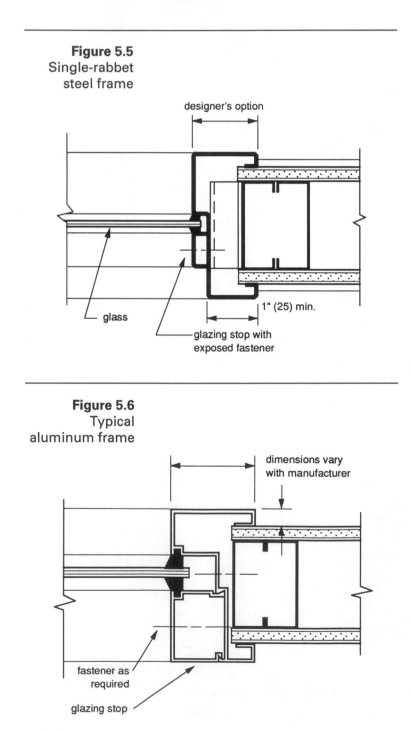

designer's option

glass

glazing stop with
exposed fastener

1" (25) min.

Figure 5.6
Typical
aluminum frame

dimensions vary
with manufacturer

fastener as
required

glazing stop

Steel framing

Interior steel glass framing (also called hollow-metal framing, like door framing) is typically required for fire-rated openings or where the designer wants to match nearby hollow-metal door framing. Frames are fabricated of 16- or 18-gage steel bent to standard or custom profiles. Because they are fabricated by bending, the corners have a slightly rounded profile. Figures 5.4 and 5.5 show two standard glass frame profiles similar to door frame profiles.

Like wood frames, there must be a removable stop to provide for glass installation and replacement. Most hollow-metal glass frames have visible screw heads where the stop is attached to the frame.

Aluminum framing

Aluminum glass frames are used where a fire rating is not required, but where the other advantages of a metal frame are needed: durability, easy fabrication, and compatibility with aluminum door framing. Because they are extruded, aluminum frames have sharp corners, which some designers prefer over the rounded corners of steel frames. In addition, glazing stops on most aluminum framing snap into place so there are no unsightly exposed fasteners. As with door frames, glass frames are available in standard anodized finishes, as well as various types of colored finishes. For large projects, custom colors can be specified.

Exact shapes, sizes, finishes, and fabrication and installation methods vary by manufacturer, but one typical aluminum frame is illustrated in Figure 5.6.

FRAMELESS GLAZING [08810]

Frameless glazing minimizes the appearance of head, sill, and jamb framing for glass. Instead, the glass seems to float within an opening with the finish materials appearing to continue uninterrupted from one side of the glass to the other. In most situations, minimal framing is provided at the sill and head and is recessed into the structure to

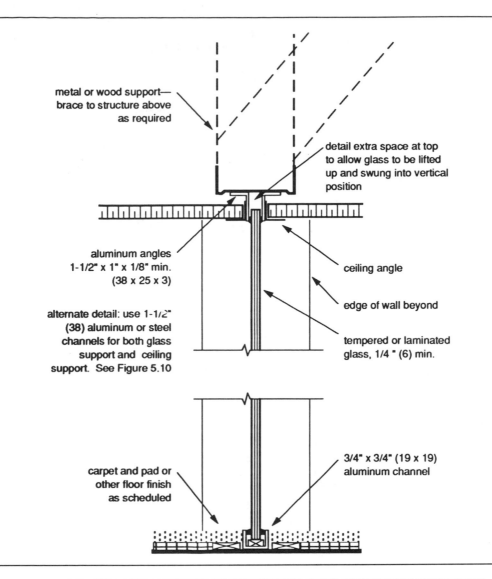

Figure 5.7
Frameless glazing at head and sill

metal or wood support—brace to structure above as required

detail extra space at top to allow glass to be lifted up and swung into vertical position

aluminum angles 1-1/2" x 1" x 1/8" min. (38 x 25 x 3)

ceiling angle

edge of wall beyond

alternate detail: use 1-1/2" (38) aluminum or steel channels for both glass support and ceiling support. See Figure 5.10

tempered or laminated glass, 1/4 " (6) min.

carpet and pad or other floor finish as scheduled

3/4" x 3/4" (19 x 19) aluminum channel

Glass thickness in. (mm)	Joint width, minimum in. (mm)	Joint width, maximum in. (mm)
⅜ (10)	⅜ (10)	⁷⁄₁₆ (11)
½ (13)	⅜ (10)	⁷⁄₁₆ (11)
⅝ (16)	⅜ (10)	½ (13)
¾ (19)	⅜ (10)	½ (13)
⅞ (22)	⅜ (10)	½ (13)

Table 5.4
Joint widths for butt-joint glazing

Reprinted with permission from *Glazing Manual,* copyright 1986, Flat Glass Marketing Association.

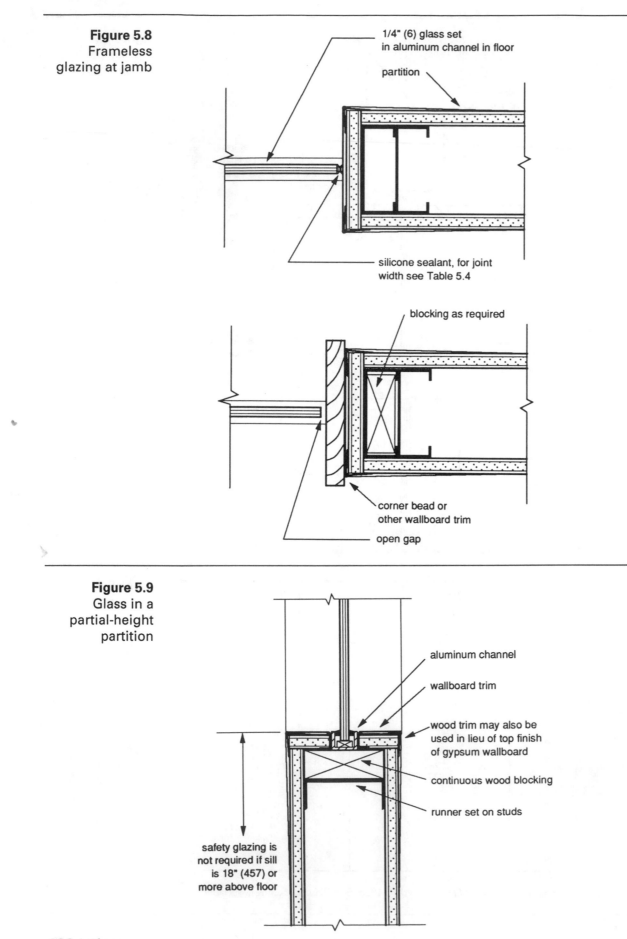

Figure 5.8
Frameless glazing at jamb

1/4" (6) glass set in aluminum channel in floor

partition

silicone sealant, for joint width see Table 5.4

blocking as required

corner bead or other wallboard trim

open gap

Figure 5.9
Glass in a partial-height partition

aluminum channel

wallboard trim

wood trim may also be used in lieu of top finish of gypsum wallboard

continuous wood blocking

runner set on studs

safety glazing is not required if sill is 18" (457) or more above floor

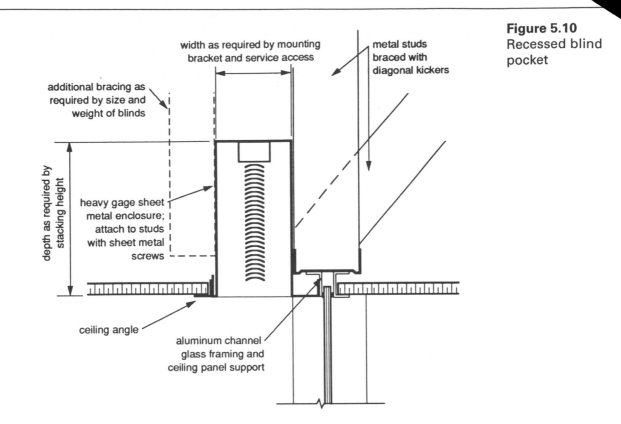

Figure 5.10
Recessed blind pocket

width as required by mounting bracket and service access

metal studs braced with diagonal kickers

additional bracing as required by size and weight of blinds

depth as required by stacking height

heavy gage sheet metal enclosure; attach to studs with sheet metal screws

ceiling angle

aluminum channel glass framing and ceiling panel support

conceal it. Jamb framing is completely eliminated and the edge of the glass is simply held away from the wall a fraction of an inch. If more than one panel of glass is required, the edges are butted together and the joint filled with silicone sealant. In some cases, where sound or draft control are not required, the joints are left open.

Figure 5.7 shows a common method of framing the sill and head of a single piece of glass that extends from the floor to a suspended ceiling. Figure 5.8 shows two possible methods of treating the jamb: by letting the wall finish continue through the plane of the glass, and by installing a simple frame without a glazing stop. If the glass is installed in a partial-height gypsum wallboard partition, a detail similar to Figure 5.9 can be used.

The thickness of the glass used depends on the size of the opening and the amount of glass "shake" that is tolerable. For most full-height glazing of 8 ft to 10 ft, a ¼-in. (6 mm) thick tempered glass is acceptable, but ⅜-in.

(10 mm) is preferred. For small openings ³⁄₁₆-in. (5 mm) thick glass may be used. If sound control is required, laminated glass should be used.

Figure 5.11
Frameless glazing joints

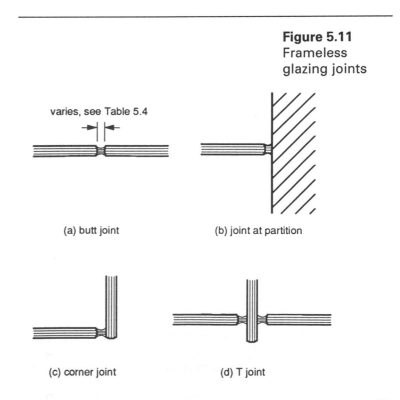

varies, see Table 5.4

(a) butt joint

(b) joint at partition

(c) corner joint

(d) T joint

For many interior design applications, full-height frameless glazing is used to create a sense of openness and to allow natural light to penetrate interior spaces. However, some provisions for privacy may be required, such as in a conference room. In this case, a recessed pocket for horizontal blinds can be installed adjacent to the glass to conceal the blinds when they are retracted. Figure 5.10 shows one method of detailing a recessed blind pocket.

When the edges of glass are butted together without any framing, minimum dimensions should be maintained to allow adequate space for filling with sealant, if it is used. Either clear or black silicone sealant can be used, but clear sealant often shows bubbles and can be visually more objectionable than black silicone. Figures 5.11(a)–5.11(d) show some common frameless joint configurations. Table 5.4 gives recommended joint widths for butt-joint glazing. The T-joint illustrated in Figure 5.11(d) shows one piece of glass extending beyond the other two. This is generally a better way to handle three intersecting pieces of glass, because it is very difficult to install sealant neatly if three edges meet at a single point.

When very large openings must be glazed without frames, or when two or more pieces of glass must be stacked on top of one another without frames, an all-glass glazing system is used. This type of glazing system consists of glass walls supported only at the top and bottom by framing with lateral support provided by glass fins mounted perpendicular to the primary glass plane. Individual pieces of glass are connected with special patch fittings and joints are sealed with silicone sealant. All-glass systems are capable of spanning vertically up to 30 ft (9 m) if the weight of the glass is carried by the base, and up to 75 ft (23 m) if the upper sections of glass are suspended from special clamps attached to an adequate structural support.

Because the vertical supports are glass and the top and bottom framing members can be recessed into the ceiling and floor, this system provides an almost completely unobstructed view opening. Glass doors can be used with the system by using special patch fittings that are similar to those described in Chapter 3 and shown in Figure 3.22.

Figures 5.12(a) and 5.12(b) show typical vertical and horizontal sections for an all-glass system. For many interior applications where the vertical span is not great,

Figure 5.12
All-glass glazing system

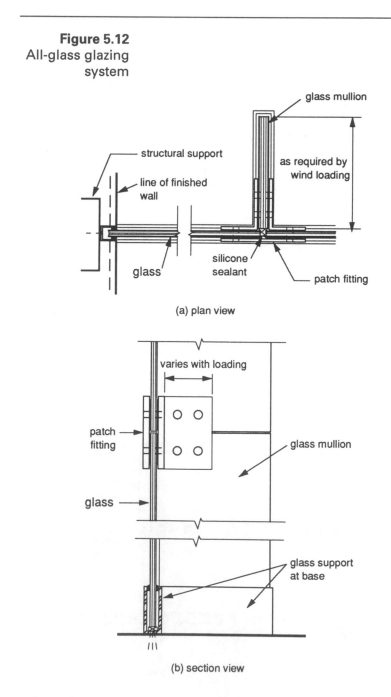

(a) plan view

(b) section view

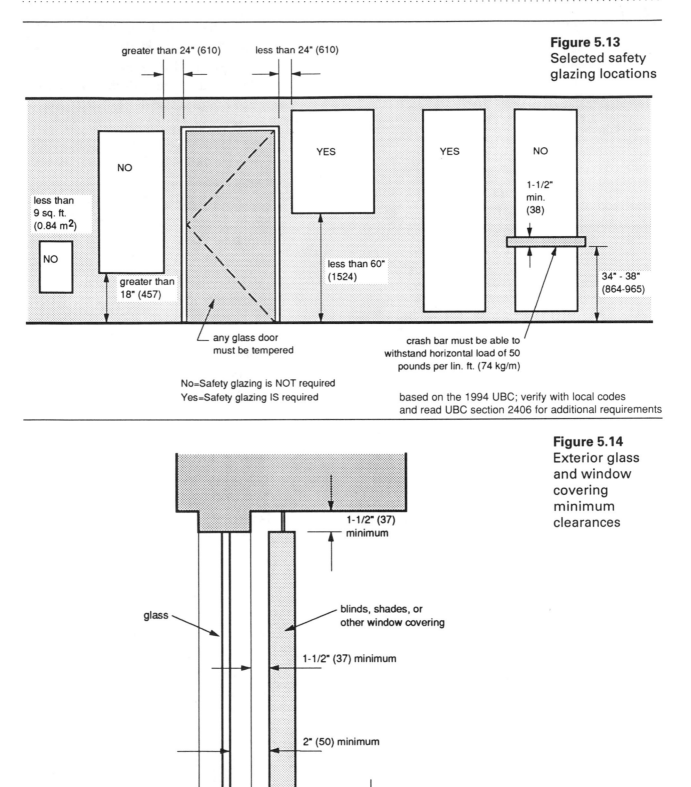

Figure 5.13
Selected safety glazing locations

greater than 24" (610)

less than 24" (610)

NO

less than
9 sq. ft.
(0.84 m^2)

NO

greater than
18" (457)

any glass door
must be tempered

YES

less than 60"
(1524)

YES

NO

1-1/2"
min.
(38)

34" - 38"
(864-965)

crash bar must be able to
withstand horizontal load of 50
pounds per lin. ft. (74 kg/m)

No=Safety glazing is NOT required
Yes=Safety glazing IS required

based on the 1994 UBC; verify with local codes
and read UBC section 2406 for additional requirements

Figure 5.14
Exterior glass
and window
covering
minimum
clearances

1-1/2" (37)
minimum

blinds, shades, or
other window covering

glass

1-1/2" (37) minimum

2" (50) minimum

1-1/2" (37)
minimum

heating/cooling supply

the glass can be supported by the floor framing and the patch fittings without using glass mullions.

SAFETY GLAZING [08810]

In addition to regulating the type and amount of glass in fire-rated assemblies, building codes and federal regulations require that safety glazing be used in hazardous areas. Hazardous locations are those subject to human impact, such as glass in doors, shower and bath enclosures, and certain locations in walls. Tempered glass and laminated glass are considered safety glazings.

A composite drawing of where safety glazing is and is not required when located in a partition is shown in Figure 5.13. These requirements are from the Uniform Building Code (UBC), but the other model codes have very similar requirements. The exact regulations are given in two references: The American National Standards Institute ANSI Z97.1, *Safety Glazing Material Used in Buildings* and the Code of Federal Regulations, 16 CFR Part 1201, *Safety Standard for Architectural Glazing Materials.* The National Building Code of Canada is a little less prescriptive. It requires tempered or laminated glass in doors, shower enclosures, and glass sidelights greater than 500 mm (1 ft 7⅝ in.) wide.

COORDINATION

- For large sheets of glass, verify the maximum size that can be transported into the building through stairways or elevators.

- Specify horizontally tempered glass to avoid visible tong marks in frameless glazing.

- If patterned or etched glass is used, include in the details which way the patterned or etched side should face.

- If frameless glazing is used adjacent to a glass door, the thickness of the glass should match the thickness of the door for the best appearance.

- Consider a design for markings on full-height glass to prevent people from running into large glazed areas. Even though the glass is tempered and strong enough to withstand impact, people are injured trying to walk through what looks like openings. Alternately, furniture, plants, or other objects can be designed for placement in front of glazing.

- Detail glass stops for the side of the partition where appearance is least important because fasteners, joints, and glazing tape or sealant on the stop side are usually not as neat as the opposite side.

- When detailing and specifying window coverings maintain sufficient clearances between the window covering and exterior glazing to avoid heat buildup, which might cause the glass to crack or break. Figure 5.14 shows minimum clearances to permit air movement around the glass. Window coverings should also be located so heating and cooling outlets are on the room side of the shading device. Verify exact requirement with the building's mechanical engineer if necessary.

6

ARCHITECTURAL WOODWORK

Architectural woodwork is custom, shop-fabricated millwork built of lumber, finished wood, and other materials. It typically includes cabinetry, paneling, custom doors and frames, shelving, stair work and handrails, blinds and shutters, custom furniture, and special interior trim. Architectural woodwork makes it possible to produce superior wood items because most of the work is done under carefully controlled factory conditions with machinery and finishing techniques that cannot be duplicated on a job site.

Two related types of woodwork are finish carpentry and modular casework. However, architectural woodwork differs from these types in that it is custom designed and fabricated for a particular job and it is built in a factory.

Finish carpentry is woodwork assembled at the job site by finish carpenters. It includes such items as installation of doors and windows, door and window trim, standard wood base, site-built stairways, and handrails. Finish carpentry is commonly used in residential construction and commercial construction where there is a limited amount of woodwork or where cost is a consideration.

Modular casework is mass-produced cabinetry from a manufacturer's standard set of details adapted for a particular project. Although it is fabricated in a factory, there are a limited number of sizes and styles from which to select. Modular casework is typically used in institutional buildings, such as schools, hospitals, and laboratories, where economy, consistent appearance, and serviceability are important considerations. On a residential scale, prefabricated kitchen and bath cabinets are a type of modular casework.

Many aspects of architectural woodwork fabrication have been standardized by the Architectural Woodwork Institute (AWI), a nonprofit trade association representing the architectural woodwork manufacturers of the United States and Canada and by the Woodwork Institute of California. They are described in great detail in the *Architectural Woodwork Quality Standards, Guide Specifications and Quality Certification Program. Quality Standards* provides information about standard construction techniques, describes standards and tests than can be used to assure compliance, and provides a means of specifying by using the *Standards* as reference specifications. Although the AWI *Quality Standards* are voluntary, they are widely used in the commercial interior construction industry.

FINISH CARPENTRY [06200]

Although finish carpentry cannot be installed with the same level of quality as factory-built architectural woodwork, it is adequate for a variety of interior finishes in residential and some commercial construction. However, the types of materials used and specification methods are different from those of architectural woodwork.

Materials and grading

Lumber used for finish carpentry is a regional material and the available species vary depending on location. Common species include Douglas fir, ponderosa pine, sugar pine, Idaho white pine, southern pine, western red cedar, poplar, oak, and redwood, among others. Local suppliers can provide information on available species and grades.

For interior construction, one of the most important aspects of specifying finish carpentry is the grade, which determines the type and number of allowable defects. Grading rules vary depending on the species and the trade organization responsible. Some of the more common grades for softwood shop lumber are summarized in Tables 6.1–6.3. For most species, B & Better is the highest

Table 6.1
Selected grades for appearance grades of western lumber

Grade category	Grades	Description
Selects	B & Better	Highest quality of select grade lumber available with many pieces absolutely clear and free of defects.
	C Select	Appearance only slightly less than B & Better. Recommended for high-quality interior trim and cabinetwork with natural stain or enamel finishes.
	D Select	Allows more defects than C Select grade but is suitable where finish requirements are less exacting.
Finish	Superior; Superior VG	Highest quality of Finish grade lumber available with many pieces absolutely clear. Used for high-quality trim and cabinetwork where natural, stain, or enamel finishes are used and the finest appearance is required. Can be specified as VG for vertical grain.
	Prime; Prime VG	Allows slightly more defects than Superior, but can be used where finishing requirements are less exacting. Can be specified as VG for vertical grain.
	E	Boards in this grade can be cut in such a way as to produce pieces of Prime or Superior grades. E-grade boards must contain two-thirds or more of such cuttings 2 in. (50 mm) or wider and 16 in. (406 mm) or longer.
Paneling	Any select or finish grade	C Select or any other grade can be used to produce paneling.
	Select 2 common for knotty paneling	Grade reserved for knotty paneling made from number 2 Common grade boards (not shown in this table).

Note: additional grades are available but they are commonly used for other architectural purposes.

available grade and is excellent for natural finishes or painted finishes. However, its supply is limited. C Select has only slightly more defects and is usually the best grade to specify for painting and some natural finishes. It is also possible with some species to specify either vertical or flat grain, which describes how the board is cut from the tree. Vertical grain wood is cut so that the annual growth rings are perpendicular, or almost perpendicular, to the face of the board. Vertical grain boards tend to warp less, are more abrasion resistant, and stain more uniformly than flat grain boards. The grades in the Finish category are similar to the Select grades and are usually used to grade Douglas fir and hem-fir.

Plywood

Plywood is a panel product made from an odd number of layers of thin veneer glued together under heat and pressure. Each adjacent ply is laid in a direction perpendicular to the ply next to it. Plywood suitable for natural, stain, and painted finishes is commonly used in finish carpentry construction. Plywood is available in several thicknesses, including ¼, ⅜, ½, ⅝, and ¾ in. (6, 10, 13, 16, and 19 mm). The standard sheet size is 4 × 8 ft (1219 × 2438 mm). Common finished surfaces are softwoods (such as fir), but surfaces of birch and oak veneer are also available where a smooth, finished surface suitable for painting or stain, respectively, is required. Medium density overlay (MDO) is also used where a smooth surface is needed for painting.

Plywood is graded based on the quality of the face veneer. The grades suitable for interior construction include N, A, and B. N grade is the highest quality and is intended for natural finishes. It is cut from one-hundred percent heartwood and is free from knots and splits, with only minor defects permitted. The veneer is well matched for color and grain continuity. Grade A is

Grades	Description
B & Better	Highest quality available. Generally clear of defects, although a limited number of pin knots are permitted. Used for finest quality for natural or stain finish.
C	Almost clear but permits limited number of small tight knots and surface checks. Excellent grade for painted or natural finish where requirements are less exacting.
C & Better	Combination of B & Better and C grades
D	More defects allowed, but usable for painted finishes where appearance is not critical.

Table 6.2 Finish lumber grades for southern pine

Grades	Description
Clear, all heart	Highest quality of redwood available. Free of defects on one face although the reverse face may have slight imperfections.
Clear	Same quality as Clear, all heart, but contains some sapwood.
B Grade	Contains limited number of knots and other imperfections not allowed in Clear, all heart or Clear.

Table 6.3 Redwood lumber grades for interior use

Note: additional grades are available but they are commonly used for structural purposes.

suitable for a smooth, painted finish. It is generally free of defects and what minor defects are allowed are patched with fillers for a uniform, smooth surface. B grade is generally not used for finished surfaces, except for utility shelving and similar uses. The surface is solid and free from open defects, but some knots, pitch streaks, and other minor imperfections are allowed.

When large, flat sheets are required for structural purposes instead of a finished surface, either plywood or particleboard is used. Particleboard is composed of small wood particles, fibers, or chips mixed together in a binder and formed under pressure into a panel. Like plywood, it is available in several thicknesses in 4×8 ft (1219 $\times$ 2438 mm) sheets. It is generally preferred for backing and framing of finish carpentry and architectural woodwork because it is less expensive and more dimensionally stable than plywood. Common thicknesses include ⅜, ½, ¾, and 1¼ in. (10, 13, 19, and 32 mm).

Molding

Molding is trim used for decorative or functional purposes. For finish carpentry construction, standard profiles of molding are available in softwood and hardwood. A few representative profiles are shown in Figure 6.1, although there are over a hundred available. In most cases, the standard molding profiles for base, casing trim, cornices, chair rails, handrails, and other applications are adequate. However, custom profiles can be detailed and specified when standard trim will not work. This is commonly done in commercial construction when molding made from a particular species of wood is not available. Refer to the section on standing and running trim for more information on custom wood molding.

Figure 6.1
Standard wood molding profiles

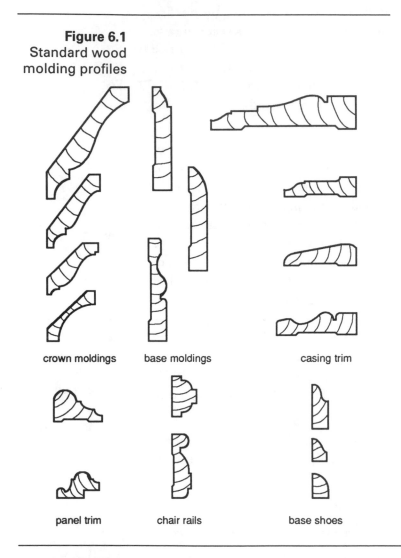

crown moldings   base moldings   casing trim

panel trim   chair rails   base shoes

Applicable standards for finish carpentry

Hardwood Plywood Manufacturers Association: NHPA HP-1 1992, *Interim Voluntary Standard for Hardwood and Decorative Plywood*

Northeast Lumber Manufacturers Association: *NeLMA Standard Grading Rules for Northeastern Lumber*

National Institute for Standards and Technology: *US Product Standard PS 1-83 for Construction and Industrial Plywood*

Western Wood Products Association: *Western Lumber Grading Rules*

Wood Moulding and Millwork Producers Association: *WM Series Moulding Patterns Catalog*

LUMBER [06400]

The raw material for architectural woodwork is broadly classified as either softwood or hardwood. Softwood refers to timber from evergreen trees, such as pine and fir; hardwood refers to timber from deciduous trees, such as oak and maple. The names are slightly misleading because many softwoods are physically quite hard and many hardwoods are actually soft.

Timber is manufactured into two forms for use in architectural woodwork: solid stock lumber and veneer. As the name implies, solid stock is a thick piece of lumber (generally ½ in. (13 mm), or thicker) used alone to form some woodwork component. A veneer is a thin piece of wood (usually less than ¹⁄₁₆ in. (1.6 mm)) sliced from a log and glued to some type of backing, usually particleboard.

Lumber sources

Wood comes from a variety of locations throughout the world including North America, Central America, South America, Africa, Europe, India, Southeast Asia, Malaysia, Indonesia, and the Philippines. Most timber for architectural woodwork is manufactured into solid stock or veneer. However, as costs rise and availability decreases, other types of manufactured lumber products may be used in interior construction. Currently, products like oriented strandboard, glued laminated timber, end-glued lumber, and composite wood beams are manufactured from wood products that were formerly considered waste.

The species of wood refers to the type of tree from which the lumber is taken. There are hundreds of species of wood that can be used for architectural woodwork and furniture, but only several dozen are used predominantly because of availability and cost. The designer's choice of a species depends on the availability and cost as well as how appropriate it is for the intended use. Some species are so rare that they are only available as a veneer and not as solid stock. Local mill shops and lumber and veneer suppliers can provide information on availability and current costs. Table 6.4 lists some common hardwood species and their characteristics.

Lumber cutting methods

The way lumber is cut from a log determines the final appearance of the grain pattern. There are three ways solid stock is cut from a log. The three methods used are plain sawing (also called flat sawing), quarter sawing, and rift sawing. These methods are illustrated in Figure 6.2.

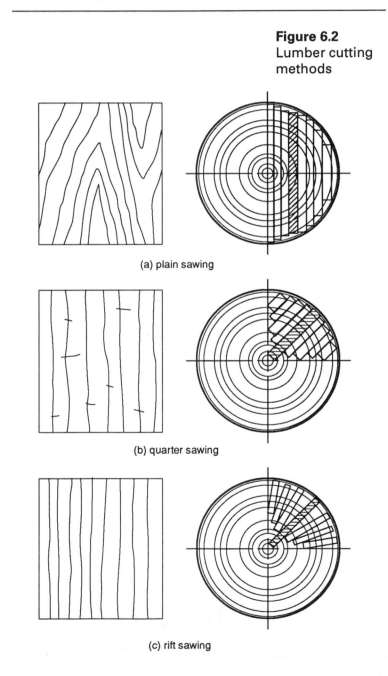

Figure 6.2
Lumber cutting methods

(a) plain sawing

(b) quarter sawing

(c) rift sawing

Table 6.4
Comparative characteristics of selected hardwood species

Common name	Common use	Veneer availability	Lumber availability	Cost range	Color
Afrormosia	P, F	L	L	3	Yellow to warm-brown; similar to teak
Ash					
Olive burl	F	A	L	3	White and brown burly pattern
White	T, C, F	A	A	2	Cream to light brown
Avodire	P, C, F	L	L	3	White to creamy gold
Beech	F	A	A	1	White to reddish-brown
Birch					
Yellow birch	P, T, C, F	A	A	1	Cream/light-brown tinged with red
Select red	P, T, C, F	A	A	2	Light-brown to reddish-brown
Select white	P, T, C, F	A	A	2	Creamy-white
Bubinga	T, C	L	A	3	Red with streaks of purple
Butternut	P, T, C, F	L	L	2	Warm buttery tan
Cherry	P, T, C, F	A	A	2	Reddish-brown
Chestnut	P, T	R	R	3	Light brown
Cypress, yellow	P, F	L	A	2	Yellowish-brown/red
Ebony, Macassar	P, F	A	L	3	Dark-brown to black; streaked with yellowish-brown
Elm					
American	P, F	A	A	2	Light grayish-brown
Slippery	P, F	A	A	2	Reddish-brown heartwood; light brown sapwood
Hickory, shagbark	F	A	A	2	Creamy to reddish heartwood
Lauan					
Red	P, C, F	A	A	1	Red to brown
White	C, F	A	A	1	Light to grayish-brown to light reddish brown
Limba	P, T, C, F	L	L	2	Pale-yellow to light brown
Mahogany					
African	P, T, C, F	L	L	2	Reddish-brown to tannish-brown
Honduras	P, T, C, F	L	L	2	Reddish-brown to tannish-brown
Maple					
Hard	C, F	L	A	2	Cream to light reddish-brown
Select white	C, F	L	A	2	Creamy
Birdseye	C, F	L	A	3	Highly figured
Soft	C, F	A	A	1	May contain dark streaks
Oak					
Red, northern	P, T, C, F	A	A	2	Light-brown with reddish tinge
White	P, T, C, F	A	A	2	Light-brown with shades of ochre
English brown	P, T, C	L	L	3	Light-tan to deep brown
Orientalwood	C, F	L	L	3	Pinkish-gray to brown
Paldao	P, T, C, F	L	L	2	Gray to reddish-brown
Pecan	P, F	A	A	2	Reddish-brown heartwood, creamy sapwood
Persimmon	F	L	L	2	Light-brown with dark stripes
Poplar, yellow	C	A	A	1	Yellowish with slight greenish cast
Rosewood					
Brazilian	P, T, C, F	L	R	3	Dark-brown with black streaks
East Indian	P, F	L	L	3	Dark-purple to ebony
Sapele	C, F	A	A	2	Dark red-brown
Teak	P, C, F	A	L	3	Tawny-yellow to light brown
Tupelo	P	A	A	1	Creamy to yellowish with brownish-streaked heartwood
Walnut, black	P, T, C, F	A	A	3	Gray-brown to dark brown
Zebrawood	P	A	L	3	Straw to dark-brown

Common uses:
P = Paneling
T = Trim
C = Cabinetry
F = Furniture
Availability:
A = Generally available
L = Limited
R = Rare
Cost range:
1 = Moderate
2 = High
3 = Expensive

Because of the limited availability of some species of wood and the expense of making certain cuts, not all types of lumber cutting are available in all species. The availability of cuts in the desired species should be verified before specifications are written.

Plain sawing

Plain sawing makes the most efficient use of the log and is the least expensive of the three methods. Because the wood is cut with various orientations to the grain of the tree, plain sawing results in a finished surface with the characteristic cathedral pattern shown in Figure 6.2(a).

Quarter sawing

Quarter sawing is produced by cutting the log into quarters and then sawing toward the center. Because the saw cut is nearly perpendicular to the grain, the resulting grain pattern is more uniformly vertical. See Figure 6.2(b). Not only does this result in a different appearance than plain sawing, but quarter sawn boards also tend to twist and cup less, shrink less in width, hold paint better, and have fewer defects. Quarter sawing is more expensive than plain sawing.

Rift sawing

Rift sawing provides an even more consistent vertical grain because the saw cuts are always made radially to the center of the tree. Because the log must be shifted after each cut and because there is a great deal of waste, rift cutting is more expensive than quarter sawing and is seldom used, except for oak and a few other species.

Lumber grading

Grading the quality of lumber for solid stock used in architectural woodwork is done differently from standard industry grading for shop lumber and plywood, which has been described in the previous section. The AWI has established three grades, Grades I, II, and III. The AWI standards establish the sizes of pieces that must be furnished free and clear of all natural or seasoning characteristics, which are considered defects. The standards also give the number of square inches per defect in boards larger than the

Nominal thickness		Finish thickness, in. (mm)	
Quarters	In. (mm)	Hardwoods in. (mm)	Softwoods in. (mm)
4/4	1 (25)	¾ (19)	¾ (19)
5/4	1¼ (32)	1¹⁄₁₆ (27)	1¹⁄₁₆ (27)
6/4	1½ (38)	1⁵⁄₁₆ (33)	1⅜ (35)
8/4	2 (51)	1½ (38)	1½ (38)
10/4	2½ (64)	2 (51)	2¼ (57)
12/4	3 (76)	2½ (64)	2½ (64)

Table 6.5 Standard sizes of hardwood lumber

required size that is free and clear of all defects. Although these three grades are not specified directly by the interior designer, the AWI *Quality Standards* do refer to them when defining the characteristics of a construction component under premium, custom, and economy grades that the designer does specify. For example, a premium grade handrail that is designed to have a transparent finish must be constructed of Grade I lumber, while Grade II lumber may be used to construct a custom grade handrail.

Standard sizes

Because architectural woodwork is custom fabricated, almost any component can be detailed to whatever size is required without using standard sizes of boards as with finish carpentry. However, lumber for woodwork is manufactured in standard thicknesses and it makes good economic sense to use these thicknesses to minimize waste, thereby reducing costs.

Figure 6.3
Gluing for width

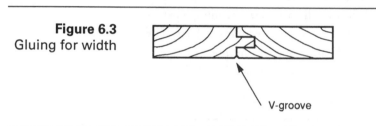

V-groove

Table 6.6
Standard
lumber widths

Nominal width, in. (mm)	Finish width, in. (mm)
2 (51)	1½ (38)
4 (102)	3½ (89)
6 (152)	5½ (140)
8 (203)	7¼ (184)
10 (254)	9¼ (235)
12 (305)	11¼ (286)

Lumber thickness for millwork is expressed in "quarters," which refers to quarter-inch increments. Thus, the thickness of a ⁵⁄₄ piece of lumber is nominally 1¼ in. (32 mm). However, this is the thickness before drying and surfacing. The actual finished thickness is less than the nominal thickness, and it is important to know the actual thicknesses to be able to economically detail woodwork. Table 6.5 gives the nominal and actual thicknesses of softwoods and hardwoods.

Although all the thicknesses may be available, for construction components that exceed 1¹⁄₁₆ in. (27 mm) in hardwoods and 1½ in. (38 mm) in softwoods, the architectural woodworker may glue two or more thinner pieces together, as described in the next section. One of the most common solid piece thicknesses is ¾ in. (19 mm), which is also the thickness of the substrate to which most veneer is applied.

Standard widths of woodwork lumber come in nominal two-in. increments and the actual widths follow the same conventions as board lumber, as listed in Table 6.6.

Built-up construction

Because fine hardwood is expensive and some species are in very short supply, most furniture and architectural woodwork are not constructed of large, solid pieces of wood as they once were. In some instances, this has actually improved the quality of furniture and woodwork. This is because contemporary veneered panels warp less and are more dimensionally stable than large pieces of solid wood. Instead of single pieces of solid wood, large expanses of flat panels or very thick trim are constructed by using veneer or gluing one or more smaller pieces of solid stock together.

Gluing for width

When a wide board is required, one or more narrower boards are glued together. This not only minimizes the cost, it also minimizes possible warping and other lumber defects. When a board is glued for width, the mill shop selects boards with similar grain patterns to make the completed piece look like one piece as much as possible. The edges are tongue and grooved or splined for a better joint and glued in the shop. See Figure 6.3.

Gluing for thickness

Although thick pieces of solid stock are available for many species, ⁴/₄ thickness is usually the thickest piece used alone. If thicker sections are required, ⁴/₄-in. (³/₄-in. actual thickness) lumber is glued together and then cut or shaped to the required profile. Because this is done in the mill shop, only a fine hairline joint is visible, and after finishing even this is not noticeable if the wood grains have been well matched. See Figure 6.4.

Detailing suggestion

In order to prevent cupping and warping of wide boards, solid stock should not be detailed to a width of more than about six times its thickness. If a wider board is required, two or more pieces can be glued together or veneer construction can be used.

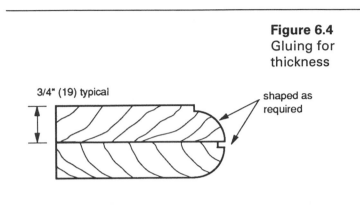

Figure 6.4
Gluing for thickness

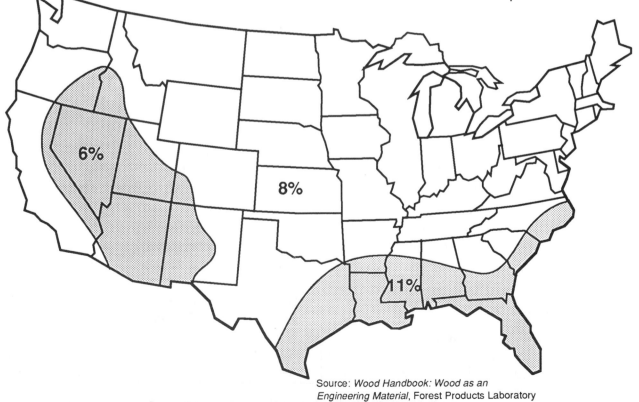

Figure 6.5
Recommended average moisture content for interior wood products

Source: *Wood Handbook: Wood as an Engineering Material*, Forest Products Laboratory

Dimensional changes due to moisture

Although detailing to allow for the expansion and contraction of wood is usually sufficient for most interior construction, when the amount of dimensional change must be known accurately, it can be calculated according to the following formula:

$$\Delta D = D_i \times [C_t \times (M_f - M_i)]$$

ΔD = change in dimension

D_i = dimension in inches or millimeters at start of change

C_t = dimensional change coefficient (C_t for shrinkage in tangential direction, C_r for radial direction; radial shrinkage is shrinkage in the dimension perpendicular to the radial lines of tree growth). See Table 6.7 for some representative coefficients

M_f = moisture content in percent at end of change

M_i = moisture content in percent at start of change

However, because of the many variables involved, the actual dimensional change based on this formula has a tolerance of 50 percent above or below the calculated distance. Any detailing based on this formula should take this into account.

Table 6.7
Coefficients for dimensional change due to shrinkage or swelling within moisture content limits of 6% to 14%

Species	Dimensional change coefficient[1]		Species	Dimensional change coefficient[1]	
	Radial, C_r	Tangential, C_t		Radial, C_r	Tangential, C_t
Ash			Iroko[2]	0.00153	0.00205
Oregon	0.00141	0.00285	Lauan		
White, green	0.00169	0.00274	Dark red	0.00133	0.00267
Avodire	0.00126	0.00226	Light red	0.00126	0.00241
Beech, American	0.00190	0.00431	Mahogany[2]	0.00172	0.00238
Birch			Maple		
Paper	0.00219	0.00304	Bigleaf	0.00126	0.00248
Yellow, sweet	0.00256	0.00338	Red	0.00137	0.00289
Cativo	0.00078	0.00183	Silver	0.00102	0.00252
Cedar			Persimmon, common	0.00278	0.00403
Eastern red	0.00106	0.00162	Red oak		
Western red[2]	0.00111	0.00234	Commercial red	0.00158	0.00369
Cherry, black	0.00126	0.00248	California black	0.00123	0.00230
Douglas fir			Redwood		
Coast-type	0.00165	0.00267	Old growth[2]	0.00120	0.00205
Interior north	0.00130	0.00241	Second growth[2]	0.00101	0.00229
Elm, American	0.00144	0.00338	Sycamore, American	0.00172	0.00296
Fir			Teak[2]	0.00101	0.00186
California red	0.00155	0.00278	Tupelo, black	0.00176	0.00308
Pacific silver	0.00151	0.00327	Walnut, European	0.00148	0.00223
Hickory			White oak		
Pecan	0.00169	0.00315	Commercial	0.00180	0.00365
True Hickory	0.00259	0.00411	Yellow poplar	0.00158	0.00289

[1] Per 1% change in moisture content, based on dimension at 10% moisture content and a straight-line relationship between the moisture content at which shrinkage starts and total shrinkage. (Shrinkage is assumed to start at 30% for all species except those indicated by footnote 2.)

[2] Shrinkage is assumed to start at 22% moisture content.

Source: *Wood Handbook: Wood as an Engineering Material,* Forest Products Laboratory.

Moisture content and shrinkage

Because all wood products shrink and swell with changes in moisture content in the air, all wood construction should be detailed to allow for this movement to take place without putting undue stress on the wood joints. Shrinkage and swelling in architectural woodwork is not as much of a problem as for site-built finish carpentry. This is because of the improved manufacturing methods and the fact that solid stock and veneer can be dried or acclimated to a particular geographical region and its prevailing humidity.

However, there are some general guidelines that should be followed. In most of the United States, and in the Canadian provinces of Ontario and Quebec, the optimum moisture content of millwork for interior applications is from 5% to 10% with an average of 8%. The relative humidity necessary to maintain this optimum level is from 25% to 55%. In the more humid southern coastal areas of the US, in Newfoundland, and in the Canadian coastal provinces, the optimum moisture content is from 8% to 13% (11% average). The required relative humidity necessary to maintain this level is from 43% to 70%. In the dry southwestern regions of the United States, and in the Canadian provinces of Alberta, Saskatchewan, and Manitoba, the corresponding values are from 4% to 9% (6% average). The relative humidity required is from 17% to 50%. See Figure 6.5.

Ecological concerns

The current concern about the deforestation of the world's tropical rain forests is causing many interior designers and architects to re-evaluate how they design and specify architectural woodwork. Because the problem is very complex and involves the supplying country's economic, political, and cultural milieu as well as worldwide economic factors, simply not specifying endangered species of timber may have very little effect on the problem. This is especially true because such a small percentage of endangered timber species is used for architectural woodwork.

One position supported by many design and furniture associations is that conservation, harvesting, and a country's local economic development need not be incompatible if the timber comes from a wisely managed plantation or agro-forest to provide sustainable yield production. Unfortunately, less than one percent of the commercial timber trade is currently produced from sustainable yield forests.

Until more is known about the problem and more countries and timber suppliers begin to produce using sustained yield management, the designer can either choose to specify woods that can be shown to come from a sustainable yield forest or select one of the hundreds of alternative domestic species that are in plentiful supply.

VENEER [06420]

A veneer is a thin slice of wood. Veneer is glued to a backing material, most commonly particleboard, to hold it flat and provide a solid substrate for installation. Most veneers are cut about $\frac{1}{28}$ in. (0.907 mm) thick, but thinner or thicker cuts can be specified to meet particular requirements. For example, a thick veneer can be specified to provide more durability or the ability to withstand the sanding and refinishing of minor nicks and scratches without showing the backing panel.

Veneer sources

As with solid stock, veneers come from timber harvested worldwide. Because of the limited supply of some species, veneer cuts may be more readily available than solid stock in the same species because veneer provides a higher yield from a tree. Some of the veneers are listed in Table 6.4. Veneers are provided to woodwork shops by veneer suppliers who buy timber from around the world and cut it into veneers.

Figure 6.6
Veneer
cutting
methods

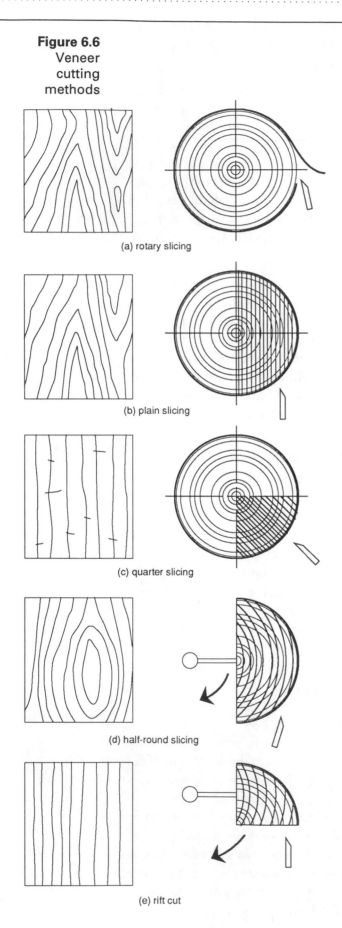

(a) rotary slicing

(b) plain slicing

(c) quarter slicing

(d) half-round slicing

(e) rift cut

Veneer cutting methods

Just as with solid stock, the way veneer is cut from a log affects its final appearance. There are five principal methods of cutting veneers, as shown in Figures 6.6(a)–6.6(e). Plain slicing and quarter slicing are accomplished the same way as cutting solid stock, except the resulting pieces are much thinner. Quarter slicing produces a more straight-grained pattern than plain slicing because the cutting knife strikes the growth rings at an angle of approximately 90°.

In the *Rotary slicing method*, the log is mounted on a lathe and turned against a knife, which peels off a continuous layer of veneer. This produces a very pronounced grain pattern that is often undesirable in fine quality wood finishes, although it does produce the most veneer with the least waste.

The *Half-round slicing method* is similar to rotary slicing, but the log is cut in half and the veneer is cut slightly across the annular growth rings. This results in a pronounced grain pattern, having characteristics of both rotary-sliced and plain-sliced veneers.

The *Rift slicing method* consists of quartering a log and cutting at a slight angle to the growth rings. Rift slicing accentuates the vertical grain pattern and minimizes the horizontal "flake" that is caused by medullary rays. These are radial cells extending from the center of the tree to its circumference. They are most commonly found in oak; therefore, rift slicing is most often specified for oak to eliminate these medullary ray markings.

Because the width of a piece of veneer is limited by the diameter of the log or the portion of the log from which it is cut, several veneers must be put together on a backing panel to make up the needed size of a finished piece. The individual veneers come from the same piece of log, which is called a *flitch*. As the veneers are sliced from the log, they are kept in sequence so they can be matched later. The methods of matching veneers are discussed in the section on panel construction.

Because veneers are very thin, they must be glued to a solid backing to hold them flat and to provide the strength needed for constructing woodwork items. There are a number of products used for veneer backing, but the most common are particleboard and plywood, with particleboard being the panel of choice among most mill shops. The thickness of the backing panel depends on the use of the final panel product and its size, but the most common thickness is ¾ in. (19 mm).

Veneer grading

The Architectural Woodwork Institute (AWI) has established three grades of architectural woodwork: Premium, Custom, and Economy. These apply to cabinetwork, paneling, doors, trim, and all other types of architectural woodwork. Premium is the highest grade available in both material and manufacturing. It is intended for the finest work. It is the most expensive grade. Custom grade is intended for high-quality, conventional work. Economy grade is the lowest grade in both materials and manufacturing. It is intended for work where cost is more important than quality or in service areas where appearance is not critical. The AWI *Quality Standards* describe the level of material and manufacture for each of the three grades for every type of construction component. Architectural woodwork can be accurately and easily specified by referring to one of the three AWI grades.

As with lumber, the Architectural Woodwork Institute defines four grades of veneers for panel surfacing. However, the designer does not specify these grades directly. Instead, the standard grades of Premium, Custom, and Economy are specified for each type of paneled product. The grade of veneer is automatically determined by the AWI *Quality Standards* according to which of these three quality level grades is specified. For example, Premium grade stile and rail paneling for transparent finish is constructed with Grade I face veneer (the highest), while Custom grade stile and rail paneling for opaque finish is constructed with Grade II face veneer.

CABINETWORK [06410]

Cabinets include custom-manufactured built-in base and upper cabinets, freestanding fixtures, and open shelving cases designed and detailed for a particular project. Cabinetwork is built predominately of wood products, but can also include other materials such as high-pressure decorative laminate, metal, glass, stone, leather, and other decorative and functional items built into the cabinet.

Various types of joints are used for millwork construction to increase the strength of the joint and improve the appearance by eliminating mechanical fasteners, such as screws. With the availability of high-strength adhesives, screws, and other concealed fasteners, visible mechanical fasteners are seldom needed for the majority of work produced in the shop. Field attachment, however, often requires the use of blind nailing or other concealed fastening to maintain the quality look of the work. Some of the common joints used in millwork are shown in Figure 6.7.

Typical cabinet construction

Although architectural woodwork can be designed and built in an almost unlimited number of ways, there are certain standard methods of construction that have been developed over time that satisfy the requirements of economy, strength, and stability. Upper and lower cabinets are common woodwork components with typical construction details. The basic construction techniques can be modified to suit individual project requirements. Figure 6.8 shows the construction of a typical base cabinet. Countertops are included in cabinet construction.

Countertop construction

Countertops are built separately from base cabinets and put in place in the field. This is because the countertops are built in single lengths that are much longer than any individual base cabinet. Building and installing the countertops separately also gives the installers the ability to precisely fit the countertop to the wall. This is most commonly done with a *scribe piece* on top of the backsplash or at the back of the countertop. A scribe piece is an oversized piece of plastic laminate or wood that can be trimmed in the field to follow any minor irregularities of the wall. As with other woodwork components, there are hundreds of possible configurations to countertops, including variations in width, materials, front edge shape and size, and backsplash size and shape. Some of the more common configurations are shown in Figures 6.9(a)–6.9(d). (Figure 6.29 shows typical plastic laminate countertop edge treatments).

Drawer and door front construction

For both base and upper cabinets there are four basic categories of door and drawer front construction: flush, flush overlay, reveal overlay, and lipped overlay. These are shown in Figures 6.10(a)–6.10(d).

Flush construction

In *flush construction,* the face of the drawers and doors are installed flush with the face frame. The primary disadvantage of this type of construction is its expense because of the extra care required to fit and align the doors and drawers within the frame. Another disadvantage is that, with use, the doors and drawers may sag. This results in nonuniform spacing between fronts and may cause some doors and drawers to bind against the frame.

A variation of flush construction is the *lipped overlay construction* in which part of the door or drawer overlaps the frame and covers the joint between the two pieces. See Figure 6.10(d).

Flush overlay

In *flush overlay construction,* the fronts of the doors and drawers overlap the face frame of the cabinet. Edges of adjacent door or drawer fronts are separated only enough to allow operation without touching, usually about

Figure 6.7
Wood joints

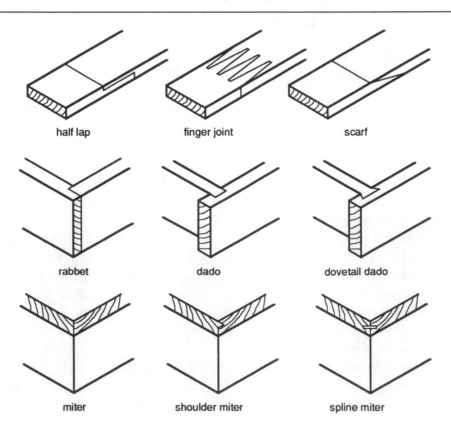

half lap   finger joint   scarf

rabbet   dado   dovetail dado

miter   shoulder miter   spline miter

Figure 6.8
Typical base
cabinet
construction

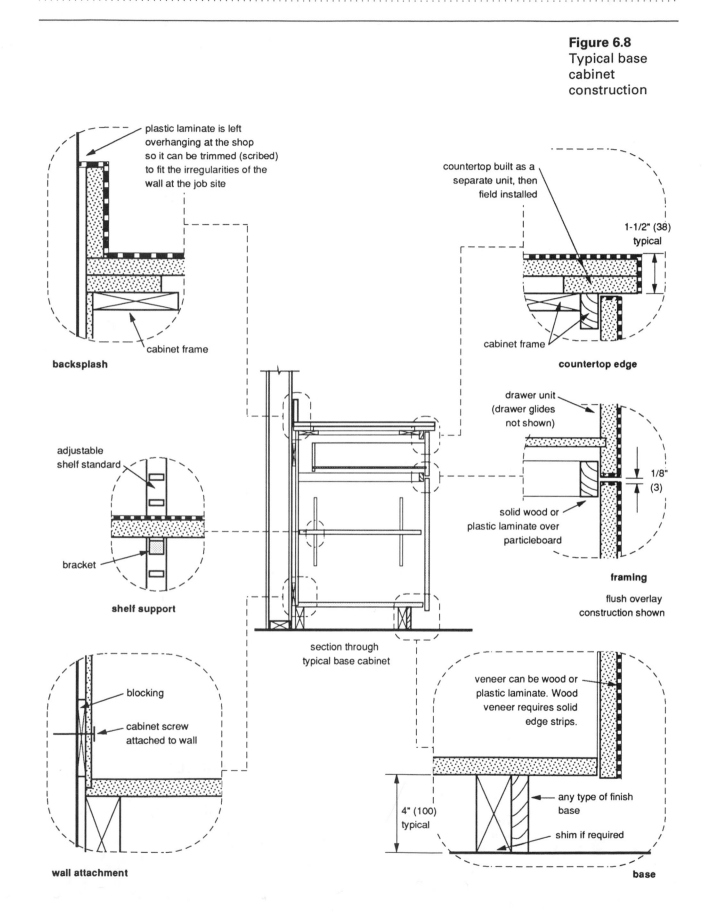

plastic laminate is left
overhanging at the shop
so it can be trimmed (scribed)
to fit the irregularities of the
wall at the job site

backsplash

cabinet frame

countertop built as a
separate unit, then
field installed

1-1/2" (38)
typical

cabinet frame

countertop edge

adjustable
shelf standard

bracket

shelf support

drawer unit
(drawer glides
not shown)

1/8"
(3)

solid wood or
plastic laminate over
particleboard

framing

flush overlay
construction shown

section through
typical base cabinet

blocking

cabinet screw
attached to wall

wall attachment

veneer can be wood or
plastic laminate. Wood
veneer requires solid
edge strips.

4" (100)
typical

any type of finish
base

shim if required

base

Figure 6.9
Typical
countertop
details

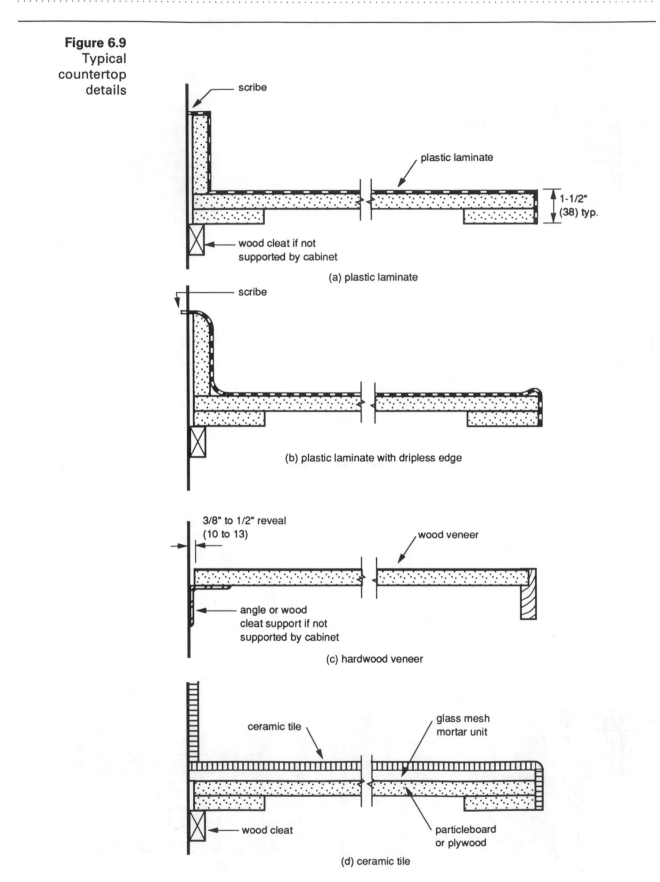

scribe

plastic laminate

1-1/2"
(38) typ.

wood cleat if not
supported by cabinet

(a) plastic laminate

scribe

(b) plastic laminate with dripless edge

3/8" to 1/2" reveal
(10 to 13)

wood veneer

angle or wood
cleat support if not
supported by cabinet

(c) hardwood veneer

ceramic tile

glass mesh
mortar unit

wood cleat

particleboard
or plywood

(d) ceramic tile

⅛ in. (3 mm), or less. Only doors and drawers are visible and they are all flush with each other. As with flush construction, the mill shop must take great care in aligning and fitting the doors and drawers so that the gap between them is uniform. As with flush construction, if the drawers and doors sag too much, problems arise. Flush overlay is typically used with high-pressure decorative laminate clad cabinets.

Reveal overlay

In *reveal overlay construction,* the edges of adjacent doors and door fronts are separated enough to reveal the face frame behind. The width of the reveal can be whatever the designer wants, subject to the width of the face frame. This construction is less expensive than flush overlay construction because minor misalignments and sagging are not as noticeable.

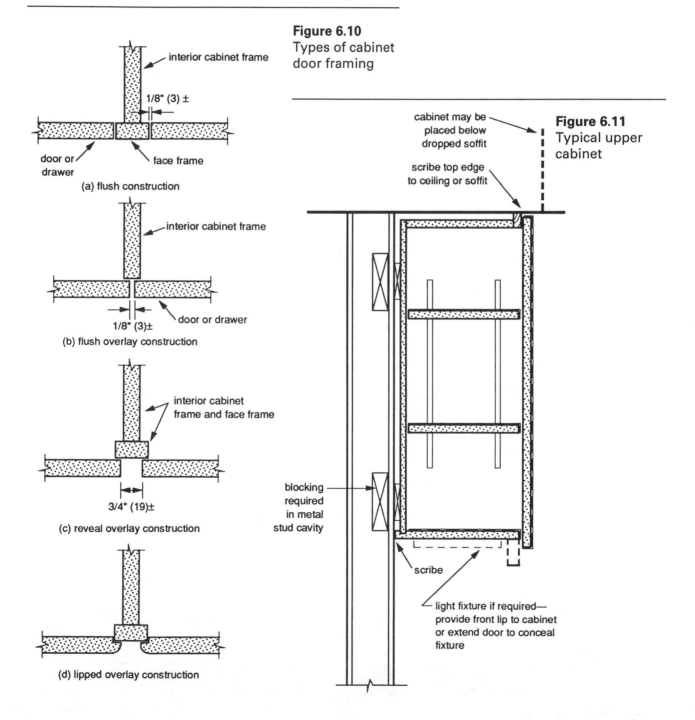

Figure 6.10
Types of cabinet door framing

(a) flush construction

(b) flush overlay construction

(c) reveal overlay construction

(d) lipped overlay construction

Figure 6.11
Typical upper cabinet

Upper cabinet construction

Upper cabinets are very similar in construction to base cabinets. The most notable exceptions are that they are not as deep as base cabinets and some design and detailing consideration must be given to the underside because it is visible. In addition, there must be some way to securely anchor the cabinet to the wall. In residential construction, the cabinet is attached to the wall by screwing through the cabinet back and wall finish into the wood studs. In commercial construction where metal studs are used, wood *blocking* is required in the stud cavity behind the wall finish. This blocking is installed as the studs are being erected and is attached to them with screws. The blocking provides a solid base for attaching the cabinets to the wall. Figure 6.11 shows a typical upper cabinet detail.

Table 6.8
Materials and thicknesses for cabinet components

Component	Material	Minimum thickness, in. (mm)
Body members—ends, divisions, bottoms and tops	Panel product	¾ (19)
Rails	Lumber or panel product	¾ (19)
Backs	Panel product	¼ (6.4)
Doors, up to 30 in. wide by 80 in. high (762 by 2032 mm)	Medium density particleboard or medium density fiberboard core panel product	¾ (19)
Drawer sides, backs and subfronts	Lumber or panel product	½ (12.7)
Drawer bottoms	Panel product	¼ (6.4)
Drawer fronts	Lumber or panel product	¾ (19)
Wood shelves (minimum thicknesses given for spans listed)	Lumber	¾ up to 36 (19 up to 914) 1¹⁄₁₆ up to 48 (27 up to 1219)
Wood shelves	Veneer core plywood	¾ up to 36 (19 up to 914) 1 up to 48 (25.4 up to 1219)
Plastic laminate clad shelves	Medium density particleboard or fiberboard	¾ up to 32 (19 up to 813) 1 up to 42 (25.4 up to 1067)

Based on information from *Architectural Woodwork Quality Standards, Sixth Edition, Version 1.0,* copyright 1993, The Architectural Woodwork Institute, used with permission.

The top of the cabinet may be detailed against the ceiling or, as is common in residential construction, the cabinet may be placed below a dropped soffit. The space between the top of the cabinet and the ceiling may also be left open. The bottom edge of the doors may extend below the cabinet bottom as shown in the detail to allow for a finger pull instead of using door pull hardware.

Cabinet materials

Depending on the grade specified, AWI standards define the materials and minimum thicknesses for the various parts of a cabinet. These are summarized in Table 6.8.

Shelving

Shelving may be mounted on adjustable metal standards attached to a partition, attached to floor-mounted cases, or built into enclosed, wall-hung cabinets. Figure 6.12 shows a common type of wall-hung shelving unit with an open front. Shelving cabinets may also be fitted with doors.

The shelves themselves may be trimmed on the front at the same thickness of the shelf or a larger edge treatment can be applied. A

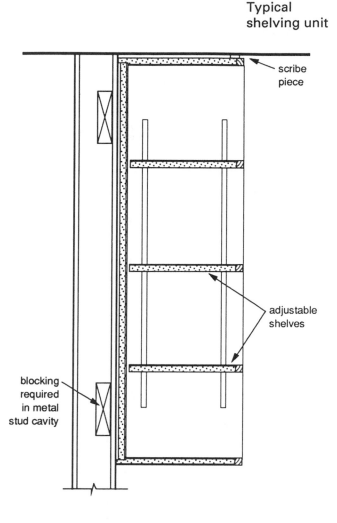

Figure 6.12
Typical shelving unit

scribe piece

adjustable shelves

blocking required in metal stud cavity

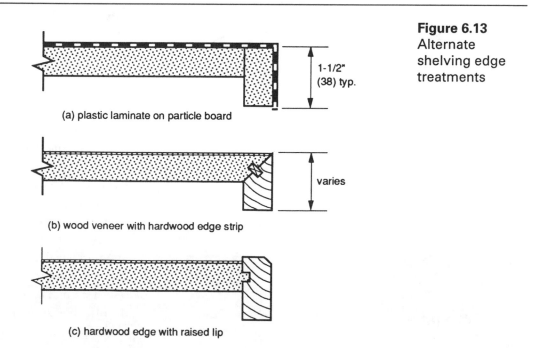

Figure 6.13
Alternate shelving edge treatments

1-1/2"
(38) typ.

(a) plastic laminate on particle board

varies

(b) wood veneer with hardwood edge strip

(c) hardwood edge with raised lip

few of these edge treatments are shown in Figures 6.13(a)–6.13(c). The edges make the shelf appear thicker and give added strength for heavy loads.

When viewed from the front, the way the shelves intersect the supports depends on the quality grade specified. For Premium grade and Custom grade shelving, stop dadoes or concealed, interlocking, fastening devices are used to attach fixed shelves to side supports. Economy grade shelving uses through dadoes. See Figures 6.14(a)–6.14(b).

Typical dimensions

Because architectural woodwork is custom designed and fabricated, any dimension of any component can be specified according to the needs of the job or the appearance

Figure 6.14
Methods of shelving attachment

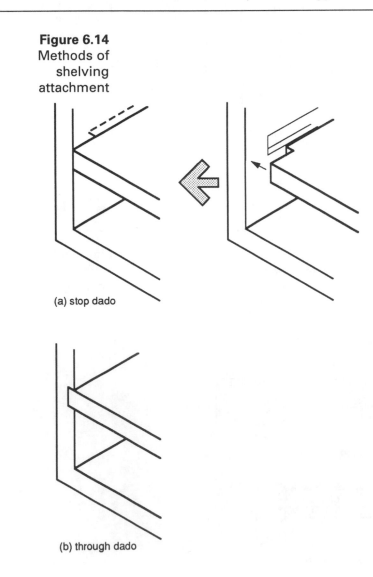

(a) stop dado

(b) through dado

desired. However, there are some standard dimensions that are common for cabinetwork and that have been found to work in most situations. Some of these are shown in Figures 6.15(a)–6.15(c).

Custom assemblies

A limitless number of designs can be developed with architectural woodwork. The details shown in this chapter are the most common and represent typical construction techniques. However, by modifying dimensions, configurations of components, trim shapes, and hardware, nearly any design concept can be realized.

Although architectural woodwork, by definition, is built from lumber products, other materials can be, and often are, incorporated into a woodwork design. Plastic laminate, metal, stone, fabric, leather, and other materials can be used to produce an endless variety of design detailing. For example, a stone top can be used on a custom reception desk or metal strips can be inlaid into wall paneling. When such materials are incidental to the primary piece of architectural woodwork, they are sometimes fabricated and usually installed by the architectural mill shop as part of the contract.

Coordination

Because architectural woodwork is fabricated to very close tolerances in the mill shop and installed in the field on, against, or within construction that is not as precise, architectural woodwork design and detailing must account for the differences in both tolerances and construction quality. Designing scribe pieces as part of the woodwork, as described for countertops, is one way of doing this. Reveals between the woodwork and other construction can also be detailed to minimize the visibility of any minor irregularities. For paneling, cabinets, and other components that must be installed plumb, space must be provided for the installers to mount wood blocking and to shim portions of the woodwork. If this produces an irregular gap between the wood-work and the wall, some acceptable method of concealing the crack is necessary. Shimming may also be required to level cabinets on uneven floors. The shim space is then covered with the finished base.

Other coordination issues include the following: anticipating and detailing for minor building movement; making woodwork finishes compatible with free-standing furniture finishes; and designing components so that they can be fabricated in pieces, which

Because one of the most common problems with shelving is excessive deflection under load, or outright collapse, the span and thickness of each shelf should be selected for minimum deflection. Shelves are simply thin, wide beams and obey the laws of statics. Therefore, any material of any size can be calculated using the standard beam equations. Table 6.9 summarizes these calculations for some common shelving materials, sizes, and spans based on a maximum deflection at the center of the shelf of ⅛ in. (3.2 mm). The table gives the maximum total load before the deflection exceeds ⅛ in.

Shelving deflection

Table 6.9
Maximum allowable total load in pounds (kg) for shelf deflection of ⅛ in. (3.2 mm) for shelves of different materials, widths, and spans

Shelf length in in. (mm)		30 (760)			36 (914)			42 (1067)		
Shelf width in in. (mm)		8 (203)	10 (254)	12 (305)	8 (203)	10 (254)	12 (305)	8 (203)	10 (254)	12 (305)
Component	Shelf thickness, in. (mm)	lb (kg)	lb (kg)	lb (kg)	lb (kg)	lb (kg)	lb (kg)	lb (kg)	lb (kg)	lb (kg)
Medium density particleboard faced with 0.05 in. plastic laminate	¾ (19)	58 (26)	73 (33)	87 (39)	34 (15)	42 (19)	51 (23)	21 (9)	27 (12)	32 (14)
	1½ (38)	388 (176)	485 (220)	583 (264)	225 (102)	281 (127)	337 (153)	142 (64)	177 (80)	212 (96)
High density particle board faced with 0.05 in. plastic laminate	¾ (19)	146 (66)	182 (83)	218 (99)	84 (38)	105 (48)	126 (57)	53 (24)	66 (30)	80 (36)
Birch-faced plywood with ¾ × ¾ in. softwood edge strip	¾ (19)	180 (81)	225 (102)	270 (122)	104 (47)	130 (59)	156 (71)	66 (30)	82 (37)	98 (44)
Birch-faced plywood with ¾ × 1½ in. softwood dropped edge	¾ (19)	366 (166)	412 (187)	458 (207)	212 (96)	238 (108)	265 (120)	133 (60)	150 (68)	167 (76)
Douglas fir, coast	¾ (19)	195 (88)	244 (111)	293 (133)	113 (51)	141 (64)	169 (77)	71 (32)	89 (40)	107 (48)
White oak	¾ (19)	178 (81)	223 (101)	267 (121)	103 (47)	129 (59)	155 (70)	65 (29)	81 (37)	97 (44)
Red oak, black cherry	¾ (19)	149 (68)	186 (84)	224 (102)	86 (39)	108 (49)	129 (59)	54 (24)	68 (31)	81 (37)
Walnut	¾ (19)	168 (76)	210 (95)	252 (114)	97 (44)	122 (55)	146 (66)	61 (28)	77 (35)	92 (42)

For calculating total loads, books weigh about 65 lb/ft³ and paper weighs about 58 lb/ft³.
Note: These values are approximate. Actual allowable loads depend on quality of materials and craftwork.

can be fit within the doors, elevators, and other openings of a completed building. Additional coordination items include the following:

• Wood blocking should be shown within metal stud partitions to provide a solid method of attaching wall-hung woodwork.

• Unless the method for providing for adjustable shelves is specifically shown on the drawings, the woodworker has the option of either using multiple holes with plastic or metal pins to support the shelves, or metal or plastic shelf standards.

• Full extension drawer slides must be specified or shown on the drawings if they are required.

• When under-cabinet lighting is provided, the exact height of the electrical conduit that connects to the fixture must be located so that it can be stubbed out accurately by the electrical contractor prior to wall finishing.

Figure 6.15
Standard cabinet dimensions

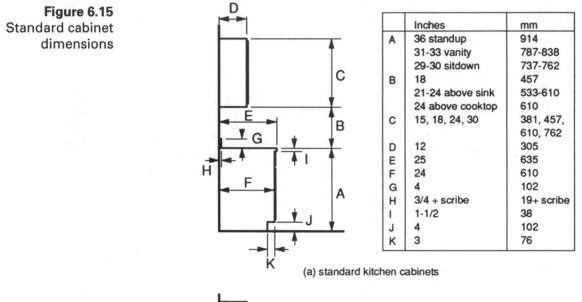

	Inches	mm
A	36 standup	914
	31-33 vanity	787-838
	29-30 sitdown	737-762
B	18	457
	21-24 above sink	533-610
	24 above cooktop	610
C	15, 18, 24, 30	381, 457, 610, 762
D	12	305
E	25	635
F	24	610
G	4	102
H	3/4 + scribe	19+ scribe
I	1-1/2	38
J	4	102
K	3	76

(a) standard kitchen cabinets

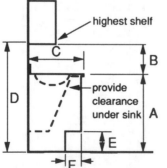

	Inches	mm
A	34 max. at sink	864
	29-31 at work	737-787
B	Varies	Varies
C	24 max.	610 max.
D	48 max.	1219 max.
E	9 max.	229 min.
F	7	178

(b) accessible kitchen cabinets

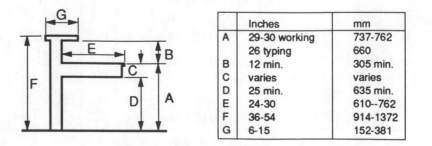

	Inches	mm
A	29-30 working	737-762
	26 typing	660
B	12 min.	305 min.
C	varies	varies
D	25 min.	635 min.
E	24-30	610--762
F	36-54	914-1372
G	6-15	152-381

(c) reception, work counter

• Scribe pieces should be provided where the cabinet touches a wall to allow for out-of-plumb or out-of-line partitions.

PANELING [06420]

Panel types

Millwork paneling includes wood-clad and laminate-clad flush paneling and stile and rail paneling. Flush paneling is built up of thin wood veneers or laminate glued to backing panels of particleboard or plywood. Raised panel construction is the more traditional type, with separate panels built within borders of solid wood rails. Flush paneling has a single, smooth surface with very little trim. Other types of paneling include fabric-covered acoustical panels, grilles, and panels covered with metal or other materials.

Typical panel construction

Flush panel construction

Flush panels are built in the mill shop in large sections and installed by hanging them to the walls with wood cleats or metal Z-clips, as shown in Figures 6.16(a)–6.16(b). In some cases the panels can be directly screwed to the wall, but the fasteners must be covered with additional trim or other decorative elements. In AWI Premium grade, veneer is applied to ¾-in. (19 mm) backing panels; in Custom grade, it is applied to ⁷⁄₁₆-in. (11 mm) panels.

The edges of each panel can be tightly butted together to give a continuous appearance or can be treated in a number of other ways, one of which is shown in Figure 6.17(b). Likewise, inside and outside corners can be tightly joined or treated like field joints. See Figures 6.17(c)–6.17(f). Whichever method is used, there should be some provision for the panels to move with changes in temperature and humidity. If a tight joint is used, as shown in Figure 6.17(a), the edges of the veneer should be beveled slightly. If the panel shrinks or moves slightly, the V-joint makes the resulting crack less noticeable. In humid climates, a slight gap may be required to allow the panel to expand.

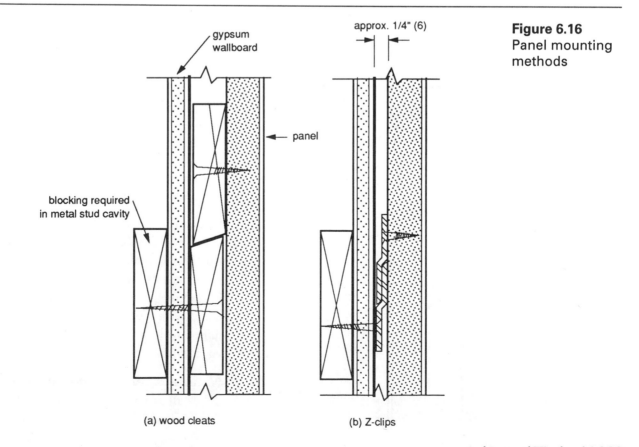

(a) wood cleats (b) Z-clips

Figure 6.16
Panel mounting methods

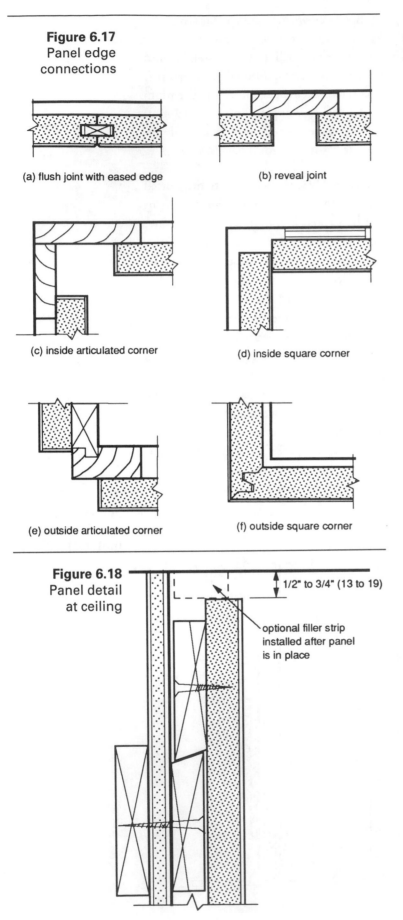

Figure 6.17
Panel edge
connections

(a) flush joint with eased edge

(b) reveal joint

(c) inside articulated corner

(d) inside square corner

(e) outside articulated corner

(f) outside square corner

Figure 6.18
Panel detail
at ceiling

1/2" to 3/4" (13 to 19)

optional filler strip
installed after panel
is in place

If panels are hung with wood cleats or Z-clips, there must be sufficient space near the ceiling for the panel to be lifted up and over the cleat or Z-clip and then lowered into place. This is usually a minimum of ¾ in. (19 mm), but the exact dimension depends on the type of mounting clip used. The resulting gap may be left as a reveal or may be filled. It can also be covered with additional wood trim, as shown in Figure 6.18.

The panel may extend to the floor or be held short of the floor so that a separate base can be installed. Several methods of doing this are illustrated in Figures 6.19(a)–6.19(c).

Stile and rail construction

Stile and rail panel construction consists of a frame of solid wood that contains individual panels. Along with various types of molding and matching doors, raised panel construction is used to detail traditional wood-paneled room interiors. See Figure 6.20. Traditionally, the panels were also made from solid wood, but today it is more common for the panels to be veneered.

As shown in Figure 6.21, the vertical frame pieces are called *stiles* and the horizontal members *rails*. The panels are held in place with grooves cut in the sides of the frames or with individual molding pieces, called *sticking*. Some of the various types of panels and methods of holding them in place are shown in Figures 6.22(a)–6.22(c). Whichever method is used, there must be sufficient room allowed for expansion and contraction with changes in the moisture content.

Stile and rail paneling may be hung on walls with wood cleats or metal Z-clips like flush paneling. If extensive molding is used, the panels can be screwed to wood blocking behind the paneling and the fasteners concealed with molding. Individual panels are joined with dowels or splines to keep the edges flush.

Matching wood veneer panels

When flush panels are finished with uniform materials such as plastic laminate, a single-color or fabric, matching adjacent panels is not a problem. However, when the flush panels are wood veneer, their matching is critical to the final appearance of the job. The methods of slicing a log to obtain veneers has been discussed in a previous section. How those individual pieces of veneer are placed on a panel and how the panels are placed within a room are discussed in this section. The three considerations, in increasing order of scale, are matching between adjacent veneer leaves, matching veneers within a panel, and matching panels within a room.

Matching veneer leaves

Matching adjacent veneer leaves may be done in three ways, as shown in Figures 6.23(a)–6.23(c). *Book matching* is the most common. As the veneers are sliced off the log, every other piece is turned over so that adjacent leaves form a symmetrical grain pattern. In *slip matching*, consecutive pieces are placed side by side with the same face sides being exposed. *Random matching* places veneers in random sequence, and even veneers from different flitches may be used.

Veneer leaves may be book-matched end to end as well as side to side if the length of the flitch is not long enough to cover the wall in a single piece. For rooms with high ceilings, the maximum length of flitch in the specified species should be determined so that the end conditions can be detailed accordingly.

Because book matching requires that every other leaf of veneer be turned over, the veneers may reflect light differently or accept stain and finishing differently depending on the species and flitch. The resulting color variations between veneers can be minimized by proper finishing techniques.

Matching veneers within a panel

Veneers must be glued to rigid panels (usually ¾-in. (19 mm) particleboard) to make installation possible. If the veneers are random-matched, they are laid up in any sequence in any width. If the veneers are slip-matched, they are laid on the panels in whatever width they are as they are sliced off the log.

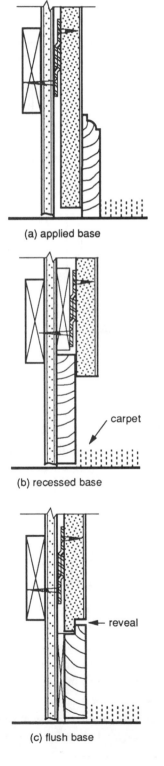

Figure 6.19
Panel details
at base

(a) applied base

carpet

(b) recessed base

reveal

(c) flush base

**Figure 6.20
Stile and
rail panel
construction**

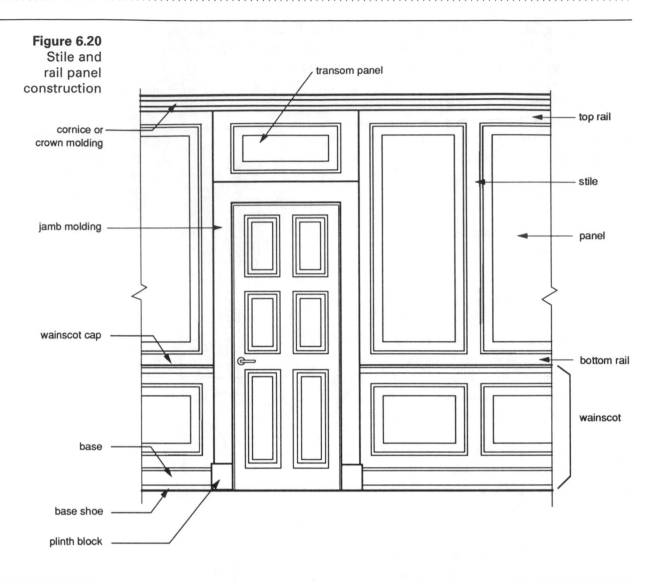

transom panel

cornice or
crown molding

top rail

stile

jamb molding

panel

wainscot cap

bottom rail

wainscot

base

base shoe

plinth block

Curved paneling

Both flush paneling and stile and rail paneling can be fabricated for inside or outside curves. Several methods may be used to produce flush paneling. One method uses several thin layers of bendable plywood, which are laid against a curved form. The veneer is then applied to the backing. Another method uses several solid pieces of lumber, with edges beveled to form the desired curve, glued together. The finish face is sanded smooth and finished. A third method uses kerfing, which is a series of sawcuts in the back of the panel made perpendicular to the direction of the bend. Because the lines of the sawcut can telegraph through to the finished surface, this method is the least desirable.

Curved molding can also be produced in a number of ways. Solid pieces of wood can be cut with a band saw to the required radius out of a large piece of flat, solid stock. The pieces are then shaped to the desired profile. A second method uses several thin plies of material laminated to one other as they are formed into the required shape. A third method uses common lumber formed into the required shape and then covered with veneers of the finish wood. The method used is selected by the architectural woodworker based on the type of profile involved, the radius of the curve, and the particular fabricating methods the woodworker prefers to use.

Figure 6.21
Stile and rail
components

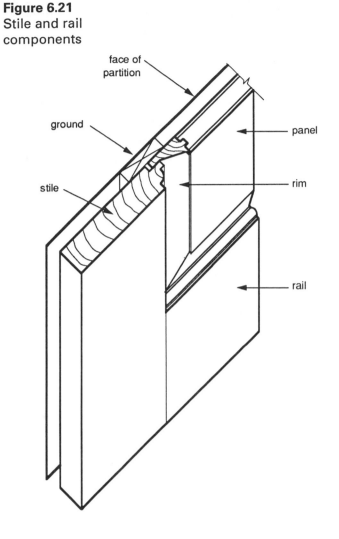

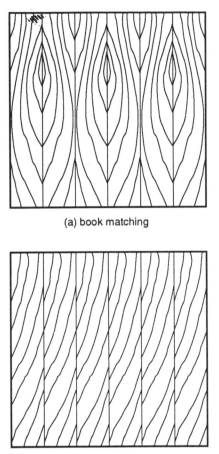

(a) book matching

(b) slip matching

Figure 6.22
Panel details

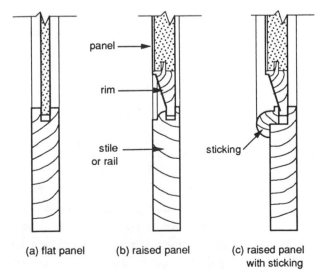

(a) flat panel   (b) raised panel   (c) raised panel
with sticking

(c) random matching

Figure 6.24
Matching
veneers within
a panel

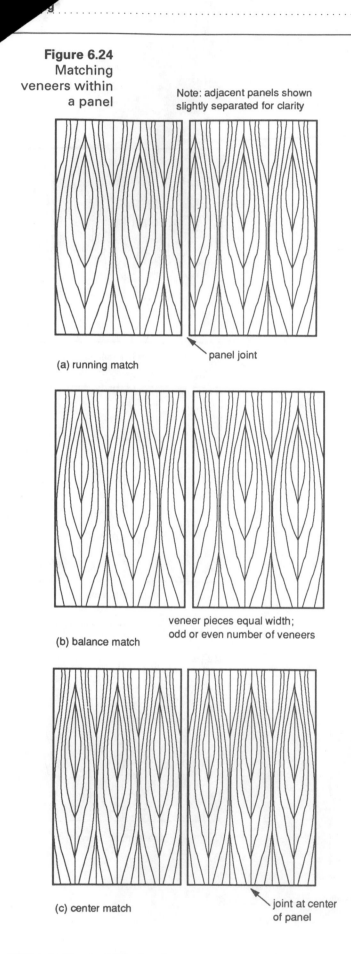

Note: adjacent panels shown
slightly separated for clarity

(a) running match

panel joint

veneer pieces equal width;
odd or even number of veneers

(b) balance match

(c) center match

joint at center
of panel

If the veneers are book-matched, there are three ways of matching veneers within a panel, as shown in Figures 6.24(a)–6.24(c). A *running match* alternates book-matched veneer pieces regardless of their width or how many must be used to complete a panel. Any portion left over from the last leaf of one panel is used as the starting piece for the next. *Balance matching* uses veneer pieces trimmed to equal widths in each panel. There may be an even or odd number of individual leaves on each panel. In *center matching* there are an even number of veneer leaves of uniform width so that there is a veneer joint in the center of the panel. Center matching is the most expensive of the three methods. Balance matching is the most common type specified and produces the most pleasing assembly of veneers.

Matching panels within a room

There are also three ways that panels can be assembled within a room to complete a project. Figures 6.25(a)–6.25(c) show these three methods by illustrating three sides of a room as though they were unfolded and the three walls laid flat.

The first and least expensive method of panel matching is called *warehouse matching*. Premanufactured panels, typically 4 ft wide by 8ft or 10 ft long (1219 mm by 2438 or 3048 mm), are assembled from a single flitch that yields from six to twelve panels. They are field cut to fit around doors, windows, and other obstructions, resulting in some loss of grain continuity. If more than one set is required, matching the grain patterns between the two sets is not possible. Doors and cabinets cannot be matched with the paneling.

The second method, called *sequence matching*, uses panels of uniform width manufactured for a specific job and with the veneers arranged in sequence. If some panels must be trimmed to fit around doors and other obstructions, there is a moderate loss of grain continuity. Doors and cabinets cannot be matched with the paneling.

Figure 6.25
Matching panels
within a room

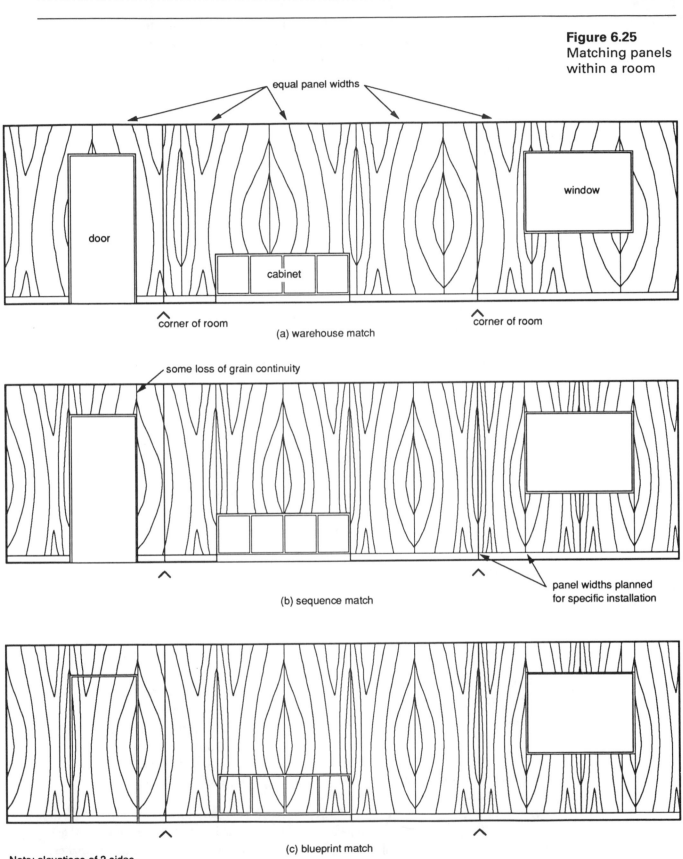

equal panel widths

door

cabinet

window

corner of room   corner of room

(a) warehouse match

some loss of grain continuity

(b) sequence match

panel widths planned
for specific installation

(c) blueprint match

Note: elevations of 3 sides
of room shown "unfolded"

The third and most expensive method is *blueprint matching*. Here, the panels are manufactured to fit the room precisely and to line up with every obstruction so that grain continuity is uninterrupted. Veneers from the same flitch are matched over doors, cabinets, and other veneer-covered items.

Coordination

As with cabinetwork, adequate provisions must be made in panel detailing for blocking, shim space, and scribe pieces, where the paneling is adjacent to other construction. Additional coordination items include the following:

• Wood blocking inside of partitions must be shown on the drawings for installation by other trades. If local construction practices require that surface backing be installed by trades other than the woodworker, the type and location of these should be verified with the woodworker and shown on the drawings.

• The location of all mechanical and electrical fixtures must be shown on the drawings so that the woodworker can make the necessary cutouts.

• Fire-retardant ratings of the finished paneling and wood blocking must be determined based on local codes and specifications. Refer to the section on fire ratings of architectural woodwork for more information.

LAMINATES [06240]

High-pressure decorative laminates

A common finishing material used with architectural woodwork is *high-pressure decorative laminate* (HPDL). This is a thin sheet material made by impregnating several layers of kraft paper with phenolic resins and overlaying the paper with a decorative melamine sheet and an alphacellulose overlay. The entire assembly is placed in a hot press under pressures as high as 1000 lb/in.^{2} (6895 kPa), or more where the various layers fuse together. Plastic laminates are used as finish surfaces for countertops, wall paneling, cabinets, doors, shelving, flooring, signs, and furniture.

Because laminates are very thin, they must be adhered to panel substrates, such as plywood or particleboard. However, special, thick laminates are available up to 1 in. (25 mm) in thickness. Smaller pieces can be glued to solid pieces of lumber.

There are several types of substrates used for plastic laminate construction. These include particleboard, medium density fiberboard (MDF), hardboard, and veneer core. Among these, 45 lb density particleboard is one of the most commonly used. It is the most dimensionally stable, provides a smooth surface for laminating, has sufficient impact resistance, and provides enough strength for holding screws and for constructing panels and casework. In recent years, there has been some concern about the outgassing of formaldehyde from particleboard. With today's particleboard manufacturing techniques, the release of formaldehyde is negligible (0.3 parts per million or less). The laminate also provides a seal on the board, preventing most long-term emissions.

Medium density fiberboard (MDF) is also a popular substrate for plastic laminate. MDF is made by breaking down wood fibers into very fine fluff no more than ⅛ in. (3 mm) long and then mixing it with glue and compressing it under high pressure. It is normally formed into 4 ft × 8 ft (1219 mm × 2438 mm) sheets from ¼ in. to 1¼ in. (6 mm to 32 mm) thick. It can also be formed into molding from 16 ft to 24 ft (4877 mm to 7315 mm) long. Its density is from 44 lb to 50 lb (708 kg/m^3 to 800 kg/m^3) per cubic foot.

MDF has a smoother surface than particleboard, which reduces the potential for telegraphing through the laminate and makes it suitable for gloss laminates. However, it is more expensive than particleboard and does not hold some types of screws as well.

In addition to being used as a substrate for laminates, MDF can be used for shelving, molding, and furniture, and as part of laminate flooring. Its dense, smooth composition allows routing and a flawless paint finish. It is dimensionally stable so it does not warp, crack, or cup. Untreated MDF has the same fire rating as plywood, but special fire-resistant MDF is available. As with particleboard, MDF made with urea-based resins does emit formaldehyde (about 0.3 parts per million), but formaldehyde-free MDF with adhesives similar to those in polyurethane glues is available.

The last two substrates that can be used for plastic laminate, hardboard, and veneer core are not as widely used as particleboard and medium density fiberboard. Like particleboard, hardboard has a smooth surface, but that can sometimes cause bonding problems. Veneer core is subject to warpage and other problems; therefore, its use is not recommended for interior applications.

Plastic laminate is available in a wide variety of finishes. The most common is the matte, or suede finish. It has a low light reflectance, is durable, and cleans easily. Another type is the mirror, or glossy, finish. This has a very high gloss finish but should only be used for vertical applications where the potential for scratching is low. Other finishes include satin, embossed, and pebbly. Individual manufacturers should be consulted for the availability of colors and finishes.

There are several types and thicknesses of plastic laminate. The five most common are listed below.

• General Purpose (GP50). This laminate is 0.050 in. (1.27 mm) thick and is used for most horizontal applications.

• General purpose for vertical use (GP28). This is a thinner material manufactured for vertical applications that receive less wear and impact than horizontal surfaces. It is 0.028 in. (0.71 mm) thick.

• Postforming (PF30, PF42). Although thin, general-purpose laminates can be bent to moderate radii (6 to 8 in.), a special postforming grade is required for tighter bends. Postforming grades of plastic laminate are heated in the shop, bent to the required form, and allowed to cool. Once this cooling takes place the laminate is set. PF30 laminate can be bent to an outside radius of ½ in. (13 mm); PF42 can be bent to an outside radius of ⅝ in. (16 mm). Inside radii of ³⁄₁₆ in. (5 mm) can also be formed.

• Cabinet liner (CL20). This laminate is 0.020 in. (0.51 mm) thick and is intended for use where a decorative finish is required, but where the surface receives little wear, such as the vertical surfaces of cabinet and bookshelf interiors.

• Backing sheet (BK20). Whenever one side of a panel is faced with plastic laminate, a backing sheet must be placed in the opposite side to prevent warping and protect against dimensional instability. Backing sheets are thin, nondecorative laminates used for this purpose.

Specialty laminates

There are several types of high-pressure decorative laminates manufactured for specific purposes. Although these generally cost more, they fill specific needs for interior construction.

• Colorthrough laminates. These laminates are manufactured with decorative papers throughout the thickness so that the resulting sheet is a solid color. This eliminates the dark line visible at the edge of sheets when they are trimmed. Colorthrough laminates are available in thickness of 0.050 in. to 0.060 in. (1.27 to 1.52 mm) and in postformed grades.

• Fire-rated laminates. These finishes comply with Class 1 or Class A ratings as long as the appropriate substrates and adhesives are selected. The performance characteristics are the same as for standard laminates, but they cannot be postformed.

• Chemical-resistant laminates. Special formulation of the laminate materials give these products additional resistance to strong chemicals found in laboratories, medical facilities, and photographic studios. They are available in horizontal as well as vertical thicknesses and can be postformed for curved surfaces.

• Static-dissipative laminates. For areas where static control is required, such as in hospital operating rooms, electronic manufacturing plants, and computer rooms, these laminates provide a conductive layer within the sheet. When connected to suitable grounding, they prevent the buildup of static charges and continuously channel them away.

• Thick laminates. Heavier, high-wear laminates are available where extra strength and impact resistance are required. Standard types include high-wear in thicknesses of 0.062 in., 0.080 in., and 0.120 in. (1.58, 2.03, and 3.05 mm) (HW62, HW80, and HW120). SP125 is a specific-purpose grade with a thickness of 0.125 in. (3.18 mm).

• Dimensional laminates. Dimensional laminates have deeply embossed finishes simulating textures, such as slate, woven fabrics, and leather. Because of the differences in high and low areas, they are a little more difficult to clean on horizontal surfaces and the high points show wear more rapidly than the low points.

• Metal-faced laminates. A limited number of metal finishes are available. They do not have the same wear resistance as real metal; therefore, they should only be used on vertical surfaces subject to little abuse. They can be fabricated with standard woodworking equipment and cost much less than real metal. However, it is difficult to fabricate small, detailed items with finely crafted edges.

• Natural wood laminates. Thin veneers of actual wood are bonded to the standard type of laminate kraft papers and resins with this product. The laminate can be specified to provide untreated wood ready for finishing or with a protective layer of melamine resin.

• Flooring laminates. These are used for access flooring in computer rooms and other areas where individual panels of a raised flooring system are required. In most cases, the available colors and patterns are limited and are part of the access flooring manufacturer's standard product line although custom orders are available.

• Tambours. Laminate-clad tambours are available from several manufacturers in colors and patterns that match other laminate sheets. Flat-sheet tambours, rounded surfaces, and other types are available.

• Engraving stock. For fabricating signs and nameplates a special engraving stock is available with black, white, or red cores in a variety of surface colors and patterns.

For large orders and additional cost, custom patterns and colors can be specified as well as custom silk-screening of logos and other graphic designs.

Thermoset decorative panels

Another type of laminate product is made by pressing a decorative overlay from a thermoset polyester or melamine, resin-impregnated, saturated sheet onto a cellulosic substrate, such as particleboard or medium-density fiberboard. They differ from high-pressure decorative laminates in that the decorative surface is fused to the substrate of particleboard, rather than being a thin veneer that must be adhesive bonded to another substrate. Because the process is usually done with pressures lower than HPDLs, these products are sometimes called "low-pressure laminates," or melamine. The manufacturers that produce thermoset decorative panels form the American Laminators Association (ALA) and use the trade name Permalam® to identify these types of panels. The standard developed by the ALA requires that thermoset panels meet or, in some cases, exceed the minimum performance standards of HPDLs.

Because the decorative surface is part of the substrate, the potential problem of delamination is eliminated and the panels come ready to be fabricated. Generally, the cost of thermoset panels is less than HPDLs in many cases. However, there are currently several disadvantages to thermoset decorative panels: they come in a limited range of colors, textures, and grades. They cannot be postformed for curves; and they should not be used for high-wear horizontal surfaces, such as countertops. In addition, only a limited number of Class I or Class A fire-rated panels are available from a few manufacturers. Thermoset panels are typically used for furniture, fixtures, and kitchen cabinets, or where resistance to heavy use is not required.

Panels are available in thickness of ¼, ⅜, ½, ⅝, ¾, 1, and 1⅛ in. (6, 10, 13, 16, 19, 25, and 29 mm) in panel sizes from 4 ft to 5 ft wide (1219 to 1524 mm) and 6 ft to 18 ft long (1829 to 5486 mm).

Detailing considerations

High-pressure decorative laminate is a very flexible material; an unlimited variety of built-in and free-standing construction can be designed. However, there are a few limitations to remember when detailing.

For panel applications, such as wall panels and cabinet fronts and sides, a balance sheet must be applied to the face opposite the finish face to prevent the panel from warping. Also, because the substrate is a wood product, panels will expand and contract with changes in temperature and humidity. There should be allowances from ¹⁄₆₄ in. to ³⁄₆₄ in. (0.397 to 1.191 mm) between adjacent large panels to provide for dimensional changes. Wall panels are mounted to partitions in the same way as wood veneer panels, with wood cleats or Z-clips as shown in Figure 6.16. As with wood panels, it is advisable to provide for slight misalignment between adjacent panels and to allow for dimensional changes. One way to do this is with a slight reveal joint, as shown in Figure 6.26. Outside and inside corners can be detailed for a precise intersection as shown in Figures 6.27(a) and 6.27(b).

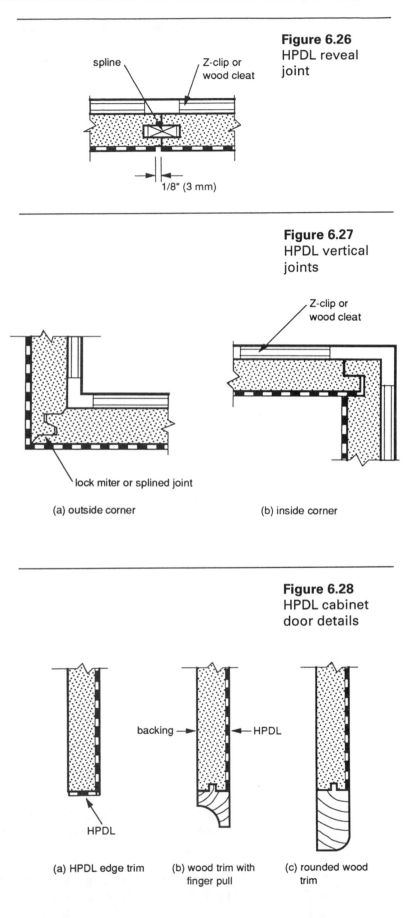

Figure 6.26
HPDL reveal joint

spline
Z-clip or wood cleat
1/8" (3 mm)

Figure 6.27
HPDL vertical joints

Z-clip or wood cleat
lock miter or splined joint
(a) outside corner
(b) inside corner

Figure 6.28
HPDL cabinet door details

backing
HPDL
HPDL
(a) HPDL edge trim
(b) wood trim with finger pull
(c) rounded wood trim

Door and drawer fronts can be detailed with the faces and edges of HPDL, or two or more materials can be combined. Figures 6.28(a)–6.28(c) show some common methods of detailing cabinet door fronts.

Countertop edges are common in all types of construction. A variety of details is possible with HPDL; some samples of detailing are illustrated in Figures 6.29(a)–6.29(d).

Figure 6.29
HPDL edge treatments

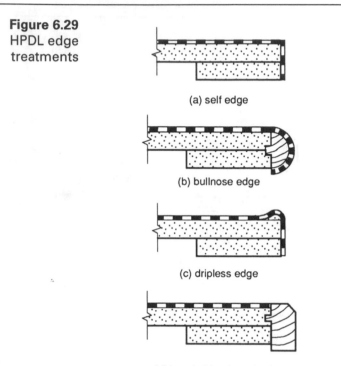

(a) self edge

(b) bullnose edge

(c) dripless edge

(d) beveled hardwood edge

STANDING AND RUNNING TRIM [06450]

Standing and running trim are items similar to standard molding sections applied as finish carpentry items. Unlike moldings, however, standing and running trim are custom fabricated to meet the requirements of a specific project.

Standing trim is woodwork of fixed length intended to be installed as a single piece of wood. Examples include door frame trim, door stops, window casing, and similar items. *Running trim* is woodwork of continuing length that must be installed in several pieces fitted end to end, such as base molding, cornices, chair rails, and soffits. *Rails* are gripping or protection surfaces on corridor walls of hospitals and the like and guard rails at glass openings.

The *profile* of trim, or its cross-sectional shape, can be identical to the many standard shapes available in premanufactured molding, or custom profiles can be milled. To create custom profiles, the mill shop makes a cutting blade with the desired profile, puts it on the molding machine, and runs solid stock through. If the profile is large or complex, more than one piece of molding may have to be run and then assembled to obtain the final trim.

Applicable standards for laminates

American National Standards Institute (ANSI):

ANSI A161.2	*Performance Standards for Fabricated High Pressure Decorative Laminate Countertops*
ANSI 208.1	*Particleboard, Mat-Formed Wood*
ANSI 208.2	*Medium Density Fiberboard for Interior Use*

Architectural Woodwork Institute (AWI):

AWI *Quality Standards*, Sections 400B, 500B, and portions of 1300

American Laminators Association (ALA):

ALA 1992	*The Performance Standard for Thermoset Decorative Panels*

American Society for Testing and Materials (ASTM):

ASTME D-1037	*Standard Methods of Evaluating the Properties of Wood Base Fiber and Particle Panel Materials*

National Electrical Manufacturers Association (NEMA):

LD 3-1995	*High Pressure Decorative Laminates*

When the size of hardwood handrails exceeds 1¹⁄₁₆ × 6½ in. (27 × 165 mm), the woodworking shop may glue for width or thickness to achieve the required size.

Differences between grades of standing and running trim

Standing and running trim can be specified in any of the three AWI grades, but only Premium or Custom should be used for most quality woodwork. Premium grade provides a smoother finish for both transparent and opaque finishes. The differences between these two grades are summarized in Table 6.10.

FIRE RATINGS OF ARCHITECTURAL WOODWORK

Although specific building code requirements for woodwork use vary slightly across the United States and in Canada, there are many similarities. Refer to Chapter 17 for information on model building codes and a more complete discussion of occupancy and use areas.

In general, most of the model building codes regulate the use of woodwork as wall or ceiling finish, but do not regulate the use of wood in furniture, cabinets, or trim. This includes cabinets attached to the structure.

Interior finish is defined in the *Uniform Building Code* (and similarly in other model codes) as wall and ceiling finish, including wainscoting, paneling, or other finish applied structurally or for decoration, acoustical correction, surface insulation, or similar purposes. Requirements do not apply to trim, defined as picture molds, chair rails, baseboards, and handrails; to doors and windows or their frames; nor to materials that are less than ¹⁄₂₈ in. (0.91 mm) thick cemented to the surface of walls or ceilings.

Item	Premium grade	Custom grade
Material for transparent finish	Grade I	Grade II
Material for opaque finish	Grade I	Grade II
Smoothness of exposed surfaces		
Transparent and opaque finshes on flat surfaces	150 grit sandpaper	120 grit sandpaper
Transparent and opaque finishes on molded surfaces	120 grit sandpaper	20 knife cuts per inch
Transparent and opaque finishes on shaped surfaces	120 grit sandpaper	20 knife cuts per inch
Transparent and opaque finishes on turned surfaces	120 grit sandpaper	100 grit sandpaper
Flushness variation of factory joints	0.015 in. (0.38 mm)	0.025 in. (0.64 mm)
Sanding cross scratches	None allowed for transparent finishes; not to exceed 0.25 in. (6 mm) for opaque surfaces	None allowed for transparent finishes; not to exceed 0.25 in. (6 mm) for opaque surfaces

Table 6.10
Differences between premium and custom grades for standing and running trim

Based on information from *Architectural Woodwork Quality Standards, Sixth Edition, Version 1.0,* copyright 1993, The Architectural Woodwork Institute, used with permission.

The model building codes regulate the use of woodwork as a finish material by first establishing different use areas in a building depending on their importance in relationship to the means of egress from the building. The three use areas include exits, corridors, and other spaces. Exits are protected escape routes and must have the lowest flame-spread classification for interior finishes. Exits are generally enclosed stairs and passageways connecting stairs to the exterior. Corridors are those areas connecting rooms and other occupied areas with the building exits. Other spaces consist of all the remaining areas in a building.

The codes also divide buildings into categories, depending on their occupancy. While specific terms vary slightly from one code to the next, the general occupancy classifications include assembly, educational, mercantile, business, institutional, and residential.

For each use area in each occupancy group, the codes then limit the flammability of finish materials. For example, an exit stairway in a nursing home is inherently a more critical area than a living room of a single family house, so its finishes must be less flammable.

Finish materials are placed in one of three classes depending on their flame-spread ratings. Flame-spread ratings indicate the flammability of a finish and are determined by subjecting the finish to a standardized laboratory test. Flame-spread ratings from 0 to 25 are considered Class I ratings (or Class A in certain codes); ratings from 26 to 75 are Class II ratings (or Class B); and ratings from 76 to 200 are Class III ratings (or Class C). Refer to Chapter 17 for more information.

All of the model building codes have tables that indicate what flame-spread classification must be met, depending on the use area and occupancy group. Exits are always the most restrictive and require Class I (or Class A) finishes. Corridors generally require Class II finishes, and other areas typically require Class III finishes. However, assembly and institutional occupancies have stricter requirements and the applicable code should be referenced to determine the exact requirements.

The model codes sometimes allow an increase of one category in the flame-spread classification of interior finishes when automatic sprinklers are installed throughout the building. For example, a corridor that requires a Class II finish in a nonsprinkler-fitted building may be allowed a Class III finish in a sprinkler-fitted building.

Most wood species without flame-retardant treatment have flame-spread ratings less than 200, and some even have ratings less than 75. This makes them appropriate for "other use" areas and some corridors without any special consideration.

The model codes do not regulate the use of wood for free-standing furniture or for cabinets and shelves attached to the building because they are not considered fixed construction. Trim is also not regulated under the Uniform Building Code and the Standard Building Code. The Building Officials Code Administrators (BOCA) National Building Code and the Life Safety Code define trim as finish that does not exceed 10 percent of the total aggregate area of the ceiling and walls of the room in which it is used. The BOCA National Building Code and the Life Safety Code allow a maximum flame-spread rating of 200 for trim in any application. Trim is not regulated in the National Building Code of Canada (NBCC) if it has a flame-spread rating less than 150 and its area does not exceed 10 percent of the area of the wall or ceiling on which it occurs.

The strictest regulation on the use of woodwork as an interior finish occurs when paneling is used on walls and ceilings. The paneling must meet the maximum flame-spread regulations of the code in force, based on occupancy and use area. However, because the codes generally do not regulate finishes less than ⅟₂₈ in. (0.91 mm) thick, veneer less than this thickness with any flame-spread rating may be used if it is placed on fire-retardant-treated material, such as particleboard.

When high-pressure decorative laminate (HPDL) is used on paneling, it is not subject to regulation if it is less than ⅟₂₈ in. (0.91 mm) thick. However, it should be applied to a substrate (usually particleboard) that is fire-retardant treated. Laminate for vertical use (GP28) is 0.028 in. (0.71 mm) thick and, therefore, does not have to be treated. When thicker laminate is used and the flame- spread rating is critical, fire-rated laminate can be used on a fire-retardant treated substrate with the appropriate adhesive.

Blocking on the outside of the partition on which paneling is applied should also be fire-retardant-treated. In addition, some codes may require that blocking within the partition also be fire-retardant treated.

SPECIAL WOODWORK ITEMS

Cabinets, shelving, paneling, and standing and running trim are some of the most common types of architectural woodwork; however, there are many other finish items that a mill shop can produce. These include custom doors and frames, upholstered wall systems, solid surfacing materials, stairwork, handrails, screens, shutters, and free-standing furniture.

Doors

When a desired type, size, or finish of door is not available as a standard or custom order from a door manufacturer, an architectural woodworking shop can custom fabricate nearly any type of door. These include flush doors as well as stile and rail doors. Usually, a custom door is required when an exotic species of wood is specified for the surface, when the door is part of a blueprint matching of interior paneling, or when additional materials are applied to the door. Custom-designed stile and rail doors, curved doors, blind doors, and oversized doors are also common items that require specialty work.

As with other custom woodwork items, doors are specified in any of the three AWI grades of Premium, Custom, or Economy. For wood veneer doors manufactured for a transparent finish, Premium grade requires that the vertical edges of the door be the same species as the face veneer and that the veneers for pairs of doors and doors with transoms be matched. These are not requirements for Custom grade doors. Refer to the AWI *Quality Standards* for other construction details based on these three grades.

For flush doors, various core and face constructions are available, but they are designated differently than stock doors using the NWWDA I.S. 1 standards described in Chapter 3. A summary of these is shown in Table 6.11, and diagrams of common door constructions are shown in Figure 3.6.

Upholstered wall systems [09520]

There are several ways to cover walls with a fabric finish. Several of these, including those using proprietary track systems, are discussed in Chapter 10. Direct application of fabric and installation of proprietary systems are performed by separate contractors. However, when acoustic fabric-wrapped panels are detailed and specified, they are often fabricated and installed by the woodwork contractor.

Figure 6.30 illustrates one method of detailing a fabric-wrapped panel (showing two possible edge conditions) for fabrication by a woodwork contractor. The panel is hung on the wall using Z-clips or wood cleats like other finish panels. The panel is made from plywood or particleboard framed on all four sides with continuous wood blocking. The edges of the frame can be milled to any

AWI symbol	Description
PC-5 ME	Particleboard core with crossband and face veneer on each side. Stiles and rails bonded to core. Vertical edge species matches face veneer species.
PC-5 CE	Particleboard core with crossband and face veneer on each side. Stiles and rails bonded to core. Vertical edge species compatible with face veneer species.
PC-7 ME	Particleboard core with two crossbands and face veneer on each side. Stiles and rails bonded to core. Vertical edge species matches face veneer species.
PC-7 CE	Particleboard core with two crossbands and face veneer on each side. Stiles and rails bonded to core. Vertical edge species compatible face veneer species.
PC-HPDL-3	Particleboard core with nominal 0.050-in. (1.27 mm) high-pressure decorative laminate each side. Stiles and rails bonded to core.
PC-HPDL-5	Nominal 0.050-in. (1.27 mm) high-pressure decorative laminate each side glued to hardwood crossbands on particleboard core assembly. Stiles and rails bonded to core.
SLC-5 ME	Staved lumber core with crossband and face veneer on each side. Stiles and rails bonded to core. Vertical edge species matches face veneer species.
SLC-5 CE	Staved lumber core with crossband and face veneer on each side. Stiles and rails bonded to core. Vertical edge species compatible with face veneer species.
SCL -7 ME and SCL-7 CE	Same as SLC-5, but with seven-ply construction.
SLC-HPDL-5	Nominal 0.050-in. (1.27 mm) high-pressure decorative laminate each side glued to hardwood crossbands on particleboard core assembly. Stiles and rails bonded to core.
	Note: particleboard core and lumber core doors also available where the stiles and rails are NOT bonded to the core. Refer to AWI standards for a complete description.
FD 1½	1½-hour-rated and labeled fire door with either wood veneer or high-pressure decorative laminate face.
FD 1	1-hour-rated and labeled fire door with either wood veneer or high-pressure decorative laminate face.
FD ¾	¾-hour-rated and labeled fire door with either wood veneer or high-pressure decorative laminate face.
FD ⅓	⅓-hour-rated and labeled fire door with either wood veneer or high-pressure decorative laminate face.
SR	Sound retardant door manufactured to conform to STC ratings prescribed in ASTM E-90. Available in thicknesses of 1¾ in., 2¼ in., 2½ in., and thicker as required (44.4, 57.1, and 63.5 mm).
LL	Lead-lined doors. Thickness of lead must be specified based on shielding rating required. May have either wood veneer or HPDL veneer and lead-lined vision panel.
ES	Electrostatic shielded door. Wire mesh embedded in center of core or between crossbanding and core. Mesh is grounded with braided wire pigtails through hinges. Number of pigtails must be specified.
IHC	Institutional hollow core. Stiles and rails wider than standard hollow core door.
SHC	Standard hollow core. Most economical door.

Based on information from *Architectural Woodwork Quality Standards, Sixth Edition, Version 1.0,* copyright 1993, The Architectural Woodwork Institute, used with permission.

desired profile. The frame should be tapered slightly toward the interior of the panel to avoid having the concealed edge telegraph through the fabric. The interior of the panel is filled with fiberglass panels or fabric batting to act as the sound-absorbent material. If a hanging strip is required for artwork or other wall-suspended material, its size and location should be indicated on the drawings. Similar edge details can be used to create blind doors within the field of the partition.

It is usually best to limit woodworker-fabricated panels to simple shapes that can be covered with a single width of fabric. For walls with curves, angles, cutouts, and complex forms, and where continuous fabric is used, it is usually best to use one of the proprietary systems described in Chapter 10.

Solid surfacing materials [06650]

Solid surfacing is a generic term for homogeneous, polymer-based surfacing materials. It is a combination of two ingredients—a filler, usually alumina trihydrate (ATH), and a clear resin binder, either acrylic or polyester—or a mixture of the two. Various colors and speckles can be added with pigments and small bits of the product itself. It can be formed into flat sheets or into shapes such as kitchen sinks. Solid surfacing is most commonly used for kitchen and bath countertops, sinks, shower enclosures, toilet partitions, bars, and other areas where high-pressure plastic laminate might be used. However, it can also be used for furniture, flooring, and various consumer products.

Sheet goods used for countertops are normally ¾ in. (19 mm) thick but newer, lower-priced products are ½ in. (12 mm) thick. There is even a ⅛-in. (3 mm) thick product that is applied as a veneer; ¹⁄₁₆-in. (2 mm) spray-on surfacing is also available. However, most fabricators still prefer to use the ¾-in. material.

Because the color is integrated throughout the thickness of the material, scratches, dents,

stains, and other types of minor damage can be sanded out or cleaned with a household abrasive cleanser. Because many of the available patterns resemble stone, solid surfacing is often used as a light-weight substitute for stone tops. One disadvantage to solid surfacing is its cost. It is about three times as expensive as high-pressure plastic laminate, but similar in cost to some granite or marble. The cost can be raised considerably if ornate inlays or decorative patterns are used.

Solid surfacing materials are easily fabricated and installed with normal woodworking tools. Edges can be routed for decorative effects. When two pieces must be butted

Figure 6.30
Fabric-wrapped panel

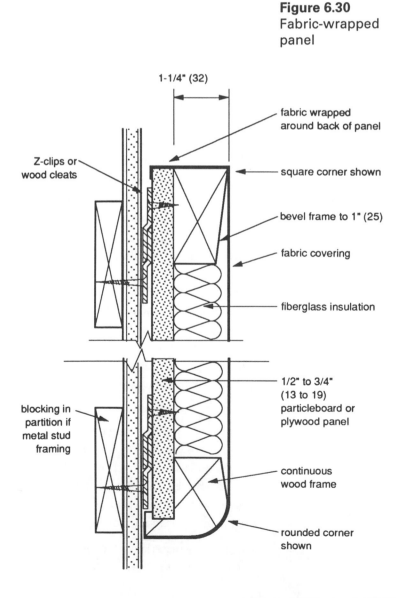

together, a two-part epoxy or liquid form of the material is used for a seamless appearance.

FINISHES [06400]

Finish is used on woodwork to protect it from moisture, chemicals, and contact, and to enhance its appearance. Woodwork can either be field finished or factory finished. Because more control can be achieved with a factory finish it is the preferred method, although minor cabinet and trim work is often field finished in single family residential construction. For high-quality woodwork, field finishing is generally limited to minor touchup and repair.

Prior to finishing, the wood must be sanded properly and filled if desired. On many opened-grain woods, such as oak, mahogany, and teak, a filler should be applied prior to finishing to give a more uniform appearance to the millwork; however, this is not required. Other types of surface preparation are also possible, depending on the aesthetic effect desired. The wood may be bleached to lighten it or to provide uniformity of color. Wood may also be mechanically or physically distressed to give it an antiqued or aged appearance. The color of the wood can also be changed in subsequent finishing operations by using shading or toning compounds.

Opaque finishes

Opaque finishes include lacquer, varnish, polyurethane, and polyester. They should only be used on closed-grain woods where solid stock is required, and on medium-density fiberboard where sheet materials are required.

Lacquer is a coating material with a high nitrocellulose content modified with resins and plasticizers dissolved in a volatile solvent. Catalyzed lacquers contain an extra ingredient that speeds drying time and gives the finish additional hardness.

Varnish is a material consisting of various types of resinous material dissolved in one of

several types of volatile liquids. Conversion varnish is produced with alkyd and urea formaldehyde resins. When a high solids content is specified, the finish becomes opaque.

Polyurethane is a synthetic finish that gives a very hard, durable finish. Although difficult to repair or refinish, polyurethane finishes offer superior resistance to water, many commercial and household chemicals, and abrasion. Opaque polyurethanes are available in sheens from dull satin to full gloss.

Polyesters are another type of synthetic finish that give the hardest, most durable finish possible. Opaque polyesters can be colored and are available only in a full gloss sheen. Like polyurethanes, polyester finishes are very difficult to repair and refinish outside the shop, but give very durable finishes with as much as 80 percent of the hardness of glass.

Transparent finishes

Transparent finishes include lacquer, varnish, vinyl, penetrating oils, polyurethane, and polyester.

Lacquer and varnish

Standard lacquers are easy to apply, easy to repair, and are relatively low in cost. However, they do not provide the chemical and wear resistance that some of the other finishes provide. Catalyzed lacquers for transparent finishes are more difficult to repair and refinish, but are more durable and resistant to commercial and household chemicals. A special water-reducible acrylic lacquer is available if local regulations prohibit the use of other types of lacquers.

Conversion varnish has many of the same advantages of lacquer but can often be applied with fewer coats.

Vinyl

Catalyzed vinyl yields a surface that has the most chemical resistance of the standard lacquer, varnish, and vinyl finishes. Vinyl is also very resistant to scratching, abrasion, and other mechanical damage.

Oils

Oil finishes are one of the traditional wood finishes. They are easily applied and give a rich look to wood, but require re-oiling periodically and tend to darken with age. The look of an oil finish can be achieved with a catalyzed vinyl.

Polyurethane and polyester

As with the opaque finishes, both polyurethane and polyester provide the most durable transparent finishes possible. They are the most expensive of the finishing systems and require skilled applicators. Transparent polyurethanes are available in sheens from dull to full gloss, while polyesters are available only in full gloss.

Stains

Prior to applying the final finish, wood may be stained to modify its color. The two types are water-based and solvent-based stains. Water-based stains yield a uniform color, but raise the grain. Solvent-based stains dry quickly and do not raise the grain, but are less uniform.

For shop-finished millwork, the American Woodwork Institute has developed 16 standard finishing systems, as listed in Table 6.12, which include both transparent and opaque finishes. These are not the only finish systems available, but they make it easy to specify and provide a common standard. Refer to the AWI *Quality Standards* for more information on these finishes.

Whichever finish is selected, the specifications should include the requirement that finish samples be provided by the woodworker and approved prior to fabrication. If specific colors of stain or sheen must be matched, samples of these must be supplied by the designer to the mill shop so that finish samples can be made for approval.

INSTALLATION OF ARCHITECTURAL WOODWORK [06400]

The mill shop is responsible for installing the woodwork they produce unless other contractual arrangements are made. Items are manufactured in sizes as large as practically possible and delivered to the job site when most of the other finish work has

Table 6.12
AWI finish systems

System No.	Type	Name
TR-0	Transparent only	Synthetic penetrating and simulated oil
TR-1/OP-1	Transparent/opaque	Standard lacquer
TR-2/OP-2	Transparent/opaque	Catalyzed lacquer
TR-3/OP-3	Transparent/opaque	Cellulose acetate butyrate (CAB) and water reducible acrylic lacquer
TR-4/OP-4	Transparent/opaque	Conversion varnish
TR-5/OP-5	Transparent/opaque	Catalyzed vinyl
TR-6/OP-6	Transparent/opaque	Catalyzed polyurethane
TR-7/OP-7	Transparent/opaque	Polyester
OP-8	Opaque only	Polyester/polyurethane

Based on information from *Architectural Woodwork Quality Standards, Sixth Edition, Version 1.0,* copyright 1993, The Architectural Woodwork Institute, used with permission.

been completed. The mill shop is responsible for determining how to prefabricate the components and for assembling them in the field. However, problems should be anticipated and very large units designed so that there are logical places where the woodworking shop can join units without compromising design intent. The shop drawings should show how the mill shop intends to break down the woodwork for shipment and install it. Potential problems should be discussed with the mill shop when the shop drawings are reviewed.

The AWI *Quality Standards* give the methods and allowable tolerances for installation of woodwork based on whether it is Premium or Custom grade.

7
ORNAMENTAL METALS

Ornamental metals include a wide variety of both functional and decorative products. These include spiral stairs, handrails, guardrails, and elevator interiors. Metal may also be used for custom doors and door facings, partition and millwork facings, building directories and kiosks, signs, custom light fixtures, ceilings, or as part of almost any construction assembly. The decorative options available to the designer are almost limitless. The most commonly used ornamental metals include stainless steel, the copper alloys of bronze and brass, and aluminum. Carbon steel, copper, iron, and porcelain enamel are used less frequently.

In addition, steel or aluminum may be required strictly for utilitarian purposes to support or brace millwork, partitions, ceilings, and other construction.

STAINLESS STEEL [05010]
Types and uses
Stainless steel is an alloy of steel containing 12 percent, or more, of chromium. For most types of stainless steel additional elements are added, such as nickel, manganese, and molybdenum to impart particular qualities. Stainless steel is used for its corrosion resistance, strength, and appearance. In some alloys it is the strongest architectural metal available. For interior construction, common uses include wall and door coverings, railings, elevator finishes, lavatory and kitchen equipment, furniture, hardware, and concealed anchors and fasteners.

There are dozens of different types of stainless steels based on the composition of alloys, but only seven are commonly used for architectural purposes. They are referred to by number and include Types 201, 301, 302, 304, 316, 410, and 430, with Types 304 and 430 used the most for interior applications. The 200 series is also referred to as chromium–nickel–manganese stainless steel because of these added elements. The 300 series is chromium–nickel and the 400 series is straight chromium. Table 7.1 summarizes the types, properties, and uses of stainless steel for interior design applications.

Standard forms
Stainless steel is available in several stock forms that metal fabricators use to construct interior components. Knowing the availability of these forms when developing custom details can help reduce costs and simplify fabrication. These forms and their

Alloy numbering systems

Stainless steel and other metals are commonly referred to by various names and numbers which, in the past, have been unique to each industry. Today, the Unified Numbering System (UNS) is used to designate all commercial metals and alloys. A typical UNS number consists of a letter prefix to designate the general type of metal and is followed by a five-digit number that identifies the specific alloy. The letter A represents aluminum; C, copper and copper alloys; N, nickel and nickel alloys; F, cast irons and cast steels; G, carbon and alloy steels; and S, stainless steel. For stainless steel and the copper alloys, the first three digits of the number are the same as the former alloy number type. For example, for Type 304 stainless steel, the UNS number is S30400. For copper alloy 280, which is also sometimes called by its previous trade name, muntz metal, the new number is C28000. The position of the old number designations in the new system makes it relatively easy to use both systems.

**Table 7.1
Types and properties of stainless steel**

Type	Properties	Uses
201	Similar to 301 and 302 but stronger and harder.	Where higher strength than 301 or 302 is required.
301	Can be cold rolled to very high tensile strengths; 300 series cannot be hardened by heat treatment; 300 series is nonmagnetic.	Structural members; roof drainage products.
302	Highly resistant to atmospheric corrosion; strong and hard.	Building exterior elements.
304	Similar to type 302 but is better for welding; most common type for architectural work and has largely replaced type 302. (302 and 304 are often referred to as 18-8 stainless because of the percentage of chromium and nickel.)	Store fronts, fascias, doors, railings, column covers, food preparation equipment, sinks, countertops; applications where welding is required.
316	Contains molybdenum for extra corrosion resistance for marine or extremely corrosive industrial environments.	Building elements where extreme corrosion is present or near saltwater locations.
410	Can be hardened by heat treatment; 400 series is magnetic.	Bolts, nuts, screws, and other fasteners in protected locations; special extruded shapes.
430	Less corrosion resistant than the 200 and 300 series; used primarily for interior applications; cannot be hardened by heat treatment.	Trim, column covers, appliances, railings, and other interior applications where lowest cost is required.

standard nomenclature include sheet, plates, strips, bars, pipes, and tubing. See Figure 7.1.

Sheet stock is considered any material less than 3/16 in. (4.8 mm) thick and 24 in. (610 mm) wide, or wider. Plates are pieces 3/16 in. thick and thicker, and over 10 in. (254 mm) wide. Strip stock is any material under 3/16 in. thick and under 24 in. wide. Bar stock includes rounds, squares, flats, octagons, and hexagons. Flat bar stock is available in thicknesses from 1/8 in. (3.2 mm) and thicker, and from 1/4 in. up to 10 in. wide (6.4 up to 254 mm). Round and square bar stock is available in diameters and sizes starting at 1/4 in. (6.4 mm).

For larger round and rectangular sections pipe or tubing can be used. Round pipe is produced with standardized sizes and wall thicknesses and is used for many structural purposes as well as for pressure applications. It is subjected to several processes and mechanical tests at the mill. Round, square, and rectangular tubing, is manufactured to exact outside diameter dimensions in a variety of diameters and wall thicknesses and is available in a wider variety of alloys and finishes not commonly available in pipe.

Both pipe and tubing are manufactured in either a welded or seamless form. Welded pipe and tubing are formed from coiled strip stock that is bent into shape and continuously welded. Seamless pipe and tubing are formed by extrusion. Tubing is much lower in cost than pipe, and "ornamental" tubing (which is formed by welding) should be specified for most ornamental interior applications. Commonly available sizes of round, square, and rectangular tubing are shown in Figures 7.2(a)–7.2(c).

Stainless steel is also available in other common shapes. Angles, channels, tees, and other structural shapes can be used in detailing; however, they are expensive because of their extra weight. Table 7.2 lists some typical sizes for small shapes used for interior detailing.

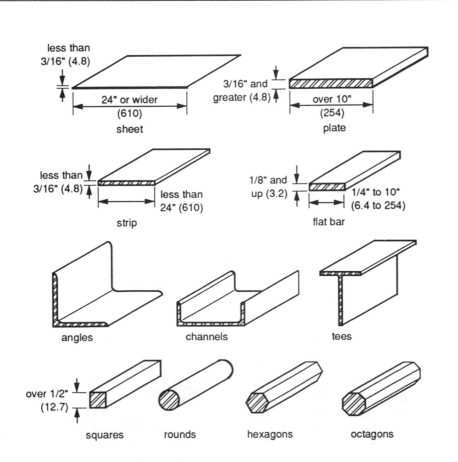

Figure 7.1
Stainless steel forms

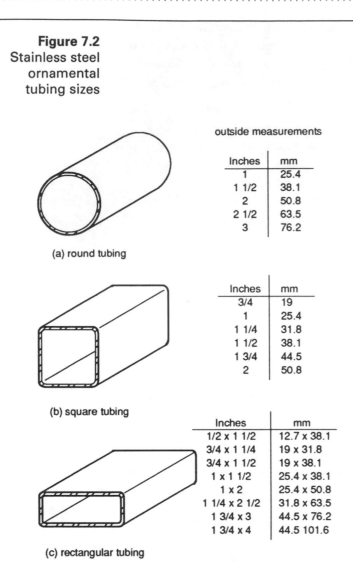

Figure 7.2
Stainless steel
ornamental
tubing sizes

outside measurements

Inches	mm
1	25.4
1 1/2	38.1
2	50.8
2 1/2	63.5
3	76.2

(a) round tubing

Inches	mm
3/4	19
1	25.4
1 1/4	31.8
1 1/2	38.1
1 3/4	44.5
2	50.8

(b) square tubing

Inches	mm
1/2 x 1 1/2	12.7 x 38.1
3/4 x 1 1/4	19 x 31.8
3/4 x 1 1/2	19 x 38.1
1 x 1 1/2	25.4 x 38.1
1 x 2	25.4 x 50.8
1 1/4 x 2 1/2	31.8 x 63.5
1 3/4 x 3	44.5 x 76.2
1 3/4 x 4	44.5 101.6

(c) rectangular tubing

Stainless steel finishes [05010]

Stainless steel is available in several finishes. These are produced either at the mill or by a metal fabricator and include rolled, polished, and etched finishes. Other types are available, but are seldom used for architectural purposes.

Rolled finishes are produced on sheet material by passing the steel between rollers under pressure at the mill. The finish of the steel depends on the finish of the rollers and can range from a bright, reflective surface to a deeply embossed pattern. Each manufacturer produces its own set of proprietary rolled finishes and should be consulted concerning availability. Rolled finishes are the least expensive of all the finishes.

Polished finishes are the most common for architectural applications. These are produced by grinding, polishing, and sometimes buffing the metal until the desired surface is obtained. There are five industry standard polished finishes for sheet and strip stock, which are described in Table 7.3. Generally, the more polished the finish, the higher the cost. Finishes for plates, bars, and tubing are specified a little differently, but all can be mechanically polished to match the sheet finishes described in Table 7.3.

Etched finishes are produced by dry or wet methods. Dry etching uses blasting with

Table 7.2
Standard sizes
of stainless
steel forms

Sizes		Thicknesses	
in.	mm	in.	mm
¾ × ¾	19.1 × 19.1	⅛	3.2
1 × 1	25.4 × 25.4	⅛ and 3/16	3.2 and 4.8
1¼ × 1¼	31.8 × 31.8	⅛ and 3/16	3.2 and 4.8
1½ × 1½	38.1 × 38.1	⅛ and 3/16	3.2 and 4.8
2 × 2	50.8 × 50.8	3/16 and ¼	4.8 and 6.4
2½ × 2½	63.5 × 63.5	3/16 and ¼	4.8 and 6.4
3 × 3	76.2 × 76.2	¼, 5/16, and ⅜	4.8, 7.9, and 9.5

abrasive grit or glass beads to wear away a defined area. Stencils, metal templates, or adhesive materials are used to mask off portions of the metal. Wet etching uses acid to wear off some of the finish. Special masking must be used to maintain sharply defined areas and prevent the acid from undercutting the protected area.

Detailing stainless steel

Custom details for stainless steel can be developed in the same way as for plain carbon steel or any other metal. Combinations of bar, plate, tubing, sheet stock, and other shapes can be detailed to nearly any configuration and in any combination. Stainless steel can be joined by welding, mechanical fasteners, and, in some cases, with adhesives. For the smoothest joint, welding is preferred. However, the finish specified must make it possible to smooth and work the weld to match the adjacent finish. Some rolled and proprietary finishes cannot be matched after shop welding. When mechanical fasteners, such as screws, bolts, and rivets, are used, they should also be stainless steel to prevent galvanic action and rust stains caused by carbon steel fasteners. Adhesives are typically used to laminate sheet stock to other materials.

In order to simplify fabrication and minimize cost, the smallest sizes and gages should be used that satisfy the application. Table 7.5 gives some commonly used gages for various interior design applications. However, these are only guidelines; local fabricating shops should be consulted to determine the most readily available and appropriate size and gage for a particular use.

Sometimes there is disagreement about whether the thickness of a metal should be spelled "gauge" or "gage." The correct spelling for technical use is "gage." This is supported by *The Random House Dictionary,* the Construction Specifications Institute, and various other industry sources, such as the *Recommended Standards on Production Procedures* published by the Northern California Chapter of the American Institute of Architects. It also has the practical value of being shorter to write and letter on drawings.

Spelling preferences for gage

Finish No.	Description	Typical uses
3	Dull finish obtained by finishing with a 100-grit abrasive.	Institutional kitchen equipment, some architectural components where dull finish and low cost are required.
4	General-purpose polished finish obtained by finishing with a 120-150 mesh abrasive. It shows a visible grain that prevents mirror reflection.	Wall panels, column covers, restaurant equipment, hospital equipment, elevator interiors and doors, and furniture.
6	Dull satin finish with low luster. Has lower reflectivity than a No. 4 finish.	Wall panels, doors, and applications where contrasted with brighter finishes.
7	Highly reflective finish, almost mirrorlike.	One of the most common finishes for ornamental architectural components.
8	Most reflective finish.	Mirror and reflectors; not commonly used for interior applications.

Table 7.3
Selected finishes of stainless steel

BRONZE AND BRASS [05010]
Types and uses

Bronze and brass are the terms commonly used to describe a range of copper alloys. There are three primary groups of copper alloys: those that are almost pure copper, those called architectural bronze or the common brasses, and the nickel–silver and silicon bronze alloys. Technically, bronze is an alloy of copper and two percent, or more, of tin. Brass is an alloy of copper and zinc. In both metals, the predominant element is copper. In practical use, however, many of the alloys that are really brass are often

Comparative metal gages

Gage sizing is commonly used to indicate the thickness of metal. Although most metal producers prefer to use decimal or metric measurements, gages are still used. Unfortunately, there are several different gage sizing systems that have developed throughout the history of the metals industry, with each gage number having a slightly different actual thickness and each system being used for different types of metal or the forms of metal produced. Table 7.4 shows four commonly used gage systems with the actual imperial and metric thickness of the gage number. When detailing and specifying metals, it is best to use the actual thickness required. Because not all thicknesses are available in all forms and from all suppliers, availability must be verified with a metal supplier or local ornamental metal shop prior to detailing.

Table 7.4
Comparative metal gages

Gage no.	Aluminum, copper, brass, bronze sheets, strips, and wire; small copper and brass tubing		Stainless steel sheets		Stainless steel, aluminum, bronze, and large copper and brass tubing; stainless strip		Steel sheets	
	B&S & AWG		USG		BWG			USG
	in.	mm	in.	mm	in.	mm	in.	mm
8	0.1285	3.264	0.1719	4.366	0.165	4.191	0.1644	4.176
10	0.1019	2.588	0.1406	3.571	0.134	3.404	0.1345	3.416
12	0.0808	2.052	0.1094	2.779	0.109	2.769	0.1046	2.657
14	0.0640	1.626	0.0781	1.984	0.083	2.108	0.0747	1.897
16	0.0508	1.290	0.0625	1.588	0.065	1.651	0.0598	1.519
18	0.0403	1.024	0.0500	1.270	0.049	1.245	0.0478	1.214
20	0.0320	0.813	0.0375	0.953	0.035	0.889	0.0359	0.912
22	0.0253	0.643	0.0312	0.792	0.028	0.711	0.0299	0.759
24	0.0201	0.511	0.0250	0.635	0.022	0.559	0.0239	0.607
26	0.0159	0.404	0.0187	0.475	0.018	0.457	0.0179	0.455
28	0.0126	0.320	0.0156	0.396	0.014	0.356	0.0149	0.378
30	0.0100	0.254	0.0125	0.318	0.012	0.305	0.0120	0.305

B & S = Brown and Sharp   AWG = American Wire Gage
USG = United States Standard Gage   BWG = Birmingham Wire Gage

Gage	Thickness, in.	Thickness, mm	Typical applications
11	0.1250	3.175	Door bumpers, thresholds, cover plates
12	0.1094	2.779	Doors, kick plates, elevator panels, items subject to abuse and wear
14	0.0781	1.984	Column covers, convector covers, large flush panels
16	0.0625	1.588	Large mullions, unbacked fascia and panels
18	0.0500	1.270	Corner guards, door sections, handrails
20	0.0375	0.953	Window sills
22	0.0312	0.792	Light mullions, stiffeners
24	0.0250	0.635	Window framing, louvers
26	0.0187	0.475	Cleats and clips, other fasteners
28	0.0156	0.396	Laminated panels
30	0.0125	0.318	Laminated panels

Table 7.5
Applications of stainless steel sheet thicknesses

Note: verify appropriate gages with metal fabricator.

Alloy no.	UNS no.	Common name	Nominal composition	Color
110	C11000	Copper	99.9% copper	Salmon-red
122	C12200	Copper	99.9% copper 0.02% phosphorous	Salmon-red
220	C22000	Commercial bronze	90% copper 10% zinc	Red-gold
230	C23000	Red brass	85% copper 15% zinc	Reddish-yellow
260	C26000	Cartridge brass	70% brass 30% zinc	Yellow
280	C28000	Muntz metal	60% copper 40% zinc	Reddish-yellow
385	C38500	Architectural bronze	57% copper 3% lead 40% zinc	Reddish-yellow
655	C65500	Silicon bronze	97% copper 3% silicone	Reddish-gold
745	C74500	Nickel silver	65% copper 25% zinc 10% nickel	Warm silver
796	C79600	Leaded nickel silver	45% copper 42% zinc 10% nickel 2% manganese 1% lead	Warm silver

Table 7.6
Types and properties of copper alloys

Source: Copper Development Association, Inc., New York, NY.

referred to as bronze. In fact, none of the most common copper alloys used in interior architectural work are true bronzes. To avoid confusion, copper alloys can be referred to by their alloy number. Table 7.6 lists the copper alloys commonly used for both interior and exterior architectural components.

For most interior design construction, any of the alloys listed in Table 7.6 can be specified subject to availability in the forms required. The choice is usually a matter of the final color and appearance required, along with the cost. However, the most commonly used alloys for interior construction include 220, 230, 260, 280, and 385. Table 7.7 summarizes the typical uses of the copper alloys. Because these alloys are true brasses and are the most frequently used for interior applications, the word "brass" will be used for the remainder of this chapter even though the information applies to copper and most of the other alloys as well.

Although the copper alloys are corrosion resistant, they all change color with age and exposure to moisture in the air. After several years of weathering, those exposed to the exterior turn green or brown. For most interior use this is usually not a problem because the metal is protected from atmospheric moisture and chemicals. However, brass will tarnish and may show some color changes after several years, unless protected with some type of coating or refinished periodically.

Standard forms

Brass is available in the standard forms of sheet, plate, bar stock, tubing, and pipe. As with stainless steel, these basic shapes are used to fabricate custom assemblies by various forming and fastening methods. Brass

Table 7.7
Uses of copper alloys for interior construction

Use	110	122	220	230	260	280	385	655	745	796
Bank equipment	•	•	•	•		•	•		•	•
Builders' hardware			•	•	•		•		•	•
Ecclesiastical equipment	•		•	•	•	•				
Elevators, escalators			•	•		•			•	•
Food service equipment	•	•			•	•		•		
Furniture	•		•	•	•			•	•	
Grilles, screens	•		•	•	•		•		•	•
Lighting fixtures	•	•	•		•		•			
Louvers	•	•	•	•			•			
Plumbing fixtures				•	•	•				
Railings		•	•	•	•	•	•		•	•
Signs	•	•	•	•	•	•	•			
Thresholds								•		•
Toilet and bath accessories				•	•	•	•			•
Wall coverings	•	•	•	•	•					
Wall panels	•	•	•	•			•			

Source: Copper Development Association, Inc., New York, NY.

can also be extruded and cast. Extrusion is common for door and window frames, railings, and trim, while casting is used to manufacture hardware and plumbing fixtures. Custom extrusions can be designed and manufactured; however, this forming method is not economical unless the amount of extrusion required is very large.

Brass can be fabricated to any size required; however, it is more economical to design and detail ornamental brass using standard shapes and sizes whenever possible. Figures 7.3(a)–7.3(d) illustrate some of these standard shapes. Tables 7.8–7.10 list standard sizes for these shapes. Hexagonal and octagonal tubing is also available on special order, as are some T-shapes, Z-shapes, and proprietary shapes. Note that square and rectangular tubing and the channels and angles have sharp corners, as contrasted with stainless steel and regular steel tubing, channels, and angles. While there are some standard shapes and sizes, several manufacturers use brass to fabricate proprietary shapes and products. These can be ordered from catalogs. For example, several manufacturers produce lines of brass railings for bars, guardrails, and handrails, including brackets and other accessories for a complete installation.

Figure 7.3
Standard brass shapes

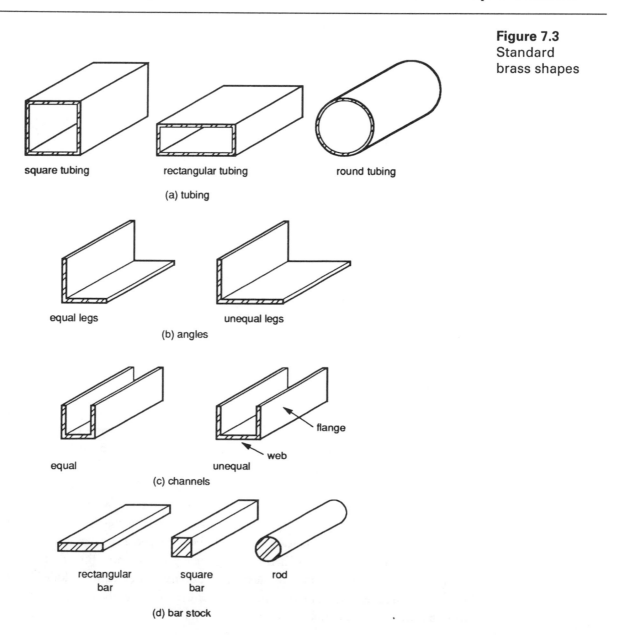

square tubing   rectangular tubing   round tubing

(a) tubing

equal legs   unequal legs

(b) angles

equal   unequal   flange   web

(c) channels

rectangular bar   square bar   rod

(d) bar stock

Table 7.8
Standard sizes
of brass tube
and pipe shapes

Square tubing[1]		Rectangular tubing[1]		Round tubing[1]		Pipe[2]			
						Nominal size		Actual outside diameter	
in.	mm	in.	mm	in.	mm	in.	mm	in.	mm
½ × ½	12.7 × 12.7	⅜ × 1	9.5 × 25.4	⅜	9.5	1	25.4	1.315	33.4
⅝ × ⅝	15.9 × 15.9	½ × 1	12.7 × 25.4	½	12.7	1¼	31.8	1.660	42.2
¾ × ¾	19.1 × 19.1	½ × 1¼	12.7 × 31.8	⅝	15.9	1½	38.1	1.900	48.3
⅞ × ⅞	22.2 × 22.2	½ × 1½	12.7 × 38.1	¾	19.1	2	50.8	2.375	60.3
1 × 1	25.4 × 25.4	½ × 2	12.7 × 50.8	⅞	22.2				
1¼ × 1¼	31.8 × 31.8	⅝ × 1¼	15.9 × 31.8	1	25.4				
1½ × 1½	38.1 × 38.1	¾ × 1	19.1 × 25.4	1¼	31.8				
1¾ × 1¾	44.5 × 44.5	¾ × 1½	19.1 × 38.1	1½	38.1				
2 × 2	50.8 × 50.8	¾ × 2	19.1 × 50.8	1¾	44.5				
2½ × 2½	63.5 × 63.5	1 × 1½	25.4 × 38.1	2	50.8				
3 × 3	76.2 × 76.2	1 × 2	25.4 × 50.8	2½	63.5				
4 × 4	101.6 × 101.6	1 × 3	25.4 × 76.2	3	76.2				
		1¼ × 2	31.8 × 50.8	3½	88.9				
		1½ × 2	38.1 × 50.8	4	101.6				
		1½ × 3	38.1 × 76.2	5	127				
		1¾ × 3	44.5 × 76.2	6	152.4				
		1¾ × 4	44.5 × 101.6	8	203.2				
		2 × 3	50.8 × 76.2						
		2 × 4	50.8 × 101.6						

(1) Tubing available in lengths up to 16 ft (4.8 m) and thicknesses from 0.016 in. to 0.125 in. (0.41 to 3.18 mm).
(2) Pipe available in lengths up to 20 ft (6.1 m).

Source: Manufacturers' catalogs.

Brass finishes [05030]

Brass is available in mechanical, chemical, and coated finishes. Mechanical finishing alters the surface of the metal by rolling or some other mechanical means. Chemical finishes alter the surface with chemical processes. Coatings are applied finishes that are formed from the metal itself through chemical or electrochemical conversion or by adding some other material. Combinations of these three basic finishing methods may be used.

Chemical conversion coatings can be used to change the color of brass or to give the appearance of natural weathering effects. Of all the conversion coatings, patinas (verde antiques) and statuary (oxidized) finishes are most often used for exterior applications. However, because chemical conversion coating processes are difficult to control, are expensive, and require a skilled finisher, they are not commonly used for interior applications.

Table 7.9
Standard sizes of brass angles and channels[1]

Angles[2]				Channels[3]					
Equal legs		Unequal legs		Equal		Unequal			
						in.		mm	
in.	mm	in.	mm	in.	mm	Flange	Web	Flange	Web
⅜ × ⅜	9.5 × 9.5	⅜ × ¾	9.5 × 19.1	¼ × ¼	6.4 × 6.4	½	⅜	12.7	9.5
½ × ½	12.7 × 12.7	½ × ¾	12.7 × 19.1	⅜ × ⅜	9.5 × 9.5	½	¾	12.7	19.1
⅝ × ⅝	15.9 × 15.9	½ × 1	12.7 × 25.4	½ × ½	12.7 × 12.7	½	1	12.7	25.4
¾ × ¾	19.1 × 19.1	½ × 1½	12.7 × 38.1	⅝ × ⅝	15.9 × 15.9	½	1¼	12.7	31.8
1 × 1	25.4 × 25.4	½ × 2	12.7 × 50.8	¾ × ¾	19.1 × 19.1	½	1½	12.7	38.1
1¼ × 1¼	31.8 × 31.8	¾ × 1	19.1 × 25.4	1 × 1	25.4 × 25.4	⅝	1¼	15.9	31.8
1½ × 1½	38.1 × 38.1	¾ × 1¼	19.1 × 31.8	1¼ × 1¼	31.8 × 31.8	⅝	1½	15.9	38.1
2 × 2	50.8 × 50.8	¾ × 1½	19.1 × 38.1	1½ × 1½	38.1 × 38.1	¾	½	19.1	12.7
2½ × 2½	63.5 × 63.5	1 × 1½	25.4 × 38.1	2 × 2	50.8 × 50.8	¾	1	19.1	25.4
3 × 3	76.2 × 76.2	1 × 2	25.4 × 50.8			¾	2	19.1	50.8
						1	¾	25.4	19.1
						1	1½	25.4	38.1
						1	2	25.4	50.8
						1	2½	25.4	63.5
						1½	2½	38.1	63.5

[1] Verify availability of sizes and alloys with fabricator.
[2] Angles typically ⅛ in. (3.2 mm) thick.
[3] Channel thickness varies with size ranging from 0.062 in. to 0.125 in. (1.58 to 3.18 mm).

Source: Manufacturers' catalogs.

The most commonly used mechanical and coating finishes for brass are summarized in Table 7.11. Where applicable, the standard number designations of these finishes assigned by the National Association of Architectural Metal Manufacturers (NAAMM) is given.

When specifying a brass finish, remember that the more highly polished a finish the more difficult it is to conceal scratches and to refinish. Also keep in mind that large, flat, highly polished surfaces tend to show varia-tions in flatness (oil canning) more than textured or figured surfaces.

DETAILING WITH BRASS [05050]

Brass can be formed into an unlimited num-ber of shapes and sizes and different pieces can be fastened to fabricate nearly any type of detail. Brass can also be combined with other materials, such as wood, plastic, and stone, to construct specialty items. How-ever, standard shapes, sizes, and metal alloys should be used to minimize cost and fabrication difficulty. The following are some general guidelines for designing and detailing with brass.

Standard sizes

Standard sizes and shapes of tubing, bar stock, and other shapes should be used whenever possible. The standard sizes given in the previous sections are some of the more commonly available. However, what is available should be verified with fabricators prior to developing details that use unusual shapes or sizes. The alloys that the required shapes are available in should also be verified. Some-

times the same alloy is not used for sheet stock as for bar or tubing.

Detailing with sheet stock

For details with large expanses of smooth, flat sheet stock, the metal gage must be thick enough to avoid oil canning or showing other surface imperfections. A minimum of 10-gage brass (0.1019 in. or 2.588 mm) should be used when large areas are unsupported or unbacked. If the sheet has an embossed pattern, thinner material can be used because the patterning imparts stiffness to the sheet. When brass is laminated to particleboard or other backing, sheets as

Table 7.10
Standard sizes of brass bar and rod stock

Rectangular bars				Square bars	Rods	
in.	mm	in.	mm	in.	in.	mm
⅛ × ¼	3.2 × 6.4	⅜ × ½	9.5 × 12.7	¼	¼	6.4
⅛ × ½	3.2 × 12.7	⅜ × ¾	9.5 × 19.1	⁵⁄₁₆	⁵⁄₁₆	7.9
⅛ × ⅝	3.2 × 15.9	⅜ × 1	9.5 × 25.4	⅜	⅜	9.5
⅛ × ¾	3.2 × 19.1	⅜ × 1½	9.5 × 38.1	½	½	12.7
⅛ × 1	3.2 × 25.4	⅜ × 2	9.5 × 50.8	⅝	⅝	15.9
⅛ × 1¼	3.2 × 31.8	½ × ¾	12.7 × 19.1	¾	¾	19.1
⅛ × 1½	3.2 × 38.1	½ × 1	12.7 × 25.4	1	1	25.4
⅛ × 2	3.2 × 50.8	½ × 1¼	12.7 × 31.8	1¼	—	31.8
³⁄₁₆ × ⅜	4.8 × 9.5	½ × 1½	12.7 × 38.1			
³⁄₁₆ × ½	4.8 × 12.7	½ × 1¾	12.7 × 44.5			
³⁄₁₆ × ¾	4.8 × 19.1	½ × 2	12.7 × 50.8			
³⁄₁₆ × 1	4.8 × 25.4	½ × 2½	12.7 × 63.5			
¼ × ½	6.4 × 12.7	½ × 3	12.7 × 76.2			
¼ × ¾	6.4 × 19.1	¾ × 1	19.1 × 25.4			
¼ × 1	6.4 × 25.4	¾ × 1½	19.1 × 38.1			
¼ × 1¼	6.4 × 31.8	¾ × 2	19.1 × 50.8			
¼ × 1½	6.4 × 38.1					
¼ × 1¾	6.4 × 44.5					
¼ × 2	6.4 × 50.8					

Source: Manufacturers' catalogs.

Table 7.11
Selected finishes
of copper alloys

NAAMM no.	Name	Description
Buffed finishes:		
M21	Smooth specular	Brightest mechanical finish available produced by grinding, polishing, and buffing to a mirrorlike surface.
M22	Specular	Bright finish produced by grinding, polishing, and only light buffing.
Directional textured:		
M31	Fine satin	Fine, velvety texture with tiny, nearly parallel scratches on the surface.
M32	Medium satin	Similar to fine satin but not as smooth.
M33	Coarse satin	Similar to medium satin but not as smooth.
M36	Uniform	Produced by a single pass of a No. 80 grit belt.
Nondirectional textured:		
M42	Fine matte	Texture produced by blasting metal with sand or metal shot. Use is limited to metal at least ¼ in. (6 mm) thick. Texture shows fingerprints and holds dirt; protective organic coatings are required.
M43	Medium matte	Similar to fine matte but not as smooth.
	Patterned	Produced by passing light-gage sheet stock between two engraved rollers or impressing patterns by stamping. Pattern varies with manufacturer. Patterning increases stiffness and eliminates distorted reflections.
Clear organic coatings:		
06x	Air-dry coatings	Most commonly used for interior ornamental metal.
07x	Thermoset	Used for hardware.
Types of clear organic coatings:		
	Acrylic	Good color retention and resistance to impact and abrasion. Air-drying type used for architectural applications. Relatively high cost.
	Cellulose acetate butyrate	Air-drying type. Used for interior applications because they tend to darken under exterior exposure. Moderate in cost and fair performance.
	Epoxy	Used for interior applications where high resistance to impact and abrasion is required. Only available in thermosetting or two-part types.
	Nitrocellulose	Used for interior applications where low cost is required. Air-drying type but must be stripped and reapplied frequently.
	Urethane	Air-drying type used for interior applications where excellent resistance to abrasion and chemicals is required. Relatively high cost.
Laminated:		
L91	Clear polyvinyl-fluoride	A 1 mil sheet of polyvinylfluoride adhesively bonded to the brass. Resists abrasion, impact, and weathering.
	Oils and waxes	Primarily used for maintenance by hand rubbing.

Note: For a complete list of finishes, refer to the *Metal Finishes Manual* published by the National Association of Architectural Metal Manufacturers.

Reprinted with permission of the National Association of Architectural Metal
Manufacturers (NAAMM), Chicago, IL.

thin as 20-gage (0.032 in. or 0.813 mm) can be used. Slightly thicker sheets of 18-gage, 16-gage, or 14-gage can also be used. Items that are fabricated of brake-formed brass should be from 14-gage or 12-gage metal (0.0640 or 0.0808 in.) (1.626 or 2.052 mm).

Methods of fastening

Brass can be joined with mechanical fasteners, adhesives, or by brazing or soldering. Mechanical fasteners include screws, bolts, rivets, and various types of clips in compatible alloys. In most cases, the appearance of interior metal work is improved if mechanical fasteners are concealed. If the installation makes it impossible to conceal fasteners, their type, size, and location should be given careful consideration based on the final installed position.

Adhesives can be used for laminating sheets onto backing material or to join smaller pieces to other materials when exposed fasteners would be objectionable. Unless some additional mechanical fastening device can be incorporated into a detail, adhesive bonding should not be used alone where the metal must support forces other than its own weight. It is usually best to verify the advisability of using adhesives for a particular detail with an ornamental metal fabricator.

Brass can be joined by brazing, soldering, or welding. Brazing is the joining of two metals at an intermediate temperature above 800°F (438°C) using a nonferrous filler metal. Soldering is the joining of two metals using lead-based or tin-based alloy solder that melts below 500°F (260°C). Welding joins two metals by using high temperatures (much higher than brazing) to heat them above their melting points either with or without a filler metal. Of the three methods, brazing is most often used for joining brass for architectural purposes. If possible, brazed joints should be concealed because the filler metal does not exactly match the brass.

OTHER METALS

Although stainless and copper alloys are the most commonly used metals for interior ornamental metalwork, others are available. These include aluminum, structural steel, and iron. Aluminum is used where existing door or interior glazing frames must be matched or where metal is required, but the color and finish of stainless steel or brass is not required. Aluminum is also used where light weight and low cost are needed. Structural steel is used where high strength is required for other construction elements and appearance is not a concern, or where a durable metal is required that can be refinished easily. Wrought iron is used in decorative work for components such as railings, balusters, and grilles.

Aluminum [05010, 05030]

Aluminum is typically used in manufactured construction products, such as door and window frames, railings, screens and grilles, and cast fittings. However, aluminum is also available in the standard forms of bars, rods, tubes, and pipe that can be detailed to form custom fabrications. In addition, aluminum can be extruded from custom-designed dies into special shapes. However, the quantity required to make this economically feasible is usually greater than most interior design projects require. In most cases, standard extruded shapes are available as stock items that can be used for custom fabrication.

Aluminum is available in several finishes including mechanical, chemical, and anodic. Mechanical finishes include buffed, which produces a smooth specular surface; directional-textured; nondirectional-textured; and patterned. Directional-textured finishes can be specified as fine satin, medium satin, coarse satin, hand rubbed, and brushed. Nondirectional-textured finishes, which cannot be used on material thinner than ¼ in. (6 mm), include extra-fine matte, fine matte, medium matte, coarse matte, and fine shot blast. Heavier textured finishes are possible, but not typically used for interior design work.

A chemical finish is usually an intermediate process for some other final finish. Chemical finishes may be used to clean, etch, or prepare the metal for a coating.

The most common type of finish is the anodic, or anodized, which is an electrochemical process that forms an oxide coating on the metal surface when placed in a bath of chemicals with an electric current. The resulting coating can be clear or one of the common bronze or black colors. Aluminum can also be painted, electroplated, covered with porcelain enamel, and powder coated.

Aluminum can be joined by screwing, bolting, concealed fasteners, welding, brazing, soldering, and adhesive bonding. Welding, brazing, and soldering should only be used when the joint is concealed or prior to final finishing. Adhesive bonding should be limited to thin material in situations where high strength is not required. Verify the preferred joining methods with the fabricator prior to developing final details.

Monel metal [05060]

Monel metal, sometimes known as Benedict nickel, is an alloy of nickel and copper with other trace elements. It has a silver-gray color similar to stainless steel but with slightly more gray. Monel metal is highly resistive to salt spray and has a slightly lower coefficient of thermal expansion than stainless steel. However, it is about twice as expensive as stainless steel.

Monel is typically used in sheet form for roof panels, wall panels, and column covers. Standard sheet widths are 30, 36, and 48 in. (760, 914, and 1220 mm) with a maximum sheet length of 144 in. (3658 mm). Standard sheet thicknesses for interior design applications are 0.018, 0.021, and 0.031 in. (0.457, 0.533, and 0.787 mm).

Monel is available in finishes ranging from a cold-rolled mill finish to mirror polish. It can also be textured and embossed as can stainless steel. Outside, monel weathers to a greenish-brown or a gray-green depending on the amount of salt in the air. Used for interior applications, monel metal develops a light tarnish that can easily be removed with metal-polishing compounds.

Structural steel [05120]

Steel is used for construction where appearance is not a prime concern or where structural support is required for floor openings, bracing for heavy loads, long spans of unsupported millwork, partial height partitions, and other areas where high strength is required. Steel is also used for standard fabrications, such as industrial railings and spiral stairs. Where major structural work is required, a structural engineer must design and detail that portion of the construction. For minor bracing, and support, simple

Anodized color standards

One of the problems with anodized aluminum is matching colors from different products or fabricators or trying to match the color of a new component with an existing anodized product of the same color. The Architectural Anodizers Council (AAC) has established standards for six of the most commonly used colors that enable designers to specify these colors with the assurance that they will be uniform and match the same colors produced by other manufacturers. Additional colors will be added as they are developed and proven for production.

The colors, along with their AAC numbers, include: champagne bronze (AAC-CB1); light bronze (AAC-LB2); medium bronze (AAC-MB3); dark bronze (AAC-DB4); deep bronze (AAC-DB5); and black (AAC-B6).

standard shapes and sizes of steel can be specified by the designer. For example, Figures 7.4 and 7.5 illustrate two situations where structural steel is used in conjunction with other interior construction. Figure 7.4

shows square steel tubing welded to a base plate, which is bolted to the floor to help support a low partition. Figure 7.5 shows one method to support lengths of countertop with open space below.

There are hundreds of standard shapes of structural steel. Like stainless steel, brass, and aluminum, steel is manufactured in sheets, plates, bars, rods, piping, square and rectangular tubing, angles, channels, and tees, as well as heavier H and I sections for structural columns and beams. For miscellaneous bracing and minor support, Table 7.12 gives some common sizes for the smaller sections. For a complete listing, refer to the *Manual of Steel Construction* published by the American Institute of Steel Construction. Note that unlike brass or aluminum, tubing, angles, channels, and other shapes have slightly rounded corners.

Steel can be bolted or welded together. When attached to concrete structural elements, it is usually bolted with expansion anchors or power-actuated fasteners. Other materials, such as metal studs, wood blocking, plywood, and particleboard, are attached to steel with screws, bolts, or power-actuated fasteners.

Iron [05700]

For ornamental work, iron is used in two forms, cast iron and wrought iron. Cast iron contains more than 1.7 percent carbon. Wrought iron is almost pure iron, with from 0.03 to 0.05% carbon, although many blacksmiths use mild steel with carbon percentages in the range of 0.05 to 0.30. Both alloys contain small amounts of other

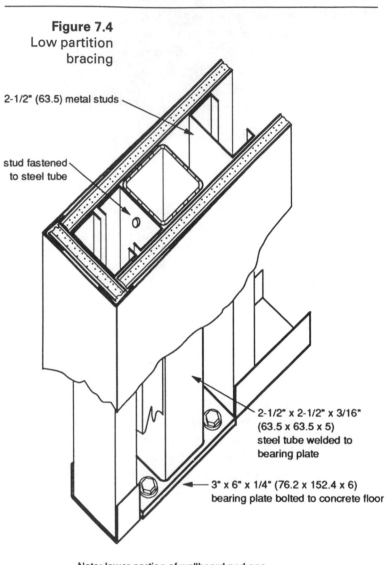

Figure 7.4
Low partition
bracing

2-1/2" (63.5) metal studs

stud fastened
to steel tube

2-1/2" x 2-1/2" x 3/16"
(63.5 x 63.5 x 5)
steel tube welded to
bearing plate

3" x 6" x 1/4" (76.2 x 152.4 x 6)
bearing plate bolted to concrete floor

Note: lower portion of wallboard and one
stud not shown for clarity; 3-5/8" studs
may also be used

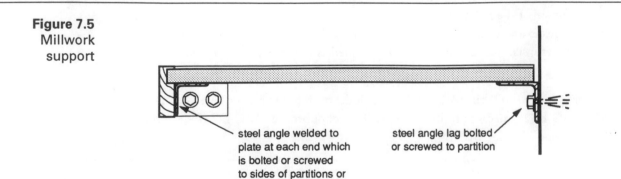

Figure 7.5
Millwork
support

steel angle welded to
plate at each end which
is bolted or screwed
to sides of partitions or
millwork

steel angle lag bolted
or screwed to partition

elements. Wrought iron and cast iron work are done by craftspersons using the historical techniques of forging, casting, stamping, and hammering to produce custom construction elements. Today, ironwork is used to fabricate railings, fences, grilles, screens, gates, lettering, room dividers, light fixtures, furniture, and other decorative elements. In many cases, wrought iron and cast iron fabrications are designed by the craftsperson or artist doing the work, with general design direction by the interior designer or architect.

Table 7.12 Standard sizes of structural steel forms used for miscellaneous bracing

Pipe[1]		Square tubing[2]	Rectangular tubing	Angles[3]	
Nominal, in. (mm)	O.D., in. (mm)	in. (mm)	in. (mm)	Equal legs, in. (mm)	Unequal legs, in. (mm)
¾ (19.1)	1.050 (26.7)	1 × 1 × ⅛ (25.4 × 25.4 × 3.2)	2 × 1 × ⅛ (50.8 × 25.4 × 3.2)	1 × 1 × ⅛ (25.4 × 25.4 × 3.2)	2 ½ × 2 × ³⁄₁₆ (63.5 × 50.4 × 4.8)
1 (25.4)	1.315 (33.4)	1½ × 1½ × ³⁄₁₆ (38.1 × 38.1 × 4.8)	3 × 2 × ³⁄₁₆ (76.2 × 50.8 × 4.8)	1¼ × 1¼ × ³⁄₁₆ (31.8 × 31.8 × 4.8)	2 ½ × 2 × ¼ (63.5 × 50.4 × 6.4)
1¼ (31.8)	1.660 (42.2)	2 × 2 × ³⁄₁₆ (50.8 × 50.8 × 4.8)	3½ × 2½ × ³⁄₁₆ (88.9 × 63.5 × 4.8)	1½ × 1½ × ³⁄₁₆ (38.1 × 38.1 × 4.8)	3 × 2 × ³⁄₁₆ (76.2 × 50.8 × 4.8)
1½ (38.1)	1.900 (48.3)	2 × 2 × ¼ (50.8 × 50.8 × 6.4)	4 × 2 × ³⁄₁₆ (101.6 × 50.8 × 4.8)	1½ × 1½ × ¼ (38.1 × 38.1 × 6.4)	3 × 2 × ¼ (76.2 × 50.8 × 6.4)
2 (50.8)	2.375 (60.3)	2½ × 2½ × ³⁄₁₆ (63.5 × 63.5 × 4.8)	4 × 2 × ¼ (101.6 × 50.8 × 6.4)	1¾ × 1¾ × ³⁄₁₆ (44.4 × 44.4 × 4.8)	3 × 2 × ⁵⁄₁₆ (76.2 × 50.8 × 7.9)
2½ (63.5)	2.875 (73.0)	2½ × 2½ × ¼ (63.5 × 63.5 × 6.4)	4 × 3 × ³⁄₁₆ (101.6 × 76.2 × 4.8)	1¾ × 1¾ × ¼ (44.4 × 44.4 × 6.4)	3 × 2½ × ³⁄₁₆ (76.2 × 63.5 × 4.8)
3 (76.2)	3.500 (88.9)	3 × 3 × ³⁄₁₆ (76.2 × 76.2 × 4.8)	4 × 3 × ¼ (101.6 × 76.2 × 6.4)	2 × 2 × ³⁄₁₆ (50.8 × 50.8 × 4.8)	3 × 2½ × ¼ (76.2 × 63.5 × 6.4)
3½ (88.9)	4.000 (101.6)	3 × 3 × ¼ (76.2 × 76.2 × 6.4)	5 × 2 × ³⁄₁₆ (127 × 50.8 × 4.8)	2 × 2 × ¼ (50.8 × 50.8 × 6.4)	3 × 2½ × ⁵⁄₁₆ (76.2 × 63.5 × 7.9)
4 (101.6)	4.500 (114.3)	3½ × 3 ½ × ³⁄₁₆ (88.9 × 88.9 × 4.8)	5 × 2 × ¼ (127 × 50.8 × 6.4)	2 × 2 × ⁵⁄₁₆ (50.8 × 50.8 × 7.9)	3½ × 2 ½ × ¼ (88.9 × 63.5 × 6.4)
		3½ × 3½ × ¼ (88.9 × 88.9 × 6.4)	5 × 3 × ³⁄₁₆ (127 × 76.2 × 4.8)	2½ × 2½ × ³⁄₁₆ (63.5 × 63.5 × 4.8)	3½ × 2½ × ⁵⁄₁₆ (88.9 × 63.5 × 7.9)
		4 × 4 × ³⁄₁₆ (101.6 × 101.6 × 4.8)	5 × 3 × ¼ (127 × 76.2 × 6.4)	2½ × 2½ × ¼ (63.5 × 63.5 × 6.4)	3½ × 3 × ¼ (88.9 × 76.2 × 6.4)
		4 × 4 × ¼ (101.6 × 101.6 × 6.4)	5 × 4 × ³⁄₁₆ (127 × 101.6 × 4.8)	3 × 3 × ¼ (76.2 × 76.2 × 6.4)	4 × 3 × ¼ (101.6 × 76.2 × 6.4)
			5 × 4 × ¼ (127 × 101.6 × 6.4)	3½ × 3½ × ¼ (88.9 × 88.9 × 6.4)	4 × 3½ × ¼ (101.6 × 88.9 × 6.4)

[1] Pipe is available in three weights. Standard weight is normally sufficient for miscellaneous interior detailing. The actual outside diameter (O.D.) is larger than the nominal size.
[2] Tubing is available in several wall thicknesses; the thinner ones are usually sufficient.
[3] Angles are designated by an L or ∠ symbol followed by the length of the legs, followed by the thickness.

Source: American Institute of Steel Construction, *Manual of Steel Construction, 9th ed.*

Because of the unique nature of the material, ironwork is fabricated differently than other ornamental metals. The finished appearance has a rough, hand-built look unique to the material and is often left unfinished or painted black. Joining techniques are different, as well, and usually emphasize the connection rather than trying to conceal it. Wrought iron is joined by forge welding, riveting, collaring, and wrapping.

OTHER SPECIALTY METALS

Perforated metal [05700]

Perforated metal is sheet metal that has been punched with a regular pattern of holes.

Figure 7.6
Perforated metal patterns

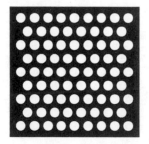

round holes, offset

round holes, straight

square perforations, straight line

square perforations, staggered

slots, side staggered

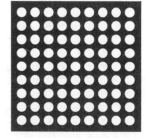

slots, straight line

Standard perforations include round and square holes as well as slots in a wide range of patterns, hole sizes, and hole spacing. For interior applications perforated metals are used for space dividers, railing guards, shelving, furniture, supply- and return-air grilles, coverings for acoustical panels, custom light fixtures, or any specialty fabrication that can be constructed with sheet metal. Some of the commonly available perforated metal patterns are shown in Figure 7.6.

Although perforated metal can be purchased in long rolls, standard stock sheet sizes for custom fabrication include 36 × 96, 36 × 120, 48 × 96, and 48 × 120 in. (900 × 2400, 900 × 3050, 1200 × 2400, and 1200 × 3050 mm). There are hundreds of available hole shapes and sizes, but not all may be as readily available as others. Availability and cost should be verified with a metal fabricator.

Architectural mesh [05700]

Architectural mesh is a specialty metal that is most often used for elevator cab interiors, but it can be creatively applied in other interior applications, such as wall panels and door facings. Architectural mesh is formed by "weaving" thin strips of metal or heavy wire and then grinding off a portion of one face to reveal a highly textured, but relatively flat, surface. The final surface appearance depends on the type of weave, the type of metal used, and how much is ground off. Stainless steel and brass are the most commonly used materials.

Spiral stairs [05715]

Spiral stairs are stairs having a closed circular form with wedge-shaped treads supported from a central, minimum diameter column (usually 4 in. or 100 mm). Standard prefabricated spiral stairs are commonly made from steel. Treads can be exposed steel, hardwood over steel supports, recessed steel stair pans for infill with concrete or stone, or particleboard over a steel support that can be finished with carpet or resilient flooring.

Handrails can be specified as steel pipe, wood, or other ornamental metal. Custom spiral stairs can be fabricated of nearly any combination of steel, wood, and other ornamental metal. Spiral stairs are available in standard diameters from 3 ft 6 in. to 7 ft in six-inch increments (1067 to 2134 mm in 152 mm increments).

Spiral stairs can be fabricated with 22.5°, 27°, and 30° treads, with 30° treads being the most common. This means that there are 12 treads in a full 360° turn or three treads for each quarter circle of the stair. The riser height is set between 7½ in. and 9½ in. (191 mm and 241mm)to make up the total floor-to-floor height, so each riser is the same and the head room restriction is satisfied. At the top of the stairs, a square landing is used to make the transition between the stairs and the rest of the floor when a square opening is used. Depending on the floor-to-floor dimension, circular stairs must be planned so that the first riser at the bottom and the last riser at the top are situated so people enter and exit the stairway traveling in the right direction.

Most building codes allow spiral stairs to be used if certain size restrictions are met, as shown in Figure 7.7. The minimum clear width must be 26 in. (660 mm). The minimum tread width measured perpendicular to the center line of the tread at a point 12 in. (100 mm) from the support column, must be at least 7½ in. (190 mm). The minimum amount of head room is 6 ft 6 in. (1981 mm) and the maximum riser height is 9½ in. (241 mm). If these minimum dimensions are met, the Uniform Building Code allows spiral stairs to be used in Group R, Division 3 occupancies (private homes) and in individual units of Group R, Division 1 occupancies (hotels and apartments). These stairs can be used as required exits only if the area served is no more than 400 ft² (37 m²).

Given these restrictions, spiral stairs must be at least 5 ft in diameter (1500 mm), with about a minimum 8 in. (200 mm) riser for

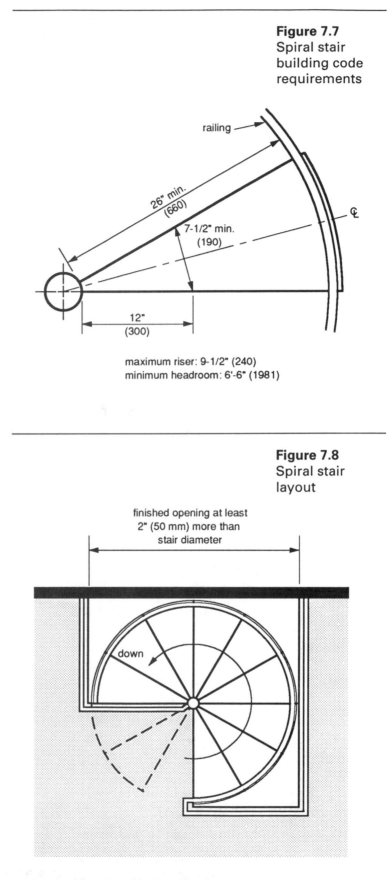

Figure 7.7
Spiral stair building code requirements

railing

26" min. (660)

7-1/2" min. (190)

12" (300)

maximum riser: 9-1/2" (240)
minimum headroom: 6'-6" (1981)

Figure 7.8
Spiral stair layout

finished opening at least 2" (50 mm) more than stair diameter

down

a 27° tread and about a minimum 9 in. (225 mm) riser for a 30° tread. This is based on having to achieve head room clearance of 6 ft 6 in. (1981 mm) plus about 2 in. (50 mm) of upper landing thickness within a three-quarter circle turn. Using a 27° tread, there are 10 treads in a three-quarter circle; using a 30° tread there are only 9 treads in the same turn.

Figure 7.8 shows one example of a 30° tread stair between two floors 9 ft (2743 mm) apart. If a full 360° turn was used, this would allow 13 risers (12 treads) to be used. If the floor-to-floor height is 9 ft (108 in. or 2743 mm), then each riser would be 8.3 in. (211 mm). However, calculating the headroom using nine risers in the three-quarter turn under the landing yields only 6 ft 3¾ in. (1900 mm), which is too low to meet code

requirements. If the riser height is increased to 9 in. (229 mm), then sufficient head room is provided as the stairs pass under the landing; however, only 12 risers are needed to make up the 108 in. total height.

GALVANIC ACTION

Galvanic action is the electrochemical process that occurs when dissimilar metals are in contact in the presence of an electrolyte, such as water. The result is the corrosion of one of the metals. Because most interior applications of metals are in relatively dry environments, galvanic action is not always a problem. However, detailing in a way such that dissimilar metals are in contact should be avoided, especially in humid climates or where moisture may be present, either as vapor or in liquid form. Certain combinations of metals are more susceptible than others to galvanic action. Table 7.13 lists some of the metals used for interior applications. The farther apart the metals are from each other in the table, the greater the possibility of corrosion. The metals are listed from the most susceptible to corrosion to the least, from top of the table down.

Galvanic action can be prevented by using the same, or compatible, metals and fasteners whenever possible. When two or more metals must be combined, they should be separated with isolators made from Teflon®, neoprene, or other suitable material. Teflon-coated screws can also be used when necessary.

Table 7.13
Galvanic series

Zinc   *most*

Galvanized steel

Aluminum alloys: 5052, 3004, 3003, 1100, 6053

Aluminum alloys: 2117, 2017, 2024

Low-carbon steel

Wrought iron

Cast iron

Type 410 stainless steel, active

Type 304 stainless steel, active

Type 316 stainless steel, active

Lead

Copper alloy 280

Copper alloy 675

Copper alloys:
    270
    230
    110
    651, 655
    923, cast

Type 410 stainless steel, passive

Type 304 stainless steel, passive

Type 316 stainless steel, passive   *LEAST*

8

FLOORING CONSTRUCTION

This chapter outlines some of the basic construction methods for flooring that is built on top of a structural floor and that is composed of several individual components. Chapter 9 discusses flooring finishes applied as a single thin material, such as resilient tile and carpet.

WOOD FLOORING [09550]

Types, uses, and grades

There are four basic types of wood flooring: strip flooring, plank flooring, block flooring, and solid block flooring. For all types of wood flooring, oak and maple are the most commonly used species. Oak and maple are hard, durable, and available. Other common hardwoods are beech and birch.

Strip flooring

Strip flooring is one of the most common types of wood flooring. It consists of thin strips from ⅜ in. (10 mm) to ²⁵⁄₃₂ in. (20 mm) thick of varying lengths, with tongue-and-groove edges. See Figure 8.1(a). Most strip flooring is 2¼ in. (57 mm) wide, but 1½-in. (38 mm) wide strips are also available. Strip flooring is used for residential and commercial wood floors for its appearance, warmth under foot, resiliency, and durability.

Plank flooring

Plank flooring comes in the same thicknesses as strip flooring, but is from 3¼ in. to 8 in. (83 to 203 mm) wide. See Figure 8.1(b). It is laid in random lengths with the end joints staggered. Plank flooring is used primarily in residential applications where a larger scale is desired. It is also used to simulate wider, authentic planking.

Block flooring

Block flooring is made of preassembled wood flooring in three configurations. Unit block flooring is standard strip flooring assembled into a unit held together with steel or wood splines. Laminated block flooring is flooring made with from three to five plies of cross-laminated wood veneer. Both types of block flooring are from ⁵⁄₁₆ in. (8 mm) to ⅝ in. (16 mm) thick and come in varying lengths depending on the manufacturer. Unit and laminated block flooring can be laid in any pattern, but herringbone is one of the most common.

Parquet flooring is made of preassembled units of several small, thin slats of wood in a variety of patterns. See Figure 8.1(c). It is available either finished or unfinished. Some manufacturers make parquet with a cellular foam backing that is resilient and has a factory-applied adhesive for residential "peel-and-stick applications." Commercial applications use nonbacked units that are field finished. Parquet flooring is usually sold in 12-in. squares that are ⁵⁄₁₆ in. thick (300 mm squares, 8 mm thick) for mastic application, although some manufacturers make other sizes. Parquet flooring is easier and less expensive to install than other types of flooring. It also can be installed in a wide range of designs.

Solid block flooring

Solid block flooring is made from solid *end grain blocks*. See Figure 8.1(d). These are solid pieces of wood 2, 2½, 3, and 4 in. thick (50, 64, 75, and 100 mm) laid on end with adhesive. Solid block floors are very durable and resistant to oils, mild chemicals, and indentation. They are used for industrial floors or other heavy-duty commercial applications.

Special flooring

There are several variations of wood floors for special uses. These include resilient and relocatable floors. Resilient floors are wood strip floors laid on one of three types of systems described in the next section. They provide extra "spring" for uses like dance, gymnasium, and theater floors. Relocatable floors are systems of modular units, usually 4 ft² (1200.37 m²), that can be quickly installed and dismantled. They are used for athletic and institutional floors, where the type of flooring needs to be changed frequently.

Grades

Wood flooring is graded differently than other wood products. Grading rules are set by the various trade associations such as the National Oak Flooring Manufacturers Association and the Maple Flooring Manufacturers Association. Unfinished oak flooring is graded as Clear, Select, No. 1 Common, and No. 2 Common. Clear is the best grade with the most uniform color. Plain sawn is standard, but quarter sawn is available on special order. Piece lengths are 1¼ ft (381 mm), and longer, with an average length of 3¾ ft (1143 mm). Other species are graded as First, Second, and Third grades, along with some combination grades. First Grade corresponds to Select in oak and Second Grade and Third Grade correspond to No. 1 Common and No. 2 Common, respectively. These are summarized in Tables 8.1–8.3.

Additional flooring species

In addition to the commonly used maple, oak, birch, and beech, there are many wood species, both domestic and imported, that can be used for flooring. Many are available in limited quantities and some are expensive, but they all offer the designer a wide variety of colors, grain patterns, and figures beyond what are available with maple and

Figure 8.1
Types of wood flooring

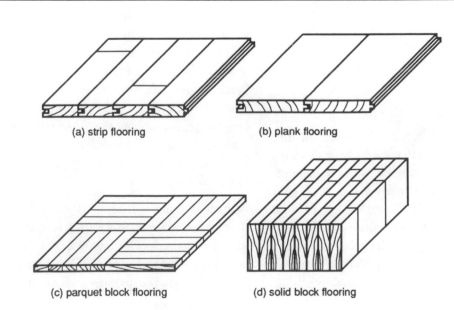

(a) strip flooring

(b) plank flooring

(c) parquet block flooring

(d) solid block flooring

Grade	Bundled lengths	Appearance description
Clear	1¼ ft and up, average length 3¾ ft (380 mm and up, average length 1140 mm)	Best grade with the most uniform color. Plain saw is standard with quarter sawn available on special order only.
Select	1¼ ft and up, average length 3¼ ft (380 mm and up, average length 990 mm)	Limited character marks, unlimited sound sap. Plain sawn is standard with quarter sawn on special order only.
No. 1 Common	1¼ ft and up, average length 2¾ ft (380 mm and up, average length 840 mm)	Variegated appearance, light and dark colors, knots, worm holes and other character marks. Imperfections are filled and finished.
No. 2 Common	1¼ ft and up, average length 2¼ ft (380 mm and up, average length 686 mm)	Rustic appearance. Has all characteristics of the species. Red and white oak may be mixed.

Combination grades: Select and Better (special order)
1¼ ft shorts (lengths of 9 to 18 in.) (225 to 457 mm) red and white oak mixed
No. 1 Common and Better

Source: National Oak Flooring Manufacturers Association.

Table 8.1
Grades of unfinished oak flooring

Grade	Bundled lengths	Appearance description
Prime	1¼ ft and up, average length 3½ ft (380 mm and up, average length 1070 mm)	Excellent appearance with natural color variations permitted. Special order.
Standard	1¼ ft and up, average length 2¾ ft (380 mm and up, average length 840 mm)	Variegated appearance with varying sound wood characteristics of species.
Tavern	1¼ ft and up, average length 2¼ ft (380 mm and up, average length 690 mm)	Rustic appearance with all wood characteristics of species. Economical floor.

Combination grades: Standard and Better, Tavern and Better

Source: National Oak Flooring Manufacturers Association.

Table 8.2
Grades of prefinished oak flooring

Grade	Bundled lengths	Appearance description
First Grade	Bundles 1¼ ft and up (380 mm and up)	Best appearance. Natural color variation, limited character marks, unlimited sap.
Second Grade	Bundles 1¼ ft and up (380 mm and up)	Variegated appearance, varying sound wood characteristics of species.
Third Grade	Bundles 1¼ ft and up (380 mm and up)	Rustic appearance, all wood characteristics of species. Serviceable economical floor after filling.

Other grades:	Second and Better	Third and Better
	First Grade white hard maple	First Grade red beech and birch

Source: National Oak Flooring Manufacturers Association.

Table 8.3
Grades of maple, beech, and birch flooring

oak. Some of these available wood species are summarized in Table 8.4.

Wood Floor Finishes

Several types of finishes are available. One of the most common is water-based urethane. It produces a durable, quick-drying finish that satisfies environmental regulations for limited volatile organic compound (VOC) content. It dries clear and inhibits color changes in certain woods. In addition, water-based urethane is the best choice for some exotic woods that contain oils and chemical compounds that adversely react with some types of solvent-based finishes.

Oil-modified polyurethane also produces a durable finish, but it may be slower drying, contain an unacceptable VOC content, and darken some woods. However, some manufacturers have reformulated their oil-modified products to comply with VOC regulations.

Other finishes include moisture-cured urethanes and acid-cured (Swedish) finishes. Both provide an extremely durable cover but produce a strong, unpleasant odor during application.

Typical installation details

Wood strip flooring must be installed over a suitable nailable base. Because wood swells when it becomes damp, provisions must be made to prevent moisture from seeping up from below and to allow for expansion of the completed floor. Strip flooring is installed by blind nailing through the tongue.

Figure 8.2 illustrates the typical installation method for residential floors on wood joists. The strip flooring is blind nailed to a suitable subfloor, either plywood or particleboard, typically ½ in. (13 mm) minimum thickness. The subflooring should be laid with the long dimension perpendicular to the joists with a ⅛-in. (3 mm) gap between the panels and with the end joints staggered by 4 ft (1200 mm). A layer of 15-lb asphalt felt may be laid to prevent squeaking and to act as a vapor barrier.

Figure 8.3 shows two methods of installing wood flooring over a concrete subfloor in commercial construction. In Figure 8.3(a), a sheet of ¾-in. (19 mm) plywood is attached to the concrete to provide the nailable base. A layer of 6-mil polyethylene film is laid down first, if moisture may be a problem. The concrete subfloor should be level to within ¼ in. in 10 ft (6.4 mm in 3050 mm) with no high spots or depressions.

In Figure 8.3(b), the wood flooring is laid on wood sleepers. This method of installation not only results in a more resilient floor that is more comfortable under foot, but also provides an air space that allows excess moisture to escape. In both instances, a gap of about ⅜ in. to ¾ in. (10 to 19 mm) is left at the perimeter to allow for expansion. This gap is concealed with the wood base. If the size of the room exceeds 20 × 20 ft (6 × 6 m), then additional expansion space may be required.

Resilient strip flooring systems can be installed in one of three ways. In the first, the flooring is nailed to wood sleepers that rest on resilient neoprene pads. See Figure 8.4. The pads are spaced 12 in. (300 mm) on center. The wood sleepers are nominal 2 × 4-in. (50 × 100 mm) pressure-treated wood 4 ft (1200 mm) long, spaced 9 in. (225 mm) on center for $^{25}/_{32}$-in. (20 mm) flooring, or spaced 12 in. (300 mm) on center for $^{33}/_{32}$-in. (26 mm) flooring. The ends of the sleepers should be laid end to end with a ¼-in. (6 mm) gap between them and with the end joints staggered a minimum of 2 ft (600 mm).

The second system uses strip flooring locked into place and to each other with steel clips attached to a resiliently mounted anchor slot that is recessed into insulation board. See Figure 8.5. Several variations are available from different manufacturers.

The third method uses spring-mounted isolation feet that support the wood sleepers to which the wood flooring is attached.

In all three methods of resiliently mounted wood flooring, the concrete subfloor must

Table 8.4
Wood flooring
species

Species	Availability	Hardness	Stability	Common coloring
Ash, white	M	3	.00274	Light color with heartwood light tan to dark brown
Beech	L	3	.00431	Reddish-brown with sapwood pale white
Birch	M	3	.00338	Light reddish-brown with white sapwood
Cherry, black	M	2	.00248	Reddish-brown heartwood with light sapwood
Cherry, Brazilian	C	5	.00300	Reddish-brown when seasoned; darkens in sunlight
Cypress, Australian	L	3	.00162	Honey-gold to brown with darker knots
Douglas fir	C	1	.00267	Yellowish-tan to light brown heartwood
Hickory	L	4	.00411	Reddish-brown with dark brown stripes
Jarrah	L	4	.00396	Dark brownish red heartwood with paler sapwood
Mahogany, santos	M	5	.00238	Dark, reddish-brown
Maple	C	3	.00353	Light color with creamy-white heartwood
Merbau	L	4	.00158	Brown to dark red-brown
Mesquite	L	5	.00129	Light brown to dark reddish-brown
Oak, red	C	3	.00369	Reddish with lighter sapwood
Oak, white	C	3	.00365	Grayish-brown heartwood with very light sapwood
Padauk	M	4	.00180	Reddish to purple-brown with cream-colored sapwood
Pine, antique heart	L	3	.00263	Recycled pine of light tan to reddish-brown
Pine, southern yellow	C	2	.00265	Light yellow to reddish- or yellowish-brown
Purpleheart	L	4	.00212	Deep purple with cream-colored sapwood
Teak	L	2	.00186	Yellow-brown to dark golden brown; cream sapwood
Walnut	M	2	.00274	Chocolate brown heartwood with tan sapwood
Wenge	L	4	.00201	Very dark brown with fine, black veins

Availability: C = commonly available
     M = moderately available
     L = limited availability

Hardness: 1 = <700
    2 = 700–1000
    3 = 1000–1500
    4 = 1500–2000
    5 = 2000+

Stability: Listed values are the dimensional change coefficient. The lower the value the more stable the wood.

Hardness based on the Janka hardness scale, which is the load required to embed an 11-mm steel ball to one-half its diameter in the wood. 5 = hardest; 1 = softest.

be depressed a distance sufficient enough to allow the finished floor to be level with the adjacent flooring. Because this distance can be anywhere from 1¼ in. to 2½ in. (32 to 64 mm), these methods are generally only used for new construction. To apply wood strip flooring over existing concrete floors, the method shown in Figure 8.3(a) should be used because it minimizes the thickness required for the flooring. Even in this case, some provision for making the transition to a lower surface-applied flooring material must be made. If this is not possible, then thinner parquet flooring or block flooring can be used.

For most residential or commercial projects, laminated and parquet flooring are glued over a stable wood subfloor or directly onto a smooth concrete subfloor if moisture is not present. Figure 8.6 shows a typical residential application of parquet flooring. If the flooring is placed on a floor above a crawl space, the crawl space should be well-ventilated and the ground covered with 6-mil polyethylene.

Coordination

• Areas below the floors on which wood flooring is installed should be ventilated to prevent passage of moisture from below.

Figure 8.2
Wood strip flooring on wood framing

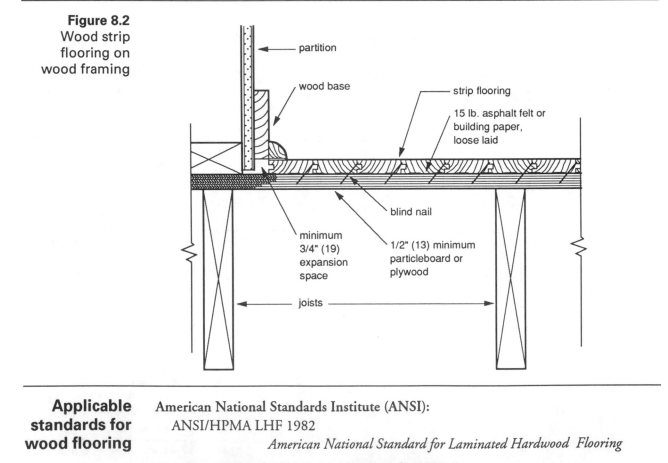

- partition
- wood base
- strip flooring
- 15 lb. asphalt felt or building paper, loose laid
- blind nail
- minimum 3/4" (19) expansion space
- 1/2" (13) minimum particleboard or plywood
- joists

Applicable standards for wood flooring

American National Standards Institute (ANSI):
　ANSI/HPMA LHF 1982
　　　　　American National Standard for Laminated Hardwood Flooring

American Society for Testing and Materials (ASTM):
　ASTM D-2394　*Methods for Simulated Service Testing of Wood and Wood-base Finish Flooring*

Maple Flooring Manufacturers Association (MFMA):
　Grading Rules for Hard Maple

National Oak Flooring Manufacturers Association (NOFMA):
　Official Flooring Grading Rules

• Concrete subfloors for parquet flooring must be level to within ¼ in. in 10 ft (6 mm in 3050 mm).

• Concrete subfloors for resilient wood flooring systems must be level to within ⅛ in. in 10 ft (3 mm in 3050 mm).

TILE [09300]

Types and uses

Tiles are small, flat finishing units made of clay or clay mixtures. The advantages of tile include durability; water resistance (if glazed); ease of installation; ease of cleaning; a wide choice of colors, sizes, and patterns; fire resistance; fade resistance; and the ability to store heat for passive solar collection. The two primary types are ceramic tile and quarry tile.

Ceramic tile is a surfacing unit, usually relatively thin in relation to facial area, made from clay or a mixture of clay and other ceramic materials. It has either a glazed or an unglazed face, and is fired above red heat during manufacture to a temperature sufficiently high to produce specific physical properties and characteristics.

Quarry tile is glazed or unglazed tile, usually with 6 in.² or more, of facial area. It is made from natural clay or shale by extrusion.

Figure 8.3
Wood strip flooring on concrete framing

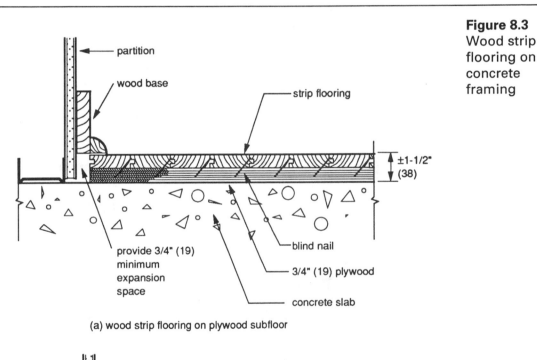

(a) wood strip flooring on plywood subfloor

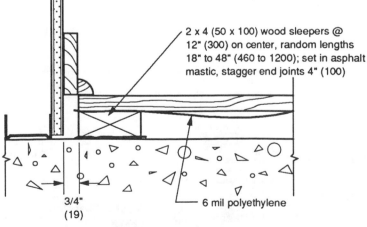

(b) wood strip flooring on sleepers

Some of the other common types of tile include glazed wall tile, unglazed tile, ceramic mosaic tile, paver tile, quarry tile (glazed or unglazed), abrasive tile, and antistatic tile.

Ceramic mosaic tile is formed by either the dust-pressed or extrusion method, ¼ in. (6 mm) to ⅜ in. (10 mm) thick, and having a facial area of less than 6 in.² (3870 mm²). Dust pressing uses large presses to shape the tile out of relatively dry clay. The extrusion process uses machines to cut tiles from a wetter and more malleable clay extruded through a die.

The United States tile industry classifies tile based on size: tile under 6 in.² (3870 mm²) is *mosaic tile*; tile over 6 in.² is *wall tile*. Glazed and unglazed nonmosaic tile made by the extrusion method is *quarry tile*. Glazed and unglazed tile over 6 in.² made by the dust-pressed method is called *paver tile*.

Tile is also classified according to its resistance to water absorption, with nonvitreous tile having a water absorption rate of more than 7.0 percent. Impervious tile has a water absorption rate of 0.5 percent, or less. In between these two tile types are semivitreous tile and vitreous tile.

Imported tile is classified differently than tile produced in the United States. European manufacturers classify tile according to its production method, either the dust-pressed or extrusion method, its degree of water absorption, its finish, and whether it is glazed or unglazed.

The classifications of abrasion resistance are: Group I, light residential; Group II, moderate residential; Group III, maximum residential; and Group IV, commercial (having the highest abrasion resistance).

Figure 8.4
Resilient wood flooring system

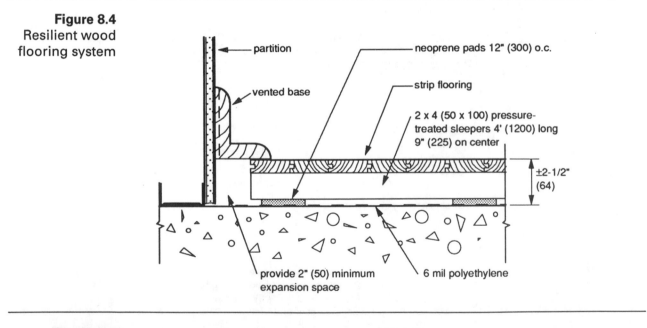

Figure 8.5
Strip flooring on resilient underlayment

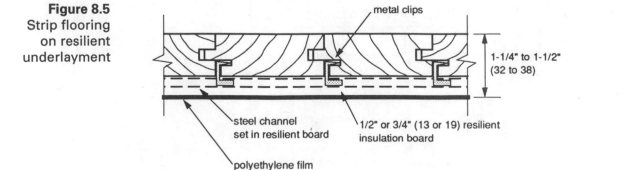

Standard forms

Ceramic mosaic tile is available in standard nominal US sizes of 1 × 1 in. and 2 × 2 in. (25 × 25 mm and 50 × 50 mm) with a nominal thickness of ¼ in. (6 mm). Some 2 × 1 in. tile is also available, as well as small hexagonal shapes. Glazed wall tile is manufactured in standard nominal sizes of 4¼ × 4¼, 6 × 4½, and 6 × 6 in. (108 × 108 mm, 152 × 114 mm, and 152 × 152 mm), with a nominal thickness of ¼ in. or 5⁄16 in. (6 or 8 mm). Individual manufacturers may produce other sizes as well.

Most manufacturers produce a complete line of trim pieces for ceramic tile installation. These include cove base, bull-nose, inside and outside corners, and other shapes that are most often required. The standard trim shapes are illustrated in Figures 8.7(a) and 8.7(b). However, some manufacturers produce only a limited number of trim shapes; their availability should be verified prior to final selection.

Quarry tile is available in nominal flat sizes of 3 × 3 in., 4 × 4 in., 6 × 6 in., 8 × 8 in., 8 × 4 in., and 6 × 3 in. (75 × 75, 100 × 100, 150 × 150, 200 × 200, 200 × 100, and 150 × 75 mm) with a nominal thickness of ½ in. (13 mm). Trim pieces are similar to those of wall tile.

Safety factors

Tile (and also terrazzo, stone, and other smooth surfaces) can be a potentially dangerous

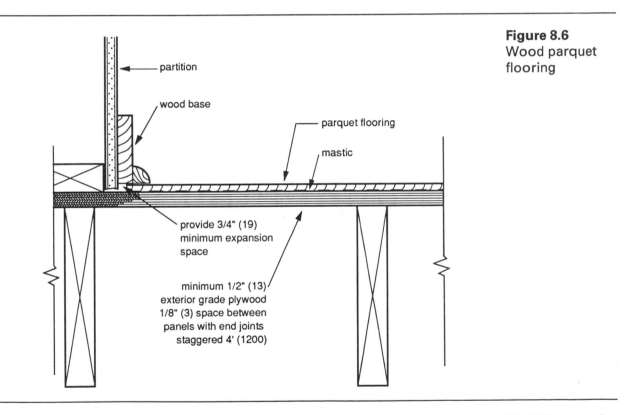

Figure 8.6
Wood parquet flooring

Wood flooring must meet the flame-spread requirements for the type of occupancy and area of the building in which they are used. For most areas where wood flooring is typically used in commercial construction this is not a problem because all flooring will meet Class I (A) requirements. For Type I and Type II construction, the applicable building code may require that the space between sleepers be filled with noncombustible material or fire-stopped so that no open space exceeds 100 ft² (9.3 m²).

Additional code requirements apply to stage floors and conventional plank flooring.

Building code requirements for wood flooring

flooring surface, especially when wet or covered with grease or other slippery materials. For tile and other materials, the American Society for Testing and Materials has a test standard to evaluate the coefficient of friction: ASTM C-1028, *Standard Test Method for Determining the Static Coefficient of Friction of Ceramic Tile, and Other Like Surfaces by the Horizontal Dynamometer Pull-meter Method*. Many manufacturers make floor tile with roughened surfaces to improve slip resistance; however, it is sometimes difficult to know what coefficient of friction a particular manufacturer's tile has or what value should be specified for any given situation. ASTM D-2047, *Standard Test Method for Static Coefficient of Friction of Polish-coated Floor Surfaces by the James Machine*, used for resilient flooring, mentions that a level of 0.5 or more has traditionally been recognized as

Applicable standards for tile

American National Standards Institute (ANSI):

ANSI A108.1   *Installation of Ceramic Tile, a Collection (Includes the A108 and A118 Series)*

ANSI A108.1a   *Specifications for Installation of Ceramic Tile in the Wet-set Method, with Portland Cement Mortar*

ANSI A108.1b   *Specifications for Installation of Ceramic Tile on a Cured Portland Cement Mortar Setting Bed with Dry-set or Latex Portland Cement Mortar*

ANSI A108.1c   *Specifications for Contractors Option: Installation of Ceramic Tile in the Wet-set Method with Portland Cement Mortar or Installation of Ceramic Tile on a Cured Portland Cement Mortar Bed with Dry-set or Latex Portland Cement Mortar*

ANSI A108.4   *Specifications for Installation of Ceramic Tile with Organic Adhesives or Water Cleanable Tile Setting Epoxy Adhesive*

ANSI A108.5   *Installation of Ceramic Tile with Dry-set Portland Cement Mortar or Latex-Portland Cement Mortar*

ANSI A108.6   *Installation of Ceramic Tile with Chemical Resistant, Water Cleanable Tile-setting and Grouting Epoxy*

ANSI A108.7   *Installation of Electrically Conductive Ceramic Tile Installed with Conductive Dry-set Portland Cement Mortar*

ANSI A108.8   *Installation of Ceramic Tile with Chemical-resistant Furan Mortar and Grout*

ANSI A108.9   *Installation of Ceramic Tile with Modified Epoxy Emulsion Mortar/Grout*

ANSI A108.10   *Installation of Grout in Tile Work*

ANSI A118.1   *Specifications for Dry-set Portland Cement Mortar*

ANSI A118.2   *Specifications for Conductive Dry-set Portland Cement Mortar*

ANSI A118.3   *Specifications for Chemical Resistant Water Cleanable Tile-setting and Grouting Epoxy*

ANSI A118.4   *Specifications for Latex-Portland Cement Mortar*

ANSI A118.5   *Specifications for Chemical-resistant Furan Mortar and Grout*

ANSI A118.6   *Specifications for Ceramic Tile Grouts*

ANSI A118.8   *Specifications for Modified Epoxy Emulsion Mortar/Grout*

ANSI A136.1   *Organic Adhesives for Installation of Ceramic Tile*

ANSI A137.1   *Specifications for Ceramic Tile*

Tile Council of America, Inc.(TCA):

Ceramic Tile: The Installation Handbook

providing nonhazardous walkway surfaces. However, this test method is not applicable for wet surfaces and does not take into account other factors such as the type of shoe material, type of contaminate on the stair, and level of surface. For wet surfaces, two other ASTM test methods can be used: ASTM F-1679, *Standard Test Method for Using a Variable Incidence Tribometer*, and ASTM F-1677, *Standard Test Method for Using a Portable Inclinable Articulated Strut Slip Tester*. Underwriters Laboratories requires a level of 0.5, or higher, as a minimum safety level based on the ASTM C-1028 test method. Some have suggested a level of 0.6 for a good slip-resistant floor. The Americans with Disabilities Act requires a minimum static coefficient of friction of 0.6 in level areas and 0.8 on ramps. Until specific,

uniform criteria are established, the designer should take into account the conditions under which floor tile will be used before selecting a particular type. For example, a public lobby where snow and rain may be tracked in may need to be more slip resistant than a residential bathroom, where people are taking smaller strides without slippery shoe material.

Typical details

Tile is laid on a suitable substrate using one of several formulations of mortar, or with adhesives. The joints are filled with grout. The particular type of mortar or adhesive and grout depends on the type of tile and the parameters of the job. The two most common methods of laying a tile floor are the thin-set method and the full mortar bed method.

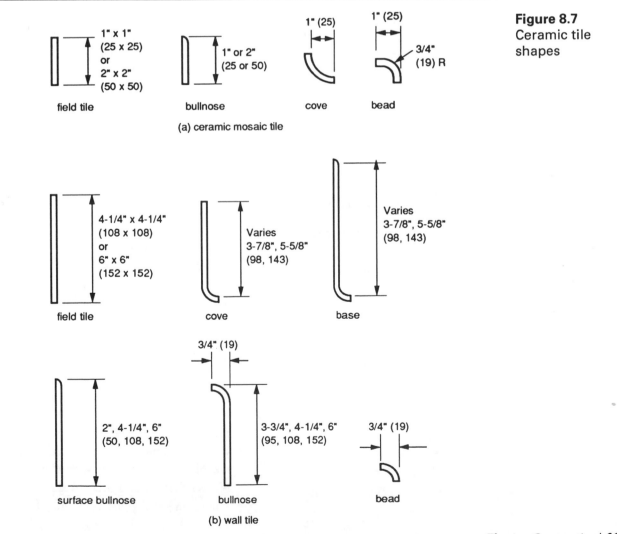

Figure 8.7
Ceramic tile shapes

The thin-set method

Thin-set tile floors are laid on a suitable substrate, commonly a glass mesh mortar unit specifically manufactured for tile installation. This is a cementitious panel nailed to the subfloor. The tile is laid on a thin coating of dry-set or latex-Portland cement mortar with latex-Portland cement grout. See Figure 8.8. A standard sand and Portland cement grout can also be used. When using thin-set tile, the subfloor must be level, free from dirt and other contaminates, and able to support the extra weight of the tile. If a subfloor deflects or moves in some way, a thin-set tile installation will probably develop cracks. If movement or deflection more than $\frac{1}{360}$ of the span is expected, then a full mortar bed with a cleavage membrane should be used.

The full mortar bed method

The full mortar bed method of laying ceramic tile floors is shown in Figures 8.9(a)

and 8.9(b). The tile and reinforced mortar bed are separated from the structural floor with a cleavage membrane (15-lb roofing felt, or 4-mil polyethylene film) to allow the two floors to move independently. This system should be used on floors where excessive deflection is expected and on precast and posttensioned concrete floors. Because the mortar bed is reinforced with 2 × 2 in. (51 × 51 mm), 16-gage welded wire fabric, the tile and bed are rigidly held together as a unit. In addition to providing for movement, the full mortar bed allows for minor variations in floor level to be corrected with the mortar. The tile can be set on the mortar bed while it is still plastic or on a cured mortar bed using a second coat of dry-set or latex-Portland cement mortar. If a waterproof floor is required, a waterproof membrane can be used in place of the cleavage membrane. This is the preferred method for tile floors in commercial showers or where continuous wetting will be present. Figure 8.9(b) shows the full mortar bed method over a concrete subfloor.

The full mortar bed method is not usually used in existing construction because of the required thickness of the mortar bed and the extra weight. Ideally, subfloors should be depressed about 1½ in. (38.1 mm) so that the level of the floor matches adjacent flooring construction.

Expansion joints

Expansion joints in ceramic tile floors are needed in some situations. They are required for large expanses of tile and where the tile abuts restraining surfaces, such as columns, walls, and pipes. They are also required where backing materials change and where dissimilar floors occur. Expansion joints are not required in small rooms or corridors less than 12 ft (3.66 m) wide. If there are existing control, isolation, construction, or building expansions joints, the tile joints must coincide with them as well. Figures 8.10(a) and 8.10(b) show two tile expansion joint applications, and Table 8.5

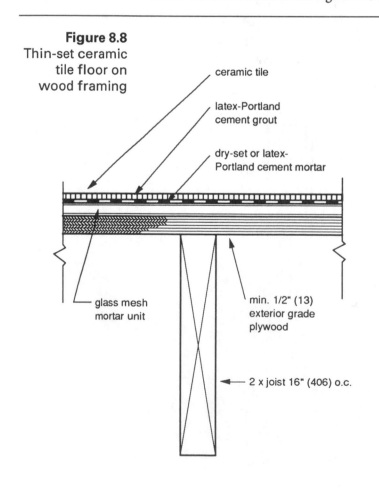

Figure 8.8
Thin-set ceramic tile floor on wood framing

ceramic tile

latex-Portland cement grout

dry-set or latex-Portland cement mortar

glass mesh mortar unit

min. 1/2" (13) exterior grade plywood

2 x joist 16" (406) o.c.

gives the recommended sizes and spacing for expansion joints.

Expansion joints must be filled with sealant rather than grout. For joints where traffic is expected, a two-part polyurethane conforming to ASTM C-920, Type M, Grade P, Class 25 should be used with a Shore A hardness of 35 or greater. For nontraffic areas a silicone, one-part polyurethane, or polysulfide sealant can be used.

Mortar for interior installations

There are several mortars and adhesives used for ceramic tile installation, each offers different characteristics for particular uses. These are summarized in Table 8.6. Compatible grouts are also available for each of the mortar types.

Italian tile

There are four types of Italian glazed tile and four types of unglazed tile:

Glazed:
Cottoforte: pink-red tile with good mechanical strength
Majolica: yellow-pink tile used for walls
White-body earthenware: used for walls and light residential floors
Monocottura: for interior and exterior floors

Unglazed:
Red stoneware: commercial tile with high mechanical strength and excellent frost and abrasion resistance
Terra cotta: for interior and exterior floors

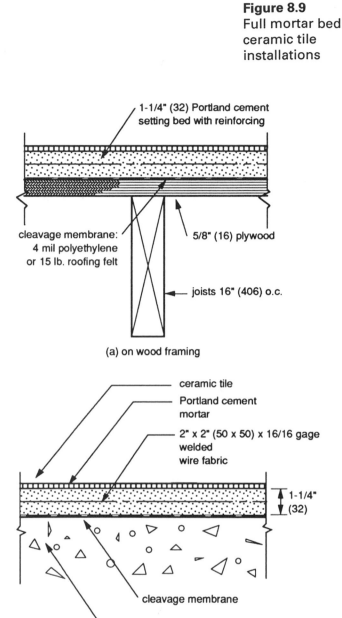

Figure 8.9
Full mortar bed ceramic tile installations

1-1/4" (32) Portland cement setting bed with reinforcing

cleavage membrane: 4 mil polyethylene or 15 lb. roofing felt

5/8" (16) plywood

joists 16" (406) o.c.

(a) on wood framing

ceramic tile
Portland cement mortar
2" x 2" (50 x 50) x 16/16 gage welded wire fabric
1-1/4" (32)
cleavage membrane
concrete subfloor

(b) on concrete

	Ceramic mosaic and glazed wall tile	Quarry and paver tile	Exposed to direct sunlight or moisture
Spacing	24 ft to 36 ft (7 to 11 m)	24 ft to 36 ft (7 to 11 m)	12 ft to 16 ft (3.5 to 5 m)
Width	⅛ in. to ¼ in.(1) (3 to 6 mm)	¼ in.(2) (6 mm)	¼ in. (6 mm)

Table 8.5
Recommended ceramic tile expansion joint width and spacing

(1) The preferred minimum is ¼ in., but the joint should never be less than ⅛ in.
(2) Same as the grout joint but not less than ¼ in.

Fully vitrified stoneware: a nonporous porcelain or china tile

Clinker tile: similar to red stoneware for walls and floors

Coordination

• For both thin-set and full mortar bed tile floors verify the load-carrying capacity of the structural floor to support the extra weight of the tile.

• For thin-set tile floors, the maximum variation in the surface of the subfloor must not exceed ⅛ in. in 10 ft (3 mm in 3050 mm).

Figure 8.10
Ceramic tile expansion joints

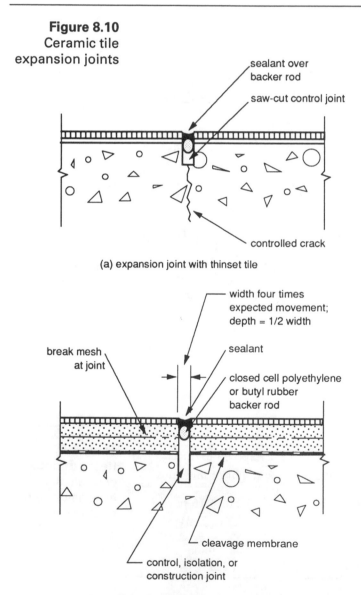

(a) expansion joint with thinset tile

(b) expansion joint with full mortar bed tile

• For full mortar bed tile floors, the maximum variation in the surface of the subfloor must not exceed ¼ in. in 10 ft (6 mm in 3050 mm).

• If a floor must slope to a drain, the slope must be in the subfloor, not in the setting bed.

• Location of joints should coordinate with wall joints and other surrounding construction elements.

• Subflooring and underlayment for ceramic tile over wood joists must be installed dry with closely spaced fasteners and with gaps between panels to allow for moisture-induced movement. The gaps must then be taped and filled prior to installing the tile.

TERRAZZO [09400]

Types and uses

Terrazzo is a composite material that is poured in place or precast. It is used for floors, and stairs and sometimes for walls. Terrazzo consists of marble, quartz, granite, or other suitable stone chips in a matrix that is cementitious, modified cementitious, or resinous. Terrazzo is poured, cured, ground, and polished to produce a smooth surface.

The advantages of terrazzo include durability, water resistance, ease of cleaning, fire resistance, and a wide choice of patterns and colors. An unlimited number of terrazzo finishes can be achieved by specifying various combinations of chips and matrix colors.

There are four basic types of terrazzo. Standard terrazzo is the most common type, using small chips no larger than ⅜ in. (9.5 mm). Venetian terrazzo uses chips larger than ⅜ in. (9.5 mm). Palladian terrazzo uses thin random-fractured slabs of marble with standard terrazzo between. Rustic terrazzo has the matrix depressed to expose the chips. It is most commonly used for exterior applications where a rough surface is required.

The most commonly used matrix is cementitious, a mixture of white Portland cement, sand, and water. Modified cementitious

Type	Characteristics	Use requirements and limitations	Applications
Portland cement	Strong, water resistant. Tile set while mortar in plastic state or on cured bed with dry-set or latex-Portland cement mortar. Poor crack resistance.	Structurally sound substrate. Proper damp curing.	Only mortar used for full mortar bed installation on new or existing construction. Applied over substrates of concrete, masonry, wood, plaster, steel stud walls, etc.
Dry set	Water resistant, impact resistant. Soaking of tiles not required.	Not a water barrier. Substrate must be true and level. Damp curing.	Thin-set applications. Applied over substrates of concrete, masonry, glass-mesh mortar units Portland cement mortar beds.
Latex-Portland cement	More water resistant than dry-set. Less rigid than Portland cement mortar. Impact resistant.	Must dry out from 14 to 60 days for areas that may not dry out completely during use. Should not be used over plywood subfloors. Damp curing.	Thin-set applications where flexibility is required to accommodate minor floor movement.
Epoxy	Chemically resistant. High bond strength. Impact resistant.	Level subfloor. Substrate must be clean and free of concrete curing compounds, oil, and sealers.	Thin-set on commercial floors where high impact and chemical resistance are needed.
Modified epoxy emulsion	High bond strength. Shrinks less than other mortars.	Not chemically resistant. Modest resistance to cracking.	Thin-set applications. For light-duty or residential use only over plywood or concrete.
Furan	Chemically resistant. High impact resistance. Excellent resistance to high temperatures.	Skilled applicators required. Expensive. Black in color.	For heavy use in commercial and industrial applications over all standard substrates, including existing tile and steel plate.
Epoxy adhesive	High bond strength. Ease of application.	Little chemical resistance.	Thin-set for residential only on floors, walls, countertops.
Organic adhesive	Ease of application. Economical.	Must have properly prepared backings for wet areas.	Thin-set for residential only on floors, walls, countertops.

Table 8.6
Mortar types and uses

matrices, which consists of mixing epoxy or polyacrylate with the Portland cement, are used when additional chemical resistance or conductivity are required or when the installation is thin-set. Resinous matrices of epoxy or polyester are used for thin-set applications. Conductive floors are used where static electricity buildup must be avoided. Conductive matrices are black due to their carbon content.

Finishes

Terrazzo is generally finished to a smooth surface with an 80-grit stone grinder. However, to achieve a more textured surface, terrazzo can be ground with a rough, 24-grit grinder. Rustic terrazzo exposes some of the stone when the matrix is washed before it has set; however, this finish is usually not appropriate for interior flooring.

Typical details

Terrazzo can be installed on walls as well as on floors. It can also be precast and poured into metal forms, such as stair pans. For floors, there are four methods of installation: sand cushion, bonded, monolithic, and thin-set. Each requires a different total thickness of material and different installation method. However, each method requires the use of divider strips placed at regular intervals to provide a controlled cracking point for the material, to facilitate leveling during installation, and for decorative purposes. Divider strips are most commonly a white alloy of zinc or brass in 12, 14, 16, or 18 (Brown and Sharp) gages (see Table 7.4). Strips ⅛-in., ¼-in., and ⅜-in. (3, 6, and 10 mm) wide can also be used. They are available in T and L shapes in various depths appropriate for the installation method. Plastic and neoprene control strips are also used, with neoprene used over expansion joints in the concrete subfloor.

The sand cushion method, shown in Figure 8.11, is the best way to avoid cracking the terrazzo. This is because the finish system is physically separated from the structural slab with a membrane, much the same as with a full mortar bed ceramic tile floor. Because the underbed is reinforced, the terrazzo system can move independently of the structure. The sand cushion method requires a total depth of 2½ in. (64 mm) and weighs about 30 lb/ft² (146 kg/m²); therefore, it is only appropriate for new construction where a structurally sound, depressed concrete floor slab can be provided. Divider strips should be located to provide areas of approximately 9 ft² to 36 ft² (0.8 to 3.3 m²). The length of each area should not exceed twice the width.

Figure 8.11
Sand cushion
terrazzo

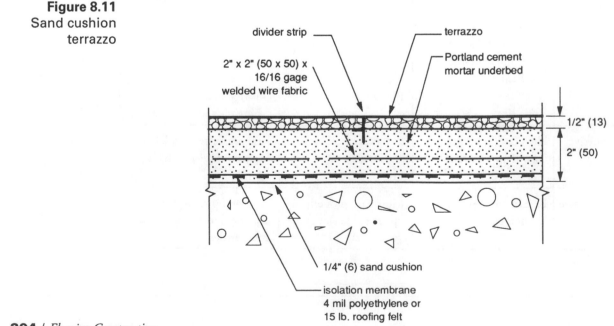

Bonded terrazzo reduces the total thickness and weight of the installation, but because the terrazzo is bonded to the concrete structural floor below, any deflection or other movement of the structure will cause the crack to telegraph through to the finished surface. See Figure 8.12. Because bonded terrazzo requires a total depth of 1¾ in. (45 mm) and weighs about 18 lb/ft² (8.8 kg/m²), it is also only appropriate for new construction where a depressed concrete subfloor can be provided. Divider strips should be located to provide areas of approximately 16 ft² to 36 ft² (1.5 to 3.3 m²). The length of each area should not exceed twice the width. A bonded terrazzo base is illustrated in Figure 8.13.

Monolithic terrazzo installations bond directly to the concrete structural floor without the use of a mortar underbed, as shown in Figures 8.14 and 8.15. Like bonded installations, they will crack if the slab below deflects. However, they are only ½ in. (13 mm) thick and weigh about 7 lb/ft² (3.4 kg/m²). This makes them suitable for new construction, as well as for some types of remodeling but only if the floor is structurally capable of supporting the extra weight without excessive deflection. The structural slab should also be level to within ⅛ in. in 10 ft (3 mm in 3050 mm). Divider strips should be located to provide areas of approximately 200 ft² to 300 ft² (19 to 28 m²) in rectangular areas. The length of each area should not be more than 50 percent longer than the width. The divider strips should also be located at column center lines and over any control and construction joints in the concrete slab. When control joints in the concrete slab do not exist where divider strips are desired, the slab can be saw cut to no more than one third its thickness to create slab control joints. Saw cutting should be verified with the building architect and engineer to be sure that the structure is not weakened or that conduit and other items embedded in the slab are not damaged.

Thin-set terrazzo is similar to monolithic, but only requires from ¼ in. to ⅜ in. (6 mm to 10 mm) thickness. It weights about 3 lb/ft² (1.5 kg/m²). Epoxy, polyester, or polyacrylate matrices must be used for thin-set applications. Expansion strips with neoprene filler must be provided at all control joints in the structural slab, and divider strips should be located where a structural crack exists or can be anticipated. Divider strips are also used to create designs or patterns in the floor.

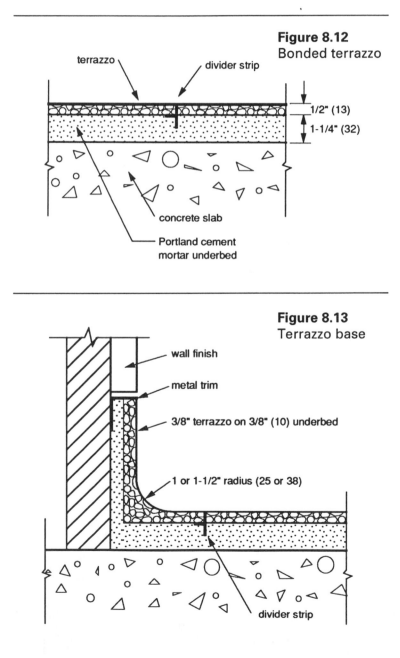

Figure 8.12
Bonded terrazzo

terrazzo

divider strip

1/2" (13)
1-1/4" (32)

concrete slab

Portland cement mortar underbed

Figure 8.13
Terrazzo base

wall finish

metal trim

3/8" terrazzo on 3/8" (10) underbed

1 or 1-1/2" radius (25 or 38)

divider strip

Coordination

• Existing floors must be capable of supporting the extra weight of terrazzo.

• For sand cushion and bonded floors the concrete subfloor must be level to within ¼ in. in 10 ft (6 mm in 3050 mm).

• The design and installation of divider strips must coincide with the expansion and control joints of the concrete subfloor.

• For custom chip and matrix combinations, a minimum 6 × 6-in. (150 × 150 mm) sample should be requested from the terrazzo contractor prior to installation.

Figure 8.14
Monolithic terrazzo

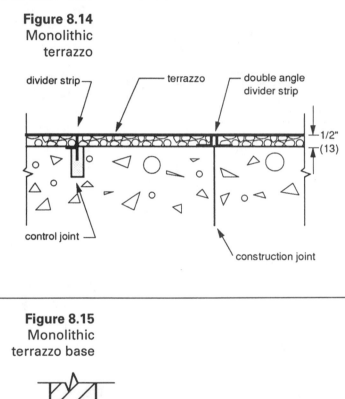

divider strip — terrazzo — double angle divider strip

1/2" (13)

control joint — construction joint

Figure 8.15
Monolithic terrazzo base

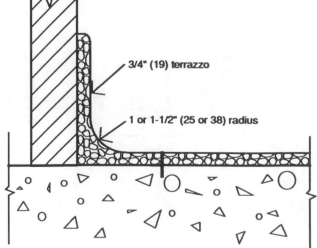

3/4" (19) terrazzo

1 or 1-1/2" (25 or 38) radius

• For bonded, monolithic, and thin-set installation, the subfloor must be free of compounds used to cure the concrete. It must also have the correct finish texture for the type of terrazzo installation: a troweled finish for bonded and a textured broom finish for monolithic floors.

STONE FLOORING [09600]

Traditionally, stone flooring was laid in slabs about ¾ in. (19 mm) thick on a thick mortar bed. While that method is still used today, new cutting and fabrication technology makes it possible to use thin tiles of natural stone. Smaller sizes of thin tiles are usually not reinforced, but some manufacturers apply backings of fiberglass or other materials to add strength. Thin natural stone tiles not only reduce cost but simplify installation. They also make possible the use of stone flooring where it once was infeasible because of weight restrictions. Installation methods are similar to those for ceramic tile.

Types and uses

There are five types of stone commonly used for flooring. These include granite, marble, limestone, slate, and sandstone. The same types of stone can be used for wall facing as described in Chapter 10.

Granite is an igneous rock that has visible grains. It is available in a wide variety of colors, including gray, beige, white, pink, red, blue, green, and black. For interior use, there are five common finishes. A polished finish has a mirror gloss with sharp reflection. A honed finish has a dull sheen, without reflections. Fine-rubbed finishes produce a smooth surface free from scratches with no sheen. A rubbed finish has a surface with occasional slight "trails" or scratches. Finally, a thermal, or flame, finish is coarse, with the exact amount of coarseness varying depending on the grain structure of the granite.

Marble is a metamorphic rock formed by layers of shells, which, under heat and pressure, formed into a composition of crystalline grains of calcite and dolomite. Like granite, marble is available in a range of colors and patterns from uniform, pure white to vivid greens and reds with wild streaked patterns. The smoothest finish for marble is polished, which produces a glossy surface that brings out the full color and character of the marble. A honed finish has a satin-smooth surface with little or no gloss. An abrasive finish has a flat, non-reflective surface that is suitable for stair treads and other nonslip surfaces. A wet-sand finish yields a smooth surface that is also usable for nonslip floors.

Limestone is most commonly used for exterior surfaces, but a type of limestone, called *travertine*, is frequently used for interior flooring. Because of the way it is naturally formed, travertine has a network of holes in it. These must be filled with an epoxy resin (which can be colored to be compatible with the stone) to make a smooth surface. Travertine has a light, creamy color and is usually finished with a polished surface.

Slate is a fine-grained metamorphic rock, that is easily split into thin slabs, making it ideal for flooring as well as roofing. Slate is available in color ranges of gray, black, green, brown, and deep red. A natural cleft finish shows the surface as it is when cleaved from the rock. The surface is rough, with levels ranging about ⅛ in. (3.2 mm). A sand-rubbed finish gives an even plane and shows a slight grain. A honed finish is semipolished, without a sheen.

Sandstone is a sedimentary rock consisting of sand combined with other substances. When cleaved from the natural rock it is called *flagstone* and has a naturally rough surface. It can be used with irregular edges, just as it comes from the rock, or it can be cut into rectangular or square shapes.

Standard forms

Thick stone for flooring is from ¾ in. to 1 in. thick (19 to 25 mm), and varies in size depending on the stone type and availability in the color specified. Granite is available in sizes up to 4 × 10 ft (1200 × 3000 mm); marble in sizes up to 5 × 7 ft (1500 × 2100 mm) for Group A stone; and travertine up to about 3 × 4 ft (900 × 1200 mm). Slate and sandstone come in smaller sizes, depending on the thickness and finish, but range from 8 × 16 in. to 24 × 36 in. (200 × 400 mm to 600 × 900 mm). However, the practical

---

Marble groups

The Marble Institute of America has developed a system that classifies marble into four groups. The groups do not represent the quality or value of the stone, but are based on the characteristics encountered in fabrication. Not all marbles in some of the groups are suitable for all applications, and the maximum size of available slabs varies depending on the group. Group C and Group D represent the most fragile stones, but are still used with the proper finishing and fabricating techniques.

Group A: Sound marbles and stones, with uniform and favorable working qualities.

Group B: Marbles and stones similar in character to Group A, but their working qualities are somewhat less favorable. They may have natural faults, and a limited amount of repair is required.

Group C: Stone with some geological flaws, voids, veins, and lines of separation. Some repair with filling, waxing, liners, and other kinds of reinforcing is done when necessary.

Group D: This group has the most variation in working qualities and contains more natural faults than Group C. More repair and reinforcing is required than Group C marbles.

maximum size for thick stone is about 36 in.² (900 mm). Beyond this size it is difficult to lay and move around the interior of a building.

Stone tile is available in thicknesses of ³⁄₁₆ in. to ⅝ in. (5 mm to 16 mm) in sizes of 1 × 1 ft, 1 × 2 ft, 2 × 2 ft, 2 × 4 ft, up to 5 × 10 ft (300 × 300 mm, 300 × 600 mm, 600 × 600 mm, 600 × 1200 mm, up to 1500 × 3000 mm) depending on the manufacturer, thickness, and reinforcing method. Other stock sizes are available from some manufacturers and all can be easily cut with standard carpentry or mason's tools.

Figure 8.16
Thin-set stone
flooring

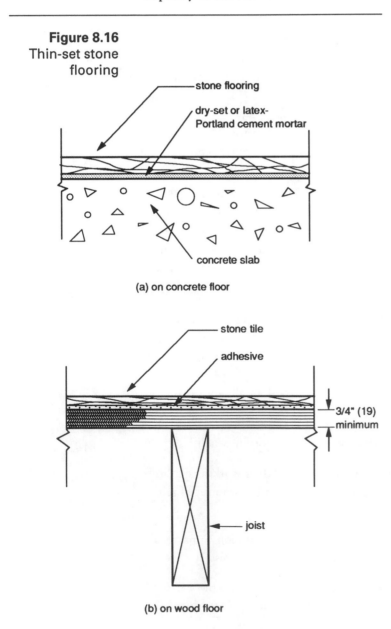

(a) on concrete floor

(b) on wood floor

Typical details

Stone flooring can be installed in two basic ways, using thin-set or a full mortar bed. Full mortar bed applications are generally the best and must be used when the subfloor is uneven or when the stone varies in thickness, as with slate or sandstone. Thin-set applications are less expensive, add much less weight to the floor, and are faster to install. They are suitable for thin stone floors cut in uniform thicknesses in either residential or commercial construction.

With thin-set installations, a uniform thickness of stone is set on the subfloor with a special thin-set mortar (about ⅛ in. or less in thickness) or with an adhesive. Figure 8.16(a) shows a thin-set application on a concrete subfloor; Figure 8.16(b) shows a thin-set application on a wood frame subfloor. Although the thin-set method is used primarily for thin stone, it can also be used for full thickness slabs if required.

A full mortar bed installation requires that a layer of mortar from ¾ in. to 1¼ in. thick be applied to a suitably prepared, structurally sound subfloor. The stone is then set either in the semiwet mortar, or the mortar is allowed to cure and the stone is set with another thin layer of dry-set mortar on top of the first. See Figure 8.17. As with tile and terrazzo full mortar bed methods, a full mortar bed stone floor is usually restricted to new construction where the subfloor can be depressed enough so that the finish floor level aligns with adjacent construction.

With the full mortar bed method, the mortar can be bonded to the subfloor or separated from it with a cleavage membrane, usually 4-mil polyethylene. When a cleavage membrane is used, steel reinforcing mesh is placed in the mortar bed, allowing the finish floor to be structurally separate from the subfloor. If the subfloor deflects or moves slightly, the stone flooring is protected from cracking because it is not bonded to the structural floor.

Stone floors can be set with the joints tightly butted together or with spaces between joints. If there is a gap in the joint, it must be filled with grout or a Portland cement/sand mixture that can be color-coordinated with the stone. Several special types of grout are available that are resistant to chemicals, fungi, and mildew. Latex grout is also available and provides some flexibility when slight movement in the floor is expected.

Coordination

• Existing floors must be capable of supporting the extra weight of stone. Structural capacities should be verified with a structural engineer.

• For thin-set applications, concrete subfloors must be level to within ¼ in. in 10 ft (6 mm in 3050 mm). Wood floors must be structurally sound and level to within 1/16 in. in 3 ft (2 mm in 900 mm).

• Polished finishes should not be used in areas where the stone might get wet or on stairs because of the potential slippage problems. Flamed finishes with granite or an abrasive finish with marble are better choices in these applications and, in fact, are required by code in some applications.

• The edges of stone flooring adjacent to other materials should be protected from chipping with stone thresholds or metal strips. Figures 8.18(a) and 8.18(b) show two methods of making this transition.

ACCESS FLOORING [10270]

Access flooring is a system of individual panels set on pedestals above a floor which allows electrical wiring, communications cabling, and small ducts to be placed between the structural floor and the raised flooring. Each panel can be removed individually to provide access to the services. Access flooring is typically used in large computer rooms where there is extensive cabling and where frequent access is needed. It is also used in recording studios, laboratories, communication centers, offices,

and anywhere flexibility and accessibility to services are required.

Floor panels are 2 × 2 ft (600 × 600 mm) set on adjustable steel or aluminum pedestals that support the panels at the corners. Some systems have stringers that connect the tops of the pedestals and provide additional lateral and gravity support. Pedestals can raise the flooring from 4 in. to 30 in. (100 to 760 mm) above the structural floor, depending on the space required for services. The panels are constructed of steel, aluminum, concrete, or particleboard, with finishes of plastic laminate, vinyl, or carpeting. Various types of pedestal systems are available from several manufacturers, depending on the loading requirements, size of installation, and height required. Perforated panels are used for air distribution and special cutouts are used to bring cable and wiring through the panels. Accessories for ramps, closure panels, and handrails are also available.

Figure 8.17
Full mortar bed stone flooring

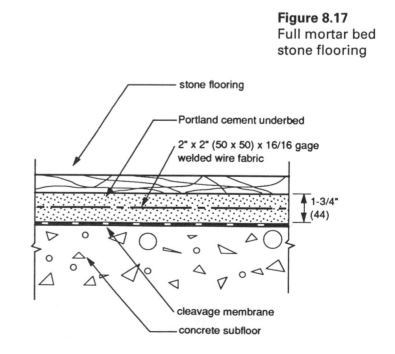

stone flooring

Portland cement underbed

2" x 2" (50 x 50) x 16/16 gage welded wire fabric

1-3/4"
(44)

cleavage membrane

concrete subfloor

Figure 8.18
Stone
flooring edges

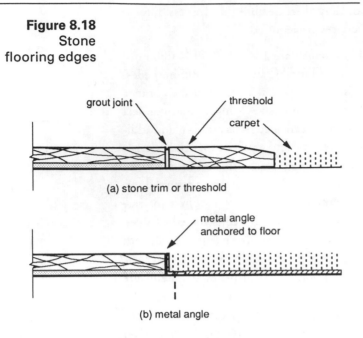

grout joint   threshold

carpet

(a) stone trim or threshold

metal angle
anchored to floor

(b) metal angle

9

APPLIED FLOOR FINISHES

This section includes flooring that is applied as a single thin material, such as resilient tile and carpet. Refer to Chapter 8 for materials and construction techniques that involve several components applied to a structural floor.

CARPET [09680]

Carpet is one of the most commonly used flooring materials. If properly selected, it is attractive, durable, quiet, easy to install, and requires less maintenance than many other types of flooring. There are three basic forms of carpet: sheet carpet, carpet tiles, and rugs. Sheet carpet is available in rolls from 2 ft 3 in. to 15 ft wide (690 mm to 4.6 m), depending on the manufacturing method, with 12 ft being a common width. Carpet tiles are individual squares of carpet. A rug is a soft floor covering laid on the floor, but not fastened to it, that does not cover the entire floor.

Carpet fibers

Carpet is made from several fibers and combinations of fibers, including wool, nylon, acrylic, modacrylic, polyester, and olefin. The construction methods and properties of each of these fibers are summarized in Table 9.1.

Wool

Wool is a natural material and, overall, is one of the best for carpet. It is very durable and resilient, wears well, has superior appearance characteristics, is flame resistant, and is moderately easy to clean and maintain. Unfortunately, it is also one of the most expensive fibers for initial cost; however, in many situations the life-cycle cost can be lower than that of other carpet fibers.

Nylon

Nylon is an economical carpet material that is very strong and wear resistant. It has high stain resistance, excellent crush resistance, can be dyed with a wide variety of colors, and cleans easily. Some nylons create static problems and have a glossy sheen; however, these problems have generally been alleviated with improved fiber construction and by blending nylon with other fibers. New improvements in fiber construction also help to conceal dirt particles by increasing the light scattering properties of individual filaments. Because of its many advantages, including cost, nylon is the most widely used fiber for both residential and commercial carpet.

Table 9.1
Carpet
properties

	Fibers					
	Wool	Nylon	Acrylic	Modacrylic	Polyester	Olefin
Manufacturing process:						
Tufted	•	•	•		•	•
Woven	•	•	•	•		
Needle punched		•				
Fusion bonded	•	•	•			
Typical construction						
Face weight, oz./yd (g/m²)	30–55 (1017–1865)	20–40 (680–1360)	25–42 (850–1420)	40 (1360)	32–55 (1080–1865)	26 (880)
Total weight, oz./yd (g/m²)	62–100 (2100–33 900)	67–85 (2270–2880)	66–80 (2240–2710)	70–80 (2370–2710)	70–104 (2370–3520)	–
Pitch	189	270	216	216	216	216
Stitches per in.	8–9	7.5–11.25	8.75–11	7–9	7–9	12
Pile height, in. (mm)	⁵⁄₁₆–⁹⁄₁₆ (8–14)	⅛–⅝ (3–16)	⁷⁄₃₂–⁷⁄₁₆ (5.5–11)	³⁄₁₆–¹⁵⁄₆₄ (5–6)	⁹⁄₁₆–¹³⁄₁₆ (14–21)	⁵⁄₁₆ (8)
Surface:						
Level loop	•	•	•		•	
Cut pile	•	•	•	•		•
Cut/loop		•	•	•		
Loop/random shear		•	•			
Flame spread	55	35	25	20	20	80
Smoke developed, max.	160	190	160	60	410	–
Resistance to:						
Abrasion	4–5	5	3	2	3–4	4
Acids	2	4–5	3	3	4	4
Alkalis	2	4–5	4	3	4	4
Burns	3	2	2	2	3	2
Crushing	4–5	3	3	3	2–3	1–2
Insects and fungi	2–5[1]	4–5	4–5	4–5	4	4–5
Moisture	2	2	3	3	3	5
Soiling	3–4	3	3–4	3–4	4	4–5
Staining	2–3	4	4	4	3	4–5
Static buildup	2–4[1]	1–4[1]	3	3	3	4–5
Sunlight	3–4	2	3	2–3	2–3	2–4
Properties:						
Durability	4–5	5	3–5	3–5	4	3
Ease of maintenance	4–5	3	3–5	3–5	3–4	5
Resilience	5	3	2	2	2	1
Appearance retention	5	3–5	3–5	3–5	3–5	3

1 = Poor
2 = Fair
3 = Good
4 = Very good
5 = Excellent

[1] Depends on treatment.

Acrylic and modacrylic

Acrylic is a synthetic fiber that has moderate abrasion resistance, but has a more wool-like appearance than nylon. Like nylon, it can be dyed with a variety of colors, has good crush resistance, and is easy to maintain. It is also resistant to sunlight fading.

Modacrylic is a modified version of acrylic, containing a lower percentage of acrylonitrile units in its polymer base. It has a lower abrasion and alkali resistance.

Polyester

Polyester carpet fiber is made from synthetic polymers and is highly abrasion resistant, cleans well, is mildew resistant, and is low in cost. It is sometimes used as a blend with nylon. However, it has only fair crushing resistance.

Olefin

Olefin (polypropylene) is used primarily for indoor-outdoor carpet and as an alternate to jute for carpet backing. It is strong, very durable, stain resistant, and cleans easily. However, it is the least attractive of the artificial fibers and has low resilience as well as a low melting point.

Manufacturing processes

Carpet is manufactured by weaving, tufting, needle punching, fusion bonding, and, less frequently, by knitting and custom tufting.

Weaving

Weaving is the traditional method of making carpet by interlacing warp and weft yarns. Warp is the yarn that runs lengthwise; weft is the yarn that runs crosswise. The number of warp lines of yarn in a 27-in. (686 mm) width is called the *pitch*. The number of weft yarns per inch is referred to as the *wires* per inch. Weaving is a method that produces a very attractive, durable carpet, but is the most expensive method of manufacturing carpet by machine. As shown in Figures 9.1(a)–9.1(c) there are three primary methods of weaving.

Wilton carpet is produced on a jacquard loom that allows complex patterns to be woven into the carpet as well as several types of surface textures, including level cut pile, level loop, cut/uncut, and multilevel loop. See Figure 9.1(a). Different colors of yarn run beneath the surface of the carpet and are pulled up only when they are needed for the pattern. Therefore, Wiltons are generally heavier and more expensive that the other woven types for the same total weight.

Velvet carpet is the simplest form of weaving and places all the pile yarn on the face of the carpet. See Figure 9.1(b). Velvet carpets are

Figure 9.1
Types of woven carpet

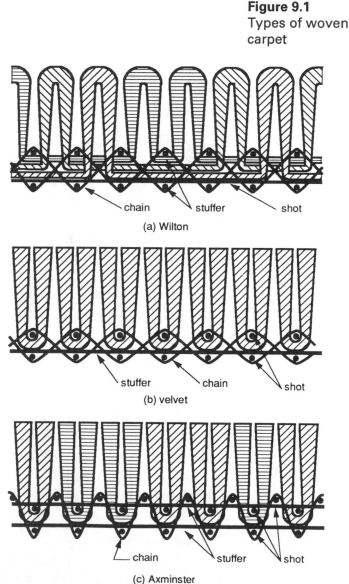

(a) Wilton

(b) velvet

(c) Axminster

generally solid colors. However, multicolored yarns can also be used in a wide variety of surface textures, including plushes, loop pile, cut pile, multilevel loop, and cut-and-loop styles.

Axminster carpets are made on a modified jacquard loom that delivers different colors of yarn at different times according to the pattern desired. See Figure 9.1(c). Because of the weaving process, Axminster carpets can be produced in a wide range of patterns and colors from geometric to floral. Unlike the Wilton process, most of the pile yarn is placed on the surface. The carpet has an even, cut-pile surface with a heavily ribbed backing.

Tufting

Tufting is a process in which the pile yarn is punched through the backing with a row of needles, much like a sewing machine. The spacing between the needles is the gage of the carpet. As the needle goes through the backing, the yarn is caught and held while the needle makes the next pass. The rate at which the backing material passes through the machine determines the distance between stitches, or the stitch rate. Once tufted, the loop of yarn can be left as is for loop carpet or cut for cut-pile carpet. Because of the speed (about 25 times as fast as weaving) and relative low cost of tufting, this process accounts for the majority of the carpet manufactured.

Needle punching

Needle punching is similar to tufting, except that the fiber is pushed and pulled through a backing with barbed needles. A secondary backing is then applied to strengthen the assembly. Needle punching produces a fairly flat carpet of limited variation in texture and accounts for a very small percentage of the total carpet market.

Fusion bonding

Fusion bonding embeds the pile yarn in a backing of liquid vinyl. When the vinyl hardens, the tufts are permanently locked into the backing. Texture and pattern types are limited in fusion bonding, and it is used primarily for carpet tiles.

Carpet properties
Appearance and durability

The appearance and durability of a carpet are affected by the amount of yarn in a given area, how tightly that yarn is packed, and the height of the yarn. The pitch of a woven carpet is the number of ends of surface yarn in a 27-in. (686-mm) width. For tufted carpet, this measurement is called the *gage*, which is the spacing in fractions of an inch between needles across the width of the carpet. Gages of 5/64 in., 1/10 in., and 1/8 in. (1.98, 2.54, and 3.2 mm) are common for contract carpet. The *stitch* (or stitch rate) is the number of lengthwise tufts in one inch. The wires per inch is the corresponding measurement in woven carpet. The higher the pitch or gage number and stitch numbers are, the denser the carpet is. The pile height is the height of the fiber from the surface of the backing to the top of the pile. Generally, shorter and more tightly packed fibers result in a more durable, and more expensive carpet.

Carpet flammability

There are two primary concerns related to the flammability of carpet: whether a carpet will ignite and sustain a fire if it is the first item ignited, and how flammable it is when subjected to the heat and flame of a fully developed fire. To prevent carpet from igniting and spreading fire when exposed to something like a dropped match, current federal law requires that all carpet manufactured and sold in the United States meet the requirements of ASTM D-2859, also known as the *Methenamine Pill Test*.

Regulations that address carpet flammability in fully developed fires are more varied. At the least, building codes regulate the maximum flame-spread rating of finish materials when tested according to ASTM E-84, *Standard Test Method for Surface*

Burning Characteristics of Building Materials. Also known as the *Steiner tunnel test,* this standard is not entirely appropriate for carpet, but is still referenced in many codes. The Steiner tunnel test is also referred to as NFPA 255 and UL 723 by the National Fire Protection Association and Underwriters Laboratories, respectively. Refer to Chapter 17 for more information on finish flammability.

Tuft density, average density, and weight density of carpet

One of the main determinants of carpet quality and durability is the density of the yarn that is exposed to wear. A carpet that has more yarn packed closer together will wear better than a looser constructed carpet. One measure of this density is the tuft density, which is the gage (or pitch for woven carpets) multiplied by the stitch (or wires per inch). This calculation gives the tufts per square inch. However, overall density is also dependent on the pile height, which is the distance from the top of the surface yarn to the top of the backing. Given two carpets with the same tuft density and face weight, the one with the lower pile height will wear better because the same amount of yarn is packed into a tighter space. The face weight is the number of ounces of yarn in the surface pile per square yard.

The average pile density, AD, takes into account the pile height and is calculated by the formula

$$AD = \frac{\text{face weight (oz./yd)} \times 36}{\text{pile height}}$$

This gives the amount of yarn per cubic yard. Generally, commercial carpet should have an average density of at least 3000.

The weight density is the average density multiplied by the face weight. This takes into account the value of pile weight on durability and resilience because two carpets with different face weights and pile heights may have the same calculated average density, but the one with the higher weight density will wear better.

Yarn weight and construction

Yarn weight refers to the thickness of the yarn and is called the yarn count. Construction is described in yarn plies and refers to the number of single yarns that are twisted together to make the yarn for tufting or weaving.

There are several methods of designating yarn count, depending on the manufacturing process and the country of manufacture. For tufted and fusion-bonded carpets two systems are used, the woolen count system and the denier system. The woolen count is the number of yards in one ounce of finished yarn and also includes the number of plies. For example, a 3/80 count means 80 yards of three-ply yarn per ounce. The denier system is used for synthetic yarns and is measured in grams per 9000 meters of yarn. For example, a yarn denier of 1250/4 means that 9000 meters of a particular four-ply yarn weighs 1250 grams.

Four systems are used for woven carpet, depending on the country: cotton count (United States), TEX (Europe, United Kingdom, New Zealand, Australia, and elsewhere), metric (Europe, United Kingdom, Japan), and Dewsbury. The cotton count and the TEX systems are the most common. The cotton count is the number of 840 yard skeins (called hanks) in a pound of yarn. The TEX system is similar to the denier system, but is a true metric count. Tex is the weight in grams of one kilometer of yarn. To keep the TEX system in the same order of magnitude as the denier system, the term decitex is sometimes used, which is the weight in grams of 10,000 meters of yarn.

A more accurate test of carpet flammability is the *flooring radiant panel test*, ASTM E-648 (also designated as NFPA 253 and NBS IR 75-950 by the National Fire Protection Association and the National Institute for Standards and Technology, respectively). This test is required by all major federal agencies for their projects and by many other state and local jurisdictions. The amount of radiant energy needed to sustain flame is measured and defined as the *critical radian flux*. It is measured in watts per square centimeter and two classes, Class I and Class II, have been established. Corridors and exit-ways in hospitals and nursing homes must have a Class I rating (minimum of 0.45 watts/cm^2). Corridors and exit-ways of all commercial buildings and hotels must have a Class II rating (0.22 watts/cm^2); however, this test only applies to carpet in corridors, not in rooms and other areas.

Other flammability tests that are required by some state and federal agencies include NFPA 258, *Standard Research Test Method for Determining Smoke Generation of Solid Materials* (NBS 708) and UL 992, *Test Method for Measuring the Surface Flame Propagation Characteristics of Flooring and Floor-Covering Materials*. The smoke density chamber test measures the smoke potential of burning materials and the amount of obscuration from that smoke. The chamber test measures flame spread as an alternate to the Steiner tunnel test.

Carpet backing and cushioning [09682]

Carpet backing both provides support for and locks in the pile yarn. It also gives added strength and dimensional stability to carpets. In woven and knitted carpets the pile yarns and backing yarns are combined during the manufacturing process. Polypropylene yarn is the most common backing for woven carpet, but others include jute, cotton, and polyester. A coating of latex is often applied to woven carpet to provide additional dimensional stability and tuft bind.

Tufted carpet is manufactured by punching the yarns through a primary backing of woven or nonwoven polypropylene or woven jute. A secondary backing is then applied to hold the tufts in place and give added stability. This is usually a coating of latex, but a foam cushion or laminated fabric backing can also be applied. Needle punched carpet is latex coated or foam backed.

An important part of carpet installation is the carpet cushion, sometimes called padding. Cushion is not appropriate for all carpet installation (such as direct glue-down installation), nor is it required; however, it is recommended. Cushioning increases the life of the carpet, provides increased resiliency and comfort, helps sound absorption, lessens impact noise, and improves thermal qualities in some situations. Common cushion materials include sponge rubber, felt, urethane, and foam rubber.

Sponge rubber is made from natural or synthetic rubber and other chemicals and fillers with a facing on the top side. It is available in flat sheets or a waffled configuration. Thicknesses range from ⅛ in. to ⁵⁄₁₆ in. (3 to 8 mm), with weights from 41 oz./yd^2 to 120 oz./yd^2 (1390 to 4070 g/m^2).

Felt is available in four forms: hair, combination, fiber, and rubberized. Hair felt is composed of one-hundred percent animal hair. Combination felt is a mixture of animal hair and other fibers. Fiber felt is composed entirely of felt. Rubberized felt is any of the other three types with a rubberized coating on one side. Felt is available in thicknesses from ¼ in. to ⁹⁄₁₆ in. (6 to 14 mm) and in weights from 32 oz./yd^2 to 86 oz./yd^2 (1080 to 2920 g/m^2).

Urethane is manufactured in three different ways to produce prime, densified, or bonded sheets. Thickness ranges from ¼ in. to ¾ in. (6 to 19 mm). Prime urethane comes in densities from 1.3 lb/ft^3 to 6 lb/ft^3 (20.8 to 96 kg/m^3). Densified urethane is available in densities from 2.7 lb/ft^3 to 6 lb/ft^3 (43 to

96 kg/m³). Bonded urethane can be specified in densities from 4 lb/ft³ to 10 lb/ft³ (64 to 160 kg/m³).

Foam rubber is commonly applied as an integral backing to some carpet. It is natural or synthetic latex rubber with additives, and a backing on one side. Its thicknesses range from ⅛ in. to ⅝ in. (3 to 16 mm), and its weights range from 28 oz./yd² to 65 oz./yd² (950 to 2200 g/m²).

All types of cushioning are available in widths of up to 12 ft (3.7 m).

Installation

Carpet is installed in one of three ways: direct glue-down, stretched-in, or double glue-down. In direct glue-down installation, the carpet is attached to the floor with adhesive. The carpet may be installed with an integrated cushion. Direct glue-down installations resist shifting in heavy traffic areas and support wheeled traffic better than the stretched-in method. The direct glue-down method is also faster and less expensive to install. However, glue-down installation without cushioning does not last as long because of the increased wear on the carpet. It is also harder underfoot. Because direct glue-down installation requires a low pile carpet, the choice of textures and construction methods is limited.

A stretched-in installation uses tackless strips attached around the perimeter of the room. These plywood strips have embedded sharp points that face toward the walls. Carpet cushion is either stapled to wood floors or glued to concrete floors after the tackless strips are in place. The carpet is then stretched against the strips, which hold the carpet in place. See Figure 9.2.

Double glue-down uses a high-density cushion glued to the subfloor. The carpet is then glued to the cushion. This method combines the advantages of both stretched-in and direct glue-down installations. It is good for high traffic areas, but is not as good as direct glue-down for rolling wheeled traffic.

Prior to installation, a seaming diagram should be submitted by the carpet installer for review. Carpet should be installed so that the nap runs in the same direction on all pieces. Seams should not run across heavy traffic areas whenever possible, nor should they be placed where people tend to change walking directions, such as at corners of corridors, in front of elevators, or at doorways. Seams should also not run perpendicular to the width of a doorway. Although not ideal, seams across a door opening are acceptable and usually necessary for an economical installation.

Carpet tile [09690]

Carpet tiles are individual pieces of carpet, typically 18 in.², that are applied to the floor with pressure-sensitive adhesive. Because of their modular design, damaged or worn pieces can be replaced without removing the entire floor covering. They are generally specified for commercial installations where frequent change in room layout is expected, where maintenance may be a problem, or where flat, undercarpet electrical and telephone cabling is used.

Coordination

• Subflooring must be suitably prepared to receive carpet. Concrete floors must be

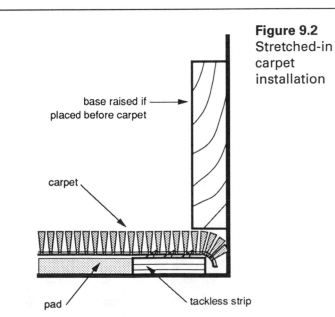

Figure 9.2
Stretched-in carpet installation

base raised if placed before carpet

carpet

pad

tackless strip

smooth, with high points or ridges ground down and depressions and cracks filled.

• For direct glue-down applications, concrete floors must be free of moisture and curing agents.

• Wood subfloors must be flooring grade plywood, particleboard, or hardboard, with joints filled and rough spots sanded smooth.

• Wood floors over crawl spaces or other damp locations should have ventilated space below with a vapor barrier placed over the earth in the crawl space.

• Edges of carpet adjacent to other flooring must be suitably terminated with standard binder bars, carpet grippers, or other custom details.

• Verify that the carpet installation meets ADA requirements. See Chapter 18.

RESILIENT TILE FLOORING [09660]

Resilient flooring is a generic term that describes several types of composition materials made from various resins, fibers, plasticizers, and fillers. It is formed under heat and pressure to produce a thin material either in sheets or tiles. This sections describes the various types of resilient tile flooring, while the next section describes sheet flooring.

Resilient flooring is applied with mastic to a subfloor of concrete, plywood, or other smooth underlayment. Some resilient floorings may only be installed on floors above grade, while others may be placed below, on, or above grade. Refer to the manufacturer's literature for specific recommendations. The types of resilient flooring

---

Applicable standards for carpet

American Society for Testing and Materials (ASTM):

ASTM D-418	*Methods of Testing Pile Yarn Floor Covering Construction*
ASTM D-2859	*Standard Test Method for Flammability of Finished Textile Floor Covering Materials*
ASTM D-4157	*Standard Test Method for Abrasion Resistance of Textile Fabrics (Oscillatory Cylinder Method)*
ASTM D-4158	*Standard Test Method for Abrasion Resistance of Textile Fabrics (Uniform Abrasion Method)*
ASTM E-84	*Standard Test Method for Surface Burning Characteristics of Building Materials*
ASTM E-162	*Standard Test Method for Surface Flammability of Materials Using a Radiant Heat Energy Source*
ASTM E-648	*Standard Test Method for Critical Radiant Flux of Floor-covering Systems Using a Radiant Heat Energy Source (NFPA 253 and NBS IR 75-950)*
ASTM E-662	*Standard Test Method for Specific Optical Density of Smoke Generated by Solid Materials (NFPA 258)*

Carpet and Rug Institute:

CRI-104	*Standard for Installation of Commercial Carpet*
CRI-105	*Standard for Installation of Residential Carpet*

National Fire Protection Association (NFPA):

NFPA 253	*Flooring Radiant Panel Test*
NFPA 258	*Standard Research Test Method for Determining Smoke Generation of Solid Materials*

Underwriters Laboratories (UL):

UL 992	*Chamber Test Method of the Flame Propagation Classification of Flooring and Floor Covering Materials*

used today include vinyl, vinyl composition, rubber, cork, vinyl-faced cork, and asphalt. Vinyl, vinyl composition, and rubber flooring are the most common. Resilient tile flooring properties are summarized in Table 9.2.

Vinyl tile

Vinyl tile is the term commonly used to refer to flooring based on polyvinylchloride (PVC). It is a good, durable, resilient flooring that is resistant to indentation, abrasion, grease, water, alkalis, and some acids. Vinyl

Table 9.2
Resilient tile flooring properties

	Vinyl	Vinyl composition	Rubber	Cork	Vinyl-faced cork	Asphalt
Common sizes, in. (mm)	9 × 9, 12 × 12, 24 × 24 (225 × 225, 300 × 300, 600 × 600)	9 × 9, 12 × 12, (225 × 225, 300 × 300)	9 × 9, 12 × 12, 18 × 18, 24 × 24 (225 × 225, 300 × 300, 450 × 450, 600 × 600)	6 × 6, 9 × 9, 12 × 12 (150 × 150, 225 × 225, 300 × 300)	9 × 9, 12 × 12 (225 × 225, 300 × 300)	9 × 9, 18 × 18 (225 × 225, 460 × 460)
Thickness, in. (mm)	$\frac{1}{16}$, $\frac{1}{8}$ (1.6, 3.2)	$\frac{3}{32}$–$\frac{5}{32}$ (2.4–4)	$\frac{3}{32}$, $\frac{1}{8}$, $\frac{3}{16}$ (2.4, 3.2, 4.8)	$\frac{1}{8}$–$\frac{5}{16}$ (3.2–8)	$\frac{1}{8}$ (3.2)	$\frac{1}{8}$ (3.2)
Use[1]	B, O, A	B, O, A	B, O, A	A	A	A
Load limit, psi (kg/cm²)	200 (14)	50–75 (3–5)	200 (14)	75 (5)	75–150 (5–10.5)	25 (2)
Flame spread	45–75	15–75	75	–	–	75
Smoke developed	425	215–450	450 or less	–	450 or less	–
Resistance to:						
Alkalis	4–5	4	4	1	4	1
Cigarette burns	1–3	1–3	4	2	2	1
Grease/oil	5	5	1	2	5	1
Indentation	3–5	2–3	4	2	3	2
Stains	2–5	2–5	4–5	1–2	2–4	2
Properties:						
Durability	4–5	3–4	4	1	2	2
Ease of maintenance	3–4	3–4	2–3	1–2	3–4	2
Resilience	1–4	1–4	4	5	3	1
Quietness	2–5	1–4	5	5	3	1

1 = Poor
2 = Fair
3 = Good
4 = Very good
5 = Excellent

[1] B = Below grade. O = On grade. A = Above grade.

comes in a variety of colors and patterns and is easy to install. It can be used below grade, on grade, or above grade. It must be installed over a clean, dry, and smooth surface. It is slightly more expensive than vinyl composition tile.

Vinyl tiles are generally 12 in.² (300 mm), although some are available in 9 in. (225 mm) squares and larger sizes. Either ¹⁄₁₆ in. or ⅛ in. (1.6 or 3.2 mm) thicknesses are available; however, for commercial use and better residential floors, the ⅛ in. thickness is preferred.

Vinyl composition

Vinyl composition tile is similar to vinyl tile but includes various types of fillers that decrease the percentage of polyvinylchloride. While composition tile costs less than homogenous vinyl, it has less flexibility and abrasion resistance. Because of this, through-grain types should be specified. These are tiles where the color and pattern extend uniformly through the tile thickness. Normally, this tile is applied with mastic; however, peel-and-stick types are available for residential applications. Tile is also available with an attached foam backing for greater resilience.

Rubber

Rubber flooring is made from synthetic rubber and offers excellent resistance to deformation under loads, providing a very comfortable, quiet, resilient floor. Rubber, however, is not very resistant to oils or grease and small objects can cause damage in the form of indentations. This flooring is available with a smooth surface or with a patterned, raised surface, which allows water and dirt to lie below the wearing surface helping to prevent slipping or excessive abrasion. Rubber flooring is available in tiles or in sheet form in several thicknesses.

Cork

Cork flooring is made from granulated pieces of bark from the cork oak tree that are bonded together under heat and pressure. Cork is available in tile form and is used where acoustical control or a high degree of resilience is desired. However, some types are not resistant to staining, fading, moisture, heavy loads, or concentrated foot traffic. Cork is usually combined with resins to improve its durability and make it easier to maintain. Generally, cork should only be used on above-grade floors, although some types can be used on grade if installed according to the manufacturer's directions.

Vinyl-faced cork

Vinyl-faced cork uses cork and thermoplastic binders as the base material with a top layer of polyvinylchloride. This improves the wear resistance and cleanability of the tile, while retaining its resilience and appearance.

Preparation of substrates

Preparation of the subfloor on which resilient tile or sheet flooring is placed is critical to a successful installation. Because moisture is the cause of most problems, concrete floors must be dry at the time of installation. For new concrete floors it may take from six to twelve weeks, or more, for the slab to thoroughly cure and dry. If there is any doubt, the slab should be tested for moisture. Below grade and on grade slabs should have a vapor barrier below them to prevent moisture from migrating from the earth. Concrete must be free of curing compounds, sealers, and hardeners that will interfere with the adhesive bonding. The slab must also be free of solvents, grease, oil, and similar compounds. The surface should be smooth and level to within ⅛ in. in 10 ft (3 mm in 3050 mm), with no abrupt transitions or depressions. Construction and control joints should be filled and leveled with a latex patching compound.

Wood subflooring should be smooth, with all boards securely fastened. Generally, underlayment of plywood, hardboard, or particleboard is recommended. The board should be underlayment grade, at least ¼ in.

(6 mm) thick and securely glued and nailed, with the joints staggered. The joints should be sanded and filled, if necessary, with all nails driven flush. Grade-level wood floors should be over a well-ventilated crawl space with a vapor barrier on the earth in the crawl space. Resilient floors may be installed over existing wood floors if they are smooth, tight, and all ridges are sanded. However, underlayment is preferred.

RESILIENT SHEET FLOORING [09665]

Resilient flooring in sheet form has several advantages over tile. Although it is more difficult to install, it provides a floor with fewer seams. That makes the floor easier to clean, more hygienic, and more resistant to moisture spills. Some types of sheet flooring even allow what seams that do exist to be sealed. There are three primary types of sheet flooring: vinyl, rubber, and linoleum, with three variations of vinyl flooring. Conductive flooring and slip-retardant flooring are also available. The properties of the primary types of sheet flooring are shown in Table 9.3.

Vinyl sheet flooring

Solid sheet vinyl, like solid vinyl tile, is a homogeneous nonlayered construction of polyvinylchloride with color and pattern extending through the entire thickness. It is very durable and resistant to indentation and rolling wheeled traffic. Because the seams can be sealed with heat welding or solvent welding, it is an excellent floor for health care facilities, clean rooms, and industrial flooring.

Inlaid vinyl is one of the most commonly used sheet floorings. It includes various fillers and is manufactured with a felt backing. It is available in wider rolls than solid sheet vinyl and the seams can be sealed with a two-part epoxy adhesive if necessary. It is also available with an integrated cushioned backing.

Clear-coated rotogravure vinyl is manufactured with colors and patterns printed on the surface, which is coated with clear vinyl. Because of the rotogravure printing process, there is an unlimited variety of patterns and colors that can be applied. However, this flooring is not as durable and resistant to indentation and abrasion as the other vinyls; therefore, it is used primarily in the residential and light commercial market.

Rubber sheet flooring

Rubber sheet flooring has the same properties as rubber tile, but with fewer seams. The decorative types of flooring with raised patterns are usually specified in sheet form.

Linoleum

Linoleum is one of the traditional types of sheet flooring. It is composed of oxidized linseed oil or other binders, pigments, and fillers applied over a backing of burlap or asphalt-saturated felt. Linoleum is available as plain or battleship linoleum, which is a single color, or inlaid linoleum, which consists of multicolored patterns that extend

---

American Society for Testing and Materials (ASTM):

ASTM F-693   *Standard Practice for Sealing Seams of Resilient Sheet Flooring Products by Use of Liquid Seam Sealers*

ASTM F-710   *Standard Practice for Preparing Concrete Floors and Other Monolithic Floors to Receive Resilient Flooring*

ASTM F-1066   *Standard Specification for Vinyl Composition Floor Tile*

ASTM F-1303   *Standard Specification for Sheet Vinyl Floor Covering With Backing*

ASTM F-1344   *Standard Specification for Rubber Floor Tile*

Applicable standards for resilient floor covering

ASTM F-1516   *Standard Practice for Sealing Seams of Resilient Flooring Products by the Heat Weld Method*

ASTM F-1700   *Standard Specification for Solid Vinyl Floor Tile*

ASTM F-1859   *Standard Specification for Rubber Sheet Floor Covering Without Backing*

ASTM F-1860   *Standard Specification for Rubber Sheet Floor Covering With Backing*

ASTM F-1861   *Standard Specification for Resilient Wall Base*

Table 9.3
Resilient sheet flooring properties

	Solid sheet vinyl	Inlaid vinyl	Clear-coated rotogravure	Rubber	Linoleum
Common widths, ft (mm)	4, 6 (1200, 1800)	9, 12, 15 (2740, 3660, 4570)	12, 15 (3660, 4570)	3, 6 (900, 1800)	6, 12 (1800, 3660)
Thickness, in. (mm)	0.08–0.1 (2,2.5)	0.071–0.10 (1.8–2.5)	0.05–0.1 (1.3–2.5)	$\frac{3}{32}$, $\frac{1}{8}$, $\frac{3}{16}$ (2.4, 3, 5)	0.065–0.125 (1.6–3)
Use[1]	B, O, A	B, O, A	B, O, A	B, O, A	A
Load limit, psi (kg/cm2)	200 (14)	75–100 (5–7)	75 (5)	200 (14)	75 (5)
Flame spread	45–75	45–75	45–75	75	–
Smoke developed	450 or less	450 or less	450 or less	100–450	–
Resistance to:					
Alkalis	4–5	4	3–4	4	2
Cigarette burns	1–3	1–3	1–4	4	1–2
Grease/oil	5	5	3–4	1	5
Indentation	3–5	2–3	2	4	2
Stains	2–5	2–5	2–5	4–5	4
Properties:					
Durability	4–5	3–4	2	4	3
Ease of maintenance	5	3–4	2–3	3–4	2
Resilience	1–4	1–4	1–4	4	2
Quietness	2–5	1–4	1–4	5	2

1 = Poor
2 = Fair
3 = Good
4 = Very good
5 = Excellent

[1] B = Below grade. O = On grade. A = Above grade.

through the thickness to the backing. Linoleum has very good abrasion and grease resistance, but has limited resistance to alkalis. Light gage is used for residential floors and heavy gage for commercial floors.

SEAMLESS FLOORING [09670]

Seamless flooring is a mixture of a resinous matrix, fillers, and decorative materials applied in a liquid or viscous form that cures to a hard, seamless surface. Depending on the type of matrix and the specific mixture, the flooring is either poured or troweled on a subfloor. Some products are self-leveling, while others must be worked to a level surface. Some products, such as epoxy terrazzo, are surface ground after they cure to produce a smooth surface.

Seamless flooring is high-performance flooring that is used where special characteristics are required, such as extreme hardness, severe stain and chemical resistance, high water resistance, and where cleanliness and ease of cleaning are required. It is used for industrial floors, commercial kitchens and food preparation plants, factories, clean rooms, laboratories, hospitals, correctional facilities, and parking garages.

The many materials used for seamless flooring are generally divided into thermosetting and thermoplastic products. Some of the more common thermosetting matrices are two-part epoxy, two-part polyurethane, polychloroprene (neoprene), and two-part polyesters. One-part mixtures are also available, but are not as good as two-part mixtures. Common thermoplastic flooring includes acrylic and mastic products. Mastics are composed of asphalt emulsion, Portland cement, and various types of sand or stone filler. Various proprietary mixtures are also on the market.

Seamless flooring is applied in thicknesses from $\frac{1}{16}$ in. to $\frac{1}{2}$ in. (2 to 13 mm), depending on the type of product. Mastics may be applied in thicknesses up to $1\frac{1}{2}$ in. (38 mm). Seamless flooring is applied over a suitable base of concrete or wood subflooring, with the material turned up at the walls to form an integrated cove base.

10

WALL FINISHES

Wall finishes include those applied as a single, thin decorative covering, such as paint, wallpaper, and vinyl wall-covering, and those composed of several construction elements that add substantial thickness to a wall, such as ceramic tile or stone. In each case, the finish is not a structural part of the wall. However, some finishes require certain types of partition construction in order to be applied correctly. Refer to Chapter 1 for partition construction.

PAINT [09900]

Paint is a generic term for a thin coating used to protect and decorate the surface to which it is applied. Paint is one of several types of coatings. Coatings are composed of a vehicle, which is the liquid part of the coating, and the body and pigments if the coating is opaque. The vehicle has a nonvolatile part called the *binder*, and a volatile part called the *solvent*. The binder, along with the body, forms the actual film of the coating, while the solvent dissolves the binder to allow for application of the coating. The solvent evaporates or dries, leaving the final finish. The body of most quality paints is titanium dioxide, which is white. Pigments give paint its color.

Paints are broadly classified into solvent-based and water-based types. Solvent-based paints have binders containing or dissolved in organic solvents; water-based paints have binders that are either soluble or dispersed in water. Epoxy, polyurethane, and other specialty coatings use special chemicals for binders to impart unique qualities to the coating that are not found in standard solvent or water-based paints.

Solvent-based paint

Clear, solvent-based coatings include varnishes, shellac, silicone, and urethane. When a small amount of pigment is added, the coating becomes a stain, which gives color to the surface, but allows the appearance of the underlying material to show through. Stains are most often used on wood. Clear coatings can be used for interior applications because it is not necessary to have a pigment to protect the surface, as is usually required for exterior applications.

Oil paints use a drying or curing oil as a binder. In the past, linseed oil was the traditional oil, but other organic oils have been used. Today, synthetic, alkyd resin is used as the drying oil. Oil paints are durable, but have a strong odor when applied and must be cleaned up with a solvent, such as mineral spirits. In addition, they cannot be painted on damp surfaces or on surfaces that may become damp from behind.

In many remodeling projects, old paint must be removed. If the building is old enough to have lead-based paint, local regulations may require that the lead paint be removed from some types of residential occupancies by a licensed company using approved methods for removal and disposal. Sometimes, resheathing the wall is an acceptable alternative.

Water-based paint

Latex paints are water-based paints that use either vinyl chloride or acrylic resins as binders. Acrylic latex is better than vinyl latex in its durability, hiding power, and resistance to bleeding of underlying stains. Both types are relatively free from odor, can be used indoors as well as outdoors, and can be thinned with water.

Epoxy paint

Epoxy is used as a very durable binder for resistance to corrosion and chemicals. Epoxies also resist abrasion and strongly adhere to concrete, metal, and wood. Epoxy is considered a high-performance coating and requires skilled applicators. The fumes are also noxious, therefore, special ventilation is usually required for on-site application.

Polyurethane paint

Urethane is considered another high-performance coating. It is used for its superior resistance to abrasion, grease, alcohol, water, and fuels. Interior applications most often include clear coverings for wood floors and clear or pigmented paint for antigraffiti coatings. Polyurethane paint is sometimes used strictly for its aesthetic qualities because it can have a very high-gloss finish with an almost glasslike sheen.

Coordination

Application

Successful application of coatings depends not only on the correct selection for the intended use, but also on the surface preparation of the substrate, the primer used, and the method of application. Surfaces must be clean, dry, and free from grease, oils, and other foreign material. Application can be done by brushing, rolling, or spraying. The amount of coating material to be applied is typically specified as either wet or dry film thickness (WFT or DFT) in mils (thousandths of an inch) for each coat needed. The coating should be applied under dry conditions when the temperature is between 55°F and 85°F. If a semigloss or gloss paint is specified for gypsum wallboard partitions, the entire surface of the partition should receive a skim coat of joint compound to provide a uniform surface for the paint. If this is not done, the difference between the paper facing of the wallboard and the joint compound over joints and screws may become visible.

Paint gloss

Most water- and solvent-based paints are available in several surface finishes, which are referred to as glosses. Gloss and semigloss paints are used for their washability and shiny appearance. However, gloss paints tend to show defects in the surfaces on which they are applied. Satin finish paints provide a dull luster, while still retaining some washability. The type of gloss is determined by

Table 10.1
Standard paint gloss ranges

Common name	Gloss range
Flat	Below 15
Eggshell	5–20
Satin	15–35
Semigloss	30–65
Gloss	Over 65

Source: ASTM D 523.
Copyright ASTM. Reprinted with permission.

the amount of light reflected from a surface according to a standard test method. The common names and their gloss range are shown in Table 10.1.

There are dozens of standards for all the available coatings and the many test procedures related to them. The standards listed below are for some of the more common paints and test methods.

WALLPAPER [09950]

Wallpaper is available in a range of colors, patterns, textures, and materials for direct application to plaster or gypsum wallboard partitions. Wallpaper is generally packaged in rolls 20½ in. (520 mm) wide by 21 ft (6.4 m) long (about 36 ft^2 or 3.3 m^2) and may be all paper or paper backed with cotton fabric or other material. Double and triple rolls are also available. Some wallpaper is available with a thin vinyl coating. Before application, a liquid sizing must be applied to the wall to seal the surface against alkali, to reduce the absorption of the paste or adhesive used, and to provide the proper surface for the wallpaper.

Most wallpaper is manufactured with a short pattern repeat. This is the distance between one point to the next repeated same point. When one length of wallpaper is aligned with the next piece in a direct horizontal line it is called a *straight match*. If the next piece must be lowered to continue the pattern it is called a *drop match*. Some wallpapers have no repeat pattern because they are strictly for texture. However, some specialty mural or trompe l'oeil wallpapers are available that have no repeats because they are designed to be applied to form an overall image.

VINYL WALLCOVERING [09950]

Vinyl wallcovering provides a durable, abrasion-resistant finish that is easy to clean and can satisfy most code requirements for flammability. It is available in a wide range of colors and patterns. Vinyl wallcovering typically comes in rolls 52 in. or 54 in. wide and 30 yd long. It can be specified either with or without an additional coating of polyvinylfluoride film, which provides added stain resistance and extra protection for the vinyl. Other types of protective films are also available, but they are not as stain resistant.

There are three grades of vinyl wallcovering: Type I is light duty, Type II is medium duty, and Type III is heavy duty. Type I has a total weight of 7 to 13 oz./yd^2 (237 to 440 g/m^2), Type II has a total weight of between

---

American Society for Testing and Materials (ASTM):

ASTM D-1005	*Standard Test Method for Measurement of Dry Film Thickness of Organic Coatings*
ASTM D-1212	*Standard Test Method for Measurement of Wet Film Thickness of Organic Coatings*
ASTM D-5146	*Guide to Testing Solvent-Borne Architectural Coatings*
ASTM D-5324	*Guide to Testing Water-Borne Architectural Coatings*

Commercial Item Descriptions (CID):

CID A-A-2246B	*Paint, Latex*
CID A-A-2247	*Paint, Latex (Semi-gloss, interior)*
CID A-A-2248	*Paint, Latex (Flat, interior)*
CID A-A-50574	*Enamel, Odorless, Alkyd, Interior, Semi-gloss, White and Tints*

Federal Specifications (FS):

TT-E-489J	*Enamel, Alkyd, Gloss, Low VOC Content*
TT-E-506K	*Enamel, Alkyd, Gloss, Tints and White (For interior use)*

Applicable standards for interior paints and coatings

13 oz./yd² and 22 oz./yd² (440 to 745 g/m²), and Type III has a weight of over 22 oz./yd² (745 g/m²). Type I is used for residential and commercial applications where little or no abuse is expected. The vinyl serves as a substitute for paint while adding texture.

Type II is used for residential, commercial, and institutional applications where a moderate amount of traffic and abrasion is expected, such as in offices, dining rooms, classrooms, and some corridors. Type III is used where extra heavy use is expected, such as public corridors, food-service areas, and hospitals.

Vinyl wallcovering is applied with mastic to properly prepared gypsum wallboard or smooth plaster walls. Primer should be used on new wallboard to prevent damage to the partition if the wallcovering is removed. Stripable adhesive is also available for use over unprimed gypsum wallboard. Two methods of seaming are used: double-cutting and butting. Double-cutting involves overlapping adjacent strips and then cutting through and removing both. This results in a very tight butt joint. Butting must be used for patterned wallcovering where matching is critical or with dark-colored or deeply embossed material where removal of adhesive is difficult.

Figure 10.1
Tuck joints for wallcoverings

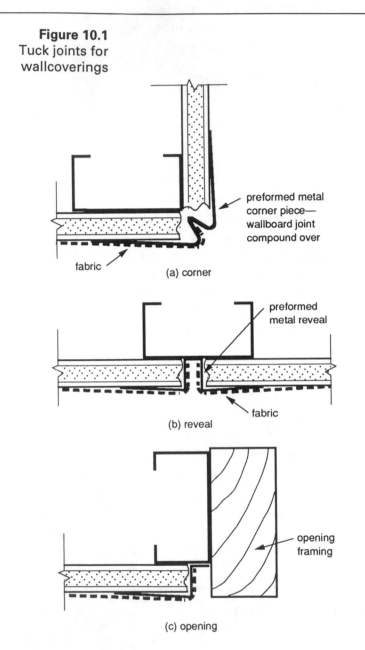

preformed metal corner piece—wallboard joint compound over

fabric

(a) corner

preformed metal reveal

fabric

(b) reveal

opening framing

(c) opening

FABRIC WALLCOVERING [09950]

Several types of fabrics can be used for wallcovering, including wool, silk, and synthetics, subject to flame-spread restrictions. If the fabric is heavy enough, it can be applied directly to the wall with adhesives. Seams are butted together to give the appearance of a continuous wall surface. In most instances, the fabric must be backed with paper or other material to prevent the adhesive from damaging the material and to give it additional dimensional stability.

When fabric is applied as a single layer of material, the terminating edges are carefully

Applicable standards for vinyl wallcovering

The Chemical Fabrics and Films Association (CFFA):

CFFA-2-1984   *Quality Standard for Vinyl-coated Fabric Wallcovering*

Federal Specifications (FS):

FS-CCC-W-408D   *Wallcovering, Vinyl Coated*
FS-L-P-1040B   *Plastic Sheets and Strips Polyvinylfluoride*

cut against the ceiling, floor base, door molding, and other trim. The adhesive is usually sufficient to hold the fabric in place. In the following situations a tuck joint should be provided: where fabric abuts other finishes; where there is a danger of people brushing against the fabric edge; or where a neat and precise line is needed. This provides a small recess where the fabric can be tucked into a small crack. This not only gives a neater edge, but conceals any minor delamination of the fabric edges from the partition should it occur. Figures 10.1(a)–10.1(c) show some common tuck joints. Tuck joints can be used for both vinyl wallcovering and fabric wallcovering.

An alternate installation method is an upholstered wall, which is fabric stretched over a frame and secured into place. Two types of upholstered walls are shown in Figure 10.2. Various proprietary stretch-fabric wall systems are available that allow fabric to be placed over inside and outside curved partitions as well as flat partitions. The edges can be straight or curved and the fabric can be placed on doors as well. Some systems provide a fiberglass batting under the fabric for nominal sound absorption.

When the fabric is placed over a thick fiberglass batting the assembly becomes an acoustic panel, as described below. In whatever way fabric wallcovering is applied, it must conform to the required fire rating for finishes either by being fire resistant, itself, or by being fire-retardant treated. Refer to Chapter 17 for flame-spread requirements of wall finishes.

ACOUSTIC PANELS [09520]

When a high degree of sound absorption is required, acoustic panels must be used. Although upholstered walls do provide some sound-absorbing qualities and can be designed to provide a high degree of sound absorption, acoustic panels differ in that they are designed as individual panels and have at least 1 in. (25 mm) of sound-absorbing material.

In addition, they are covered with a permeable material, such as a loose-weave fabric, so that the sound energy can pass through the fabric and be dissipated in the material underneath.

Acoustic panels can be purchased with a manufacturer's standard fabric, a customer's own material (COM), or they can be custom fabricated. Refer to Chapter 6 for information on how custom acoustic panels are constructed and attached to partitions. Refer to Chapter 11 for information on the fundamentals of acoustic control. When sound control is critical or when the room sounds will be either very high or low frequencies, an acoustical engineer should be consulted.

Two important decisions have to be made with acoustic panels. The first concerns fabric type, and the second concerns core material. As mentioned, the fabric must be permeable to allow for sound energy to pass through. This also means that the fabric should not be backed. In addition, fabrics should be hydrophobic; those that do not

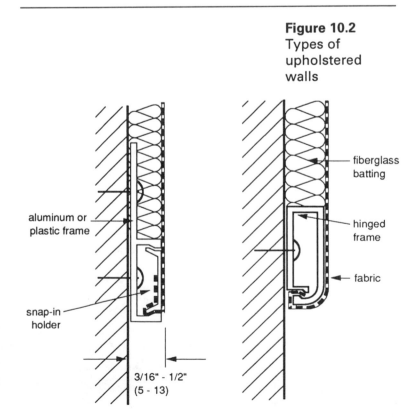

Figure 10.2
Types of upholstered walls

aluminum or plastic frame

snap-in holder

3/16" - 1/2" (5 - 13)

fiberglass batting

hinged frame

fabric

absorb and hold moisture that could cause sagging and distortion. Hydrophobic fabrics include modacrylics, polyesters, cotton, linen, olefin, and wool. Hydrophilic fabrics (those that absorb and retain moisture) should be avoided or be limited to 25 percent of the fabric's contents. These include silk, rayon, nylon, and acetate. Weaves that are balanced, such as jacquards and damasks, should be used; unbalanced weaves, such as satin, taffetas, and basket weaves, should be avoided.

Core material can be a loose material such as fiberglass or polyester batting, or a tackable material such as mineral fiberboard or

Table 10.2
Typical maximum sizes of building stone

Type	Variety	Maximum size, ft-in. (mm)
Marble	Group A[1]	5 ft × 7 ft (1500 × 2130)
	Group B	2 ft 6 in. to 4 ft wide 4 ft to 7 ft long (760 to 1200) (1200 to 2130)
	Group C[2] (for ¾ in. and ⅞ in. stone the smaller sizes should be used)	2 ft 6 in. to 4 ft wide 4 ft to 7 ft long (760 to 1200) (1200 to 2130)
	Group D[2]	2 ft 6 in. to 4 ft wide 4 ft to 7 ft long (760 to 1200) (1200 to 2130)
Granite		4 ft × 10 ft (1200 × 3050)
Slate	Panels	4 ft × 6 ft 6 in. (1200 × 2000)
Slate, natural finish	Green or gray, ⅜ in. thick (10 mm) Blue black Green or gray 3/4 in. thick (19 mm)	8 in. × 16 in. (200 × 400) 18 in. × 30 in. (460 × 760) 15 in. × 24 in. (380 × 600)
Slate	Honed or sanded finish	3 ft × 5 ft (900 x 1500)
Limestone	2 in. thickness	3 ft × 5 ft (900 × 1500)

These dimensions are general guidelines only. Maximum sizes depend on the type of stone, the quarry, and the quantities needed. Check with the quarry and the local supplier before deciding on final sizes.

[1] Refer to Chapter 8 for a description of marble groups.

[2] A maximum size of 20 ft^2 (1.9 m^2) per piece is recommended for Groups C and D marble.

Source: Marble Institute of America; National Building Granite Quarries Association, Inc.; Indiana Limestone Institute of America, Inc.

tackable, acoustic fiberglass. Mineral fiber-board is a dimensionally stable composite of inorganic mineral fibers with a microper-forated surface. Tackable acoustic fiberglass is noncombustible fibrous glass mat bonded with a resinous binder and formed into a rigid board with a finish face of thin, rigid fiberglass mesh. Avoid pressed, recycled paper products because these tend to absorb moisture and do not have good dimensional stability.

STONE WALL FINISHES [09600]

Types

As with flooring, stone commonly used for partition finishes includes granite, marble, limestone, slate, and sandstone. Because porosity is not a problem with interior vertical applications, travertine and other limestones are sometimes used for interior walls without being filled. In addition, cast stone and other artificial wall coverings are used and installed like stone. Cast stone is a mixture of cement, sand, and light aggregates cast in forms to look like stone. Refer to Chapter 8 for a description of the various types of natural stone.

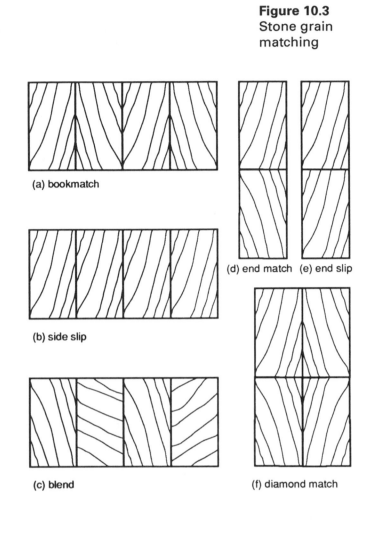

Figure 10.3
Stone grain matching

(a) bookmatch

(b) side slip

(c) blend

(d) end match   (e) end slip

(f) diamond match

Most code requirements related to stone veneer are for exterior applications. However, the *Uniform Building Code* provisions that commonly apply to interior stone include the following. Other codes have similar provisions.

• Stone wainscots not exceeding 4 ft (1200 mm) high above the finished floor may be exempted from the provisions of Chapter 14 of the UBC if approved by the building official.

• Stone veneer cannot support any load other than its own weight and the vertical dead load of the veneer above.

• Stone up to 2 in. (50 mm) thick must be supported with corrosion-resistant ties no smaller in diameter than no. 9 gage wire or no. 22 gage by 1 in. (25 mm) if they are sheet metal. Corrosion-resistant dowels may also be used.

• Individual veneer units between 3 and 15 lb/ft² (14.6 and 73.2 kg/m²) adhered to backing with cement or mastic cannot exceed 36 in. (900 mm) in the greatest dimension or be more than 720 in.² (.46 m²) in total area. Individual units less than 3 lb/ft² are not limited in dimension or area.

• Additional anchoring or special details may be required in areas of high seismic risk.

Building code requirements for stone veneer

Figure 10.4
Interior stone
veneer

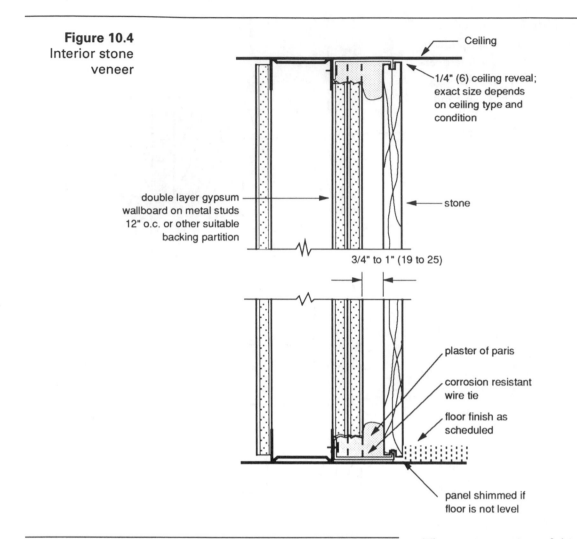

Ceiling

1/4" (6) ceiling reveal;
exact size depends
on ceiling type and
condition

double layer gypsum
wallboard on metal studs
12" o.c. or other suitable
backing partition

stone

3/4" to 1" (19 to 25)

plaster of paris

corrosion resistant
wire tie

floor finish as
scheduled

panel shimmed if
floor is not level

Figure 10.5
Veneer at
vertical joint

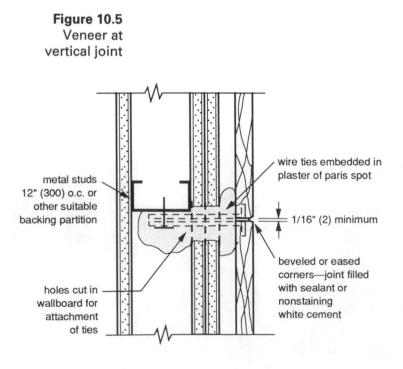

metal studs
12" (300) o.c. or
other suitable
backing partition

wire ties embedded in
plaster of paris spot

1/16" (2) minimum

beveled or eased
corners—joint filled
with sealant or
nonstaining
white cement

holes cut in
wallboard for
attachment
of ties

The maximum sizes of thick-cut stone depend on the type and thickness used. These are summarized in Table 10.2. Stone tile is discussed in the next section.

Typical details

Like flooring, stone partition finishes can be constructed using thick slabs or thinly cut sheets. With the traditional, standard set method of applying stone, slabs about ¾ in. to ⅞ in. (19 to 22 mm) thick are attached to wall substrates (either masonry or gypsum wallboard) in large sheets with stainless steel wires or flat metal ties. Some stones, notably marble, have definite grain patterns, and because thick stone can be set using large slabs, the method of matching adjacent slabs must be specified. Like wood paneling, the grains can be matched in different ways. Figures 10.3(a)–10.3(f) show some of the common methods.

The wires or ties are attached to the stone by being set in holes or slots cut into the back or sides of the panel. The other end is attached to the metal stud or masonry backup wall. See Figure 10.4. Lumps of plaster of paris, called *spots*, are placed between the substrate and the back of the stone panel at each anchor. The spots hold the slab in place and allow for precise alignment before they harden. For rooms with normal ceiling heights, the stone rests on the floor and the anchors simply serve to hold each panel in place. The joints can be filled with nonstaining Portland cement mortar, or sealant, or can be left open. As shown in Figure 10.5, vertical joints show a slight gap and usually contain additional wire ties.

Where outside corners occur, a variety of details may be used. Some of these are illustrated in Figure 10.6. When more than one level of stone is required in high spaces or where a horizontal joint is desired, one of the anchoring methods shown in Figure 10.7(a)–10.7(c) can be used. If additional support is required, steel angles can be used as shown in Figure 10.7(d).

With the new technology for cutting and laminating stone to various types of reinforcing backing, thin stone tiles are largely replacing the traditional thick slab construction. These tiles are about ⅜ in. thick and come in sizes of 1 × 1 ft, 1 × 2 ft, and 2 × 2 ft (300 × 300, 300 × 600, and 600 × 600 mm), although other sizes and thicknesses are available, depending on the manufacturer. In many cases the stone is simply mastic applied to a suitable substrate, usually gypsum wallboard on metal studs.

See Figure 10.8. Some manufacturers provide special clips that hold the stone in place against the backup wall.

Coordination

• The substrate must be sufficiently strong and stiff to carry the additional weight of stone. This is especially true of thick, standard set stone.

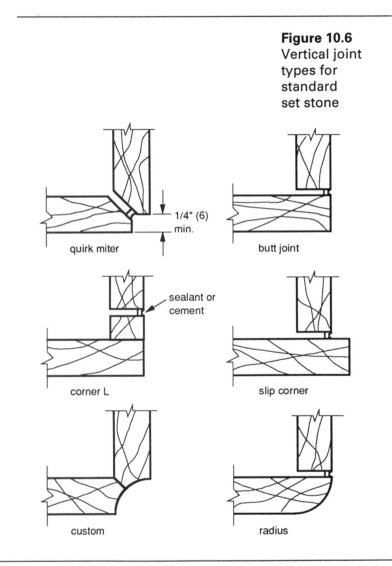

Figure 10.6
Vertical joint types for standard set stone

quirk miter

1/4" (6) min.

butt joint

sealant or cement

corner L

slip corner

custom

radius

Applicable standards for stone

American Society for Testing and Materials (ASTM):

ASTM C-119   *Standard Definitions of Terms Relating to Natural Building Stones*
ASTM C-503   *Standard Specification for Marble Dimension Stone (Exterior)*
ASTM C-568   *Standard Specification for Limestone Dimension Stone*
ASTM C-615   *Standard Specification for Granite Dimension Stone*
ASTM C-616   *Standard Specification for Quartz-based Dimension Stone*
ASTM C-629   *Standard Specification for Slate Dimension Stone*

Figure 10.7
Anchoring
methods for
horizontal
joints

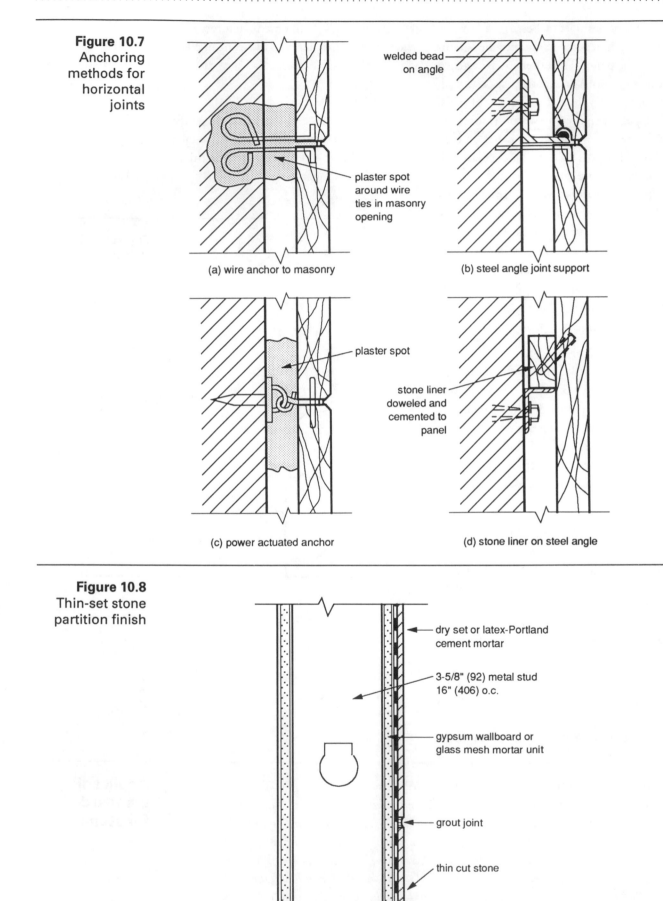

welded bead
on angle

plaster spot
around wire
ties in masonry
opening

(a) wire anchor to masonry

(b) steel angle joint support

plaster spot

stone liner
doweled and
cemented to
panel

(c) power actuated anchor

(d) stone liner on steel angle

Figure 10.8
Thin-set stone
partition finish

dry set or latex-Portland
cement mortar

3-5/8" (92) metal stud
16" (406) o.c.

gypsum wallboard or
glass mesh mortar unit

grout joint

thin cut stone

• Because cutting and fitting for light switches, thermostats, and other wall-mounted items adds to the cost and interrupts the appearance of stone facings, these items should be given careful design consideration and, whenever possible, located where stone is not used.

• The size tolerances and squareness of surrounding construction must be sufficient to receive accurately cut stone.

• If stone is set to the floor without a base, the floor should be checked for level. The bottom of the stone may need to be cut to follow the floor line.

• If stone is placed on fire-rated partitions, anchoring requirements must be verified with the applicable building code.

• The maximum slab size for thick stone may be limited by the sizes of elevators, doors, and other limitations of the existing building.

CERAMIC TILE WALL FINISHES [09310]

The types, sizes, and standards for ceramic wall tile and other vertical applications are the same as those described in Chapter 8 for floor construction. Like flooring, although there are many variations of installation methods, there are basically two methods of installing wall tile: thin-set and full mortar bed.

The thin-set method

The thin-set method is used for residential and light commercial installations in areas such as kitchens, toilet rooms, and showers, as well as in dry areas. However, it should not be used in areas subject to continuous wetting, such as commercial shower rooms, pool areas, and the like. It is an appropriate application when weight and wall thickness must be kept to a minimum and where moderate cost is a consideration.

In the thin-set method, the supporting partition may be masonry or wood or metal studs. If the tile will be subject to only occasional wetting, a water-resistant gypsum

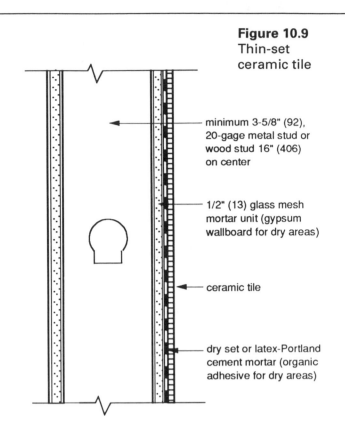

Figure 10.9
Thin-set ceramic tile

minimum 3-5/8" (92), 20-gage metal stud or wood stud 16" (406) on center

1/2" (13) glass mesh mortar unit (gypsum wallboard for dry areas)

ceramic tile

dry set or latex-Portland cement mortar (organic adhesive for dry areas)

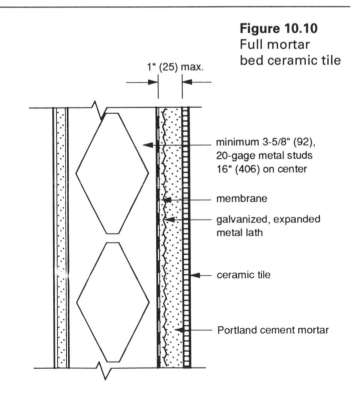

Figure 10.10
Full mortar bed ceramic tile

1" (25) max.

minimum 3-5/8" (92), 20-gage metal studs 16" (406) on center

membrane

galvanized, expanded metal lath

ceramic tile

Portland cement mortar

wallboard may be used over wood or metal studs. This includes areas such as residential kitchens, powder rooms, and walls outside a residential tub or shower enclosure. If the tile will be subject to more intense wet conditions, then glass mesh mortar units (or cement boards, as they are sometimes called) must be used on the studs. Areas where these backer boards are appropriate include residential tub and bath enclosures, gang showers, janitors' closets, and indoor pools.

For thin-set applications, a dry-set or latex-portland cement mortar is used. In dry areas, tile may be applied over standard gypsum wallboard with organic adhesive. See Figure 10.9. Some types of organic adhesive are also acceptable for light-use wet areas such as kitchens and areas outside tub or shower surrounds.

The full mortar bed method

Like ceramic tile flooring, the full mortar bed method is one of the most durable of the wall tile setting systems. It uses a thick bed of cured mortar as the base for the application of tile using a bond coat of dry-set or latex-Portland cement mortar. It is typically used in commercial construction, either in dry or limited water-exposure areas or in continuously wet areas, such as gang showers, laundries, pools, and tubs. If the tile will be continuously wet, a waterproof membrane must be used. Although Figure 10.10 shows an application over metal studs, a full mortar bed may also be used on masonry, concrete, or wood stud partitions as long as they can support the extra weight, which is approximately 18 to 20 lb/ft^2 (88 to 98 kg/m^2).

11
ACOUSTICS

The acoustic quality of a room or space can affect its usability and the way it is perceived, as much as its furniture, finishes, colors, and shape can. Spaces that are too noisy or reverberant are distracting, at best, and unusable, at worst. In some cases, such as in classrooms, when some sounds are not audible the situation is equally distracting.

There is a direct relationship between many interior construction design decisions and the resulting acoustic quality of a space. Room shapes and sizes, space planning, finish materials, construction techniques, and even furniture all influence the acoustic properties of a space, depending on the room's use and the sound sources within it and adjacent to it.

For most common situations, a basic knowledge of acoustics can help the interior designer make the best decisions. Complex designs, such as concert halls or recording studios, or where particularly troublesome noise sources exist, require the services of a qualified acoustical consultant.

ACOUSTIC FUNDAMENTALS
Qualities of sound

Sound travels in waves that consist of a high-pressure front followed by a low-pressure front. When the ear perceives a series of these pressure fronts of equal spacing, a tone is heard. Sound waves have four basic qualities: frequency, velocity, wavelength, and power.

Frequency is the number of successive pressure fronts that pass a given point in one second, and is measured in hertz (Hz). (One Hz equals one cycle per second.) The sounds that we call high notes or high-pitch sounds have high frequencies; base notes have low frequencies.

Velocity depends on the medium in which the sound is traveling and the temperature of the medium. In air at normal room temperature this is about 1130 ft/sec (345 m/sec).

Wavelength is the distance between the pressure fronts measured in feet and inches (meters and millimeters). There is a direct relationship between frequency and wavelength based on the speed of sound. For sound in air at room temperature that relationship is given by

$$\lambda = \frac{1130}{f}$$

in SI units: $\lambda = \frac{345}{f}$ Equation 11.1

λ is the wavelength in feet and f is the frequency in Hertz. It is an inverse relationship; as the frequency increases the wavelength decreases and as the frequency decreases the wavelength increases. This has a significant bearing on design because the size of architectural and finish components influence the behavior of sounds depending on their frequency.

Power is the quality of acoustic energy as measured in watts. It is this power that people perceive as loudness.

Loudness

The human ear is sensitive to a large range of sound power, from about 10^{-16} watts/cm^2 to 10^{-3} watts/cm^2. Because of this and the fact that the sensation of hearing is proportional to the logarithm of the source intensity, the decibel (abbreviated dB) is used in acoustic descriptions and calculations. The decibel conveniently relates actual sound intensity to the way humans experience sound. By definition, zero decibels is the threshold of human hearing and 130 decibels is the threshold of pain. Some common sound intensity levels and their subjective evaluations are shown in Table 11.1.

Changes in loudness are subjective, but some common guidelines are shown in Table 11.2. These are useful for evaluating the effects of increased or decreased decibel levels in design situations. For example, spending money to modify a partition to increase its sound transmission class (defined later in this chapter) by three decibels would not be worth the expense because it would hardly be noticeable.

Intensity level, dB	Example	Subjective evaluation	Intensity, w/cm^2
140	Jet plane takeoff		
130	Gunfire	Threshold of pain	10^{-3}
120	Hard rock band, siren at 100 ft	Deafening	10^{-4}
110	Accelerating motorcycle	Sound can be felt	10^{-5}
100	Auto horn at 10 ft	Conversation difficult to hear	10^{-6}
90	Loud street noise, kitchen blender	Very loud	10^{-7}
80	Noisy office, average factory	Difficult to use phone	10^{-8}
70	Average street noise, quiet typewriter, average radio	Loud	10^{-9}
60	Average office, noisy home	Usual background	10^{-10}
50	Average conversation, quiet radio	Moderate	10^{-11}
40	Quiet home, private office	Noticeably quiet	10^{-12}
30	Quiet conversation	Faint	10^{-13}
20	Whisper		10^{-14}
10	Rustling leaves, soundproof room	Very faint	10^{-15}
0	Threshold of hearing		10^{-16}

Table 11.1 Common sound intensity levels

Human sensitivity to sound

Although human response to sound is subjective and varies with age, physical condition of the ear, and other factors, the following guidelines are useful.

• A healthy young person can hear sounds ranging from about 20 Hz to 20,000 Hz, while most adults hear sounds ranging from about 20 Hz to 16,000 Hz. People are most sensitive to frequencies in the 3000 Hz to 4000 Hz range. Speech is composed of sounds primarily ranging from 150 Hz to 5000 Hz, with most ranging from 500 Hz to 3000 Hz.

• The human ear is less sensitive to low frequencies than to middle and high frequencies, for sounds of equal energy.

• Most common sound sources contain energy over a wide range of frequencies. Because frequency is an important variable in how a sound is transmitted or absorbed (because of its wavelength), it must be taken into account in building acoustics. For convenience, measurement and analysis are often divided into eight octave frequency bands identified by their center frequency. These are 63, 125, 250, 500, 1000, 2000, 4000, and 8000 Hz. For detailed acoustic design, smaller bands are often used.

SOUND TRANSMISSION

There are two basic problems in controlling noise (any unwanted sound): preventing or minimizing the transmission of sound from one space (or noise source) to another space, and reducing the noise within a space. This section discusses sound transmission; the next section outlines the basics of sound absorption as the primary means of reducing noise in a space.

Change in intensity level, dB	Change in apparent loudness
1	Almost imperceptible
3	Just perceptible
5	Clearly noticeable
6	Change when distance to source in a free field is doubled or halved
10	Twice or half as loud
18	Very much louder or quieter
20	Four times or one-fourth as loud

Table 11.2
Subjective change in loudness based on decibel level change

When there are two or more sound sources in a space, it is often useful to know what the combined decibel level is. Because decibels are logarithmic, they cannot be added directly. There is a complex formula for adding two or more decibels, but for practical purposes the values in Table 11.3 can be used to give results accurate to within one percent. For three or more sources, first add two, then the result to the third number, and so on.

Addition of decibels

When difference between the two values is:	Add this value to the higher value
0 or 1 dB	3 dB
2 or 3 dB	2 dB
4 to 8 dB	1 dB
9 dB or more	0 dB

Table 11.3
Addition of decibels

Transmission loss and noise reduction

Reducing sound transmission from one space to another to an acceptable level is one of the primary considerations in selecting construction elements and detailing barrier assemblies. Transmission of sound through a barrier is primarily retarded by the mass of the barrier. To a lesser extent the stiffness, or rigidity, of the barrier retards sound transmission. Given two barriers of the same weight per square foot, the one with less stiffness will perform better than the other. For construction, barriers may be partitions, floors, doors, glass, or anything that separates one room from another.

There are two important concepts in noise reduction: transmission loss and actual noise reduction between two spaces. Transmission loss only takes into account the loss through a barrier. Transmission loss is the difference, in decibels, between the sound power incident on a barrier in a source room and the sound power radiated into a receiving room on the opposite side of the barrier. This is a measurement typically derived in a testing laboratory when evaluating a particular construction assembly or component at various octave band frequencies.

Noise reduction is the arithmetic difference, in decibels, between the intensity levels in two rooms separated by a barrier of a given

Applicable standards for acoustics

Ceiling & Interior Systems Construction Association (CISCA):

AMA I-II	*Ceiling Sound Transmission Test by the Two-room Method*

American Society for Testing and Materials (ASTM):

ASTM E-90	*Test Method for Laboratory Measurement of Airborne Sound Transmission Loss of Building Partitions*
ASTM E-413	*Classification for Rating Sound Insulation*
ASTM E-336	*Test Method for Measurement of Airborne Sound Insulation in Buildings*
ASTM E-492	*Test Method for Laboratory Measurement of Impact Sound Transmission Through Floor-ceiling Assemblies Using the Tapping Machine*
ASTM E-497	*Standard Practice for Installing Sound-isolating Lightweight Partitions*
ASTM E-989	*Standard Classification for Determination of Impact Insulation Class*
ASTM E-1041	*Guide for Measurement of Masking Sound in Open Offices*
ASTM E-1110	*Classification for Determination of Articulation Class*
ASTM E-1111	*Test Method for Measuring the Interzone Attenuation of Ceiling Systems*
ASTM E-1130	*Test Method for Objective Measurement of Speech Privacy in Open Offices Using Articulation Index*
ASTM E-1264	*Classification for Acoustical Ceiling Products*
ASTM E-1374	*Guide to Open Office Acoustics and Applicable ASTM Standards*
ASTM E-1375	*Test Method for Measuring the Interzone Attenuation of Furniture Panels as Acoustical Barriers*
ASTM E-1376	*Test Method for Measuring the Interzone Attenuation of Sound Reflected by Wall Finishes and Furniture Panels*
ASTM E-1408	*Standard Test Method for Laboratory Measurement of the Sound Transmission Loss of Door Panels and Door Systems*
ASTM E-1414	*Standard Test Method for Airborne Sound Attenuation Between Rooms Sharing a Common Ceiling Plenum*

American National Standards Institute (ANSI):

ANSI S3.5	*Methods for the Calculation of the Articulation Index*

transmission loss. Noise reduction depends not only on the transmission loss of the barrier but also on the area of the barrier separating the two rooms and the absorption of the surfaces in the "quiet" room. Noise reduction can be increased by increasing the transmission loss of the barrier, by increasing the absorption in the "quiet" room (the one not producing the noise), by decreasing the area of the barrier separating the rooms, or by some combination of all three.

To simplify the selection of construction walls and other building components, a single-number rating system is often used to rate the transmission loss of the construction averaged across all octave band frequencies. This is the sound transmission class (STC). The higher the STC rating, the better the barrier is (theoretically) in stopping sound. Table 11.4 shows some STC ratings and their effects on hearing.

STC ratings represent the ideal loss through a barrier under laboratory conditions. Partitions, floors, and other construction components built in the field are seldom constructed as well as those in the laboratory. Also, breaks in the barrier, such as cracks, electrical outlets, doors, and the like, significantly reduce the overall noise reduction.

In critical situations, transmission loss and selection of barriers should be calculated using the values for various frequencies rather than the single STC average value. Some materials may allow an acoustic "hole," stopping most frequencies but allowing transmission of a certain range of frequencies. However, for preliminary design purposes in noncritical situations, the STC value is adequate.

The transmission loss or noise reduction that a partition or floor/ceiling assembly should have depends on the use of the adjacent rooms, the expected noise sources, the sensitivity of the occupants, and the amount of money available to spend on sound control. In some situations, model building codes or local, state, or federal regulations set minimum criteria for sound isolation. Tables 11.5–11.7 give some suggested sound insulation criteria for common building uses. The US Department of Housing and Urban Development (HUD) guidelines give minimum STC values for three grades, with Grade I having the best sound isolation.

Noise criteria curves

All normally occupied spaces have some amount of background noise. This is undesirable because some noise is necessary to avoid the feeling of a "dead" space and to help mask other sounds. However, the acceptable amount of background noise varies with the type of space and the frequency of sound. For example, people are generally less tolerant of background noise in bedrooms than they are of noise in public lobbies, and they are generally more tolerant of higher levels of low-frequency sound than of high-frequency sound.

These variables have been consolidated into a set of noise criteria curves relating frequency in eight octave bands to noise level. See Figure 11.1. Accompanying these curves are noise criteria ratings for various types of spaces and listening requirements. A representative sampling is shown in Table 11.8.

STC	Subjective effect
25	Normal speech can be clearly heard through the barrier.
30	Loud speech can be heard and understood fairly well.
35	Loud speech is not intelligible but can be heard.
42–45	Loud speech can only be faintly heard. Normal speech cannot be heard.
46–50	Loud speech not audible. Loud sounds other than speech can only be heard faintly if at all.

Table 11.4
Effect of barrier STC on hearing

Table 11.5
Sound isolation criteria

Type of occupancy	Area considered (source)	Adjacent area (receiving room)	Minimum STC[1]
Single-family residential	Bedrooms and living rooms	Bedrooms	40–48
		Living rooms	42–50
		Bathrooms	45–52
		Kitchens	45–52
Multifamily residential	See Tables 11.6 and 11.7		
Offices—normal privacy	Offices	Adjacent offices	45
		General office areas	45
		Conference rooms	45
		Toilets	47
		Corridors	45
		Kitchen/dining rooms	47
		Mechanical equipment	52+[2]
Offices—confidential, privacy required	Offices	Adjacent offices	52
		Conference rooms	52
		Other areas	52
Offices—large general areas	General office areas	Corridors, lobby	37
		Data processing	42
		Kitchen/dining areas	42
Hotels/motels	Bedrooms	Adjacent bedrooms	48+
		Bathrooms	52+
		Corridor, public areas	48+
		Mechanical rooms	52+[2]
Apartments	See Tables 11.6 and 11.7		
Schools	Classrooms	Adjacent classrooms	42–48
		Corridors/public area	42
		Shops	52+
		Music rooms	52+
		Toilets	47
		Kitchen/lunchroom	47
	Music rooms	Corridors	52

[1] These are minimum values for actual in-field service. Assemblies with laboratory ratings should be higher.
[2] Some mechanical rooms may require special treatment, especially if there is large, commercial equipment or unusual noise producing situations.

Source: *Architect's Handbook of Formulas, Tables, & Mathematical Calculations.* David Kent Ballast. Englewood Cliffs, NJ: Prentice-Hall, 1988.

Partition function between dwellings		Grade I	Grade II	Grade III
Apartment A	Apartment B	STC	STC	STC
Bedroom	Bedroom	55	52	48
Living room	Bedroom[1, 2]	57	54	50
Kitchen[3]	Bedroom[1, 2]	58	55	52
Bathroom	Bedroom[1, 2]	59	56	52
Corridor	Bedroom[2, 4]	55	52	48
Living room	Living room	55	52	48
Kitchen[3]	Living room[1, 2]	55	52	48
Bathroom	Living room[1]	57	54	50
Corridor	Living room[2, 4, 5]	55	52	48
Kitchen	Kitchen[6, 7]	52	50	46
Bathroom	Kitchen[1, 7]	55	52	48
Corridor	Kitchen[2, 4, 5]	55	52	48
Bathroom	Bathroom[7]	52	50	46
Corridor	Bathroom[2, 4]	50	48	46

Table 11.6
Sound isolation criteria of partitions between dwelling units

[1] The most desirable plan is to have the partition separating spaces with equivalent functions; for example, living room opposite living room. When this arrangement is not feasible, the partition must have greater sound-insulating properties.
[2] Whenever a partition wall might serve to separate several functional spaces, the highest criterion must prevail.
[3] Or dining, or family, or recreation room.
[4] Assuming there is no entrance door leading from corridor to living unit.
[5] If a door is part of the corridor partition, it must have the same rating as the corridor. The most desirable arrangement has the entrance door leading from the corridor to a partially enclosed vestibule or foyer in the living unit.
[6] Double-wall construction is recommended to provide, in addition to airborne sound insulation, isolation from impact noises generated by the placement of articles on pantry shelves and the slamming of cabinet doors.
[7] Special detailing is required for vibration isolation of plumbing in kitchens and bathrooms.

Source: *"A Guide to Airborne, Impact, and Structureborne Noise Control in Multifamily Dwellings,"*
U.S. Dept. of Housing and Urban Development, HUD-TS-24 (1974).

Partition function between dwellings		Grade I STC	Grade II STC	Grade III STC
Bedroom	Bedroom[1, 2]	48	44	40
Living room	Bedroom[1, 2]	50	46	42
Bathroom	Bedroom[1, 2, 3]	52	48	45
Kitchen	Bedroom[1, 2, 3]	52	48	45
Bathroom	Living room[2, 3]	52	48	45
Mechanical room	Sensitive areas	65	62	58
Mechanical room	Less sensitive areas (kitchens, family rooms, etc.)	60	58	54

Table 11.7
Sound isolation criteria within a dwelling unit

[1] Closets may be profitably used as "buffer" zones, provided unlouvered doors are used.
[2] Doors leading to bedrooms and bathrooms preferably should be of solid-core construction and gasketed to assure a comfortable degree of privacy.
[3] Special detailing is required for vibration isolation of plumbing in kitchens and bathrooms.

Source: *"A Guide to Airborne, Impact, and Structureborne Noise Control in Multifamily Dwellings,"*
U.S. Dept. of Housing and Urban Development, HUD-TS-24 (1974).

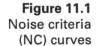

Figure 11.1
Noise criteria
(NC) curves

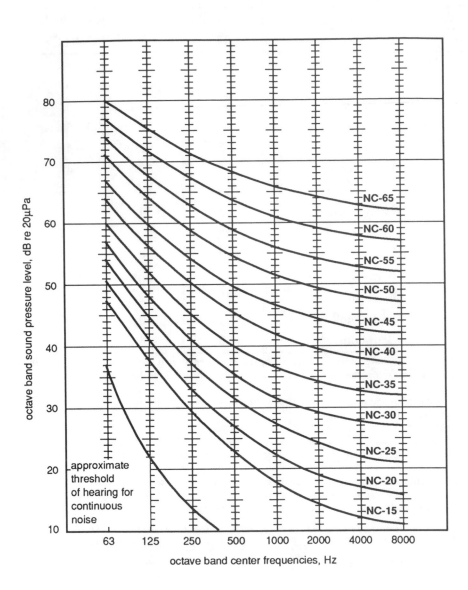

Figure 11.1 Noise Criteria (NC) Curves

Table 11.8	Type of space	Preferred range of noise criteria (dB)
Representative noise criteria	Concert halls, opera houses, recording studios	15–20
	Bedrooms, apartments, hospitals	20–30
	Private offices, small conference rooms	30–35
	Large offices, retail stores, restaurants	35–40
	Lobbies, drafting rooms, laboratory work spaces	40–45
	Kitchens, computer rooms, light maintenance shops	45–50

Noise criteria (NC) curves can be used to specify the maximum amount of continuous background noise allowable in a space, to establish a minimum amount of noise desired to help mask sounds, and to evaluate an existing condition. When an NC rating is specified for a particular space it means that the noise in each of the eight octave bands cannot exceed the sound-pressure level shown on the left of the chart.

When background noise conforms to a noise criteria curve, it usually still contains too many low-frequency and high-frequency sounds to be comfortable. A modification of the NC curves, called the preferred noise criteria (PNC), has been established that has sound-pressure levels lower than the NC curves in the low- and high-frequency ends of the chart.

SOUND ABSORPTION

Controlling sound transmission is only part of good acoustic design. The proper amount of sound absorption must also be included. Although sound intensity levels decrease about 6 dB for each doubling of distance from the source in free space, this is not the case in a room. In a room, the sound level decreases very near the source as it does in free space, but then it begins to reflect and levels out at a particular intensity. Of course, the *source* of the noise can be reduced, but this is not always possible. Sound absorption, then, is used to reduce the intensity level of sound within a space, to control unwanted sound reflections, to improve speech privacy, and to decrease reverberation.

Fundamentals of sound absorption

The absorption of a material is defined by the coefficient of absorption, α, which is the ratio of the sound intensity absorbed by the material to the total intensity reaching the material. Therefore, the maximum absorption possible is 1, that of free space because no sound is reflected. Generally, a material with a coefficient below 0.2 is considered to be sound reflective and one with a coefficient above 0.2 is considered to be sound absorbing. These coefficients are published in the manufacturer's technical literature.

There are three basic types of materials and construction components that absorb sound in different ways. These include porous materials, volume resonators, and vibrating panels.

Porous materials are the most common types and include items such as acoustic panels (described in Chapters 6 and 10) and acoustic ceiling tiles. In porous material, the sound energy is converted to heat by friction (absorbed) as it travels among the tiny fibers in the material.

Volume resonators (sometimes called Helmholtz resonators) are construction elements that have a small slot leading to a larger chamber. The chamber may be lined with porous material. A common commercial product of this type uses a concrete block with slits opening onto the cavity of the block. Volume resonators are designed to absorb low-frequency sound. The sound energy is converted to heat by friction at the

---

The Uniform Building Code requires that in Group R occupancies (residential) wall and floor/ceiling assemblies separating dwelling units or guest rooms from each other and from public space provide airborne sound insulation for walls and both airborne and impact sound insulation for floor/ceiling assemblies. Walls and floor/ceiling assemblies must meet a sound transmission class (STC) of 50 if the assembly has been laboratory tested and 45 if the assembly is field tested. Floor/ceiling assemblies must meet an impact insulation class (IIC) of 50 if the assembly has been laboratory tested and 45 if the assembly is field tested. Entrance doors from interior corridors together with their perimeter seals must have an STC rating of not less than 26.

Building code requirements for sound transmission

opening and decreases in energy as it bounces around inside the cavity. If porous material is applied in the cavity, additional energy is lost as friction.

Vibrating panels are also designed to absorb low-frequency sound by converting sound energy to vibrational energy. They are usually designed with air space behind them with or without porous material, depending on the frequencies they are designed to absorb.

The coefficient of absorption varies with the frequency of the sound, and some materials and construction elements are better at absorbing some frequencies than others. This is because of the varying wavelengths of all the frequencies according to equation 11.1. For example, a sound with a frequency of 3000 Hz has a wavelength of 0.38 ft (115 mm) while a sound with a frequency of 200 Hz has a wavelength of about 5.6 ft (1700 mm). This is a significant fact when selecting absorbing materials. For example, a 1-in. (25 mm) layer of fiberglass covered with

porous fabric has a coefficient of absorption of 0.99 for 1000 Hz frequencies, but a coefficient of absorption of only 0.10 for 125 Hz frequencies. Because the wavelength of the higher frequency is closer to the small size of the fiberglass matrix, there is more opportunity for the sound to move against the absorbing material and be converted to heat. The longer wavelengths mostly travel right through the material without being absorbed and are reflected back into the room by the rigid partition behind. Volume resonators and vibrating panels are designed to overcome this inherent problem in thin porous materials.

Because of the relationship between absorption efficiency and frequency, the coefficient of absorption for a material should be reviewed in all of the octave bands in critical applications. However, for convenience in noncritical applications, a single-number rating system is often used. This is the noise reduction coefficient (NRC). The NRC is the average of a material's absorption coefficients at the four frequencies of 250, 500, 1000, and 2000 Hz, rounded to the nearest multiple of 0.05. Where low-frequency absorption is not critical, the NRC rating is a useful index for selecting materials. Some typical NRC ratings are shown in Table 11.9.

Noise reduction within a space

The total absorption of a material depends on its coefficient of absorption and the area of the material. The unit used for this quantity is called the *sabin*, which is the absorption value of one square foot of material with a perfect absorption of 1.0. (A metric sabin equals 10.76 English sabins.) Because most rooms have several materials with different areas, the total absorption in a room is the sum of the various individual material absorptions. Finishes and construction detailing should be balanced to provide the best overall room absorption. For example, depending on the use of the room, hard, nonabsorbing materials used on the floor and the ceiling may have to be balanced with

Table 11.9
Noise reduction coefficients

Material	NRC
Vinyl tile on concrete	0.05
Wood strip flooring	0.10
Carpet, ½ in. pile on concrete	0.50
Carpet, direct glue to concrete	0.30
Gypsum board walls	0.05
Heavy plate glass	0.05
Marble or glazed tile	0.00
Fiberglass wall panel measuring 1 in. with fabric cover	0.80
Plywood paneling	0.15
Heavy velour fabric (18 oz.), draped to half area	0.60
Suspended acoustic tile measuring ⅝ in.	0.60
Suspended acoustic tile measuring 1 in.	0.90

absorbing materials on the walls. Although noise reduction can be calculated with formulas in critical situations, for most interior design the following rules of thumb may suffice:

- Avoid designing rooms with hard, reflective surfaces on the walls, floor, and ceiling. The space could be too "live" and noisy.
- The average absorption coefficient of a room should be at least 0.20. An average absorption above 0.50 is usually not desirable, nor is it economically justified. A lower value is suitable for large rooms; larger values are suitable for small or noisy rooms.
- Each doubling of the amount of absorption in a room results in a noise reduction of only 3 dB, which is hardly noticeable. To make any difference, the total absorption must be increased by at least three times to reduce the noise by 5 dB, which is noticeable.
- Although absorptive materials can be placed anywhere, ceiling treatment for sound absorption is more effective in large rooms, while wall treatment is more effective in small rooms.
- Generally, absorption increases with an increase in thickness of a porous absorber, except for low-frequency sounds that require special design treatment.
- If a corridor is appreciably higher than its width, some absorptive material should be placed on the walls as well as the ceiling, especially if the floor is hard-surfaced. If the corridor is wider than it is high, ceiling treatment is usually enough.
- The amount of absorption of a porous type of sound absorber, such as fiberglass or mineral wool, depends on (1) material thickness, (2) material density, (3) material porosity, and (4) the orientation of the material's fibers. A porous sound absorber should be composed of open, interconnected voids.

Calculating noise reduction within a space

In some situations, it may be necessary to increase noise reduction by increasing the sound absorption in a room. The effect of doing this can be calculated to see if the change is both sufficient and economically justified. To do this, the total absorption of the room before the change is calculated. This is the sum of all the individual absorptions of the different materials. Then, the total absorption after the change is calculated and the noise reduction calculated. Because of the logarithmic relationship of sounds, the formula includes using a common logarithm.

The total absorption of a material is calculated according to the equation

$$A = S\alpha \qquad \text{Equation 11.2}$$

A = the absorption in sabins
 (metric sabin = 10.76 English sabins)

S = the area of the material in square feet
 (m^2)

α = the coefficient of absorption

This calculation is performed for each of the materials in the room and added together.

Next, the total absorption after the change is calculated and compared with the original value according to the equation

$$NR = 10 \log \left(\frac{A_2}{A_1} \right) \qquad \text{Equation 11.3}$$

then

NR = the noise reduction in decibels

A_1 = total original room absorption in sabins

A_2 = total room absorption after the increase of absorption

This formula relates to the overall reverberant noise level in a room and does not affect the noise level very near the source.

Reverberation

Reverberation is the prolongation of sound as it repeatedly bounces off hard surfaces. It is an important part of the acoustic environment because it affects the intelligibility of speech and the quality of music. Technically, reverberation time is the time it takes the sound level to decrease 60 dB after the source has stopped producing the sound.

It is a desirable quality if the reverberation time is appropriate for the use of the space. For example, the recommended time for offices and small rooms for speech is 0.3 seconds to 0.6 seconds, while for auditoriums it is 1.5 seconds to 1.8 seconds. Reverberation can be controlled by modifying the amount of absorptive or reflective finishes in a space. Each doubling of the absorption in a room reduces reverberation time by half.

SOUND CONTROL

This section reviews some of the specific design and construction strategies that can be used to control sound and noise in various circumstances.

Space planning for acoustic control

There are many ways the acoustic performance of a group of spaces or an individual room can be affected by floor plan layout and the size and shape of the room itself.

In addition to designing walls and floors to retard sound transmission and proper use of sound absorption, there are several ways to help minimize acoustic problems with interior space planning. These are diagrammed in Figure 11.2 and summarized below.

• Zone activities of similar noise levels and plan areas of similar use next to each other. See Figure 11.2(a). For example, placing bedrooms next to each other is better than placing a bedroom next to a noisy space like the kitchen.

• Use quiet or semiquiet utility spaces as buffers between a noisy area and a quiet area. See Figure 11.2(b).

• Use closets, bookshelves, and similar functions on a common wall to help separate two rooms. See Figure 11.2(c). This not only helps add distance and mass to the common partition, but also keeps furniture and other noise-producing objects away from the common wall. Using closets between

---

Example: Calculating noise reduction

A room 15 × 20 ft with a 9-ft ceiling has a carpeted floor with a 44-oz. carpet on a pad ($\alpha = 0.40$), gypsum wallboard, and a gypsum board ceiling ($\alpha = 0.05$). What would be the noise reduction achieved by directly attaching acoustical tile with a given NRC of 0.70 to the ceiling?

Original total absorption of the room:

floor:	15 × 20 = 300 × 0.40 =	120
walls:	2 × 15 × 9 = 270 × 0.05 =	14
	2 × 20 × 9 = 360 × 0.05 =	18
ceiling:	15 × 20 = 300 × 0.05 =	15
	Total =	167 sabins

Absorption after treatment:

ceiling = 15 × 20 = 300 × 0.70 = 210 sabins

Subtracting 15 from the old value and adding 210 as a new value, the net total is 362 sabins.

$$NR = 10 \log \left(\frac{362}{167} \right)$$

$$= 10 \log (2.17)$$

$$= 3.4 \text{ dB}$$

Increasing the absorption by this amount helps a little, but the difference is just perceptible (see Table 11.2). Tripling the absorption would be clearly noticeable.

---

bedrooms at a common wall is one example of this technique.

• Stagger doorways in halls and other areas to avoid providing a straight-line path for noise. See Figure 11.2(d).

• Minimize the area of the common wall between two rooms where a reduction in sound transmission is desired. See Figure 11.2(e). This is one of the variables of noise reduction discussed previously.

• Avoid room shapes that focus sound. See Figure 11.2(f). Barrel vaulted hallways and circular rooms, for example, produce undesirable focused sounds. Rooms that focus sound in some places and not others may also deprive some listeners of useful reflections.

Control of room noise

There are three ways sound can be controlled within a space: by reducing the loudness of the sound source, by modifying the absorption in the space, and by introducing nonintrusive background sound to mask the unwanted sound.

Reducing loudness

Reducing the level of the sound source is not always possible if the sound is created by a fixed piece of machinery, people, or some similar situation. However, if the source is noise from the outside or an adjacent room, the transmission loss of the enclosing walls can be improved. If a machine is producing the noise, it can often be enclosed or modified to reduce its noise output.

Modifying absorption

Modifying the absorption of the space can achieve some noise reduction. However, there are practical limits to adding absorptive materials. This approach is most useful

Figure 11.2
Acoustic control with space planning

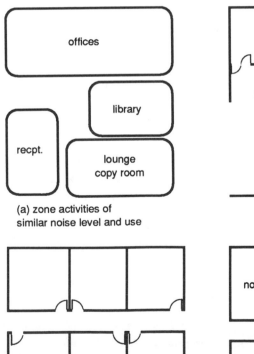

(a) zone activities of similar noise level and use

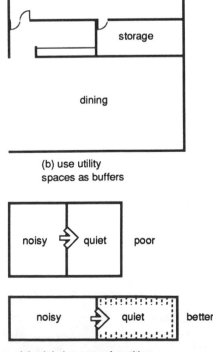

(b) use utility spaces as buffers

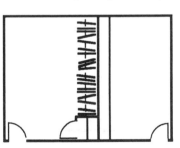

(c) use closets and bookshelves to separate activities and to keep furniture away from common walls

(d) offset doors

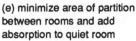

(e) minimize area of partition between rooms and add absorption to quiet room

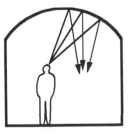

(f) avoid shapes that concentrate sound

when the problem room has a large percentage of hard, reflective surfaces.

Introducing background sound

In most cases, introducing nonintrusive background sound is desirable because it can mask unwanted noise. Some amount of background noise is always present. This may come from the steady hum of HVAC (heating, ventilating, and air conditioning) systems, business machines, traffic, conversation, or other sources. For example, if the sound level on one side (the noisy side) of a partition with an STC rating of 45 is 75 dB and the background noise on the quiet side of the partition is 35 dB, the noise coming through the partition will not be heard (theoretically) on the "quiet" side. See Figure 11.3. The transmitted sound is 30 dB (75 − 45), which is below the background sound of 35 dB. If the background noise level is decreased to 25 dB, then transmitted sounds will be heard. Of course, this is only a general guideline; the frequency of the noise and the background sounds will affect what is actually heard.

This phenomenon is used to purposely introduce carefully controlled sound into a space rather than to rely only on random background noise. Often called white sound, random noise, or acoustic perfume, speakers are placed in the ceiling of a space and connected to a sound generator, which produces a continuous, unnoticeable sound at particular levels across the frequency spectrum. The sound generator can be tuned to produce the frequencies and sound levels appropriate to mask the desired sounds. White sound is often used in open offices to provide speech privacy and to help mask office machine noise.

Speech privacy

In many spaces, the critical acoustic concern is not eliminating all noise or designing a room for music, but providing for a certain level of privacy while still allowing people to talk at a normal level. In many cases, speech privacy is regarded as a condition in which talking may be heard as a general background sound but not easily understood. This is most often required in open plan offices.

Speech privacy in areas divided by full-height partitions is usually achieved by sound loss through the partitions and, to a lesser extent, by the proper use of sound-absorbing surfaces. In open areas, such as an open-plan office, speech privacy is more difficult to achieve. There are five important factors in designing for speech privacy in an open area. All of these must be present to achieve the optimum acoustic environment.

1. The ceiling must be highly absorptive. The ideal is to create, as closely as possible, a "clear sky" condition so that sounds are not reflected from their sources to other parts of the space.

2. There must be space dividers that help reduce the transmission of sound from one space to the adjacent spaces. The dividers should have a combination of absorptive surfaces placed over a solid liner called a

Figure 11.3
Effect of
background
sound on noise
perception

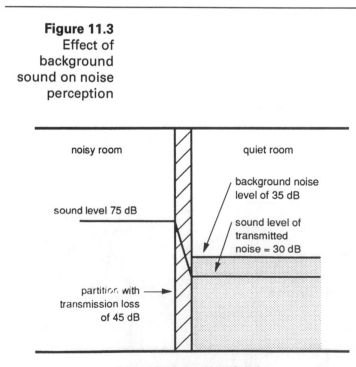

if transmitted sound level is below
the background level, the sound
is not perceptible.

septum. The absorptive surfaces minimize sound reflections and the septum reduces direct transmission of sound through the divider.

3. Other surfaces, such as the floor, furniture, windows, and light fixtures, must be designed or arranged to minimize sound reflections. A window, for example, can provide a clear path for reflected noise around a partial height partition.

4. If possible, activities should be distanced to take advantage of the normal attenuation of sound with distance.

5. There should be a properly designed background masking system. If the right amount of sound-absorbing surfaces is provided, the surfaces absorb all sounds in the space, not just the unwanted sounds. Background sound must then be reintroduced to maintain the right balance between speech sound and the background masking sound.

DETAILING FOR REDUCING SOUND TRANSMISSION

The control of sound transmission through a barrier depends primarily on the barrier's

---

Articulation index (AI) and articulation class (AC)

Because speech privacy in open offices depends on a complex interaction of many variables, two measures are used to evaluate open office acoustics: the articulation class (AC) and the articulation index (AI). Both of these test methods and rating systems have replaced the Speech Privacy Noise Isolation Class (NIC) and the Speech Privacy Potential (SPP) that were formerly used. The articulation class is determined by ASTM E-1110, *Classification for Determination of Articulation Class* and the articulation index is determined by ASTM E-1130, *Standard Test Method for Objective Measurement of Speech Privacy in Open Offices Using Articulation Index.*

The AC gives a rating of system component performance and does not account for masking sound. The AI measures the performance of all the elements of a particular configuration working together: ceiling absorption, space dividers, furniture, light fixtures, partitions, background masking systems, and HVAC systems. It is used to objectively test speech privacy of open office spaces, either in the actual space or in a laboratory mock-up of the space.

The articulation index can be used to (1) compare the relative privacy between different pairs of workstations or areas, (2) evaluate how changes in open office components affect speech privacy, and (3) measure speech privacy objectively for correlation with subjective responses. It has the potential for being a method to specify required levels of speech privacy; however, more research is needed in this area.

The articulation index predicts the intelligibility of speech for a group of talkers and listeners. The result of the test is a single-number rating. The AI rating can range from 0.00 to 1.00, with 0.00 being complete privacy and 1.00 being absolutely no privacy where all individual spoken words can be understood. Confidential speech privacy exists when speech cannot be understood and occurs when the articulation index is at or below 0.05. Normal speech privacy means concentrated effort is required to understand intruding speech and exists when the AI is from 0.05 to 0.20. Above an AI of 0.20, speech becomes readily understood. Unacceptable privacy exists when the AI is above 0.30.

Both the articulation index and articulation class are intended only for open office situations where speech is the sound source of concern. However, the articulation index can be adapted for other open plans, such as in schools, and can be applied to measure speech privacy between enclosed and open spaces and between two enclosed rooms.

Figure 11.4
Components
of a partition
resistant to
sound
transmission

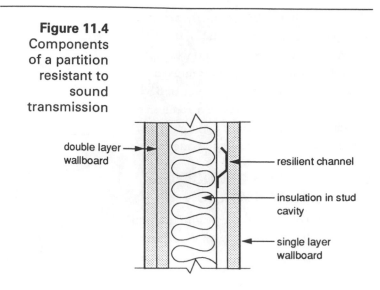

double layer wallboard →

→ resilient channel

→ insulation in stud cavity

← single layer wallboard

mass and, to a lesser extent, on its stiffness. Walls and floors are generally rated by their STC value; the higher the STC rating, the better the barrier is in reducing transmitted sound. Manufacturer's literature, testing laboratories, and reference literature typically give the transmission loss at different frequencies. Some representative STC values for gypsum wallboard partitions are given in Figure 1.21.

Partitions

There are several methods used to build a sound-resistant partition. These are shown diagrammatically in Figure 11.4. The first technique simply adds mass to the wall. This

Table 11.10
Transmission
loss data for
typical partition
types

Construction description	STC
Gypsum wallboard, ⅝ in. (15.9 mm) thick, each side 3⅝ in. (92.1 mm) metal studs	42
Same as above with 3 in. (75 mm) sound attenuation blankets in cavity	48
Two layers ½ in. (13 mm) gypsum wallboard, each side 2½ in. (63.5 mm) metal studs with 1½ in. (38 mm) sound attenuation blankets in cavity	54
Same as above except only one layer drywall on one side of partitions	50
Gypsum wallboard, ⅝ in. (15.9 mm) thick, each side 2 × 4 in. (50 × 100 mm) wood studs	34
Same as above using resilient channels on wood studs	45
Gypsum wallboard, ⅝ in. (15.9 mm) thick, on 2 × 4 in. staggered wood studs on common 2 × 6 in. plate with 2 in. (50 mm) sound attenuation blanket in cavity	45
Two layers ½ in. gypsum wallboard each side 2 × 4 in. studs, gypsum wallboard mounted on one side on resilient clips, 3 in. (75 mm) sound attenuation blanket in cavity	59
Four-inch brick with ½ in. (13 mm) plaster one side	50
Lightweight concrete block measuring 4 in. (100 mm)	40
Standard weight concrete block measuring 4 in. (100 mm)	45
Standard concrete block measuring 4 in. (100 mm), with ½ in. (13 mm) gypsum wallboard on each side	48
Lightweight concrete block measuring 8 in. (200 mm)	49

Note: partition STC ratings include fully calked perimeter and no flanking loss due to ceiling construction.

Source: *Architect's Handbook of Formulas, Tables, & Mathematical Calculations.* David Kent Ballast. Englewood Cliffs, NJ: Prentice-Hall, 1988.

can be done by using a heavy material for the partition, such as masonry, or by using more than one layer of gypsum wallboard. Partitions with high STC ratings commonly have a double layer of wallboard on one or both sides of the stud. The second technique is to place insulation within the stud cavity. This absorbs sound (reduces its energy) that is transmitted through one layer of the wall before it reaches the other. Finally, resilient channels can be used as furring strips on one side of the partition. Because of their design, only one leg of the channel touches the stud so that the wallboard "floats" and dampens sound striking it rather than transmitting it to the stud and through the partition.

Some representative STC ratings for various types of partitions are shown in Table 11.10.

However, constructing a partition with these elements is not enough. There are many ways sound can pass through, over, and around an otherwise well-built partition. These are shown in Figure 11.5. Gaps in the barrier must be sealed. Edges at the floor,

ceiling, and the intersecting walls must be calked; as shown in Figure 11.6. Penetrations of the barrier should be avoided; however, if they are absolutely necessary, they should also be sealed. For example, electrical outlets should not be placed back to back, but staggered in separate stud spaces and calked. See Figure 11.7. Pipes, ducts, and similar penetrations provide a path for both airborne sound and mechanical vibration and, therefore, should not be rigidly connected to the barrier. Any gaps between ducts, pipes, and a partition should also be sealed and calked.

It is critical to make sure that all cracks in a partition or other barrier are sealed. A hairline crack will decrease a partition's transmission loss by about 6 dB. A 1-in.^{2} (645 mm^2) opening in a 100-ft^2 (9.3 m^2) gypsum wallboard partition can transmit as much sound as the entire partition. A wall with 0.1 percent open area (from cracks, holes, undercut doors, and so on) can have only a maximum transmission loss of about

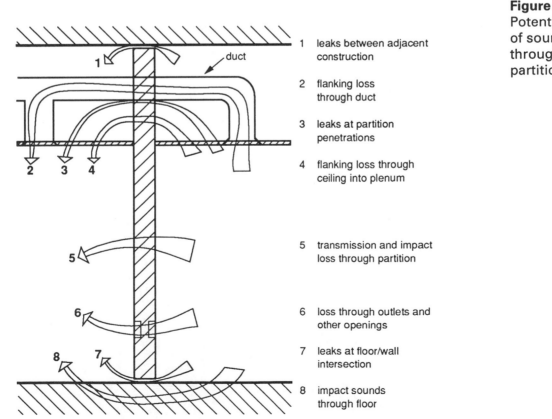

Figure 11.5
Potential sources of sound leaks through partitions

1   leaks between adjacent construction

2   flanking loss through duct

3   leaks at partition penetrations

4   flanking loss through ceiling into plenum

5   transmission and impact loss through partition

6   loss through outlets and other openings

7   leaks at floor/wall intersection

8   impact sounds through floor

Figure 11.6
Partition
sealing detail

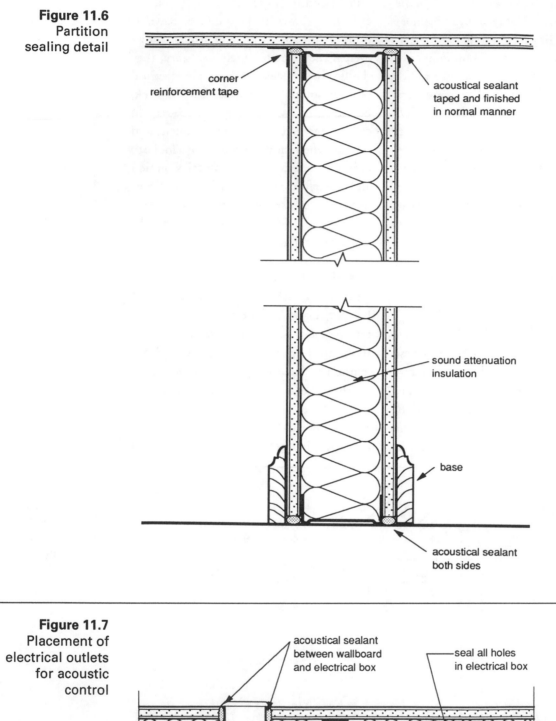

corner
reinforcement tape

acoustical sealant
taped and finished
in normal manner

sound attenuation
insulation

base

acoustical sealant
both sides

Figure 11.7
Placement of
electrical outlets
for acoustic
control

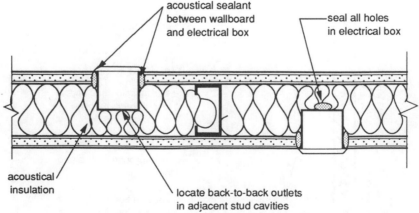

acoustical sealant
between wallboard
and electrical box

seal all holes
in electrical box

acoustical
insulation

locate back-to-back outlets
in adjacent stud cavities

30 dB, no matter how solidly it is constructed. A wall with 1 percent open area can have only a maximum loss of about 20 dB.

Construction with a lower STC rating than the barrier itself should be avoided or given special treatment because it will decrease the overall rating of the barrier. Doors placed in an otherwise well-built sound wall are a common problem. For example, a partition 9 ft high by 15 ft long (2700 × 4600 mm) with an STC of 54 and a door in it measuring 3 ft by 7 ft (900 x 2100 mm) with an STC of 29 and sealed around its perimeter only has an overall STC of 37 dB.

However, the problem can be dealt with in several ways. The perimeter should be completely sealed with weather stripping specifically designed for sound sealing at the jamb and head and with a threshold or automatic door bottom at the sill. See Figure 11.8. An automatic door bottom is a piece of hardware that drops a seal from the door to the floor or threshold as the door closes. Typical head and jamb seal details are shown in Figures 4.12 and 4.13, while automatic door bottoms are illustrated in Figure 4.14. The numbers in Table 11.11 illustrate the wide range of STC ratings for doors depending

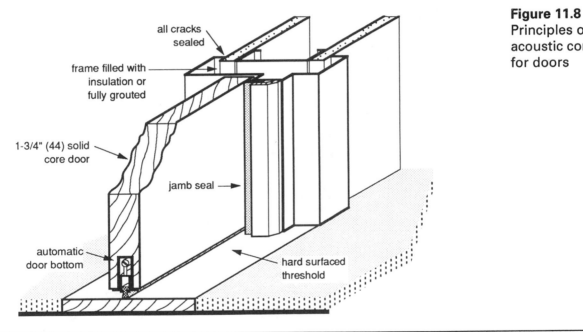

Figure 11.8
Principles of acoustic control for doors

all cracks sealed

frame filled with insulation or fully grouted

1-3/4" (44) solid core door

jamb seal

automatic door bottom

hard surfaced threshold

Door assembly	STC
Hollow core 1¾ in. (44 mm) thick with ¼ in. (6 mm) gap at sill	17
Solid core wood 1¾ in. (44 mm) thick with no seal	20
Solid core wood 1¾ in. (44 mm) thick with perimeter seal and automatic door bottom	29
Steel door 1¾ in. (44 mm) thick with compressible perimeter seal and automatic door bottom	44
Two 1¾ in. (44 mm) solid core doors with full seals separated by 3 ft (900 mm) air space	47

Table 11.11
Transmission loss data for typical door assemblies

Note: these figures were compiled from various industry sources and represent typical ratings useful for preliminary design decisions. Refer to manufacturers' literature for more detailed data.

on the type of construction assembly. Refer to the manufacturer's literature for STC ratings for specific applications of the various types of available door seals.

Figure 11.9
Glazing assembly for sound control

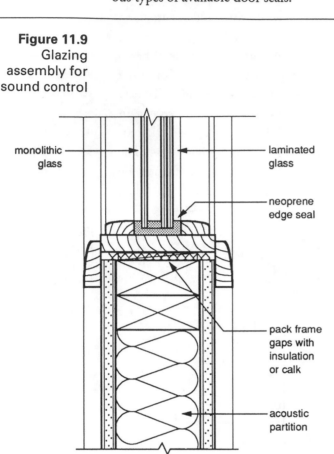

monolithic glass

laminated glass

neoprene edge seal

pack frame gaps with insulation or calk

acoustic partition

The door itself should be as heavy as possible, preferably a solid core wood door or an insulated steel door. Solid core wood doors 1¾ in. (44 mm) thick with correctly installed perimeter seals can achieve STC ratings in the low 30s. When higher STC ratings are required, insulated steel doors with double seals should be used. When an STC door rating over 49 is required, 2¼-in. (57 mm) thick doors are used. Often, two sealed doors are used, separated by an air gap. For extremely critical installations, such as recording studios and concert halls, special prepackaged, sound-rated door assemblies should be used.

Interior glass lights pose another problem for sound transmission. As shown in Table 11.12, single thickness glass does not provide much sound attenuation. When higher ratings are required, laminated glass set in resilient framing should be used. See Figure 11.9. Laminated glass provides more mass and the plastic interlayer improves the damping characteristics of the barrier. Alternately, double- or triple-pane assemblies can be used or double layers of laminated glass.

In addition to correctly detailing doors and glazed openings in partitions, all flanking paths should be eliminated or treated

Table 11.12
Transmission loss data for glass

Glazing assembly	STC
Single strength float glass	26
Float glass ¼ in. (6 mm) thick	29
Float glass ½ in. (13 mm) thick	33
Laminated glass ¼ in. (6 mm) thick (0.030 in. interlayer)	35
Laminated glass ½ in. (13 mm) thick (0.060 in. interlayer)	38
Laminated glass ¾ in. (19 mm) thick (two, 0.060 in. interlayers)	41
Float glass ¼ in. and ½ in. thick with 2 in. (50 mm) air space between	39
Laminated glass ¼ in. and ½ in. thick with 6 in. (150 mm) air space	44

Note: In critical situations to achieve the above ratings, glass panels must be sealed at all edges. When using two layers of glass separated by an air space, the thicknesses of the glass lights should not be the same.

Source: *Architect's Handbook of Formulas, Tables, & Mathematical Calculations.* David Kent Ballast. Englewood Cliffs, NJ: Prentice-Hall, 1988.

appropriately. These include plenum spaces above ceilings, heating registers that pass from one room to the next, air conditioning ducts, pipes, and other penetrations. In many commercial projects, partitions extend only to the suspended ceiling, allowing sound to travel from one room, through the ceiling tile into the plenum, and into the adjacent room. Ideally, the partition should extend to the structural floor above. When this is not possible, some type of plenum barrier should be constructed. Two of these are illustrated in Figures 11.10(a) and 11.10(b).

Floor/ceiling assemblies

For floor/ceiling assemblies, a high STC rating is not enough to evaluate the effectiveness of transmission loss. Impact noise, or sound resulting from direct contact of an object with a sound barrier, can occur on any surface, but it generally occurs on a floor/ceiling assembly. It is usually caused by footfalls, shuffled furniture, and dropped objects on hard-surfaced floors, such as ceramic tile, hardwood, or resilient tile.

The result of impact noise caused by these kinds of activities is quantified by the impact

Figure 11.10
Plenum barriers

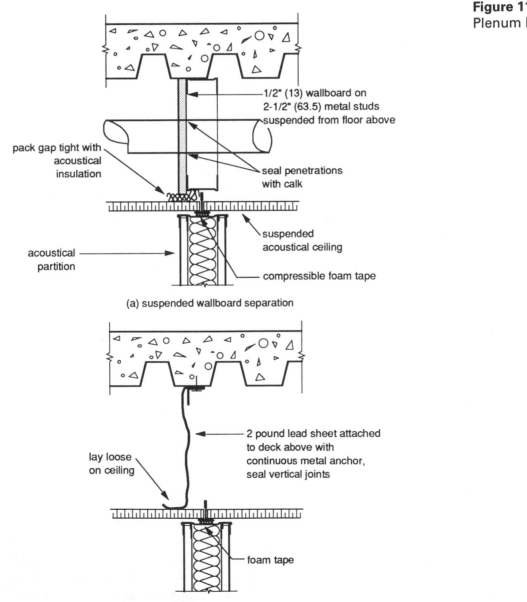

1/2" (13) wallboard on
2-1/2" (63.5) metal studs
suspended from floor above

pack gap tight with acoustical insulation

seal penetrations with calk

acoustical partition

suspended acoustical ceiling

compressible foam tape

(a) suspended wallboard separation

2 pound lead sheet attached to deck above with continuous metal anchor, seal vertical joints

lay loose on ceiling

foam tape

(b) lead sheet separation

insulation class (IIC) number, a single-number rating of a floor/ceiling assembly's impact sound performance. The higher the IIC rating, the better the floor performs in reducing impact sounds in the test frequency range.

In most cases, the construction of floors is already determined by the architectural design of a building, either existing or new. Fortunately, the IIC value of a floor depends mostly on its finish and can most easily be increased by adding carpeting. In critical situations, the ICC rating can also be improved by providing a resiliently suspended ceiling below, floating a finished floor on resilient pads over the structural floor, or by providing sound-absorbing material (insulation) in the air space between the floor and the finished ceiling below.

Structure-borne noise

Most problems with noise transmission occur when the source vibrates the air in the noisy space, which in turn strikes a partition or ceiling and travels through the construction assembly into another space. Noise can also be transmitted by a source directly through the structure of a building. Dropped objects and footfalls on hard-surfaced floors as described previously are one example. The most troublesome structure-borne noises are produced by machines, HVAC systems, plumbing fixtures, and water flowing through pipes.

To control structure-borne noise, machines should be mounted on resilient pads or on special-spring supported mountings. Plumbing pipes should not be rigidly attached to studs, joists, and other structural elements. Instead, the pipe should be wrapped with insulation and then clamped to the supporting structure. Ducts should be lined with insulation and connections between vibrating equipment and the ducts attached to it should not be rigid. Although it is nearly impossible to isolate plumbing fixtures from the structure, they can be planned so they are not adjacent to quiet areas. If this is not possible, insulated chase walls can separate areas with plumbing from other rooms.

DETAILING FOR NOISE REDUCTION

As mentioned previously, there are three ways of controlling room noise, one of which is to increase the absorption. This is typically done with sound-absorbent finishes on walls, ceilings, and floors, although in large spaces, separate sound absorbers or reflectors can be suspended from the ceiling. In most situations acoustical ceiling tile, carpeting, furniture, and other construction elements are usually sufficient to provide an adequate amount of absorption for typical residential and commercial uses. These include homes, offices, retail stores, restaurants, and the like.

Figure 11.11
Details for low-frequency sound absorption

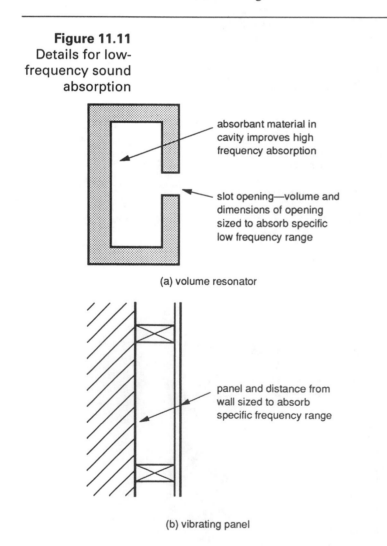

absorbant material in cavity improves high frequency absorption

slot opening—volume and dimensions of opening sized to absorb specific low frequency range

(a) volume resonator

panel and distance from wall sized to absorb specific frequency range

(b) vibrating panel

If additional absorption is required, partitions are usually treated with acoustic panels or upholstered walls as shown in Figures 6.30 and 10.2. Acoustical panels that are part of furniture systems can also provide additional absorption. However, these types of panels are only effective for the higher frequencies and for speech. Controlling low-frequency and very high-frequency sounds within a room requires construction elements that can trap the longer, low-frequency wavelengths or control the very short high-frequency wavelengths. Low-frequency control usually requires an allowance for thicker partitions or more space to apply detailing that absorbs low-frequency sound. Various details can be developed to meet the particular requirements of the project and the specific frequencies that must be controlled. In critical situations, an acoustical consultant should assist in developing these types of details. Two typical methods for absorbing low-frequency sounds are shown in Figures 11.11(a) and 11.11(b).

REFLECTION, DIFFUSION, AND DIFFRACTION

Reflection is the return of sound waves from a surface. Sometimes, reflection rather than absorption is the goal, such as in concert halls, lecture auditoriums, and large conference rooms. The reflectivity of a surface depends on its size, smoothness, and the wavelengths of the sounds striking it. If the size of a surface is greater than or equal to four times the wavelength of a sound striking it, the angle of incidence equals the angle of reflection, just as with light. For example, in order to reflect a 1000 Hz sound with a wavelength of about 1.13 ft (344 mm) a reflector should be at least 4½ × 4½ ft (1.4 × 1.4 m) wide. Similarly, if the texture of the surface is rough, with the individual surface variations about equal to the wavelength striking it, the sound will tend to be scattered rather than reflected like a mirror.

Reflection can be useful for reinforcing sound in lecture rooms and similar spaces. It can also be annoying if it produces echoes, which occur when a reflected sound reaches a listener later than about ¹/₁₇ second after the direct sound. Assuming a sound speed of 1130 ft/sec, an echo will occur whenever the reflected sound path exceeds the direct sound path by 70 ft or more.

Diffusion is the random distribution of sound from a surface. It occurs when the surface dimension of a reflector is about equal to the wavelength of the sound striking it, or when the individual textures on a large surface are equal to the wavelength.

Diffraction is the bending of sound waves around an object or through an opening. Diffraction can occur when a reflecting surface is small compared with the wavelength of the sound striking it. Diffraction explains why sounds can be heard around corners and why even small holes in partitions allow so much sound to be transmitted.

12

STAIR DESIGN AND CONSTRUCTION

Stairways may be classified into two broad types: those used for strictly utilitarian purposes, such as exit stairs, and monumental stairs designed to be a prominent design feature as well as providing vertical access. Interior design projects in both residential and commercial construction often require that new stairs be planned or that existing stairs be remodeled. For example, this can occur when a commercial tenant wants a private stairway connecting floors, when new mezzanines are planned, or when the existing stair configuration must be remodeled to meet current building codes.

This chapter discusses design guidelines for planning stairs and reviews construction requirements for common stair types. Although some code requirements are summarized in this chapter, refer to Chapter 17 for detailed building code requirements for exiting and stairway enclosure construction and to Chapter 18 for accessibility and Americans with Disabilities Act (ADA) requirements.

STAIRWAY LAYOUT

Configuration

The design and detailing of a stair begins with deciding on its basic configuration and shape, the approximate amount of space required, and the geometry of its layout. Some of the most common configurations are shown in Figures 12.1(a)–12.1(h). Each of these types has many variations. For example, a simple straight run stair may be enclosed or partially open, may be interrupted with several landings, or the landings may project from the face of the open side of the stair. L-shaped stairs can have equal or unequal legs. Monumental stairs can be designed in an unlimited number of configurations, sizes, and materials. The configuration of stairs is based on the space available and where the top and bottom of the stair must end.

Horizontal layout

Once the basic configuration of a stairway has been determined, the width, total run, and landing depths and widths determine

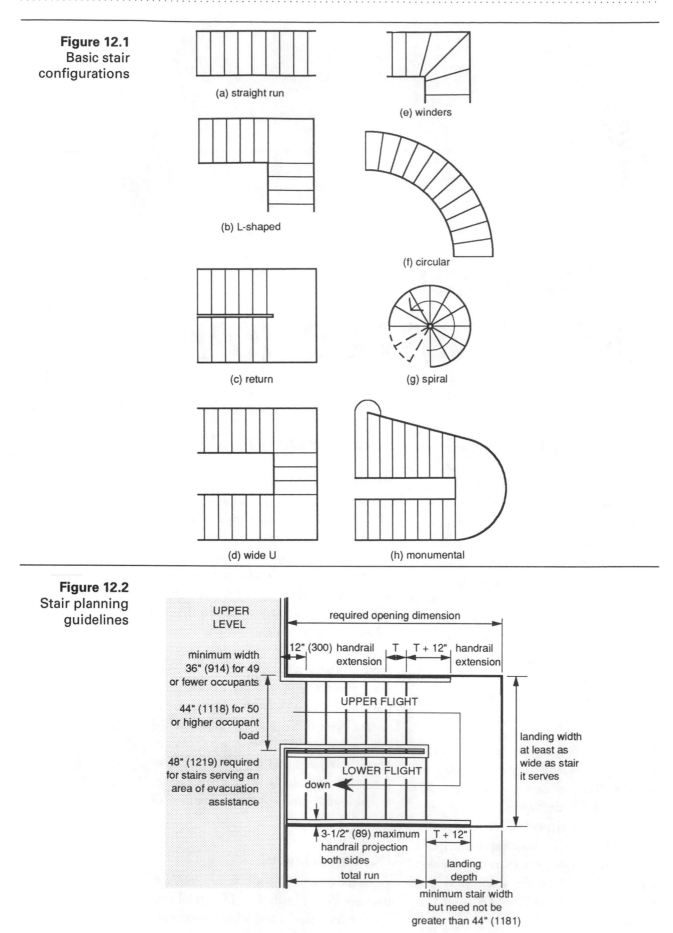

Figure 12.1
Basic stair configurations

(a) straight run

(b) L-shaped

(c) return

(d) wide U

(e) winders

(f) circular

(g) spiral

(h) monumental

Figure 12.2
Stair planning guidelines

UPPER LEVEL

minimum width 36" (914) for 49 or fewer occupants

44" (1118) for 50 or higher occupant load

48" (1219) required for stairs serving an area of evacuation assistance

required opening dimension

12" (300) handrail extension

T

T + 12"

handrail extension

UPPER FLIGHT

LOWER FLIGHT

down

landing width at least as wide as stair it serves

3-1/2" (89) maximum handrail projection both sides

total run

T + 12"

landing depth

minimum stair width but need not be greater than 44" (1181)

how much space is required. Figure 12.2 shows the minimum dimensions for laying out a stairway in plan view, including a landing. The total run depends on the depth of the treads and the number of risers and landings that will be used. Calculating stair risers and treads and total run is discussed in the next section.

The minimum width of any stair is 36 in. (914 mm) and is 44 in. (1118 mm) when the occupant load exceeds 50. Handrails may project a maximum of 3½ in. (89 mm) on both sides of a stairway. Stringers, trim, and similar decorative features can project a maximum of 1½ in. (38 mm) on each side.

The layout of return stairs or wide U-shaped stairs requires a slight adjustment in the relationship between the lower flight and the upper flight in order for the center railing to make a smooth switchback. As

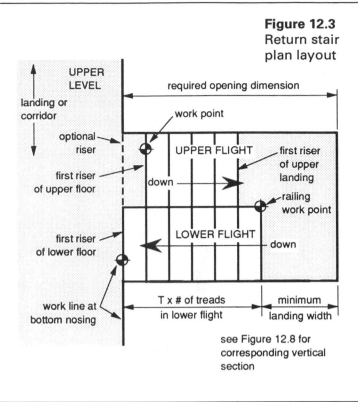

Figure 12.3
Return stair plan layout

see Figure 12.8 for corresponding vertical section

Building code requirements for horizontal layout

In addition to the requirements shown in Figure 12.2, building codes limit the use of special types of stairs. These include winding, circular, and spiral stairways. They are only allowed as private stairways in homes, apartments, condominiums, and the like.

Winding stairways have tapered treads that are wider at one end than the other. See Figure 12.4(a). When circular stairways have a smaller radius than required by code (see below), they are classified as winding stairways. When winders are used, they should all be the same shape and size, if possible.

Circular stairways have sides whose shape is a circular arc. The inside, or smaller arc, cannot be less than twice the width of the stair. See Figure 12.4(b). If it is, then it is considered a winding stairway. The Uniform Building Code and Standard Building Code limit the least dimension of the tread at the smallest point to 10 in. (254 mm), while the National Building Code requires a dimension of 11 in. (279 mm).

Spiral stairs use wedge-shaped treads that radiate from a center support column. Spiral stairs are discussed in Chapter 7, but the code requirements are repeated in Figure 12.4(c) for convenience. The allowable riser height is greater than for other stairs; it must be enough to provide a minimum headroom height of 6 ft 6 in. (1981 mm) but cannot be greater than 9½ in. (241 mm).

For enclosed exit stairways with doors adjacent to landings the codes require that the door not encroach into the required exit path more than a certain distance, either as the door is opening or when the door is fully opened. UBC requirements are shown in Figure 12.5. However, the dimensions in Figure 12.5 do not include any allowance for evacuation assistance space, if it is required. However, these areas are normally provided in the building exit stairways.

Figure 12.4
Building code
requirements
for nonstraight
stairs

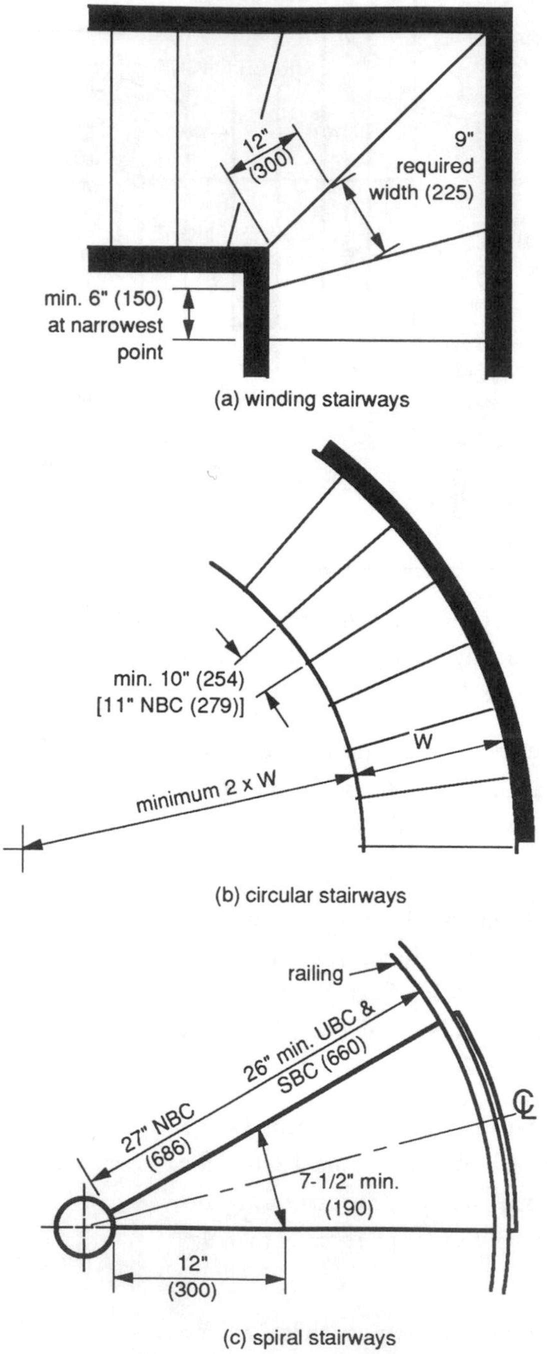

(a) winding stairways

(b) circular stairways

(c) spiral stairways

Note:
UBC = Uniform Building Code
NBC = National Building Code
SBC = Southern Building Code

shown in Figure 12.3, the first riser of the upper flight of steps at the intermediate landing is offset from the last tread of the lower flight by one tread dimension. Because of the angular geometry, this allows the handrail to turn back at one point instead of jogging vertically at the landing. This relationship is also shown in elevation view in Figures 12.8 and 12.10.

If the last riser of the upper flight of steps ends one tread dimension short of the stairway opening, then the handrail can be extended the required 12 in. (300 mm) without intruding into the upper level. Figure 12.11 shows a detailed schematic elevation view of this relationship.

Vertical layout

The basic design and code requirements for vertical dimensions of stairs are shown in Figure 12.6. Handrails must be provided on both sides of stairs 44 in. wide, or wider and must run continuously for the full length of the stair, and (except for private stairways) at least one handrail must extend beyond the upper and lower riser by at least 12 in. (300 mm). For conformance to accessibility regulations, the handrail at the bottom must extend 12 in. beyond a point one tread width from the lowest riser.

There has been extensive research into the best dimensions for the rise and treads of stairs and the safest and most comfortable proportion between the two. The maximum rise and minimum tread dimensions of 7 in. and 11 in., respectively, represent some of the most current research, including considerations for the physically disabled. See Figure 12.7. Some researchers recommend that treads should be even wider, from 12 in. to 14 in. The tread of a stair is considered the horizontal projection of the distance from the edge of one nosing to the next. It does not include any part of the tread under the nosing.

Because stair dimensions are based on the normal stride of a person while ascending and descending a stair, various formulas have been used to determine one dimension based on the other. This is typically the case when the total rise is known and the number of risers must be a whole number without exceeding 7 in. (178 mm) or 8 in. (203 mm) on private stairways. Some of these equations include the following (R equals riser height and T equals tread depth):

$$2R + T = 25 \qquad \text{Equation 12.1}$$

$$R \times T = 75 \qquad \text{Equation 12.2}$$

$$R + T = 17 \qquad \text{Equation 12.3}$$

$$T = 20 - \frac{4R}{3} \qquad \text{Equation 12.4}$$

Some of these formulas are rather old and represent proportions that were comfortable for people who, on average, were slightly smaller than the average size of people today. Equation 12.1, for example, was developed in the seventeenth century and originally stipulated that twice the riser plus the tread should be between 24 and 25. Now the minimum should be 25 and may be increased to 26. Of the four equations, 12.1 gives the widest tread based on a given riser height if the value of 25 is used, and can be

Figure 12.5
Planning guidelines for enclosed exit stairs

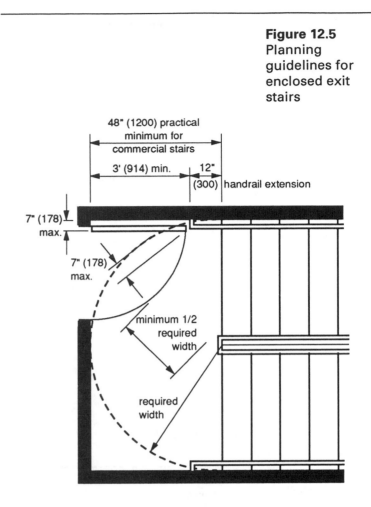

Figure 12.6
Stair section design guidelines

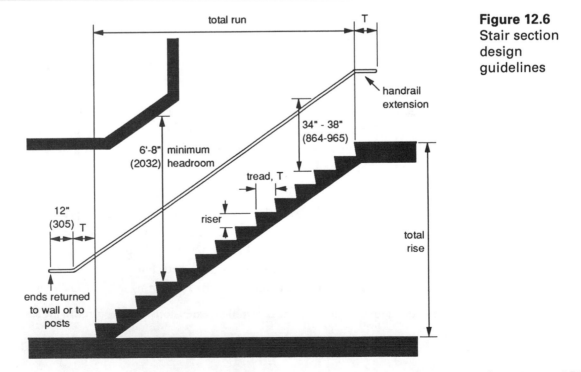

used in most designs. A wider tread is generally the safest, especially when descending stairs.

Stairs consisting of just one or two risers are especially dangerous because people have a more difficult time recognizing the change in level. For these types of stairs the recommended minimum tread depth is 13 in. (330 mm). In addition, there should be some means of making the level change more apparent, such as with riser lights or warning strips. Handrails should also be used as a visual cue to indicate that there is a level change and to give people something to hold on to as they traverse the steps.

The total run of a stair is calculated by taking the total rise in in. (mm) and dividing by an estimated riser height, usually 7 in. (178 mm). If the result is not a round number, then the required number of risers is the next highest full number. This is then divided into the total rise to obtain the actual required riser. The number of treads for a straight run stair is one less than the number of risers, and this number is multiplied by the tread dimension to obtain the total required run.

The maximum distance between landings is 12 ft (3660 mm); however, some research suggests that 9 ft (2740 mm) is a better dimension, especially for the physically disabled.

As noted in the previous section, the treads in return stairs or wide-U stairs should be set in a particular relationship so that the switchback of the center handrail occurs at a single point rather than being vertically offset. In addition, the top riser in the upper flight can be set back from the stair opening to allow for the required 12-in. (300 mm) extension without interfering with the landing space or to make the transition from handrail height to guardrail height (42 in.). This geometry is illustrated in Figure 12.8 and shown in more detail in Figures 12.9–12.11.

Figure 12.7
Riser and tread dimensions

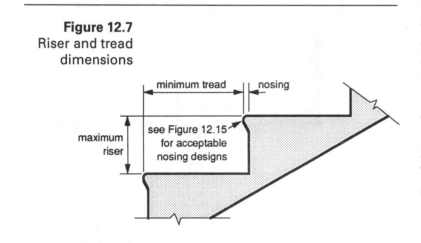

Example: Calculating total straight stair run

What is the required total run for a straight stair if the floor-to-floor height is 8 ft 6 in. and the tread dimension is 11 in.?

Assume that the riser height is 7 in. Divide 8 ft 6 in., or 102 in., by 7 to get 14.57 risers. Round up to 15 risers and divide 15 into 102 to get a riser height of about 6¾ in. In a straight run stair, 15 risers requires 14 treads. Using a tread of 11 in., multiply 14 times 11 to get a total run of 154 in., or 12 ft 10 in.

Building code requirements for vertical layout

The Uniform Building Code requires that every stairway having two or more risers must have risers with a minimum dimension of 4 in. (100 mm) and a maximum dimension of 7 in. (178 mm). Treads must be at least 11 in. (279 mm) deep. These are consistent with the Americans with Disabilities Act (ADA) requirements. For private stairs serving an occupant load of less than 10, the rise and tread may be 8 in. (203 mm) and 9 in. (229 mm), respectively.

The code requirements for handrails, railing extensions, and headroom are shown in Figure 12.6.

The illustrations show the critical working points for designing a stair with any material and in any dimensions. For multiple floor stair layouts, the upper flight in Figure 12.8 should be increased by two risers. Then, the stairway can be stacked as many times as required, and the return flight will always lead the lower flight by one tread. For L-shaped stairways, the first riser of the upper flight should also begin one tread distance from the nosing of the last riser of the lower flight so that the handrail makes a direct 90° turn without a vertical offset rise.

As shown in Figure 12.11, if the top of the handrail is placed 34 in. (864 mm) above the nosing line, the railing will intersect a 42-in. (1067 mm) guardrail in the location shown. Another method of making the transition from the handrail to the guardrail without the extra top tread is to locate the handrail at the required height and attach it to a separate railing that is higher than the handrail.

STAIR DESIGN AND CONSTRUCTION

Wood stairs [06430]

Wood stairs can be constructed in an almost unlimited number of styles and details from simple, utilitarian stairs to elaborate, custom-fabricated monumental staircases. Basic, straight run, U-shaped, and L-shaped stairs with little decorative features are normally site-built by finish carpenters. Decorative, prefabricated railings, balusters, and newel posts may be used in conjunction with the basic structure and the treads and

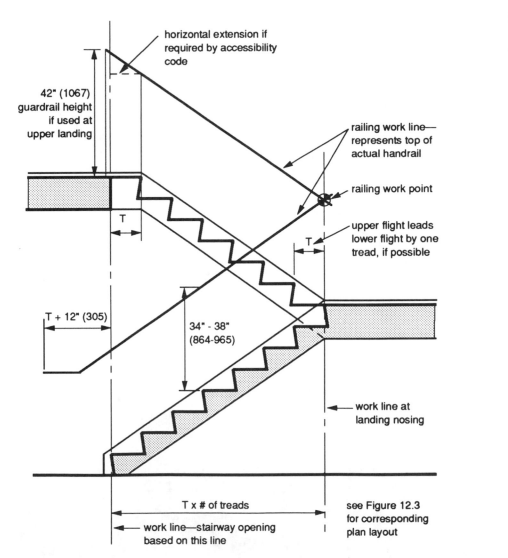

Figure 12.8
Return stair vertical layout

horizontal extension if required by accessibility code

42" (1067) guardrail height if used at upper landing

railing work line— represents top of actual handrail

railing work point

T

upper flight leads lower flight by one tread, if possible

T

T + 12" (305)

34" - 38" (864-965)

work line at landing nosing

T x # of treads

work line—stairway opening based on this line

see Figure 12.3 for corresponding plan layout

Figure 12.9
Stair layout at
lower floor

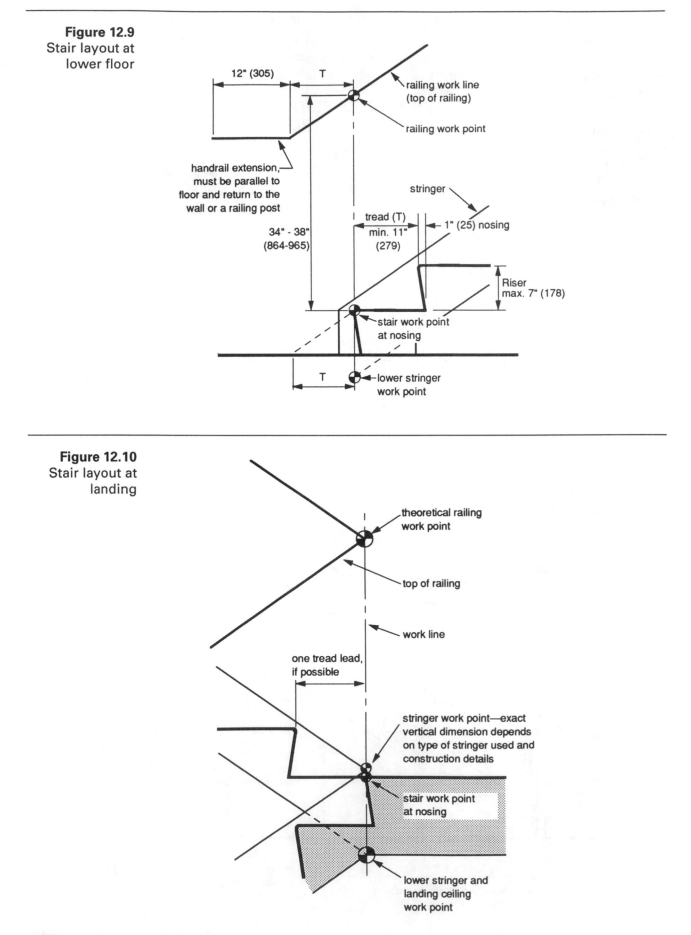

12" (305)   T

railing work line
(top of railing)

railing work point

handrail extension,
must be parallel to
floor and return to the
wall or a railing post

stringer

tread (T)
min. 11"
(279)

1" (25) nosing

34" - 38"
(864-965)

Riser
max. 7" (178)

stair work point
at nosing

T

lower stringer
work point

Figure 12.10
Stair layout at
landing

theoretical railing
work point

top of railing

work line

one tread lead,
if possible

stringer work point—exact
vertical dimension depends
on type of stringer used and
construction details

stair work point
at nosing

lower stringer and
landing ceiling
work point

risers of the stair. Open staircases with custom detailing, winding stairs, and spiral stairs are usually built in a mill shop and assembled on the site.

Figure 12.12 illustrates a typical site-built stairway and the common construction components. An opening in the floor is framed with double joists. Wood carriages are cut out of 2 × 12 in. members to form the supports for the treads and risers. For narrow stairs there are usually three carriages, one on each side and one in the center of the stair. If carpeting is used, the treads and risers are finished with plywood or particleboard. If exposed hardwood is used, either the treads can be finished with prebuilt treads with rounded nosings or strip flooring can be applied over an underlayment of particleboard. Open stairs can have any type of railing and baluster configuration as long as minimum code requirements are satisfied.

Steel and metal stairs [05510]

Steel stairs are prefabricated assemblies made to fit the dimensions required by the opening in which they are placed. As shown in Figure 12.13, they are constructed of preformed steel risers and treads welded to a supporting framework of steel channels and

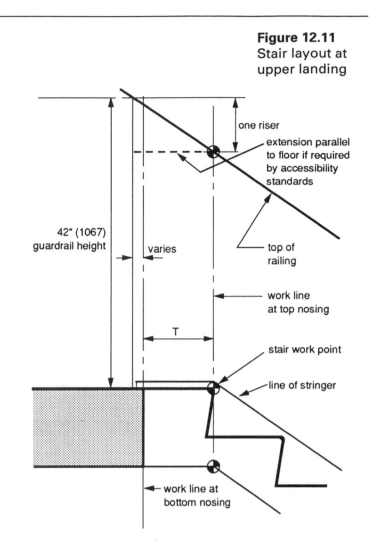

Figure 12.11
Stair layout at upper landing

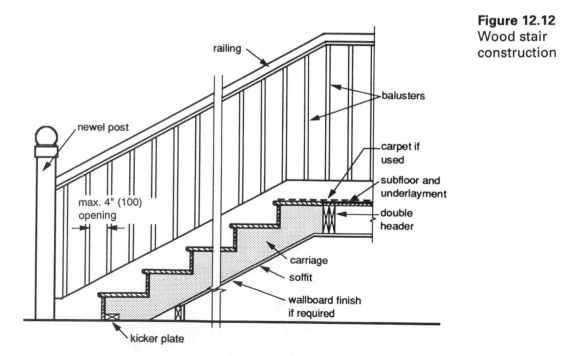

Figure 12.12
Wood stair construction

angles. For utility stairs, the stringers are normally steel channels with the flange of the channel on each side pointing away from the stairs. Landings are constructed of steel plate supported on channels and stiffening angles. The treads and landings are filled with 1½ to 2 in. (38 to 50 mm) of concrete. Any finish material used is applied over this supporting framework. If the underside of the stair needs to be finished, metal studs may be attached to the steel framework and covered with gypsum wallboard or other material. Balusters and railings of utility stairs are also steel welded to each other and to the stringers or attached to the sides of the stairway opening. See Figures 12.14(a) and 12.14(b).

More decorative steel or ornamental metal stairs are fabricated using similar techniques. The railing is made from ornamental metal or wood and the railing support can be metal, tempered glass, or other type of custom-designed assembly. When tempered glass railing supports are specified, a detail similar to Figure 12.19 is used.

Tread design

The important parts of treads include their depth, material, and nosing design. The depth of treads must be sufficient to provide safe footing for both ascending and descending, as discussed in a previous section. The material should be a nonslip surface, but not so rough that feet may be caught on the nosing upon descending. Any nonslip material designed into the nosing should be level with the rest of the tread.

Traditionally, a coefficient of friction of 0.5 or greater has been a widely accepted standard for slip resistance. This number is developed in accordance with ASTM D 2047, *Standard Test Method for Static Coefficient of Friction of Polish-coated Floor Surfaces as Measured by the James Machine.*

Figure 12.13
Steel stair construction

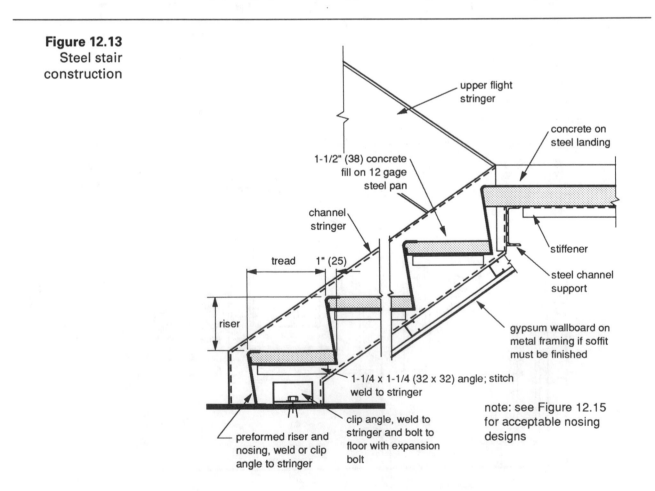

However, this test method is not applicable for wet surfaces and does not take into account other factors such as the type of shoe material, the type of contaminate on the stair, and the level of the surface. For wet surfaces two other ASTM test methods can be used: ASTM F 1679, *Standard Test Method for Using a Variable Incidence Tribometer*, and ASTM F 1677, *Standard Test Method for Using a Portable Inclinable Articulated Strut Slip Tester*. In some cases, a coefficient of 0.6 is a better minimum figure to use on stairways.

Safe and accessible design requires that nosings not be abrupt and have a maximum rounded edge of ½ in. (13 mm). Figures 12.15(a)–12.15(c) show three possible nosing designs. Open risers should not be used.

Tread and riser finishes may include carpet, hardwood flooring, vinyl tile, concrete,

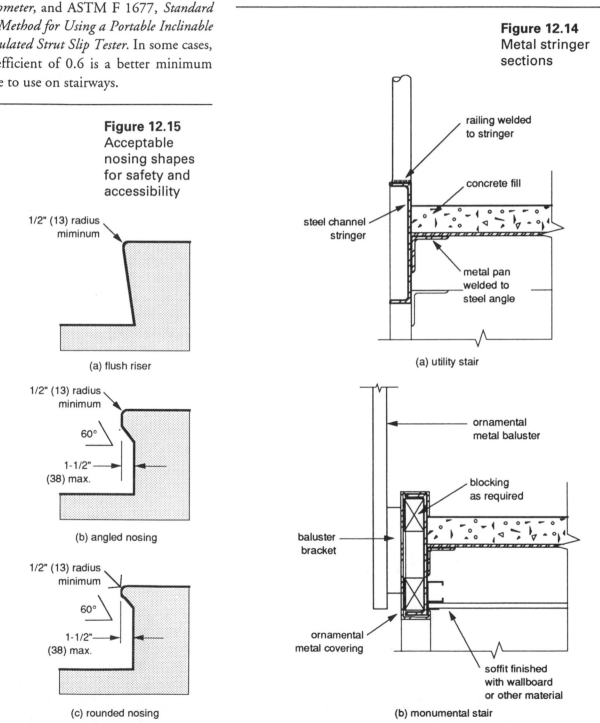

Figure 12.15
Acceptable nosing shapes for safety and accessibility

1/2" (13) radius miminum

(a) flush riser

1/2" (13) radius minimum

60°

1-1/2" (38) max.

(b) angled nosing

1/2" (13) radius minimum

60°

1-1/2" (38) max.

(c) rounded nosing

Figure 12.14
Metal stringer sections

railing welded to stringer

concrete fill

steel channel stringer

metal pan welded to steel angle

(a) utility stair

ornamental metal baluster

blocking as required

baluster bracket

ornamental metal covering

soffit finished with wallboard or other material

(b) monumental stair

ceramic tile, terrazzo, glass, special glass block pavers, or exposed steel plate. Ceramic tile and terrazzo stair finishes are illustrated in Figures 12.16(a) and 12.16(b).

Handrail design

Handrails are provided in stairways for many purposes: to help a user prevent loss of balance; to maintain stability in case of a fall; to guide with visual or balance problems; and in some cases to help a user pull himself up when climbing a stair.

Because handrails help reduce the number of accidents and their severity, they are important design elements. Handrails should be designed so that people can both grip them with maximum effect and hold them by friction when pulling up or descending.

Figure 12.16
Ceramic tile and
terrazzo stairs

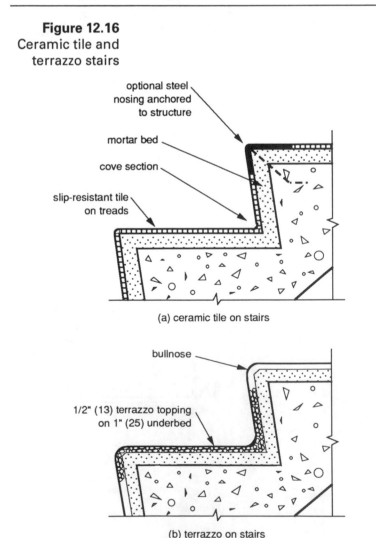

(a) ceramic tile on stairs

(b) terrazzo on stairs

Studies have shown that a circular shape is best for gripping and a 1½-in. (38 mm) diameter is the best size. For children, an additional handrail should be about 1⅛ in. to 1¼ in. (29 to 32 mm) in diameter and mounted 22 in. to 24 in. (560 to 600 mm) above the nosing line.

Building and accessibility codes require standard handrails to be mounted from 34 in. to 38 in. (865 to 965 mm) above the nosings. Some research studies have shown that the higher end of the range is best for safety, especially when descending. In open stairs, the Uniform Building Code and other codes allow the handrail mounting height to also serve as a guardrail. However, even if codes allow this, for safety reasons a separate guardrail or low wall in addition to the handrail should be provided at 42 in. (1067 mm) above the height of the nosing.

By code there must be a space of at least 1½ in. (38 mm) between the wall and the handrail. Some studies have suggested that this should be increased to anywhere from 1.6 in. (41 mm) to 2¼ in. (57 mm) to over 3½ in. (89 mm) to allow sufficient space for people to grip the handrail in case of a slip. However, some codes do not allow a space larger than 1½ in. (38 mm), and others limit the total maximum projection of the handrail into the required stairway width.

Combining all the code requirements and most current research, the best compromise for a handrail may be a 1½-in. (38 mm) round handrail with a 2-in. (51 mm) space between the wall and the rail. This makes the total projection 3½ in. (89 mm), which is the allowable encroachment into the required exit stairway width. For monumental stairs and stairs that are not a minimum width, the space between the handrail and the wall should be increased, if not specifically prohibited by the local building code. The handrail should be mounted on the higher side of the allowable height range, from 36 in. to 38 in. (914 to 965 mm).

The Uniform Building Code requires handrails to be sized from 1½ in. to 2 in. (38 to 51 mm) and have a shape that is easily gripped. There must be at least 1½ in. between the inside of the handrail and the adjacent surface. Four acceptable designs are shown in Figure 12.17. Handrails must be located from 34 in. to 38 in. above the nosing of the stairway. (See Figure 12.6.) However, the Americans with Disabilities Act (ADA) requires that handrails be sized between 1¼ in. and 1½ in. (32 to 38 mm). This effectively leaves 1½ in. as the only acceptable dimension.

Building code requirements for handrails

Because codes require that handrails be securely anchored, the adjacent partitions or rails should be detailed accordingly. For example, the UBC requires that guardrails be capable of withstanding a load of 200 lb (90 kg) applied in any direction at any point along the handrail. Other model codes may have different requirements. Wood stud partitions are usually sufficient to hold handrail brackets if they are attached directly to the studs. For metal stud partitions, solid wood blocking must be provided.

Note: most building codes require handrails to have a gripping surface between 1-1/2" and 2" in diameter while accessibility guidelines require a dimension from 1-1/4" to 1-1/2" in diameter; therefore, 1-1/2" (38 mm) is the best dimension to use to satisfy both regulations.

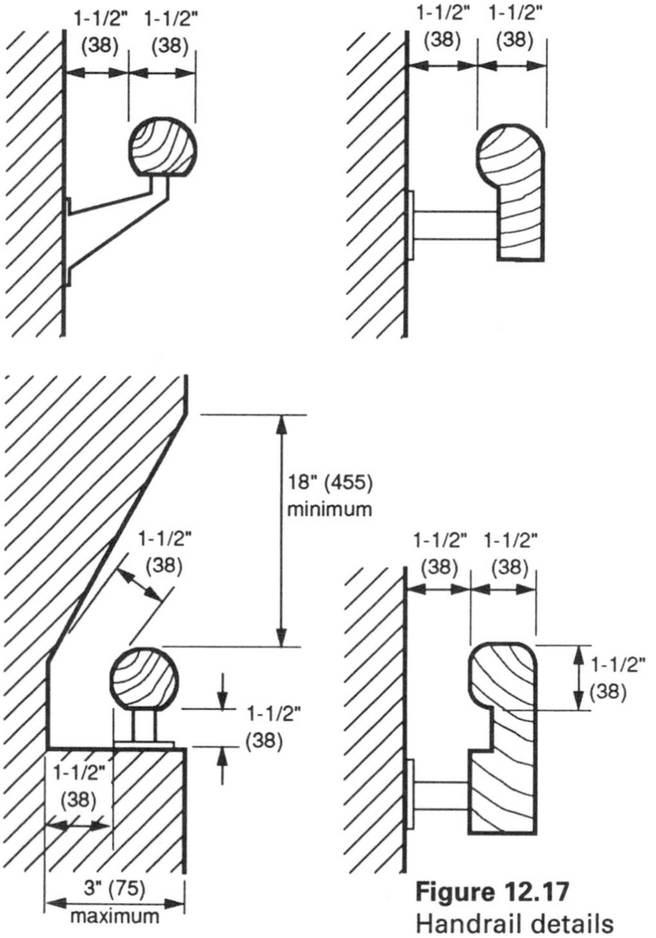

Figure 12.17
Handrail details

Building code requirements for guardrails

Guardrails are required around unenclosed openings, landings, ramps, and balconies that are more than 30 in. (760 mm) above the floor below. Guardrails must be no lower than 42 in. (1067 mm) above the adjacent finished walking surface. A 36 in. (914 mm) height is allowed for guardrails in Group R-3 occupancies and interior guardrails in guest rooms of Group R-1 occupancies.

Open guardrails must have intermediate rails or an ornamental pattern such that a sphere 4 in. (100 mm) in diameter cannot pass through.

The Uniform Building Code requires that guardrails be capable of withstanding a load of 50 lb/linear foot (75 kg/m) applied horizontally at right angles to the top rail.

The materials for handrails should provide a surface with enough coefficient of friction to allow gripping parallel to the handrail, while not being so rough that it would discourage use or abrade skin.

For wide stairs the UBC and the Standard Building Code allow one handrail for stairs less than 44 in. (1118 mm) and two handrails for stairs from 44 in. to 88 in. (1118 to 2235 mm). Research suggests that the maximum practical limit for one handrail is closer to 35 in. (890 mm), and for two handrails the maximum stair width should be only 47 in. (1200 mm). Beyond this distance, intermediate handrails should be provided to allow people to be close enough to a handrail to use it or grab it if necessary.

The National Building Code and the International Building Code (to be published in the year 2000 and which will ultimately replace the current three model codes) require that intermediate handrails be within

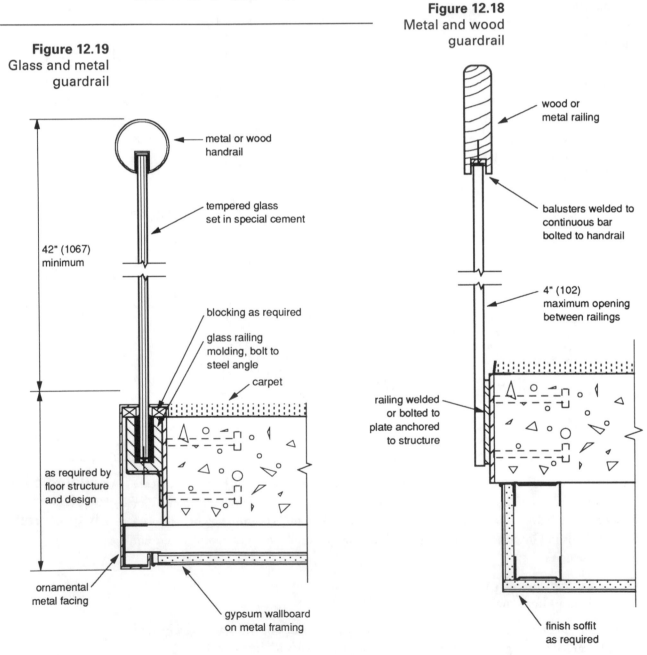

Figure 12.19
Glass and metal guardrail

metal or wood handrail

tempered glass set in special cement

42" (1067) minimum

blocking as required

glass railing molding, bolt to steel angle

carpet

as required by floor structure and design

ornamental metal facing

gypsum wallboard on metal framing

Figure 12.18
Metal and wood guardrail

wood or metal railing

balusters welded to continuous bar bolted to handrail

4" (102) maximum opening between railings

railing welded or bolted to plate anchored to structure

finish soffit as required

30 in. (762 mm) of all portions of the required egress width of a stairway.

Guardrail design
[05520, 06450, 08810]

Guardrails protect people from falling into a floor opening. As such, they must be high enough to resist the center of gravity of the majority of people. This dimension is about 42 in. (1067 mm) and is the height required by building codes. Although most codes do not require guardrails if the fall to the adjacent lower floor level is below a certain distance (30 in. in the case of the UBC), even low areas should have guardrails for safety. Even a short fall can be dangerous.

In addition to a minimum height, the top portion of a handrail should be designed to discourage people from sitting on it if the situation suggests. For example, high school students would be more likely to sit on a handrail than elderly people in a nursing home.

When the space below the guardrail is open, it must be filled in some way to prevent small children from climbing through. Most codes now require a maximum spacing so a sphere 4 in. (102 mm) in diameter cannot pass through. If there is a danger of objects falling off the floor, a toe board should also be provided. Bottom rails near the floor should be avoided if it is likely that people will climb on the rail, thus lowering the effective height of the guardrail.

Guardrails can be designed in a variety of ways, depending on the structure of the opening, the materials used, and the design style desired. Figure 12.18 shows a typical guardrail with steel balusters and a wood railing. Figure 12.19 illustrates a common method for supporting an ornamental metal rail with a tempered glass panel.

SIGNAGE SYSTEMS

Signage system design includes planning the types of signs required, determining their location, designing and detailing custom signs, and specifying standard manufactured signs. For most commercial projects, a coherent and easily understood signage system is critical for identification, direction, and exiting. This is especially true for large, public buildings where users are not familiar with the layout.

A discussion of the theory and implementation of wayfinding and signage system design is beyond the scope of this book. Rather, this chapter includes general information on signage system design that can affect the work of the interior designer or that must be coordinated with the interior construction.

There are many manufacturers that make complete lines of signage, from exterior signs to building directories to individual room plaques. In many instances, purchasing signs directly from a catalog is sufficient. A building owner or individual tenant may even assume the responsibility of providing signs themselves without any assistance from a designer. However, signage should be coordinated with the design and detailing of the space in which it is used, and this is often the

responsibility of the interior designer. When custom signs are required or special construction is required for built-in signs provided by someone else, the designer must plan and develop appropriate details.

PLANNING SIGNAGE

The design of a signage system actually begins with space planning and interior design. Space planning, circulation path layout, entry and exit locations, and visual clues and reference points are all critical to a coherent wayfinding and signage system.

A plan with a complicated layout of rooms, corridors, and spaces will require a more extensive system of signage to help people find their way and make sense of a confusing organization of space. In the worst case, no amount of signage may be able to completely overcome a poorly planned layout.

The three-dimensional form of space and its colors, finishes, and furnishings can also provide reference points and visual clues to help people orient themselves and identify where they want to go.

The next step after designing a clearly organized space plan is to determine the types of signs required and their locations. There are

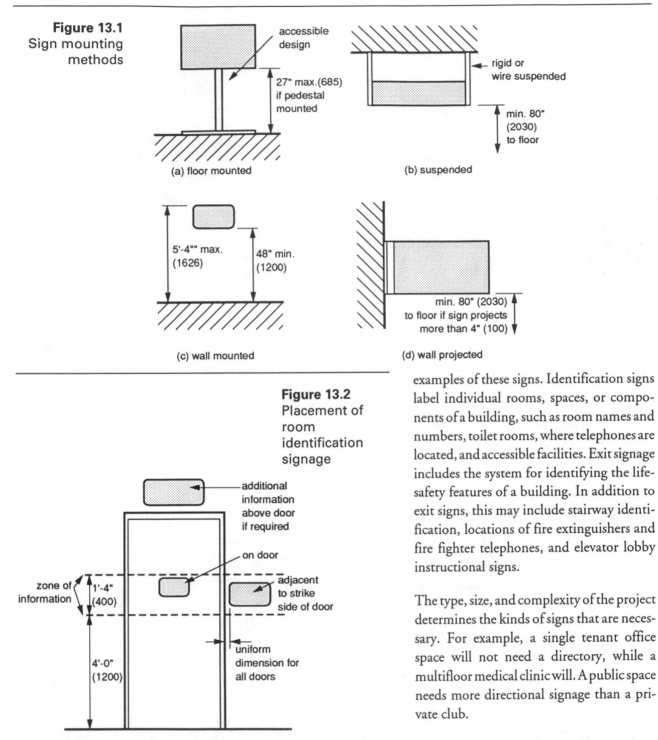

Figure 13.1
Sign mounting methods

accessible design

27" max.(685)
if pedestal
mounted

(a) floor mounted

rigid or
wire suspended

min. 80"
(2030)
to floor

(b) suspended

5'-4"" max.
(1626)

48" min.
(1200)

(c) wall mounted

min. 80" (2030)
to floor if sign projects
more than 4" (100)

(d) wall projected

Figure 13.2
Placement of room identification signage

additional
information
above door
if required

on door

zone of
information

1'-4"
(400)

adjacent
to strike
side of door

uniform
dimension for
all doors

4'-0"
(1200)

examples of these signs. Identification signs label individual rooms, spaces, or components of a building, such as room names and numbers, toilet rooms, where telephones are located, and accessible facilities. Exit signage includes the system for identifying the life-safety features of a building. In addition to exit signs, this may include stairway identification, locations of fire extinguishers and fire fighter telephones, and elevator lobby instructional signs.

The type, size, and complexity of the project determines the kinds of signs that are necessary. For example, a single tenant office space will not need a directory, while a multifloor medical clinic will. A public space needs more directional signage than a private club.

four basic categories of interior signs: informational, directional, identification, and exit. Informational signs provide the building user with data about the building or space. These include building directories, kiosks, location maps, and how-to-use signs. Directional signs help people find their way around the building or space. Arrows, directional labels, and even stripes on the floor are

Informational signs should be located where people are most likely to need the information the signs contain. Building directories, for example, should be near the entrances to the building or the elevators. Directional signs should be located where people need to make decisions about which way to go. Identification signs should be on or directly adjacent to the room, space, or element they identify and placed in a consistent relationship with that room, space, or element. For instance, all room names and numbers may be placed adjacent to the strike side of door jambs. If this is the case, then some signs should not be placed on the door itself.

Next, a consistent method and position of mounting signs should be established. Signs can be mounted in a number of ways, as shown in Figures 13.1(a)–13.1(d). In each case, once a placement has been established, the position, dimensions, and relationship to other building elements should be maintained so that people know where they can expect to find information.

For example, Figure 13.2 shows suggested locations for the placement of room identification signs. In most cases it is preferable to place these types of signs within a horizontal band between 4 ft and 4 ft 4 in. (1200 to 1300 mm) above the floor. This is about eye level for most people, and where it is still easily accessible for children and persons in wheelchairs. Additional identification or information can be placed above the door if required.

Overhead signs are best located either in the center of the circulation path or directly over the room or object they identify. The lowest edge must be at least 80 in. (2030 mm)

Building code requirements for signage

Most building code requirements referring to signage relate to exiting. The Uniform Building Code specifies regulations for exit signs, stairway identification, and door identification, as well as one reference to accessibility signage.

Exit signs must be located at stair enclosure doors, and other required exits. They must also be placed at the required exits from a room or area when two or more exits are required. In corridors, they must be located where necessary to clearly indicate the direction of egress. The exact number and location of exit signs often depend on the local building department's policy and what the field inspectors require. Usually, signs should be located so that people can always see two exit signs indicating two methods of egress. This means that exit signs may need to be placed at intersections and turns in corridors, as well as on exit doors.

Exit signs are required to be illuminated and connected to a separate power supply. The lettering must be in high contrast with the background with block letters 6 in. (150 mm) high with a stroke width of not less than ¾ in. (19 mm).

Corridors serving guest rooms in hotels in Group R-1 occupancies must also have floor-level exit signs with the bottom of the sign not less than 6 in. or more than 8 in. (150 to 200 mm) above the floor. When identifying an exit door, the exit signs must be on the door or within 4 in. (100 mm) of the latch door jamb.

When egress control devices are used on exit doors (those that sound an alarm and do not unlatch for a given time delay) there must be an accompanying sign that reads: KEEP PUSHING. THIS DOOR WILL OPEN IN __ SECONDS. ALARM WILL SOUND.

Room capacity postings are required in classrooms, assembly rooms and similar areas with an occupant load of 50 or more where fixed seats are not installed. The sign must be located near the main exit from the room, be legible, and indicate the number of occupants permitted for the room's use.

Other exit signage requirements relate to exit doors and stairway identification.

The UBC also requires that all accessible toilet rooms and bathing facilities be identified by the international symbol of accessibility.

above the floor. Projected signs and free-standing signs must also conform to accessibility guidelines, as described in Chapter 18.

SIGNAGE MATERIALS [10440]

Almost any material can be used for interior signage because it does not have to resist temperature extremes, weathering, moisture, snow loading, and other abuse that exterior signs are subject to. However, some materials are used more frequently because of their availability, ease of fabrication, and coordination with existing premanufactured sign systems. This section briefly outlines some of the more common materials used.

Plastics

Plastic is one of the most common materials for interior signage. It is durable, easy to fabricate, relatively inexpensive, can be formed in a variety of ways, and can be colored to produce an almost unlimited variety of sign types. Plastics are used by nearly every sign manufacturer to produce their lines of standard sign systems.

Several types of plastics are available for manufacturing signs; however, only a few are commonly used. These include acrylic, polycarbonate, butyrate, fiber-reinforced polyester, and polyvinylchloride.

Acrylic is the most commonly used type of plastic for signage. It is available clear or colored, in opaque or semi-opaque forms. Acrylic is easily formable and can be mounted in a number of ways. It can be scratched easily and will crack and shatter if struck hard enough. One type, called DR, has a higher impact strength than regular acrylic. Acrylics are available in a variety of thicknesses depending on the size of the sign and rigidity required. Thicknesses of 1/16, 1/8, 3/16, and 1/4 in. (1.6, 3, 5, and 6 mm) are common.

Polycarbonate has a very high impact resistance (in thicker, laminated constructions it is used for bullet-resistant glazing) and can be used where vandalism is a problem. Films are available from 0.005 in. to 0.025 in.

thick and sheets are available in thicknesses from 0.030 in. to 0.500 in. (0.127 to 0.635 mm and 0.762 to 13 mm). Clear polycarbonate is available, as is a limited range of colors.

Butyrate is used for vacuum-formed signs and letters because of its easy formability. It has a high impact resistance; however, it is only available in a limited range of transparent and translucent colors.

Fiber-reinforced polyester is also known as fiberglass. It has high impact strength but shows some graininess because of the glass fibers in the material. It is a durable material and has good light-diffusing properties.

Polyvinylchloride (PVC) is seldom used for interior signage. Exceptions are where extreme moisture resistance is required and where exposure to sunlight is not present.

Metals

While any type of metal can be used for signage, the most common materials are aluminum, stainless steel, brass, and bronze. Aluminum is lightweight, strong, durable, easily cut, and does not rust. It can be used in thin sheet form as a backing for applied lettering, or letters can be cut out of the sheet, leaving a negative image that can show other materials laminated beneath the aluminum. Cut-out aluminum sheet is also used for internally illuminated signs when backed with light-diffusing plastic. Individual letters can also be cut from thicker sheet stock and applied individually on other backing materials. Die stamping, embossing, and engraving can also be done on aluminum. Aluminum is available in natural mill finishes, anodized colors, baked enamel colors, or adhesive films.

Stainless steel can be fabricated in forms similar to aluminum. It can be used in thin sheet form as a backing for applied lettering, or letters can be cut out of the sheet. Stainless steel is also used for individually cut letters from thicker sheet stock, or as enclosures for large signs. In addition, die stamping, embossing, and engraving can be used with stainless steel.

Brass and bronze are most commonly used for either individual cut letters or cast plaques. Brass and bronze for signs are available in many of the alloys discussed in Chapter 7.

Other materials

Some interior signs are made from adhesive film, photographic film, and direct painting. Other less used materials include wood, neon, and electronic signs, which are generally employed in special applications rather than for standard identification and directional signage.

Adhesive films

Adhesive films are thin plastic or vinyl letters and symbols with an adhesive backing. Vinyl letters are die cut on a removable backing sheet. They are applied by removing the backing and placing the letters on a smooth, clean surface. Removable and permanent adhesives are available. Transfer lettering is a less expensive type in which the letters are printed on the back of a carrier sheet and then transferred to a surface by burnishing. These letters are very susceptible to damage and must be protected with some type of transparent covering.

Photographic films

Photographic films are produced by exposing art work to light sensitive photographic films and producing either a negative or positive image of the original art work. The images may be printed on film or paper. Because of the photographic process, extremely accurate enlargements or reductions can be made of the original art. Negative film is often used for internally illuminated signs by sandwiching the negative film image between a clear outer covering of glass or plastic and an inner layer of light-diffusing plastic. See Figure 13.3(a). Positive images printed on paper must be mounted on some other material, such as plastic, hardboard, or

medium density overlay plywood to keep them flat. See Figure 13.3(b). For permanent signs, a protective outer covering should be added.

Electronic signage

Electronic signs are being used more frequently for informational signage. Touch-screen video display units, for example, are used for building directories. These display units allow people to proceed through a menu-driven sequence of displays to find what they need. The displays can be reprogrammed as information changes.

Figure 13.3
Photographic film signs

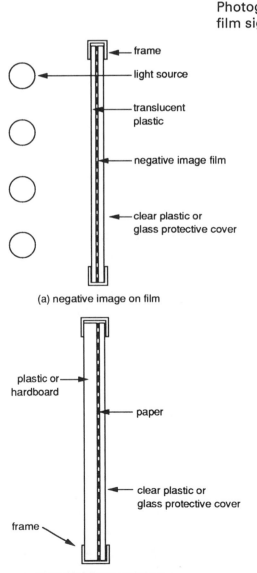

(a) negative image on film

— frame
— light source
— translucent plastic
— negative image film
— clear plastic or glass protective cover

plastic or hardboard —
— paper
— clear plastic or glass protective cover
frame —

(b) positive image on paper

SIGN CONSTRUCTION [10440]

Plastic signs

Plastic signs are available in a variety of forms from simple, engraved plaques adhesively applied to walls, to large, three-dimensional custom fabrications. Most plastic signs for interior use are purchased as part of a manufacturer's standard product line with specific messages imprinted, engraved, or otherwise lettered as required by the job. Signs that need to be changed frequently are printed on inserts that are slipped into grooves on a carrier plaque or applied with a magnetic backing.

Signs are mounted to walls in a variety of ways, depending on the size, weight, and partition material. Several of the most common methods are shown in Figures 13.4(a)–13.4(f).

Small, lightweight signs are mounted with double-face tape, adhesive, or Velcro fasteners. Heavier signs must be mechanically fastened to the partition. The fasteners can be exposed, as shown in Figure 13.4(d), or concealed. For signs thicker than 3⁄16 in. (5 mm), rods are fastened to the wall and fit within predrilled holes in the back of the sign. For very large or heavy signs, separate hanger angles may have to be bolted to the partition and the sign hung from them. If necessary, metal stud partitions should have wood blocking installed so that a rigid attachment of the angles can be made.

Overhead signs are fastened to the ceiling with bolts or screws. Lightweight signs may be bolted through the ceiling tile or screwed directly to the ceiling grid. Heavy, overhead signs attached to a suspended acoustical

---

ADA signage requirements

The Americans with Disabilities Act (ADA) requires that certain accessible rooms and features be clearly identified with the symbol for accessibility and that identification, directional, and informational signs meet certain specifications.

Permanent rooms and spaces must be identified with signs having lettering from 5⁄8 in. to 2 in. (16 to 50 mm) high raised 1⁄32 in. (0.8 mm) above the surface of the sign. Lettering must be all upper case, in sans serif or simple serif type, accompanied with Grade 2 Braille. If pictograms are used, they must be at least 6 in. (152 mm) high and must be accompanied with the equivalent verbal description placed directly below. Signs must be eggshell matte or other nonglare finish, with characters contrasting with their background. Permanent identification signs must be mounted on the wall adjacent to the latch side of the door such that a person can approach to within 3 in. (76 mm) of the signage without encountering protruding objects or standing within the door swing. Mounting height to the center line of the sign must be 60 in. (1525 mm).

Directional and informational signs must have lettering at least 3 in. (75 mm) high with a width-to-height ratio between 3:5 and 1:1. The stroke width-to-height ratio must be between 1:5 and 1:10. Contrast and finish requirements are the same as for permanent room identification.

The international symbol for accessibility is required on parking spaces, passenger loading zones, accessible entrances, and toilet and bathing facilities when not all are accessible. Building directories and temporary signs do not have to comply with the requirements. In addition, the international telecommunications devices for the deaf (TDD) symbol is required to identify text telephones, and volume control telephones must have this symbol. In assembly areas, permanently installed assistive listening systems must have the international symbol of access for hearing loss.

Refer to Chapter 18 for more information and diagrams.

ceiling may require a backing plate resting on the ceiling grid. Very heavy signs should be suspended separately from the structure above with threaded rods or other adequate support.

When detailing custom signs with plastic components, there must be adequate space for the plastic to expand and contract. Although interior temperature extremes are not great, large plastic panels need room to move.

Metal signs

Custom metal signs can be fabricated in an unlimited number of ways. Lightweight metal signs are mounted using the same methods shown in Figures 13.4(a)–13.4(f). For very large metal signs or plastic signs with a structural metal framework, such as wall-suspended signs, additional steel support may be required. Free-standing floor-mounted signs may need to be fastened to steel plates bolted into the structural floor.

For most interior signage, metal signs usually consist of individual letters or symbols. If the letters are small and lightweight, they can be adhesively applied directly to the partition finish. Heavy metal letters have pins welded, brazed, or soldered to their backs. The letters are then cemented to the partition by setting the pins in predrilled holes in the finish material. See Figure 13.5. This mounting method works well for applying letters or cast bronze plaques to hard materials, such as stone or tile. However, changing the sign means replacing the finish as well.

Illuminated signs

Illuminated signs are used when ambient lighting is insufficient to provide clear visibility of a sign or when special emphasis is required. Signs can be lit two ways: internally or externally. Internally illuminated signs either profile the letter forms with a bright background or the letter forms themselves are bright against a dark background. In most cases, the letter forms and other symbols are cut out of other material, such as metal or opaque plastic, and light shines through a translucent plastic face covering the cut-out areas. Fluorescent lamps are typically used because they provide even illumination and are not as hot as other sources.

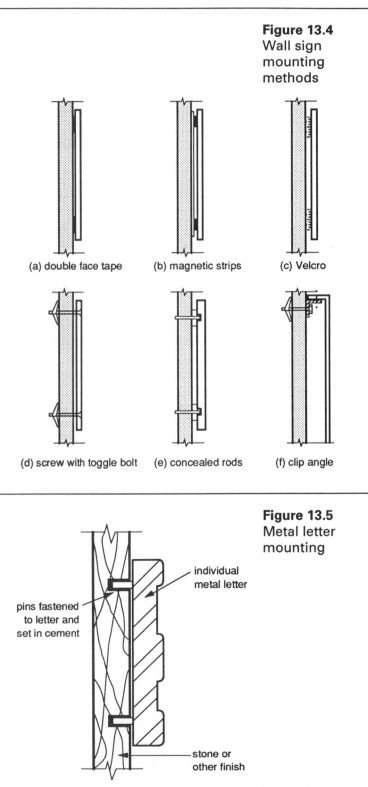

Figure 13.4
Wall sign mounting methods

(a) double face tape

(b) magnetic strips

(c) Velcro

(d) screw with toggle bolt

(e) concealed rods

(f) clip angle

Figure 13.5
Metal letter mounting

pins fastened to letter and set in cement

individual metal letter

stone or other finish

In order to achieve even illumination, the lamps must be placed a sufficient distance behind the sign face. See Figure 13.6. This distance should be a minimum of 4 in. (100 mm), and more if possible. The spacing between lamps should ideally be no more than the distance from the lamps to the sign face.

Illuminated signs must be ventilated and detailed, and must be mounted so that lamps can be replaced and other routine maintenance can be performed. The interior designer must coordinate the location of the sign with the electrical engineer so that adequate power is available at the point where required by the sign manufacturer.

Externally illuminated signs use ambient light, dedicated spotlights, or other light sources to provide highlighting. These signs are easier to fabricate and maintain than internally illuminated signs. In addition, the colors of signs illuminated from the exterior are usually truer than those of internally illuminated signs. However, if more than normal ambient light is required, a special fixture needs to be dedicated for the sign and a clear line of sight maintained for uniform illumination. External lighting must be carefully designed to prevent glare, which can make it difficult, or even impossible, to read the sign.

SIGN TYPES

Informational signs [10410]

The most common types of interior informational signs are building directories and floor directories. Building directories provide the names and locations of companies within a building and sometimes the names of people within each company. Floor directories provide the names and locations of office or spaces on a specific floor or within a particular area on the floor.

Building or floor directories may be mounted flat on a wall, cantilevered from a wall, freestanding, or recessed into a wall. See Figures 13.7(a)–13.7(d). In any case, adequate space must be provided in front of the sign so that people can refer to it without blocking other circulation or interfering with the required exit width. There must also be sufficient space for changing names, replacing lights, cleaning, and other maintenance.

Internally illuminated directories or those that use cathode ray tubes, such as touch-screen directories, need power, and ventilation. They also must be mounted at a comfortable height.

Directional signs [10440]

Because directional signs are so common to commercial interiors, the design should be planned to accommodate the variety of signs that are usually required. Directional signs are typically required at the entrance to a building or use area, at elevator lobbies and stairs, and at decision points in the circulation system. Several may be required at each point. Figures 13.8(a)–13.8(c) show the ideal locations for wall-mounted directional signage in some common plan configurations. Overhead signs can be used in some instances, but they still have to provide directions when viewed from any position and must have adequate clearance below.

Figure 13.6
Guidelines for
internally
illuminated signs

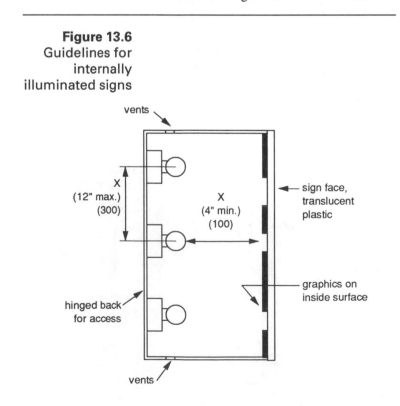

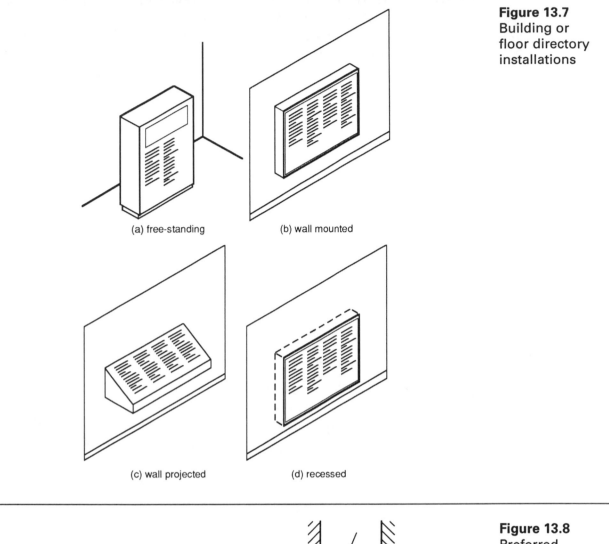

Figure 13.7
Building or
floor directory
installations

(a) free-standing

(b) wall mounted

(c) wall projected

(d) recessed

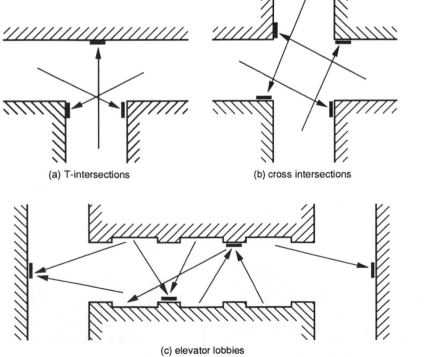

Figure 13.8
Preferred
locations of
corridor signs

(a) T-intersections

(b) cross intersections

(c) elevator lobbies

Identification signs [10440]

Identification signs must be placed on or near the room or object they identify. Room signs should be placed in a consistent location, as shown previously in Figure 13.2. Signs identifying open areas or counters may need to be suspended or floor mounted when there is no partition for direct attachment. Identification signage is usually a combination of permanent signs, such as those identifying rest rooms, and temporary signs, such as those giving the name of an office occupant. As with directional signage, identification signage may require varied amounts of information on different signs. This need is usually accommodated by using a modular system of sign sizes mounted in a uniform position, as shown in Figure 13.9, so that all signs are coordinated in their size, shape, and placement.

Exit signs [10440, 16535]

The requirements for exit signs are determined by the applicable building code; however, the designer does have some choice of mounting styles and finishes. For example, an exit sign can be ceiling mounted or wall mounted, as long as its location satisfies the building code and provides sufficient headroom clearance. Manufacturer's catalogs show specific types and styles that are available. Figures 13.10(a)–13.10(d) illustrate some of the typical types and installation methods.

Coordination with other design and construction features

Although a signage system may be developed by a signage company or graphic designer, the interior designer must coordinate design and construction features with the signage needs. These include the following:

• During initial space planning, circulation paths and room layout should be kept as direct as possible to minimize the reliance on directional signs.

• Space planning and circulation paths should include distinct identifying landmarks so that people can get their bearings by using the landmarks in addition to referring to signage.

• Partitions must be detailed sufficiently thick when necessary to accommodate recessed directories or other large, recessed signs.

• Wood blocking must be provided in metal stud partitions to facilitate the mounting of large or heavy signs. Extra bracing above suspended ceilings may also be required for suspended signs.

Figure 13.9
Modular sign sizes

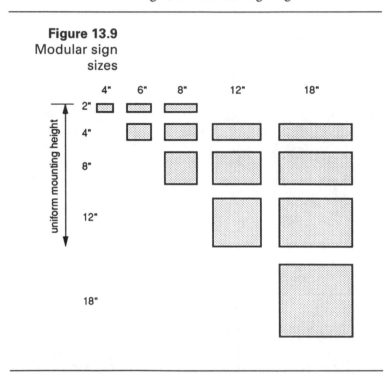

Figure 13.10
Exit signs

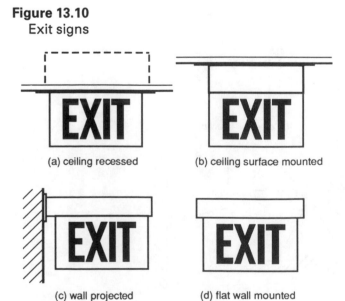

(a) ceiling recessed   (b) ceiling surface mounted

(c) wall projected   (d) flat wall mounted

• No other fixtures, finishes, or furnishings (such as plants, furniture, or HVAC equipment) should be planned that might interfere with sign visibility.

• Extra space in front of a sign should be provided if it includes a tactile map for the blind.

• Light switches, thermostats, and other wall-mounted devices and equipment should be planned so that they do not interfere with standard locations for signage.

• Partition finishes should be specified and detailed in such a way that it is not impossible to mount signs. For example, fabric wallcovering may prevent adhesion of double stick tape.

• Adequate space, power, and telecommunication lines must be provided for TDDs (telecommunications devices for the deaf) if they are used.

• The power supply for illuminated and electronic signs must be adequate for the requirements of the specified sign.

• Lighting must be controlled to avoid glare, while still providing enough light for visibility, including that required for the elderly and visually impaired. In addition, ambient light should not conflict with illuminated signs.

14

SECURITY SYSTEMS

Security is required for any type of interior design project. It may be as simple as a front door lock for a residence or as complex and sophisticated as a combination of physical barriers and an electronic surveillance, detection, and control system for a bank. Clients are demanding more security for their projects; therefore, interior designers must be aware of the types of systems and equipment that are available along with the kinds of coordination and support they, as designers, must provide.

Common security problems include residential and commercial burglary, employee pilferage, vandalism, sabotage or theft of company records and property, confinement of prisoners, protection of personnel, safety and confinement in psychiatric wards, abduction, and, in extreme instances, terrorism. Full security analysis, design of systems, and specification of equipment is beyond the scope of this book and must be performed by a knowledgeable security consultant or specialized vendor of security equipment. This chapter briefly outlines some of the basics of security planning for projects with low-level security needs and describes the typical areas where an interior

designer must coordinate with the security specialist working on the job.

The interior designer should be a part of the team involved with security planning and specification. Depending on the complexity of the project, this team may include the building architect, a security consultant, equipment vendors, the client, the electrical engineer, and others. Lack of coordination and involvement on the part of the interior designer usually results in the security equipment appearing as though it were installed as an afterthought, without regard for the other materials and finishes. In some cases, poor coordination can result in additional construction time and costs for the client.

SPACE PLANNING FOR SECURITY

Good security begins with a clear definition of the problem. Part of the programming document must include a clear statement by the client concerning the level of security required and a list of the potential threats. For some clients, such as large corporations and banks, security requirements are usually well defined. For others, such as small retail stores and offices, the client may not have given much thought to security beyond basic locks. The designer should raise the question and help these clients define security needs and possible responses. If the security problem is complex, the designer may suggest that a security specialist be included on the project team.

Good security involves physical as well as electronic barriers. The physical layout and construction of a space can have a profound effect on fundamental security as well as on how easy or difficult it is to plan and install monitoring and access devices.

During space planning, rooms, areas, and circulation paths should be designed to take advantage of proximity, line of sight, and location. Proximity refers to the location of one space near another. Line of sight allows either human or electronic surveillance of a given area. Location refers to where secure areas are planned in relation to the building perimeter, services, and other rooms. The following guidelines should be reviewed:

• Locate spaces together that have similar security requirements. This makes it easier to enclose the area with physical barriers, such as partitions and doors and provide monitoring, along with minimizing the number of electronic devices needed to control the area. This can reduce both construction complexity and costs.

• Plan for permanently stationed personnel to be in a central location with a clear line of sight to as many secure areas as possible. These may be security guards or other staff, such as secretaries, clerks, and nurses. This makes visual surveillance easier and can reduce the number and cost of electronic monitoring devices.

• Locate personnel at entries and other control points as a backup to locks and other electronic access and monitoring control devices.

• If required, lay out spaces and circulation to provide a clear line of sight for electronic surveillance, such as cameras and photoelectric, microwave, or infrared detection.

• Locate sensitive areas, such as computer rooms and private conference rooms, away from windows and the building's perimeter.

• If service is required to secure areas, locate them near separate entrances or the service elevator so that separation from public access can be maintained and travel distance is minimized.

• Plan for security areas to be near existing secure walls. These may be a building's concrete core wall or masonry walls. This can minimize construction costs if special, high-security partitions need to be built.

In addition to these basic space planning guidelines, a separate room may be required for a security control center. The size depends on the complexity of building and may be integrated with equipment for monitoring and controlling fire detection and suppression, mechanical systems, and communications systems. For small installations, the security equipment may be installed at the guard's desk or at a central control station. Large areas near entrances may also be required for X-ray or magnetic screening devices. In these instances, the client's security consultant will provide the required dimensions for space planning.

SECURITY EQUIPMENT

In addition to physical barriers, security systems include methods for preventing entry, detecting intruders, controlling access to secure areas, and notification in the event of unauthorized entry or other emergencies. The types of hardware and electronic devices that are used depend on the nature of the threat, the level of security desired, and the amount of money that can be devoted to the system. This section outlines some of the more common devices with which designers should be familiar.

Intrusion detection [16720]

Security derived from intrusion detection devices can be classified into three types:

perimeter protection, area or room protection, and object protection.

Perimeter protection

Perimeter protection secures the entry points to a space or building. These include doors, windows, skylights, and can also include ducts, tunnels, and other service entrances. Some of the more common types of perimeter protection include the following:

• Magnetic contacts. These are used on doors and windows to either sound an alarm when the contact is broken (the door or window is opened) or send a signal to a central monitoring and control station. These can be surface mounted, recessed into the door and frame, or concealed in special hinges. The hinges may only be available in certain sizes and finishes; therefore, the other hardware used on the job must be coordinated with them.

• Glass break detectors. These sense when a window has been broken or cut either by using metallic foil or with a small vibration detector mounted on the glass.

• Window screens. These screens have fine wires embedded in them that can be used to set off an alarm when they are cut or broken.

• Photoelectric cells. These cells detect when the beam has been broken, either by a door opening or by someone passing through an opening. These can be surface mounted, but are more secure and look better if provisions are made to recess them in the partition or other construction.

Area or room protection

Area or room protection devices sense when someone is in a room or an area within the field of coverage. These devices have the advantage of warning of unauthorized entry when perimeter sensors have not been activated. Area intrusion devices include the following:

• Photoelectric beams. These beams warn of intrusion by sending a pulsed infrared beam across a space. If the beam is broken the device either sounds an alarm or sends a signal to a monitoring station. Photoelectric beams can be focused in both large and small areas. The equipment is small and usually can be recessed or concealed.

• Infrared detectors. These detectors sense sources of infrared radiation, such as the human body, compared with the normal room radiation. They are unobtrusive, but must have a clear field of view of the area they are protecting.

• Audio detectors. These detectors listen for unusual sounds in a space at levels above what is normally encountered. When that level is exceeded, an alarm is sounded. Microphones can also be used to continuously monitor all sounds in a space through a speaker at a central monitoring station.

• Pressure sensors. These sensors detect weight on a floor or other surfaces. Sensor mats can be separate fixtures laid over the existing floor finish or placed under carpet or other building materials.

• Ultrasonic detectors. These detectors emit a very high-frequency sound wave. When this is interrupted by an intruder, an alarm signal is activated. The range of ultrasonic detectors is limited to a space about 12 ft (3.7 m) high and 20 ft × 30 ft in area (6.1 × 9.1 m).

• Microwave detectors. These detectors sense interruptions in the field of microwave radiation that they emit. Their use is limited in interior construction, however, because the microwave radiation can penetrate most building materials and can be reflected by metal.

Object protection

Object protection is used to sense movement or tampering with individual objects, such as safes, art work, file cabinets, or other equipment. Capacitance proximity detectors detect when metal objects are touched. Vibration detectors sense a disturbance of the object. Infrared motion detectors determine if the space around an object is violated.

Electronic surveillance

Electronic surveillance is the interception of sound and electromagnetic signals with remote sensing devices. For example, with readily obtainable, relatively inexpensive technology it is possible to listen in on conversations from outside a building or pick up signals being emitted from a computer screen at a remote distance. For organizations that require security from this type of intrusion, special rooms are required that have electromagnetic or radio frequency shielding.

Sensitive government installations have used such shielding for some time. It is just recently that many companies are realizing they must protect themselves from corporate espionage as well as from other types of theft.

The basic principle behind electronic shielding involves building a "cage" of continuously conductive material that catches signals and conducts them to the ground. The type of cage depends on the amount of protection required and the bandwidth that must be shielded. The rating of protection is measured in decibels (dB) of attenuation. Many government and military facilities are designed for 100-dB attenuation across a broad bandwidth of signals. Theoretically, this level provides 100 percent protection. However, this level of protection requires heavy steel plate and expensive special construction. For most corporate needs, an attenuation of 60 dB stops more than 99.9 percent of the electronic signals coming from office computers and other sources.

To achieve acceptable levels of protection for most corporate uses, there are several products available. Copper foils can be used, but these are difficult to install and require soldered connections. There is also non-woven fabric that is covered with an electronically conductive metallic coating. As with copper foil, this is placed behind the finished wall surface so it is not obtrusive. Other types of fabric material are also available as is metallic shielding paint. For windows, fine metal screens can be used,

but special shielded glass is also available that looks like normal glass. Doors designed for radio frequency or electromagnetic shielding are also required. In addition to the conductive cage, filters must be provided for electrical, telephone, and computer cabling where they penetrate the shielding membrane.

In most cases, detailing rooms protected from electronic surveillance is straightforward and unobtrusive, but a security expert should be consulted for specific product specifications and detailing requirements.

Access control [16720]
Access control devices

Access to secure areas can be controlled with a number of devices. The simplest is the traditional mechanical lock. The various types of locksets are described in Chapter 4. High-security locksets are available that provide an additional level of security through the use of key types that are difficult to duplicate, special tumbler mechanisms, and long-throw dead bolts. There are also interlocking dead bolts that secure the door bolt to the strike so that the door jamb cannot be spread to disengage the bolt from the frame. To prevent knobs or lever handles from being torqued apart, or otherwise opened by brute force or jimmying, most lock manufacturers provide security strikes, cover plates, cylinder guards, and other devices to make it more difficult to open a locked door.

Because access and duplication of keys can be a problem even for the most secure mechanical lock, various types of electronic locks are available. Not only can these selectively control access better than keys, but they can monitor who enters and exits a door and record the date and time of the access.

Card readers are common electronic access control devices. A plastic card containing a coded magnetic strip is used that unlocks the door when a valid card is passed through the reader. Card readers can be connected to a central monitoring computer that keeps a log of which person's card was used to open which door and when that door was opened. The computer can be programmed to only allow certain cards to operate certain doors. Operation can be further limited to specific hours during the day and specific days of the week. If a card is lost or stolen, its access code can be quickly and easily removed from the system.

In most instances, card readers are mounted on the partition adjacent to the door. Proximity readers are also available that can be completely concealed behind a wall to prevent tampering and minimize the visual impact of the reader. The user simply has to place the card near the reader for it to operate. Some readers will sense the card in a person's wallet or purse when it is within a few feet of the device.

Numbered keyboards operate in the same way by unlocking a door when the user enters the correct numerical code. However, numbered keyboards do not provide the same flexibility as magnetic cards. Numbered keypads can also be purchased integrated with a knob or lever handle. These are not connected to a central station, but do eliminate the problem with key control of standard locksets.

A variation on the magnetic card reader is the punched card access system used by many hotels. The key code can be changed each time a new person checks into a room; therefore, a previous occupant cannot copy or reuse a key.

New biometric devices are now available that can read individual biological features, such as the retina of the eye or a hand print, providing a counterfeit-proof method of identification. Although expensive, these devices are feasible when a very high level of security is required. Work is continuing on developing commercially available devices that can recognize voice prints and fingerprints.

Ballistic threat levels

The security industry uses standard methods of referring to and specifying construction designed to resist ballistic attack. There are several test methods that use standard firearms and ammunition to test and rate products and construction assemblies, such as glazing and doors. Because not every installation requires the same amount of protection, it is useful to be aware of these standard protection levels so that construction is not over- or under-specified. Manufacturers of security equipment for interior construction refer to these protection levels in their literature. It is also good to be aware of the terms that clients and security consultants may use.

One of the most common standards is Underwriters Laboratories' ANSI/UL 752, *Standard for Bullet-resisting Equipment*, which sets eight ballistic threat levels (from lowest to highest or UL-Level 1 to UL-Level 8, respectively). Construction can be listed based on what threat level it provides protection from. Ballistic threat Level 1, for example, provides protection from a 9 × 19 mm Parabellum round fired from a semi-automatic pistol with a 5 in. barrel fired at a velocity of 1175 ft/sec. Ballistic threat Level 8 provides protection from a 7.62 mm NATO round fired from a combat rifle at a velocity of 2750 ft/sec.

Similar types of performance requirements have also been established by the National Institute for Justice, the US Department of Defense, US Department of State, and the Naval Civil Engineering Laboratory. The Naval Civil Engineering Laboratory, for example, has classifications for higher ballistic threats, including small arms multiple-impact threat (SAMIT) and small arms multiple-impact threat armor piercing (SAMITAP).

Specifics on the various standards and threat classification levels are listed later in this chapter.

Locking mechanisms

Card readers and other devices control the operation of one of several types of locking mechanisms. One type is the electric lock, which retracts the bolt when activated from the secure side of the door. Unlatching from the inside is by a button or switch or by mechanical retraction of the bolt with the lever handle. Electric locks require an electric hinge or other power-transfer device to carry the low-voltage wiring from the control device to the door and then to the lock.

Electric strikes are also used. These replace the standard door strike and consist of a movable mechanism that is mortised into the frame. The latch bolt is fixed from the secure side of the door. On activation the electric strike retracts, allowing the door to be opened. On the inside, the latch bolt can be retracted by mechanical means with the lever handle.

Electric bolts are available that drop into a mortised fitting in the top or side of a door. On activation the bolt retracts, allowing

Figure 14.1
Security partitions

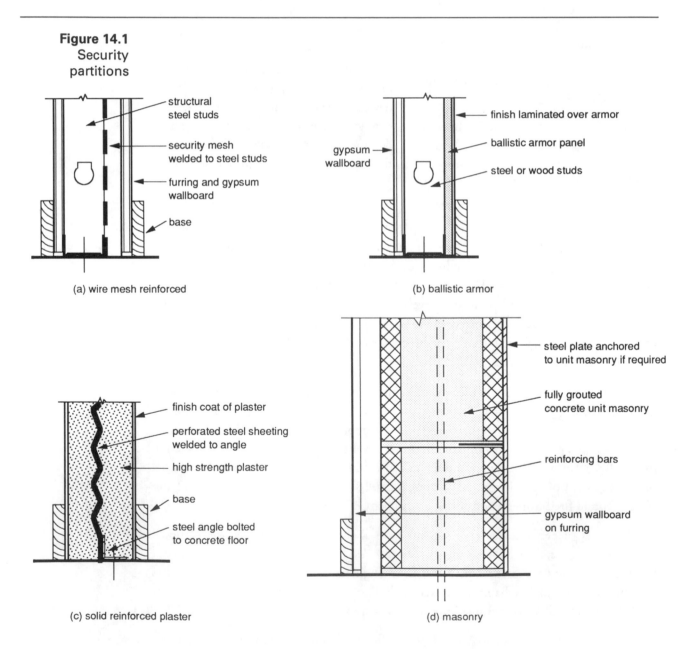

(a) wire mesh reinforced

- structural steel studs
- security mesh welded to steel studs
- furring and gypsum wallboard
- base

(b) ballistic armor

- gypsum wallboard
- finish laminated over armor
- ballistic armor panel
- steel or wood studs

(c) solid reinforced plaster

- finish coat of plaster
- perforated steel sheeting welded to angle
- high strength plaster
- base
- steel angle bolted to concrete floor

(d) masonry

- steel plate anchored to unit masonry if required
- fully grouted concrete unit masonry
- reinforcing bars
- gypsum wallboard on furring

normal operation of the door. A fail-safe feature retracts the bolt if there is a power failure or on activation of a fire alarm. Electric bolts are limited to use on nonexit doors because most building codes now require electronically controlled exit doors to be operable from the inside by purely mechanical means.

Doors can also be secured with electromagnetic locks. When activated, the lock holds the door closed with a powerful magnetic force. Card readers, keypads, buttons, or other devices deactivate the electromagnet. These can be designed to open on activation of a fire alarm or power failure.

Notification systems [16720]

When intrusion is detected, an alarm signal is triggered. This signal can activate an alarm, such as a bell or horn, turn on lights, alert an attendant at a central control station, or be relayed over phone lines to a central security service. Combinations of all three notifications are also possible. If an office building has a central station, a building tenant may be able to connect special lease-space security with the central station. When a central station is notified, the alarms are automatically recorded in the system.

DETAILING REQUIREMENTS

Interior construction design and detailing typically interfaces with security systems in four areas: physical barriers, such as partitions, doors, and glazing; hardware; millwork enclosures for security equipment; and miscellaneous support for wall- and ceiling-mounted equipment.

Partitions

Standard interior partition, door, and glazing construction provide very little protection from someone determined to break into a building or room or from ballistic attack. For most interior projects, standard construction is used with intrusion alarms to discourage and impede unauthorized entry and to notify someone at a central monitoring

station. If a higher level of security is required, gypsum wallboard partitions may need to be reinforced or other partition types constructed. These are often reinforced and protected gypsum wallboard partitions, reinforced plaster, reinforced masonry, or concrete. Some common types of security partitions are shown in Figures 14.1(a)–14.1(d).

If the threat is from ballistic attack rather than physical break in, ballistic armor can be used. This is a fiberglass-reinforced composite material available in rigid sheets like plywood. It is available in thicknesses from ¼ in. to ½ in. (6 to 12 mm). It is easily cut and applied to studs and can be covered with plastic laminate, wood veneer, vinyl wall covering, wall paper, or simply painted.

Very high security partitions, such as vault enclosures, are beyond the scope of this book and are not typically encountered on most interior design projects. Regardless of what type of partition is constructed, it should be backed up with adequate intrusion alarms.

Security doors [08320]

Doors are one of the weakest points in security construction. This is because there are several vulnerable components including the door itself, the attachment of the door to the frame, the frame, and the hardware. Any of these components can be compromised to gain entry. Although methods for detailing and specifying very high security doors are beyond the scope of this chapter, the following suggestions can be used to increase the security of interior doors for most common applications. The construction of the door should be combined with appropriate access controls and intrusion alarms.

- For low-security residential construction, use solid core wood doors with heavy wood frames securely anchored to the partition. Mortise locksets with long-throw dead bolts (minimum 1 in., or 25 mm) should be used that latch to a reinforced strike plate, which is securely anchored to the partition framing with long screws.

• Moderate-security doors can be constructed of 14-gage steel with 2-in. wide (51mm) hollow metal frames. Additional security can be provided by using hollow metal steel doors with a minimum 12-gage face, with internal channel stiffeners mounted in a frame of 16-gage or heavier steel, fully grouted and securely anchored to the partition.

• If possible, plan doors so that they open away from the security threat. This places the hinges on the secure side of the door.

• Specify nonremovable hinge pins or hinges with safety studs to prevent removal of the door from the hinge side.

• Avoid the use of glazing. If necessary, use small lights of laminated glass or polycarbonate.

• Doors with electric locks or other types of electrical devices on the door leaf require a power-transfer connection. Security power transfers are mortised into the frame and hinge edge of the door and are only visible when the door is opened. A flexible, pivoting mechanism within the mortised enclosure boxes allows the door to be operated

freely. Electric hinges are also available that completely conceal the wiring, even when the door is open.

• If louvers are required, they should be steel reinforced and covered with a strong wire mesh. Most manufacturers provide security louvers as part of their standard product line.

• For high-security doors, the locking mechanism and strike should be protected with ⅛ in. (3 mm) steel plate to prevent jimmying and prying. Most hardware manufacturers supply these protective plates when specified.

• Most building codes require that exit doors be operable from the inside by purely mechanical motion without any reliance on electronics or power. There are electric latchsets and panic hardware devices that can be connected to a building's security system to serve as access control with monitoring signals while still allowing emergency exit.

Security glazing [08660]

Depending on the application, security glazing must resist physical attack or ballistic attack, or both. There is a difference between physical-attack-resistant and bullet-resistant glazing. Laminated glass can prevent some small arms fire from penetrating, but can be broken through with various tools. Other types, primarily laminations of polycarbonate covered with glass can resist both ballistic and forced-entry attack.

Bullet-resistant glazing made of laminated glass varies between 1³⁄₁₆ in. (30.2 mm) and 2 in. (51 mm) thick, or thicker. It is fabricated of layers of annealed glass and polyvinylbutyrate (PVB) film. The number of layers and thickness of the PVB film varies depending on the degree of protection required. Each manufacturer has their standard assemblies tested for various types of attack. For store fronts and display cases that must resist simple "smash-and-grab" attacks, two plies of ⅛-in. (3 mm) thick tempered glass may be sufficient. Other

Figure 14.2
Security glazing

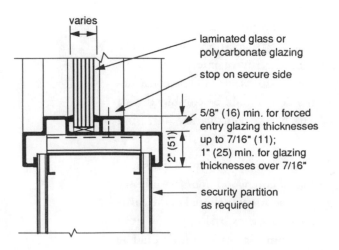

varies

laminated glass or polycarbonate glazing

stop on secure side

5/8" (16) min. for forced entry glazing thicknesses up to 7/16" (11);
1" (25) min. for glazing thicknesses over 7/16"

2" (51)

security partition as required

installations may require multiple layers of thicker glass.

When additional strength and resistance to prolonged break-in attack is required, polycarbonate glazing should be used. This is polycarbonate plastic sandwiched between outer protective layers of annealed or heat-strengthened glass. The exact thickness and lamination construction depends on the size of the ballistic threat and the degree of attack resistance required, but ranges from about 1 in. to 3 in. (25 to 76 mm). This must be accommodated in the framing and partition detailing. In addition, the surrounding partition should have at least an equal amount of protection. It does little good to have a high-security door or piece of glazing in a partition that can easily be broken through. See Figure 14.2 for common security glazing details. Framed glass doors can also be fabricated with polycarbonate glazing.

Other detailing requirements

Additional areas of coordination required between interior construction and security systems design include hardware specification, millwork design, and support for recessed or surface-mounted equipment.

Because specialized security hardware often is not available in as many styles and finishes as standard hardware, the security types may dictate what styles and finishes are used in the remainder of a room, space, or on an entire project. Consultation with the client, architect, and security consultant should begin as soon as possible so that informed choices can be made as detailed interior design is progressing.

Millwork design for guard stations, security rooms, and equipment enclosures depends on the exact type, size, and weight of the equipment to be accommodated. This information is available from the equipment vendors or the security consultant. When the interior designer is the prime design consultant, the designer is usually the person who coordinates the millwork design with equipment requirements, client needs, and the work of the electrical consultant.

American Society for Testing and Materials (ASTM):
- ASTM F-476   *Standard Test Methods for Security of Swinging Door Assemblies*
- ASTM F-571   *Standard Practice for Installation of Exit Devices in Security Areas*
- ASTM F-588   *Standard Test Methods for Resistance of Window Assemblies to Forced Entry Excluding Glass*
- ASTM F-1029   *Guide for Selection of Physical Security Measures for a Facility*
- ASTM F-1233   *Standard Test Method for Security Glazing Materials and Systems*

Military Specifications:
- MIL-B-11352F   *Block, Vision: Bullet-resistant*

National Institute for Justice (NIJ):
- NIJ Std. 0108.01 *Ballistic-resistant Protective Materials*

Underwriters Laboratories (UL):
- UL 752   *Bullet-resisting Equipment*
- UL 972   *Standard for Safety Burglary Resisting Glazing Material*
- UL 1034   *Burglary Resistant Electric Locking Mechanisms*

US Department of State, standards SD-STD-01.01 and SD-STD-01.02

Applicable standards for security glazing and doors

The type of physical support required for equipment also depends on the nature of the security system. The interior designer may need to show on the design drawings items such as blocking in partitions; hangers and support framing above ceilings; built-in enclosures in partitions and millwork; and precisely dimensioned openings for cameras, monitors, and other security equipment.

COORDINATION WITH ELECTRICAL AND SIGNAL SYSTEMS

Although the security consultant, equipment vendor, electrical engineering consultant, and contractor are responsible for designing and installing security systems and the power they need to operate, the interior designer is often the person who must coordinate the efforts of these team members so that their work fits within the overall interior design and construction of the project. In most cases this involves making sure necessary information is transmitted between the members of the team and that all required data and details are shown on the final set of drawings. It also requires that the interior designer design and detail portions of the construction to accommodate the security equipment. Some of the important elements of electrical and signal system coordination include the following:

• Lighting required for surveillance and deterrence should be compatible with the general ambient lighting whenever possible.

• The closed circuit television (CCTV) vendor needs to know what type of lighting will be used to select the best type of camera tube. Conversely, the electrical engineer may need to provide a particular type of lighting for specific types of cameras.

• The interior designer must provide adequate space and support for video cameras, monitors, access devices, and control equipment. The electrical engineer needs to design power supply to these devices as well.

• Speakers may be required for public address and communication within secured areas and near doors. These should be coordinated with the other elements of the designer's reflected ceiling plan or partition detailing.

• Conduit must be shown on the electrical consultant's drawings to accommodate signal system wiring for remote-controlled locks, CCTV, and other security equipment.

• Power transfers for doors should be specified to meet the necessary level of security, but should be concealed whenever possible.

15

AUDIOVISUAL SYSTEMS

Audiovisual (AV) systems are being used more than ever for education, business presentations, and communication as well as entertainment. People are accustomed to seeing video images, computer screens, and other advanced display technologies, and thus have come to expect it in everyday life. As a result, the spaces in which these systems are used are becoming a more important part of interior design than they ever have been. Spaces must be designed for the technology, rather than forcing the equipment into a room as an afterthought.

This chapter provides basic guidelines for space planning and designing rooms used for common types of AV equipment in commercial projects. However, it does not include the design of large auditoriums, nor does it cover the specifics of equipment selection, acoustical and speaker design, wiring, or preparing AV presentations. If a project requires a sophisticated AV system, an AV consultant should be part of the design team.

SLIDE PROJECTION

Despite new display technologies and sophisticated multimedia, slides are still widely used. They have the advantages of relatively low cost, easy portability, and are suitable for both small and large audiences. Used as a part of a multiprojector, multiscreen presentation with sound and music, a well-produced program can be as dramatic as other types of media.

However, for maximum impact, the physical layout of the room in which slides are shown must be appropriate for the audience size, seating arrangement, equipment used, projection methods, and location of the speaker.

Planning guidelines

Planning for slide projection, and AV spaces in general, requires balancing several variables, including seating capacity, room size and shape, projection distances, type of projection media, screen size and type, viewing angles, and seating layout.

In most cases, the client's program defines the type of projection medium that will be used and the size of the audience. The size and shape of the room, screen size, and specific equipment are then based on those parameters. For slide projection (as well as film projection) there are some common planning guidelines for arranging seating in relationship to the screen. These are illustrated in Figure 15.1 and include the closest viewer, the farthest viewer, and the angle of view of the screen. Guidelines for vertical dimensions are shown in Figure 15.2.

Commonly used rules of thumb suggest that the closest viewer be no closer than a minimum of two times the screen height and the most distant viewer no farther than eight times the screen height. The preferred closest distance is 2½ times the screen height, but this is not always possible when space is limited. The top of the screen should be no more than 30° above the closest viewer's horizontal line of sight. The preferred viewing angle for a matte screen is 60° on both sides of the screen from lines representing the angles of reflection on each side of the

screen. See Figure 15.1. The preferred viewing angle for a beaded screen is 50°. Seating should be laid out within this ideal field of vision so that the screen viewing angle suggests the ideal shape of the room. The angles are based on the ability of the screen to scatter the projected light back to the audience as it is reflected.

Because ideal viewing distances (including the most distant viewer) depend on the screen height, they are therefore dependent on the ceiling height of the room and the lowest edge of the screen. As shown in Figure 15.2, the absolute lowest edge of the screen should be no less than 48 in. (1200 mm) above the floor for a room with a flat floor. However, the average eye level of a seated person is about 50 in. (1270 mm).

Figure 15.1
Seating
guidelines for
front projection

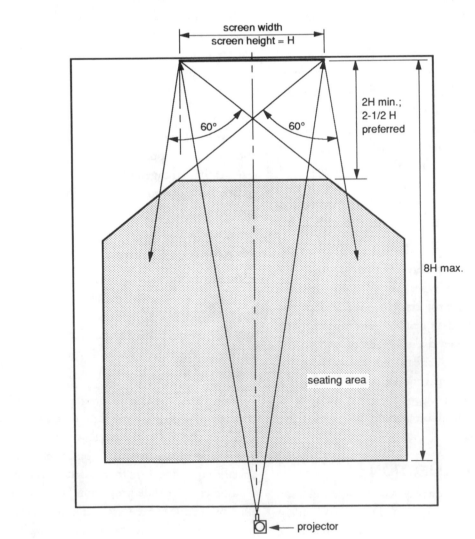

With head height added to this dimension, a screen with its lowest edge 48 in. above the floor will still cause viewing problems, especially for larger audiences. Depending on the seating layout, there will be about 10 in. to 12 in. (250 to 300 mm) of interference near the bottom of the screen.

Because many business and educational AV spaces are planned in existing or new buildings where the ceiling height has already been established, the ceiling height may dictate the screen size which, in turn, will dictate the maximum number of viewers based on the type of seating used. If the ceiling is a suspended acoustical ceiling, it is sometimes possible to relocate lights, conduit, and some mechanical duct work to allow the ceiling to be raised in an AV room.

The example on page 298 shows how to calculate maximum audience size, but it only deals with the maximum screen height and seating capacity and configuration. The exact size of the slides, projection distance, and screen shape were not considered. All of these parameters can also affect the planning of the space.

For example, because most slides are rectangular (the common 35-mm slide), some slides could be shown in the vertical orientation and some in the horizontal orientation. If some were shown vertically, the limiting screen height of 4 ft 6 in. (1372 mm) in the previous example would apply to the *long* dimension of the image.

The ratio of the length of an image to its height is called the *aspect ratio*. For a 35-mm slide the aspect ratio is 1.49 (see Table 15.1); therefore, a horizontally projected slide would only be 3 ft (900 mm) on the same screen (4 ft 6 in. divided by 1.49). Because screen height is usually the limiting factor in visibility, this 3-ft height would really determine the farthest viewer. Screen height usually determines visibility because of the height of lettering, numbers, and symbols on the screen for most business and educational purposes. Using the same situation as in calculating a maximum audience, the distance to the farthest viewer would be only 3 ft (900 mm) times 8 ft, or 24 ft (7.3 m). This would reduce the maximum audience size by one row. Therefore, it is critical to know if slides will be projected both horizontally and vertically when planning AV rooms for rectangular slides.

Equipment requirements

Planning an AV room also requires knowing what type of equipment will be used or purchasing the equipment to fit the limitations of the space plan. For projection media, such as slides and film, there is a definite relationship between the four variables of the size of the image on the screen, the size of the projected image (the actual film size), the focal length of the projection lens, and the projection distance. The image can also be projected either from in front of the screen or from behind a translucent screen (rear screen projection).

Because the four variables are related by simple rules of optics, if three of the variables are known, then the fourth can be calculated:

$$T = \frac{fH}{h} \qquad \text{Equation 15.1}$$

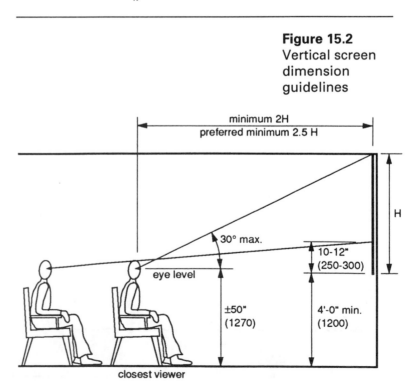

Figure 15.2
Vertical screen dimension guidelines

Example
Calculating a maximum audience size

Figure 15.3
Seating layout for calculating a maximum audience

A client wants to show slides in a room 30 ft (9.1 m) wide with a matte screen and a ceiling height of 9 ft (2740 mm), where the audience will be seated at tables 2 ft (600 mm) deep. To minimize interference, the bottom of the screen will be located at 4 ft 6 in. (1372 mm) above the floor. Standard slides will be used so that the ratio of screen width to height is about 1.5. (See Table 15.1.) Assuming the tables are 5 ft (1500 mm) long and two people are seated per table, what is the maximum size of the audience?

As shown in Figures 15.3(a) and 15.3(b), the maximum screen height is 4 ft 6 in. (1372 mm). This means that the farthest viewer should be no more than 36 ft (11 m) from the screen and the closest viewer should be no less than 9 ft (2.7 m) from the screen. See Figure 15.3(a). This gives a total seating depth of 27 ft (8.3 m). Assuming a spacing of 3 ft (900 mm) from the front edge of one table to the back edge of the next, the seat-to-seat spacing will be 5 ft (1500 mm). Dividing this spacing dimension into 27 ft (8.3 m) means that six rows of tables can be laid out in front of the screen.

The width of the screen is 1.5 times the height, or 6 ft 9 in. (2057 mm). The tables can then be planned within a 60° viewing angle, as shown in Figure 15.3(b). Counting the number of chairs gives a maximum audience of 48 people. Because of the length of the tables, the room width must be at least 28 ft to 30 ft (8.5 to 9.1 m) wide (including side aisles) to accommodate this layout. If other rooms, columns, or space planning requirements encroached into the width of the room, it would further limit the maximum audience size. If theater style seating was used, more people could be accommodated within the same viewing area.

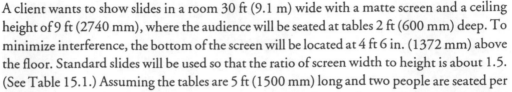

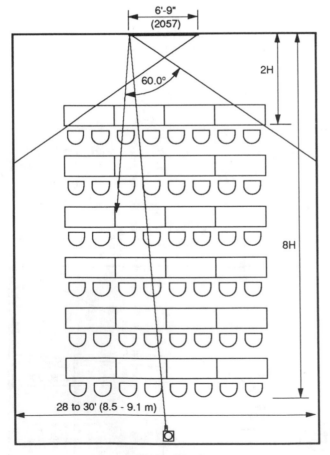

(a) determination of depth of seating area

(b) plan layout

Other variations can be derived from this basic formula, as shown below:

$$f = \frac{Th}{H} \qquad \text{Equation 15.2}$$

$$H = \frac{hT}{f} \qquad \text{Equation 15.3}$$

$$W = \frac{wT}{f} \qquad \text{Equation 15.4}$$

$$T = \frac{fW}{w} \qquad \text{Equation 15.5}$$

$$f = \frac{Tw}{W} \qquad \text{Equation 15.6}$$

T = projection distance (throw) in feet (m)

f = focal length of lens in inches (mm)

w = width of frame of projection media (film) in inches (mm)

h = height of frame of projection media in inches (mm)

W = width of image size on screen (or the screen itself if full coverage is desired) in feet (m)

H = height of image (or screen) in feet (m)

Note that when using SI units converted from English units, the conversions must be exact and not rounded.

Projection media	Frame size, in.		Aspect ratio	Frame size, mm	
	height, h	width, w	w/h	height, h	width, w
Slide media					
Standard 35-mm slide	0.902	1.346	1.49	22.9	34.2
2 × 2 super slide	1.496	1.496	1.00	38.0	38.0
126 (Instamatic) slide	1.043	1.043	1.00	26.5	26.5
35-mm filmstrip	0.668	0.885	1.32	16.9	22.5
35-mm half-frame slide	0.626	0.902	1.44	15.9	22.9
2¼ × 2¼ slide	2.031	2.031	1.00	51.6	51.6
Overhead projector	7.5	10.0	1.33	190.0	254.0
Overhead projector	1.00	10.0	1.00	254.0	254.0
Film media					
8-mm motion picture	0.129	0.172	1.33	3.28	4.37
Super 8	0.158	0.211	1.33	4.01	5.36
16-mm motion picture	0.284	0.380	1.33	7.21	9.65
35-mm motion picture	0.600	0.823	1.37	15.2	20.9
35-mm wide screen	0.446	0.825	1.85	11.3	20.9

Table 15.1
Frame sizes of common projection media

Projector type	Focal lengths, in.	Focal lengths, mm
35-mm slide projector	1 to 12	25 to 1200
16-mm movie projector	2 standard; 1 to 4 available	50; 25 to 100 available
Super 8 movie projector	½ standard	13
Super slide projector	5 standard; others available	125; others available
35-mm movie projector	approx. 1; others available	50; others available

Table 15.2
Typical focal lengths of common projection lenses

The frame sizes of common slide and film projection media are shown in Table 15.1. Some typical focal lengths of common projection lenses are given in Table 15.2.

In some cases, a particular focal length of lens must be used in order to project a maximum screen size image as determined in calculating a maximum audience if the location of the projector is fixed. In other cases, limitations in throw distance caused by small rear screen projection rooms may dictate the focal length of the lens. Sometimes, the size of the screen and projection

Figure 15.4
Projection ratios
for 35-mm slides

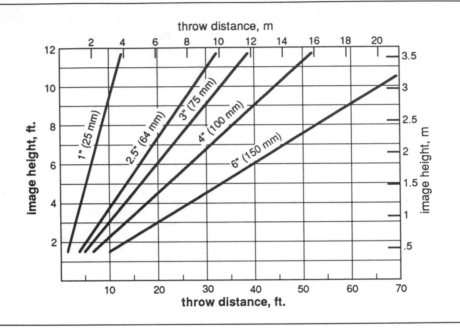

Example
Calculating
the projection
lens size

Using the same plan as determined in calculating a maximum audience, assume that slides will only be projected horizontally. What size projection lens would be required for front projection allowing for a 5 ft (1500 mm) aisle behind the last row of seats and a distance of about 2 ft from the back of the aisle to the projection lens itself?

The most distant viewer is 36 ft (11 m) from the screen. Adding this distance to a 5-ft (1.5m) back aisle and 2 ft (0.6 m) to the projector gives a total throw distance, T, of 43 ft (13.1 m). Using Equation 15.2, a screen height, H, of 4 ft 6 in. (1.372 m), and a frame size, h, of 0.902 in. (22.9 mm) from Table 15.1,

$$f = \frac{Th}{H}$$

$$= \frac{(43)(0.902)}{4.5}$$

$$= 8.6 \text{ in.}$$

In SI units the solution is

$$f = \frac{Th}{H}$$

$$= \frac{(13.1)(22.9)}{1.372}$$

$$= 218 \text{ mm}$$

lens are fixed and the throw length must be determined to plan the position of the projector or the projection room.

Although this is not one of the standard slide projection lenses, a longer focal length zoom lens could be used and adjusted so that the image would completely fill the screen.

The equations listed above and the values in Table 15.1 can be used to calculate variables exactly. However, because there is a direct relationship between all four variables, they are easily graphed. Figure 15.4 can be used to determine approximate screen height, throw distances, or focal lengths for the common frame size of 35-mm slides when two of the variables are known.

Rear projection

For many permanent AV rooms, rear projection screens are used. These have the advantage of concealing the equipment, avoiding interference with the projection beam from fixed obstructions or the audience, and reducing the amount of space required behind the audience. Rear projection screens are also preferable when there will be a relatively high level of ambient light in the audience. This is because these screens tend to reflect less of the ambient light than front projection screens. For business and educational purposes, some ambient light is desirable so that the audience can take notes, read text, or see the speaker. In contrast, front projection AV rooms require a lower ambient light level so that the image on the screen is not degraded.

The major disadvantage of rear projection is that an extra room is required behind the screen. However, by using short focal length lenses and mirrors, the depth of the room can be minimized. Another disadvantage is that the ideal audience seating area is smaller with rear projection than with front projection. This is because the light is transmitted through a screen rather than being reflected, and the effective angle at which the screen can bend the light to all viewers in the

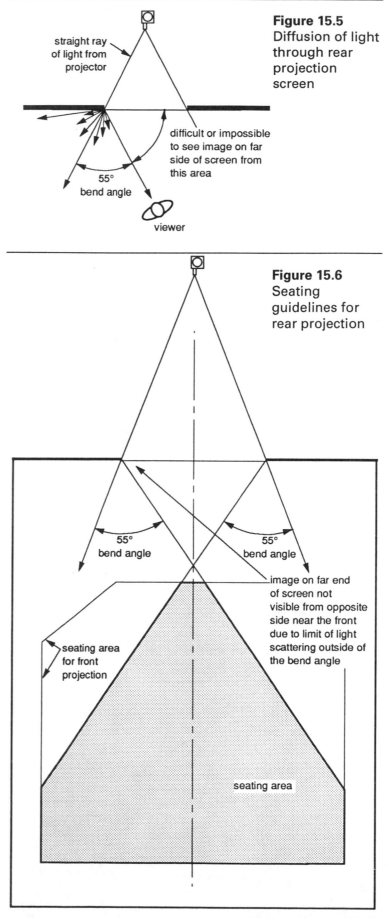

Figure 15.5
Diffusion of light through rear projection screen

straight ray of light from projector

difficult or impossible to see image on far side of screen from this area

55° bend angle

viewer

Figure 15.6
Seating guidelines for rear projection

55° bend angle

55° bend angle

image on far end of screen not visible from opposite side near the front due to limit of light scattering outside of the bend angle

seating area for front projection

seating area

audience is smaller than for front projection screens. Figure 15.5 shows this optical principle. When applied to an entire rear projection screen for the full width of an audience, the geometry appears as shown in Figure 15.6. Compare this with the projection lines in Figure 15.1 and superimposed in Figure 15.6.

The exact location of the edges of the seating area depends on the angle at which the image strikes the screen (which depends on the focal length of the lens used) and the type of screen used, which determines the amount of light bending (the bend angle shown in Figure 15.5). For very preliminary planning, seating should be limited to an area

within a 45° line on either side of a line perpendicular to the screen. Note that if two screens are used side by side for multiple projector presentations, the desirable seating area decreases for both rear and front projection because of this effect.

Although short focal length lenses can decrease the space required for rear screen projection, they have three disadvantages. One is that the overall amount of light transmitted decreases as the focal length decreases, resulting in a decrease in screen brightness. The second is that as the focal length decreases, the difference in brightness between the center and the edge of someone's view increases. As a result, the center of view appears as a hot spot and the edges of the image appear noticeably darker. The third disadvantage is that the size of the desirable viewing area decreases because of the geometry of light diffusion, as illustrated in Figure 15.6. All three of these problems can be solved by using a longer focal length lens and using mirrors to bend the projection distance. This minimizes the depth of the room required and maintains the other advantages of rear screen projection.

Figure 15.7 shows a rear projection layout using a single image screen with both straight projection and mirrored projection. Using the same screen limitations in calculating a maximum audience, but using a 2½-in. projection lens, Figure 15.7(a) shows how the depth of room can be reduced. Several mirrors can also be used to bend the beam several times (Figure 15.7(b)) although the number of mirrors should be minimized because there is some loss of brightness every time the image is reflected.

Sound transmission of noisy projectors through thin rear projection screens can be another disadvantage. However, this disadvantage can be mitigated by detailing a clear piece of glass about ½ in. to 1 in. (12 to 25 mm) behind the actual projection screen to serve as a sound barrier.

Figure 15.7
Use of mirrors
for rear screen
projection

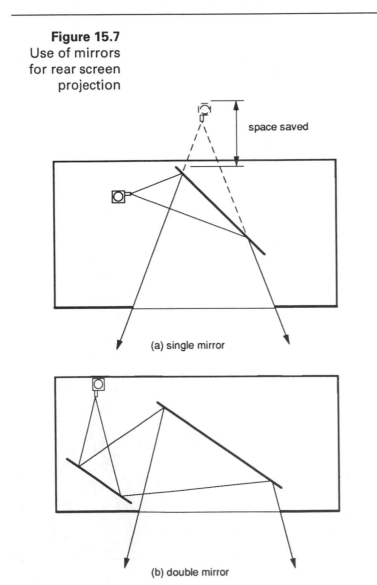

space saved

(a) single mirror

(b) double mirror

FILM PROJECTION

Planning guidelines

As an audiovisual medium, motion picture film is not used as much as it once was except for professionally produced entertainment films. For most business and educational purposes it has been largely replaced by video. However, there are some instances where film must be shown. This is especially true for production educational films and multimedia shows that mix film with slides. In these instances, one of the most commonly used formats is 16-mm film.

Many of the planning requirements for film projection are the same as for slides for both front and rear projection. Minimum and maximum viewing distances and recommended viewing angles are the same as previously discussed for slides. As with slides, these dimensions depend on the screen size which, in turn, depends on the size of the projection media and the throw distance. Equations 15.1–15.6 still apply, and some common film projection media are given in

Table 15.1. Typical focal lengths of lenses are given in Table 15.2.

There are some differences, however, that must be considered in planning for film projection. This is especially true when the film will be shown on the same screen as slides or when slides and film projection will be mixed in the same presentation.

The first difference is the aspect ratio of different types of films. As previously mentioned, the aspect ratio is the ratio of the width of a projection medium to its height. These are shown for common film media in Table 15.1. For example, for a standard 16-mm film the aspect ratio is 1.33. If 16-mm film is projected on a screen exactly sized for a 35-mm slide and the heights of the image are matched, the film will not completely fill the same screen.

The second difference is that most lenses for film projectors, especially the low cost, portable projectors used for business and education purposes, are often of fixed focal

---

Although most dedicated auditoriums for audiovisual (AV) purposes are designed as part of the architecture of a building, there can be instances when large capacity rooms are designed as part of the interior design work in either new or remodeled construction. Depending on the exact use, these AV rooms may be classified as business occupancy, educational occupancy, or assembly occupancy. (Refer to Chapter 17 for a discussion of occupancy groups.) Regardless of the classification, the higher occupant load requires a minimum of two exits from the room. These exits must be separated a distance apart, as dictated by the prevailing code.

The Uniform Building Code (UBC), for example, requires than any assembly area with an occupant load greater than 50 have at least two exits. These must be separated a distance apart not less than half the distance of the diagonal dimension of the room. For auditoriums and other rooms with a concentrated use, the UBC occupant load factor is 7 ft²/person, meaning that any AV room larger than 350 ft² (50 times 7) must have two exits.

If a large AV room is classified as an assembly occupancy, additional code requirements apply. If fixed seats are used, main and side exits, aisle widths, ramp slopes, steps, and handrails must be constructed according to the prevailing code requirements. Assembly occupancies also require the use of panic hardware on exit doors. The Americans with Disabilities Act (ADA) requires that a certain number of spaces be provided for persons in wheelchairs whether or not fixed seating is used. Assisted listening devices may also be required for the hearing impaired. Refer to Chapter 18 for more information on ADA requirements.

Building code requirements for auditoriums

length. This means that locating the projector to fit the required screen size may be more difficult than with slide projectors. Although zoom lenses are available, they are not always purchased as part of a business or educational installation.

A third difference is that the light output of standard portable projectors limits the image size to about a 13-ft (4 m) wide screen. The larger the image size, the lower the brightness on the screen; therefore, room darkening is critical for large images.

A fourth difference concerns rear projection. Because film can only be placed in the projector one way, using only one mirror would reverse the image on the screen. Slide projection can overcome this problem with simple reversal of the slide, but rear screen film projection must use an even number of mirrors, generally two. Special right angle projection lenses are available that include a mirror. If these lenses are used, only one more mirror is required.

Finally, most films have an associated sound track that requires a sound system. For most professional purposes, the built-in speakers of portable projectors are not acceptable; therefore, a separate sound system of amplifiers, speakers, and associated controls is required.

Equipment requirements

As with slide projection, if three of the four variables of projection are known (screen image size, film size, focal length, and projection distance), then the fourth can be calculated. It is also possible to chart the relationships for some of the common focal length lenses. These are shown in Figure 15.8.

TELEVISION

Planning guidelines

The use of video images for AV presentation has increased greatly in recent years, primarily due to the easy and low-cost availability of video cassette recorders and program material available on video tape. For many situations, video tape is a much more convenient way to distribute and view moving images than standard movie film. Video presentations are even replacing many types of multimedia shows that were previously done with slides and recorded sound. Because the methods of recording images and displaying them are different for video than for slides or film, different planning and design guidelines are required.

There are two basic types of video displays: video receivers and monitors where the picture is generated by a tube within the set (like a standard home television) and

Figure 15.8
Projection ratios
for 16-mm
motion picture
projection

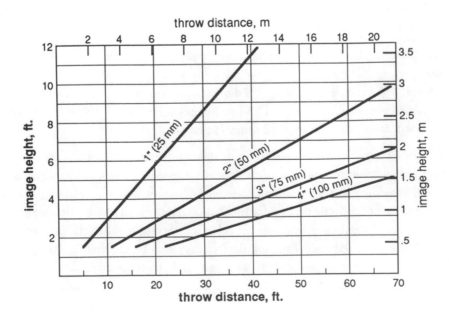

projection video where multiple color beams are projected onto a screen (like most large screen televisions). New, single lens liquid crystal projectors are also being perfected that mix the three basic television colors inside the unit. These are relatively small and can use zoom lenses to project the image. Each type of display requires different planning and has limits on viewing positions and distances.

Video monitors and receivers

Video monitors and receivers are available in a variety of sizes. Both use a screen and a picture tube to generate an image. A video monitor only displays a picture from an electronic source from a camera, a video tape recorder, or a receiver tuned to an off-the-air broadcast. A receiver is equipped with a tuner that can select one of the off-the-air channels of television broadcasts. The size of screen is referred to by its diagonal dimension.

The viewing distances and angles of television screens basically depend on the resolution of the screen (the number of lines per inch) and the distance from the screen to the viewer. Recommended viewing angles and distances for standard video monitors or receivers for viewing general programming images are shown in Figure 15.9. When the screen is displaying detailed text or graphics, viewers must be closer, in the range of three to six times the diagonal screen dimension.

The number of people who can view a screen of a given dimension depends on the seating method. The variation in audience size for two seating arrangements using a 20-in. (508 mm) screen is illustrated in Figures 15.10(a) and 15.10(b). The approximate number of views that can be accommodated with various sizes of screens is listed in Table 15.3. Figure 15.11 illustrates some guidelines for mounting heights of monitors.

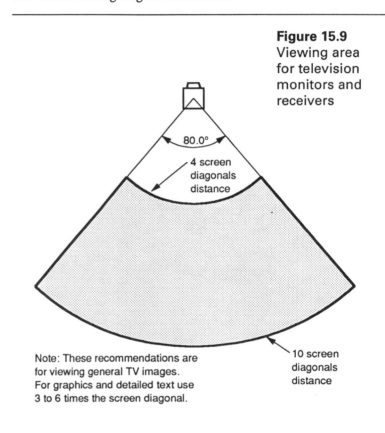

Figure 15.9
Viewing area for television monitors and receivers

80.0°

4 screen diagonals distance

10 screen diagonals distance

Note: These recommendations are for viewing general TV images. For graphics and detailed text use 3 to 6 times the screen diagonal.

Screen size		No. of viewers, theater style		
in.	mm	8 ft²/person with 5D minimum seating distance	6 ft²/person with 4D minimum seating distance	No. of viewers at desks
12	305	7	12	4
20	508	18	30	12
25	635	28	54	20
35	890	45	84	44

Table 15.3
Number of viewers of a single television screen

Note: based on maximum viewing distances of 10 times the screen diagonal.

Projection video and screens

Projection video uses equipment that projects three different colored beams of red, green, and blue light onto a screen. Smaller units, commonly used in the home, are self-contained and have a screen about 4 ft (1200 mm) in diagonal dimension. Larger screen sizes require that a separate projector be placed either in front of or behind the screen. The required throw of fixed-lens projectors is 1½ times the image width, with a maximum tilt from the horizontal of 12°. When front projection is used, the projector is normally suspended from the ceiling. Rear projection onto a translucent screen allows the equipment to be completely concealed and mounted so that the axis of projection is perpendicular to the screen.

There are several types of screens for projection video. Because current video standards produce a picture with an aspect ratio of 1.33:1 (ratio of 4 to 3), the screen should be in the same proportion. Although some projectors can produce an image up to 21 ft (6.6 m) wide, the maximum practical limit for good brightness and appearance is about 8 ft (2400 mm) wide.

Many video projection systems and screens result in a narrow viewing angle. However, good, high-gain screens allow viewing up to 45° on either side of an axis perpendicular to the screen. Minimum and maximum viewing distances are about the same as for monitors and receivers. When high definition television (HDTV) becomes common it will have a different set of optimum viewing criteria.

Equipment requirements

The equipment required for video presentations varies widely. In the simplest setup only a single monitor and video cassette recorder are required. Complex video presentation rooms require large projectors, monitors, a sound system, control equipment, and possibly cameras and special lighting. For these installations, an AV consultant is required.

COMPUTER SCREEN PROJECTION

There are two general approaches to displaying computer data: the data and on-screen images are converted to another medium that is then projected; or the computer images are displayed directly. The first approach includes making slides with a film recorder from computer programs that

Figure 15.10
Seating capacities for a 20-in. screen

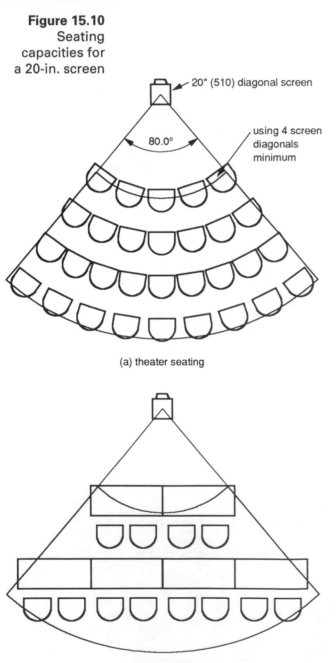

20" (510) diagonal screen

80.0°

using 4 screen diagonals minimum

(a) theater seating

(b) table seating

generate slides; converting the computer data to standard television format and recording it on video tape; and printing or plotting the data on transparencies and using a standard overhead projector. All of these are acceptable options, depending on the size of audience, the available budget, and the quality desired.

Direct projection from a computer

There are times, however, when computer output must be projected directly to a screen for a large audience. There are three ways to do this.

Large screen monitors

The first is to use a large screen monitor. Resolution and color rendition are excellent; however, as with television screens, the size of the audience is limited by the visibility of screen resolution, size of text, graphics, other images on the screen, and the viewing distance. Large screen color monitors are also very expensive. If a computer-generated display is designed correctly with large type and graphic images, the same planning guidelines apply as those used for presentations with television monitors and receivers. However, as the size of the on-screen image decreases, maximum viewing distances also decrease.

Liquid crystal displays

The second method is to use a liquid crystal display (LCD) placed on a standard overhead projector. LCDs are devices that are connected directly to a computer and act as a transparent computer screen. The light and lens in the overhead projector is used to project the image onto a screen. Anything that would normally be seen on the computer screen is projected. LCDs are less expensive than data projectors and are easier to transport. However, all the limitations of overhead projectors apply. For instance, the aspect ratio is limited to 1.33 or 1.00 (see Table 15.1) and keystoning may be a problem. Keystoning is the effect of a

projected image being wider at the top than the bottom because the projection beam is not perpendicular to the screen. This can be avoided by tilting the screen to be perpendicular to the projected beam.

Data projects

The third way to show computer images is to use a data projector. Like video projectors, these convert the computer output into light beams projected onto a screen. Because a computer uses digital signals and different scanning methods, standard video projectors will not work unless reformatting hardware and software are used. The same planning guidelines used for television projection can be applied to data projection, assuming the computer output has been designed to be large enough to be seen from the farthest anticipated part of the presentation room.

TELECONFERENCING
Planning guidelines

Teleconferencing is the communication between two or more geographically separate meetings. The communication can be as simple as the standard conference call

Figure 15.11
Television monitor mounting heights

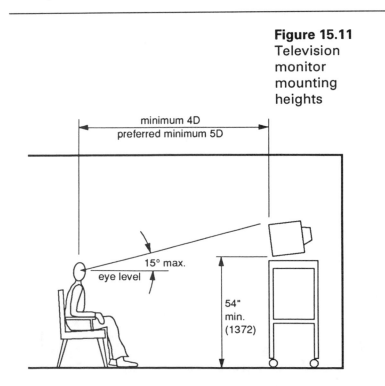

minimum 4D
preferred minimum 5D

15° max.
eye level

54" min. (1372)

over telephone lines, or as complex as a satellite linkup of full-motion video conferencing with additional communication of computer graphics and facsimile. This

section discusses preliminary planning for video teleconferencing, the type using television cameras and monitors with sound and possibly other graphic display devices.

Because video teleconferencing requires a complex mix of communications equipment, cameras, monitors, microphones, control equipment, lighting, and acoustics, a teleconferencing consultant is required to provide detailed design and specifications for the equipment and final layout of the space. However, much of the preliminary space planning and construction detailing is the responsibility of the interior designer.

Video teleconferencing is expensive to install and operate and is usually limited to larger companies that can afford the initial installation cost and for whom the cost savings in travel expenses justifies the use of such facilities. However, it is becoming more affordable because of technical advances in hardware design and signal compression; the use of digital information on dial-up digital circuits instead of satellite transmission or dedicated phone lines; and the increasing standardization of transmission standards.

A teleconferencing facility requires a dedicated space to contain the conference table, cameras, and monitors; the equipment and control room; the space for other equipment, such as facsimile units and graphic display screens; additional seating; and possibly a coffee bar. The relationship of the conference table to the cameras and monitors is especially important and determines the basic size and shape of the room. In the simplest setup for very small groups, one camera and one monitor can be used. However, it is more common to use two or more cameras and two or more monitors so that overall views of larger groups can be shown as well as close shots of individual participants.

Figures 15.12(a)–5.12(c) show some common table shapes used for video teleconferencing. Each has advantages and disadvantages. The straight table arrangement

Figure 15.12
Table shapes
for video
teleconferencing

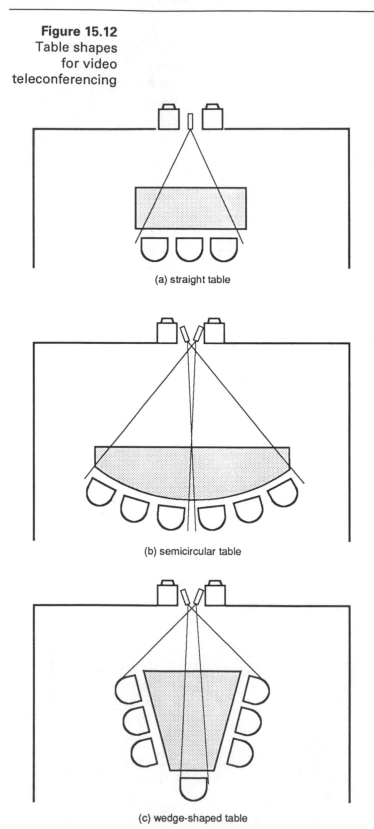

(a) straight table

(b) semicircular table

(c) wedge-shaped table

is simple and requires little space; however, it is only good for very small groups of three or four people, each of them must lean forward to see the others in the room. The semicircular table allows each person to be equidistant from the cameras and monitors, but often appears too formal. The wedge-shaped table looks more like a conference table and allows eye contact across the table. However, it makes camera placement difficult and requires people to lean forward to see someone on the same side of the table.

The conference table usually contains microphones and controls and establishes the participant's chair location in relation to the cameras, monitors, and lighting. Therefore, it is usually fixed in place and custom-designed for the particular needs of the facility. The primary participants sit at the table, but additional seating can be included behind the table if a larger group needs to be accommodated occasionally.

As with standard television monitor viewing, there is a limit to the maximum viewing distance for visibility. See Figure 15.13. Generally used rules of thumb require that the closest viewer be no closer than two times the screen width and the farthest viewer be no farther than five times the screen width. This is to allow for visibility of type and graphics displayed on the screen. General views of people can be seen from greater distances. For example, a 21-in. (530 mm) diagonal monitor has a width of about 15 in. (377 mm); therefore, the maximum viewing distance would only be about 74 in. or 6 ft 2 in. (1880 mm). Because of these visibility requirements, large monitors are usually required for groups over five or six.

The number of cameras required depends on the number of people. One camera is sufficient for up to four people. More than four people requires at least two cameras so images of individual people are large enough to see. Additional cameras may be required in the ceiling or elsewhere for viewing documents.

Room requirements

Regardless of the type of equipment used and the size of the table, video teleconferencing rooms must be designed and detailed for the best acoustics, lighting, and comfort. The perimeter partitions must be detailed to control sound transmission from the surrounding spaces. This requires partitions that extend from the floor to the structure with all cracks sealed. If constructed of wallboard, a double layer on each side can be used with acoustical insulation in the stud cavity. Refer to Chapters 1 and 11 for more information on acoustics and partition construction. HVAC equipment and duct work should also be separated or insulated to control sound transmission and structure-borne sound from other spaces. The room finishes must also limit reverberation and echo that could interfere with speech intelligibility. This is easily done by using carpeted floors and acoustical ceilings. Acoustic wall panels can also be used if additional absorption is required.

Figure 15.13
Seating distances for video teleconferencing

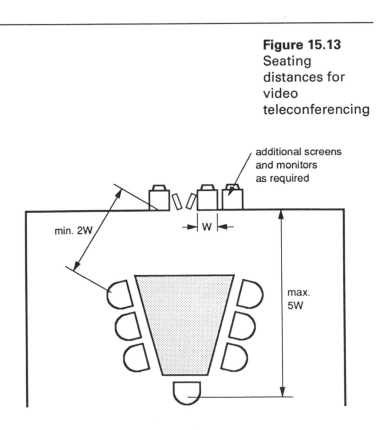

Lighting should consist of general room illumination with additional spotlighting on the faces of the participants and some backlighting to visually separate the participants from the background. A teleconferencing consultant or lighting consultant can recommend specific lighting types and positions for best visibility and picture quality.

Good colors to use include grays and blues. White walls should be avoided as they tend to be too bright. The table color should not be too dark or too light. Dark tables absorb too much light while light tables reflect too much unflattering light under the faces of the participants. Also, avoid patterned wall finishes because these can produce an annoying moiré effect on the screen.

16

MECHANICAL & ELECTRICAL SYSTEMS COORDINATION

This chapter reviews construction design and detailing that must be coordinated with mechanical and electrical systems. Although the interior designer is not responsible for designing building systems or producing construction drawings for them, he or she must often coordinate with consulting engineers and the architect concerning the location of plumbing fixtures, air diffusers, sprinklers, and other mechanical and electrical elements.

In many cases, existing mechanical and electrical services are fixed, thereby dictating the location of interior design elements. In other cases, the interior designer has some flexibility in suggesting the location of certain mechanical fixtures. For new construction, the interior designer often works with an architect or engineer to coordinate the desired location of mechanical and electrical equipment based on space planning requirements.

HVAC EQUIPMENT [15500]

HVAC is the acronym for *heating, ventilating, and air conditioning* and includes all the equipment used for these purposes. One system may combine all three, or there may be two or more systems used to heat, ventilate, and cool a building.

Types of systems

HVAC systems are often classified by the medium used to heat or cool the building. The two primary methods of heating and cooling use air or water. In some parts of the country, electricity is also used for heating. Some systems use a combination of media.

All-air systems

All-air systems cool or heat spaces by conditioned air alone. Heat or cool air is transported to the space with supply- and return-air ducts. A common example of an all-air system is a residential forced-hot-air furnace. A boiler powered by oil or gas heats air that is distributed throughout the house in duct work. In each room there are also return-air ducts that collect the cooled air and return it to the furnace for reheating. If necessary, an air conditioning unit is connected to the same duct work to provide cooled and humidified or dehumidified air.

For commercial buildings, there are several variations of systems including variable air volume, high-velocity dual duct, constant volume with reheat, and multizone systems. Each type requires supply-air duct work, registers, and return-air grilles in all spaces. Registers are connected to the supply-air duct work and can be adjusted to control the direction of air flow and the volume of air coming through them. In many instances, separate duct work is not used for return air; rather, grilles are placed in the suspended ceiling to collect return air. The space above the suspended ceiling and the structural floor above is called the *plenum*. The mechanical system draws the return air back through the plenum to a central collecting point on each floor, where it is then returned through ducts to the building's heating plant.

In commercial construction, if fire-rated partitions extend through the suspended ceiling, supply-air ducts and openings for return air must penetrate the partitions. At the locations where the penetrations occur, fire dampers are required that automatically close in the event of a fire.

Supply-air registers are often connected to the main duct work with flexible ducting. This allows some adjustability in the exact location of an air register if its location conflicts with some other ceiling-mounted item, such as a light fixture. Because return-air grilles are generally not connected to ducts in commercial construction, they may also be relocated if overall air circulation is maintained. The mechanical engineer should be consulted to determine how much the registers can be moved.

All-water systems

All-water heating systems use a convector in each space through which hot water is circulated. The hot water heats the fins of the convector. As air is drawn over the fins, it is heated. The air may be circulated by convection as with most residential baseboard fin-tube radiators or by forced circulation created with a fan. Figures 16.1(a) and 16.1(b) illustrate two common types of convectors. When commercial convectors are used for heating there is usually an additional forced-air system with diffusers in the ceiling to provide conditioned air.

There are also combination systems that use duct work for supplying fresh air, but also use water to heat or cool the air before it is introduced into the conditioned space. These are called *terminal reheat systems* and the equipment is located in the plenum. Other installations use an all-water system for heating and a separate duct system for ventilation and cooling. In geographical areas where electric heat is economical, radiant panels

Figure 16.1
Convectors

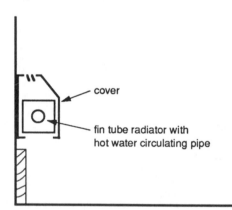

(a) residential baseboard convector

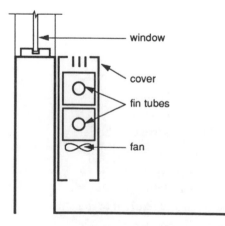

(b) commercial wall-mounted convector

can be used. They are mounted in the walls or created by running cables in the ceiling. Sometimes electric panels are used to overcome localized drafts.

System requirements

HVAC systems can affect interior construction detailing in several ways. These include the following:

Space for ducts and pipes

In residential construction, small ducts and plumbing pipes are typically run within the walls and floor joists or in crawl spaces or attics. Larger horizontal ducts in a house must be run below the floor joists and a dropped ceiling built to conceal them.

In commercial construction, horizontal ducts are typically run in the plenum space and vertical ducts within their own chases. Large ducts may occupy most of the vertical distance between a suspended ceiling and the structure above making it difficult, if not impossible, to recess light fixtures. The size and location of duct work should be verified before designing the location of light fixtures. Some commercial construction uses access flooring, which is a false floor of individual panels raised above the structural floor with pedestals. This provides space to run electrical and communication wiring, as well as HVAC duct work. Refer to Chapter 8 for more information on access flooring.

Small pipes can be run within walls in commercial construction, but larger pipes need to be placed in thicker walls or in chase walls that provide space between two widely spaced partitions. Figures 16.2(a) and 16.2(b) illustrate some of the types and sizes of pipes and the minimum partition space required.

Plenum requirements

In commercial construction when the plenum is used for return air, building codes prohibit the use of combustible materials, such as wood or exposed plastic-sheathed wire, within the space. However, some special types of telephone and communication

wiring are plenum-rated, and these may be used in a plenum without running them in steel conduit.

Access

Building codes require that access be provided to certain components of mechanical and electrical systems. These include valves, fire dampers, heating coils, mechanical equipment, and electrical junction boxes. If these components are located above a suspended acoustical ceiling, access is provided by simply removing a ceiling tile. In other locations, such as in gypsum wallboard ceilings and within partitions, access doors are required.

Figure 16.2
Pipe chases and partitions

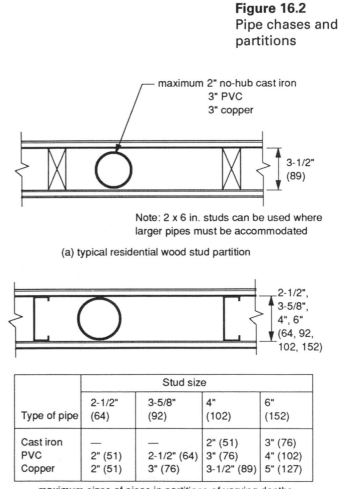

maximum 2" no-hub cast iron
3" PVC
3" copper

3-1/2"
(89)

Note: 2 x 6 in. studs can be used where larger pipes must be accommodated

(a) typical residential wood stud partition

2-1/2",
3-5/8",
4", 6"
(64, 92,
102, 152)

Type of pipe	Stud size			
	2-1/2" (64)	3-5/8" (92)	4" (102)	6" (152)
Cast iron	—	—	2" (51)	3" (76)
PVC	2" (51)	2-1/2" (64)	3" (76)	4" (102)
Copper	2" (51)	3" (76)	3-1/2" (89)	5" (127)

maximum sizes of pipes in partitions of varying depths

(b) commercial metal stud partition

Thermostats

The positions of thermostats are usually determined by the mechanical engineer. They are typically placed away from exterior walls, heat producing sources, or other areas that may adversely affect their operation. They are usually located 48 in. above the floor; however, the location should be coordinated with light switches, other nearby control devices, trim, and wall finishes.

Coordination with other ceiling items

The interior designer should coordinate the location of supply- and return-air diffusers with other ceiling items, such as lights, sprinkler heads, smoke detectors, and speakers, so that the ceiling is as well-planned as possible. However, the mechanical engineer must be consulted to verify that the desired locations do not adversely affect the operation of the HVAC system. Generally speaking, air-supply registers should be placed near windows and other sources of heat loss or heat gain, while return-air grilles should be placed away from the supply points to provide good heat and air circulation throughout the space.

Window coverings

Because window coverings can affect the heating and air conditioning load in a space and may interfere with supply-air diffusers or other heating units near the window, the interior designer should have the mechanical engineer or architect check the proposed type, size, and mounting of window coverings to verify that they will not create a problem with the HVAC system. In commercial construction, for example, there should be at least 2 in. (50 mm) between the glass and any window covering to avoid excessive heat buildup, which might cause the glass to crack or break. Refer to Figure 5.14.

Furniture placement

Most HVAC systems are designed to work independently of furniture placement. However, in some cases the interior designer may want to consider the location of floor registers, fin-tube baseboard radiators, electrical outlets, and other equipment as it affects the placement of furniture and built-in woodwork.

Air-supply options [15940]

There are several types of air-supply diffusers available, depending on the requirements of the HVAC system, the type of wall or ceiling in which they are mounted, and the appearance desired. Some of the more common types are shown in Figures 16.3(a)–16.3(c).

Air diffusers 1-ft or 2-ft (300 or 600 mm) square are commonly used in suspended acoustical ceilings because they fit within standard ceiling grids, are easy to install, and are inexpensive. They simply lay onto the gridlike ceiling tile as shown in Figure 16.3(a). Similar types are available for gypsum wallboard and plaster ceilings. These usually have a trim flange that snaps onto the diffuser and covers the rough cut opening in the ceiling, as shown in Figure 16.3(b).

Slot air diffusers can be used when the appearance of the air distribution device needs to be minimized or when the available space does not allow a square diffuser. As shown in Figure 16.3(c), these diffusers are long and narrow and contain from two to eight slots, resulting in a finished opening of about 3 in. to 8 in. (75 to 200 mm) in width. They can be purchased in any length and used for either supply or return air. There is a box above that is as long as the slots. Air is supplied by a flexible round duct attached to the side of the box. Slot air diffusers are available for either suspended acoustical ceilings or gypsum wallboard and plaster ceilings. However, they are usually used with wallboard ceilings to provide a trim, unobtrusive method of distributing air.

POWER AND COMMUNICATION

Power system requirements [16050]

Electrical systems include power for lighting (discussed in the next section), convenience outlets, and fixed equipment. As with lighting, the electrical engineer (or electrical contractor on some residential work) designs and specifies the exact type of circuiting, wire sizes, and other technical aspects of the electrical systems. The interior designer, however, is often responsible for schematically showing the desired location of outlets and switches, where power is required for special built-in equipment, and the appearance of cover plates and other visible electrical devices.

There are several types of conductors that supply power throughout a building. These extend from the electrical service entrance to the circuit breaker boxes to the individual switches, lights, and outlets. Nonmetallic sheathed cable, sometimes referred to by the trade name Romex®, consists of two or more plastic-insulated conductors and ground wire surrounded by a moisture-resistant plastic jacket. This type of cable can be used in wood or metal-stud residential buildings and those not exceeding three floors, as long as it is used with wood studs (or metal studs with the holes through which the cable passes protected by bushings or grommets) and is protected from damage by being concealed behind walls and ceilings.

Flexible metalclad cable, also known by the trade name BX® (or the common term "flex"), consists of two or more plastic-insulated conductors encased in a continuous spiral-wound strip of steel tape. It is often used in remodeling work because it can be pulled through existing spaces within a building. It is also used to connect commercial light fixtures to junction boxes so that the fixtures can be easily relocated in a suspended acoustical ceiling.

For commercial construction and large multifamily residential construction, individual plastic-insulated conductors must be placed in metal conduit or other approved carriers. Conduit supports and protects the wiring, serves as a system ground, and protects surrounding construction from fire if the wire overheats or shorts. Another type of cabling is under-carpet wiring. This is thin,

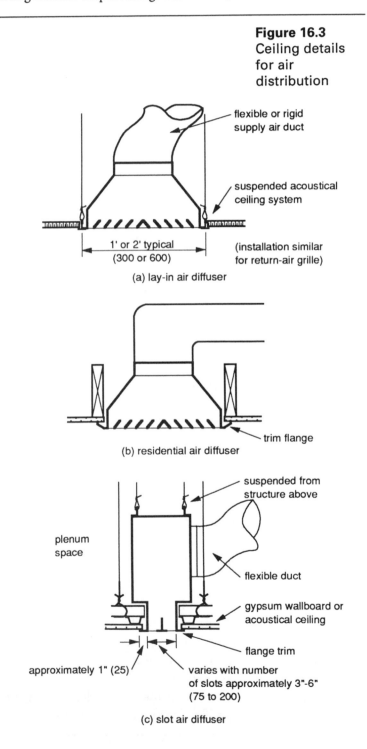

Figure 16.3 Ceiling details for air distribution

flexible or rigid supply air duct

suspended acoustical ceiling system

1' or 2' typical (300 or 600)

(installation similar for return-air grille)

(a) lay-in air diffuser

trim flange

(b) residential air diffuser

suspended from structure above

plenum space

flexible duct

gypsum wallboard or acoustical ceiling

flange trim

approximately 1" (25)

varies with number of slots approximately 3"-6" (75 to 200)

(c) slot air diffuser

flat, protected wire that can be laid under carpet without protruding. Cable for both 120-volt circuits and telephone lines is available; however, it must be used with carpet tiles so it is readily accessible. Under-carpet wiring connects pedestals in the middle of the room that contain electrical outlets and telephone connections to junction boxes in nearby walls, where the wiring is connected to standard conduit-enclosed cable.

For some remodeling work, it may be very difficult or impossible to install new conduit or armored cable. In such cases, surface-mounted metal raceways can be used. These are thin conduits, usually rectangular in shape, that are fastened to the wall or ceiling. Plastic-sheathed cable is installed, then a protective cap that encloses the conduit is applied. Outlet and switch boxes are available as part of each manufacturer's system.

Outlets, switches, and other types of connections to the power supply must be made in junction boxes. For single switches and duplex outlets, they measure about 2 in. × 4 in. (50 × 100 mm). Larger boxes are 4 in.² or 4½ in.² (100 or 114 mm). Longer boxes are available, or several can be connected if there are more than two switches or two duplex outlets. Boxes are about 1½ in. or 2⅛ in. deep (38 or 54 mm). Junction boxes are also required where light fixtures are connected to the electrical system.

Telephone and communication system requirements [16700]

Interior design drawings usually show telephone and communication systems on the same plan as the power outlets. The interior designer is responsible for indicating the location of such items as telephones, intercommunication systems, public address speakers, buzzers, and computer terminals. The locations are also shown on the electrical engineer's drawings. As with power outlets, the actual circuiting, wire sizes, and connections to central equipment are usually determined by the electrical engineer or the contractor responsible for installing the equipment.

Because telephone and communication systems are low-voltage systems, the requirements for conduit and other protection are not quite as stringent as for standard voltage power. In many cases, an outlet box is provided at the connection in the wall and the wire is run within the walls and ceiling spaces without conduit. However, in some commercial construction, all cable is required to be protected in conduit. As previously described, special plenum-rated cable is available that does not require conduit; however, it is more expensive than standard cable.

Circuit protection

In addition to the protection provided by circuit breakers in the panel boxes that trip off if the circuit is overloaded, there are two other types of protection provided in electrical wiring. The first is grounding, which is a separate wire in addition to the two that provide power. The grounding of an electrical system prevents a dangerous shock if someone touches an appliance with a short circuit and simultaneously touches a ground path, such as a water pipe. The ground wire provides a path for the fault.

A ground fault, however, can create other problems, because the current required to trip a circuit breaker is high and small leaks of current can continue unnoticed until someone receives a dangerous shock or a fire develops. Ground fault interrupters (GFIs) are devices that detect small current leaks and disconnect the power to the circuit or appliance. GFIs can be a part of a circuit breaker or installed as part of an outlet. Ground fault interrupters are required for outdoor outlets and in bathrooms and kitchens as well as other locations specified in the National Electrical Code.

There are three types of steel conduit: electrical metallic tubing (EMT), intermediate metal conduit (IMC), and rigid steel conduit (RS). EMT is the most commonly used because it is lightweight and can be easily bent on the job site.

For some detailing where electrical service is required and space is limited, it is necessary to know the outside diameter of the conduit and what the minimum bend can be for a given size of conduit. The size of the conduit depends on the number of conductors within it, which is regulated by the National Electrical Code. Conduit size can be determined by referring to the electrical engineer's drawings. Table 16.1 gives the outside diameters of some of the smaller sizes of conduit that are likely to be encountered in interior construction work.

Steel conduit types and sizes

Nominal size		EMT		IMC		RS	
in.	mm	in.	mm	in.	mm	in.	mm
½	13	0.71	18	0.82	21	0.84	21
¾	19	0.92	23	1.03	26	1.05	27
1	25	1.16	30	1.29	33	1.32	33
1¼	32	1.51	38	1.64	42	1.66	42
1½	38	1.74	44	1.88	48	1.90	48
2	50	2.20	56	2.37	60	2.38	60
2½	64	2.88	73	2.87	73	2.88	73

Table 16.1 Outside diameters of conduit

EMT   Electrical metallic tubing
IMC   Intermediate metal conduit
RS   Rigid steel conduit

This material is reproduced with permission from *American National Standard C80.1-1990, C80.3-1991,* and *C80.6-1986,* copyright 1990, 1991, and 1986 by the American National Standards Institute. Copies of these standards may be purchased from the American National Standards Institute at 11 West 42nd Street, New York, NY 10036.

Figure 16.4 shows the minimum field bends for smaller sizes of conduit so that adequate clearance can be provided when space is limited.

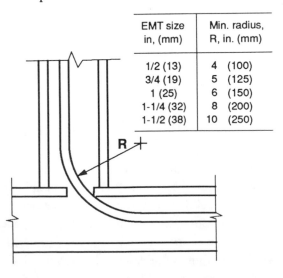

EMT size in, (mm)	Min. radius, R, in. (mm)
1/2 (13)	4 (100)
3/4 (19)	5 (125)
1 (25)	6 (150)
1-1/4 (32)	8 (200)
1-1/2 (38)	10 (250)

Figure 16.4 Minimum conduit bends

LIGHTING

Light sources [16510]

Light sources can affect construction detailing because of their size, weight, location, method of mounting, and heat output. For example, cove lighting requires a continuous piece of construction that is large enough and strong enough to support and conceal the luminaires. Recessed downlights require coordination with other mechanical and electrical systems to insure that sufficient clearance is available above the ceiling. The following briefly describes some of the typical light sources.

Incandescent

An incandescent lamp consists of a tungsten filament placed within a sealed bulb containing an inert gas. Several types and shapes are used in surface-mounted lights, recessed downlights, and other types of fixtures.

Common incandescent lamps are used in many types of luminaires. Depending on the wattage and size of the lamp, the housing can be fairly large, sometimes requiring substantial clearance above the ceiling for recessed downlights. Reflector lamps, such as types R, ER, and PAR, require similar large clearances and may require separation from combustible materials because of their heat output if the luminaire is not specially designed and rated for use near combustible materials.

When space is limited, miniature, low-voltage MR lamps and housings can be used. They not only require less space but also produce less heat than standard line voltage lamps, although their operating temperature near the lamp can be high.

Incandescent lamps are used in many standard and custom installations because they are inexpensive, compact, easy to dim, can be repeatedly started without a decrease in lamp life, and have a warm color rendition. In addition, their light output can be easily controlled with reflectors and lenses. Their disadvantages include low efficacy, short lamp life, and high heat output.

Fluorescent

Fluorescent lamps are used where a more efficient source than incandescent lamps is required, or where a linear source of light is needed. Because fluorescent lamps are larger than incandescent lamps, it is more difficult to control their light output precisely; therefore, they are usually more suitable for general illumination. Compact fluorescents are available that fit within a reflector housing similar to incandescent downlights and wall washers. However, these types of luminaires still require more space than small incandescent lamps or low-voltage reflector lamps. Fluorescent lamps are ideal for continuous lighting, such as cove lighting used to illuminate a ceiling, or downlighting used to uniformly wash a partition with light.

All fluorescent lamps have a ballast, a device that supplies the proper starting and operating voltages to the lamp. When detailing custom fluorescent installations or fixtures (as well as low-voltage incandescent installations), the detail must provide a space for the ballast, either near the lamp or remotely located.

High-intensity discharge

High-intensity discharge (HID) lamps include mercury vapor, metal halide, and high-pressure sodium. Although these lamps are very efficient, their use in interior applications is usually limited to general illumination of large spaces, such as gymnasiums, parking garages, and industrial applications.

Neon and cold-cathode lamps

In addition to the three basic types of lamps, there are also neon and cold-cathode lamps. Neon lamps can be formed into an unlimited number of shapes and are used for signs and specialty accent lighting. By varying the gases within the tube, a variety of colors can be produced. Cold-cathode lamps are similar to neon in that they can be produced in long runs of thin tubing bent to shape. They have a higher efficacy than neon lamps, are slightly larger (about 1 in. (25 mm) in diameter), and can produce several shades of white as well as many colors. Both types require small metal brackets to hold the lamp in place. Both types also require a transformer.

Lighting systems

The type of lighting system selected determines the required construction detailing. For recessed lighting there must be sufficient clear space above the ceiling to install the specified fixtures. For most standard recessed fluorescent troffers used in commercial construction this is not a problem. For some large, recessed incandescent downlights, it may be necessary to relocate HVAC duct work, conduit, and plumbing pipes to accommodate the location and spacing of fixtures. Because this usually increases construction cost, it should be avoided when

possible. An alternate is to select low-clearance fixtures.

Before design begins, the available clearances should be verified by reviewing the architectural and mechanical drawings and by viewing the actual installation of the above-ceiling construction. Although exact sizes depend on the particular luminaire used, Figures 16.5(a)–16.5(e) show some typical size ranges of various recessed fixtures.

For cove lighting, the exact configuration of the supporting construction depends on the size of the luminaire, the sight lines to conceal the fixture, the particular photometric characteristics of the lamp, and the desired design of the cove strip. If a luminaire specifically built for cove lighting is used, the manufacturer's catalogue should be consulted for any critical placement dimensions. Figures 16.6(a)–16.6(d) show some of the common shapes for cove lighting and the important dimensions for detailing.

Figure 16.5
Typical clearances for recessed luminaires

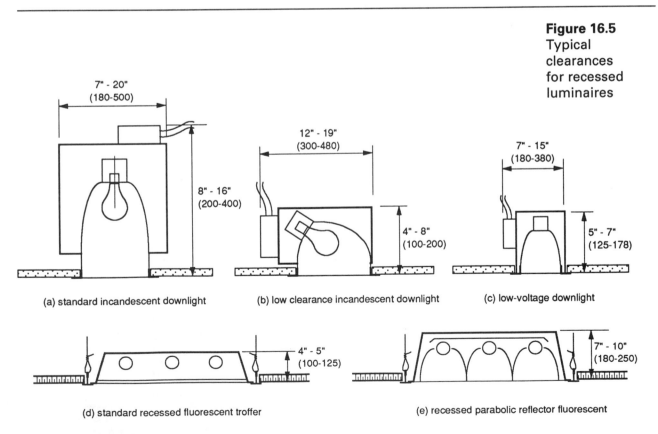

(a) standard incandescent downlight

(b) low clearance incandescent downlight

(c) low-voltage downlight

(d) standard recessed fluorescent troffer

(e) recessed parabolic reflector fluorescent

For all lighting, the ability to easily relamp fixtures should be considered when developing details. Clear access should be maintained around the lamp. Sufficient clearance also should be provided for removal of the lamps, especially large lamps such as fluorescent tubes.

Control devices [16915]

The interior designer should decide how the lights in a space will be switched. This decision is based on the function of the lighting, how much individual control is required, where the switches are best located, energy conservation needs, and the maximum electrical load requirements on any one circuit.

The function of a space may simply require one on/off switch for all the lights in the space. In a lecture room, for example, it may be necessary to provide several circuits and switches so that some lights can be turned off while some remain on. Multiple switching also gives users the flexibility of saving energy by turning off some lights when they are not required.

Switches should be located at the door that is primarily used to enter a space so that they can easily be turned on and off as people enter or leave the room. If there are two doors or the space is very large, three- or four-way switches can be used. These allow a light to be switched at two or three different locations, respectively.

The circuiting of lights also depends on the type of control required. A group of lights connected to a dimmer switch must be on its own circuit. Both incandescent and fluorescent lights can be dimmed. However, fluorescent dimmers are more expensive and special fixtures are required to minimize flicker as they are dimmed. Incandescent lights should be on a circuit separate from fluorescent lights. In commercial installations this is often mandatory because incandescent lights are on 120-volt circuits and fluorescent lights are usually connected to 277-volt circuits. Large commercial installations use 277-volt

Figure 16.6
Types of cove lighting

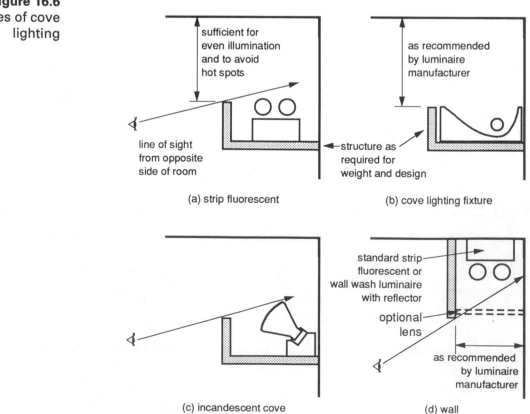

(a) strip fluorescent

(b) cove lighting fixture

(c) incandescent cove

(d) wall

circuits because they are more efficient. Lights can also be switched by low-voltage relay switching, automatic time clocks, and proximity devices that sense when people enter or leave a room.

Finally, the number of switches depends on electrical load limitations. This is determined by the electrical engineering consultant or, on small projects, by the electrical contractor. Electrical codes limit the total wattage that can be connected to any one circuit, therefore, a large space with a great deal of lighting will have several switches. Wall space near doors and other detailing should make provisions for multiple switches, if necessary.

Custom detailing for lighting

For many projects, the light fixtures available from manufacturers' catalogues may not be appropriate for a particular design. In these cases, custom fixtures can be designed and fabricated. Although the interior designer may develop the general design parameters for size, shape, and finishes, a qualified lighting designer should develop the actual details for fabrication. If Underwriters Laboratories (UL)-approved components are used in a custom fixture, the unit can usually be installed without further approvals. If custom components are

designed, the entire custom luminaire may have to undergo lengthy and expensive testing before it is approved by code officials for use.

PLUMBING
Plumbing system requirements [15410]

Plumbing systems consist of two major components: hot and cold water supply and drainage. In all plumbing installations, residential or commercial, water is supplied under pressure to individual plumbing fixtures. Because of this and because the pipes are generally small, it is relatively easy to locate pipes within wall cavities, ceiling structures, and other areas in order to supply a fixture, even if it is some distance from the main source of water. However, the closer the fixture is to the source, the less costly it is to run piping to it.

Drainage systems present a more difficult problem. Because they work by gravity, drain pipes must be sloped downward to carry away wastes. In addition, vent pipes are required. Figure 16.7 shows a simplified diagram of the several components of a typical drainage and vent system.

The first component attached to the fixture is the trap. With a few exceptions, traps are

The Uniform Building Code, the National Electrical Code, the Life Safety Code, and Canadian codes include provisions for emergency lighting in commercial buildings. Because each jurisdiction differs slightly in its requirements, the local codes in force must be reviewed. Generally, however, all codes require that in the event of a power failure, sufficient lighting must be available to safely evacuate building occupants.

Emergency lighting is required in exit stairs and corridors as well as in such occupancies as places of assembly, educational facilities, hazardous locations, and other places where occupancy loads exceed a given number. The usual minimum lighting level required is one footcandle (10.8 lux) at floor level. Illuminated exit signs are also required in most commercial buildings. There must be an exit sign at each exit door and at each door leading to an exit-way. There also must be directional exit signs at corridor intersections and where a corridor changes direction. Emergency lighting circuits and exit lights are usually a part of the original architectural design of a building. However, extensive remodeling must also include proper connection to the emergency circuits and installation or relocation of exit signs. It must always be evident to the occupants where the exits are.

Emergency lighting

located at every fixture and are designed to catch and hold a quantity of water to provide a seal that prevents gases from the sewage system from entering the building. The locations where traps are not installed include fixtures that have traps as an integral part of their design (for example, toilets) and where two or three adjacent fixtures are connected (for example, a double kitchen sink).

Traps are connected to the actual drainage piping and must also be connected to vents. Vents are pipes connected to the drainage system at various locations, open to outside air, and designed to serve two purposes. First, they allow built-up sewage gases to escape, instead of bubbling through the water in the traps. Second, they allow pressure in the system to equalize so that discharging waste does not create a siphon that would drain the water out of the traps.

From the trap, sewage travels to a vertical stack via fixture branch lines. If the stack carries human waste from toilets, it is called a *soil stack*. If the stack only carries wastes other than human waste, it is known as a *waste stack*.

Vents from individual fixtures are connected above the fixtures in two ways. If a vent connects to a soil or waste stack above the highest fixture in the system, the portion of the stack above this point is known as a *stack vent*. The stack vent extends through the roof. In multistory buildings, there is a separate pipe used for venting called a *vent stack*. It either extends through the roof or connects with the stack vent above the highest fixture, as shown in Figure 16.7.

Locating plumbing fixtures

Because of the cost of plumbing and the necessity of sloping drainage pipes, fixtures should be located as close to existing plumbing lines as possible. These include horizontal lines or vertical risers that run continuously through a multistory building. Drains must be sloped a minimum of ¼ in./ft (6 mm/300 mm) (⅛ in./ft is allowed

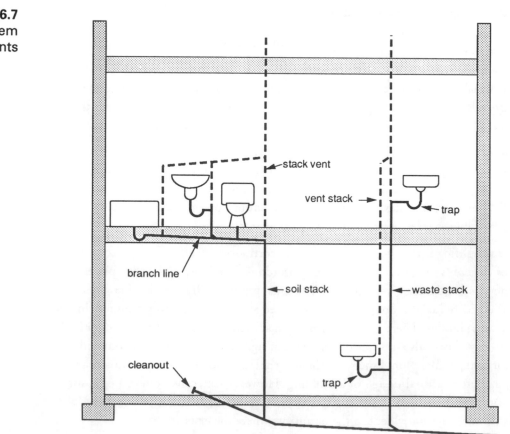

Figure 16.7
Drainage system components

for pipes larger than 3 in.). Therefore, if a pipe must be concealed within a floor space, the slope and the size of the pipe itself will limit the distance from the fixture to a connection with a riser. Figure 16.8 illustrates these principles.

The maximum distance from a fixture and a vertical or horizontal waste line usually depends on the space available to maintain a ¼-in.(6 mm) slope. This is the case when the vent is located adjacent to the fixture. However, there are some instances when there is no wall or other construction directly behind the fixture in which to conceal vertical piping (for example, a sink in a peninsula cabinet). The vent must be located some distance away from the fixture's trap. Plumbing codes limit the maximum distance from

Trap drain size, in.	Maximum distance to trap, ft-in.	Trap drain size, mm	Maximum distance to trap, mm
1¼	2 ft 6 in.	31.8	760
1½	3 ft 6 in.	38.1	1070
2	5 ft	50.8	1520
3	6 ft	76.2	1830
4 +	10 ft	101.6+	3050

Table 16.2 Horizontal distance of trap arms to vents

¼ in./ft (20.9 mm/m)

Reproduced from the 1991 edition of the *Uniform Plumbing Code*, copyright 1991, with the permission of the publishers, the International Association of Plumbing and Mechanical Officials.

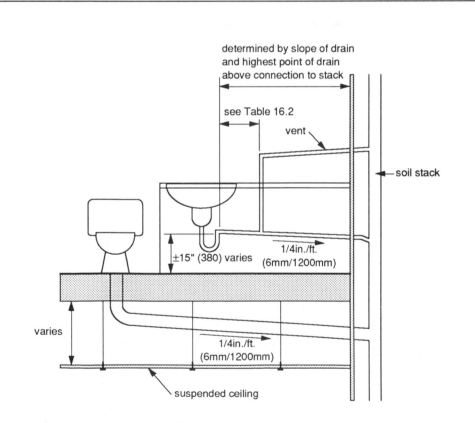

Figure 16.8 Planning for drainage lines

a trap to the nearest vent. This depends on the size of the pipe. Table 16.2 gives the maximum distances allowed by the Uniform Plumbing Code.

In commercial buildings, most plumbing is concentrated in one area near the core where it serves the toilet rooms, drinking fountains, and similar fixtures. To provide service to sinks, private toilets, and the like, wet columns are sometimes included in the building. These are areas, usually at a structural column location, where hot and cold supply and drainage risers are located. Individual tenants can easily tap into these lines, if desired, without having to connect to more remote plumbing.

If extensive plumbing work is required, the necessary pipes may not fit within the space provided by standard partitions. A soil stack from a toilet, for example, requires a 3-in.

(76 mm) diameter pipe that has an actual outside diameter somewhat larger than 3 in. In some instances, a 4-in. (100 mm) pipe is required. In this case, either thicker partitions or plumbing chases are required. Some common pipe sizes and partitions required to accommodate them are shown in Figure 16.2. Chase walls are used to conceal very large pipes or groups of pipes, such as between two back-to-back toilet rooms. Chase walls are constructed with two sets of studs with a space between large enough for the pipes. Figure 1.13 illustrates typical chase wall construction.

FIRE PROTECTION [15300]

Fire protection systems include detection devices, such as smoke and heat detectors; alarm, communication, and annunciation equipment; and fire suppression systems. Sometimes only one or two of these components

Figure 16.9
Sprinkler
spacing

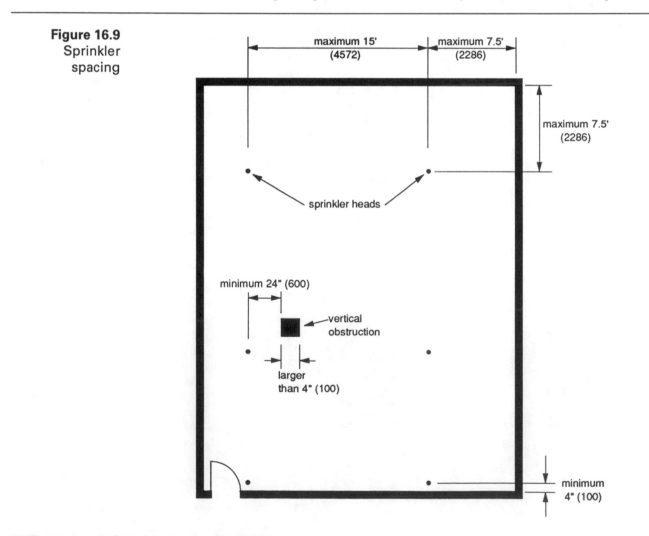

are used, such as smoke detectors in homes. In commercial construction, all of these components are present and interconnected into a complete fire protection system.

The most common component of a fire protection system that the interior designer may need to coordinate with is the sprinkler system. Although the designer does not design sprinkler systems, the location of sprinkler heads may be suggested by the designer to coordinate with other ceiling-mounted items.

Sprinkler locations [15330]

The design and installation of sprinkler systems are governed by local building codes. However, most codes refer to the standard published by the National Fire Protection Association, NFPA-13, which classifies the relative fire hazard of buildings into three groups: light, ordinary, and extra hazard. Light hazard occupancies include the type of uses most interior designers deal with. They include residences, offices, hospitals, schools, other institutions, museums, retail space, auditoriums, and restaurants.

The hazard classification and other requirements determine the required spacing of sprinklers. When designing reflected ceiling plans for most occupancies the following guidelines can be used.

In light hazard occupancies there must be one sprinkler for each 200 ft^2 (18.6 m^2) if the system is not hydraulically designed, or 225 ft^2 (20.9 m^2) if the system is hydraulically designed. Most sprinkler systems for commercial buildings are hydraulically designed either by the fire protection engineer or the fire protection contractor, so that the maximum coverage of 225 ft^2 is typically used in light hazard occupancies. However, for open wood joist ceilings, the maximum area drops to 130 ft^2 (12.1 m^2).

The maximum spacing between sprinkler heads is 15 ft (4570 mm) for the 225-ft^2 coverage requirement, with the maximum

distance from a wall being half the required spacing, or 7½ ft (2285 mm). The minimum distance from partitions to the nearest sprinkler is 4 in. (100 mm). Sprinklers near vertical obstructions (such as columns) over 4-in. (100 mm) wide must be located at least 24 in. (600 mm) from the obstruction. See Figure 16.9.

There is also the small room rule. A small room is defined as a room with a smooth ceiling area not exceeding 800 ft^2 (74 m^2) of light hazard occupancy classification. Within a small room, sprinklers may be located not more than 9 ft (2740 mm) from any single wall, as long as the sprinkler spacing and area limitations are not exceeded.

Figure 16.10
Sprinklers near obstructions

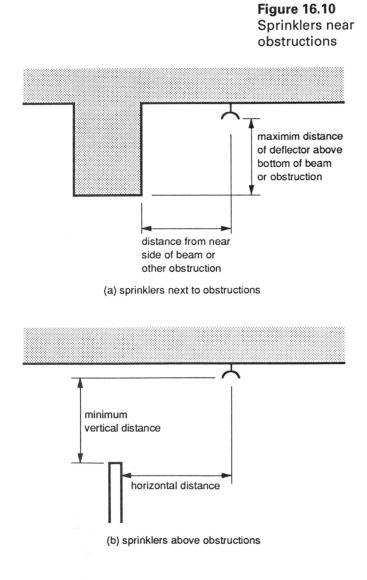

distance from near side of beam or other obstruction

maximim distance of deflector above bottom of beam or obstruction

(a) sprinklers next to obstructions

minimum vertical distance

horizontal distance

(b) sprinklers above obstructions

Table 16.3
Position of sprinkler near beams or dropped ceilings

Distance from sprinkler to side of beam or obstruction (ft-in.)	Maximum allowable distance from deflector to bottom of beam or obstruction (in.)	Distance from sprinkler to side of beam or obstruction (mm)	Maximum allowable distance from deflector to bottom of beam or obstruction (mm)
less than 1 ft	0	less than 305	0
1 ft to less than 2 ft	1	305 to less than 610	25
2 ft to less than 2 ft 6 in.	2	610 to less than 762	51
2 ft 6 in. to less than 3 ft	3	762 to less than 914	76
3 ft to less than 3 ft 6 in.	4	914 to less than 1067	102
3 ft 6 in. to less than 4 ft	6	1067 to less than 1219	152
4 ft to less than 4 ft 6 in.	7	1219 to less than 1372	178
4 ft 6 in. to less than 5 ft	9	1372 to less than 1524	229
5 ft to less than 5 ft 6 in.	11	1524 to less than 1676	279
5 ft 6 in. to less than 6 ft	14	1676 to less than 1830	356

Reprinted with permission from NFPA 13, *Installation of Sprinkler Systems,* Copyright © 1991, National Fire Protection Association, Quincy, MA 02269. This reprinted material is not the complete and official position of the National Fire Protection Association on the referenced subject which is represented only by the standard in its entirety.

Table 16.4
Position of sprinkler near room dividers and similar obstructions

Horizontal distance from sprinkler to obstruction (in.)	Minimum vertical distance (in.)	Horizontal distance from sprinkler to obstruction (mm)	Minimum vertical distance (mm)
6 or less	3	152 or less	76
more than 6 to 9	4	more than 152 to 229	102
more than 9 to 12	6	more than 229 to 305	152
more than 12 to 15	8	more than 305 to 381	203
more than 15 to 18	9.5	more than 381 to 457	241
more than 18 to 24	12.5	more than 457 to 610	318
more than 24 to 30	15.5	more than 610 to 762	394
more than 30	18	more than 762	457

Reprinted with permission from NFPA 13, *Installation of Sprinkler Systems,* Copyright © 1991, National Fire Protection Association, Quincy, MA 02269. This reprinted material is not the complete and official position of the National Fire Protection Association on the referenced subject which is represented only by the standard in its entirety.

When beams, dropped ceilings, or other obstructions project below the main ceiling where the sprinklers are located, they must be located a certain distance away from the projection so that the water stream is not deflected. See Figure 16.10(a). Table 16.3 gives the maximum distance above the bottom of the beam or obstruction based on the distance from the sprinkler to the obstruction, as shown in Figures 16.10(a) and 16.10(b).

When sprinklers are installed in rooms with furniture systems, free-standing partitions, privacy curtains, or room dividers, there must be a minimum distance between the sprinkler and the top of the obstruction. This is diagrammed in Figure 16.10(b), and the minimum distances are given in Table 16.4.

Sprinkler heads [15330]

In most construction, only the sprinkler heads are visible, and several styles are available, including recessed, upright, pendent, and sidewall. Recessed types have a smooth cover that is flush with the ceiling. When there is a fire, the cover falls away and the sprinkler head activates. Upright heads are used where there is exposed plumbing and high, unfinished ceilings. Pendent sprinklers are the traditional types for finished ceilings, where the head extends a few inches below the ceiling. Sidewall heads are used for corridors and small rooms when one row of sprinklers will provide adequate coverage for narrow spaces. Horizontal sidewall sprinklers also can be plumbed from the walls instead of from the ceiling, which makes them useful for remodeling work.

17

BUILDING CODES

This chapter discusses the major provisions common to most building codes as they affect interior construction. However, because each jurisdiction has its own requirements and amendments to model codes, the applicable code specific to each jurisdiction must be reviewed to determine complete requirements. In addition to the information in this chapter, refer to individual sidebars in previous chapters, which discuss building code requirements as they pertain to the topic of each chapter.

TYPES OF CODES

Building codes are only one type of regulation affecting the construction of architecture and interior spaces. Additional requirements that may be applicable include rules and regulations administered by local agencies that control schools, restaurants, and hospitals, in addition to state codes, and federal agency regulations, such as those of the Federal Housing Authority (FHA) and the Occupational Safety and Health Administration (OSHA), and federal laws, such as the Americans with Disabilities Act (ADA).

Building codes are usually adopted and enforced by local governments, either by a municipality or, in the case of sparsely populated areas, a county or district. In some areas of the country, a statewide building code is used. Codes are enacted as laws just like any other regulation. Before construction, a building code is enforced through the permit process, which requires that the builder submit plans and specifications for checking and approval before a building permit is issued. During construction, the department responsible for enforcement conducts inspections to verify that building proceeds according to the approved plans. However, the design professional is ultimately responsible for making sure that the design meets all applicable codes.

Model building codes

Local jurisdictions (including states) may write their own building codes, but in most cases one of the model codes is adopted into law by reference. A model code is one that has been written by a group comprised of experts knowledgeable in the field, without reference to any particular geographical area. Adopting a model code allows a city, county, or district to have a complete, workable building code without the difficulty and expense of writing its own. If certain provisions need to be added or changed to suit the particular requirements of a municipality, the model code is enacted with modifications. Even when a city or state writes its own code, it is usually based on one of the model codes. Exceptions include some large cities, such as New York and Chicago, and a few states that have adopted the *Life Safety Code* or have their own.

Three model codes are used in most of the United States:

1. The *Uniform Building Code* (UBC) is used in the western and central portions of the US. The UBC is published by the International Conference of Building Officials (ICBO).

2. The *BOCA National Building Code* is used in the northeastern part of the US. The BOCA code is published by the Building Officials and Code Administrators International (BOCA).

3. The *Standard Building Code* (SBC) is used in much of the southeastern US. The SBC is published by the Southern Building Code Congress International (SBCCI).

The primary code for Canadian provinces is the *National Building Code of Canada* (NBCC). Other Canadian codes regulate plumbing, housing, fire safety, and other specific areas of construction.

The *Uniform Building Code* (UBC) is used by the majority of the states and is the code on which the information in this chapter is based. Because all three codes and the NBCC have very similar provisions, most of the basic concepts of the UBC can be applied to most interior construction and detailing situations. However, the exact provisions of local codes must be determined before final design and detailing is complete.

In addition to building codes, there are companion codes and standards that govern other aspects of construction. With the exception of the electrical code, these are published by the same groups that publish the model building codes. For example, the International Conference of Building Officials also publishes the *Uniform Mechanical Code* and

the *Uniform Plumbing Code*. The electrical code used by all groups is the *National Electrical Code,* published by the National Fire Protection Association (NFPA).

In 2000, the International Code Council (ICC) published the *International Building Code (IBC),* which will eventually replace the three model codes in the United States. The ICC also publishes the *International Plumbing Code,* the *International Mechanical Code,* and the *International Private Sewage Disposal Code.*

Local codes

Local codes may include amendments to the model building code in use. These amendments usually pertain to specific concerns or needs of a geographical region or are provisions designed to alleviate local problems that are not addressed in the model codes.

Local codes may also include requirements of agencies that govern hospitals, nursing homes, prisons, restaurants, schools, and similar institutions, as well as rules of local fire departments.

State and federal regulations

Most states have agencies that also regulate building in some way. In addition to state building codes, state government may enforce energy codes, fabric flammability standards, and specific rules relating to state government buildings, institutions, and other facilities.

At the national level, several federal agencies may regulate a construction project, ranging from military construction to building federal prisons. Certain federal agencies may also regulate or issue rules covering a specific part of construction, such as the safety glazing requirements issued by the Consumer Product Safety Commission (CPSC).

For interior designers the most notable national federal-level law is the Americans with Disabilities Act (ADA), which regulates, among other things, removal of barriers for the physically disabled. The ADA requirements are based on the American National Standard Institute's (ANSI)

A117.1, *American National Standard for Buildings and Facilities Providing Accessibility and Usability for Physically Handicapped People.* However, additional provisions are provided in the ADA regulations. Chapter 18 covers requirements for barrier-free design.

Model codes also make extensive use of industry standards that are developed by trade association, government agencies, and standards-writing agencies, such as the American Society for Testing and Materials (ASTM), the American National Standards Institute (ANSI), and the National Fire Protection Association (NFPA). These are made a part of building codes by reference.

OCCUPANCY REQUIREMENTS

Occupancy refers to the type of use of the building or interior space, such as an office, a restaurant, a private residence, or a school.

Types of occupancy

Every building or portion of a building is classified according to its use and is assigned an occupancy group. This is true of all three model codes and specific city and state/province codes, although the lettering system may vary somewhat. The philosophy behind occupancy classification is that some building uses are more hazardous than others. For example, a building where flammable liquids are used is more dangerous than a single-family residence. Similarly, a large auditorium holding hundreds of people has exiting requirements different than a meeting room that only holds a few dozen people. The Uniform Building Code, for example, classifies occupancies into ten major groups:

A	assembly
B	business
E	educational
F	factory and industrial
H	hazardous
I	institutional
M	mercantile
R	residential
S	storage
U	utility

Each of these classifications is divided into categories, called divisions, to distinguish subgroups that define the relative hazard of the occupancy. For example, in the residential group, an R-1 occupancy includes hotels and apartments, while an R-3 occupancy includes dwellings.

Knowing the occupancy classification is important in determining other building code requirements, many of which relate to the architectural design of a building, such as the maximum area, the number of floors allowed, and how the building is separated from other structures. For interior design, occupancy classification affects the calculation of occupant load, ventilation and sanitation requirements, and other special restrictions particular to any given classification.

Occupancy separation

When a building contains two or more occupancies, it is considered to be mixed occupancy. This is quite common in architectural and interior design. For instance, the design of a large office space can include office occupancy adjacent to an auditorium used for training, which would be an assembly occupancy. Commercial interior design often involves planning a new space of one occupancy that is next to an existing space of another occupancy. Each occupancy must be separated from other occupancies with a fire-resistive separation of the hourly rating as defined by the particular code that applies. The required hourly rating determines the specific design and detailing of the partition separating the two spaces.

CONSTRUCTION TYPES

Construction type refers to the fire resistance of certain building components. These include critical elements, such as exterior bearing walls, columns, stair and elevator enclosures, permanent partitions, and floors. Every building is classified into one of several types of construction. The Uniform Building Code has five types, Types I through V, with several subgroups. Type I buildings are the most fire resistive and Type V are the least. For example, shaft enclosures, such as stairways, must be protected with 2-hour-rated walls in a Type I or II building, while only a 1-hour rating is required in Type III buildings.

The purpose of classifying buildings in this way is to protect the structural elements from fire and collapse and to divide the building into compartments so that a fire in one area will be contained long enough to allow people to evacuate the building and to give fire fighters time to arrive before the fire spreads. Like occupancy classification, construction type takes into account the relative hazard of buildings constructed with varying degrees of fire resistance. For example, a very large high-rise building in an urban area is potentially more dangerous than a house in the suburbs.

There are several interrelated variables concerning construction type, most of which have already been determined by the architect when designing the building. For existing buildings, the construction type is already established. To determine the construction type of a building, consult the local building official or the building's architect.

Knowing the construction type is important for interior design work, especially if major changes are being made. If the occupancy type of an existing building is being changed, the interior designer must know the construction type to verify that the maximum allowable floor area is not exceeded. In addition, construction type can affect the required fire ratings of permanent partitions; new shaft enclosures; coverings of structural elements; ceilings; opening assemblies, such as doors and glazing; and corridors in high-rise buildings.

TESTING STANDARDS

All approved materials and construction assemblies referred to in building codes are required to be tested by approved agencies according to standardized testing procedures. There are hundreds of standardized tests for building materials and constructions. Some of the more common ones are listed in this section.

Testing agencies

Any approved testing laboratory can perform tests on building materials as long as it follows standardized procedures. The American Society for Testing and Materials is one agency that publishes thousands of test procedures that prescribe, in detail, such

Underwriters Laboratories

One of the most well-known testing agencies is Underwriters Laboratories (UL). Among other activities, UL develops standards and tests products for safety. When a product successfully passes the prescribed test, it is given a UL label. There are several types of UL labels, and each means something different. When a complete and total product is successfully tested, it is *listed*. This means that the product passed the safety test and is manufactured under the UL follow-up services program. Such a product receives a listed label.

Another type of label is the classified label. This means that samples of the product were tested for certain types of uses only. In addition to the classified label, the product must also carry a statement specifying the conditions that were tested for. This allows field inspectors and others to determine if the product is being used correctly.

Other types of labels include the Component Recognition Mark (indicated by RU, with the R printed backwards) and the Field Evaluated Product Mark. The Component Recognition Mark is applied to a component of a total assembly that will later be tested. The Field Evaluated Product Mark indicates that the product was tested in the field by a UL engineer because it was not tested in the laboratory.

Results of UL tests and products that are listed are published in *UL's Building Materials Directory*.

things as how the test apparatus must be set up, how materials must be prepared for the test, the length of the test, and other requirements. If a product manufacturer has one of its materials successfully tested, it will indicate what tests the material has passed in the product literature.

Types of tests

Material testing for interior design components can be broadly classified into two groups: tests that rate the ability of a construction assembly to prevent the passage of fire and smoke from one space to another, and tests that rate the degree of flammability of a finish material. The following summaries include testing for building products and finishes. Flammability standards for carpet are described in Chapter 9.

One of the most commonly used tests of the first type is ASTM E-119, *Standard Methods of Fire Tests of Building Construction and Materials*. This test involves building a sample of the wall or floor/ceiling assembly in the laboratory and setting a standard fire on one side of it. Monitoring devices measure heat and other aspects of the test as it proceeds. In some cases, a standard fire hose stream is applied to the assembly to see how well it holds up to fire fighting efforts. The test evaluates an assembly's ability to prevent the passage of fire, heat, and hot gases. A similar test for doors is NFPA 252, *Fire Tests of Door Assemblies*.

Flammability tests for building and finish materials are more numerous. These tests determine the following:

(1) If a material is flammable, and if so, if it simply burns with applied heat or if it supports combustion (adds fuel to the fire);

(2) The degree of flammability (how fast fire spreads across it); and

(3) How much smoke and toxic gas it produces when ignited.

ASTM E-84, *Standard Test Method for Surface Burning Characteristics of Building Materials* is one of the most common fire testing standards. It is also known as the *Steiner tunnel test* and rates the surface burning characteristics of interior finishes and other building materials by testing a sample piece in a tunnel test chamber that has a controlled flame at one end. The primary result is a material's *flame-spread rating* compared to cement-asbestos board (with a rating of 0) and red oak flooring (with an arbitrary rating of 100).

The *smoke density chamber test* (NFPA 258) measures the smoke that develops from both flaming and nonflaming (smoldering) solid materials. The result is a measure of optical density on a scale of 0 to 800. Many codes require a smoke-developed rating of 450, or less, for finish materials.

Flame-spread ratings

After a material is subjected to one of the standard tests, it is given a rating based on its performance during the test. With the ASTM E-84 test, the Steiner tunnel test, materials are classified into one of three groups based on their tested flame-spread characteristics. These groups and their flame-spread indexes are given in Table 17.1.

Class I is the most fire resistant. Product literature generally indicates the flame spread of the material, either by class (Roman numeral or letter) or by numerical value. Building codes specify the minimum flame-spread requirement for various occupancies in specific areas of the building. For example, Table 17.2 gives the maximum allowable flame-spread rating for three areas of a building based on occupancy, as required by the UBC. In some cases, the building code allows a reduction of one class rating if an

Class	Flame-spread index
I (A)	0–25
II (B)	26–75
III (C)	76–200

Table 17.1
Flame-spread ratings

approved sprinkler system is provided. However, this may not apply to certain critical areas, such as enclosed vertical exit-ways, or in certain occupancies.

Fire-resistive assembly ratings

For construction assemblies tested according to ASTM E-119, the rating given is according to time—that is, the amount of time an assembly can resist a standard test fire without failing. The ratings are 1-hour, 2-hour, 3-hour, and 4-hour. Doors and other opening assemblies can also be given 20-minute, 30-minute, and 45-minute ratings. The assemblies that interior designers are most often concerned with include permanent partitions, doors, glazed openings, and portions of floor/ceiling constructions. Occasionally, if a project involves build-out of two or more floors, shaft enclosures, such as stairways, must also be detailed to meet the applicable fire-resistive requirements.

Building codes typically have tables showing the kinds of construction that meet various hourly ratings. Other sources for acceptable construction assemblies include Underwriters Laboratories' *Building Materials Directory*, manufacturer's proprietary product literature, and other reference sources. Construction of fire-rated gypsum wallboard partitions is discussed in Chapter 1, but masonry and plaster partitions can also meet the requirements for rated walls.

FIRE-RESISTIVE STANDARDS

Building codes recognize that there is no such thing as a fireproof building; there are only degrees of fire resistance. Because of this, building codes specify requirements for two broad classifications of fire resistance: resistance of construction materials and assemblies, and surface burning characteristics of finish materials.

Assemblies

In the first classification, the amount of fire resistance that a material or construction assembly must have is specified. For instance, exit-access corridors are often required to have at least a 1-hour rating and the door assemblies in such a corridor may be required to have a 20-minute rating. The method of testing materials and rating them has been discussed earlier in this chapter.

It is important to note that many materials by themselves do not create a fire-rated barrier. It is the construction assembly of which they are a part that is fire resistant. A 1-hour-rated suspended ceiling, for example, must use rated ceiling tile, but it is the assembly of tile, suspension system, and the structural floor above that carries the 1-hour rating. In a similar way, a 1-hour-rated partition may consist of a layer of ⅝-in. (15.9 mm) Type X gypsum board attached to both sides of a wood or metal

Table 17.2 Maximum flame-spread class for selected occupancies	Occupancy group	Enclosed vertical exit-ways	Other exit-ways	Rooms or areas
	A	I	II	II
	E	I	II	III
	F	II	III	III
	I-1.1, I-1.2, I-2	I	I	II
	I-3	I	I	I
	B, M, and S	I	II	III
	R-1	I	II	III
	R-3	III	III	III

stud according to certain conditions. A single piece of gypsum board cannot have a fire-resistance rating by itself.

Finishes

In the second broad classification, single layers of finish materials are rated, and their use is restricted to certain areas of buildings based on the rating they have. See Table 17.2. The most common test standard used to rate materials is ASTM E-84, or the Steiner tunnel test, which has been discussed earlier. The purposes of this type of regulation are to control the flame-spread rate along the surface of a material and to limit the amount of combustible material in a building.

The materials tested and rated according to surface burning characteristics include finishes, such as wainscoting, paneling, heavy wall covering, or other finish applied structurally or for decoration, acoustical correction, surface insulation, or similar purposes. In most cases, the restrictions do not apply to trim, such as chair rails, base, and handrails, or to doors, windows or their frames, or to materials that are less than $\frac{1}{28}$-in. (0.9 mm) thick cemented to the surface of non-combustible walls or ceilings.

Refer to Chapter 9 for a discussion of carpet flammability and tests specifically related to carpet.

EXITING

Although exiting provisions of the model building codes and specific state and local codes vary in details, they are all based on similar concepts. The information in this chapter is based on the Uniform Building Code. Exact exiting requirements should be reviewed for designs regulated by the local applicable code.

The egress system

The UBC and other codes divide the means of egress into a system comprised of three parts: the exit access, the exit, and the exit discharge. These must lead to a public way.

The exit access is the portion of the egress system that leads to the entrance to an exit. Exit-access areas may or may not be protected, depending on the specific requirements of the code based on occupancy and construction type. They may include components such as rooms, spaces, aisles, intervening rooms, hallways, corridors, ramps, and doorways. In concept, exit access is the least protected of the entire egress system.

The exit is the portion of the egress system between the exit access and the exit discharge. Exits are fully enclosed and protected. They may be as simple as an exterior exit door or may include exit passageways, exit enclosures for stairs, and horizontal exits. Depending on building height, construction type, and passageway length, exits must have either a 1- or 2-hour rating.

The exit discharge is the portion of the egress system between the exit and the public way. Exit-discharge areas typically include portions outside the exterior walls such as exterior exit balconys, exterior exit stairways, and exit courts, but may also include building lobbies.

Occupant load and number of exits

The occupant load is the number of people that a building code assumes will occupy a given building or portion of a building. It is based on the occupancy classification as discussed previously, including assembly, business, educational, and the other categories. Occupant load assumes that certain types of use will be more densely packed with people than others, and that exiting provisions should respond accordingly. For example, an auditorium needs more exits to allow safe evacuation than an office space with the same floor area.

Occupant load is determined by taking the area in square feet assigned to a particular use and dividing by an *occupant load factor* as given in the code. In the UBC the occupant load factor is given in Table 10-A, which

Figure 17.1
Minimum egress requirements of the UBC

TABLE 10-A—MINIMUM EGRESS REQUIREMENTS[1]

USE[2]	MINIMUM OF TWO MEANS OF EGRESS ARE REQUIRED WHERE NUMBER OF OCCUPANTS IS AT LEAST	OCCUPANT LOAD FACTOR[3] (square feet) × 0.0929 for m²
1. Aircraft hangars (no repair)	10	500
2. Auction rooms	30	7
3. Assembly areas, concentrated use (without fixed seats)	50	7
Auditoriums		
Churches and chapels		
Dance floors		
Lobby accessory to assembly occupancy		
Lodge rooms		
Reviewing stands		
Stadiums		
Waiting area	50	3
4. Assembly areas, less-concentrated use		
Conference rooms	50	15
Dining rooms		
Drinking establishments		
Exhibit rooms		
Gymnasiums		
Lounges		
Stages		
Gaming: keno, slot machine and live games area	50	11
5. Bowling alley (assume no occupant load for bowling lanes)	50	[4]
6. Children's homes and homes for the aged	6	80
7. Classrooms	50	20
8. Congregate residences	10	200
9. Courtrooms	50	40
10. Dormitories	10	50
11. Dwellings	10	300
12. Exercising rooms	50	50
13. Garages, parking	30	200
14. Health care facilities—		
Sleeping rooms	8	120
Treatment rooms	10	240
15. Hotels and apartments	10	200
16. Kitchens—commercial	30	200
17. Libraries—		
Reading rooms	50	50
Stack areas	30	100
18. Locker rooms	30	50
19. Malls (see Chapter 4)	—	—
20. Manufacturing areas	30	200
21. Mechanical equipment rooms	30	300
22. Nurseries for children (day care)	7	35
23. Offices	30	100
24. School shops and vocational rooms	50	50
25. Skating rinks	50	50 on the skating area; 15 on the deck
26. Storage and stock rooms	30	300
27. Stores—retail sales rooms		
Basements and ground floor	50	30
Upper floors	50	60
28. Swimming pools	50	50 for the pool area; 15 on the deck
29. Warehouses[5]	30	500
30. All others	50	100

[1]Access to, and egress from, buildings for persons with disabilities shall be provided as specified in Chapter 11.
[2]For additional provisions on number of exits from Groups H and I Occupancies and from rooms containing fuel-fired equipment or cellulose nitrate, see Sections 1018, 1019 and 1020, respectively.
[3]This table shall not be used to determine working space requirements per person.
[4]Occupant load based on five persons for each alley, including 15 feet (4572 mm) of runway.
[5]Occupant load for warehouses containing approved high rack storage systems designed for mechanical handling may be based on the floor area exclusive of the rack area rather than the gross floor area.

Reproduced from the 1997 edition of the *Uniform Building Code*™, Volume 1, copyright © 1997, with the permission of the publisher, the International Conference of Building Officials.

also includes other requirements for providing two exits and barrier-free access. See Figure 17.1. These load factors range from a low of 3 ft^2/person (0.28 m^2) for waiting areas to a high of 500 ft^2/person (46.4 m^2) for warehouses. These numbers mean that for the purposes of estimating exiting requirements, one person is occupying, on average, the number of square feet is listed in the occupant load factor column of the table. In determining the occupant load, all portions of the building are presumed to be occupied at the same time. If there are mixed occupancies, each area is calculated with its respective occupant load factor and then all loads are added together.

The number of exits from a space, a group of spaces, or an entire building is determined based on the occupant load. All buildings or portions of a building must, of course, have at least one exit. When the number of occupants of a use exceeds the number given in the building code (such as in the second column of Figure 17.1), then at least two exits must be provided. The idea is to have an alternate way out of a room, group of rooms, or building if one exit is blocked. Areas above the first floor must always have at least two exits if the occupant load is 10 or more, although there are some exceptions for residential occupancies. In addition, three exits are required when the occupant load is

Example
Calculating restaurant occupant load

What is the occupant load for a restaurant dining room that is 2500 ft^2 (232.5 m^2) in area?

In Figure 17.1, dining rooms are listed under the use of "Assembly areas, less-concentrated use," with an occupant load factor of 15 ft^2. Dividing 15 into 2500 gives an occupant load of 167 persons (166.67 rounded up to 167).

Example
Calculating office occupant load

What is the occupant load for an office with 3700 ft^2 that also has two training classrooms of 1200 ft^2 each?

An office has an occupant load factor of 100, so 3700 divided by 100 gives an occupant load of 37 persons. Classrooms have an occupant load factor of 20. Two classrooms of 1200 gives a total of 2400 ft^2. 2400 divided by 20 gives an occupant load for the classrooms of 120. The total occupant load of all the spaces, therefore, is 37 plus 120, or 157 persons.

from 501 to 1000 persons, and four exits are required for occupant loads over 1001.

In calculating restaurant occupant load described previously, the restaurant dining room would have to have two exits because 167 persons exceeds the number of 50 given in Figure 17.1 (Table 10-A of the UBC). In calculating office occupant load, the total area of the offices and classrooms would have to have two exits. In addition, note that each classroom would have to have two exits because the occupant load for each is 60 (1200 divided by 20 ft²/occupant). This is more than the 50 occupants given in the second column of the table, which is the trigger point for requiring a minimum of two exits.

Arrangement and size of exits

Once the number of exits required for each room, space, or group of rooms is known, the arrangement and width of those exits can be determined. When two exits are required, they must be placed a distance apart equal to not less than one-half the length of the maximum overall diagonal dimension of the building or area to be served, as measured in a straight line between the

Figure 17.2
Arrangement of exits

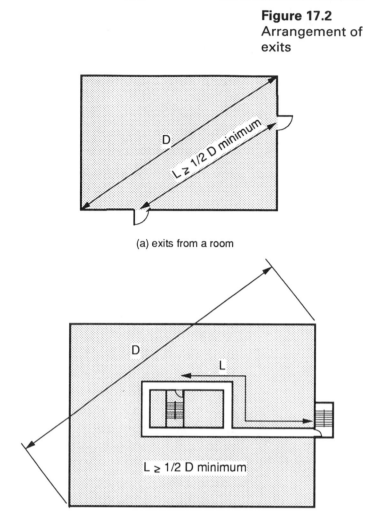

(a) exits from a room

(b) exits from a building or group of rooms

The Uniform Building Code requires at least two exits from a second story or basement when the occupant load exceeds 10. However, there are several exceptions. (Similar exceptions should be reviewed in other codes.)

Exceptions to the two-exit requirement for residential occupancies

1. Two or more dwelling units on the second floor or basement may have access to only one common exit when the total occupant load does not exceed 10.

2. Only one exit is required from the second floor or basement within an individual dwelling unit or a Group R, Division 3 congregate residence.

3. Only one exit is required from the third floor of an individual dwelling unit or a Group R, Division 3 congregate residence if the floor area does not exceed 500 ft² (46.4 m²).

4. Only one exit is required from floors and basements used exclusively for service of the building. However, storage rooms, laundry rooms, maintenance offices, and similar uses are not considered as providing service to the building.

5. Storage rooms, laundry rooms, and maintenance offices not exceeding 300 ft² (27.9 m²) may be provided with only one exit.

6. Only one exit is permissible from elevator lobbies if the exit door does not require keys, tools, or special knowledge or effort to operate.

exits. This rule is shown diagrammatically in Figures 17.2(a) and 17.2(b). This requirement is intended to prevent a fire or other emergency from blocking both exits because they have been positioned too close together.

If three or more exits are required, two exits must be placed a distance apart equal to and not less than (or ≥) half the length of the maximum overall diagonal dimension of the building or area to be served measured in a straight line. The additional exit or exits must be arranged a reasonable distance apart so that if one is blocked the others will be available.

The maximum distances from any point to the door of the nearest exit are 200 ft (61 m) in an unsprinklered building and 250 ft (76.2 m) in a sprinklered building. See Figure 17.3. These distances may be increased up to 100 ft (30.5 m) when such increases are within a 1-hour-rated exit corridor.

For most occupancies, the total width of exits in inches is determined by multiplying the occupant load by 0.3 for stairways and by 0.2 for other exits. If a greater width is specified elsewhere in the code, the larger

number must be used. This total width must be divided approximately equally among the separate exits. For instance, using calculating office occupant load again, the occupant load of 157 multiplied by 0.2 gives 31.4 in. The corridor serving this occupancy would have to be at least this wide. However, as described in the next section, the minimum corridor width is 44 in. (1118 mm) anyway. For the doors, because at least two exits are required in this example, the total required exit width would be more than satisfied with two 3-ft (915 mm) wide doors, which gives a total exit width of 6 ft (1830 mm).

Most codes allow a room to have one exit through an adjoining or intervening room if it provides a direct, obvious, and unobstructed means of travel to an exit corridor or other exit as long as the total maximum travel distances described above is not exceeded. However, exiting is *not* permitted through kitchens, store rooms, rest rooms, closets, or spaces used for similar purposes. In the UBC, foyers, lobbies, and reception rooms constructed as required for corridors (with a 1-hour-rated partition) are not considered intervening rooms, therefore, exiting can take place through these spaces.

Figure 17.3
Distances
to exits

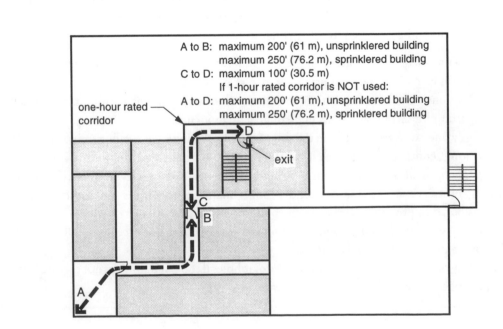

A to B: maximum 200' (61 m), unsprinklered building
maximum 250' (76.2 m), sprinklered building
C to D: maximum 100' (30.5 m)
If 1-hour rated corridor is NOT used:
A to D: maximum 200' (61 m), unsprinklered building
maximum 250' (76.2 m), sprinklered building

one-hour rated corridor

exit

Corridor construction

A corridor is a fully enclosed portion of an exit access that creates a single path of travel. With a few exceptions, corridors must be built of 1-hour fire-resistive construction with protected openings. The purpose of a corridor is to provide a safe means of egress from a room or space to a building exit or to another approved exitway, such as a stairway. When two exits are required, corridors must be laid out so that it is possible to travel in two directions to an exit. If one path is blocked, occupants always have an alternate way out. Dead-end corridors (those with only one means of exit) are limited to a maximum length of 20 ft (6.1 m) in the UBC.

As discussed in the previous section, the minimum width of a corridor in inches is determined by taking the occupant load it serves and multiplying by 0.2 or 0.3. However, the absolute minimum width for most occupancies is 44 in. (1118 mm) if the corridor serves an occupant load of 50 or more. For occupant loads less than 50, the minimum width is 36 in. (914 mm). However, the minimum width of a corridor as determined by a building code should be verified with the minimum width required by ADA requirements, as discussed in Chapter 18.

For certain occupancies, most notably educational and institutional, the UBC requires wider corridors. For instance, the UBC requires that corridors in schools must be 2 ft wider than the width as determined by the calculation described in the previous section, but no less than 6 ft (1830 mm) wide.

The width of a corridor must be unobstructed except that handrails and fully opened doors can protrude a maximum of 7 in. Other projections, such as trim, may extend into the width a maximum of 1½ in. on each side. See Figure 17.4.

With a few exceptions, corridors must be built of 1-hour fire-resistive construction when serving an occupant load of 10 or more in R-1 and I occupancies, and when serving an occupant load of 30 or more in other occupancies. This must include the walls and ceilings. If the ceiling of the entire story is 1-hour rated, then the rated corridor walls may terminate at the ceiling. Otherwise, the 1-hour-rated corridor must extend through the ceiling to the rated floor or roof above.

OPENING ASSEMBLIES

Requirements for doors and frames

Doors placed in 1-hour corridors must have a fire rating of at least 20 minutes and include approved smoke- and draft-control seals around the door. Doors in 1-hour exit passageways must have a fire rating of at least 1 hour with approved smoke- and draft-control seals. An exit passageway is an enclosed exit connecting a required exit or exit court with a public way or exit discharge. Exit doors must be maintained self-closing (with a door closer) or be automatic-closing by actuation of a smoke detector. Both the door and frame must bear the label of an approved testing agency, such as Underwriters Laboratories (UL).

Building code provisions apply to exit doors serving an area with an occupant load of 10 or more. Exit doors must be pivoted or side-hinged and must swing in the direction of travel when the area served has an occupant

Figure 17.4
Allowable projections into exit corridors

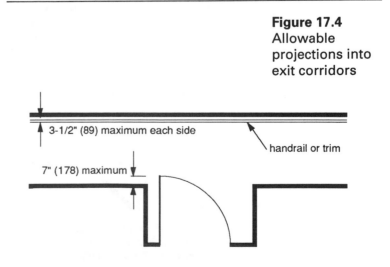

3-1/2" (89) maximum each side

handrail or trim

7" (178) maximum

load of 50 or more. This is to prevent a door from being blocked when people are trying to get out in a panic. See Figure 17.5(a). Doors must also not swing into a required travel path such as a corridor. In many instances, exit doors must be recessed as shown in Figure 17.5(b).

Exit doors must be a minimum of 3 ft (914 mm) wide and 6 ft 8 in. (2032 mm) high. The maximum width of an individual leaf is 4 ft (1219 mm).

When closed, exit doors must provide a tight seal against smoke and drafts. Glass in exit doors must be wired glass, and the total area of the glass is limited depending on the door's fire rating.

In most cases, special doors (such as revolving, sliding, and overhead doors) are not considered as required exits. Power-operated doors and revolving doors are sometimes allowed if they meet certain requirements. Revolving doors, for example, must have leaves that collapse under opposing pressure and must have a diameter of at least 6 ft 6 in.

(1981 mm). There must also be at least one conforming exit door adjacent to each revolving door.

For additional code requirements for exit doors, refer to Chapter 3.

Requirements for hardware

Exit doors must have automatic closers on them, and all hardware must be tested and approved for use on fire exits. Exit doors must be operable from the inside without the use of any special knowledge or effort, and for certain occupancies, such as educational and assembly, panic hardware is required. This is hardware that unlatches the door when pressure is applied against it rather than requiring a turning motion as with a door knob or lever handle. The door must swing to a full-open position under a maximum opening force of 30 lb (133.45 N).

For additional code requirements of exit door hardware, refer to Chapter 4.

Requirements for glazing in doors

When glass is installed in fire-rated exit doors it must be wired glass set in metal frames or special fire-rated glass. The maximum area is limited by the hour rating of the door. Wired glass in 1- or 1½-hour-rated B-label door is limited to a maximum area of 100 in.² (0.64 m²), with a maximum width of 10 in. (250 mm) and a maximum height of 33 in. (838 mm). Glass lights in 45-minute and 20-minute doors are limited to 1296 in.² (0.84 m²) with a maximum height or width of 54 in. (1372 mm).

STAIRWAY CONSTRUCTION REQUIREMENTS

Stairways serving an occupant load of 50 or more must be at least 44 in. (1118 mm) wide or as wide as determined by multiplying the occupant load by 0.3 as discussed previously. Those serving an occupant load of 49 or less must not be less than 36 in. (914 mm)

Figure 17.5
Exit door swing

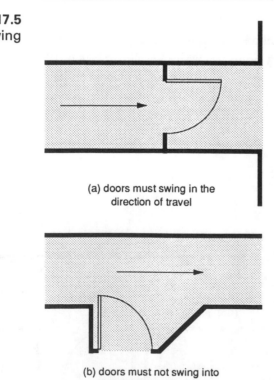

(a) doors must swing in the direction of travel

(b) doors must not swing into the required exit path more than 7 inches (178) wide. Handrails may project into the required width 3½ in. (89 mm) on each side.

Stair risers cannot measure less than 4 in. (102 mm) or more than 7 in. (178 mm), and the tread must be no less than 11 in. (279 mm). Risers for barrier-free stairs cannot exceed 7 in.; treads must have an acceptable nosing design as discussed in Chapters 12 and 18. For residential occupancies and private stairways serving an occupant load less than 10, the maximum riser may be 8 in. (203 mm) and the minimum tread may be 9 in. (229 mm).

Winding, circular, and spiral stairways may be used as exits in R-3 occupancies and in private stairways of R-1 occupancies only if they meet certain design conditions as described in Chapter 12.

Landings must be provided at the top and bottom of every stairway, and the minimum dimension in the direction of travel must not be less than the width of the stair but need not be more than 44 in. (1118 mm) if the stair is a straight run.

Handrails must be provided on both sides of the stair. Stairways less than 44 in. (1118 mm) wide in residential occupancies only need one handrail. Stairways more than 88 in. (2235 mm) wide need one intermediate handrail for each 88 in. of width. The top of the handrail must be between 34 in. and 38 in. (864 and 962 mm) above the nosing of the treads and must extend not less than 12 in. (300 mm) beyond the top and bottom risers. The ends must be returned or terminate in a newel post. The gripping portion cannot be less than 1¼ in. (32 mm) or more than 2 in. (51 mm) in cross-sectional dimension. There must be a space at least 1½ in. (38 mm) wide between the wall and the handrail.

Refer to Chapter 12 for additional discussion of building code requirements for stairway layout, handrails, and guardrails, as well as diagrams of the code requirements described above. Refer to Chapter 18 for accessibility requirements.

GLAZING

Code requirements for glazing focus on two basic issues: its use in fire-rated assemblies such as partitions and doors and its use in hazardous locations.

Glass may be used in 1-hour-rated corridor walls if it is a minimum of ¼-in. (6 mm) thick wired glass set in steel frames and the total area does not exceed 25 percent of the area of the wall separating the room from the corridor. Special fire-rated glass, as discussed in Chapter 5, may be used in lieu of wired glass as long as it is installed according to the manufacturer's details and conforms to UL listing requirements.

When glass is installed in hazardous locations—that is, where it is subject to human impact—it must be safety glazing. This is tempered glass or laminated glass. The exact locations where safety glazing is required are shown in Figure 5.13 and discussed in Chapter 5.

For additional code requirements of glazing and a discussion of topics including fire-rated glazing, wired glass, and safety glazing, refer to Chapter 5.

OTHER REQUIREMENTS

In addition to the provisions mentioned in the previous sections, all the model building codes regulate many other aspects of construction. These include the use and structural design of individual materials, excavations, demolition, and elevators, and many other construction aspects. In addition to the model codes, there are local, state, and federal codes that regulate projects. For example, some states have specific flammability codes that regulate the specification of furniture fabrics and other interior materials. Specific requirements for barrier-free design are discussed in the next chapter.

Special occupancy requirements

Building codes also specify special requirements for each occupancy type based on the needs unique to that occupancy. For example, the Uniform Building Code requires storage areas of wholesale or retail stores of business occupancies to be separated from the public areas with a 1-hour-rated fire-resistive occupancy separation. Educational occupancies must have wider corridors than those specified in Chapter 33 of the UBC. In residential occupancies basements and bedrooms must have special emergency escape windows of a particular size and height above the floor. The applicable building code should be consulted to determine special occupancy requirements that are applicable.

Plumbing systems

Model codes specify in great detail how a plumbing system must be designed. They also specify the number of sanitary fixtures required based on the type of occupancy. In most cases, satisfying the requirements is the responsibility of the mechanical engineer and architect. However, in some cases, the interior designer may be involved with remodeling toilet rooms in commercial buildings. In this case, it is helpful to know how many fixtures are required when preliminary design layouts are being developed. For example, the *Uniform Plumbing Code* (UPC), which is a companion volume to the UBC, gives the minimum number of toilets, lavatories, drinking fountains, and other fixtures required in a building.

Sound ratings

A building code may require that wall and floor/ceiling assemblies in residential occupancies separating dwelling units or guest rooms from each other and from public spaces be insulated to provide for sound-transmission control. If this is the case, the code specifies the minimum sound transmission class (STC) for walls or impact insulation class (IIC) for floors. Construction details must then be selected that satisfy these requirements.

Refer to Chapter 11 for more information on acoustics.

18

BARRIER-FREE DESIGN

Barrier-free design, or *universal design,* should be an integral part of every building and interior space. Although building codes and many federal and state agencies require accessibility, the overriding regulation today is the Americans with Disabilities Act (ADA). This federal law requires, among other things, that all commercial and public accommodations be accessible to people with disabilities. Although the ADA is not a national building code and does not depend on inspection for its enforcement, building owners must either comply with the requirements or be liable for civil suits. The ADA does not cover single- or multifamily housing; however, such housing is regulated by local building codes and by other federal and local codes so that these building types must also be accessible. ADA regulations follow most of the standards set forth in CABO/ANSI A117.1, *American National Standard for Buildings and Facilities Providing Accessibility and Usability for Physically Handicapped People.* In addition, the ADA includes provisions regarding such things as the minimum numbers of facilities and accommodations. In some cases, the *Uniform Federal Accessibility Standards* may govern,

but these are almost identical to ADA and CABO/ANSI A117.1 standards.

The standards discussed in this chapter include the basic requirements for accessibility related to interior design as defined in the ADA and by CABO/ANSI A117.1. The full text of the ADA should be consulted for additional detailed requirements, including special requirements for restaurants, medical care facilities, business uses, libraries, and lodging facilities.

ACCESSIBLE ROUTES

An *accessible route* is a continuous unobstructed path connecting all accessible elements and spaces in a building or facility. (For the purposes of this book, exterior requirements are not covered.) It includes corridors, doorways, floors, ramps, elevators, lifts, and clear floor space at fixtures. The standards for accessible routes are designed to accommodate persons with severe disabilities using wheelchairs, but are also intended to provide ease of use for people with other disabilities.

Accessible routes and other clearances are based on basic dimensional requirements of wheelchairs. The minimum clear floor space

Figure 18.1
Maneuvering
clearances

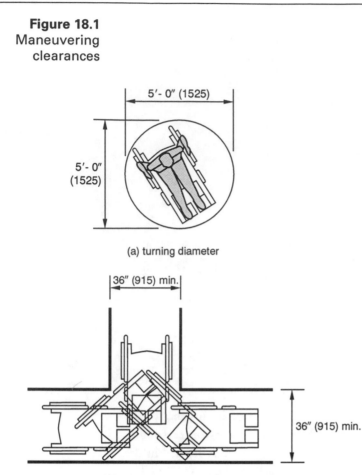

(a) turning diameter

(b) T-shaped space for 180° turns

Figure 18.2
Wheelchair
clearances

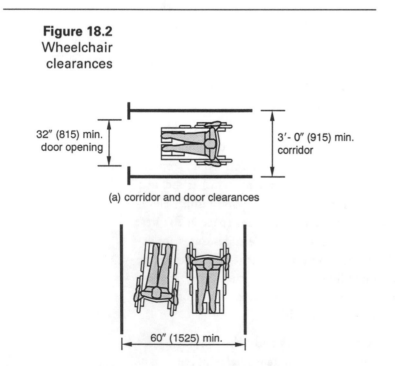

(a) corridor and door clearances

(b) minimum clear width for two wheelchairs

required to accommodate one stationary wheelchair is 30 in. × 48 in. (760 × 1220 mm). For maneuverability, a minimum 60-in. (1525 mm) diameter circle is required for a wheelchair to make a 180° turn, as shown in Figure 18.1(a). In place of this, a T-shaped space may be provided, as shown in Figure 18.1(b).

The minimum clear width for an accessible route is 36 in. (915 mm) continuously and 32 in. (815 mm) at a passage point, such as a doorway. The passage point cannot be more than 24 in. (610 mm) long. The minimum passage width for two wheelchairs is 60 in. (1525 mm). If an accessible route is less than 60 in. wide, then passing spaces at least 60 × 60 in. (1525 × 1525 mm) must be provided at intervals not to exceed 200 ft (61 m). These requirements are shown in Figures 18.2(a) and 18.2(b).

In toilet rooms the turning space may overlap with the required clear floor space at fixtures and controls and with the accessible route. The minimum dimensions for turns in corridors or around obstructions are shown in Figures 18.3(a) and 18.3(b).

An accessible route may have a slope of up to 1:20 [1-in. rise for every 20 in. in distance (25.4 for 508 mm)]. Slopes any greater than this are classified as ramps and must meet the requirements given later in this chapter.

DOORWAYS

Width and arrangement

Doors must have a minimum clear opening width of 32 in. (815 mm) when the door is opened at 90°. The maximum depth of a doorway 32 in. (813 mm) wide is 24 in. (610 mm). If the area is deeper than this, the width must be increased to 36 in. (915 mm). See Figures 18.4(a) and 18.4(b).

Maneuvering clearances are required at standard swinging doors to allow easy operation of the latch and provide for a clear swing. For single doors, the clearances are shown in Figure 18.6. For two doors in a series, the minimum space is shown in Figures 18.6(a) and 18.6(b). Note the 48 in. (1220 mm) space requirement. If sufficient clearance is not provided, then the doors must have power-assisted mechanisms or be automatic-opening doors.

Opening force

The maximum opening force required to push or pull open an interior hinged door cannot be more than 5 pound-ft (22.2 N). This force does not include the force required to retract the latch bolts or disengage other devices that may hold the door closed. Automatic doors and power-assisted doors may also be used if they comply with ANSI/ BHMA (Builders Hardware Manufacturers Association) standard A156.10 (automatic doors) or ANSI/BHMA 156.19 (low-powered, automatic doors).

When closers are used the sweep period of the door must be adjusted so that from an open position of 70°, the door will take at least 3 seconds to move to a point 3 in. (75 mm) from the latch, as measured to the leading edge of the door.

Hardware

Thresholds at doorways cannot exceed ½ in. (13 mm) in height and must be beveled so that no slope of the threshold is greater than 1:2. Operating devices must have a shape that is easy to grasp. This includes lever handles, push-type mechanisms, and U-shaped handles. Round-shaped door knobs are not allowed. If door closers are provided, they must be adjusted to slow the closing time. Hardware for accessible doors cannot be mounted more than 48 in. (1220 mm) above the finished floor.

PLUMBING FIXTURES AND TOILET ROOMS

CABO/ANSI A117.1 and the ADA govern the design of the components of toilet rooms as well as individual elements, such as drinking fountains, bathtubs, and showers. As mentioned in a previous section, toilet rooms

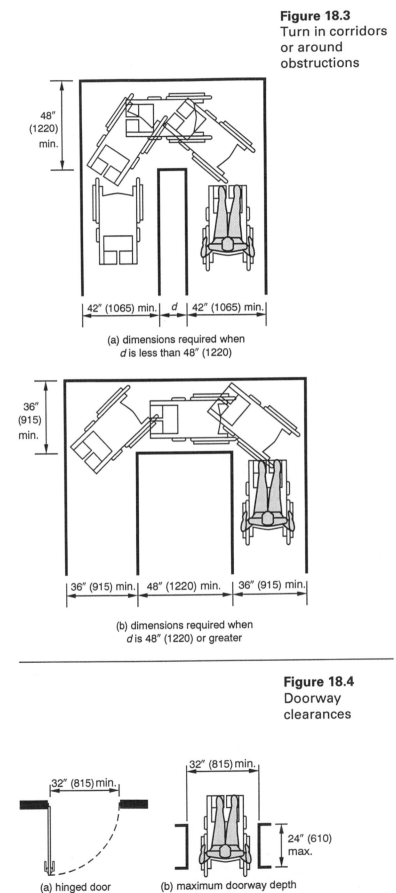

Figure 18.3
Turn in corridors or around obstructions

48″ (1220) min.

42″ (1065) min. d 42″ (1065) min.

(a) dimensions required when d is less than 48″ (1220)

36″ (915) min.

36″ (915) min. 48″ (1220) min. 36″ (915) min.

(b) dimensions required when d is 48″ (1220) or greater

Figure 18.4
Doorway clearances

32″ (815) min.

32″ (815) min.

24″ (610) max.

(a) hinged door

(b) maximum doorway depth

Figure 18.5
Maneuvering
clearances at
doors

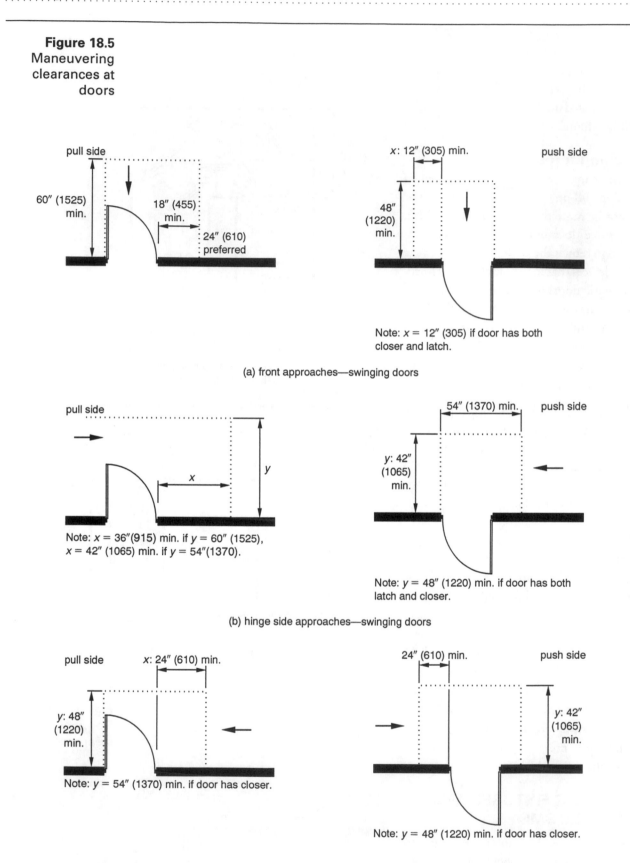

pull side

60″ (1525)
min.

18″ (455)
min.

24″ (610)
preferred

x: 12″ (305) min.   push side

48″
(1220)
min.

Note: *x* = 12″ (305) if door has both
closer and latch.

(a) front approaches—swinging doors

pull side

x

y

Note: *x* = 36″(915) min. if *y* = 60″ (1525),
x = 42″ (1065) min. if *y* = 54″(1370).

54″ (1370) min.   push side

y: 42″
(1065)
min.

Note: *y* = 48″ (1220) min. if door has both
latch and closer.

(b) hinge side approaches—swinging doors

pull side   *x*: 24″ (610) min.

y: 48″
(1220)
min.

Note: *y* = 54″ (1370) min. if door has closer.

24″ (610) min.   push side

y: 42″
(1065)
min.

Note: *y* = 48″ (1220) min. if door has closer.

(c) latch side approaches—swinging doors

must have a minimum clear turning space of a 5-ft (1525 mm) diameter circle in addition to the minimum access areas required at each type of fixture. The 5-ft circle can overlap with required access at controls and fixtures and with the accessible route.

Toilet stalls

There are several acceptable layouts for toilet stalls. Minimum clearances for two standard stall layouts are shown in Figures 18.7(a) and 18.7(b). When toilet rooms are being remodeled and it is technically infeasible to put in a standard stall, alternate layouts are also acceptable, as shown in Figure 18.8. In all cases, the clearance depth varies depending on whether a wall-hung or floor-mounted water closet is used. If the depth is increased by 3 in. (76 mm), a floor-mounted water closet can be used. In most cases, the door must provide a minimum clear opening of 32 in. and must swing out, away from the stall enclosure. Grab bars must also be provided, as shown in the illustrations, mounted from 33 in. to 36 in. (840 to 915 mm) above the floor.

If toilet stalls are not used, the center line of the toilet must still be 18 in. (455 mm) from a wall with grab bars at both the back and side of the water closet. A clear space in front of and beside open water closets should be provided, as shown in Figure 18.9. The dimension from the center line of the toilet is 18 in. (457 mm) to both an adjacent wall and the closest edge of a lavatory. Toilet paper dispensers must be installed within reach, with the center of the dispenser a minimum of 19 in. (485 mm) above the floor.

Urinals

Urinals must be either of the stall- or wall-hung type, with an elongated rim at a maximum height of 17 in. (430 mm) above the floor. A clear floor space of 30 × 48 in. (760 × 1220 mm) must be provided in front of the urinal, which may adjoin or overlap an accessible route. Urinal shields that do not extend beyond the front edge of the rim may

be provided with 29 in. (735 mm) clearance between them.

Lavatories and sinks

Lavatories must be designed to allow someone in a wheelchair to move under the sink to allow easy use of the basin and water controls. The required dimensions are shown in Figures 18.10(a) and 18.10(b). Note that because of these clearances, wall-hung lavatories are the best type to use when accessibility is a concern. If pipes are exposed below the lavatory, they must be insulated or otherwise protected and there must not be any sharp or abrasive surfaces under lavatories or sinks. Faucets must be operable with one hand and cannot require tight grasping, pinching, or twisting of the wrist. Lever-operated, push-type, and automatically controlled mechanisms are acceptable types.

Figure 18.6
Double door clearances

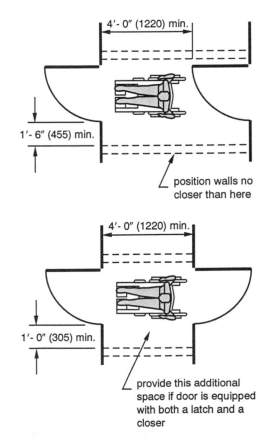

4'- 0" (1220) min.

1'- 6" (455) min.

position walls no closer than here

4'- 0" (1220) min.

1'- 0" (305) min.

provide this additional space if door is equipped with both a latch and a closer

Figure 18.7
Toilet stall
dimensions

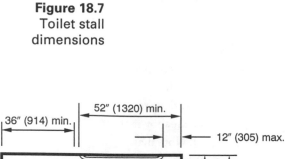

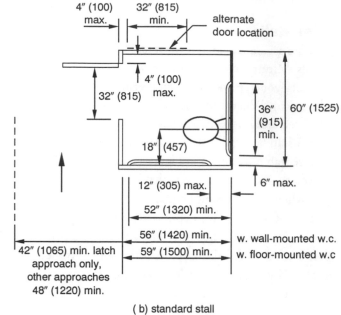

(a) standard stall (end of row)

(b) standard stall

Figure 18.8
Alternate toilet
stall dimensions

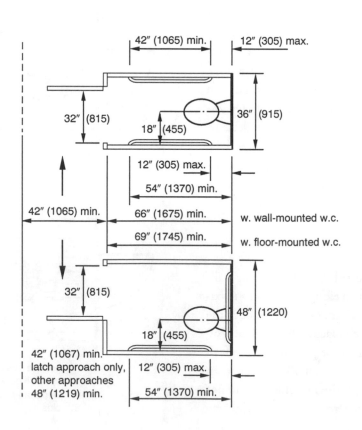

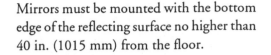

Figure 18.9
Clear floor space
at water closets

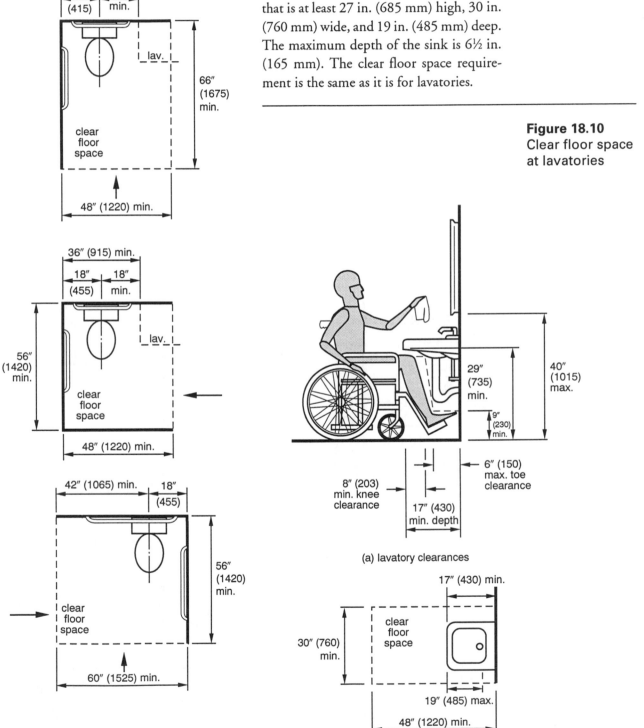

Mirrors must be mounted with the bottom edge of the reflecting surface no higher than 40 in. (1015 mm) from the floor.

Requirements for sinks are similar, except that the 29 in. (735 mm) clearance to the underside of the apron is not required. Instead, a clear space under the sink is required that is at least 27 in. (685 mm) high, 30 in. (760 mm) wide, and 19 in. (485 mm) deep. The maximum depth of the sink is 6½ in. (165 mm). The clear floor space requirement is the same as it is for lavatories.

Figure 18.10
Clear floor space
at lavatories

(a) lavatory clearances

(b) clear floor space at lavatories

Drinking fountains

Requirements for drinking fountains with a front approach are shown in Figures 18.11(a) and 18.11(b). Free-standing or built-in drinking fountains without clear space below must have a clear floor space in front of them at least 30 in. deep by 48 in. wide (760 × 1220 mm), with the long dimension parallel to the fountain, to allow a person in a wheelchair to make a parallel approach.

Bathtubs

Bathtubs must be configured as shown in Figures 18.12(a)–18.12(c). An in-tub seat or a seat at the head of the tub must be provided, as shown in the drawing. Grab bars must be provided, as illustrated in Figures 18.13(a) and 18.13(b). If an enclosure is provided, it cannot obstruct the controls or transfer from wheelchairs onto seats or into the tub. Enclosure tracks cannot be mounted on the rim of the tub.

Figure 18.11
Water fountain
access

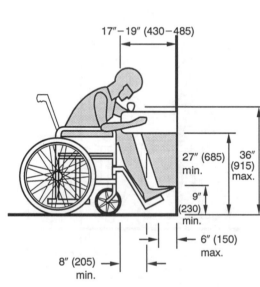

(a) spout height and knee clearance

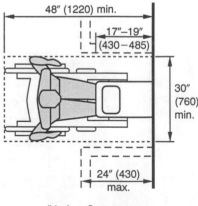

(b) clear floor space

Figure 18.12
Clear floor space
at bathtubs

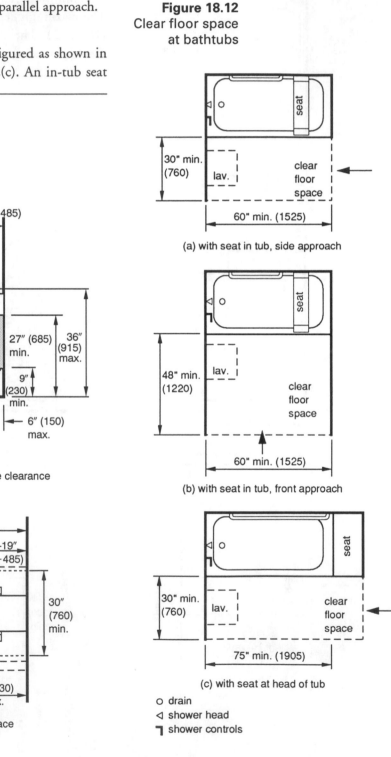

(a) with seat in tub, side approach

(b) with seat in tub, front approach

(c) with seat at head of tub

o drain
◁ shower head
⌐ shower controls

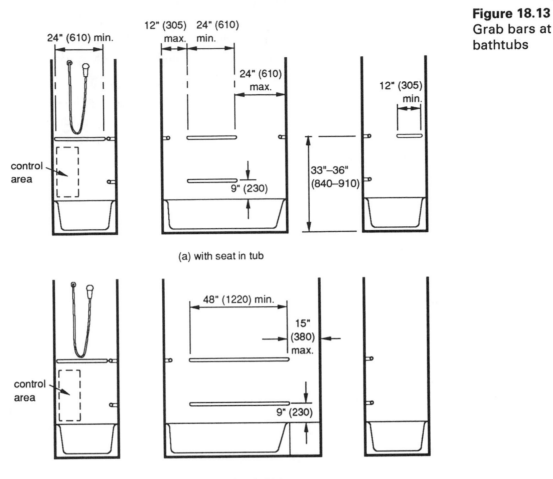

Figure 18.13
Grab bars at bathtubs

(a) with seat in tub

(b) with seat at head of tub

Showers

Shower stalls may be one of two basic types, as shown in Figures 18.14(a) and 18.14(b). When facilities with accessible sleeping rooms or suites are provided, a minimum number of rooms are required that have roll-in showers, as specified in the ADA requirements. A seat is required in the smaller shower stall configuration, while a folding seat is required in the larger configuration if a permanent seat is provided. Grab bars must be provided and mounted from 33 in. to 36 in. (840 to 915 mm) above the floor.

FLOOR SURFACES

Floor surfaces must be stable, firm, and slip-resistant. If there is a change in level, the transition must meet the following requirements. If the change is less than ¼ in.

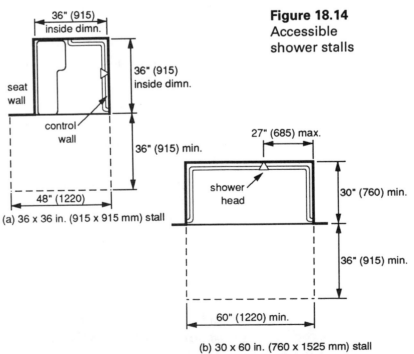

Figure 18.14
Accessible shower stalls

(a) 36 x 36 in. (915 x 915 mm) stall

(b) 30 x 60 in. (760 x 1525 mm) stall

(6 mm), it may be vertical and without edge treatment. If the change is between ¼ in. and ½ in. (6 to 13 mm), it must be beveled with a slope no greater than 1:2 [a ½-in. rise requires 1 in. length (13 mm requires 26 mm), for example]. Changes greater than ½ in. (13 mm) must be accomplished with a ramp that meets the requirements in the next section.

If carpeting is used, it must have a firm cushion or backing, or no cushion. It must also have a level loop, textured loop, level cut-pile, or level cut/uncut pile texture with a maximum pile height of ½ in. (13 mm). It must be securely attached to the floor and have trim along all lengths of exposed edges.

RAMPS AND STAIRS

Ramps are required to provide a smooth transition between changes in elevation for wheelchair-bound persons, as well as those whose mobility is otherwise restricted. In general, the least possible slope should be used. However, in no case can a ramp have a slope greater than 1:12 [1-in. rise for every 12 in. in run (25 mm for 300 mm)]. The maximum rise for any ramp is limited to 30 in. (760 mm). Changes in elevation greater than this require a level landing before the next run of ramp is encountered. In some cases where existing conditions prevent the 1:12 slope, a 1:10 slope is permitted if the maximum rise does not exceed 6 in. (150 mm) and a 1:8 slope is permitted if the maximum rise does not exceed 3 in. (75 mm).

The minimum clear ramp width is 36 in. (915 mm), with landings at least as wide as the widest ramp leading to them. Landing lengths must be a minimum of 60 in. (1525 mm). If ramps change direction at a landing, then the landing must be at least 60 in. square.

Ramps with rises greater than 6 in. (150 mm) or lengths greater than 72 in. (1830 mm) must have handrails on both sides, with the top of the handrail from 34 in. to 38 in. (865 to 965 mm) above the ramp surface. They must extend at least 12 in. (305 mm) beyond the top and bottom of the

ramp segment and have a diameter or width of gripping surface from 1¼ in. to 1½ in. (32 to 38 mm). Handrails are not required for ramps adjacent to seating in assembly areas.

Stairs that are required as a means of egress and stairs between floors not connected by an elevator must be designed according to certain standards specifying the configuration of treads, risers, nosings, and handrails. The maximum riser height is 7 in. (180 mm), and the treads must be a minimum of 11 in. (280 mm) as measured from riser to riser, as shown in Figure 12.9. Open risers are not permitted. The undersides of the nosings must not be abrupt and must conform to one of the styles shown in Figure 12.15.

Stairway handrails must be continuous on both sides of the stairs. The inside handrail on switchback or dogleg stairs must always be continuous as it changes direction. Other handrails must extend beyond the top and bottom riser, as shown in Figure 12.6. The top of the gripping surface must be between 34 in. and 38 in. (865 to 965 mm) above stair nosings. The handrail must have a diameter or width of gripping surface from 1¼ in. to 1½ in. (32 to 38 mm). There must be a clear space between the handrail and the wall of at least 1½ in. (38 mm). Some acceptable handrail configurations are shown in Figure 12.17.

When an exit stairway is part of an accessible route in an unsprinklered building (not including houses), there must be a clear width of 48 in. (1220 mm) between handrails.

PROTRUDING OBJECTS

There are restrictions on the size and configuration of objects and building elements that project into corridors and other walkways because they present hazards for the visually impaired. These restrictions are shown in Figures 18.15(a) and 18.15(b); they are based on the use of a cane by someone with severe vision impairment. Protruding objects with their lower edge less than 27 in. (685 mm) above the floor can be detected, therefore they may project by any amount.

Regardless of the situation, protruding objects cannot reduce the clear width required for an accessible route or maneuvering space. In addition, if vertical clearance of an area adjacent to an accessible route is reduced to less than 80 in. (2030 mm), a guardrail or other barrier must be provided.

DETECTABLE WARNINGS

Detectable warning surfaces are required on walking surfaces in front of stairs, hazardous vehicular areas, and other places where a hazard may exist without a guardrail or other method of warning. The surfaces must consist of exposed aggregate concrete,

Figure 18.15
Requirements for protruding objects

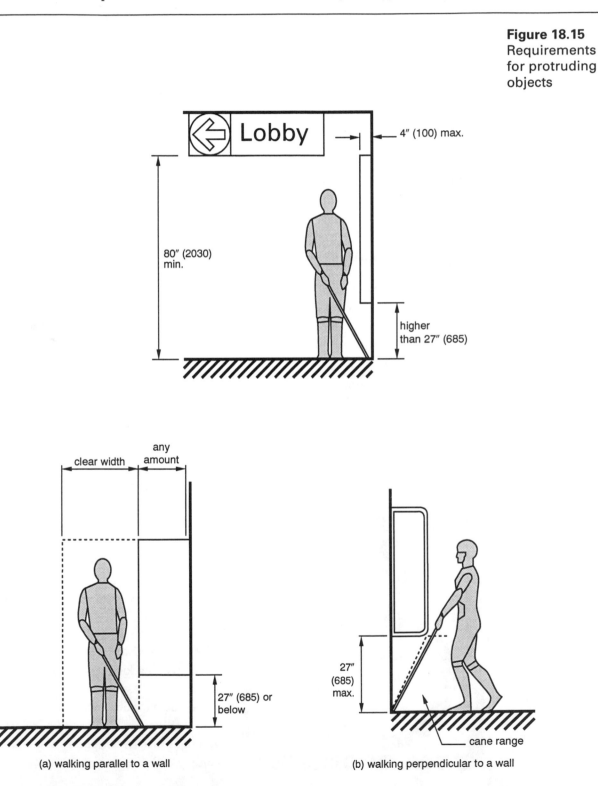

(a) walking parallel to a wall

(b) walking perpendicular to a wall

cushioned surfaces of rubber or plastic, raised strips, or grooves. Such textures must contrast with that of the surrounding surface. At the time of this writing, the detectable warning provisions of ADA have been temporarily suspended pending further study, but local codes or other state and federal regulations should be verified to determine what rules apply to a particular design project.

Door handles are also required to have textured surfaces if they are part of a door that leads to an area that might prove dangerous to a blind person, such as doors to loading platforms, boiler rooms, and stages.

SIGNAGE AND ALARMS

Signage for visually impaired people must be provided that gives emergency information and general circulation directions. Signage is also required for elevators.

Emergency warning systems are required that provide both a visual and audible alarm. Audible alarms must produce a sound that exceeds the prevailing sound level in the room or space by at least 15 dB. Visual alarms must be flashing lights that have a flashing frequency of about one cycle per second.

The Americans with Disabilities Act requires that certain accessible rooms and features be clearly identified with the symbol for accessibility. The ADA also requires that identification, directional, and informational signs meet certain specifications.

Permanent rooms and spaces must be identified with signs having lettering from ⅝ in. to 2 in. (16 to 50 mm) high, raised ¹⁄₃₂ in. (0.8 mm) above the surface of the sign. Lettering must be all upper case, in sans serif or simple serif type accompanied with Grade 2 Braille. If pictograms are used, they must be at least 6 in. (152 mm) high and must be accompanied with the equivalent verbal description placed directly below the pictogram. Signs must be eggshell matte or other nonglare finish with characters and symbols contrasting with their background. Permanent identification signs must be wall-mounted adjacent to the latch side of the door such that a person can approach to within 3 in. (76 mm) of the signage without encountering protruding objects or standing within the door swing. Mounting height to the center line of the sign must be 60 in. (1525 mm). When there is no wall space to the latch side of the door, including double-leaf doors, the sign must be placed on the nearest adjacent wall.

Directional and informational signs must have lettering at least 3 in. (75 mm) high (measured as a capital X) with a width-to-height ratio between 3:5 and 1:1. The stroke width-to-height ratio must be between 1:5 and 1:10. Contrast and finish requirements are the same as for permanent room identification.

The international symbol for accessibility is required on parking spaces, passenger loading zones, accessible entrances, and toilet and bathing facilities when not all are accessible. See Figure 18.16. Building directories and signs that are temporary do not have to comply with the requirements.

Figure 18.16
International symbol for accessibility

TELEPHONES

If public telephones are provided, then there must be at least one telephone per floor conforming to the requirements as shown in Figures 18.17(a) and 18.17(b) and as specified in the ADA requirements. If there are two or more banks of telephones, there must be at least one conforming telephone per bank. When four or more public pay telephones are provided, at least one interior public text telephone is required.

Accessible telephones may be designed for either front or side access. The dimensions required for both of these types are shown in Figures 18.17(a) and 18.17(b). In either case, a clear floor space of at least 30 × 48 in. (760 × 1220 mm) must be provided. The telephones should have push-button controls and telephone directories within reach of a person in a wheelchair.

The international TDD (text telephone) is required to identify the location of those phones and volume control telephones must have a sign depicting a telephone handset with radiating sound waves. In assembly areas, permanently installed assistive listening systems must have the international symbol of access for hearing loss. See Figures 18.18(a) and 18.18(b).

Refer to the ADA requirements and local codes for detailed rules on telephone types and installation requirements.

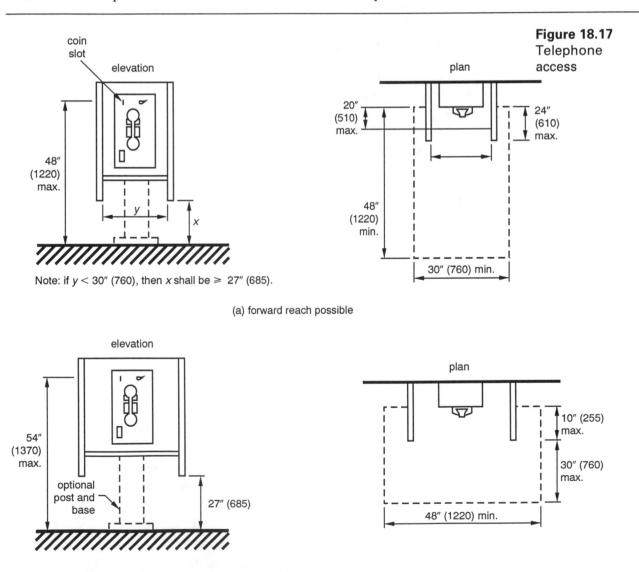

Figure 18.17
Telephone access

Note: if y < 30″ (760), then x shall be ≥ 27″ (685).

(a) forward reach possible

(b) side reach possible

Figure 18.18
International
TDD and hearing
loss symbols

(a) TDD symbol

(b) access for hearing loss symbol

Table 18.1
Minimum
number of
wheelchair
spaces for
assembly
areas

Capacity of seating in assembly areas	Number of required wheelchair locations
4 to 25	1
26 to 50	2
51 to 300	4
301 to 500	6
over 500	6, plus 1 additional space for each total capacity increase of 100

SEATING

If fixed or built-in seating or tables are provided in accessible public- or common-use areas, then at least 5 percent, but not less than one, of the seating areas must be accessible. This includes such facilities as restaurants, nightclubs, and similar spaces. In new construction and when possible in remodeling, the number of tables should be dispersed throughout the facility. If smoking and nonsmoking areas are provided, the required number of seating spaces must be proportioned among the smoking and nonsmoking areas. The area for this type of seating must comply with the dimensions shown in Figure 18.19.

In places of assembly with fixed seating, the minimum number of wheelchair locations is given in Table 18.1. At least 1 percent, but not less than one, of all fixed seats must be aisle seats with no armrests on the aisle side, or with removable or folding armrests on the aisle side. Signs notifying people of the availability of these seats must be posted at the ticket office. The wheelchair areas must be an integral part of the overall seating plan and must be provided so that people have a choice of admission prices and lines of sight comparable to those available for members of the general public. At least one companion seat must be provided next to each wheelchair area. Wheelchair areas must adjoin an accessible route that also serves as a means of emergency egress. Space for wheelchair areas must conform to Figures 18.20(a) and 18.20(b).

When assembly areas are part of a remodeling project and it is not feasible to disperse the seating areas throughout, the accessible seating areas may be clustered. These clustered areas must have provisions for companion seating and must be located on an accessible route that also serves as a means of emergency egress.

Refer to the complete text of the ADA for requirements for audio-amplification systems and assisted listening devices and signage required for assembly areas.

Figure 18.19
Minimum
clearances for
seating and
tables

Figure 18.20
Wheelchair
seating spaces

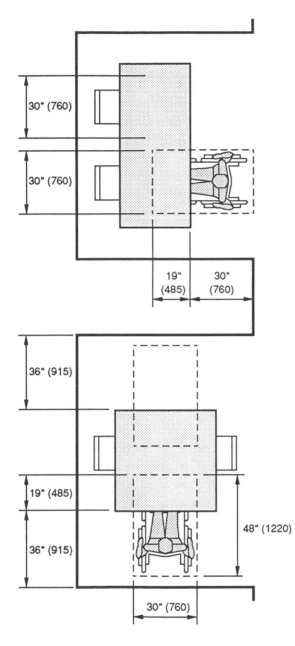

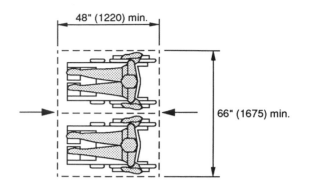

(a) front or rear access

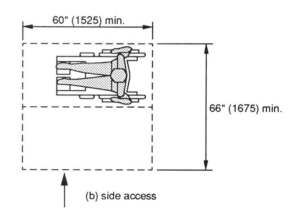

(b) side access

APPENDIX A-1:
SUMMARY OF LATCHSET AND LOCKSET FUNCTIONS

	Types: 1000: Mortise; 2000: Preassembled; 4000: Bored; 5000: Interconnected						Function					
	1000	2000	4000	4000	4000	5000						
	Grades						Operating component		Method of locking		Method of unlocking	
Description	1,2,3	1	1	2	3	1,2,3	Out	In	Outside	Inside	Outside	Inside
Passage	F01	F36	F75	F75	F75	—	K	K	—	—	—	—
Privacy, bedroom, or bath	F02	—	—	—	—	—	K/R	—	—	Turn	Emergency release	Turn
Communicating	F03	—	—	—	—	—	K	K	Turn	Turn	Turn	Turn
Entry	F04	—	—	—	—	—	K	K	Stop or mechanical means		Key	Knob
Classroom	F05	F42	F84	F84	—	—	K	K	Key	—	Key	Knob
Classroom or hospital	F06	—	—	—	—	—	K	K	Key for knob	—	Key	Knob
Holdback	—	F43	F85	—	—	—	K	K	Key for knob (latchbolt may be locked in retracted position)		Key	Knob
Storeroom or closet	F07	F44	F86	F86	F86	—	K/F	K	—	—	Key	Knob
Front door	F08	—	—	—	—	—	K	K	Stop or mechanical means for outside; turn (DB)		Key (BB)	Knob
Apartment, exit, or public toilet	F09	F45	F88	—	—	—	K	K	—	Key	Key	Knob
Apartment corridor	F10	—	—	—	—	—	K	K	Stop or mechanical means for outside; turn (DB)		Key (BB)	Knob

	Types: 1000: Mortise; 2000: Preassembled; 4000: Bored; 5000: Interconnected						Function					
	1000	2000	4000	4000	4000	5000	Operating component		Method of locking		Method of unlocking	
	Grades						Out	In	Outside	Inside	Outside	Inside
Description	1,2,3	1	1	2	3	1,2,3	Out	In	Outside	Inside	Outside	Inside
Dormitory or exit	F11	—	—	—	—	—	K	K	Stop or mechanical means for outside; key (DB)		Key (latchbolt)	Knob (BB)
Dormitory or exit	F12	—	—	—	—	—	K	K	Stop or mechanical means for outside; key (DB) outside; turn (DB) inside		Key (DB)	Knob (BB); turn (DB)
Dormitory or exit	F13	—	—	—	—	—	K	K	Key (DB)	Turn (DB)	Key (DB)	Knob (BB)
Store door	F14	F47	—	—	—	—	K	K	Key (DB)	Key (DB)	Key (DB)	Key (DB)
Hotel guest room	F15	—	—	—	—	—	K/F	K	—	Turn (DB) (restricts all keys except emergency)	Key (latchbolt)	Knob (latchbolt; turn (DB) or knob on both)
Dead lock	F16	—	—	—	—	—	C	C	Key	Key	Key	Key
Dead lock	F17	—	—	—	—	—	C	T	Key	Turn	Key	Turn
Dead lock	F18	—	—	—	—	—	C	—	Key	—	Key	—
Privacy, bedroom, or bath	F19	—	—	—	—	—	K	K	—	Turn (DB)	Emergency release	Knob (BB)
Apartment corridor	F20	—	—	—	—	—	K	K	Stop or mechanical means for outside; key (DB) outside; turn (DB) inside		Key (BB)	Knob (BB)
Room door	F21	—	—	—	—	—	K	K	Key (DB)	Turn (DB)	Key (DB)	Turn (DB)
Privacy, bedroom or bath	F22	F37	F76	—	—	—	K	K	—	PB on all; turn for F22	Emergency release	Knob
Privacy, bedroom or bath	—	—	—	F76	F76	—	K	K	—	LD	Emergency release	Knob or LD in unlocked position
Apartment or store door	F24	—	—	—	—	—	TP	TP	—	Key for outside; key (DB)	Key (latchbolt)	TP
Store door	F25	—	—	—	—	—	TP	TP	Key (DB)	Key (DB)	Key (DB)	Key (DB)
Patio or privacy	—	F38	F77	—	—	—	K	K	—	PB for all; LD for F77	—	Knob
Patio or privacy	—	—	—	F77	F77	—	K	K	—	LD	—	Knob or LD in unlocked position
Communicating	—	F39	F78	F78	—	—	K	K	TB in knob	TB in knob	TB in knob	TB in knob
Entrance or storeroom	—	F40	F81	F81	F81	—	K	K	—	TB for all; LD for F81	Key	Knob
Entry	—	F41	F82	—	—	—	K	K	—	PB for all; LD for F82	Key	Knob

	Types: 1000: Mortise; 2000: Preassembled; 4000: Bored; 5000: Interconnected						Function					
	1000	2000	4000	4000	4000	5000	Operating component		Method of locking		Method of unlocking	
	Grades						Out	In	Outside	Inside	Outside	Inside
Description	1,2,3	1	1	2	3	1,2,3	Out	In	Outside	Inside	Outside	Inside
Entry	—	—	—	F82	F82	—	K	K	—	LD	Key	Knob or LD in unlocked position
Store door	—	F46	F91	—	—	—	K	K	Key (both knobs)	Key (both knobs)	Key (both knobs)	Key (both knobs)
Hotel guest, clubhouse, dormitory, apartment	—	F48	F93	F93	—	—	K/F	K	—	PB for all; LD for F93 (restricts all keys except emergency)	Key	Knob
Communicating (knob and turn simultaneously locked)	—	—	F79	F79	—	—	K	T	TB in knob; LD	—	TB in knob; LD	—
Communicating	—	—	F80	F80	—	—	K	K	Key	Key	Key	Key
Exit (manually operated TB or LD unlocks outside knob)	—	—	F83	F83	F83	—	K	K	—	TB; LD	—	Knob
Asylum, Institutional	—	—	F87	—	—	—	K/F	K/F	—	—	Key	Key
Exit	—	—	F89	F89	F89	—	K/F	K	—	—	—	Knob
Corridor (closing door releases PB or LD)	—	—	F90	F90	—	—	K	K	Key	PB; LD	Key	Knob (releases PB or locking device)
Service station	—	—	F92	F92	—	—	K	K	—	PB; LD	Key (releases PB or LD except when locked)	Knob (releases PB or LD except when locked)
Exit	—	—	F89	F89	F89	—	K/F	K	—	—	—	Knob
Entry	—	—	—	—	—	F95	K	K	Key	Turn	Key	Knob
Entry (key restores inside LD to unlocked position)	—	—	—	—	—	F96	K	K	Key (DB)	LD for outside knob; turn (DB)	Key (latchbolt); key (DB)	Knob (BB)
Entry (manually operated LD unlocks outside knob)	—	—	—	—	—	F97	K	K	Key (DB)	LD for outside knob; turn (DB)	Key (latchbolt); key (DB)	Knob (BB)
Storeroom	—	—	—	—	—	F98	K/R	K	Key (DB)	—	Key (BB)	Knob
Dormitory (closing door releases LD)	—	—	—	—	—	F99	K	K	Key (DB)	LD for outside knob; turn (DB)	Key (LD, DB)	Knob (BB)
Hotel/motel (indicator and shut out feature released by rotating knob)	—	—	—	—	—	F100	K/R	K	Key (DB)	Turn (DB) (restricts all keys except emergency)	Key (BB)	Knob (BB); turn (DB)

	Types: 1000: Mortise; 2000: Preassembled; 4000: Bored; 5000: Interconnected						Function					
	1000	2000	4000	4000	4000	5000	Operating component		Method of locking		Method of unlocking	
	Grades											
Description	1,2,3	1	1	2	3	1,2,3	Out	In	Outside	Inside	Outside	Inside
Hotel/motel	—	—	—	—	—	F101	K/R	K	—	Turn (DB)	Key (latchbolt)	Knob (BB); turn (DB)
Handle set trim	—	—	—	—	—	F102	TP	K	Key (DB)	Turn (DB)	Key (DB)	Knob (BB)
Handle trim set	—	—	—	—	—	F103	TP	K	Key (thumb piece and DB)	LD (thumb piece); turn (DB)	Key (BB)	Knob (BB)
Entry (key restores inside LD to locked position)	—	—	—	—	—	F104	K	K	Key (DB)	LD for outside knob; turn (DB)	Key (BB)	Knob; turn
Entry (manually operated LD unlocks outside knob)	—	—	—	—	—	F105	K	K	Key (DB)	LD for outside knob; turn (DB)	Key (BB)	Knob; turn
Dormitory (closing door releases LD)	—	—	—	—	—	F106	K	K	Key (DB)	LD for outside knob; turn (DB)	Key (LD, BB)	Knob (BB)

K	Knob or lever handle
T	Turn
K/F	Knob, always fixed
K/R	Knob, always rigid or free spinning
TP	Thumb piece
C	Cylinder only
K/DB	Key, deadbolt
DB	Deadbolt
BB	Both bolts
LD	Locking device
PB	Push button
TB	Turn button

Note: See Appendix A-2 for a full description of all lock functions.

Source: Based on information from ANSI A156.2, A156.12, A156.13.

APPENDIX A-2: HARDWARE LOCK FUNCTIONS

SERIES 1000 MORTISE LOCK FUNCTIONS

F01   *Passage or closet latch.* Latch bolt operated by knob from either side at all times.

F02   *Privacy, bedroom, or bath lock.* Latch bolt operated by knob from either side. Dead bolt is operated by turn from inside and by emergency release from outside.

F03   *Communicating lock.* Latch bolt operated by knob from either side. Two dead bolts or split dead bolt are operated independently by turns from both sides. This function should not be used on doors in rooms that have no other entrance.

F04   *Entry lock.* Latch bolt operated by knob from either side except when outside knob is made inoperative by a stop or mechanical means other than key. When outside knob is locked, latch bolt is retracted by key from outside or by rotating inside knob. Auxiliary dead latch.

F05   *Classroom lock.* Latch bolt operated by knob from either side except when outside knob is locked from outside by key. When outside knob is locked, latch bolt is retracted by key from outside or by rotating inside knob. Auxiliary dead latch.

F06   *Classroom or hospital lock.* Latch bolt operated by knob from either side except when outside knob is locked from outside by key. Latch bolt can be locked in a retracted position by key. When outside knob is locked, latch bolt is retracted by key from outside or by rotating inside knob, unless latch bolt has been locked in a retracted position. Auxiliary dead latch.

F07   *Storeroom or closet lock.* Latch bolt operated by key from outside or by rotating inside knob. Outside knob is always inoperative. Auxiliary dead latch.

F08   *Front door lock.* Latch bolt operated by knob from either side except when outside knob is made inoperative by a stop or mechanical means other than key. Dead bolt is operated by turn inside. Key outside operates both bolts.

F09   *Apartment, exit, or public toilet lock.* Latch bolt operated by knob from either side, except when outside knob is locked by key from inside. When outside knob is locked, latch bolt is retracted by key from outside or by rotating inside knob. Auxiliary dead latch.

F10   *Apartment corridor door lock.* Latch bolt operated by knob from either side, except when outside knob is made inoperative by a stop or mechanical means other than key. Dead bolt operated by turn inside. Key outside operates both bolts. Dead bolt has 1-in. (25.4 mm) throw.

F11   *Dormitory or exit lock.* Latch bolt operated by knob from either side except when outside knob is made inoperative by a stop or mechanical means other than key. Dead bolt projected by key from either side. Dead bolt retracted by key from outside. Both bolts retracted by inside knob.

F12   *Dormitory or exit lock.* Latch bolt operated by knob from either side, except when outside knob is made inoperative by a stop or mechanical means other than key. Dead bolt projected by key from outside and by turn from inside. Dead bolt retracted by key from outside and by turn from inside. Rotating inside knob retracts both bolts.

F13   *Dormitory or exit lock.* Latch bolt operated by knob from either side. Dead bolt projected by key from outside and turn from inside. Rotating inside knob retracts both bolts.

F14   *Store door lock.* Latch bolt operated by knob from either side. Dead bolt operated by key from either side.

F15   *Hotel guest lock.* Latch bolt operated by key from outside or by rotating inside knob. Outside knob is always inoperative. Dead bolt projected by turn from inside and all keys except emergency and display key are shut out. Auxiliary dead latch. Indicator button. When so specified, rotating inside knob retracts both bolts.

F16   *Dead lock.* Dead bolt operated by key from either side.

F17   *Dead lock.* Dead bolt operated by key from outside only and by turn from inside.

F18   *Dead lock.* Dead bolt operated by key from outside only.

F19   *Privacy, bedroom, or bath lock.* Latch bolt operated by knob from either side. Dead bolt operated by turn from inside and emergency release from outside. Rotating inside knob retracts both bolts.

F20   *Apartment corridor door lock.* Latch bolt operated by knob from either side, except when outside knob is made inoperative by a stop or mechanical means other than key. Dead bolt operated by key outside or turn inside. Key outside operates both bolts. Dead bolt has 1 in. (25.4 mm) throw. Rotating inside knob retracts both bolts. Latch bolt is deadlocked when outside knob is made inoperative or when the dead bolt is projected. When dead bolt is retracted, knob is unlocked by stop or mechanical means other than key.

F21   *Room door lock.* Latch bolt operated by knob from either side. Dead bolt operated by key from outside and turn from inside.

F22   *Privacy, bedroom, or bath lock.* Latch bolt operated by knob from either side except when outside knob is locked by inside turn or button. Operating inside knob, closing door, or operating outside emergency release unlocks outside knob.

F24   *Apartment or store door handle lock.* Latch bolt operated by thumb piece on both sides, except when outside thumb piece is locked by key from inside. When outside thumb piece is locked, latch bolt is retracted by key outside or by thumb piece inside. Auxiliary dead latch.

F25   *Store door handle lock.* Latch bolt operated by thumb piece from either side. Dead bolt operated by key from either side.

SERIES 2000 PREASSEMBLED LOCK FUNCTIONS

F36   *Passage or closet latch.* Latch bolt operated by knob from either side at all times.

F37   *Privacy, bedroom, or bath lock.* Latch bolt operated by knob from either side. Outside knob is locked by push button inside and unlocked by emergency release outside, rotating inside knob, or closing door.

F38   *Patio or privacy lock.* Latch bolt operated by knob from either side. Outside knob is locked by push button inside and unlocked by rotating inside knob or closing door. Auxiliary dead latch. This lock should not be used in rooms that have no other entrance.

F39   *Communicating lock.* Latch bolt operated by knob from either side. Turn button in either knob locks or unlocks opposite knob. Auxiliary dead latch. This lock should not be used in rooms that have no other entrance.

F40   *Entrance or store room lock.* Latch bolt operated by knob from either side except when outside knob is locked by turn button in inside knob. When outside knob is locked, latch bolt may be retracted by key from outside or by rotating inside knob. Turn button must be manually rotated to unlock outside knob. Auxiliary dead latch.

F41   *Entry lock.* Latch bolt operated by knob from either side except when outside knob is locked by push button in inside knob. When outside knob is locked, operating key from outside or rotating inside knob retracts latch bolt and releases push button. Closing door does not release push button. Auxiliary dead latch.

F42   *Classroom lock.* Latch bolt operated by knob from either side except when outside knob is locked from outside by key. When outside knob is locked, latch bolt may be retracted by key from outside or by rotating inside knob. Auxiliary dead latch.

F43   *Holdback lock.* Latch bolt operated by knob from either side except when outside knob is locked from outside by key. Latch bolt may be locked in a retracted position by key. When outside knob is locked, latch bolt may be retracted by key from outside or by rotating inside knob, unless latch bolt has been locked in a retracted position. Auxiliary dead latch.

F44   *Storeroom or closet lock.* Latch bolt operated by key from outside or by rotating inside knob. Outside knob is always fixed. Auxiliary dead latch.

F45   *Apartment, exit, or public toilet lock.* Latch bolt operated by knob from either side, except when outside knob is locked by key from inside. When outside knob is locked, latch bolt may be retracted by key from outside or by rotating inside knob. Auxiliary dead latch.

F46   *Store door lock.* Latch bolt operated by knob from either side except when both knobs are locked by key from either side. Auxiliary dead latch.

F47   *Store door lock.* Latch bolt operated by knob from either side. Dead bolt operated by key from either side.

F48   *Hotel guest room, clubhouse, dormitory, or apartment entrance lock.* Latch bolt operated by knob from inside at all times. Outside knob always fixed. Latch bolt operated by key from outside except when push button inside is depressed thus shutting out all keys except the emergency key. Depressing push button operates visual indicator in face of cylinder showing the room is occupied. Turning inside knob or closing door releases indicator and shut out feature except when shut out is activated by a special procedure that shuts out all keys except emergency keys. Auxiliary dead latch.

SERIES 4000 BORED LOCK FUNCTIONS

F75   Grades 1, 2, and 3. *Passage or closet latch.* Latch bolt operated by knob from either side at all times.

F76   Grade 1. *Privacy, bedroom, or bath lock.* Latch bolt operated by knob from either side. Outside knob is locked by push button or other locking device inside and unlocked by emergency release outside, rotating inside knob or closing door.

F76   Grades 2 and 3. *Privacy, bedroom, or bath lock.* Latch bolt operated by knob from either side except when outside knob is locked by locking device inside. Locking device shall automatically release when inside knob is turned or be in unlocked position before inside knob can be operated. Emergency release on outside permits outside knob to operate latch bolt.

F77   Grade 1. *Patio or privacy lock.* Dead locking latch bolt operated by knob from either side. Outside knob is locked by push button or other locking device inside and unlocked by rotating inside knob or closing door. This lock should not be used on doors in rooms that have no other entrance.

F77   Grades 2 and 3. *Patio and privacy lock.* Dead locking latch bolt operated by knob from either side except when outside knob is locked by locking device inside. Locking device shall automatically release when inside knob is turned or must be in the unlocked position before the knob can be operated.

F78   Grades 1 and 2. *Communicating lock.* Dead locking latch bolt operated by knob from either side. Turn button in either knob or locking device on either side locks or unlocks opposite knob. This lock should not be used on doors in rooms that have no other entrance.

F79   Grades 1 and 2. *Communicating lock.* Dead locking latch bolt operated from outside by knob and from inside by thumb turn. Turning button in knob or operating locking device locks both knob and thumb turn. Button or other locking device does not release unless manually restored to unlocked position.

F80   Grades 1 and 2. *Communicating lock.* Dead locking latch bolt operated by knob from either side. Turning key in either knob locks or unlocks its own knob independently. This lock should not be used on doors in rooms that have no other entrance.

F81   Grades 1, 2, and 3. *Entrance or store room lock.* Dead locking latch bolt operated by knob from either side except when outside knob is locked by turn button or other locking device inside. When outside knob is locked, latch bolt is operated by key in outside knob or by rotating inside knob. Turn button or other locking device must be manually operated to unlock outside knob.

F82   Grade 1. *Entry lock.* Dead locking latch bolt operated by knob from either side except when outside knob is locked by push button or other locking device on inside. When outside knob is locked, operating key in outside knob or rotating inside knob unlocks push button or other locking device and retracts latch bolt. Closing door does not release push button or other locking device.

F82   Grades 2 and 3. *Entry lock.* Dead locking latch bolt operated by knob from either side except when outside knob is locked by locking device on inside. When outside knob is locked, operating key in outside knob unlocks locking device. Locking device automatically releases when inside knob is turned or is in the unlocked position before the inside knob can be operated.

F83   Grades 1, 2, and 3. *Exit lock.* Dead locking latch bolt operated by knob from either side except when outside knob is locked by turn button or other locking device in inside. Turn button or other locking device manually operates to unlock outside knob. Rotating inside knob always operates latch bolt.

F84   Grades 1 and 2. *Classroom lock.* Dead locking latch bolt operated by knob from either side except when outside knob is locked from outside by key. When outside knob is locked, latch bolt is operated by key in outside knob or by rotating inside knob.

F85   Grade 1. *Holdback lock.* Dead locking latch bolt operated by knob from either side except when outside knob is locked from outside by key. Latch bolt may be locked in a retracted position by key. When outside knob is locked, latch bolt is operated by key in outside knob or by rotating inside knob unless latch bolt has been locked in a retracted position.

F86   Grades 1, 2, and 3. *Store room or closet lock.* Dead locking latch bolt operated by key in outside knob or by rotating inside knob. Outside knob is always fixed.

F87   Grade 1. *Utility, asylum, or institutional lock.* Dead locking latch bolt operated by key in knob from either side. Both knobs are always fixed.

F88   Grade 1. *Apartment, exit, or public toilet lock.* Dead locking latch bolt operated by knob from either side except when outside knob is locked by key room inside. When outside knob is locked, latch bolt may be retracted by key in outside knob or by rotating inside knob.

F89   Grades 1, 2, and 3. *Exit latch.* Dead locking latch bolt retracted by knob from inside at all times. Outside knob is always fixed.

F90   Grades 1 and 2. *Corridor lock.* Dead locking latch bolt operated by knob from either side except when outside knob is locked by key in outside knob or by push button or other locking device in inside. Key in outside knob locks or unlocks outside knob. Rotating inside knob releases push button or other locking device placed in a locked position. Closing door releases push button or other inside locking device. Inside knob always operates.

F91   Grade 1. *Store door lock.* Dead locking latch bolt operated by knob from either side except when both knobs are locked by key in knob from either side.

F92   Grades 1 and 2. *Service station lock.* Dead locking latch bolt operated by knob from either side except when outside knob is locked by push button or other locking device inside. Key outside, rotating inside knob, or closing door releases push button or other locking device unlocking outside knob except when slotted push button or other locking device is in a locked position. Inside knob always operates.

F93   Grades 1 and 2. *Hotel guest room, clubhouse, dormitory, or apartment entrance lock.* Dead locking latch bolt operated by knob from inside at all times. Outside knob always fixed or inoperable. Latch bolt operated by key from outside except when push button or other locking device inside is operated thus shutting out all keys except emergency key. Operating push button or other locking device operates visual indicator outside showing room is occupied. Turning inside knob or closing door releases indicator and shut out feature except when shut out is activated by a special procedure which shuts out all keys except emergency or display key.

SERIES 5000 INTERCONNECTED FUNCTIONS

F95   *Entry lock.* Latch bolt operated by knob from either side. Rotating thumbturn from inside or key from outside will extend dead bolt to locked position. Both dead bolt and latch bolt are retracted to the unlocked position by rotating inside knob.

F96   *Entry lock.* Dead locking latch bolt is operated by knob on either side except when outside knob is made rigid or free spinning by locking device inside. When outside knob is locked, dead locking latch bolt is operated by key outside. Inside locking device must be manually operated to unlock outside knob. Rotating thumbturn from inside or key from outside extends the dead bolt to the locked position. Both dead bolt and dead locking latch bolt are retracted by rotating the inside knob. Closing the door does not release locking device inside.

F97   *Entry lock.* Dead locking latch bolt is operated by knob from either side except when outside knob is made rigid or free spinning by locking device inside. When outside knob is locked, dead locking latch bolt is operated by key outside. Inside locking device must be manually operated to unlock outside knob. Rotating thumbturn from the inside or key from the outside extends the dead bolt to the locked position. Both dead bolt and dead locking latch bolt are retracted by rotating the inside knob. Closing the door does not release locking device inside.

F98   *Storeroom lock.* Dead locking latch bolt is operated by key outside or rotating inside knob. Outside knob is always rigid or free spinning. Key outside projects or retracts dead bolt. Rotating inside knob or key outside retracts both the dead bolt and the dead locking latch bolt.

F99   *Dormitory lock.* Dead locking latch bolt is operated by knob from either side except when outside knob is made rigid or free spinning by locking device inside. When outside knob is locked, dead locking latch bolt is operated by key outside restoring inside locking device to the unlocked position. Rotating thumbturn from inside or key from outside extends dead bolt to the locked position. Both dead bolt and dead locking latch bolt are retracted by rotating the inside knob. Closing door releases locking device inside.

F100   *Hotel/motel lock.* Dead locking latch bolt is operated by key outside or rotating inside knob. Outside knob is always rigid or free spinning. Rotating thumbturn from the inside or key from outside extends the dead bolt to the locked position. Both dead bolt and dead locking latch bolt are retracted by key outside or by rotating the inside knob. A visual occupancy indicator is operated from the inside and shuts out all keys except an emergency key. Rotating the inside knob releases the indicator and shut out feature unless fixed in a shut out position by a special tool.

F101   *Hotel/motel lock.* Dead locking latch bolt is operated by key outside or rotating inside knob. Outside knob is always rigid or free spinning. Rotating thumbturn from inside extends dead bolt to the locked position and indicates occupancy on the outside. Both dead bolt and dead locking latch bolt are retracted by rotating the inside knob. The occupancy indicator is released from the outside with a special key.

F102   *Handle set trim.* Latch bolt is retracted by thumbpiece on the outside and knob on inside. Rotating thumbturn from inside or key from outside extends the dead bolt to locked position. Both dead bolt and latch bolt are retracted to the unlocked position by rotating inside knob.

F103   *Handle trim set.* Dead locking latch bolt is operated by thumbpiece outside or knob inside except when outside thumbpiece is locked or made inoperative by locking device inside or by key outside. When outside thumbpiece is locked or inoperative, dead locking latch bolt and dead bolt are retracted by key or key and thumbpiece operation outside by rotating inside knob. Rotating thumbpiece inside or key outside extends dead bolt to locked position. Thumbpiece outside remains locked or inoperative until unlocked by locking device inside or by key outside.

F104   *Entry lock.* Dead locking latch bolt is operated by knob from either side except when outside knob is made rigid or free spinning by locking device inside. When outside knob is locked, dead locking latch bolt is operated by key outside, restoring inside locking device to unlocked position. Rotating thumbturn from inside or key from outside extends the dead bolt to the locked position. Both dead bolt and dead locking latch bolt retract by rotating inside knob, key outside and thumbturn inside. Closing door does not release locking device inside.

F105   *Entry lock.* Dead locking latch bolt is operated by knob from either side except when outside knob is made rigid or free spinning by locking device inside. When outside knob is locked, dead locking latch bolt is operated by key outside. Inside locking device must be manually operated to unlock outside knob. Rotating thumbturn from inside or key from outside extends the dead bolt to the locked position. Both dead bolt and dead locking latch bolt are retracted by rotating inside knob, key outside, and thumbturn inside. Closing door does not release locking device inside.

F106   *Dormitory lock.* Dead locking latch bolt is operated by knob from either side except when outside knob is made rigid or free spinning by locking device inside. When outside knob is locked, dead locking latch bolt is operated by key outside, restoring inside locking device to unlocked position. Rotating thumbturn from inside or key from outside extends dead bolt to the locked position. Both dead bolt and dead locking latch bolt are retracted by rotating inside knob, key outside, and thumbturn inside. Closing door releases locking device inside.

APPENDIX B: ABBREVIATIONS FOR INTERIOR DESIGN DRAWINGS

Above finished floor	AFF	Alternate	ALT
Above raised floor	ARF	Alternating current	AC
Above suspended		Aluminum	AL
ceiling	ASC	American National	
Abrasive	ABRSV	Standards Institute	ANSI
Access door	AD	American wire gage	AWG
Access floor	AF	Ampere	AMP
Access panel	AP	Anchor	AHR
Acoustical	ACOUS	Anchor bolt	AB
Acoustical insulation	ACOUS INSUL	Anodized	ANOD
Acoustical panel	ACOUS PNL	Antenna	ANT
Acoustical plaster	ACOUS PLAS	Apartment	APT
Acoustical plaster		Approved	APPD
ceiling	APC	Approximately	APPROX
Acoustical tile	ACOUS TILE	Architect	ARCH
Acoustical wall		Architect-Engineer	A-E
treatment	ACWT	Architectural terra cotta	ATC
Adhesive	ADH	Area	A
Adjacent	ADJ	Area drain	AD
Adjustable	ADJ	Assembly	ASSY
Aggregate	AGGR	Association	ASSN
Air conditioning	AC	Asymmetrical	ASYM
Air conditioning unit	ACU	Attachment	ATCH
Air vent	AV	Audiovisual	AV
Alarm	ALM	Automatic door closer	ADC
Alarm annunciator		Automatic door seal	ADS
panel	AAP	Automatic sprinkler	AS
Alteration	ALTRN	Average	AVG

Back to back	B/B	Ceiling height	CLG HT
Balcony	BALC	Ceiling register	CLG REG
Base line	BL	Center line	CL
Base plate	BP	Center to center	C TO C
Baseboard	BB	Centimeter	CM
Baseboard radiation	BBRR	Ceramic	CER
Basement	BSMT	Ceramic tile	CER TILE
Beam	BM	Chalkboard	CH BD
Bearing	BRG	Chamfer	CHAM
Bedroom	BR	Change order	CO
Below	BLW	Channel	CHAN
Below ceiling	BLW CLG	Chrome plated	CHR PL
Below finish floor	BLW FFLR	Circle	CIR
Bench mark	BM	Circuit	CKT
Between	BETW	Circuit breaker	CKT BKR
Bevel	BEV	Circular	CIRC
Beveled plate glass	BPG	Classroom	CLRM
Bituminous	BITUM	Cleanout	CO
Black iron	BI	Clear	CLR
Block	BLK	Closed circuit	
Blocking	BLKG	television	CCTV
Board	BD	Closet	CLO
Bookshelves	BK SH	Cold water	CW
Both faces	BF	Cold-rolled	CR
Both sides	BS	Cold-rolled steel	CRS
Both ways	BW	Column	COL
Bottom	BOT	Column line	CLL
Bottom face	BF	Combination towel	
Bracing	BRCG	dispenser &	
Bracket	BRKT	receptacle	CTD&R
Brass	BRS	Common	COM
Brick	BRK	Communication	COMM
Bronze	BRZ	Compartment	COMPT
Brown and Sharpe gage	B&S	Compressible	CPRS
Building	BLDG	Compressor	CPRSR
Bulletin board	BB	Concrete masonry unit	CMU
Burglar alarm	BA	Concrete	CONC
		Concrete floor	CONC FL
Cabinet	CAB	Conference	CONF
Cabinet heater	CAB H	Connection	CONN
Cable television	CTV	Construction	CONSTR
Calking	CLKG	Construction joint	CJ
Canvas	CANV	Continuous	CONT
Carpet	CARP	Contract limit line	CLL
Casework	CSWK	Contractor	CONTR
Casing	CSG	Control joint	CLJ
Casing bead	CSB	Convector	CONV
Cast iron	CI	Cool white	CW
Cast stone	CS	Cool white delux	CWX
Ceiling	CLG	Coordinate	COORD
Ceiling diffuser	CLG DIFF	Corner	CNR
Ceiling grille	CG	Corner bead	COR BD

Corner guard	CG	Electrical	ELEC
Corridor	CORR	Electrical water cooler	EWC
Countersunk	CSK	Electrical water heater	EWH
Cover	COV	Elevation	EL
Cover plate	COV PL	Elevator	ELEV
Cross arm	X ARM	Enamel	ENAM
Cubicle	CUB	Enclosure	ENCL
Cylinder	CYL	Entrance	ENTR
Cylinder lock	CYL L	Equal	EQ
		Equally spaced	EQL SP
Damper	DMPR	Equipment	EQUIP
Datum	DAT	Escalator	ESCAL
Degree	DEG	Exhaust	EXH
Deluxe white	DW	Exhaust air	EXH A
Demolition	DEMO	Exhaust duct	EXH DT
Department	DEPT	Exhaust fan	EXH FN
Detail	DET	Exhaust grille	EXH GR
Detector	DET	Exhaust hood	EXH HD
Diagonal	DIAG	Existing	EXST
Diameter	DIAM	Expansion bolt	EXP BT
Diffuser	DIFF	Expansion joint	EXP JT
Dimension	DIM	Extrusion	EXTR
Dimmer control panel	DCP		
Dining room	DR	Fabric wallcovering	FWC
Dishwasher	DW	Fabricate	FAB
Distribution panel	DISTR PNL	Face of concrete	FOC
Ditto	DO	Face of finish	FOF
Division	DIV	Face of masonry	FOM
Domestic water heater	DWH	Face of studs	FOS
Door closer	DCL	Face to face	F/F
Door frame	DFR	Far side	FS
Door louver	DLV	Fiberglass	FGL
Door stop	DST	Finish	FIN
Double	DBL	Finish floor	FIN FL
Double acting	DBL ACT	Fire damper	FDMPR
Double-acting door	DAD	Fire extinguisher	FEXT
Double glazing	DBL GLZ	Fire extinguisher	
Down	DN	cabinet	FEC
Downspout	DS	Fire hose cabinet	FHC
Drain waste & vent	DWV	Fireplace	FPL
Drawer	DWR	Fireproofing	FPRF
Drawing	DWG	Fixture	FXTR
Drinking fountain	DF	Float glass	FLT GL
Dumbwaiter	DWTR	Floor	FL
Duplex	DX	Floor drain	FD
Duplicate	DUP	Floor finish	FLR FIN
Dutch door	DD	Floor register	FLR REG
		Flooring	FLG
Each face	EF	Fluorescent	FLUOR
Each way	EW	Folding	FLDG
Eased edges	EE	Framed mirror	FR MIR
East	E	From floor above	FFA
Eccentric	ECC		

From floor below	FFB	Hollow metal	HM
Front	FRT	Hollow metal door	HMD
Furnace	FUR	Hollow metal frame	HMF
Furniture	FURN	Horizontal	HORIZ
Furring	FURR	Hot water	HW
Future	FUT		
		Incandescent	INCAND
Gage	GA	Inside diameter	ID
Galvanized	GALV	Inside face	IF
Galvanized iron	GI	Instantaneous water	
Galvanized steel	GALVS	heater	IWH
Garage	GAR	Insulate	INS
Gas	G	Insulated panel	INSUL PNL
General	GENL	Insulation	INSUL
General contractor	GC	Intercommunication	INTERCOM
Glass	GL	Interior	INTR
Glass block	GLB		
Glaze, Glazing	GLZ	Janitor	JAN
Glazed	GLZD	Janitor's closet	JC
Glazed concrete		Joint	JT
masonry unit	GLZ CMU	Joist	JST
Glued laminated	GLU LAM	Junction box	JB
Grab bar	GB		
Grade	GR	Kiln–dried	KD
Grille	GRL	Kilogram	KG
Ground	GND	Kilovolt	KV
Ground fault interrupter	GFI	Kilovolt ampere	KVA
Grout	GT	Kitchen	KIT
Guardrail	GDR	Knock down	KD
Gypsum	GYP	Knockout	KO
Gypsum board	GYP BD		
Gypsum plaster	GYP PLAS	Laboratory	LAB
		Ladder	LAD
Hand dryer	HD	Lamination	LAM
Handrail	HNDRL	Landing	LDG
Hanger	HGR	Large	LRG
Hardboard	HDBD	Lateral	LATL
Hardware	HDW	Lath and plaster	L&P
Hardwood	HDWD	Laundry	LAU
Head	HD	Lavatory	LAV
Heater	HTR	Left	L
Heating	HTG	Left hand	LH
Height	HGT	Left hand reverse	LHR
Hertz	HZ	Length overall	LOA
Hexagonal	HEX	Library	LIB
High	H	Light	LT
High-intensity		Light pole	LP
discharge	HID	Lighting	LTG
High output	HO	Lightproof	LP
Hold-open	HO	Lightweight	LT WT
Hollow concrete		Linear	LIN
masonry unit	HCMU	Linear ceiling diffuser	LCD
Hollow core	HC	Linear diffuser	LD

Linear foot	LF	Nominal	NOM
Lintel	LNTL	North	N
Living room	LR	Not applicable	NA
Load bearing	LD BRG	Not in contract	NIC
Locker	LKR	Not to scale	NTS
Locker room	LKR RM	Number	NO
Long leg horizontal	LLH		
Long leg vertical	LLV	Obscure	OBS
Louver	LVR	Obscure glass	OGL
Low voltage	LV	Obscure wire glass	OWGL
Lumber	LBR	Office	OFF
		On center	OC
Manfacturing	MFG	Opening	OPNG
Marble	MARB	Opposite	OPP
Mark	MK	Out to out	O/O
Masonry	MAS	Outside diameter	OD
Masonry opening	MO	Outside dimension	OD
Master bedroom	MBR	Outside face	OF
Material	MATL	Outside radius	OR
Maximum	MAX	Overall	OA
Mechanical	MECH	Overhead	OVHD
Medicine cabinet	MC	Owner furnished-	
Medium density overlay	MDO	contractor installed	OFCI
Metal	MET	Owner furnished-	
Metal lath	ML	owner installed	OFOI
Meter	M		
Mezzanine	MEZZ	Paint	PNT
Millwork	MLWK	Painted	PTD
Minimum	MIN	Pair	PR
Minute	MIN	Panel	PNL
Mirror	MIR	Panic bar	PB
Miscellaneous	MISC	Paper cup dispenser	PCD
Molding	MLDG	Paper towel dispenser	PTD
Mortar	MTR	Paper towel receptacle	PTR
Mounted	MTD	Parallel	PAR
Mounting	MTG	Particleboard	PBD
Movable	MVBL	Partition	PTN
Mullion	MULL	Passenger	PASS
Multiple	MULT	Perforated	PERF
		Perimeter	PERIM
Nameplate	NPL	Permanent	PERM
National Electric Code	NEC	Perpendicular	PERP
National Fire Protection		Plaster	PLAS
Association	NFPA	Plastic laminate	PLAM
Natural	NAT	Plate	PL
Near face	NF	Platform	PLAT
Near side	NS	Plumbing	PLMB
Negative	NEG	Plywood	PLYWD
No paint	NP	Polished	POL
Noise criterion	NC	Precast	PRCST
Noise reduction	NR	Prefabricated	PREFAB
Noise reduction		Prefinished	PREFIN
coefficient	NRC	Property line	PL

Public address	PA	Speaker	SPKR
Pull box	PB	Specification	SPEC
Pull chain	PC	Sprinkler	SPKLR
Purse shelf	PSH	Square	SQ
Push button	PB	Square foot	SQ FT
		Square inch	SQ IN
Quarry tile	QT	Square kilometer	SQ KM
Quarter	QTR	Square meter	SQ M
		Square yard	SQ YD
Rabbet	RAB	Stainless steel	SST
Radiator	RAD	Steel	STL
Radius	R	Steel plate	STL PL
Receptacle	RCPT	Storage	STOR
Recessed	REC	Supply air	SA
Rectangular	RECT	Supply-air grille	SAG
Reference	REF	Supply diffuser	SD
Refrigerator	REFR	Surface	SURF
Register	REG	Surfaced four sides	S4S
Remote control	RC	Surfaced two sides	S2S
Removable	REM	Suspended	SUSP
Required	REQD	Suspended ceiling	SUSP CLG
Resilient	RESIL	Switch	SW
Return	RET	Symmetrical	SYMM
Right hand	RH	System	SYS
Right hand reverse	RHR		
Riser	R	Tackboard	TK BD
Room	RM	Tee	T
Rough opening	RO	Telephone	TEL
Round	RND	Television	TV
		Temperature	TEMP
Sanitary	SAN	Tempered glass	TMPD GL
Schedule	SCHED	Temporary	TEMP
Screen	SCRN	Terra cotta	TC
Section	SECT	Terrazzo	TER
Service sink	SSK	Thermostat	T
Sheating	SHTHG	Thickness	THK
Sheet	SH	Thousand	M
Sheet metal	SM	Threshold	THRES
Shelving	SHV	To floor above	TFA
Shower	SHR	To floor below	TFB
Similar	SIM	Toilet paper holder	TPH
Single	SGL	Tolerance	TOL
Sink	SK	Tongue and groove	T&G
Sliding	SL	Top and bottom	T&B
Sliding door	SLD	Top of beam	TB
Sliding glass door	SGD	Top of concrete	TC
Slip joint	SJ	Top of finished floor	TFF
Soap dispenser	SD	Top of joist	TJ
Solid core	SC	Top of pavement	TP
Sound transmission		Top of slab	TSL
class	STC	Top of steel	TST
South	S	Top of wall	TW
Space	SP		

Total	TOT	Vinyl tile	VT
Towel bar	TB	Vinyl wallcovering	VWC
Towel dispenser	TD	Vitreous	VIT
Towel dispenser/		Volt	V
receptacle	TDR	Wainscot	WSCT
Tread	T	Wall to wall	W/W
Typical	TYP	Warm white	WW
		Warm white deluxe	WWX
Underwriters		Waste	W
Laboratories, Inc.	UL	Waste receptacle	WR
Unfinished	UNFIN	Water closet	WC
United States gage	USG	Water heater	WH
Unless otherwise noted	UON	Water resistant	WR
Utility	UTIL	Waterproof	WP
		Watt	W
Variable air volume	VAV	Weather stripping	WS
Veneer	VNR	Weight	WT
Vent pipe	VP	Welded	WLD
Vertical	VERT	West	W
Vertical grain	VG	Width	WD
Very high output	VHO	Wire glass	WGL
Vestibule	VEST	With	W/
Video display		Without	W/O
terminal	VDT	Wood	WD
Vinyl	VIN	Working point	WP
Vinyl base	VB		

READING LIST

CHAPTER 1

Gypsum Association. *Fire Resistance Design Manual.* Evanston, IL: Gyspum Association, 1997.

Gypsum Association. *Levels of Gypsum Board Finish.* Evanston, IL: Gyspum Association, 1996.

Gorman, J.R., Sam Jaffe, Walter F. Pruter, and James J. Rose. *Plaster and Drywall Systems Manual, 3rd. ed.* New York, NY: McGraw-Hill, 1988.

United States Gypsum. *Gypsum Construction Handbook.* Chicago, IL: United States Gypsum Company, 1992.

CHAPTER 2

American Society for Testing and Materials. ASTM C-635, *Metal Suspension Systems for Acoustical Tile and Lay-in Panel Systems.* Philadelphia, PA: American Society for Testing and Materials, 1991.

American Society for Testing and Materials. ASTM C-636, *Installation of Metal Ceiling Suspension Systems for Acoustical Tile and Lay-in Panels.* Philadelphia, PA: American Society for Testing and Materials, 1991.

American Society for Testing and Materials. ASTM E-580, *Recommended Practice for Application of Ceiling Suspension Systems for Acoustical Tile and Lay-in Panels in Areas Requiring Seismic Restraint.* Philadelphia, PA: American Society for Testing and Materials, 1991.

Ceilings & Interior Systems Construction Association. *Guidelines for Seismic Restraint Direct-hung Suspended Ceiling Assemblies, Seismic Zones 3 & 4.* Skokie, IL: Ceilings & Interior Systems Construction Association, 1991.

Ceilings & Interior Systems Construction Association. *Recommendations for Direct-hung Acoustical Tile and Lay-in Panel Ceilings, Seismic Zones 0–2.* Skokie, IL: Ceilings & Interior Systems Construction Association, 1991.

CHAPTER 3

National Wood Window and Door Association. *Architectural Wood Flush Doors*. Des Plaines, IL: National Wood Window and Door Association, 1993.

National Wood Window and Door Association. *Wood Stile and Rail Doors*. Des Plaines, IL: National Wood Window and Door Association, 1991.

Steel Door Institute. SDI 108, *Recommended Selection and Usage Guide for Standard Steel Doors and Frames*. Cleveland, OH: Steel Door Institute, 1990.

Steel Door Institute. ANSI/SDI 100, *Recommended Specifications, Standard Steel Doors and Frames*. Cleveland, OH: Steel Door Institute, 1991.

Steel Door Institute. SDI 111, *Recommended Standard Details for Steel Doors and Frames*. Cleveland, OH: Steel Door Institute, 1991.

CHAPTER 4

Door and Hardware Institute. *Basic Architectural Hardware*. Chantilly, VA: Door and Hardware Institute, 1985.

Steel Door Institute. *Hardware for Standard Steel Doors and Frames*. Cleveland, OH: Steel Door Institute, 1988.

CHAPTER 5

Amstock, Joseph S. *Handbook of Glass in Construction*. New York: McGraw-Hill, 1997.

Flat Glass Marketing Association (FGMA). *Glazing Manual*. Topeka, KA: Flat Glass Marketing Association, 1990.

CHAPTER 6

Architectural Woodwork Institute. *Architectural Woodwork Quality Standards, Guide Specifications and Quality Certification Program, 7th ed.* Arlington, VA: The Architectural Woodwork Institute, 1997.

Architectural Woodwork Institute. *Fire Code Summary.* Arlington, VA: The Architectural Woodwork Institute, 1992.

Schneidwind, Arno P., ed. *Concise Encyclopedia of Wood and Wood Based Materials*. New York: Pergamon Press, 1989.

CHAPTER 7

American Iron and Steel Institute. *Finishes for Stainless Steel.* Washington, DC: Committee of Stainless Steel Producers, American Iron and Steel Institute, 1983.

Copper Development Association. *Copper Brass Bronze Design Handbook*. Greenwich, CT: Copper Development Association, n.d.

Zahner, L. William. *Architectural Metals*. New York: John Wiley & Sons, 1995.

CHAPTER 8

Corbella, Lucio Enrico, and Renato Calenzani. *The Architect's Handbook of Marble, Granite and Stone*. New York: Van Nostrand Reinhold, 1989.

National Terrazzo & Mosaic Association. *Handbook.* Des Plaines, IL: The National Terrazzo & Mosaic Association, n.d.

Tile Council of America. *Handbook for Ceramic Tile Installation.* Princeton, NJ: Tile Council of America, 1996.

CHAPTER 10

Amrhein, James E., and Michael W. Merrigan. *Marble and Stone Slab Veneer.* Los Angeles, CA: Masonry Institute of America, 1986.

Banov, Abel. *Paints & Coatings Handbook for Contractors, Architects, Builders and Engineers.* Farmington, MI: Structures Publishing Company, 1978.

Corbella, Lucio Enrico, and Renato Calenzani. *The Architect's Handbook of Marble, Granite and Stone.* New York: Van Nostrand Reinhold, 1989.

Jackman, Dianne R., and Mary K. Dixon. *The Guide to Textiles for Interior Designers, 2nd ed.* Winnipeg: Peguis Publishers, 1990.

Marble Instiue of America. *Design Manual IV.* Farmington, MI: Marble Institute of America, 1990.

Morgans, W. M. *Outlines of Paint Technology, Vol 1. Materials.* New York: John Wiley, 1984.

Tile Council of America. *Handbook for Ceramic Tile Installation.* Princeton, NJ: Tile Council of America, 1996.

Weismantel, Guy E., ed. *Paint Handbook.* New York: McGraw-Hill, 1981.

CHAPTER 11

Cremer, Lothar. *Principles and Applications of Room Acoustics.* New York: Applied Science, 1982.

Egan, M. David. *Architectural Acoustics.* New York: McGraw-Hill, 1988.

Jones, Robert St. Claire. *Noise and Vibration Control in Buildings.* New York: McGraw-Hill, 1984.

Templeton, Duncan, and David Saunders. *Acoustic Design.* London: Architectural Press, 1987.

CHAPTER 12

Templer, John. *The Staircase, Studies of Hazards, Falls, and Safer Design.* Cambridge, MA: The MIT Press, 1992.

CHAPTER 13

Davies, Alan. *Signage.* New York: Roof, 1987.

McLendon, Charles B., and Mick Blackistone. *Signage: Graphic Communications in the Built World.* New York: McGraw-Hill, 1982.

Arthur, Paul, and Romedi Passini. *Wayfinding: People, Signs, and Architecture.* New York: McGraw-Hill, 1992.

CHAPTER 14

Fennelly, Lawrence J. *Effective Physical Security: Design, Equipment, and Operations.* Boston, MA: Butterworth-Heinmann, 1992.

Gigliotti, Richard, and Ronald Jason. *Security Design for Maximum Protection.* Stoneham, MA: Butterworth, 1984.

Cherry, Don T. *Total Facility Control.* Stoneham, MA: Butterworth, 1986.

CHAPTER 15

Wadsworth, Raymond H. *Basics of Audio and Visual Systems Design.* Indianapolis, IN: Howard W. Sams, 1983.

Simpson, Robert S. *Effective Audio-Visual, A User's Handbook, 2nd ed.* Oxford, England: Focal Press, 1992.

CHAPTER 16

Ambrose, James. *Building Construction: Interior Systems.* New York: Van Nostrand Reinhold, 1991.

Babbitt, Harold E. *Plumbing.* New York: McGraw-Hill, 1986.

Flynn, John E., Arthur W. Segil, Jack A. Kremers, and Gary R. Steffy. *Architectural Interior Systems, 3rd ed.* New York: Van Nostrand Reinhold, 1992.

Gordon, Gary, and James L. Nuckolls. *Interior Lighting for Environmental Designers, 3rd ed.* New York: John Wiley, 1992.

Smith, Fran Kellogg, and Fred J. Bertolone. *Bringing Interiors to Light: The Principles and Practices of Lighting Design for Interior Designers.* New York: Whitney Library of Design, 1986.

Sorcar, Prafulla C. *Architectural Lighting for Commercial Interiors.* New York: John Wiley, 1987.

Stein, Benjamin M., and Frederick H. Reynolds. *Mechanical and Electrical Equipment for Buildings, 8th ed.* New York: John Wiley, 1991.

CHAPTER 17

Building Officials and Code Administrators International, Inc. *National Building Code.* Country Club Hills, IL: Building Officials and Code Administrators International, Inc., 1996.

Egan, M. David. *Concepts in Building Fire Safety.* Malabar, FL: Robert Krieger, 1986.

Harmon, Sharon Koomen. *The Codes Guidebook for Interiors.* New York: John Wiley & Sons, 1994.

International Conference of Building Officials. *Uniform Building Code.* Whittier, CA: International Conference of Building Officials, 1997.

Liebing, Ralph W. *Construction Regulations Handbook.* New York: John Wiley, 1987.

National Association of Home Builders of the United States. *Understanding Building Codes and Standards in the United States.* Washington, DC: National Association of Home Builders of the United States, 1986.

Southern Building Code Congress International, Inc. *Standard Building Code.* Birmingham, AL: Southern Building Code Congress International, Inc., 1997.

CHAPTER 18

American National Standards Institute. ANSI 117.1, *Specifications for Making Buildings and Facilities Accessible to and Usable by Physically Handicapped People.* New York: American National Standards Institute, 1986.

Department of Justice, Office of the Attorney General. *Nondiscrimination on the Basis of Disability by Public Accommodations and in Commercial Facilities.* 28 CFR Part 36, 1991.

General Services Administration. *Uniform Federal Accessibility Standards.* Fed. Std. 795, U.S. Government Printing Office, April 1, 1988.

Evan Terry Associates. *ADA Facilities Compliance Workbook.* New York: John Wiley, 1992.

Thompson Publishing Group. *Facility Guide to the ADA.* Salisbury, MD: Thompson Publishing Group, 1993.

Perritt, Henry H., Jr. *Americans with Disabilities Act Handbook.* New York: John Wiley, 1990.

GENERAL REFERENCE SOURCES

Ching, Francis D. K. *Interior Design Illustrated.* New York: Van Nostrand Reinhold, 1987.

Cowan, Henry J., ed. *Handbook of Architectural Technology.* New York: Van Nostrand Reinhold, 1991.

Olin, Harold Bennett. *Construction Principles, Materials, and Methods, 5th ed.* Chicago: Institute of Financial Education, 1983.

Reznikoff, S. C. *Interior Graphic and Design Standards.* New York: Whitney Library of Design, 1986.

———. *Specifications for Commercial Interiors.* New York: Whitney Library of Design, 1989.

Rupp, William, and Arnold Friedmann. *Construction Materials for Interior Design.* New York: Whitney Library of Design, 1989.

Staebler, Wendy W. *Architectural Detailing in Contract Interiors.* New York, NY: The Whitney Library of Design, 1988.

INDEX

Entries from tables are indicated by page numbers in italic.

MASTERFORMAT® INDEX

Masterformat®

Masterformat® is a registered trademark of the Construction Specifications Institute, Inc. (CSI) and Construction Specifications Canada (CSC).